D1548110

Bridging
Two
Eras

Bridging

Two
Eras

The

Autobiography of

Emily Newell Blair

1877–1951

Edited by
Virginia Jeans Laas

University of Missouri Press
Columbia and London

Copyright © 1999 by
The Curators of the University of Missouri
University of Missouri Press, Columbia, Missouri 65201
Printed and bound in the United States of America
All rights reserved
5 4 3 2 1   03 02 01 00 99

Library of Congress Cataloging-in-Publication Data

Blair, Emily Newell, b. 1877.
  Bridging two eras : the autobiography of Emily Newell Blair,
1877–1951 / edited by Virginia Jeans Laas.
      p.   cm.
  Includes bibliographical references and index.
  ISBN 0-8262-1254-9 (alk. paper)
  1. Blair, Emily Newell, b. 1877.   2. Women politicians—United
States Biography.   3. Politicians—United States Biography.
4. Democratic Party (U.S.) Biography.   5. Feminists—United States
Biography.   6. United States—Politics and government—1919–1933.
7. United States— Politics and government—1933–1945.   8. Carthage
(Mo.) Biography.   9. Women authors—United States Biography.
I. Laas, Virginia Jeans.   II. Title.
E748.B623A3   1999
973.91'092—dc21
[B]   99-42688
                                                                        CIP

⊗™ This paper meets the requirements of the
American National Standard for Permanence of Paper
for Printed Library Materials, Z39.48, 1984.

Designer: Elizabeth K. Young
Typesetter: BookComp, Inc.
Printer and Binder: Thomson-Shore, Inc.
Typefaces: Jansen Text, Nuptial Script

The University of Missouri Press offers its grateful acknowledgment to
Newell Blair for his generous contribution in support of the publication of
this volume.

For my beamish boys
Andrew, Matthew, and Gilbert

Contents

Acknowledgments   ix
Introduction: Emily Newell Blair   xi
The Autobiography   xvix
Chronology   xxiii

✽   BOOK 1   *Nineteenth-Century Life*

1 "Go West, Young Man"   *3*
2 Mover's Blood   *9*
3 Waiting for Her Carriage   *14*
4 School Days in the Eighties   *18*
5 Midwest   *25*
6 More of the Midwest   *32*
7 Our Droll Generation   *36*
8 Adolescent Mixture   *43*
9 Girlhood   *52*
10 Grown Up at Last   *61*
11 Broken Circle   *68*
12 Young Lady   *73*
13 Blessed Be the Dabblers   *81*
14 On to Matrimony   *90*
15 Role of Wife   *98*
16 Bleacher Seat   *102*

✽   BOOK 2   *Twentieth-Century Life*

1 The Fertile Years   *131*
2 Small-Town Writer   *142*
3 Woman's Suffrage—1914 Style   *156*

4 The Middle of the Bridge *168*

5 World War I *179*

6 Point and Counterpoint *185*

7 Edging into Politics *197*

8 Standing the Gaff *215*

9 The "Outs" Were the "Ins" *222*

10 Wooing the Minority *231*

11 My Fairy Godmother *235*

12 Campaigning for Congress *249*

13 Tug of War *258*

14 The Dog's Tail *266*

15 Women's Way of Winning *274*

16 Tickets, Please! *282*

17 Emotional Spectacle *290*

18 Magnificent—but Not Winning *299*

19 Printer's Ink *306*

20 Stomping Ground *311*

21 Republican Game and Democratic Religious Revival *318*

22 All Things to All Men *327*

23 Democratic Stock *332*

24 Political Swan Song *342*

25 So Far *349*

Bibliography 359
Index 373

Acknowledgments

Many people and institutions have given me important help in bringing this volume to print. At the top of the list are ENB's son, Newell Blair, and his wife, Greta. Both have been supportive, hospitable, and delightful in every way throughout this project. It was Newell who began the modern-day push to publish his mother's autobiography, and he was the first to contact me to edit it. He has spent many an hour with me discussing various aspects of his mother's life. I took special delight in watching his lawyer's training take over as he chose the exact word or modified his statement to reflect his precise meaning. A close second on my list is ENB's granddaughter and namesake, Emily Blair Forsythe Warren. Every historian should be so lucky as to have Emily as a keeper. On my visits to Cleveland, she housed, fed, and watered me during unconscionably long stays, shared her friends and family, and made me feel that I was not imposing. Gracious and wise, she has become a treasured friend.

Many archivists and librarians have lightened my load. At Missouri Southern, Gaye Pate in Interlibrary Loan and Robert Black in Reference have answered my queries and filled my requests with consummate skill and extraordinary speed. At the Powers Museum, Michele Hansford has been a valued resource, sharing her knowledge of ENB and Carthage with great humor. Jeanie Hill at the Carthage Library has been a sure guide through local resources, and the volunteers in the Joplin Public Library Genealogy Room have been willing assistants. In the final stages of the preparation of this manuscript I have benefited from the skills of a wonderful work-study student, Catherine Brown. As always, I am grateful to my departmental colleagues who listen with patience and forbearance.

I have been fortunate to have found great help throughout Missouri. I thank the staffs of the State Historical Society of Missouri in Columbia; the Western Historical Manuscripts Collections in Columbia, St. Louis, and Kansas City; and, in St. Louis, the Missouri Historical Society, the University of Missouri–St. Louis, and Washington University. I am thankful for and have depended upon the advice, encouragement, and support of Lawrence Christensen at the University of Missouri–Rolla and both James Goodrich and Lynn Gentzler of the State Historical Society of Missouri. My trips to St. Louis have been made easier by the hospitality of and golf matches with my friend Barbara Beuckman.

Beyond Missouri, I am grateful to archivists and librarians at the Library of Congress, the National Archives, the University of Virginia, and the Historical Society of Washington, D.C. Of special note are those at the Western Reserve Historical Society in Cleveland and Jewell Fenzi at the Woman's National Democratic Club in Washington. I am convinced that I am blessed with the world's best daughter-in-law. No matter how long I stay or how short the notice of my pending arrival, Cindy Laas makes me feel welcome in her home located so conventiently close to the D.C. Metro.

Institutions have been generous in their grants, allowing me to complete necessary research. My thanks for the State Historical Society of Missouri Richard Brownlee Research Grant, the Franklin and Eleanor Roosevelt Institute Grant, and several faculty-development grants from Missouri Southern.

My family, as always, has been most supportive. My brother, Buck, is always in my corner, and I count on him being there; my husband, Fred, never lets me down. This book is dedicated to our three sons. They have given me the greatest joy. I cherish the memories of their childhoods and admire the fine men they have become.

Introduction

Emily Newell Blair

In the 1930s, Emily Newell Blair was a household name to women across the nation. She was the author of several books, many short stories, innumerable articles on politics, and a monthly book-review column in *Good Housekeeping*. She had also proved that women could matter in politics, serving for seven years as the first fully equal woman vice chairman of the Democratic National Committee. A key player in Franklin Roosevelt's presidential campaign, she was one of the women rewarded for her contributions to his election. Her remarkable career offers especially valuable insights into the changing life experiences and expectations of women in the early decades of the twentieth century. "Bridging two eras" provides an appropriate metaphor for her life on several levels, for she exemplifies transition in time, place, and role: from Victorian to modern America, from small town to the nation's capital, and from private life to public stage. Blair moved from a conventional, middle-class, midwestern wife and mother to a feminist known nationally in literary and political circles.

Born on January 8, 1877, in Joplin, Missouri, Emily Newell was the first child of Anna Gray and James Patten Newell. Her father, the son of a Presbyterian minister, served in the Union army during the Civil War as a first lieutenant in the Thirtieth Regiment of the Iowa Volunteer Infantry. Her mother's roots reached back to Alexander McDowell, an early settler and leading citizen of Franklin, Pennsylvania. The Newell family expanded in typical nineteenth-century fashion. Brother Jim was born in 1878, only a year and a half after Emily; thereafter her sisters arrived in two-year intervals: Anna (1881), Julia (1883), Margaretta (1885), and Ella (1887).

In 1883, after her father's election to a four-year term as county recorder, the family moved from the rough, untamed mining town of Joplin to Carthage, the older, more sedate county seat only fifteen miles away. In that small midwestern town of some nine thousand residents, Emily and her siblings grew to maturity, while her father initiated his business as a mortgage broker. Relatively new to the town and, therefore, outside the elite of Carthage society, the Newells soon became a respected part of the community.

Emily used the small-town atmosphere and the freedom it provided to explore her surroundings and meet a variety of townsfolk. Unlike the anonymity of a city, the personalism of a small town gave individuality to those who were different. In walking to and from the city square or church, she encountered day laborers, skilled craftsmen, saloon keepers, and even drunks. At the same time, reared in a solidly middle-class family, she witnessed the more refined social circle of her parents, observing her mother's Shakespeare Club, teas, luncheons, and card parties. Typical of many small towns, Carthage exhibited a rather rigid sense of social stratification, yet classes separated by social distance lived in close physical proximity. A perceptive child, Emily gained some sense of differences while retaining a feeling of community.

The booming mining industry drew investment and people from many parts of the country, moderating the provincialism that might have been expected in rural southwest Missouri. The Newells' neighbors hailed from Cincinnati, Virginia, Iowa, New York, Indiana, and even Germany. Indeed, Emily's own family never overcame the feeling that they were eastern transplants, immigrants from afar. That inclination to perceive themselves as Pennsylvanians permeated their thinking and shaped their attitudes. Whether it was their eager anticipation of visits to their "home" in Pennsylvania or Mrs. Newell's determination to dress her daughters in eastern hand-me-downs, Emily absorbed that frame of mind. In fact, not until she went to Goucher College in Baltimore did she realize that she was actually a midwesterner.

Public school was yet another broadening experience for Emily Newell. Playing with and competing against children of all classes was a democratizing experience from which Emily gained an appreciation of those whose lives were different from hers. That inclusiveness did not, however, extend to all children. Strongly influenced by southern culture, Carthage did not allow black children to attend school with whites, and her mother encouraged friendships only with children in their social circle. As with other aspects of her childhood, her education was broadening yet limited.

A plump, assertive child, she thought she was not especially popular with her classmates or teachers. To compensate, she excelled in her schoolwork and was the leader of her siblings at home, organizing plays, games, and family activities. Her memories of inadequacy, however, affected Emily's behavior for many years. It took her a long time to overcome those feelings from her childhood that had left her, she wrote, with "an undue emphasis on the importance of clothes, a painful diffidence, and the feeling that people did not like me."

Because her oldest children were so near in age, Mrs. Newell insisted that Jim and Emily do almost everything together; others referred to the brother and sister as Jimily and Emily. From their close association, Emily learned to play with boys, and as a result she was never uncomfortable working with men.

Her parents provided additional educational opportunities. W. L. Calhoun offered not only piano lessons but also instruction in music history, theory, and composition. Summer art classes were taught by J. S. Ankeney who had studied in Paris and Italy. Mr. and Mrs. Newell made sure that their children were always aware of the world beyond Carthage. Her father traveled a good deal to Pennsylvania and New York on business trips and always brought home exciting tales and gifts. Her parents often took the train to St. Louis to attend the theater and musical performances, and they normally talked of business, politics, and public events in their children's presence. Reading good literature aloud was a regular family activity. Perhaps not the ideal maternal figure, Mrs. Newell was a lifelong student, setting an excellent example for her children of the importance of intellectual pursuits. Many years later, Emily's sister Julia commented: "As children the 'Newell girls' formed the idea that 'God's country' was somewhere else than in Missouri" (*Washington Star*, undated, probably late 1930s).

Emily's autobiography shows that as a child she had developed a keen ability to observe people. Her youthful years in Carthage established her sense of self, provided the fundamentals of education, gave her modest exposure to a variety of types of people, and grounded her within a loving and affectionate family. Although her family attempted to broaden her experience, her formative years were spent, after all, in the atmosphere of a small midwestern town with its parochial view of the wider world.

After graduating from Carthage High School in 1894, Emily attended Goucher College in Baltimore for one year. Her collegiate career was cut short, however, by the death of her father on June 4, 1895. She returned home to look after her younger sisters, while her mother and brother tried to hold the family business together. Eighteen-year-old Emily took charge of running the household and caring for Anna (14), Julia (12), Margaretta (9), and Ella (almost 6). The family struggled to convince people to entrust their financial assets to a sixteen-year-old boy and his forty-two-year-old mother. And they did. The business continued under the new name of A. G. Newell and Son, and the family survived its devastating loss.

In 1898, Emily added to the family income when she accepted a teaching position in Sarcoxie, Missouri. With only a year of college and a summer session at the University of Missouri, she taught physical geography, literature, and rhetoric in the high school. The following year she moved to a fifth- and sixth-grade class where she took charge of sixty-two students ranging in age from ten to seventeen.

On Christmas Eve 1900, Emily married her high school classmate, Harry Blair, and the couple moved to Joplin where he was employed as the circuit court reporter. The next year he resigned, and the couple moved to Washington so that he could attend Columbian Law School (now George Washington University). After his graduation in 1904, they returned to Carthage where Harry practiced law and Emily tended their two children (Harriet, born in 1903, and Newell, born in 1907). Theirs was a conventional, small-town, middle-class life, filled for Emily with children, friends, club work, civic projects, and extended families.

Three events moved Emily Newell Blair from her insulated life in the Midwest to national prominence. First, she began writing. With the surprising publication of her unsolicited manuscript "Letters of a Contented Wife" in *Cosmopolitan*, she launched her writing career in 1910. Her articles appeared in *Outlook, Lippincott, Woman's Home Companion, Harper's Bazaar*, and again in *Cosmopolitan*—all within the next year. Remarkably, she had established herself as a professional writer with a national reputation.

Second, the suffrage campaign propelled Blair to a wider stage. Active in her local suffrage association, she quickly became an important statewide leader, speaking to groups throughout Missouri. In 1914, she took the job as the first editor of *Missouri Woman*, the suffrage organization's monthly magazine. Through her activities at the state level, she became known to national suffrage leaders; it was she who suggested to Carrie Chapman Catt, for example, the famous Golden Lane: the walkless, talkless suffrage demonstration at the 1916 Democratic convention in St. Louis.

Third, after Harry went overseas for the YMCA during World War I, Emily Blair accepted a position working for Anna Howard Shaw and Ida Tarbell on the Woman's Committee of the Council of National Defense. She took on the task of writing an interpretive history of the women's committee that was published in 1920. Living in Washington, working with the most important and well-known women of the country, Blair was transformed. From that time forward, she knew that she need not be limited in her ambition and that there was a place for her in the world beyond southwest Missouri.

After the Nineteenth Amendment to the Constitution was passed in 1920, giving women the right to vote, Blair participated in local and state League of Women Voters activities. Looking for the most effective way to fulfill her ideals of Wilsonian progressivism, Blair chose partisan politics over the neutrality of the League of Women Voters. When Missouri's first national committeewoman, Mattie (Mrs. Burris) Jenkins of Kansas City, resigned after serving only a few months, women statewide backed Blair for the position. Her national reputation as a writer and her renown within state suffrage circles provided broad-based support among women. She had gained additional notoriety for her stand against Missouri senator James A. Reed. His opposition to woman suffrage and the League of Nations, coupled with his strong ties to the Pendergast machine in Kansas City, had led to an even wider circle of Democrats, both men and women, who favored Blair's candidacy for the national committee.

In February 1922, national-committee chairman Cordell Hull called Blair to Washington to take charge of organizing Democratic women. She went to work with a will and within six months had created more than seven hundred Democratic women's clubs across the country. Founding a newsletter, traveling extensively, giving speeches incessantly, and contributing articles to magazines regularly, she fought to make women equal partners within the party. To reward her efforts and clarify her position, Hull recommended her successful election as a vice chairman of the national committee in August 1922.

Her most lasting contribution in these years was the founding of the Woman's National Democratic Club in Washington. As the party out of power, Democrats had no gathering place in the nation's capital. They needed a space where they could host social gatherings for Democrats, sponsor educational programs for women, present speakers, and cultivate publicity for the party. Blair, with the help of Mrs. J. Borden (Daisy) Harriman, who had the important social and political contacts necessary, began a campaign to establish a Democratic women's clubhouse. Their organizational meeting was held in Harriman's home on November 24, 1922, and they hosted their first reception on January 15, 1924, in permanent quarters at 820 Connecticut Avenue. Blair remained a guiding force of the club for many years.

Reelected vice chairman of the Democratic National Committee (DNC) in 1924, Blair continued her fight to gain equality for women within the party structure. After the 1928 convention, she resigned her position, devoting the remaining years of the decade to her writing career. During this period she began her autobiography. From 1926 until 1933, as an associate editor of *Good Housekeeping*, she produced a monthly book-review column. She also regularly contributed short stories and articles on politics to a variety of magazines. She published two books: *The Creation of a Home: A Mother Advises a Daughter* in 1930 and a novel, *A Woman of Courage*, in 1931.

Throughout the 1920s and into the 1930s, Blair's most important publications dealt with women in politics. A feminist from her early days of local civic projects, she had joined partisan politics in the belief that women could gain equality with men by working within the system as equal partners. Never an advocate of a separate woman's party, she recognized that women had a special interest in certain issues, such as mothers and children, education, and women workers. She was also aware that women had developed their own style of organizing and advocacy, a cooperative and systematic approach to solving problems. She had gone into politics with the idea that her party could benefit from including women's methods and issues. By the late 1920s, her experience on the DNC had left Blair discouraged because women had made little progress in gaining meaningful power within the party. Men had recovered from an initial fear of women voting as a bloc and were unwilling to share policy-making powers. In the early 1930s, Blair shifted her position to advocate gender solidarity but always within the two-party system. She saw that women could gain equality in party politics only if they supported women for power positions and for public office. Although she never solved the problem of power sharing, her intelligent discussions gave voice to the issue and explored a variety of approaches to thinking about women and men and political power.

As the depression deepened and President Herbert Hoover's policies made no appreciable inroads on public misery, the Democratic Party saw a chance to end the twelve-year domination of national politics by the Republicans. And Emily Newell Blair saw a way out for her own family's financial troubles. With the mining industry nearly at a standstill, economic hard times had come to southwest Missouri; Harry's legal practice had suffered accordingly. For many years Emily had sought to move her family east to further her own career. Convinced that her writing career would profit by her presence closer to editors and publishers, she had previously tried (without success) to convince Harry to move to Washington or New York.

As early as 1930, she had recognized the potential of a Franklin Roosevelt presidential candidacy. Although she had become inactive in partisan politics after the 1928 election, she had never dropped her interest in or connections to the Democratic Party. The possibility of a Roosevelt candidacy stirred Blair's progressive idealism and drew her back to the political fray. Working hard during the convention, Blair helped secure the nomination for Roosevelt, and during the campaign she was one of four women sent by the DNC on speaking tours across the country.

When it was time to reap her reward for serving the party, Blair chose not to seek a job for herself. She wanted a position for Harry. For too many years her career had outshone his, and she knew that Harry would leave Missouri only if he were offered a job. Because of her long service to the party, various rumors linked Emily to important positions, such as the Employees' Compensation Commission, the Civil Service Commission, and even assistant secretary of state. If Harry were to collect her reward, she wanted a comparably important position for him. It was a struggle. Securing appointment for herself would have been much easier. She was a known quantity to the politicians; Harry was not. And he did not make a particularly effective case for himself. After considerable turmoil, however, Harry was appointed assistant attorney general in charge of the Lands Division where he served until he resigned in 1937 to establish a private law practice.

Emily eventually accepted a position on the Consumers' Advisory Board (CAB) of the National Recovery Administration (NRA), and in 1935 she became chairman, overseeing its operation until the demise of the NRA in 1936. With her job at the CAB completed, Emily, at age fifty-nine, retired. It was then that she began work again on her autobiography and contributed a few articles to popular magazines.

In October 1941, with war again looming on the horizon, Blair accepted a position on the Women's Advisory Council created by the War Department. Its purpose was to distribute information to American women on the welfare of their fathers, sons, and husbands serving in the armed forces. The War

Department then created the Women's Interest Section of the Bureau of Public Relations to develop written materials on the welfare of soldiers that would then be distributed to the memberships of the women's organizations represented on the Advisory Council. At age sixty-five, Blair became chief of the Women's Interest Section in 1942 after Mrs. Oveta Culp Hobby resigned to take charge of the Women's Army Auxiliary Corps. After suffering a debilitating stroke, Blair resigned in February 1944. She died in Alexandria, Virginia, on August 3, 1951.

The Autobiography

Emily Newell Blair's "Bridging Two Eras" exhibits characteristics common to women's autobiographies. Most women have tended to justify autobiographical writing by emphasizing its utility to others. Certainly, Blair thought her life story was worth telling to explain why feminism was important, to encourage women's participation in public life, and to show how women could succeed in the public realm. Women have also tended to deny their ambition and to present their successes as lucky accidents or the result of someone else's efforts on their behalf. Blair's original title, "Transcript of a Lucky Life," was a classic expression of that reluctance to admit her active role in promoting her own career and in seeking power and influence. It was, she claimed, her husband's idea that she begin writing; it was her husband who would have been unhappy if she had confined her activities to domestic duties.

At the same time, Blair was justified in choosing the title "Bridging Two Eras" for her autobiography. Born in the last quarter of the nineteenth century, she had lived and understood Victorian culture; yet, she was driven to seek a career outside the home. Younger than the original suffrage leaders but older than many of the new college-educated career women, she represented a middle ground between club woman activists and professional reformers. In another sense, she became a bridge: physically, she moved from small-town, out-state Missouri, which always struggled against the power of Kansas City and St. Louis, to the nation's capital, the center of national political power.

Blair's autobiography was a conscious attempt to create a public image of herself. It was a means to present an explanation and justification of her life. As such, it sometimes smooths over rough spots and makes light of what were difficult situations. Her account of getting Harry a job in the New Deal glosses over what were heart-wrenching months for the couple. On occasion, Blair stretches the truth in order to make a point. Her son, for example, has no memory of his mother ever cooking a late-night breakfast for his fraternity brothers at Sewanee. It is, nevertheless, a fundamentally honest and evocative portrait of one woman's attempt not only to expand the boundaries of her own life but also to enlarge the playing field for all women. When Blair first wrote this autobiography, she was discouraged at the meager progress women had made in public life. She felt the need to use her experience to encourage others and to demonstrate the importance of women in public life. She was no radical. A proper, feminine wife and mother, she could show that sharing political power with such a woman should not threaten any man. Blair saw this autobiography as a message to both men and women.

In 1931, Blair submitted the first version of her autobiography, titled "Middle Westerner: Transcript of a Lucky Life," to Farrar and Rinehart for publication. The height of the depression, however, was not a good time to bring out a new book, especially one with such an optimistic title. The publisher rejected it. The manuscript was put aside when Blair returned to politics and remained neglected during her years of participation in the New Deal. In 1937, Blair revised it, this time calling it "Our Droll Generation," and tried to sell it to *Ladies Home Journal* for serialization. It was once again rejected. In the fall of 1949, Blair's twin granddaughters discovered the manuscript in her attic. Blair, incapacitated by a stroke, took renewed interest in it and with the help of another granddaughter, Emily Forsythe Warren, embarked on a total revision. In April 1951, they again sent it off to a publisher, Rinehart and Company. Once again, nothing came of the effort. And so it sat until recent years when Blair's son, Newell, renewed the effort to publish his mother's autobiography. With the help of secretaries, he set about putting together a publishable manuscript, which is the only version of the autobiography that exists as an entity.

Editorial Method

In the Papers of Emily Newell Blair at the Western Reserve Historical Society, there are twenty archival boxes of typed pages of drafts of the autobiography. In addition, Newell Blair has two cardboard boxes of draft pages of typescript. There is no original document. From the thousands of pages of drafts, there is no way to distinguish absolutely what is original, what was done in the 1930s or 1950s or 1980s, or what changes were made by whom. Family members maintain that Emily's sisters removed portions of the original manuscript that they believed inappropriate, and those parts may have been lost forever. Moreover, there are scattered notations on some of the pages indicating that secretaries perhaps did more than simply retype the pages. On one page, for example, is a note stating that the person had "used my imagination on this chapter title."

In putting together this document, I began with the version created by Newell Blair and compared it with every extant page of rough draft. I have been guided by several principles. First, I have tried to remain true to what I think were Blair's original thoughts. Occasionally, there were instances in which sentences or phrases were deleted, toning down the presentation of feelings or dissatisfactions. For instance, in describing her difficulties in returning to Joplin after her years on the Democratic National Committee (DNC), one version stated: "It was not easy to go back to Joplin. But I belonged to a club which has always stuck by me, I had friends, and I set to work to make a life for myself there." In another rendering, between those two sentences was the following:

> I did not see myself sinking into a life of domesticity, and it offered nothing else. But neither did I see myself breaking the bonds that made it my home. I knew my husband was aware of my feelings. Not one to accept a sacrificial wife, he was not happy over it. My sister Ella had moved us, before I came, into another house. She had even curtained it for me. I was not as grateful as I might have been. Joplin did not any more know what to do with me than I how to fit in. I was a maverick, half admired, a little suspected and somewhat feared.

In this edition, I have restored the deletion.

Second, I have been guided by the thought that Blair intended to publish her autobiography. Therefore, I have corrected all spelling, including misspelled proper names. It has been impossible to determine if Blair or a transcriber made the mistakes; in these instances, I have played the role of copy editor. Occasionally, spelling errors caused particularly knotty problems in identification of people; for example, the name Richard Victor Culahan appeared for Richard Victor Oulahan. I have created titles for Books 1 and 2.

I have condensed Book 1 by combining very short chapters and deleting repetitious and extremely local material. In this endeavor, I have used my own judgment after reading a great many draft pages. My intention was to preserve the color, feeling, and experience of growing up in Joplin and Carthage. Blair's goal, after all, was to explain her life—not to provide a local history of Carthage or Joplin. I have been guided by the words of Emily Newell Blair herself. As a professional writer, she knew the importance of keeping her work focused. On one draft page, she commented, "To reminisce is so tempting that it is hard to discriminate between those incidents which are pertinent to my purpose and those which are merely self-pleasing." On another occasion, when discussing the intricacies of the suffrage movement, she stopped her narrative and cautioned, "[B]ut this is not a history of the suffrage movement, it is only how it affected one life of one woman." I have taken her statements at her word and attempted to keep this work focused on the experiences, thoughts, and feelings of Emily Newell Blair. As a result, this edition of Book 1 is 14 percent shorter than the family version. Book 2, however, is somewhat longer.

Just as there are many draft pages of the autobiography, there is also more than one attempt at an introduction. All offer insight into Blair's motivation for writing her autobiography. A fragment of what appears to be an introduction suggests her desire to foster a sense of feminism among women. Given that many of her publications from 1928 to 1931 called for women to support women within the political parties, perhaps the following was her earliest justification for her autobiography:

It is the story of a feminist. She did not start out as a feminist. She had no theory of feminism to test by experiment. Experience developed the feminism. Her theories were the result of her experiments. They were not fixed theories. They changed with the years. She passed through many phases. Now she sees that each phase was necessary to the conception of feminism that she now holds. And by feminism I had perhaps better say here, I mean women's having a part in the making of the world.

Another fragment suggests the relationship Blair saw between her childhood and her later ambition: "[I]t is the story of how this child, here thwarted by environment and there helped by it, here hampered by her temperament and there prodded by it, here fighting her period and there prodded by it, sometimes baffled, often stopped and again aided by Fate, managed to pursue those interests." In a foreword that she wrote for one version of the autobiography, granddaughter Emily Forsythe Warren stated that Blair had explained her motivation: "[L]ong ago she had thought of writing an autobiography, mainly for the purpose of encouraging women from small towns everywhere to take part in public affairs and not be backward or discouraged because they were small town people."

Blair's introduction to her 1937 revision, the only one positively dated, should stand as the best summary:

It is with no delusions as to my importance that I set down the story of my life, but it has been an interesting one to live and it will be interesting to me to review it. I happened, moreover, to fall in that historic period when women were bridging two eras: that in which to be a good wife and mother was career enough for any woman, and that in which women reach outside the home, even to the Cabinet of the President and the United States Senate. It fell to my lot to walk that bridge, even sometimes to straddle it, a foot on each end. My story should, therefore, present a picture of what life was like for women in that transition time, a time that will probably never come again, at least with the same background, or in just the same way. It may thus prove of interest to others beside myself.

If only I can put it down as I lived it. Let us see!

Chronology

1877	January 9, ENB's birth
	July 7, Harry's birth
1883	Newells moved to Carthage
1894	Graduation from Carthage High School
1894	Attended Goucher College
1895	June 4, father's death
1898–1900	Taught school in Sarcoxie
1900	December 24, married Harry Blair
1902	Moved to Washington, D.C.; Harry to Columbian College Law School
1903	October 7, Harriet born in Washington
1904	Harry graduated from law school
1905	Blairs returned to Carthage
1907	April 5, Newell born in Joplin
1908	Harry ran for circuit judge
1910	First articles published
1913	Elected president of Missouri Women's Press Association
1914	Jasper County Almshouse Campaign
	First suffrage speech (in St. Louis)
1915	First editor of *Missouri Woman*
	Organization of Missouri Writers' Guild, ENB elected second vice president
1916	June 14, Golden Lane at St. Louis Democratic Convention
1917	Vice chairman of Missouri Woman's Committee, Council of National Defense
	President, Carthage Equal Suffrage Association
1918	Harry went to France
	ENB went to Washington, worked for Woman's Committee, Council of National Defense
	First public argument with Sen. James Reed

1919   Harry returned from France

Blairs moved to Joplin

1920   Published history of Woman's Committee, Council of National Defense

Helped found League of Women Voters

Democratic National Convention in San Francisco

1921   Elected national committeewoman

1922   Elected vice chairman of the Democratic National Committee (DNC)

Founded Woman's National Democratic Club

1924   Reelected to DNC

1926–1933   Associate editor of *Good Houskeeping*

1926   President of Woman's National Democratic Club

1928   Resigned from national committee after national convention

1930   Publication of *The Creation of a Home*

1931   First submission of autobiography to Farrar and Rinehart

Published *A Woman of Courage*

1932   Campaigned for FDR

1933   Appointed to Consumers' Advisory Board

Harry appointed assistant attorney general in charge of Lands Division

1935   Chairman of Consumers' Advisory Board

1937   Tried to sell autobiography to *Ladies Home Journal*

Harry resigned from attorney general's office

1942   Chief of Women's Interest Section of the Bureau of Public Relations

1944   Stroke

1951   August 3, died

BOOK 1

Nineteenth-Century Life

1 "Go West, Young Man"

I waken suddenly in a lamp-lighted room and hear someone say, "You've a new little sister." I stand in a Sunday school room, a rag doll in my arms, and recite "For This Is My Oldest Dolly and I Love Her Best of All." I hang on a gate and see hacks pass by, my father's name printed in black letters on the white sheets tacked on them.

These are the incidents that spring first to my mind when I think of the little girl that was once me. I was four years old when Annie was born, four and a half when I spoke that first "piece," and five the election day when Father ran for a county office. The outstanding events of my childhood they must have been to take first place in my memory; prophetic of what were to become the major interests of my life: family, public performance, and politics. Did they fix in my mind those interests, or did I already lean toward these interests?

"Ginx," my father called me, the name of a character in a current book, as applicable to a round-faced, fat little girl who chattered incessantly.

A short, quick-actioned man, my father, with a brick-red moustache, bright black eyes, and black hair, a lock of which was brushed meticulously across a large bald top.

I early became acquainted with his story, though it has probably been pieced out by later knowledge. A storybook story, it has always seemed to me who sees facts romantically. He had come West from the town of Franklin, Pennsylvania. Before that he had, as a young man, made a fortune in lumber and oil. Unfortunately, he explored for more oil and lost the fortune. When he met my mother, he was a bachelor-about-town waiting for something to turn up. Both were "otherwise engaged" at the time, but as my father said, "It was all up with us; whenever we two would have met, it would inevitably have been the same."

My mother had no intention of marrying a man with a past and no future, and she knew he would never make good in the place where he had been rich; so she urged him to take Horace Greeley's advice and go west. He went, equipped with expensive tastes, a disregard for the value of money, a classical education begun at the age of nine, a lawyer's license, and a gay-hearted, generous spirit. He started for Topeka, Kansas, with a letter to the governor. But at Westport Landing, as what became Kansas City was then called, he heard of the discovery of lead at the new mining camp at Joplin, Missouri, and went there instead. This was in 1874.[1]

My father loved to tell of his first night in Joplin. Main Street, with its shacks and saloons, was thronged with a mob hunting a horse thief with intent to "string him up." Thinking that an unknown man might be suspected, my father betook himself to his room in the hotel, not realizing that his long, dark-blue tailored broadcloth coat with its silver buttons and his tall, gray hat would furnish him all the alibi needed.

How he found any more money to lose I do not know, but he managed to drop some into a lead mine. Long afterward the same mine paid handsomely. Perhaps it was his fate, for with remarkable consistency all my forebears— from those who came to this country in 1620 down to the present—have muffed their opportunities to make money in this land of great resources. A great-great-grandfather once owned much of the land in Pennsylvania on which oil was later discovered. My grandfather was manager of the ironworks that started the fortunes of his clerk, the Peter White who built the Pere Marquette Railway. Even my own generation, as we shall see, has this habit of wealth evasion.

Down to no dollar at all, Father appealed for work to the camp king, Pat Murphy, only to be told that there was none.[2] But as he lingered, Father overheard Mr. Murphy say: "If I could find a man for the job I'd sink a shaft on that forty."

Father stepped up again. "What about me?"

Pat Murphy looked at Father's hands and laughed.

"I said anything," said Father, "and I meant just that."

So he put down the shaft, ran the hoist, and changed the texture of his hands.

Six months later my mother, with a recklessness I have never understood in one of her cautious nature, married him.[3] She had gone to Maysville, Kentucky, to visit an aunt. Father went on to see her. After the impromptu wedding she went back to Franklin to break the news to a disapproving family and get together a belated trousseau before she joined Father in Joplin.

---

1. In 1870, E. R. Moffet and John B. Sergeant struck a rich vein of lead ore that brought miners flocking to the area. Two rival camps developed and finally incorporated as the town of Joplin in 1873. For a brief history of the founding of Joplin, see Dolph Shaner, *The Story of Joplin*, 1–33.

2. Patrick Murphy emigrated from Ireland in 1850. After running a freighting business between Colorado and Nebraska, he established a mercantile concern in Fort Scott, Kansas, moving to Carthage in 1866. When lead was discovered in the area, he helped lay out the town of Murphysburg, which later combined with Joplin. He was a founder of the West Joplin Mining and Smelting Company and was instrumental in founding Miners' Bank and Joplin Water Works. He was mayor of Joplin in 1875 (Malcolm G. McGregor, *The Biographical Record of Jasper County, Missouri*, 65–66).

3. Anna Gray married James Newell on June 4, 1875, in Maysville, Kentucky.

She has described to us the Joplin she first saw. One rough, uneven street. Plank sidewalks, the planks set together endwise. Every other shack a saloon with the door wide open. Signs above these doors: "Faro tonight" or "Roulette." Men swaggering along with guns on their hips.

On Saturday nights the gangs from Granby, from Baxter Springs, even from Southwest City and Indian Territory, came to town.[4] Shots rang out. Horses dashed up and down the streets. For safety, miners were paid off in the saloons. Somehow they seemed to have protection from the highwaymen. Probably they paid for it. No operators had offices. All business was transacted in saloons. For a long time Saturday was man's night in Joplin. No wife expected to see her husband on that evening.

A prospector needed little capital. He staked a pick and shoveler. If "shines" were found, he took a partner in for enough money to sink a shaft. This indeed continued down to my own days. Even after it was necessary to put up big mills, the money was gotten by selling off shares in the mine. Many the pick and shoveler by this method became a millionaire, or what passed for it then.[5]

Father and Mother lived in the "Brick Hotel," the only two-story building in the town. Father still worked in the mine, and Mother carried his noon dinner pail across the deep-grass prairie that came to the town street. A queer figure she must have looked on such an errand in her ruffled and fringed silk dresses brought out from Franklin. I have a picture of her now in one of them. It shows a high-cheeked, oval face, long curls, steady eyes, and lips set in a purpose never to compromise with her standards.

"Most of us," said one of her Joplin friends to me when she died, "let things go when we came to Joplin, but not your mother. We used to smile at the way she fussed over your white dresses and starched petticoats."

To the mining camp she brought her books and her silver-bound writing desk. She kept up her French reading, made out a study course, and practiced daily on the hotel piano. She did such things until the day of her death. At sixty she was taking an extension course from Chicago University, and she played the organ at church until her death. When she died at seventy-two, her Spanish textbook was found open on the table.

A schoolteacher resigned, and without telling my father, my mother applied for the position and got it. It was a two-room school, the other teacher being

---

4. From Joplin, Granby, Missouri, is about twenty-five miles to the southeast; Baxter Springs, Kansas, is fifteen miles west; Southwest City, Missouri, in the corner where Indian Territory, Missouri, and Arkansas meet, is forty miles south; and Indian Territory is ten miles to the southwest.

5. Until the turn of the century, mining operations in the Tri-State District were relatively simple affairs; the shallow deposits could be worked inexpensively by two men. Anyone with a strong back, minimal equipment, and a strong work ethic could become an operator. For a brief overview of mining in the area, see Virginia Laas, Everett Ritchie, and Daniel Stewart, *An Introduction to the Tri-State Mineral Museum*, 1–4, 18–24.

the principal, Phil Arnold, who became one of Joplin's leaders and a lifelong friend of hers.[6]

By the time I came, January 9, 1877, they had moved into a little house around the corner from the hotel. My father waded in mud to his knees to call the doctor, and I made my first cries to the accompaniment of pistol shots from the gambling hall across the alley. Aunt Emily, who came out from Franklin with the layette, has told me about it. Mother went back to Pennsylvania when Jim was born and must have taken me, for I was then only a year and a half old.[7] Mother has said that on her return Father was so glad to see me, he paid no attention to Jim. If so, that was the only time I was more important than he.

Father's finances improved. The hotel bookkeeper, after a spree, asked Father to straighten out his books, and when he was discharged because of too many sprees, Father became the bookkeeper. He was made city clerk, went into the implement business, and, in 1882, was elected county recorder of deeds, the first Democrat to be elected in Jasper County since the Civil War.[8]

Times must have changed since the first Democratic convention that was held after the war. It had convened in the deep woods, sentinels were posted with guns, and two Democrats from eastern states were made to give an account of themselves before they were admitted.

During the war Father was at Vicksburg and there became very ill. He was sent north and went to Davenport, Iowa, where his father had been minister at the time Father went into the army.[9] But my grandfather had left Davenport, and my father on his return was taken care of by a member of Grandfather's former congregation. One day on the street in Joplin a stranger in town approached him and said, "Why you must be the little redheaded captain who came to us in Davenport during the war and was very sick. I thought you were dead by now." They renewed the acquaintance, and the Iowa man

---

6. Philip Arnold had been one of the first teachers hired in Joplin in 1873. In 1874 the school board appointed him principal. Later, Arnold was superintendent of the Joplin schools, in 1880–1881; he was elected county school commissioner in 1885 and served until 1887. Anna Newell was employed for a time as a teacher, probably in 1876 (F. A. North, *The History of Jasper County, Missouri, Including a Condensed History of the State, a Complete History of Carthage and Joplin, Other Towns and Townships*, 437–38; Joel T. Livingston, *A History of Jasper County, Missouri, and Its People*, 1:231).

7. ENB's aunt Emily Gray Fleming was her mother's oldest sister. She was born on May 18, 1851, and married Joseph Allen Fleming on May 1, 1872, in Franklin, Pennsylvania. ENB's brother, James, was born in Franklin on August 8, 1878.

8. In 1877, ENB's father, James P. Newell, was city clerk of Joplin; in 1880, he began an agricultural implement business in partnership with W. S. Paul; in February 1883, Paul bought out Newell (North, *History of Jasper County . . . Townships*, 412, 568).

9. ENB's father had served as a first lieutenant in Company F, 30 Regiment, Iowa Volunteer Infantry (Anna G. Newell, Certificate of Pension, #434173, November 28, 1896, Bureau of Pensions, Department of Interior).

suggested that Father ought to have a pension. Father hadn't thought of that but applied for and was granted a pension, and it was this pension money that tided over some of the difficult times for Father and Mother in Joplin.

Joplin had changed since Mother had come there seven years before. The first railroad had come in, brick sidewalks had replaced the plank ones, ground gravel the mud of the streets, and galvanized iron fronts ornamented the store and saloon buildings, but still the Saturday night crowds surged, still outlaws came to shoot up the town. Periodically they came to Joplin and took what they wanted. When at last a sheriff tried to stop a man who was holding up a store, the outlaw bit the sheriff's hand until he dropped his gun, and then walked nonchalantly out of the store.

Once, the James boys came down to rob a bank. But when a cashier, who had formerly been a comrade in Quantrill's band, told them that it would embarrass him, they gave it up and rode away.[10]

Such a place as Joplin had no stability. Men made money and spent it. They came and they went. Few ever expected to stay. I have often heard some woman who has lived there twenty years say to a stranger: "I? Oh, my home is in _____," and she would name Buffalo or Wilkes-Barre, for Harrisburg-Joplin was a way station, not a home, and what Mother wanted was a home, such a home as her people had lived in "back East" for a hundred years.

One night in Joplin she never forgot. A shot came through the window, tore down the blind, put out the lamp; and she sat for two hours with a child on each arm until my father returned. No, Joplin was not the place for that home.

Carthage was a village before the Civil War. It was almost entirely burned down during the war, but was soon rebuilt.[11] It had been settled largely by people from small towns of New York and Pennsylvania with here and there a New Englander, and almost no southerners. Some of these people had come with money and had come to stay. They had therefore built substantial square houses set back in wide lawns, some with an acre or more about them. Characteristically, there isn't a house of this vintage in Joplin. The settlers brought with them their furniture, their manners and customs. They drove

---

10. Dolph Shaner tells of an attempt by the James boys to rob John H. Taylor's bank in East Joplin. The banker's brother, Fletch Taylor, recognized the men as old friends from William Quantrill's gang; when he invited them to meet his brother, Jesse James called off the robbery. The gang spent the evening in Joplin saloons. Shaner indicates that Fletch had been a member of the Quantrill band, not Charles W. Glover, the nephew and bank cashier. While the story varies in detail, Shaner is convinced that the attempted robbery did indeed occur (*Story of Joplin*, 50–51).

11. In March 1842, Carthage was designated the county seat of Jasper County. Because of guerrilla activity during the Civil War, the county was virtually depopulated. With peace, settlers returned, and Carthage became an incorporated town in 1868 and a chartered city in 1873 (North, *History of Jasper County . . . Townships*, 221–37).

old-fashioned surreys and had old Negro coachmen. They kept servants. They had an assembly whose members were old-fashioned enough to be shocked at the bride who appeared in a Parisian low-cut neck of the eighties but demanded a difference between an evening and a daytime frock. They had a Public Library and an Academy and Shakespeare societies and were greatly given to parties with escalloped oysters, lemon gelatine, chicken salad, and hot biscuits. Although most of the people were northerners, the menus, recipes, and social habits were by way of a southern genesis. I have never understood this. It may be that before my time some southern family, or families, who later moved away set the pattern and the northerners who moved in conformed to it, or it may be that the few southerners were so insistent that the other pattern gave way before that of a more gracious one.

Once before we moved there I had seen Carthage. When my father was elected county recorder of deeds he invited me to go there with him for the day. It took us an hour to cover the eighteen miles by train. From the depot, we went up a long street in a funny bus called a herdic filled with strange men and were at "the Square."[12] All around it stores. In the center a green place with posts around it. To them were hitched horses trailing wagons into the street. Trees in the square, large trees, oaks. There were no trees in Joplin, but I did not know that then. We had lunch at the Karr Hotel in a dining room that seemed all tablecloths, my first acquaintance with a hotel. And in Rose's Store at the corner I bought Mother a silk handkerchief.

This was the end of my childhood in Joplin, but I was to return and live there in later years.

---

12. In 1882, J. P. Newell was elected to a four-year term as county recorder (ibid., 208). A herdic is a two-wheeled, horse-drawn carriage with side seats and a rear entrance.

2 Mover's Blood

Before we moved to Carthage we went back East for a visit—my parents, my brother, Jim, my baby sister Annie, and I.[1] Though I remember nothing of two previous visits, this stands out in my mind in detail. The wide Allegheny River, into which I fell. We crossed it on a houseboat on which a fat woman and a plump, yellow-haired girl made so much of me that I was loathe to leave them until they promised me I could come again. The landing in front of a small frame house. My grandfather Newell, a tall, gaunt man, a little fearsome, Grandmother Newell with her placid smile, her dark hair parted and worn in a knot at her neck. These two people were always to seem to me the oldest I ever knew, although they must then have been but little over sixty. With them was my uncle Dave with his scarred face.[2]

Father had explained to me about this Uncle Dave. When he was twenty-five, then a student of law, an accident at the oil wells had torn his face to shreds and left him sightless. But he must be treated exactly as if he saw. He ran the oil wells on his farm, decided where to put down new ones, employed and bossed the men. Uncle Dave showed me these wells himself, pointing out to me the derricks, explaining the pump and how the oil ran through to the tanks.

"Take care, little girl," he would say. "There is a pipe there." And "Look out for that step." Queerly, I have no memory of my first acquaintance with mine shafts, but I can see those derricks and the engine house clearly.

Once, so Father told me, Uncle Dave's clothes had caught on fire, and he had run straight to the water tank and jumped in. He was to me a storybook person. And always his courage and his patience have made me ashamed to complain at any quips of fortune.

My grandfather Newell was a Presbyterian minister, one of the old school to whom doctrine was more important than grace. He was a powerful man physically, saying with pride that it took a double dose of medicine to affect

---

1. ENB's sister Anna Gray Newell was born on February 8, 1881, in Joplin.
2. ENB's paternal grandfather was Presbyterian minister Huey Newell (1811–1892) (Folder 104, Emily Newell Blair Papers; hereafter cited as ENB Papers). Her paternal grandmother was Louisa Hoosey Newell (1812–1900) (ibid.). Uncle Dave Newell (b. 1848) had been an oil producer in Pennsylvania (1900 Population Schedule, Venango County, Pennsylvania, T623, Roll 1491).

him. His will was adamant. Born of Scotch-Irish ancestry (his father had emigrated from Ulster in 1775), Grandfather early impressed on me the difference between the Protestant Irish and the Catholic Irish. Scotch-Irish we were, with the emphasis on the Scotch to stress its superiority to other brands of Irish. How shocked he would be if he could know my opinion today of those Cromwellians who stole the Irishmen's land! How pained at my suspicion that the pug noses, the round faces, and wit that appear in our family may be a heritage from some Catholic Irish lassie who captured some tall, lean, long-faced, high-browed, gray-eyed Ulsterman and left her strain in the blood my grandfather liked to think so Scotch and Presbyterian. And what would he have said of my feminist glee that however her in-laws may have thought they absorbed her she has had the last word.

At the time I visited Franklin, my grandfather had retired from active ministry although occasionally preaching powerful sermons on doctrine. Intellect was really his God, and to that he gave unvarying service. His choice of the ministry was influenced by the social pattern of his day. It offered him the place he yearned for, theology the opportunity for play of intellect and pastorates the power he would wield. In another day he would have gone into politics.

While Mother and Father went on a belated wedding trip to New York City, Jim and I went to stay with my father's sister, "Aunt Jennie," in Oil City. My aunt was a brisk, dark-skinned, dark-eyed little woman with quick speech, a tart tongue, an intense loyalty to family, a love of the fashionable and stylish, and an energy and ambition that was not content to sit at home leaving the business of the world to men. As early as 1886 she set out to put the kindergarten in the public schools of Franklin. My feminist leanings as well as my interest in clothes and furnishing I trace, I suspect, to her. Her brothers—she was the only girl among three boys—teased her interminably, but she ruled them all and they adored her. I thought of her even then as daring and valiant in Oil City, and held her life as far more colorful and exciting than my mother's.

My maternal grandparents also first loom in my consciousness in this visit to Franklin.[3] They lived on the second floor of a business building downtown, and this was to me as glamorous a way of living as a houseboat or an oil farm. The immense living room had windows all at the front curtained with heavy draperies; there was a large patterned wallpaper, and heavy large walnut furniture.

When Mother and Father returned from New York to Franklin, we gathered around with the relations to hear about it: the aunt's house on Staten

---

3. ENB's maternal grandparents were Margaretta Rachel McDowell (born July 11, 1827) and Elisha Burritt Gray (born April 20, 1823). They had married in Franklin on August 1, 1850.

Island, the hotel called "The Hoftman House," the theatres.[4] And there were Mother's new clothes to see. A black lace bonnet with blue forget-me-nots on it and pink velvet ties was especially praised by the aunts. Justification, all of this was to her, I can imagine, for her disapproved marriage. To me they only added to the glamour the whole trip had for me.

One of my maternal great-great-grandfathers, Col. Alexander McDowell, had founded the town of Franklin, and the woods were full of his descendants.[5] To have so many strange people calling me "cousin" was a new experience. We did not have "relations" in Joplin. To hear my father called "James" and my mother "Anna" was also new. No one in all their life out West ever so addressed them. Sometimes, Father was addressed as "Captain," and I learned that he had been in a war.

My grandmother, Margaretta McDowell Gray, afterward came to live with us. I was myself a mother when she died. In appearance she was what a duchess is supposed to be and never is. Portly, yet never considered fat, she moved with grace and dignity. This because, as a young girl, she was required to go up and down stairs with a basket on her head to train her in deportment. She was a very beautiful woman. Even to the day of her death people would turn to look at her on the street. She had a peaches-and-cream complexion, the pink still showing under her fair skin after it had become completely crossed with tiny fine wrinkles. Her hair turned white at thirty-five. After I knew her, she wore it parted and drawn down in smooth waves to her ears. Her eyes were a pure childlike blue, her nose finely chiseled. Her expression was quite gentle, a combination of sweetness and serenity except when her wide mouth parted in a rather dazzling smile. When dressed for occasions she wore folds of white illusions inside her V-cut neck pinned with an old seed-pearl brooch that conveyed an impression of elegance. What was always amazing to me was that in a calico morning dress, her skirt caught up at the side because she had been gardening (she loved flowers passionately), her collar open over a wrinkled throat, and her hair in curlers, she could enter a room in such a manner that everyone in it rose to do obeisance to her. She inspired devotion and reverence in everyone.

Her life had been tragic, but apparently she never realized it. She simply moved majestically through the part handed her. She was the eldest of the children born to Emily Ayres and Thomas Skelley McDowell. Emily's sister

---

4. Margaretta Gray (born May 24, 1858) was Anna Gray Newell's youngest sister, thus ENB's aunt. She and her husband, Henry Church, lived on Staten Island.

5. Alexander McDowell, born in 1760, died in Franklin, Pennsylvania, in 1816. He had come to Franklin in 1794 as a surveyor for the Holland Land Company. A friend of the Indian chief Corn Planter, he held numerous offices in Franklin: justice of the peace in 1796; trustee of Venango County, 1800; first postmaster, 1801; and first county treasurer, 1805. He also served in the Revolutionary War (plaque in Franklin Cemetery; S. J. M. Eaton, "City of Franklin," Folder 103, ENB Papers).

Amy had made a better marriage. William Galbraith of Erie was first a judge, then a congressman, then again a judge, and constantly growing richer. Amy and William had but two children, a son and a daughter, and they offered to take Emily's eldest, who was my grandmother, and educate her with their own daughter. So it was in Erie at her Aunt Amy's that Margaretta McDowell learned how to enter a room, how to manage a well-appointed house, the importance of food and service. I can imagine she found it hard when she came back to her mother's cluttered household from her aunt's well-run house, but I am sure she never showed it as never in all her life did she register annoyance, disappointment, or embarrassment although she had occasion enough for all three.

When Grandmother Margaretta McDowell married Elisha Burritt Gray he was considered a catch. He was a distinguished-looking man, tall and slim with the lean, long face of the aristocrat. The high brow of the intellectual and the pale-brown coloring that is alluring to women. Years afterward one of the most courtly men I ever saw, Arnold Plumer, said to my father, "To us younger men Mr. Gray was the ideal of what a gentleman should be."[6] Unfortunately, he was periodically driven to drinking too much. First there would be a fine position, a sufficient income to maintain it, a social life, and then an attack would come, the position would be lost, the income gone, and disgrace would follow. First he would be a kind and generous father; then threatening to throw a baby out of the window. They lived in many places, always starting with high hopes but ending usually with an embarrassed return to Franklin. He was what now would be called a mechanical engineer. Once he built several bridges across the Ohio River.

When I came to visit my grandparents in Franklin at the age of six, Grandfather had a small insurance business.[7] But one could never guess, watching my grandmother, that she was a victim of blighted hopes or faith denied. A stranger looking at her would have said: "Here is one woman for whom life has always been smooth and pleasant," and even today I do not know whether it was the result of that face to the world that was expected of a lady or of a stupidity that never knew how tragic her life was. She had the gift of getting joy out of small things, neighborliness, flowers, a fine dish, a compliment, hospitality given and received, little children. Perhaps they most of all compensated her for tragedy.

I learned that Grandfather Gray came from a line who had moved from Massachusetts to Connecticut in 1632 and from there to Dutchess County, New York, to Shelbourne, New York, to Ohio, and finally to Kentucky. Each one married in the place where he grew up, and each of these wives in turn

---

6. Arnold Plumer (b. 1839) was a banker in Franklin, Pennsylvania (1900 Population Schedule, Venango County, Pennsylvania, T623, Roll 1490).

7. The business was the E. B. Gray Insurance Agency in Franklin.

was descended from a father who had moved from the locality in which he was born. In me converge, therefore, a line that comes from Upper Marlboro, Maryland, a line from Tarvin in Virginia, a line from Kentucky, a line drawn from Connecticut, one from Massachusetts, and one from Pennsylvania.

This then is what it is to be of mover's stock. We in the Middle West, some of us, come from every place at once. Small wonder we do not develop along any one tradition. When I was vice chairman of the Democratic National Committee, I used to say laughingly that one of my qualifications for a national office was that I represented so many localities. I could tell my hearers in Connecticut with what an emotion I found myself back in the old home state. With equal honesty and emotion I could say the same thing to listeners in Maryland, Virginia, Kentucky, Ohio, Pennsylvania, New York, and Massachusetts. Of course I did not mention the date at which my family had left home.

I write at such length about these forefathers because they are typical of the middle westerner who is the product of this urge toward the frontier. Much has been written of the melting pot in large cities of different nationalities; much of the New Englander and Virginian, the Puritan and Cavalier, but little recognition has been made of the mingling in the middle westerner of all these so-called American strains, and yet this very mingling may perchance be the reason for his lack of distinction, of his failure to produce a culture of his own. Perhaps the elements are so mixed in him that nature could not produce a distinct type. I note it for another reason. A eugenist once told me that in America such a complete record of a family extending through so many lines over a period of almost three hundred years was so rare that mine offered unusual opportunity for study. I myself, as I have indicated, find it suggestive of many questions.

Emigrants are of two kinds: those who with their migration cut the umbilical cord that connects them with their past and those who hold it as taut as possible. Mother and Father were of the latter. Exiles they felt themselves to be and so did we children—a feeling that was fed by Father's trips East on business that, as the years passed, became more frequent. For he always reported them in detail, with accounts of the old friends, their new houses, their trips to Europe, their dinner tables. And there were, furthermore, those evidences of its superiority in the presents he brought back: bronze ladies, Oriental rugs, Chinese bowls, Bohemian glass vases, even dresses, and once a New York bonnet for Mother. I was seventeen years old before I realized that I was a Missourian and glad of it.

3 *Waiting for Her Carriage*

When we left Franklin we went straight to Carthage.[1] I did not see Joplin again for several years though I was to live there again and again. We went to "the Boardinghouse." If it had any other name I never knew it. A rambling, added-onto-house of which one side was all windows. In the backyard were two cabins where the Negro servants lived. In the dusk Jim and I would creep down to them and listen to their soft voices and queer expressions until Father put a stop to it. This was my first experience with the colored race, and I think that it gave me an understanding of them that my parents never had, and that has been of lasting value in my life.

Soon, all too soon for me, a house was found, and we left this enchanting boardinghouse in which for a long time I placed those stories with which I put myself to sleep.

Our house was down a side street, a story-and-a-half white house, crowded in between two others. On one side of us lived a bad boy. At least I thought he was bad, for his mother kept him tied up to a tree and we were not permitted to play with him. On the other side lived a nice boy who did not play much with us. Across the street was a wood yard. Away down the street was a park, at least they called it that, "Carter's Park." To go there Sunday afternoons with my father was a great treat. You entered a grove of trees under which grew violets, and came to a clear spring of water that bubbled out from the bottom of a high bluff of limestone. There was a hole beside it that led to a cave. My father was too dignified to take any interest in caves. Jim and I were later to explore it at the cost of some good clothes and a sound switching. Soldiers were said to have camped there during the Civil War, for across this park had been fought the first part of the Battle of Carthage.[2]

To reach this park we had to pass the houses where the Negroes lived. They were little rundown houses with the paint worn off, rags stuck in broken windows, chickens under the open porches, with never a blade of grass in the front yards, but often gay flowers at the back. In the doorways sat fat Negro

---

1. After J. P. Newell's election as county recorder of deeds in 1882, the family moved to the county seat of Carthage in 1883 (Livingston, *History of Jasper County . . . People*, 1:227).

2. Carter's Park is located at the east end of Chestnut Avenue. The Civil War engagement at Carthage took place on July 5, 1861.

women "resting" their bare feet, calling across to each other. It was not ugly or forlorn. Great trees, locusts and maples, filled the front yards and lined the streets. The houses were not cabins, but the discarded "first houses" of the settlers. There was something mysterious to me about this part of town. I was strictly forbidden to go there alone, but more than once I disobeyed.

I was asked to take part in a little home talent play given for our church. The play was *Cinderella*, and I was to be one of the fairies in the Maypole dance. I believed in fairies. I believed in Cinderella. I loved the white tarlatan dress with silver stars on it. We practiced one afternoon on Major Harding's lawn between the beds of tulips and the iron fence.[3] A sudden rain drove us into the parlor of the big, square house, the largest parlor I had ever seen, with a crystal chandelier and long mirrors. Across the hall was a "liberry" with books all over the walls. It all seemed part of the play, the pretty young lady playing at the piano, the tall lady talking to me as if I were a "grown-up."

Colored coachmen arrived, and then the doorbell rang. "I've come for Anna Brinkerhoff." Through the open door I could see the colored coachman with the big umbrella, standing on the wide porch. I tiptoed to the door and watched him as he escorted Anna to the waiting surrey with the curtains all about it. Came another colored driver for "Miss Bessie," came Jessie's mother for Jessie and Sallie, someone for Byrd, and so on, until one by one the other girls had gone each in a curtained surrey. But no one came for Emily, and so I waited. Miss Stella and Miss Fannie took me into the library.[4] They talked to me. Dishes rattled in the dining room, the gas lights were turned on, and still I waited. At last I heard my father's voice at the front door. "Where's Emily?"

"She's here," said Miss Fannie.

"But why hasn't she come home? The rain's over a long time. Her mother's been worried to death, but she'd no one to send until I came."

---

3. Grace Episcopal Church, at 820 Howard Street, was organized in 1870 (Diocese of West Missouri, *Diocesan Bulletin* 15:8 [May 1946]: 6–11, in Grace Episcopal Church File). H. H. Harding, who had served as Carthage mayor in 1875–1876, was a leading lawyer of the town. He lived at 813 Clinton (1888–1889 Carthage City Directory, 81; 1900 Population Schedule, Twelfth Census of the United States, Jasper County, Missouri, 1409).

4. Anna Brinkerhoff, daughter of First National Bank of Carthage president W. E. Brinkerhoff, lived with her family at 1141 Grand. Miss Bessie was possibly Bessie Hunt, in the Carthage High School class of 1898. Jessie Caffee was the daughter of Dr. Amos and Lacie Caffee, a doctor and druggist in Carthage (1900 Population Schedule, Jasper County, 1323). Sallie Boon (b. December 1878) was the daughter of a widow, Sallie W. Boon; she graduated from high school three years after ENB (ibid., 1391; Livingston, *History of Jasper County . . . People*, 1:543). Byrd Cunningham graduated from Carthage High School in 1891, three years ahead of ENB (Livingston, *A History of Jasper County . . . People*, 1:542). In 1900, the Hardings had two servants who lived in: Fannie Jackson and Sadie Ross (1900 Population Schedule, Jasper County, 1409).

"She's waiting, so she says, for her carriage," explained Miss Fannie.

"Her carriage!" and how my father laughed. "Her carriage! Why, she knows we haven't one!"

What my thoughts were as I trudged the three short blocks home beside my father I do not recall, for though the thoughts of children, as the poet says, may be long, long ones, they seem to leave no record. It is not only the incident that remains. It was many a day before I heard the last of that incident.

Thus rudely was my faith in pumpkin coaches betrayed. Nor was I allowed to forget it. Whenever I refused to accept some limitations of fact, someone of the family would say, "She is waiting for her carriage."

At Christmastime there arrived another sister, Julia, her best baby, Mother always insisted.[5] I remember a doll that said "Mama," a piano, and a set of red and yellow velvet furniture for the parlor that appeared as a "surprise" for Mother. When she saw them she sat down and cried. Why, I did not know, but I can imagine now that it was joy at attaining something she had long yearned for.

During this period the "Big Annie" who is so closely associated with my early life came to live with us. A tall, thin, dusty-blond Dane, she came to us straight from the old country knowing no word of English. Hardly had she arrived when she fell ill of typhoid fever, and Mother, since there were no hospitals, had to nurse her. When Annie recovered, her gratitude knew no bounds, and for twelve years she was Mother's faithful slave. Not only did she do the cooking and cleaning, but she took each child in turn under her care and even acted as Mother's personal maid.

Well educated in Danish, she looked down upon the other servants of the town, scorning to know them; and as others looked down on her, she had no friends, went nowhere, had no interests apart from ours. She had one friend who was a very fine dressmaker. She was also from Denmark, and probably told Mother about Annie. Her only knowledge of English or American was what she learned from us.

Since Mother was a born teacher, Big Annie's English was good, and she added to her vocabulary by listening when Mother read aloud in the evenings.

In the twelve years she lived with us the only money that she spent was the small amount she spent on birthday and Christmas gifts, with which she was most generous. She had left home provided apparently with enough underclothing to last her natural lifetime, some of it red woolen and some white cotton, and the two black silk dresses she brought over were quite enough to suffice her pride. These she made over periodically. She also retrimmed her two hats occasionally. I suppose she wore these on her rare trips downtown, but I do not remember having seen her in them. She may

---

5. Julia Porter Newell was born on December 21, 1883.

have bought her black cotton stockings and must sometimes have had to get new shoes, although those she wore were such queer flat ones that I doubt if she could have purchased them in Carthage. Her striped blue gingham dresses and large white aprons Mother provided, as she did the big eiderdown bathrobe and felt slippers she wore when she nursed a croupy child. Other needs she apparently did not have, for she refused to draw any cash wages, preferring to trust their accumulation in Father's hands, an accumulation that should have taught me a lesson in thrift, for when she went home on a visit ten years later, she had an opportunity to buy the little farm her father worked on, and sending home for her money, had enough at compound interest to purchase it. And this though her wages were two and a half dollars a week!

Our life would have been very different if it had not been for this "Big Annie." Long afterward when I was married and was complaining to Mother at my inability to accomplish all the things that she with her six children had managed to do, she said, "But you have not an Anna Anderson."

Every evening a tall slim young man and a short plump young lady sauntered down the street. I don't know how I knew it, some remark of my father's or some joke of his to the young man, but I did know somehow that they were lovers, that he was walking home with her, and someday they would be married. And every evening that I could, I would perch myself on the gate—yes, there was a gate with a picket fence—to wait for them and watch them out of sight.

Do all children see their childhood in such a romantic haze? Everything in those days seemed to me rare and momentous, and so I remember them.

4 School Days in the Eighties

My first school was a private one taught in the Little Holiness Church building some six blocks from our house.[1] The pupils, so it was said, were children who could not get along in public schools. I do not know about this. Mother chose it because she wanted Jim and me to start school together, and he, eighteen months younger than I, was not old enough to enter the public schools. For some reason, for either protection or restraint, she encouraged our doing everything together, with the result that for years, even after he had dropped behind me in school, we were known as "Jimily and Emily."

This comradeship with my brother accustomed me early to a masculine code. It enabled me to know boys as too few girls do. And since Jim dominated our little world, my sisters, too, lived under and by the same code. I was surprised in later years when I met the feminine substitute, subterfuge; the circuitous route was unknown to us. Lying, cowardice, cheating were held in scorn. Ability to take punishment was a test of character. Loyalty a supreme virtue. On the other hand, we sisters stood together against the privileged one, and thus sex loyalty and solidarity that so many women never know was accepted by us as natural. We never knew it was not common to all women until experience taught us so.

To me who had not been permitted to go outside our own yard except for Sunday school or an occasional downtown trip with Mother, the school building was in an intriguing spot. Not only was there a hotel to one side of it and a wood yard on the other, but across from it stood the county jail with men looking through the iron-barred windows. It was beyond the vacant lot where the courthouse had been before it burned. We were not permitted to go near it, but, fascinated, Jim and I would go home through the alley so that we could get a closer view of those faces whenever possible.

I remember only one of the pupils in that tiny school, a girl of fifteen, who was the undisputed leader. I stood in awe of her and with good reason. She was a witch, and could discover crime.

---

1. Miss Sarah Brooks established her school at 600 Maple in 1872 when she purchased a brick chapel from the Congregational Church for eight hundred dollars (1888 Carthage City Directory; North, *History of Jasper County . . . Townships*, 288–89).

It was the custom of the children to bring candy, peanuts, and popcorn and pass them around at recess to favored friends. Jim and I never had any to share. But one day I saw two dimes in Mother's bureau drawer. The amount of popcorn they bought was enough to treat the whole school.

I was enjoying myself hugely when Sallie said to me: "Emily, where did you get the money for that popcorn?"

"Mother gave it to me," I said.

"No, she didn't. Turn over your hands."

I turned them over, and she pointed to two white spots on my fingernails. "See those? They show that you have told a lie. Your mother never gave you that money. You stole it."

So my sin had found me out. I looked up at the barred windows of the jail, and without another word turned and ran home. Mother was not there. I crept under the bed and waited for her. When at last she came, I confessed what I had done. Sternly she gave me a lesson in "meum and tuum" that I have never forgotten. But she did not explain the white spots on my nails. For years whenever one came, I tried to remember what lie I had told.

The next year Jim and I were sent to public school and placed in room number two. To economize on textbooks, Mother asked that we be allowed to sit together. The smirks of the others at a boy and a girl sitting together were hard to bear.

We spent six winters in those schoolrooms, all alike, although we changed school buildings when we moved from one house to another. Those schoolrooms! Square, high ceilings—a dado painted an ugly gray—blackboards above it—chalk dust filling the troughs at the bottom of the blackboards where erasers rested—above them a dyspeptic brown, mottled paper. Bleak narrow windows—bare unpainted floors, desks always too large or too small. Teacher's platform with its pine table covered with green rep cloth hanging down. Two battered office chairs. A pine cupboard for books and pencils. Teacher in her sateen apron. A big, round, iron stove in the corner, coal box behind. The cold halls and cloakrooms. No flowers, pictures, or books.

We had calisthenics twice a day, before each session singing "Three Black Kittens," "Row, Sailor, Row," "We'll Meet at That Beautiful Shore," and "Scotland's Burning." Teacher read to us from *Bittersweet* or *Arthur Bonnicastle*. One finger must be held up to go to the outside privy, two for a drink of water. Monitors to spy on us when teacher was called out. One teacher came to us from St. Louis. She had never heard of apple showers. We all adored her and planned one for a Monday morning to show our appreciation for all she had done for us. But she misunderstood, and when forty apples came rolling across the floor to her desk she was furious. She gave us a sound lecture on respect and said we had hurt her feelings. None of us could move we were so shocked and heartbroken. How the superintendent laughed when she told him how she had been "insulted."[2]

Once a year we had Speaking Day. Teacher's desk was covered with glass vases of every size and kind with stiff bouquets in them—bleeding hearts, lilacs, hardy roses. Branches hung around the blackboard. Parents sat in chairs around the room. The children were in Sunday dresses and suits, the boys wearing neckties at other times regarded as too sissy. There were recitations, "Baby Bell," "Curfew Shall Not Ring Tonight," and "The One Hoss Shay"; dialogues; and once in a long time a solo.

Lessons? The multiplication tables backward and forward. Speed in adding columns. Long and short division. Writing? Yes, the Spencerian system—page after page of circles, ovals, and curlicues. Geography? The soil, products, the climate, the capitals of every nation. First elementary geography, and next year the same thing over again in longer words. Nothing about the beauty of old-world architecture, the mystery of the East, the charm of scenery. Nothing to stimulate our imagination and arouse our curiosity or make us want to travel. Facts. Dull, colorless facts. Heights of mountains, amount of tea produced in 1850, totals of population. Every country measured by America and found wanting. History? Dates, the number of troops in battles, the plan of campaigns, men's names. Our country always right and noble, the enemy always wrong, contemptible, and vicious. Grammar? Endless parsing and diagramming, mangling lovely things like "That orbed maiden with white fire laden, that mortals call the moon." Well, at least I can remember it! Reading? *The Wreck of the Hesperus, Snow-bound, The Vision of Sir Launfal.* Oh, we were very patriotic in our literature, with exceptions made for *Marmion* and *The Cataract of Lodore* [sic].[3] Drawing? Books in which to copy the squares and circles and angles on the opposite page. Examinations and report cards.

So I learned to read, write, and figure, though the latter never well enough to keep the stubs of my checkbook accurately. As for the unassorted lot of facts that were left with me, fortunately I have forgotten most of them, for in the world in which I lived they would have been of very little service. What, for example, did it matter in 1917, when a revolution in Russia stirred the world, how many square miles that country had covered in 1888 or what its boundaries? The articles by George Kennan in the old *Century* magazine, which I overheard Mother read to Father, had given me, at least, some notion

---

2. Professor Daniel Matthews was superintendent of the Carthage School in the first half of the decade of the 1880s; Professor J. M. White held the position in the latter years (Livingston, *History of Jasper County . . . People*, 1:236).

3. Henry Wadsworth Longfellow, *The Wreck of the Hesperus;* John Greenleaf Whittier, *Snow-bound: A Winter Idyl;* James Russell Lowell, *The Vision of Sir Launfal;* Sir Walter Scott, *Marmion: A Tale of Flodden Field;* Mary Wollstonecraft Shelley, *Lodore.*

of what the rebellion was all about.[4] I did not accept placidly this by-rote education. When I was nine my parents took me on a trip to California where I saw the Indians with their pottery at Albuquerque, walked across the Mojave Desert where our engine was stalled toward a mountain that seemed only a block away and proved to be miles, looked out through the Golden Gate, at the rocks covered with seals, played in the galleries of the old Palace Hotel with the son of a member of the first Chinese Commission to this country who still wore his native dress, went out to the new ostrich farm in Los Angeles. Reciting a geography lesson on California, I tried to tell my schoolmates about these things.

"That will do," said my teacher. "We've heard enough about that trip of yours."

Yet, thirty years later, when I met one of those schoolmates, he exclaimed, "You were the girl who went to California and told us all about it." Does he, I wonder, remember how long and wide the state is?

Jim and I traveled in a pair. Across the street from us was a grocery store where we were sent sometimes to get something wanted in a hurry. On one of these visits the grocer's son jumped on Jim and began to pummel him. Before I thought, I snatched a broom out of the rack and hit him on the head. When Jim got into a fight, I was usually there. Often I took a hand in it. Not that I kept to any Queensbury rules. If a broom was not handy, I used my nails and pulled hair. Nor can I charge this off to a maternal instinct. To this day I cannot see a person coerced by another without something in me rising up in protest.

When we were in the fourth grade Jim, one day, jumped pick-a-back on another boy as they entered the room. In punishment the teacher called the boys to the platform, made Jim climb on the other's back, and every time Jim's legs touched the floor switched them. This performance continued for some time, the pupils looking on with a mixture of amusement and horror. I stood it as long as I could and then advanced up the aisle saying: "You ought to be ashamed of yourself. You're a bully, that's what you are, a bully."

The teacher told me to sit down and keep still, and he would attend to me later. After school he did attend to me, but not with a switch. He turned to argument and soon had subdued me, for I was no Amazon, but an extremely diffident child. Only when I was outraged did combativeness overcome this diffidence.

I was not a favorite with my teachers. Jim always was. "Impertinent," they called me. "It is the way she looks at you," said one to my mother. Defense mechanisms had not, unfortunately for me, been heard of.

---

4. George Kennan (1845–1924) had traveled extensively in Russia and was a popular writer and lecturer, publishing numerous magazine and newspaper articles *(Dictionary of American Biography*, s.v. "Kennan, George"; hereafter cited as *DAB).*

Two boys who delighted to tease me would wait each day at the schoolyard gate and, as I passed through, pull the ribbons from my two pigtails. I had to retrieve the bows, for there was Mother to reckon with if I lost them, but I never spoke to the boys. Little did I dream that I would one day marry one of them.

Nor was I popular on the playground. Occasionally I was allowed to have the star part when we played "Little Red Riding Hood" because I had a red-lined coat. But usually I had to lend the cloak to someone else. I was never once a bride, and "wedding" was our favorite game. By going out of our way we could go home by the Baptist church. The steps of the old white frame building with its square tower furnished just the setting for one. So every evening we staged one there—Jim and his rival, Henry Cowgill, took turns at being the groom, and Jessie Caffee and some of the other girls at being the bride (Jim later married Jessie), but Joe Beebe was always the preacher, and I was always the bridesmaid—which indicates our appraisal by the others![5]

This pleasant diversion was suddenly stopped. The church steps no longer called forth visions of brides and flowers. They were the scene of a real crime. A highwayman held up a man there one night and shot him, leaving his body in a pool of blood. We went to see the bloodstains, gazed at them awestruck and tried to imagine how it had happened. We eagerly read all the papers and learned that the murdered man was a blacksmith, discovered by a hammer he had left on a pile of lumber nearby. We followed his murderer's trial with great interest—an interest never disclosed to Mother.

For my unimportance at school, I made up at home. There I was the oldest sister; and I could choose any game and take any part I wished. So I began early and continued late each day. Before Mother called us downstairs for breakfast, I threw my sisters into stares of horror by acting the last moments of Mary, Queen of Scots, as depicted by Abbot in the little red history, my red-lined coat for her dress, the bed for the scaffold; or, using the little tin bathtub, perform on Jim the heroic act of Charlotte Corday. With a chair for a tumbrel I would ride as Marie Antoinette to the guillotine, or turn away as a heartbroken Josephine from a stony-eyed Napoleon.[6] And when the lights were out at night, I would in whispers (for we were not allowed to talk) describe the latest experiences of Rollo in his many wanderings.

My second year at school was spent in room number eleven in a large square three-story brick building, four rooms to a floor, with one set of stairs

5. Henry Cowgill, born in 1877, was a classmate and childhood friend of Jim Newell.

6. Jacob Abbott, *History of Mary, Queen of Scots* (New York: Harper, 1876). French patriot Charlotte Corday (1768–1793) assassinated the revolutionary leader Jean Paul Marat in 1793. A tumbril is a two-wheeled cart used to carry prisoners to their execution.

for the girls and another for the boys.[7] The building was set in the center of grounds that covered a block. An invisible line separated the playground of the boys from that of the girls. In this room I received my only switching. I had whispered. Sent to the long, narrow, cold cloakroom to await the operation I put on my cloak. Other pupils similarly afflicted, I knew, reported to their parents who made indignant protests, but my parents had told me that if I were switched at school I could expect another one at home. So I kept mum and swore Jim to secrecy.

When we moved from Sixth Street, I entered room 3 of a ward school that had four grades.[8] It was a brick building, like a short-armed cross, ungainly in its height and with a flat-topped roof. Here the boys and girls could play together on the grassless, treeless yard. Water in fiber buckets with dippers tied to their pails sat on the uncovered platform entrances.

I was promoted to the fifth grade and thereafter had to go a mile straight up Main Street, across the square, to the building where I had before attended number 2. Attendance and promptness were the cardinal virtues, unexcused absences and tardiness the worst crimes. The big bell rang each morning at eight-thirty to tell the children all over town to start. It rang again at nine—for them to enter the building. There was five minutes' grace. Anyone arriving after that was a culprit. The room having the highest percentage of promptness and attendance for the month was awarded a half holiday, and competition was fierce. Once our room was slated for it, and then, on the last day, Jim and I were tardy. One tardiness might have been forgiven, but still traveling in a pair, we made two. Our room lost the holiday. Our fellow students ostracized us, the teacher lectured us, and we were sent to the superintendent of whom we stood in such awe that we considered the advisability of going home instead. But once in his office the twinkle in his eye mitigated the severity of his words.

I do not criticize the schools of Carthage of that day. As schools went in towns like ours, they were very good. The superintendent was an understanding, progressive man, and later was to exercise an influence in my life. But that was the way schools were. Today with the advent of modern techniques and child psychology the whole approach to education has been revamped.

For one thing, however, I am glad that I went to those public schools: the democracy of its playground. Among our playmates were the children of the saloon keepers, and in those days no one ranked below them. There were two children whose clothes denoted poverty, but it made no difference.

---

7. Central School, located on South Main between Seventh and Chestnut Streets, was built in 1870 on two and a half acres of land (Livingston, *History of Jasper County . . . People*, 1:128).

8. ENB had entered the Benton School at Mound and McGregor Streets.

There was no distinction in dress unless it was that some girls wore white aprons over their woolen or gingham dresses and others colored ones. We never heard the word *foreigner,* or *Jew,* or *Catholic.* The boys all went barefoot, weather permitting, and only one wore a tie. Only one little girl held aloof, a Bostonian, exiled in these strange surroundings. Today I meet these old schoolmates on the street or in towns where I speak. They are in every walk of life, failures and successes. Yet there is always a bond of memory.

We were expected by our mothers to confine our extra-school friendships to girls whose mothers they knew. But sometimes I went home with others more friendly. I found their houses interesting, their mothers' hands in the suds. These mothers wore Mother Hubbards. The backyards had cinders and bottles strewn about. There were beds in the sitting room. Dining tables in the kitchen stood with soiled white cloths making hills and mountains over the dishes beneath. I was switched for this if discovered. But as my own daughter told me after a similar punishment long afterward, "Well, it was worth a whipping."

What I learned about people made up perhaps for what school did to the clean white sheet of my mind. Long afterward I was to take a college course in sociology, only to discover with surprise that I had learned all it had to teach me in the old ward school and in our neighborhood surroundings.

My education, what I have, was gained around our family dinner table. We children were to be seen and not heard, and so we listened while Mother and Father talked to each other. And they talked about everything. His business, politics, the news of the day. As soon as he entered the front door and called "Anna" she came running, and thereafter, as long as he was in the house, they were not to be interrupted for anything short of the imminent death of one of the children.

5 Midwest

The summer after my first year at public school we moved into another house. Its location, I thought, enchanting.[1] The neighborhood might have seemed to elders to offer little to tempt the imagination, but I dramatized it all. In the first place it was on a street that ran from the square to the depot, and so people were passing constantly. In the second, it stood on a high terrace held back by a stone embankment on which we children could sit, dangling our legs, to watch the herdics and cabs dash to and from the trains. The circus parades passed us twice going to and from their lot down by the depot, and at election time there were the flambeau parades with men carrying oil torches. When the "transparencies" showed the words *Cleveland and Hendricks*, we waived our little caps with those names on the red bands; when they showed *Blaine and Logan* we kept discreetly silent. And when news came that Cleveland had lost I cried only to find next morning that he had won.[2]

Some houses had been planted there years before when the residential section promised to go in that direction. How glad I am the contractors were wrong! For otherwise I might never have learned about the "economic phases" of existence. The most interesting thing of all to me about our house was its nearness to the mills and factories that had taken over the street and left these houses an alien group dropped in their midst.

Between our house and the square were two blocks of stores, grocery, second-hand, two-story buildings in the upper part of which people lived with their back porches perched in midair. Crowded in between were little buildings where friendly men in shirtsleeves and aprons sat in doorways with nothing inside their shops but a counter with tin cans scattered on them and a table or two covered with dirty oilcloth. I never saw anyone in these shops and do not know what they were for. Probably quick-order places—the word *café* had not yet been adopted—where one could get a stew made of cove oysters or ham and eggs in a hurry.

---

1. The Newells moved to 222 North Main Street in Carthage.
2. In 1884 Grover Cleveland of New York and Thomas Hendricks of Indiana were the Democratic nominees for president and vice president. The Republicans ran James G. Blaine of Maine and John A. Logan of Illinois. In the popular vote, Cleveland's margin of victory was less than thirty thousand votes.

A block below was a woolen mill with a spring behind it filled with watercress.[3] Standing on the sidewalk I could peer down and watch the workers walking back and forth before their looms in the gaslit basement, and perched on our stone terrace I would drop into conversation with some of them as they went by in the evening. Certainly these workers passing every day with their buckets made me aware of a life that was different from our own in a not entirely pleasant way. I remember particularly a nice large woman who told me how she had to get up at four o'clock to get her housework done, and about the baby she had to leave at home.

Beyond the woolen mill was a cracker factory that made a glorious blaze one night while we children stood shivering in the yard and the firemen put wet blankets on our roof to save us from the flying sparks. Beyond that was the ice factory, the apple evaporator, and the flour mills. I learned something of them all and thus knew early that this is a work world as well as a play one. On the way to school I passed a shop where a friendly blacksmith in a leather apron and blackened face let me watch him turn the horseshoes in his forge, where the charcoal glowed, and pound them on the anvil, while his assistant pared the horses' hooves. There were also a lumberyard and a wagon factory that I examined in detail.[4] No need, for me at least, of a teacher-conducted tour to industries. The work of the world was done under our eyes daily and knit into our conception of it.

Nor were the darker phases of existence hidden from us. There was a "Last Chance Saloon" down by the factories, and often we saw men reeling noisily away from it. On the way to school we passed another saloon. I always walked slowly past its swinging doors in an effort to catch a glimpse of the inside, but all I could see was a patch of mirror above and men's shoes below. We knew about saloons though, for our washwoman's husband was the town drunkard. Mystical places of wickedness they appeared to be.

We learned about disaster, too. A few blocks up a side street was a high railroad trestle over a river. One Sunday two adults and three children were caught there when the train came. The mother held on by her hands until rescued, but the children were killed. We ran off to gaze at the place in horror.

Our house was not at all attractive, but it had a deep backyard that made

---

3. The Carthage Woolen Mill was at 398 North Main Street.

4. The Carthage Cracker Factory and Bakery, Grag and Durfee proprietors, was located on North Main Street (1888 Carthage Carthage City Directory). N. F. Cheadle was an ice dealer at 329 South Main Street; Magree and Kendrick's Fruit Evaporator was at the corner of Vine and Meridian Streets; the Cowgill and Hill Flour Mill was north of the railroad tracks; Rubetti Mills was located at 327 North Main Street. Tangner-Brosius Livery and Construction Company, founded in 1885, was located at Fifth and Lincoln Streets; McLees and Caffee, Blacksmith and Carriage Makers, was at 414 South Grant Street (ibid.). See *Carthage, Missouri, Souvenir: Past and Present, Progress and Prosperity* (Kansas City: Freeman Publishing, c. 1910), 35.

up for everything. At first we hung on the terrace a large part of the time. But not all the time. For in the side yard was a queer pile of limestone rocks with little fossils in them, arranged in a large circle with a large one in the center. A perfect place for games. It could be a castle, a Druid altar, anything we wanted. The backyard was divided into two parts. The front part was just an ordinary backyard, rough and pebbly. But at the edge of it was a row of lilacs and behind them an undiscovered country grown thick with weeds. It could be a forest, or the plains. And we cut out of the weeds rooms, one opening off another. We could cook in them and eat provisions sneaked when Anna was not looking, and imagine for days on end that we lived there and only went into the house at night and mealtime for visits. There was a lady named "Clarabelle" who wrote each week in the St. Louis paper about the gay doings at Newport and other summer resorts. I read her column avidly, and we laid out, behind the lilacs, a summer resort for our dolls, with a bathing bench made out of a tub, a box for a dancing pavilion, and dressed them properly for each occasion. "Samanthy at Saratoga" helped us in that. We had a cemetery there for a brood of swallows that had tumbled down our chimney, and a jewelry store where burdock-burr jewelry was sold for pins.

I learned early that it was easier to get a nickel from Father than from Mother—also that it was easier to get one from him if I asked for it when some of his friends were present. So, often on my way home from school I would stop at his office on "the Square."

To go to this office we had to mount a flight of stairs, the risers placarded with signs: McReynolds and Halliburton, Attorneys at Law.[5] Then we passed down a long hall and down some other steps. At the second door a shingle hung on a rod over the doorway: County Recorder of Deeds. The walls of the office were lined with brown-stained shelves holding books two feet long, bound in sheepskin with squares of shiny red leather on the backs for the title. In one corner was a crudely made walnut cupboard with pigeonholes filled with papers. An old iron safe stood in another. And near the window was a high, flat desk on which stood open the recording book of the moment, with a high stool in front of it. Sometimes I perched there and Father would let me register some deeds. Abstractors must have wondered when they came across that wobbly, childish hand. My curiosity was aroused by the big yellow cork jars sitting conveniently about the room. "Cuspidors" I was told they were, and their use was explained to me. I was glad Father didn't use them. Frequently the office was filled with men, their chairs tilted back on two legs, their feet high, cigars in their mouths. I stood by the hour in a corner listening to them talk.

---

5. J. W. Halliburton and Samuel McReynolds had been law partners since 1877 (McGregor, *Biographical Record of Jasper County*, 112–17).

Among them was a Colonel Phelps, the lawyer for the Missouri Pacific Railroad, who was said to rule the state through a little black bag filled with passes.[6] Years afterward, when working for suffrage, I was to have my own experience with him, but as a little girl I knew him only as Father's friend who sent us the passes on which we—and everyone else in Carthage—traveled. He was an elegant, unapproachable man who never forgot a wedding present or a funeral wreath.

He was one of the most brilliant lawyers in the state, and also our most distinguished citizen, to whom delegations periodically presented a gold-headed cane or a watch. To me he was a most romantic figure. Not only did he have what we considered great wealth, and what I know now to be the air of power, but the aura of tragedy hung over him. As a young man he had been shot in the courtroom and still carried the bullet in his head. As I watched the crooked eye it had left, I would wonder just where the bullet lay.

He had gone down into history as the author of a story pointed at William Stone, Missouri's United States senator who was chairman of the Foreign Relations Committee during World War I.[7] Senator Stone had twitted Colonel Phelps with being a lobbyist. For answer the colonel told a story about two dogs on his father's farm. Chicken eggs had been disappearing at a great rate. One of the dogs was caught sucking them and punished. The other was considered innocent. Then one day the second dog was discovered pushing the earth over a heap of eggshells. "We are like those dogs, Senator Stone and I," the colonel explained. "We both suck eggs, only he hides the shells; I don't."

This was long after those days when I watched the colonel with such interest in Father's office. At that time, William Stone was only a little-known lawyer in the neighboring town of Nevada, seeking his first election to Congress. Father and Mr. Phelps were supporting his candidacy; others were opposed to him. Listening at the office I overheard many of their discussions and plans. My most vivid memory of the campaign is of Father coming home one night with a black eye, having been, so he said, "thrown out of the chair" and Mother putting beefsteak on his bruise and sending him off on the midnight train to preside at the congressional convention.

Long afterward when I was in politics myself and men would say to me, "When you have been in politics longer, Mrs. Blair, you will understand how these things are done," I would remember this campaign of Mr. Stone's and the long discussions in that old office. Their assumption that I had never

---

6. William Phelps had come to Carthage in 1867 (ibid., 88–89).

7. William J. Stone, from Nevada, Missouri, was first elected to Congress in 1884. He was reelected twice, in 1886 and 1888. He was governor from 1893 to 1897. In 1903, he was elected U.S. senator and reelected twice. He died in office in 1918 (David D. March, *The History of Missouri*, 2:1182, 1626, and 1628).

heard anything about politics until after women were made voters always amused me.

Beyond Father's office the back stairs led to a wide street. There stood the open doors of the fire department. You had to scurry past, or the huge black horses might rush out over you. They were standing inside with great heavy collars suspended above them ready to drop at the sound of the bell. Sometimes you had to wait until the big two-wheeled hose carts and the hook and ladder wagon roared by. It was exciting to watch: the firemen in their wide-rimmed oilskin hats and blue flannel shirts clinging to the sides. Next to the fire department was the calaboose with its barred windows—by standing on tiptoe you could even see the barred doors into the cells.

I can see no later Carthage as clearly as I do that one when I was eight years old.

I adored my father, day after day going all the long way uptown just for the joy of walking home with him. My jerky steps I have always attributed to my efforts to make my short, chubby legs keep up with his. When I was older he often took me with him on an all-day drive to look at some farms. As we drove along, he would tell me the history of that western Missouri border during the Civil War when Order Number Eleven laid it bare; of the runaway legislature that sat at Cassville; of the battles of Wilson's Creek and Carthage.[8] When I was laid up with sore eyes for a time, he sat and read to me stories of Darius and Alexander and Cyrus, or again his favorite passages from his little, thickly marked copy of Shakespeare that I still have.

He was a queer mixture of urbane dignity and friendly joviality. His quick temper frequently made enemies for him, but after he died, we were surprised at the number of men and women who came to tell us of money loaned to them in an emergency, of something done to save their homes from foreclosure, or of bills never collected from them. He also had a quick wit that always kept the house gay when he was there. When he was away on one of his frequent trips, life seemed suddenly very dull.

A few memories of that time stand out especially dearly. One is my mother going fishing with my brother. My brother had reached the age of tadpole and frog interest. He wanted to go down to the river with the boys. Whether Mother feared the companionship of the boys or the water I don't know.

---

8. After the Battle of Carthage on July 5, 1861, Confederate forces defeated Union general Nathaniel Lyon at Wilson's Creek near Springfield on August 10. Confederate Sterling Price then raided north, putting Lexington under siege from mid-September until his withdrawal south in early October. On October 29, the pro-Confederate legislature moved from Neosho to Cassville. For Missouri in the Civil War, see William Parrish, *Turbulent Partnership: Missouri and the Union, 1861–1865*. On August 25, 1863, Federal general Thomas Ewing issued Order Number 11, removing most of the population from Jackson, Cass, and Bates Counties (see William Parrish, *A History of Missouri: Volume III, 1860–1875*, 100–101).

But down to the river she went with the motley bare-legged crew, and an incongruous figure she must have looked in her tailored dress and dignified hat as she sat on the bank watching the old Negro who lived down there in a shack show them the mysteries of putting worms on hooks and catching tadpoles with a net. A tub of tadpoles sat in our yard where we watched their metamorphoses.

Another memory is the walk from church at night. Our church was clear across the town. As far as the square we had for company "Aunt Lacie," the portly godmother of the church who never missed a service, supplied the altar with flowers, laundered the vestments, and, when necessary, swept the church and cut the grass in the large churchyard. An energetic person, the church was her recreation and dissipation. Under her wing she always had the neighbors' children and her daughters. Mother and she walked together, my brother, Jim, with her daughter Jessie, and one of the neighbors, Sallie Boon, and I. Next to her church in her loyalties came the Republican Party. In later years her dignified, silent doctor husband, a type more common in those days than now who never seemed to see you yet missed nothing of what went on, became a Silver Democrat. But no such apostasy for "Aunt Lacie." She was a great gardener, and chrysanthemums were her specialty. With these chrysanthemums she and her husband waged a silent political battle that the town watched with interest. When there was a Bryan meeting or rally, the doctor would string the white chrysanthemums along the porch.[9] As soon as he had left, "Aunt Lacie" would replace them with the yellow chrysanthemums. When he came home to dinner, he put the white ones back. After he left, she changed them again. During the afternoon when she would leave on one of her almost daily visits of charity, he changed them again. And when there was a McKinley meeting or rally, the whole performance was gone through once more.

But to continue our walk from church. As far as the square all were safe. But there Aunt Lacie left us. And the journey down Main Street to our house from the square in the dark was fearsome. Weird shapes seemed to lurk in the lumberyard. Lurching men sometimes passed us. Every corner seemed to conceal a possible adventure. We drew close together, Mother, Jim, and I, and conversed fast and furiously to keep our courage up.

One summer I was laid up with boils. As a result of which *Huckleberry Finn, Tom Sawyer, Little Women,* and *The Old-Fashioned Girl* have always been

---

9. William Jennings Bryan (1860–1925) was first elected to Congress in 1890. He served until 1894 when he unsuccessfully attempted to gain a Senate seat. He then was editor of the *Omaha World-Herald* until his nomination for president at the Chicago Democratic convention in 1896. In that election, he waged a fervent, but losing, "free silver" campaign against conservative Republican William McKinley (*DAB*, s.v. "Bryan, William Jennings"). The white chrysanthemums symbolized Bryan's advocacy of free silver; the yellow flowers stood for the Republican belief in the gold standard.

associated in my mind with a prone position and the odor of oil-seed poultices. Convalescence is associated with a tea party to which I wore a Prussian-blue hat, concave-shaped with scarlet flowers upon the top, and at which I was the tea pourer at one of the small tables.

I came home one day from school and found the house full of children who sprang out at me screaming, "Surprise, surprise!" There was a table full of presents and ice cream with pink cake. And when the children left saying properly and primly, "I've had a nice time. Thank you," I answered. "Isn't that funny, so have I."

6 More of the Midwest

All this time I was not unaware of what was going on at home. I did not reason out then that Mother was making her way in Carthage and getting great satisfaction out of it, but the incidents that stand out now in my mind could have been fixed there only because of the significance I attached to them at the time. The luncheon she gave for twelve ladies who had first invited her marked a milestone. It was probably the first formal party she had given since she had moved, and involved the purchase of new table linen and some dishes. A centerpiece of flowers came from a florist eighteen miles away. The menu was important and so, I realized, were the guests.

There were sets in Carthage. One never called them classes. There was the Presbyterian set, steady substantial people who frowned on dancing and card playing and lived in the square brick houses set back on lawns behind iron fences with iron urns beside the long walks to the front door. They had sewing parties and "receptions." Then there was the Methodist set, some of whom lived in square houses also but houses usually built of wood. They had fewer receptions and got their social life out of prayer meetings and missionary societies. And there was the society set who lived in all kinds of houses, some of them very small. They gave evening parties and luncheons and played cards at both, danced at the Assembly, and went every Thanksgiving to a ball given by the local militia organization, the Carthage Light Guard.[1] The sets overlapped a little, especially among the young married people. There were Presbyterians in the society set, but their "in" was frequently interrupted by revivals when they would eschew cards and dancing for a while or, defying the elders, be disciplined by them. There were Episcopalians and Methodists at the Presbyterian receptions, but at the society luncheons or evening parties few Methodists, for they regarded the society crowd as just as wild and wicked as the straightlaced today do the gay young crowd at the country club dances.

The children of all intermingled. It couldn't be helped when we all went to public school. Later, some of the Presbyterian children withdrew from the others and formed a circle of their own that scorned the younger society

---

1. The Carthage Light Guard was officially formed in January 1876. It was as much a social as a military organization. For its history, see Ward Schranz, "The Story of the Carthage Light Guard: Some Historical Facts about a Famous Organization of This City."

crowd. But there were always some who, to their parents' dismay, could not be retrieved. Among them there were even a few Methodists. But never, to my knowledge, a Baptist.

I have little knowledge of how the other sets lived. But in the society set there were a few who set the pace, the others keeping up with them according to their means. Among these, three women stand out in my memory. Of one of them I became in later years a great friend and admirer. She was a Kentucky woman with a southern drawl and an olive complexion dotted here and there with flat moles.[2] To her I owe a great deal. Not only did she make me at home in her book-lined library, but she showed me a composed home, developed slowly to satisfy aesthetic tastes instead of bought to indicate success, or merely organized to serve utilitarian purposes. In her small way she had a salon, for she was in the tradition of the women who have made civilization. But her remark when I was a diffident awkward fat girl of twelve, "Will says that you are a picture of me when I was your age," made up for much overlooking on the part of boys and girls, for it prophesied a future.

The other two were sisters, young married women whose enormously rich brother in St. Louis (he later founded Brookings Institute in Washington) had built them an English cottage out in exclusive Cassil Place.[3] Stanford White designed the house. Gay young women, full of fun, they simply carried on in Carthage the social life to which they were accustomed. Leadership of Carthage society would have seemed amusing to them. But the weight of the money back of them, the legend of their life in St. Louis, gave their every act authority. Their unassuming elegance drew those who envied or aspired to it, as well as those who saw in their irresponsible lightheartedness a new way of enjoying life. So all unbeknownst to them, the social set imitated them. They were crusaders of a new standard.

These were by no means the only women who mattered socially. There were older women whose friendship and recognition my mother valued even more. They lived in the brick houses I have mentioned.

Well, all these women were at this luncheon. That I remember this tells its own story.

---

2. Anna Belle Caffee, wife of drug wholesaler Dr. William K. Caffee, was born in 1860 in Kentucky. The Caffees lived at 705 South Main Street (1888 Carthage City Directory; 1900 Population Schedule, Jasper County, 1392).

3. Mr. and Mrs. R. A. Montgomery and Mr. and Mrs. Fred B. Houston moved to Carthage in the late 1880s. The brother of the two women was Robert Brookings of St. Louis. Brookings financed the home at Cassil Place, which was a development on land owned by G. A. Cassil northwest of the city square at Blanche and Central Streets (1888 Carthage City Directory; *Carthage Evening Press*, January 7, 1956, in Beimdiek Family Folder).

There was a Shakespeare Society "annual," an open meeting to which husbands were invited. My mother appeared as Queen Katherine in a brocaded black velvet dress with a wired "real lace" collar, which had been sent out by one of her sisters in Franklin.

"Aren't you proud of your mother?" everyone asked me. And I was. It was not the words she spoke. I could have said them myself in just the same accents, so often had I heard her rehearse them in the parlor at home. But it was different seeing her admired, acclaimed. It made her into something very important.

Sometime during this period I organized my first club made up of Annie, three Clarkson girls who lived across the street, and myself.[4] We had an open session for our parents and put on a program made up, I am afraid, of an essay on Longfellow and a dialogue, and Mother, wise woman that she was, instead of laughing at us, surprised us with ice cream and cake.

One winter a recently widowed aunt came to visit us and stayed a year in Carthage. Aunt Margaretta—only her sisters dared to call her "Maggie"— wore a sweeping black widow's veil that hung almost to the floor, and she looked very beautiful under it. Her two children had the most unbelievable clothes; the boy in a black velvet suit with lace collars, and the girl, whose long hair hung in curls, white cashmere dresses trimmed in lace.[5] Aunt Margaretta had sung in New York church choirs and concerts. She had velvet-framed photographs, heavy carved silver soup spoons, a rug she hung on the wall, and she insisted that Father buy finger bowls and bread and butter plates. Everyone said such nice things about her and sent her flowers. It seemed queer to me that she should cry so much.

This aunt was responsible for my first suspicion that Santa Claus did not come down a chimney, for shortly before Christmas I found some little bits of blue silk on the parlor floor that later matched the dress of my new doll. I forgave her this, however, when for Christmas dinner we had ice cream sent down from the hotel, the first time we had ice cream during the winter.

Twice a peculiar thing happened through these years. Jim, Annie, and I were invited to spend a day with a friend of Mother's. We recognized such a visit as an event, especially as our hostess devoted herself so completely to us. But strangely we did not associate the two visits with each other. So we were

---

4. James D. Clarkson, a real estate agent and the owner of farm implement stores, and his wife, Ida Cornell, had three daughters: Pearl (b. 1878), Edna (b. 1881), and May (b. 1884). They lived at 227 North Main Street (1888 Carthage City Directory; 1900 Population Schedule, Jasper County, 1455; North, *History of Jasper County . . . Townships*, 330).

5. Henry Church, ENB's aunt Margaretta's husband, died on March 15, 1885. They had two children: Katherine Gray Church, born in New York City on May 6, 1881, and Henry Seymore Church, born in New Brighton, Staten Island, on April 12, 1883. Margaretta remarried on August 6, 1891, to Albert J. Bothwell.

as surprised the second time as the first when Father came to announce that we had another little sister.[6]

Perhaps we were too interested in the baby, overwhelmed by the strangeness of Mother's illness, or awed by the nurse for questions to occur to us. Or perhaps we were just young. I was ten when the second came. When I was fourteen another was expected. Mother then took me into her confidence.

"Something lovely is going to happen to us," she said, explaining that the birth of a baby was a wonderful thing, normal, yet a miracle, too. That a child was the consummation of the most beautiful thing in a woman's life, a man's love for her, and that motherhood was the greatest thing that could happen to a woman. More, she shared with me her plans for the layette, and took me with her to Rose's Store to select the batistes, embroideries, and laces for the little dresses, the soft flannels to be made into petticoats. We went in the evening, the store kept open just for us by "Miss Jennie," as Mother could not appear in the daytime "in her condition."[7] "Miss Jennie" was an old friend of mine who always asked me, when I went for a spool of thread, how my mother was and before I left knew exactly where the garment I wore was bought and how much it had cost.

The child was stillborn. And that, too, was explained to me by Mother when Father took the little casket to the new lot in the cemetery.

Was my mother cloaking a fact of life in sentimentality when she talked of her joy in a seventh child? Perhaps. Yet she gave me a sane attitude toward nature's reproductive process for which I was grateful when I saw the revulsion of other girls. The sentimentality was to slough off when I had my own experiences. The sanity remained.

For another thing I am grateful to my mother. Although we always had a baby in the house, I never remember having had to take care of one. When I asked her about this many years later she said, "I had seen older children made drudges of when I was young, and made up my mind that mine should never be so penalized. The babies were my responsibility, not yours."

Yet when they were two or three years old, Annie and I took a great interest in them, assuming as a game that Ella was her child and Getta mine. Sometimes we kept up the myth for weeks. If Mother was behind it, she must have been very clever, for never did we suspect it.

---

6. Margaretta Louise Newell was born on October 26, 1885, and Ella Rebecca was born on June 26, 1887.

7. R. H. Rose's Dry Goods Store, established in 1873, was located on the north side of the square. Jeannie Sheffield clerked in Rose's (1895 Carthage City Directory; special edition of the *Carthage Evening Press* edited by women, October 9, 1895).

7 *Our Droll Generation*

When I was eleven we moved into "the new house."[1] This move was momentous. I felt it to be a great event, for the house had been months in the building. I knew this because I had heard it all discussed at home, board by board, and watched it grow out of a hole in the ground as we visited it each Sunday. This was our very own. And always when I speak of "the old home," it is of this house I think. For here my father was to lie in death. I was to be married there. One February day I was to open that front door, my first baby in my arms, and see my mother turn from the piano in surprise. Years later it was to be abandoned in sorrow. But I could not foresee these things then anymore than I could know all the economies that had gone into its making, or suspect the pride with which my mother must have surveyed it as a goal she had set long before. But I did know it marked a new epoch in our lives.

How grand it was to us with its square tower set on a corner, its narrow verandas on front and side, its carpeted rooms, its fireplace with bracketed overmantel and shiny green tiles, its folding doors that slipped into walls, its square reception hall, its china closet, its furnace, its laundry tubs, and most of all, its one bathroom. All of these things were new to us. Not one of them had we had in the house left behind, square room opening out of square room. And these things meant then what owning two cars did forty years later, or buying an electric refrigerator in 1930. They fixed you. You had them or you did not, and just a few did. Only a few years before had I first heard that mystical word *bathroom*. A friend, describing another's new house, had said to my mother, "And what do you think! It has a bathroom." Years later when my sisters and I went back to look at our mansion we were amazed at how it had shrunk!

The new house closed over us, absorbed us into it. We had found a happy haven. All the other houses had been ports of entry. While they undoubtedly left their marks upon us in many ways, still I think of myself and the childhood experiences while I lived in them as apart from the inside of a house. Thereafter the two were indefinably but inextricably wound together.

What interested me most, however, were the neighbors. Across the street was the big house of Major Harding, with tulip beds and a greenhouse, where

---

1. Their new address was 826 Clinton Street.

I had waited for my carriage. From Ohio the major. Next was the southern, one-story house of "Mom Betts." From Cincinnati, Mrs. Betts. Up the street lived a Judge Harrison from Virginia. On the corner below, Mr. Roessler from Germany. On our side of the street were the Allens from Iowa, a lady from Indiana, and one from New York. Only one native Missourian among the lot.[2]

The "new house" was on a two-block street. We thought of these two blocks only as "our street" because at each end was a jog beyond which there were no sidewalks. At one end was the corner grocery store with everything in it from a spool of thread to red-hots, all jumbled together and a thick, musty, spicy smell, and Mrs. Embree, tall, cadaverous, in a belted-in calico Mother Hubbard.[3] The route "uptown" turned there. At the other jog was a small white house set back in a whole block of green grass and oak trees—Colonel Phelps lived here.

On the corner above us stood the Catholic church with the priest's house beside it. As Father acted as financial adviser to the priests, being passed on from incumbent to incumbent, we had a very friendly feeling toward them. Some of them were scholars of whom Father had a high opinion, passed on, of course, to us. The church, too, fascinated me. A small, white-painted building into which we sneaked sometimes to see the candles and the blue and gold statue and again on Saturday evenings to see the priest pray before the pictures on the wall. On Sundays we hung upon the front gate exchanging friendly pleasantries with the Catholics whom we came to know by sight on their way to church. Queerly, we had no personal friends among them. I was quite grown before I ever knew well a member of that church. That and the candles and the statues made it seem quite extraneous to us, a little exotic and mystical, and yet I had a certain sense of fellowship with these Catholics due to the fact that the church to which I belonged also observed Lent and did not take part in revivals. Later this feeling of fellowship was increased when my history teacher in high school always managed to slur the Protestant Episcopal Church and the Roman Catholic Church together. What she evidently felt was expressed to me years later by a woman who came

---

2. H. H. Harding, who lived at 813 Clinton Street, was born in Ohio. Nannie P. Betts, born in Kentucky in 1846, was the mother-in-law in the household of Herbert Wolcott. Lawyer D. A. Harrison was born in 1823 in Ohio and lived at 845 Clinton. Reuben Roessler was born in Ohio in 1828, though both of his parents were from Germany; he lived at 803 Clinton. Merchant B. B. Allen and his wife, Elizabeth, were both from Iowa and lived at 820 South Clinton (1888–1889 and 1895 City Directories; 1900 Population Schedule, Jasper County, 1413).

3. Frances Embree was wife of general merchant Thomas J. Embree. They lived at 313 South Lyon Street (1888 Carthage City Directory; 1900 Population Schedule, Jasper County, 1402). Their Groceries and Dry Goods store was located at 415 East Chestnut Street (1895 Carthage City Directory).

to ask me, as vice chairman of the Democratic National Committee, what to her was evidently an important question: "Is Mr. McAdoo a Catholic?"[4]

"No," I said to her. "I think he is an Episcopalian." "Almost as bad," she said as, unaware of my religion, she leveled a long forefinger to emphasize our dreadfulness.

In after years when I was giving lectures on books, and someone would object to some recommended book because "life is not like that," I was always to recall this short street of ours. In the block above us a man walked into the home of his best friend one morning and shot him dead, making two children orphans and dragging them together with his own young wife and children through all the horrors of his murder trial. Another man, liked and respected, left town suddenly one night after a murder with which his name was always to be connected. A woman divorced her husband that he might marry her sister and, when her only child was almost grown, let her go to the husband because he could give her more advantages. Two women divorced their husbands after twenty-five years of married life, one for drunkenness, the other for unfaithfulness. A boy did time in jail.

Yet this was not regarded as an unusually unfortunate neighborhood. On the contrary, it was considered a privileged one. These things happened over a period of years. Only when I gather them together do I realize how many were the dark threads through the small pattern.

In the old house we had on the ground floor a parlor, Mother's bedroom, and a dining room—which was also the sitting room. In the new house all the bedrooms were upstairs, and downstairs was an entrance hall and a parlor, and a room we pridefully called the library though it contained only three or four small bookcases.

I can see Mother now sitting by the center light reading aloud, Father sinking back in his easy chair, my sister Annie trying to read her own book and listen too, Jim playing some game and listening, and I sitting by, all ears, while Big Annie sat in the edge of the dining room with the family darning, making there her first acquaintance with the English language. When our bedtime came we silently rose, kissed our parents, and went up the stairs into the dark, calling back again and again "Goodnight" to reassure ourselves until our lights were on. If we overstayed the appointed hour, we well knew we would go earlier the next night. Of course we missed the part of the book read after our departure, but our imaginations bridged that gap as best they could. We at least grew accustomed to good English, had an idea of the plots of the novels, and became acquainted with the styles of the various authors. If we wanted to pick up the books at other times we could do so, and increasingly as we grew older we did.

---

4. William Gibbs McAdoo, Woodrow Wilson's secretary of treasury and also his son-in-law, was a Democratic presidential contender during the 1920s.

I made the acquaintance of such writers of the late eighties and nineties as Hardy, Meredith, Tolstoy, Mark Twain, and the Victorians such as Dickens, Thackeray, Ruskin, Eliot, Hawthorne, and caught snatches of Macaulay's *English History*, Carlyle's *French Revolution*, Guizot's *French History*, Gibbon's *Rise and Fall of the Roman Empire*.[5]

Father and Mother were especially fond of drama and read and reread aloud, my father taking part, Shakespeare and the Elizabethan dramatists. My father had a small copy of Shakespeare, I remember, so worn that it almost fell to pieces, the margins dark with penciled notes. Dante, Milton, Spenser, and many more of those writers considered by the twentieth century as indispensable concomitants to culture were read and overheard by us. My mother was a born student and was never content until they had thoroughly covered an author or a period. For each she arranged a bibliography of collateral reading all her own, made up of biographies, essays of criticism, histories. Her lists would not meet professional standards. For those with universities at their back doors today this amateurish pursuit of self-improvement may seem pathetic. Yet it sprang from a real desire for knowledge, and was an attempt to satisfy tastes and longings, untainted by the vanity that wishes to impress others or the commercialism that acquires knowledge for practical purposes.

And certainly it fixed standards and raised ideals for us children growing up in a new country where the pursuit of wealth was the real concern of life and where the first come, regardless of their ability to use English correctly, were the first families. It had its disadvantages. I've never quite forgiven Carlyle and Macaulay for their effect on my writing style. The long, encumbered sentences will fall from my pen, even today, though I have fought valiantly for terseness and brevity. The instinct for connectives still bedevils me. The argumentative spirit will intrude. Living physically in the end of the century we were mentally in the first feeling of rebellion against superficiality that this later period inevitably produced.

It has always been difficult for me to understand the strength of that rebellion in later literature. We were spared the revulsion of those middle westerners, such as Ruth Suckow and Sinclair Lewis, against the crass materialism, the dead level of mediocrity, the lack of all cultural values in a pioneer community, because we never suffered these things.[6] Inside our own walls was another world built upon the standards and ideas of a little town in

---

5. Thomas Babington Macaulay, *The History of England from the Accession of James II;* Thomas Carlyle, *The French Revolution;* M. (François) Guizot and Madame Guizot de Witt, *History of France from the Earliest Time to 1848;* Edward Gibbon, *History of the Decline and Fall of the Roman Empire.*

6. Writer Ruth Suckow (1892–1960) earned both a B.A. in 1917 and an M.A. in 1918 from the University of Denver. She began her career writing short stories in Iowa City, Iowa. H. L. Mencken published more than twenty of her stories in his periodicals, *Smart*

Pennsylvania where "the pleasures of the mind" were considered enjoyable and the development of the intellect an interesting pursuit. And this, though the standards were perhaps low and the ideas outmoded by the measure of these rebels, did free us from the environment that they so resent. But on the other hand it was a wide chasm to bridge, that between these old standards and the modern, and I at least have always felt that I missed something in skipping it.

Queer books for a child, these may seem, but Mother had an idea that what we did not already know about life we would not understand, and what we knew already it would not hurt us to read about. In my case, at least, this was to prove correct. For one of my school friends whose mother would not let her read Scott's *Betrothed* lest it spoil her innocence appealed to me to find out what was in it and, though I searched it carefully for the dangerous knowledge, I had no success at all.

One book only was forbidden me, a paperback novel *Wedded but Not Married*, which found its way into the house. I was enjoying it immensely when Mother discovered me in the attic and burned it. I have forgotten the plots of many classics that I have laboriously finished, but I will always be able to tell that plot in detail, though never will I know if the man who secretly married the girl ever acknowledged her publicly.

The new home was, I understood even then, a step up.

When Father's term as county recorder was over, he had gone back to Franklin, walked into a bank, and handed the president a check for several thousand dollars.[7]

"What's this for?" asked the banker.

"You probably never expected to see it," replied Father, "but that's the money I owed you when I left here in seventy-four. I'm here to pay you."

When I learned this story—and we children learned everything—I understood those economies of Mother's that I had always so resented: a lean Christmas with only a book apiece for us three older children, dolls for the younger ones; a shabby dress at school, no candy, and few toys. Thus I saw she recouped after Father's extravagances. For Mother worked always toward a goal she had set long before, the goal we would now call "economic security." Through the years we were always to seesaw between her economies and Father's extravagances, so that sometimes I felt poverty stricken and again affluent.

Whether or not Father's payment of this outlawed debt was responsible for his new business I do not know. But soon he was lending the money of his

---

Set and *American Mercury*. From 1924 through 1936, she published nearly a novel a year, writing mainly of small-town, middle-class, midwestern life (*Dictionary of Literary Biography*, vol. 9, *American Novelists, 1910–1945*, s.v. "Suckow, Ruth").

7. J. P. Newell's term as county recorder of deeds ended in 1886.

Franklin friends on farm lands. The interest was 8 percent, his commissions high, and evidences of prosperity appeared. Little by little new furniture was added to our house. The carpets from wall to wall in time gave way to hardwood floors with parquet borders. Father's trips East came more frequently, trips that were always interesting to us not only because of the accounts we listened to of theatres and dinners, but also because of the wonderful packages he brought.

We had a surrey and a dapper horse, Trump. Trump was not temperamental, but he had his own way of distinguishing himself. One day his tongue was found in the stall next to his. What Trump's tongue was doing there we could not know, but there were indications that the neighboring horse had caught it, and Trump, to get away, had sawed it off with his teeth. At any rate Trump was without a tongue, and we had visions of his starving to death. But no, Trump learned to hold his oats in his mouth with a wisp of hay, and people came from far and near to see him eat. Now at last I had my carriage. And we were able to join the procession of vehicles that drove round and round the square Saturday nights listening to the band, which played in the center under gasoline flares. All the stores were kept open. And the sidewalks were thronged with people, girls and boys walking four abreast, mothers with children tagging on behind, often whimpering with weariness, fathers walking sturdily ahead. People sat at the upstairs office windows listening. Sometime during the evening everyone who could entered an ice cream parlor for a five- or ten-cent dish of ice cream. Later on they took an ice cream soda, strawberry or lemon, or a cherry phosphate. The chocolate soda of today and the Coca-Cola were not invented.

With his new prosperity Father suffered a relapse of the mining fever to which everyone in a mining district is subject every so often. He sank a shaft. Around the dinner table we followed him through the various stages of the disease. The Tuesday to Friday discouragement. The Saturday-night prospects that made it foolish not to try at least one more week. So the disease ran its course, reached its crisis, and the mine was abandoned. Yet, so true to form did our performance run that this same mine, in a later day, became one of the richest producers of the district.

After that, for a time Father bought farms. Later, he promoted a bank and became its vice president.[8] When the depression of 1893 struck the country, he went back to Franklin and returned carrying a little bag. In it was the cash to carry the bank through a "run." To those who live their lives apart from any knowledge or thought of where their money comes from, or those whose family activities can proceed without reference to it, it may seem strange to bring Father's business life into my story. But to write of my own life apart

---

8. In July 1890, the Central National Bank was chartered with A. H. Caffee as president and J. P. Newell as vice president (Livingston, *History of Jasper County . . . People*, 1:352).

from that would be to leave the story untold. For life unfolded as the money came, it retracted when it did not, and so apparent was the connection between the two that never could we forget its importance. Thinking of my parents' lives, and even of my own, money seems to have been life. Yet never were there people who cared less for money per se.

8 *Adolescent Mixture*

Things did not go so well with me at school. Jim had always made our friends for us. In the "Central School" for older children the boys played on one side of the school grounds, and the girls did not, apparently, care for me. I thought it was because Mother, carrying on one of her eastern traditions, did not permit me to attend evening parties. That was not true, for another girl who was not permitted to go out with the boys was all the more sought after because she could not. I should have known the cause when writing a note to a girl whom I much admired, I rhapsodized over a poem of Robert Burns I had just read and in her answer she ignored him! The real trouble was that I didn't know what to talk to them about. They thought me stiff and priggish, and probably I was. But this made it no easier.

My defense was to shine at school, although not always successfully. The teacher suggested that I do a "soliloquy" for an open session in our Assembly Hall. With intent to be amusing I poked fun at some of the older boys. This did not increase my popularity.

Fortunately, there were two children, a brother and a sister, whose mother had the same queer ideas as mine, Leigh and Sybil Hodges.[1] Sybil and I both endured martyrdom over our clothes; hers came to her by way of some rich relations who owned the C and A Railroad, mine from a friend of Mother's in Franklin. One winter we appeared in little jackets exactly alike, sage-green reps heavily braided. That they had originally come from Paris made no difference to us when all the other girls wore plaid cloaks.

It was not economy that made Mother fix these dresses over for me so much as her belief that they were nicer than anything she could buy in Carthage. For she was extravagant about my hats. Once, she even had maroon-colored kid gloves made to order for me in New York. But neither gloves nor hats compensated me for those horrible dresses. One I particularly hated had an old-gold brown velveteen plaid skirt and a blouse of brown cashmere. I complained so much about it that Mother let me choose a dress myself at Rose's Store and plan its making. After I surveyed myself in the mirror and

---

1. Leigh and Sybil Hodges were the children of Charles and Elizabeth Hodges. They lived at 616 Howard Street. Leigh, a classmate of ENB, graduated from high school in 1894; Sybil was a member of the 1897 class (ibid., 542; 1900 Population Schedule, Jasper County, 1399; 1888 Carthage City Directory).

saw my round figure in the full gathered skirt, the full gathered waist, and the full gathered sleeves of the black and white challis, I was more tractable.

While Sibyl and I suffered together over clothes, Jim and Leigh shared the ignominy of being tied to their sisters, our parents having the idea that we girls would keep them out of mischief. Drawn thus together by our common trials, we did everything as a foursome. Long Sunday-afternoon walks in the fields, picking flowers; games in our large backyard; church and Sunday school.

One summer vacation the four of us were required to spend our mornings in a studio making charcoal drawings of plaster casts. Our teachers were artists, considered "queer" in Carthage. Mr. Ankeney wore a long cape and high hat, late from the Latin Quarter in Paris. "Miss Lou," a romantic young lady, wore her hair parted when all the others' went back high on the head.[2] We learned a lot besides drawing as we listened to discussions about art for art's sake and all that. There was a man named "Oscar Wilde," who wore white satin and sunflowers. He engaged much of their attention. Our knowledge of drawing we put to use by flooding our friends and relations at Easter and Christmas with cards and booklets on which pen and ink Easter lilies and holly bushes sprouted. We spent our Sunday afternoons on long walks into the country, Leigh and Jim always walking together, Sybil and I. Jim was the privileged one in our family, Sybil in theirs.

We, Leigh and Sybil, Jim and I, shared also a common adoration for one of the belles of the town, with a strain of Indian blood in her veins. She sang in a baritone voice—it really was baritone, not alto—"Let me tangle my hands in your hair, Jeannette" to a guitar accompaniment. She gave us parties, treating us as contemporaries. Her beaux would drop in on her, and we watched her technique in rapt admiration. Her girl chum would also come, a dashing black-eyed girl who kept the town gasping. For instance, she drove a high-stepping horse with jangling silver chains stretching from harness to shafts. When Jim Corbett came to perform at the local Opera House, she met him at the depot and, uninvited, showed him the town. Later, she ran off with a ten-, twenty-, thirty-cent show, lived a tragic life, and came to a tragic end. But a beautiful soul. I loved her deeply.

Miss Emily Linst [Test?] taught us to dance, and later we went to dancing school, the four of us. Our teacher was a little wisp of a widow in rusty black, and kinky hair, clicking castanets to tap the time. In everything we vied with each other, in our report cards, in compositions, in recitations. I owe much to this rivalry. Leigh and Sybil had exquisite, almost old-world manners, which I imitated as best I could. In later days this rivalry pushed us apart, a

---

2. J. S. Ankeney lived at 705 Olive Street. He had studied in Paris and Italy before opening his studio in the Central School building (*Carthage Evening Press*, October 10, 1895, February 8, 1896; 1888 Carthage City Directory). Miss Lou Brown, a teacher at Central School, gave drawing classes (1888 Carthage City Directory).

mild family feud resulting from it, and then again we came together, drawn by our common memories of a childhood friendship, when Leigh became a well-known columnist—he was known to thousands as the Optimist of the *Philadelphia North American*—and Sybil had married a southern congressman. They were my mother's best allies in making me the kind of girl she would have me be. It meant everything to me that I was not alone in being considered "queer" by others. For "queer" I certainly thought I was.

This enforced companionship was harder for Jim than for me. Roguish and daring, he had always some plan afoot, and would have preferred for companions more exciting, uncontrolled boys. He did manage often to get away from us, swearing me to secrecy by telling me what had happened. Among his many interests was bird-egg collecting, which, as it was educational, was excused, although my parents thought we accompanied him on his expeditions oftener than we did. There were also his game chickens. He was allowed to keep them on the promise that he would not fight them. Nor can I swear that he did, although I had my suspicions, which Mother never did. That he was her favorite was well understood between us.

I was Father's favorite. Jim and I, therefore, used our judgment as to which one of us made the excuses when we had done something culpable.

And there was church. Mother, as I have said, was an Episcopalian. Her grandmother had given the ground for the old church in Pennsylvania by the chicken-supper method. And when we moved to Carthage she went at once to the little brown church with the deep-pitched roof. Not continuously, however, did it have a rector. Then my mother insisted on our going to the Presbyterian Sunday school because it was Grandfather's church. For his part Father ignored religion, as did so many men of his day and type in Carthage. But he approved it for women and children. He was as insistent as Mother on Sunday school for us. When the building craze struck Carthage it included churches. The old frame buildings gave way to brick and stone ones. Our church, too, caught the fever, and Father was one of the first to make a contribution. He took pride in the little stone building with its sloping eaves and buttresses, surmounted by the stone cross, and even served on the vestry.[3] Although the congregation was made up mostly of women, the vestry was composed entirely of men who (with a few exceptions) rarely entered church.

At Sunday school we received little illuminated cards for attendance. When we had ten small ones we exchanged them for a larger one, and for five of those we got a still larger one. But we really needed no such encouragement.

---

3. Grace Episcopal Church held its first service in its new church at 820 Howard Street on December 22, 1889. J. P. Newell at that time served on the vestry (Diocese of West Missouri, *Diocesan Bulletin* 15:8 [May 1946]: 6–11, in Grace Episcopal Church File; typescript history of church in Archives, Grace Episcopal Church).

For Sunday school was a social occasion. We met our friends. We wore our best clothes. In the primary class we learned the answers to the questions in the old *Calvary Catechism* with the ewe lamb and the crook on the cover. "Who was the first man?" "Who was the oldest man?" "Who ate grass like an ox?"

When older we learned the collect for each Sunday. Jim and Jessie had good memories and could rattle them off perfectly. It was not so easy for me. One Lent the rector said he had a wonderful prize for the students who could recite letter-perfect before Easter the entire church catechism in the prayer book. We studied earnestly and were, one by one, closeted with him in his dim, book-lined study in the rectory next to the church. Jim and I, Leigh and Sybil, and Jessie passed the test. We awaited Easter Day impatiently. What form would the so-much desired prize take? We could hardly stand it. At last the great day came. We were shown our names printed on a card hanging in the vestry! Some prize!

Lent was always meticulously observed with us. Each of the children chose some one thing to deny himself. We were excused from school to attend afternoon services. On Good Friday we stayed away from school for the morning service. Episcopalians were greatly in the minority in school, Catholics even more so. To be excused to attend Lenten services pleased our snobbish little souls, giving us a feeling of exclusiveness, if not superiority. And Easter Day found us happy, exultant in new dresses and hats in a flower-decked church. Condescendingly we found the places in the prayer books for the stranger who came in to hear the music and see the flowers. Sometimes the Knight Templars attended in a body, with white plumes on their hats and swords clanking as they got up and down. At all other times (except when the bishop came to hold confirmation service) there was only a handful of people in the pews.

Traditional Episcopalians were the ones who kept the church going in places like Carthage. There was no missionary spirit. Few outsiders came to us. I was grown before I realized that our little parish was part of a great institution that was supposed to save the world, and it was only when I came to need religion that its message took on any meaning for me. Goodness and badness had little connection in my mind with church. They had to do with parents and policemen. And this, although each Sunday I confessed "those things we have left undone which we ought to have done and those things we have done which we ought not to have done" and asked God "to have mercy upon us, miserable offenders." Church was simply something to which you belonged as you did your country and your political party.

Once I went with a friend in curiosity to a revival in the Armory. A man passing down the aisle stopped to ask me if I was a Christian. "Oh, no," I said. "I'm an Episcopalian."

And yet our church had an influence in our lives. We grew to have an intimacy with Jesus after those many Lenten services. He was a real person. The words of the Psalmist that we recited Sunday after Sunday suggested a relationship to a God not far off. The prayers did furnish spiritual exercises, the sacraments were an evidence of things not seen but felt. I am not sure that this is not after all the best way for a child to come to a realization of God. Undefined and unexplained, there is no need for him to alter his ideas with experience and years. God simply is—the X that stands for that instinctive desire for a First Cause. And prayers said for ages, as these have been, establish a communion with Him without painful searchings for words.

We were never taught about a God of wrath who punished people for their sins. We were told about a God of love with whom it was our business to establish contact. In some incomprehensible way He was all-power, but not all-powerful and therefore not to be blamed for our troubles.

The knowledge that people hold Him responsible for their tribulations came to me later as a shock. When I was fourteen, or thereabout, I was persuaded to read the thirteenth chapter of 1 Corinthians daily.[4] It established my idea of the good life. As we grew up we gossiped as others did, we disliked people, we resented them, but when we did it we felt that we did wrong. I was grown before I learned that many professional Christians did not feel that way about it. We were encouraged to put our faith into practice.

A sister-in-law was to say to me in time to come when I refused to drop from my visiting list a woman who had scandalized local society, "You are fastidious for yourself, Emily, but you have no moral sense."

Another reason I welcomed Lent was that during it Mother would not go to any entertainment, so Father would take me in her place to the plays in our little Opera House. As the best shows of the year came to small towns like Carthage at that season, I occasionally saw something really good, like the elder Sothern, and Clara Morris.[5] My theatre going at other times was limited to the matinees of the ten-, twenty-, and thirty-cent companies that, after much pleading, I was sometimes permitted to attend. A performance of

---

4. ENB's mother probably wanted her to especially heed these verses of 1 Cor. 13: "Love is patient and kind; love is not jealous or boastful; it is not arrogant or rude. Love does not insist on its own way; it is not irritable or resentful; it does not rejoice at wrong, but rejoices in the right. Love bears all things, believes all things, hopes all things, endures all things."

5. Edward Askew Sothern (1826–1881) made his American debut in 1852. A leading comedian, he was best known for his portrayal of Lord Dundreary in Tom Taylor's play *Our American Cousin* (William C. Young, *Famous Actors and Actresses on the American Stage: Documents of American Theater History*, 2:1023–28). Clara Morris (1847?–1925) was an acclaimed nineteenth-century star of melodrama. In the 1880s, she toured with her own company (Alice M. Robinson, Vera Moury Roberts, and Milly S. Barranger, eds., *Notable Women in the American Theatre*, 669–71).

Little Lord Fauntleroy and later *Katinka* Mother really grew enthusiastic about, taking us herself.

To go to the church fairs was an event to us children, almost as great as going to the county fair in August. But at the county fair the pleasure of seeing displays of fancywork and fruits and corn and vegetables and pickles and jams and jellies and preserves, even of watching the horse races, was increased by the satisfaction of being decorated with a huge dangling ticket of a special color that announced to the world that we had gone in free—our father was a director!

There were church socials to which we were permitted to go, also the home talent plays given for the church. In these we were occasionally permitted to take part, though Mother, to my sorrow, objected to my being in some extravaganzas where the girls wore short skirts and kicked their feet. Once there was a kermis, and the Italian and Dutch dances were rehearsed in our parlor.[6] As the participants were young ladies and gentlemen, I was enthralled.

Somewhere during this time we made the acquaintance of country life. Across the street lived the Daughertys, who spent their summers on their large farm about twenty miles away. Mrs. Daugherty asked Jim and me to come out at threshing time and see what it was like. At haying time, too, we drove with Father to one of his farms at Waco to spend the day.[7] I was, however, far more interested in what the people did than in the countryside. But if I did not notice the Jasper County countryside, I can remember the old threshing machines and the men in their blue jeans wiping the sweat off their foreheads with their forefingers; washing with much spluttering at the troughs on the back porches, and then sitting down at the long tables laden with platters of fried chicken, bowls of mashed potatoes and gravy, plates of huge biscuits, and countless dishes of pickles and jelly and preserves. Hired men, the threshing crew, and neighbors came to help, thirty of them. I remember, too, the women in their calico dresses with large aprons who waited on them. Portly, competent-looking women who themselves ate after the men had finished. Women who laughed deeply and took the men's compliments on their food with dignified pleasure. It was a robust and pleasant way of mixing work and hospitality. I could not have explained it this way then, but I felt it and thought life on a farm must be fun.

Back of our house, beyond an empty pasture, was a hill, James Hill. Snuggled down against it were cottages, some of them almost huts. Sometimes their occupants would appeal to Mother, or she would hear about some particular case of destitution and go down, with old quilts and baskets of food. Thus I learned about poverty.

---

6. A kermis is a low-country outdoor fair.

7. The James F. Daugherty family lived at 831 Clinton Street. Waco is close to the Kansas state line, about twenty-three miles west of Carthage.

Frequently I walked home from school with one of the girls who lived up on this hill. One day she said to me, "I should think you would wear silk dresses—you are so rich."

I can remember now my amazement. We were not rich, and I knew it. Some of our economies would amaze a WPA worker today. Mother managed carefully. Out of her house allowance of two hundred dollars a month, I remember, she saved with great pride enough money to buy a gold watch for Father at Christmas. And there were eight of us to feed and clothe. But I did not know then that poverty and riches are a matter of comparison, and I probably felt some pride that our house with its large yard created the impression of wealth.

So many and different the incidents that crowd the memory of one's youth that one is amazed that any definite character ever emerged. Here I am remembering Mother's old-fashioned standards carried over from her own girlhood and how I felt about parties and clothes. But I remember lying long afternoons on a spindle bed in the attic reading *Les Misérables*, *Vanity Fair*, *The Wandering Jew*, Bulwer Lytton's three-decker novels; a mystical debauch with Marie Corelli, and a sentimental one with Edna Lyall. There were the talks around the dinner table about Mr. Rockefeller and the Standard Oil. Mother and Father were naturally interested in them. Father had studied law in the office of the S. C. T. Dodd who drew up the first trust agreement and became the Standard Oil attorney at 36 Broadway; he was still Father's dearest friend.[8] But his critics were old friends of Father's, and Father had been an oil producer himself. Their discussions of the effect of monopoly tactics on consumers and producers were not lost on me. I even read some of the books about it myself. What I felt was expressed when on a visit to Franklin—I was fourteen—I saw a Standard Oil tank on fire and said to Uncle Dave, "This is one fire at least you can enjoy; you know they can afford it."

It was during this visit to Franklin that I made my first acquaintance with the labor problem. The Homestead strike near Pittsburgh was on. Daily I read the newspaper accounts of it to Uncle Dave. General Snowdon, the head of the state militia that had been called out, was a Franklin man and a friend of Father's. He was a charming gentleman of much importance in the town, and I felt for him, as for all these old friends of Father's, a romantic admiration. Then one day he ordered a soldier hung up by his thumbs for shouting,

---

8. Samuel Calvin Tate Dodd (1836–1907) was born in Franklin, Pennsylvania. Admitted to the bar in 1859, the year of great oil discoveries in western Pennsylvania, he became counsel to numerous independent oil operators in opposition to Rockefeller. In 1881, he became solicitor for Standard Oil, and the next year he organized the Standard Oil Trust. In 1899, he devised the plan of organization for Standard Oil of New Jersey (*DAB*, s.v. "Dodd, Samuel Calvin Tate").

"Down with Henry Frick."[9] My revulsion and horror were instantaneous. From that time derives my sympathy with labor unions.

When I started home Aunt Fanny took me up to Meadville and put me on my train.[10] We stayed overnight in a hotel and went to call on an old friend of Mother's. I sat entranced while she poured tea and reminisced about their school days.

I realized why these houses, the teas and suppers in "the East" seemed so much nicer than anything we had at home. Our house was as nice—in some ways better—our equipment was more profuse, and food and service more elaborate. But they had an ease of living we lacked. Everything they had was old, had been used innumerable times, and they did things as they had always done them. Nothing was an effort, a performance, it was just part of a routine so familiar they did not even have to think of it. The result was an informality, a naturalness we did not have. With us, newness of acquisition and continuous improvement made for strain and tenseness. The difference was that ours was a pattern in the making; they used one already finished.

I made the trip home alone—the two days and a night on the train with a change of connections at Cincinnati and the instructions not to speak to anyone making me feel it a great adventure. And so it was regarded, Father meeting me in St. Louis with evident relief. For a long time I plumed myself on it as an achievement.

There were, too, the family events: the time Uncle Ed's sleeves caught on a piece of machinery at one of Father's mines and his arm was wrapped around a wheel.[11] Father was in Kansas City attending federal court, and Mother went down to Webb City and brought Uncle Ed home on a stretcher. His arm had not been properly set, and for weeks we tiptoed, the horrible smell of disinfectants in the air and more horrible cloths carried out of the room.

And the night I awoke and thought I heard Father say in the next room, "She will not die, Doctor?" and Mother in bed the next morning white and smiling.

---

9. In June 1892, the workers at the Carnegie Steel Mill in Homestead, Pennsylvania, went on strike after company president Henry Frick refused to continue to recognize their union, the Amalgamated Association of Iron and Steel Workers. When Frick locked them out, there ensued a bloody confrontation between workers and Pinkerton detectives hired by the company, and the strike was brutally broken. At the direction of Gov. Robert E. Patterson, Maj. Gen. George R. Snowden mobilized eight thousand National Guardsmen, which helped to break the strike (Sidney Lens, *The Labor Wars: From the Molly Maguires to the Sitdowns*, 75). Henry Frick (1849–1919) became chairman of Carnegie Steel after Carnegie bought out his H. C. Frick Coke Company (*DAB*, s.v. "Frick, Henry").

10. Frances Galbraith McDowell (1846–1910) was actually ENB's great-aunt, sister of her grandmother Margaretta McDowell Gray (Folder 104, ENB Papers).

11. C. Edward Newell (b. 1851) had been a petroleum producer in Pennsylvania (1900 Population Schedule, Venango County, Pennsylvania, T623, Roll 1490, 182).

Such are the incidents stacked in my mind. Life at that age seems a procession of them, all unrelated but each with a part in making you what you turn out to be. In presenting the character of a book one can select the incidents that will present a consistent picture. It is not so in life, at least not when you are adolescent. You are a mixture, a silly girl longing for fun and a social life, a romantic bookworm, a person concerned over social injustices, a child emotionally wrought up over illness and suffering.

9 *Girlhood*

I had two great friendships: Florence Fabyan and Sallie Boon.[1] Florence was a New Englander, a descendant of Cotton Mather. A serious-minded girl, she always knew just what she wanted and planned ahead, waiting until the plan developed, as it always did, just as she desired it. To me, who was never patient and never knew what was ahead, this was almost miraculous. When she came back from a trip East one September, engaged to be married the next June, she knew exactly every detail of the wedding and had even picked out her linens and furniture. Florence had a real gift as an artist and took our drawing instructions seriously, becoming for a few years the drawing instructor of the Carthage schools.

Sallie was a beautiful girl, very popular with the boys. She had extremely slender ankles like those of a racehorse, beautiful legs and wrists. One of her brothers was a cripple who had to lie facedown on a wheelchair. The care and tenderness she had for him made a deep impression on me. I have sometimes wondered if this early experience in helpfulness did not account for her becoming the good angel of everyone in our town who met misfortune.

Nearly all the friends of my own age were born away from Carthage, coming from different states, each bringing a different background. Two only, I think, were true Carthaginians: Jessie Caffee, who became my sister-in-law, and Winifred Whitsett, who came to me by way of Anna, whose chum she was.[2] Winifred is said to have the distinction of being the only one outside the family who ever acquired the Newell knack of listening and talking at the same time.

I looked on myself during these years as a social Ishmael, all the more so because the other girls went with the boys and had a range of interests I did not share. Mother tried to help me out of this feeling by prophesying the

---

1. Florence Fabyan was a member of the Carthage High School class of 1895 with James Newell. She attended the Cooper Art Institution in New York and opened a kindergarten in Carthage. Her father, B. D. Fabyan, owned the Hotel Porter in Aurora, Missouri. The Fabyans lived at 1152 Grand Street. In 1901, Florence married Richmond F. Bingham who worked for the Interstate Commerce Commission (Livingston, *History of Jasper County . . . People*, 1:543; 1888 Carthage City Directory; *Carthage Evening Press*, June 13, 1901).

2. Winifred Whitsett, daughter of attorney George P. Whitsett, was in the high school class of 1898. The family lived at 610 Howard Street (Livingston, *History of Jasper County . . . People*, 1:543; 1895 Carthage City Directory).

glamorous time to come when I would suddenly burst into young ladyhood. To give me some idea of what was in store for me in that much prophesied "someday," she took me to look on at one of the balls given each Thanksgiving night by the Carthage Light Guard, the name given to our local militia, a town pride. All the young men who aspired to social recognition enlisted in it. They wore gray uniforms with funny caps set high on their foreheads. Competitive drills were held, and to wear the Capt. Carl R. Gray medal for a month was a great distinction.[3] The winter season was opened by this ball, and attendance at it announced a young lady's entrance into formal society. Thus she "came out." Young and old joined in the grand march. In addition to the waltzes there were polkas, schottisches, lancers, and a Virginia reel, and the costumes were reported in detail in the town paper: to this day I remember exactly how these young ladies looked. Dusky "Miss Emily" wore a gray and black velvet. "Miss Lucille" wore a pale-blue silk with the overskirt caught at the side with a silver chain. Daring "Miss Mayme," the first accordion-pleated skirt to make its appearance, of turquoise-blue silk edged with a Greek key design in gold. Her bare back was much criticized by the ladies beside whom I sat. They wore high-necked black silk dresses. Though I can still describe the elegant gowns worn at that ball by the lovely young ladies, I remember I identified myself with a dumpy little woman already called an "old maid."

After I had been married ten years and had two children I wrote a story, "The Heart of a Wallflower," which so expressed my feelings at this period that my mail contained more than one proposal of marriage. Years later, as I stood in a receiving line at a tea, a lady paused to say to me, "I've been wanting to tell you that my children came across a story of yours in an old magazine last summer, and you should have heard them shout—they enjoyed it so much that they made a play out of it and it brought down the house." She thought it was meant to be funny! What is one generation's romance is another's ridicule.

Jim and I had our parties, too. Suppers during the holidays served at seven, and afternoon lawn parties in the summer, parties that were to become a bone of contention in a few years between Mother and me. For other children had their parties in the evening. But true to her tradition, she meant to make no compromises with the ways of the new country.

---

3. The Carthage Light Guard formed in January 1876 and became part of the National Guard. In 1894, Carl R. Gray was elected captain of the company, and the medal he gave to be presented to the winner of the manual of arms competition was used until 1910 (Schranz, "Story of the Carthage Light Guard"). Gray (1867–1939) began his career in railroading in 1883 when he went to work for the St. Louis and San Francisco Railroad as a telegraph operator and agent. In 1912, he became president of the Great Northern. During World War I, he was director of operations of the Railroad Administration. In 1920, he became president of Union Pacific (*DAB*, s.v. "Gray, Carl R.").

Always practical, my mother would not fail to utilize me in her own entertainments, although cleverly she made me feel that such part as I took was an honor. And methodical was the course set for me. My premier performance was to stand at the door of the dining room and pin little bows of ribbon upon the women as they came out from their "refreshments" of chicken salad, coffee, sandwiches, ice cream, and cake. They ate seated around the edge of the room, twenty-four at a shift. In the center of the white-covered table would be a mound of flowers—arranged at some city florist's—but no sign of food. The plates were brought in from the pantry already served. I've often wondered if this ticketing fashion was a hangover from the thrift of pioneer days. Sometimes roses or carnations would be used instead of ribbons.

For the earlier "receptions" everything was prepared at home: the chicken salad in enormous stone jars, the ice cream frozen in the basement, and the several kinds of cake baked the day before. But after a time brick ice cream arrived and the town achieved a caterer who wore a white jacket with "Briles" embroidered in red letters in the corner.[4] It was at about the same time that competition as to varieties went out of fashion, and there came in sheets of white- and pink-iced cake to be cut in squares. It was a proud hostess who finally added a marshmallow to the top of each square and an even prouder one who thought of icing the sides of each square. Angel food and gold cake (to utilize the yolks) came still later.

Once Mr. Briles—we always called him Mr., and no wonder, considering his dignity and importance—underestimated the number of bricks required, and the irate hostess made him appear in the dining room and state that the mistake was his. A young bride from the East, on the other hand, thinking that the molds were individual ones instead of bricks to be sliced into eight pieces, found herself with 124 bricks for 124 guests. What a feast the poor of the town had that night!

From ticketing the guests I was promoted to standing behind the enormous pressed-glass punch bowl rented from the "Queensware" store and ladling out a pinkish concoction. The bowl stood under an arbor of roses fitted into the square bay window in the corner of the parlor. From that I graduated into the dining room where "misses" of sixteen dressed in their best white organdies were honored by being asked to wear out their best dresses and their feet serving the one or two hundred guests. Some girls were so popular that this distinction was accorded them two or three times a week. Later, these girls were replaced by colored waitresses who had discovered that they could make more "helping" at a party at a dollar a day than working in our kitchens at two and a half a week. As the demand for them increased, they raised their prices first to thirty-five cents an hour and then to fifty. The dean

---

4. B. S. Briles ran Briles Restaurant at 317 1/2 South Main Street (1895 Carthage City Directory).

of them, who once prepared, served, and cleaned up after a dinner for fifty cents, was able to earn five dollars a day by the time she was seventy-five.

But that was later, when we had become so elegant that no one could think of giving a party without Mal's assistance. The only difficulty was that her repertoire was limited. I've often wondered what out-of-town visitors who were so elaborately and generously entertained thought as they sat down day after day at luncheon and at dinner to the same menu served by the same "maid." The first time they must have been impressed, for her broiled chicken, making such inroads on the butter budget, her light biscuits or rolls, her stuffed tomato salad, and whipped-cream desserts were delicious, and her service style could not be surpassed. But even such delectable fare does pall. Of course the roast turkey, quail, and strawberry-shortcake seasons helped.

After a round of such entertainment a guest of ours once said, "Oh, for a beefsteak and onions!"

Sometimes I was permitted to assist at a luncheon or a dinner where twelve or eighteen guests sat about the long square table and were served five or six courses, beginning with oysters set in square cakes of ice (no cocktail sauce in those days) and ending with Edam cheese and crackers (the last word). My part was to trail Mal with the hot bread, the jam, olives, and cake.

And when the "Drive Whist Club" met (why "Drive" I do not know, unless it was so-called because the players progressed from table to table) I helped mother, Mal, and others bring the high-heaped dinner plates to the twelve or fifteen card tables scattered all over the first floor. The entertainment of this club taxed all our domestic resources. The tables and chairs could be rented, but china, silver, and glasses had to be borrowed.

For some unknown reason there must be a creamer and sugar on each table, and no one owned twelve or fifteen creamers and sugars. The result was that the same twelve appeared at many houses. "I'd like to know," said one of the members once, "who really owns this set," pointing to one she especially admired. "I've seen it in every house on the block."

Often regrets came at the last moment, occasioning much embarrassment to the hostess, for nearly all the card players who could be socially recognized were members. It was a proud moment for me when at last Mother fell back on me "to fill in." I had imbibed whist as I had books, by watching my parents at their frequent foursomes before I was sent to bed. A copy of Pole's *Whist* had come West with my mother, sharing importance with Shakespeare and Milton.[5] So I felt fairly well prepared until a bald-headed old gentleman nearly reduced me to tears with his criticisms and instructions. I was telling Father about it afterward. "Now if they all played like Mr. Deutsch," I said, "it would

---

5. William Pole, *The Evolution of Whist: A Study of the Progressive Changes which the Game Passed through from Its Origin to the Present.*

be easy. He doesn't care how you play at all. He takes it all as a joke."[6] How Father laughed. Mr. Deutsch was almost a professional, it seemed, and the bald-headed gentleman not quite all there in the head.

Mother was always avid for knowledge, not for any practical purpose, but for some inner satisfaction it brought her. Whenever she came across a reference to something unknown to her she always looked it up, and having a good memory never forgot it. In later years I marveled at her appetite for facts. To me they are only stepping-stones to conclusions. For her they had a value in themselves. Yet she never displayed her knowledge. It was never for effect. When my son was a child, people would express surprise at his store of information. They thought it showed precociousness. "Not at all," I said. "The only difference between him and other children is that his questions have been answered." It was my mother who had answered them.

Once Father said an open meeting of the club that he had attended was so good that it should be written up for the newspapers. Very well, Mother said, she would do it. The mere idea of seeing her name in print so scandalized him that he objected violently. But unbeknownst to him she wrote the article and sent it in unsigned. He read it with delight. "Whoever did this can write," he said. "It's clever and sparkling. Who could it be?" And then she told him. And he thought the joke on him so good and was so thoroughly proud that he then had to tell all his friends.

While "Big Anna" held sway over our kitchen, we children were never permitted inside. When she went back to Denmark for a year's vacation, Mother decided that here was our opportunity to learn what all girls should know: how to cook and serve a meal. So she did without a cook that summer and divided the work among us.

This meant a sacrifice for Mother because she had to oversee us, and she hated cooking. She was not really domestic. Never for pleasure did she do any domestic task, either embroidery, or cooking, or cleaning. But her sense of duty was keen. And not until the time had come when she need not do any did I realize this. When she thought a thing desirable she could punish herself ruthlessly.

She was the last woman in the world to have had a large family. When we children tagged after her as she went to a neighbor's, she sent us back, saying, "I won't look like a hen and chickens." Yet never for a moment did she neglect either us or the house. When I've seen other mothers playing with their children as if they were dolls, and then neglecting them as they grow older, I've remembered how systematically she cared for us, and been inclined to discount the value placed on the maternal spirit. She was primarily a wife and a student. Yet for years she made eight persons comfortable and happy

---

6. Albert Deutsch, a clothing merchant, was born in 1850 in Bohemia (1900 Population Schedule, Jasper County, 1349).

on a small income. And for thirty years after my father died her children were her most intimate friends.

It was her custom to map out our vacation days on written programs, reminiscent of the old "West Point Manual for Cadets" in their detail and use of every moment. One of her ideas was that the early morning hours are always best for study. With me it has always been the other way around. But I was never able to persuade her of this. Even when as a "young lady" I was humored in many ways, she insisted that I appear at the family breakfast table at eight o'clock. To make sure I was awake she would come into my room and ask me questions about the party of the evening before. In time I could answer them without waking at all or at least knowing that I had.

She went at our cooking course systematically. One day I helped her in the kitchen while Jim and Annie took over the front of the house; the next they helped while I did the other work. Once she had shown us, we had to do the tasks by ourselves. At the end of the summer some visitors stopped over for a day, and while Mother drove them about and entertained them we three managed all the housework and prepared a company dinner with such success as to win the condescending commendation of the guest who herself had three servants.

I liked the cooking but hated the washing of the dishes and pans, and was always on the lookout for some way to postpone the doing of them. Once I even pressed the possibility of a cyclone into service. "If the dishes blow away, it won't make any difference if they're dirty," I said to Annie, as we watched the angry clouds. "Let's sit down to wait and see."

Cooking was different. You had something to show for your efforts, if only for a time, and too it brought rewards. Father gave me five dollars for my first good loaf of bread, and my cakes were so successful that Mother's friends asked me to make some for their parties, paying me a dollar a cake. At the end of summer I had twenty-five dollars. But alas, when Big Annie returned, I was not allowed inside her kitchen, and when I tried again, the knack had left me. I have never made a good cake since.

At any rate I learned to cook, and much pride I took in it. Years and years later when I was preparing scrambled eggs and bacon for forty young people in my son's fraternity house at Sewanee, Tennessee, one boy's father said to me, "I never expected to see a political lady like you doing this."

"My dear sir," I retorted, "I learned to do this many years before I ever wrote a line or made a public speech."

Sewing I learned at an early age at a class conducted in a YMCA room downtown by a lady who did her charity stint by teaching poor children on Saturday afternoons. How they chose the girls and just what degree of poorness was theirs I do not know, but Mother and some of her friends had persuaded this teacher to include their children at a small tuition that paid for all of the materials. So by means of little quilt patches I mastered whipping, half-back, and backstitching and running so well that even today I can make almost infinitesimal stitches.

This teacher was very small, very precise, and had a tart humor. One thing she said to me I have always remembered. I had been giggling. "Those dimples are all very well now, Emily, but they will only be wrinkles someday."

In the summer of '93 Chicago was celebrating a postponed centennial with a World's Fair. The papers and magazines were full of it, and great was our joy when Mother decided that we three older children must see it. Never did we Newells do anything for mere pleasure. There had always to be a good reason, although Winifred did say that we merely found an excuse for what we really wanted to do. The reason for this trip was the educational advantage it would offer.

So Mother planned each day, noting just what we were to see and in what order. The only leeway permitted was as to our choice of what we ate at the various restaurants. Our selections were characteristic. Jim and Annie chose the familiar. I was all for investigating strange names until at some French café I chose a high-sounding dish only to find it was what we knew as "wash-day pudding" because we always had it when the top of the stove was occupied by the wash boiler.

Father had promised me another five dollars if I kept a diary during the trip. So I put down each night what I had seen that day: the silver statue of Modjeska from Montana, the old locomotives, the miniature gold mine from South Africa, the Sèvres jars, and so on.[7] I have the book now, my first literary effort.

The Chicago World's Fair architecture may have been entirely imitative and the buildings shoddy reproductions, but it burst upon the middle westerner like myself as a vision of loveliness. That buildings could be beautiful as well as useful had never occurred to me. Not yet, however, had I learned that they could be colorful. That was to be disclosed to me years after when I first saw a colored print of St. Mark's, Venice. In my youth indiscretion in color was left to nature. Houses were painted a drab gray, brown, tan, green, or an occasional pale yellow. A pink stucco house like mine in 1932 would have argued immorality in its owner. As for the filling stations that dot the land today, they would have seemed shocking, not because of their ugliness but for their gaiety.

---

7. Montana's exhibit in the Mines and Mining Building was a seven-foot silver statue of Justice riding an eagle. The model for the statue had been Ada Rehan, not Helena Modjeska. Both were well-known actresses of the period. Rehan (1857–1916) was a leading comedienne in the Augustin Daly Company. Modjeska (1840–1909) had fled Poland and become a popular star of the American stage (David F. Burg, *Chicago's White City of 1893*, 206–7; Robinson, Roberts, and Barranger, *Notable Women in the American Theatre*, 739–40; Young, *Famous Actors and Actresses*, 2:804–10).

Among the pictures in the art gallery—and these were the first real paintings I had ever seen, except the few drab landscapes and the family portraits that hung in the larger parlors in Carthage—I must confess that the ones that most interested me were those that told a story like the horrible flagellants and the boy smoking his first cigar. I remember, however, what a surprise the Corot was to me. I had taken it for granted that the soft grays of the prints hanging in our library were Corot's own idea of the color of trees. Strange and unfamiliar looked the greens and pale yellows.

The Massachusetts Building, a reproduction of John Hancock's house in Boston, made a great impression on me. And I can still see the pink poppies in the silver bowl on the dining room table of the New York building. Next to these things the china and the real lace collections held my attention. I recall an exquisite wedding veil my mother much admired. "Your admiration gives me pleasure, Madam," said the French guard. "You're the only one who has stopped here who has not asked how much it cost." My most vivid memory, however, is of painfully aching, hurting, burning feet!

Strange what determines our development. Mother's spartan discipline did not avail to make me thrifty, systematic, or neat when once I got away from her. But an undue emphasis on the importance of clothes, a painful diffidence, and the feeling that people did not like me were to ride me for years. This feeling no amount of evidence to the contrary could dissipate until years afterward, by what seemed a miracle, it left me completely.

The Halloween before I was seventeen Mother permitted me to go to my first evening party. Unfortunately an escort of my own was not included in the permission. I had to tag along with Jim and the girl he was taking who was so unenthusiastic for my company that she did not speak to me. But I found compensation for this in the knowledge that the handsomest boy in the crowd had asked me, even if I could not accept.

I had a queer feeling about boys. Part of me, that trained by Mother, scorned the idea of beaux, and the boys I knew did seem to measure up poorly beside Bulwer Lytton's *Harley Lestrange* with whom I was secretly in love. But another part of me longed for admiring glances. I knew I was not pretty, even thought of myself as ugly. The tall, broad-shouldered Gibson girl was the type, and I was overplump even in the days when slimness had not become a cult, with straight hair and a pug nose. Still, in the books the ugly girls sometimes had their innings, and I hoped for the best.

With the Halloween party I thought I was launched. But nothing more happened. At Christmas the cooking club of eight girls to which I did not belong gave a dinner for eight boys, Jim among them. This was just too much. I decided to organize a club of my own. There was Sibyl Hodges, Florence Fabyan, and Sallie Boon and Annie to begin with, and, carrying the war into the enemy's country, we invited the four most popular girls in the other club.

I had an asset in Jim. As Mother preferred him to do his playing at home and he was popular, the other boys were often in our yard.

Some of these boys had made me their confidante, a fact that rankled, revealing as it did that they did not place me in the same category as the girls they confided about. But now I saw they could be utilized. With the boys playing in the yard and the girls at the club meeting in the parlor, it was not long before our house was the rallying ground of the crowd.

My next step was to look about for a boy not yet attached to some girl. The boy who sat in front of me at school seemed a good prospect; the same boy, it happened, who had pulled my hair ribbons off at the gate. He was not a member of "the crowd," but he was eligible if he would be brought in. When I mentioned his name casually to Jim he said that the boy hated girls. Undiscouraged I asked his help with my Latin. In exchange I slipped him translations in his hour of need. Then one morning the teacher announced that she had intercepted a note between a girl and a boy. I was horror struck until she read out the names. The boy's was that of the boy in front; the girl's name was not mine. To make it worse the boy turned to me for consolation.

This disappointment was mitigated by some trade-lasts from the Lothario of the crowd and finally a note. Wonder of wonders, I was permitted to go with him to a party. It was not as thrilling as I had expected. I did not know what to talk about, my remarks on literature bringing no response. At last somehow we got home. But when I opened the front door, relieved to be there, a voice sounded from the stairway, "If you're Emily's beau, why don't you kiss her?" My youngest sister's curly head leaned over the banisters.

In spite of such a beginning, a few escorts offered themselves.

Girlhood is not, I think, a happy time for most girls, and the kindest of parents make mistakes. Yet after I went through my own experience of motherhood I was to realize that all any parent can do is the best she knows, and leave the results to fate.

10 Grown Up at Last

My preparation for college was woefully inadequate. Since I had only one year of Latin composition, I had to pass off three years of this, which, with the help of daily tutoring, I managed to do by Easter. The only French I had was what Mother had taught me during vacations, and my grammar was much better than my pronunciation.

For the first time I realized I was a westerner, more, a Missourian. I had always thought of myself as a Pennsylvanian. For childlike, I had taken over my parents' loyalties. But now I found myself classed as a westerner. And we westerners, it seemed, were a curious sort of people, talking a special dialect, unaccustomed to the usages of society. I was supposed to associate daily with Indians and cowboys. All this and more I discovered from the questions and compliments put to me by fellow students from Connecticut, Ohio, South Carolina, and New York City. "But where did you stop and buy your clothes?" "You don't speak like a westerner." "You've really nice manners." Listening to such remarks, loyalty to the West, to Missouri, was suddenly born in me.

I have never forgotten the pledge day when I waited vainly for an invitation to join a sorority. But though looked over at a number of teas, I had apparently been found wanting. Years later, my own daughter was to be one of the most rushed freshmen at the same college. Wives of ambassadors, women prominent in public life, were to write me urging me to influence her to join their sorority or their daughters'. I did not influence her one way or the other, but I was not sorry when finally she broke her pledge and chose to remain a "barb."

I did enjoy the Christmas and Easter vacations spent with some relatives in Elizabeth, New Jersey. There were several boy cousins in the family and a girl my own age, also named "Emily."[1] Servants in the household, cotillions that began at nine, to which you went with chaperons and in evening gowns. Fearful I would do something wrong, I felt myself to be a "western cousin" on probation, so much so that I said to an older cousin, "You must not hesitate to tell me if I do anything wrong or would better do it differently." Amusing and slightly ridiculous all this seems to me today when I know that these cousins

---

1. ENB's great aunt, Josephine Cecelia McDowell had married Philander E. Gray in 1862. They had eleven children (including eight boys), one of whom was named Emily Jane, born on February 11, 1877, just a month after ENB.

valued Mother and Father highly and have always been fond of me, but it indicates the mingled admiration and fear with which I approached eastern ways and people.

Yet in spite of all my discomfort I really enjoyed this visit. I saw New York for the first time, met Macy's and Stern's whence some of my clothes had come, and, what I liked best of all, went to several plays: Ada Rehan and John Drew in *Taming of the Shrew;* Mrs. Kendal; Lillie Langtry.[2]

One performance of mine this family never forgot, though whether they attributed it to my western upbringing or a personal daredeviltry I do not know. When Emily came down to the train to see me off, I persuaded her to go with me as far as Philadelphia. Although she had a brother and cousins there, she had never made this two-and-a-half-hour trip. To me, accustomed to my parents taking a night trip up to St. Louis just to attend the theatre, this little jaunt seemed nothing. We made a lark of it, I insisting on taking her into the dining car and ordering an elaborate lunch. I felt, I suppose, on my own ground and wanted to show off. When we reached Philadelphia, the cousins and brother were horrified, and a telegram to the effect that Emily was "safe" was immediately dispatched to Elizabeth. We seemed to have done something very wild and inexplicable.

On my way to Baltimore, I had stopped at my aunt Fanny's in Washington for a week, and I went over often for the weekend.[3] This great-aunt, a younger sister of my beautiful grandmother, was in the government service. Of a type long since passed, she lived in a hall bedroom overflowing with photographs and keepsakes, and went each morning to her office shabbily dressed, carrying her lunch in a paper sack; but when she was invited out socially, she donned the one elegant dress she always kept ready, put on her diamonds, and brought out a grand manner, determined that never should anyone suspect her occupation.

She was, I know now, waging a continuous battle to maintain her status as a lady against the belittling effect of being "only a government clerk." She was helped in this by the romantic devotion of three old beaux to each of whom in turn she had been engaged in her younger days. Unable to decide

---

2. Ada Rehan (1857–1916) was a star in Augustin Daly's Company for twenty years. Known as one of the most popular comediennes of the stage, she became famous for her role of Katherine in *The Taming of the Shrew* (Robinson, Roberts, and Barranger, *Notable Women in the American Theatre*, 739–40). John Drew II (1853–1927), also a leading actor in Daly's company, was called "the first gentleman of the stage" (Young, *Famous Actors and Actresses*, 1:306–15). Madge Kendal (1849–1935) had been a famous actress in England before coming to the United States. Teamed with her husband, William H. Kendal, she was a skillful comedienne as well as a good dramatic actress (Young, *Famous Actors and Actresses*, 2:637–41). Lillie Langtry (1852–1929) debuted in New York in 1882. Called "the most beautiful woman of her time," she was very popular, though not as fine an actress as Kendal or Rehan (Young, *Famous Actors and Actresses*, 2:655–59).

3. Fanny McDowell was a clerk in the Treasury Department.

between them she had remained an old maid and for thirty years had been for each of them the only woman. Each man had his appointed night for calling, the old lawyer, the old doctor, and the retired capitalist. They brought her flowers and candy, and on Christmas and birthdays gave her beautiful presents.

She had her patrons, now a senator, now a congressman. She attended the receptions of their wives meticulously, went to their less important dinners, and depended on them to take care of her in case of the always imminent shake-up in her department. An ardent Republican herself, she was not without appreciation of my father's Democracy in case the calamity of a Democratic administration should come. To question man's right to all the political plums and authority would never have occurred to her, yet she had taken care of herself since her youth, and, at times, several men besides. Today, she would be a woman bachelor and proud of it!

Of the boardinghouse she was dean, dressing every evening for dinner and sitting at the head of the table. She had a fund of anecdotes, never allowing anyone, as she said, to tell a better story than she; and she bossed everyone, sugarcoating it with kindnesses.

Often I spent weekends with her in this boardinghouse, always more interested in people than lessons. So I came to know the Washington boarding-house of that day, with its snobberies and its tragedies. An aged ex-governor of Maryland with white waxed mustache and tannish toupee, to whom the rest bowed and scraped, seemed to find a schoolgirl just the right age for company, which I knew even then was funny. I heard one of the ladies weep on Aunt Fanny's shoulder because of the husband, so tall and distinguished looking, who gambled every Saturday night and reeled home early Sunday morning. "Outlet," said Aunt Fanny briskly. "What can you expect when a man like that is bullied daily by a chief with half his brains." I watched the writer of *Kentucky Cardinal*, enraptured to see a real author.[4] And I listened to the descendant of the Washington family, the wife of an army officer, the querulous old ladies in departments, and the pretty young one just entering the treadmill of which the old ladies were the result.

Aunt Fanny made me "see" Washington. Not a monument did we miss, not a historic picture. She even told me who had lived in the houses we passed, adding sometimes a quip of her own.

Senator Sherman had just built a large yellow brick house on Franklin Square.[5] "I just couldn't imagine why he wanted a house that size, with no

---

4. James Lane Allen, *A Kentucky Cardinal: A Story* (New York: Harper, 1894).

5. John Sherman, brother of William Tecumseh Sherman, was an Ohio Republican. He served in the House from 1855 to 1861 and in the Senate from 1861 to 1877. He was secretary of the treasury in Hayes's cabinet, from 1877 to 1881, then returned to the Senate from 1881 to 1887. His final governmental service was as President William McKinley's

children," she said, "until I heard the other day that he had never destroyed a letter he had received. Then I knew it was just a brick-front letter file he wanted." When years afterward I was entertained in this house by the Chinese ambassador I told Madam Sze.

No ballyhooer in the rubberneck wagons could surpass Aunt Fanny for information. When I have sometimes had trouble finding some house to which I was invited, I may have thought how disgusted she would be with a niece who did not know where a cabinet member lived. I little dreamed then of the times I was to come there to live and so know another Washington. But always I think of that sleepy old Washington with its plethora of Civil War statues and its shabby Pennsylvania Avenue with affection. I have never been able to think of Washington in any other way.

Even to the boardinghouse I took my feeling that people did not like me. "She seems," wrote Aunt Fanny to my mother, "almost marked," the word that preceded "complex" as an excuse for queer reactions. Looking back and thinking of the young girls of a later day, natural with boys, sure of themselves, and looking at life objectively, it seems incredible that I should have been so young, so naive, so self-dramatizing and ingrowing, but I was. And whether it was just me, or that was the way with girls then, I do not know.

Aunt Fanny chaperoned me and Lula Frick, who was a classmate at Goucher College, to an Easter hop at Annapolis, where a cousin cadet was at the Naval Academy.[6] We stayed in a house with a wide staircase that divided at the landing, and long halls with steps up and down. I saw forsythia in bloom for the first time, and old carved doorways, rode in the funny cabs on the cobble-paved streets, explored the circles and the old statehouse, saw the McDowell Hall of St. John's College, named for the John McDowell whose yellow letters I had read.[7]

There is a wistfulness about the middle westerner's love of these old things not understandable to those who have always known them. It gives him a sort of homecoming that he cannot put into words. They may not mean the same thing that they do to those who have grown up with them, but they mean something only the westerners know. I have always understood the Kansan who moved the old Maryland house rock by rock to his prairie farm. He was

---

secretary of state (*Biographical Directory of the American Congress* [Washington, D.C.: U.S. Government Printing Office, 1961], 1593).

6. Lulu Frick, daughter of Jacob Frick of Wooster, Ohio, was in the Goucher class of 1889 (Sydney Roby, archivist, Goucher College, to editor, October 30, 1998). Willis McDowell had entered the Naval Academy in May 1893 (Edward Callahan, ed., *List of Officers of the Navy of the United States and of the Marine Corps from 1775 to 1900*).

7. John McDowell (1751–1820) was born in Franklin, Pennsylvania, and graduated from the College of Philadelphia in 1771. After studying law in Maryland, he became a mathematics professor at the new St. Johns College in Annapolis in 1789. He was the first principal of the college, serving in that post for sixteen years (*DAB*, s.v. "McDowell, John").

trying to retrieve something he felt he had lost, not knowing that it cannot be done that way.

The hop in the old boathouse was fun, of course—the excitement, the fear that the blind date might not like me. I had a new dress, I remember—an organdy with tiny morning glories in it over pale-green silk, with enormous sleeves to the elbows, a full skin, and double-faced satin bows at elbows, shoulders, and waist. I had learned something about clothes at college, if nothing else. Clothes here were at once more simple and more elegant than the ones we had at home. In fact their simplicity was their elegance. A large part of my allowance went into replacing the old ones with new. I have always loved clothes. I have sometimes wondered if the self-consciousness induced by those made-over clothes from Franklin could be responsible for my obsession with them. Page Mr. Freud again! The queer thing about this complex, if it is one, is that I admire people who are superior to clothes, but lean heavily on them myself. A gown has more than once given me confidence to face a situation I would otherwise have shirked.

A friend in Carthage once trying to explain my widening opportunities away from Carthage said: "Well, one thing, she always has a good dress." And she was right. But not in the way she meant it. It was what the clothes did to me, not what they did to others, that counted.

Aunt Fanny's cousin—my mother's, too—was in Congress from Pennsylvania. Cousin Alex was a Republican, part of Matt Quay's machine.[8] He found my interest in politics amusing, and introduced me to the other congressmen as "the girl politician." They were rarer than they were to become.

"You've a mess of new congressmen here from Missouri now," he said. "Butchers and bakers and candlestick makers."

"Of course," I answered. "They're Republicans."

"That's the trouble," he said, "when there's a turnover. Men we elected who would never have been nominated if they had been expected to win."

"But you're a Republican," I said, thinking he should be glad the Republicans had won these normally Democratic districts.

"Sure, but I'd rather see a smart Democrat here than these second-rate Republicans—provided, of course, there are not too many Democrats."

This was a new idea to me that Republicans could prefer good Democrats to poor Republicans.

---

8. Cousin Alexander McDowell was a Republican representative from Pennsylvania, from 1893 to 1895. Not a candidate for reelection, he was chosen clerk of the House in 1895, serving until March 1911 (*Biographical Directory of the American Congress*, 1295). Matthew S. Quay (1833–1904) had served in the Pennsylvania House of Representatives (1865–1867) and had been secretary of the commonwealth (1872–1878, 1879–1882) before being elected state treasurer in 1885. He was also Pennsylvania's senator from 1887 to 1889 and from 1901 to 1904. From 1885, he was the boss of the machine in Pennsylvania and controlled state politics (*DAB*, s.v. "McDowell, Alexander").

All this was not what I was sent to college to learn, but it was what I did learn. If I had gone back to college another year, it might have been different, but it was not to be. Just before examinations there came a telegram from Jim. Father was ill. I was to come at once. I reached Carthage Thursday. Father was better and was hoping to leave in ten days for Carlsbad for a cure. On Monday he died.[9]

I hesitate to write about that deathbed, and yet it affected all my afterlife. And now so far in the past is it that I see it objectively, as if it had no connection at all with the young girl who hung over it, facing reality for the first time in her life.

My mother, dry-eyed with the quietness that terrifies, called Jim and me into the hall and told us that the doctors gave no hope. It was only a matter of hours.

"And now let's stay with him while we can."

So the hours, two only, passed by, she at his head holding his hand and looking steadily into his eyes that stared straight up as a child's looking into sudden darkness. "There's nothing to be afraid of, James. We've talked it over so many times. We're right here with you. You're not alone. It's all right. Perfectly all right."

Jim was beside him. "Don't worry, Father. I'll take care of them."

"It's all right," said Mother again. "Perfectly all right." When it was over she took us with her into the other room. We sat about in our library, Mother in her chair, we older children grouped beside her, and six-year-old Ella, playing with Father's bedroom slippers, trying by her antics to lighten the gloom that she felt but could not understand.

Behind the closed folding doors was the casket. Never once did my mother look inside it. Kind neighbors urged her to do so, lest she regret it afterward. She took a few steps toward it and stopped midway of the room. "No, no, I can't."

And then in explanation to me, "I've never looked at him once in all these years, waking or sleeping, that he hasn't smiled at me. No, no, I couldn't."

For the ceremony at the grave she prepared us. "It is a necessary form. But it means nothing. It is not your father they're putting there." And when we left it she said firmly, dry-eyed, "Now let's go home. That is where he is—not here."

And that was where we felt him to be, felt it so strongly that sometimes I looked up, expecting him to come in at the door. Once, indeed, I dreamed that he was standing by my bedside and waked thinking I saw him there.

---

9. J. P. Newell died on June 4, 1895. His obituary stated that he had been ill for eighteen months with "neuralgia of the stomach accompanied by sorosis [sic] of the liver" (*Carthage Evening Press*, June 4, 1895).

Our neighbor, who was a psychic, an involuntary one, said she saw him standing by the steps one night as she came out onto the porch. No, we were not spiritualists; neither was this neighbor. The feeling that Mother gave me has nothing to do with a religious belief. It is not faith. It simply is there. Something that all my life has kept me from connecting the person I have known with his body after life has gone.

There is something about sorrow that those who have never experienced it cannot accept and those who have cannot put into words. It is as if another dimension of life were suddenly added, as if one moved upon another plane of existence and all he had hitherto thought real was but a shadow of reality. There comes a distaste for material things and satisfactions. One feels terribly alive, tortured yet uplifted, too. Strangely, although he would not willingly seek sorrow, though he regrets what caused it, he does not envy those who know it not.

I do not say this on the evidence of my own experience only. Those who have suffered far more deeply than I tell me that it is so. Why? How shall I say? Perhaps psychologists would say that it is because emotions usually stilled are suddenly roused, nerves tensely stretched. I do not know. But it does open something up to one, makes the seen seem less important than the unseen, lets in a breath of Infinity. Christ was a Man of Sorrows.

I have tried to express something of what I experienced. A gulf opened up between me and the other girls, between me and the things that once interested me. For a long year I dwelt in another world, and then, slowly, mentally and spiritually, I began to come back into the old one.

For problems before Mother and us required immediate solution.

11 *Broken Circle*

Though we were not of the world about us then, we were most surely in it. My father died on Monday. He was buried on Saturday. And on Monday morning my mother went down to his office and took charge of his business. The old sign—J. P. Newell—was taken down. And a new one was put up: A. G. Newell and Son. I can imagine the dismay of banker, clients, mortgagee and mortgagor. How could a woman with no previous experience of business operate a loan business involving three hundred thousand dollars? And what could a sixteen-year-old boy do?

But two things about Mother they did not know. First, her will to do what she thought she should, and second, how my father had always talked over his every business move with her. I could have told them about the latter, for I knew, of course—indeed took it for granted that it was the customary way of a husband with a wife—that he reported every client's failure to pay his obligations, and kept her informed daily as to the state of his income and his prospects. For what was his interest was hers and what filled his mind found its way into hers. I had heard him daily in those conversations *à deux* at the dining table that ran from politics to literature and from literature to business.

But even I was not prepared for the courage with which my mother faced the man's world. For hers had been the part of the quiescent listener. My father's was a dominant personality, a very masculine one. His ideal of the feminine was the clinging vine, and she played that role perfectly. It was indeed the one she was fitted for by nature. Timid, without self-reliance or conceit, she appreciated fully the shade and support the sturdy oak offered her. In a way her confidence, her economy, her encouragement had made my father, but it was the business of the vine, she felt, to provide that in return for support. To inspire a man was one thing, to assume responsibility another, and my mother loathed responsibility. Her inclusion of the sixteen-year-old boy on the sign indicated her approval of the masculine importance. If he had been of age, the "A. G." would probably never have gone on it. Indeed, she transferred her tendrils to him unconsciously. He became her oak.

I know now that she was fearful, and business was not to her liking. To her last day she held that a married woman's place was in the home. She returned to it as soon as she could. "I have tried both a woman's and a man's job," she once said. "I would choose the woman's job every time."

Yet when she was left with six children and an estate that invested would not produce enough to support them in that station in life to which she meant them to be called, she did the only thing she knew to get it for them.

The panic of '93 had lowered farm values.[1] Some of the mortgagors had been unable to pay their interest, and the properties were not worth the principal and accrued interest. It was a point of honor with Mother to see that none of Father's eastern friends who had entrusted their money to him without bond should lose a cent. So she sold our farms here and there and used the equity and Father's insurance to buy in the properties, holding them until she could get her money back. It was an intricate and involved business.

She carried on the insurance business. She was not without experience of men who took advantage of a woman in her situation. Some of them surprised us greatly, men whom Father had helped. I remember our amazement at the number of men who took their insurance away because they thought it would profit them more to favor a man who might return the favor than a woman who was sure to fail. Others did the same because they did not approve of a woman in business. One man who had been a trusted friend of Father's even tried to keep her from getting the insurance agencies. If all this did not turn my mother into a feminist, it was not without its effect on me.

I did not return to school. I managed the house. And then and there my relationship to my younger sisters changed. I went maternal. Without birth pangs I experienced motherhood. A sorry job I made of it, too. Big Annie had left us, and I had for servants untrained girls from the country who resented so young a mistress. Mother's mind was concentrated on the business. She, who had been a meticulous housekeeper, noticed nothing. The children resented my assumption of authority. By common consent Mother was to be spared annoyance, so tale-bearing to her was ruled out. But we divided into two camps, Annie and I in one, Julia, Ella, and Getta in the other, and feeling at times ran high between us.

A neighbor afterward told me that she came upon me one day lying on the floor, my head in my arms, sobbing, "I can't do it. I can't do it. I'll have to give it up." I have forgotten the incident and have no idea what led up to it. But it is altogether likely that it was merely an emotional release on my part after a not unjustified rebellion of the younger group.

Yet our home life was never again the same. It was a broken circle, and the gap made a difference. Nor was it exactly normal. The children took the lead more and more. A sixteen-year-old boy was treated as the head of the family, which was bad for him and for us, accustoming him to unearned authority and us to wrong values. The maternal attitude I had acquired toward my sisters and always thereafter continued to have was not wholly good for me

---

1. In February 1893, the Philadelphia and Reading Railroad failed, beginning a panic on Wall Street that led to one of the worst depressions in U.S. history.

or for them. True, it kept me young, bridged the period between my own girlhood and that of my daughter's, making my ideas move with the times. So I was spared that withdrawal from contact with youth that so many women experience in the first ten years of marriage. But it is not natural for a girl of that age to be maternal, and it makes her own motherhood when it comes no novelty to her. She has used up some of the emotion. Nor was it well for Jim and me to be so free of discipline as we naturally were when we assumed responsibility. For Mother deferred to us on many matters.

In the past I had been concerned with my own life and pursuits and had not had much to do with the children. Suddenly they became my responsibility, and it was my job to look after them and take complete charge. Someone once remarked on the number of people I could keep busy for an apparently indeterminate length of time, and I explained that I had had practice in doing it as the eldest of a large family. For the development of an executive there is nothing equal to it.

Annie and I thought of a way of getting the younger sisters together. We organized the "Society of the Vines," so named because our ugly porches and tower had become hung with them. Its purpose was "to form a more perfect union, to establish justice, and to insure domestic tranquility in the Newell family." The older sisters wanted to keep it pure Newell, but the younger ones insisted on including their neighbor chum, using the unanswerable argument, "She will come anyway, so we might as well invite her."[2]

We issued a weekly newspaper, the *Family Looking-Glass*, to which each member contributed a story. I have a copy by me now. In it I began a serial never to be finished, "The Little Pilgrims," in which five little heathen princesses—Thressa, Gwenivere, Dianthus, Angeline, and Thybis—all patterned after my sisters and myself, lived in a castle with a dear brother, Eugeneoff de Vanticier. I evidently pictured my idea of myself in "Thressa." She loved her little sisters and tried to help them, but she didn't know how to help herself and so, of course, could not help others. She was passing bright, but girls were not supposed to study, and she did not contradict the general idea. She was, and pictured herself, wise and beautiful. She wondered how she came to be alive and wished she could die sometimes. She used to ask people about the world and imagined herself out in it.

Anna, who afterward became a deaconess, wrote the "Story of a Soul." "The soul was that of a morning glory waving in the bright sunshine on its slim, green stem. It was helped up by a vine to which it owed its life and which also owed its life to a seed and the sun and the rain which all owe their

---

2. A copy of the minutes of their first meeting on July 18, 1895, confirms the purpose of the Society of the Vines. Officers elected were: Emily as president; Anna as secretary; Getta as vice president; Ella as treasurer; and Julia as sergeant-at-arms (Folder 114, ENB Papers).

life to something behind it all. I wonder if the little soul knew that." A little boy picked it for a sick sister and the morning glory was glad, "for was it not best to give some pleasure to this little girl who, no matter how rich she was, could never move from her chair," and "Who would say that something was not accomplished by this soul and that it was not worthy to pass on?"

Julia, the middle girl who felt herself left out in the cold because of the natural intimacy of the two older and the younger, told about a little orphan girl's first picnic, promising to finish it "next time."

Getta, a model child, reported "Ethel's Visit," Ethel being a naughty girl who when her uncle asked her if she had a nice time said: "No, I haven't, and I don't want one," and when she got home "had nothing nice to tell of."

And Ella, the youngest, always in mischief of some kind, wrote under the title "A Selfish Child": "Wonce upon a time there was a little girl that was offel stingy and her papa was away and he had just come home and he brought her a box of candy and her mama asked her for a peas of it and she said it was herse candy and it isnt yourse and when papa came home from town he asked her for a peas and she said no and ran across the room and ran against the side board and knocked her mama's glass dish and broak it and then she said Ill give you a peas now."

The club constitution required that each member should choose some failing to conquer, and that should be her mission until cured, the president hearing reports of progress at each meeting. The minutes for the second meeting report that Ella has made no progress in curing her sudden tempers as she has forgotten what her mission was, Julia is laboring under the same difficulty, Getta pronounces hers entirely cured, and Emily and Annie are both struggling with theirs but can see little progress so far.

The news items report the Mysterious Disappearance of our beautiful maltese kitty and the information that it would greatly rejoice us if we were able to sing "And the cat came back"; also the illness of the children Julia, Getta, and Ella, from what the attending physician, Anna Newell, declared was "sawdust disease," or a skin eruption.

My mother, I know now, was, after my father's death, a lamed personality. I did not realize then all his loss meant to her. Their companionship had been complete on every plane. Nor did I understand what it meant to a woman of forty who had lived for twenty years in an intense emotional relationship to have one part of her nature atrophy. She was the wife type, rather than the mother. Later I understood that she compensated with religion. With the years she gave more and more thought to it. She took up in turn Christian Science, several brands of mental science, and theosophy. But there was nothing of the fanatic in her, and deep sanity enabled her to study each of these and many other "isms" and philosophies, not excluding Swedenborgianism, Buddhism, and Mohammedanism, without relaxing her satisfaction in the rites of her church. She seemed to feel that such an anchor was desirable. Her beliefs would certainly have been suspect by orthodox clergymen, but they never knew how she had taken what she needed out of all of the "isms" she studied and arrived at a doctrine all her own. They knew her only as a regular and devout communicant, a thorough student of the Bible and comparative religion.

12 Young Lady

After one year and a half of mourning, my old friend, the Kentucky lady with the drawl, became my social godmother.[1] And an excellent one she was. She forced me to my first party, a dinner at her house. I felt strange and lonely at first. This was different from my girlhood gaieties. The young men were all older—but she drew me out. She made the young men talk to me.

She chaperoned me to the Thanksgiving Ball—one of the older men was my escort. My dress was of heavy blue silk with mousseline shooting at least twelve inches beyond the shoulders from wide straps of pink velvet on which a linen passementerie had been applied, and the gored skirt edged with tiny ruffles swept out into a long train at the back.

I was afraid my dance card would not be filled and I should be ashamed for life by having to sit out against a balustrade, a hundred eyes upon me. It was not quite what I had pictured. Party followed party, and soon I had forgotten to worry about dance cards. Once during a seven-day visit from a girl in Hannibal, we had thirty Sunday-afternoon callers, attended seven dinners, seven luncheons, three breakfasts, five teas, four dances, and one evening of cards. This was my record week.

Followed a conventional young ladyhood. It was a profession in those days. The number of young gentlemen callers Sunday afternoon, the number of invitations to dances, and the number of extras on a dance card, the color and variety of evening gowns, the height of the pompadour were matters of prime importance.

As young ladies we had a role to act, the contra-players young men. The more to each girl the more successful she. We had our technique, of course. Something we called "jollying" instead of conversation, the use of eyes to express our feelings. For men were glamour beings to be attracted and entertained—never to be treated as human. The men, I fancy, felt the same way about girls. We made a game out of our contacts and saw each other only on arranged occasions, dressed and ready for a conquest. Sports of course we had none, except occasional tennis when the girls, dressed in high collars and stiff pique skirts, amused the boys by throwing the balls as high over the net as they could.

---

1. Anna Belle Caffee, wife of William K. Caffee.

We might play with the boys as children, but at a certain age a gap seemed to widen between us. Thereafter we approached each other only over the bridge of sex. All we had known about boys as playmates seemed forgotten. They became queer, exotic creatures of our imagination to be wooed, or lured, but not to be treated as human beings. I had known boys well as a child, sharing as I did my brother's games and friends. Then I had been their confidante, accepted by them on the same grounds. I got, in fact, in those early years, my first taste of equality and liked it. Perhaps that was why I resented its loss afterward. Later when I came to work with men in politics, I was to retrieve the knowledge and understanding these early associations had given me, and enjoy with men friendships untainted with sex.

It was reported to me not long ago that a political coworker had said: "She is the only woman I know who can enter a conference of men as one of them with no one ever thinking of her as a woman." Many women, perhaps, would not take that as a compliment—but I did. Nor would some men I know mean it so. Perry Belmont once gave me as his reason for opposing suffrage: "I would not want a woman on a congressional committee with me, for if she was an attractive woman she would distract me from the work in hand, and if she was not attractive I would not want her there."[2]

Even during those years of my girlhood devoted to the game of sex there were occasional essays into friendship. One of the boys in our crowd refused to be drawn into this game.[3] No sentiment for him. Girls made good companions at a dance, on a walk or drive, if they talked sense, not otherwise. As he knew where the largest, most beautiful dogwood and redbud trees blossomed, could discover the hidden home of the rare lady's slipper in the deep woods, could recognize every bird and tell us all about its habits, a drive or walk with him became a thrilling event. True, he had a disconcerting interest in field mice and even snakes, but only rarely did he insist on taking them home with us. So, adaptability being our middle name, we dropped the game with him and asked intelligent questions that when answered led to a discussion of biological theories. By him I was first introduced to Darwin, and many were the talks we had over the warfare between science and religion as we drove off the beaten track into lacy lanes and sat by lovely springs he alone seemed to have discovered.

Three other girls had his friendship, and he divided himself impartially between us. One summer he joined some government expedition into northern

---

2. Perry Belmont (1851–1947) was a Democratic congressman from New York, from 1881 to 1888. He then served one year as U.S. minister to Spain (*Biographical Directory of the American Congress*, 540).

3. Probably John Brown, who was in the 1895 high school class and went to the University of Minnesota. Jim later described him as a well-known naturalist (*Carthage High School Star*, June 15, 1895; *Carthage Evening Press*, June 6, 1898, January 7, 1931).

Minnesota, the members of which took turns in naming the lakes, the hills, the streams discovered. John adopted the policy of commemorating the name of the girl he had last heard from. If I am not mistaken, on some government map in some archive there is today a "Lake Emily."

The day I was married he came to see me down at my brother's house where I had gone to rest while all the family, including my sister-in-law and her servant, were busily decorating my mother's house. We rummaged in the refrigerator and ate a pickup lunch together and then sat for three hours talking. When he left me at the door he said a little grimly, "Well, good-bye, chum" and to my surprise kissed me. It was the only touch of sentiment I ever saw in him.

Occasionally the technique of our game would get a rude jar from some unexpected injection of sense. I remember once I had been discussing with a boy, whom I was trying to please, the gold and silver question. How I had the temerity I do not know, but he was always one to have opinions, and the question was uppermost just then, so probably he introduced it. My brother had been a sergeant at arms—great honor he thought it—at the Chicago convention, had stood quite near to Mr. Bryan when he made his cross-of-gold speech, and afterward repeated it to us, word for word. So when Henry expressed himself vehemently, after his fashion, I probably could not keep still.[4] Then, thinking I had gone too far for maidenly modesty, I raised my eyes depreciatingly, and deferred to his masculine superiority. "But it's foolish for me to oppose my views to yours. Of course you know so much more about it."

"I don't know why I should," he said bluntly. "You always stood ahead of me at school."

I hope I had the grace to feel ashamed. But it was not until long afterward that I realized what a deserved rebuke I had gotten for my silly flattery of the male by feminine depreciation.

Evidently I continued to do some serious reading and to have an interest in affairs, however sub rosa I managed to keep it. During my first gay summer I remember I spent long afternoons with *Vanity Fair*, and was so delighted that I went on to all of Thackeray's other books. *The Wandering Jew* and Victor Hugo were read that same year. Even at my giddiest and gayest I spent the night each week reading Carlyle in a small group led by the superintendent of our schools, all the others older than I. However, I certainly kept quiet about all this when with my young friends. Yet when it came to falling really

---

4. At the 1896 Chicago Democratic convention, William Jennings Bryan came to national attention with his defense of the free-silver issue in his "Cross of Gold" keynote speech in which he said: "You shall not press down upon the brow of labor this crown of thorns, you shall not crucify mankind upon a cross of gold." ENB is probably referring to Henry Cowgill, who was a year behind her, in her brother Jim's class.

in love it was with a boy who loaned me Kidd's *Social Evolution*, to whom in return I loaned Hudson's *Law of Psychic Phenomena*, and with whom I discussed Huxley, Arnold, and Spencer.[5]

During this time I had my first taste of publicity. Every fall there was held in Kansas City a Fall Festival, with a queen chosen from the local belles. This particular year the promoters thought to stimulate attendance from surrounding towns—the increase of fall shopping of course was the motive for this festival—by giving her twelve maids of honor from twelve towns in western Missouri and twelve maids from twelve towns in eastern Kansas. These maids were to be elected by means of votes printed in the town newspapers.

Some of my beaux nominated me. The contest grew intense. Extra newspapers were printed and sold in hundred lots. Beaux expressed their devotion by buying them, and I was elected, owing, I always suspected, to political manipulation by my brother.

The maids were to be the guests of Kansas City. They were to be entertained in the hotels, dined and lunched, given a ball, and—here was the rub to my mother—to ride in a float in a parade!

The question was, would I be allowed to go? The very idea outraged those ideals of propriety my mother had brought from Franklin so long before. Finally she succumbed to the argument that refusal would insult my friends who had supported me. For besides the beaux, who did not count with her, old farmer friends of my father's had ridden in with bundles of votes, grocery clerks had contributed theirs, people that I did not know but who knew who I was had electioneered for me, not to mention schoolmates and social friends. There was a proviso. She must go with me to chaperon me.

Having once given in, she capitulated handsomely. I had some beautiful clothes. One outfit I remember distinctly; it was my first suit, and to top it off I had a large hat covered with many plumes. We maids of honor were presented with a long gold chain that hung below the waist on which hung a long crystal bottle with a handsome jeweled top in which to carry our smelling salts!

Mother took a room next to mine, accepting responsibility for other girls who came unchaperoned, and really enjoyed it. All, that is, except the publicity. The morning after my election my picture appeared in the local paper. She was indignant. Ladies did not have their pictures in the papers.

---

5. William Makepeace Thackeray (1811–1863) published *Vanity Fair* in 1848. Eugene Sue's (1804–1857) *Wandering Jew* was first published in 1845. ENB probably read Victor Hugo's (1802–1885) *Les Miserables*, first published in 1862. All three works contain generous amounts of social criticism. Benjamin Kidd, *Social Evolution* (New York: Macmillan, 1894), and Thomas Jay Hudson, *The Law of Psychic Phenomena: A Working Hypothesis for the Systematic Study of Hypnotism, Spiritism, Mental Therapeutics, etc.* (Chicago: A. C. McClurg, 1893).

Where had they gotten it? It had in fact been secured from one of my friends, but I never dared tell her which one. I still treasure that first newspaper clipping, for never, I must confess, has there been another so eulogistic.[6] Many times in the past ten years, when I have seen in various newspapers a stout, pompous lady bearing my name, I have agreed with my mother that ladies ought not have their pictures in the papers. More than once, through some mistake in the filing system of the newspaper morgue, it was not even mine. I do not ask much of the photographer—to look neither pretty nor young—but I would like to appear my size and type, a wish that has seldom been granted.

"Oh, I thought you were a large woman," strangers almost always say to me.

And once a friend who had not seen me since I was a child said: "I told them you might have grown to look like that. You never can tell. Why, you look as if all the world could come and lay its troubles on your bosom."

There would not be much room for them.

The sisters were all agog over my clothes and experiences. They might rebel at my authority, but they accepted unquestionably the code by which all the best went to the young-lady sister, finding, if not full compensation for their own privations, at least a satisfaction in her appearance and success.

I have often looked back on these years and regretted the waste of them, especially when I see around me young girls of today using them wisely to train themselves for some useful work in life, or serving an apprenticeship in the business world. My lack of college education I have never regretted half so much as those frittered years I spent conforming to a pattern for which I was not fitted by nature. For it consumed time to be a "young lady." It meant not only parties but also clothes, many of them, guests from out of town, evening after evening spent listening to a young man—a hard way sometimes to earn a corsage or a box of candy. We had no movies to go to, no radio to turn on, no night clubs where we might dance—nothing but our wits.

But when I see women, as I too often do, of thirty-five or forty suddenly break loose, learn dancing, take up cards, throw themselves madly into the social game, fishing for the admiration of men and sometimes even playing disastrously at love, I think it wasn't such a bad system for a girl to get all this out of her system early.

---

6. Emily probably participated in Queen Karnation's Kourt in the fall of 1896. The *Carthage Evening Press* reported that there were six candidates, and Emily received 2,432 votes; the next closest candidate received 954. "Miss Newell is a most estimable young lady who will do the honors of the occasion with most becoming grace and modesty. She is not only popular and very pretty but she is accomplished and dignified, most familiar with the forms and ceremonies of society. . . . Miss Newell's friends are found among all classes. Therein lay her great strength" (Folder 115, ENB Papers).

My social godmother's husband was colonel of his regiment. She took me with her to its Annual Encampment. In those days these encampments were not a serious part of the national defense program. They were never associated in our minds with the possibility of war. They offered the enlisted men an opportunity for a free camping trip with lots of fun on the side, the officers an opportunity to parade in becoming uniforms and assume a temporary importance, and young ladies a rare good time, house parties in the towns near the encampment grounds, callers morning and afternoon, a change of dress four or five times a day, balls, of which there were always several, with at least five men to one girl, band music, luncheons at officers' mess, and flirtations. Dresses were important at these encampments. A fresh one for each dance, each afternoon, and evening. For they were organdy dresses, or swiss, or dimity, or linen, with only one wearing in each. Once, I remember, a visiting girl was expecting a parcel that contained a new frock. She had talked a lot about it. The newest thing, she said. And then a flat box appeared, not more than twenty inches long.

"My new dress!" she exclaimed. "It's the latest thing!"

"Your new dress?" We were aghast. How could a full gored skirt, with ruffles upon ruffles, full puffed sleeves, a wide berth get into that? She opened it. And there it lay, a narrow skirt with flat knife pleatings about the bottom, no sleeves at all, and only a ruching of lace at the neck. That a dress! It couldn't be. More like a nightgown, and an immodest one at that. Yet the skirt was two yards wide, and the neck not more than five inches below the neck line. Little did we imagine how full and stuffy it would look to her daughter. But then, sun backs and knee lengths were beyond the reach of our wildest imaginations.

Dusty grounds, burnt-out whiskey barrels for water tanks, high grass and weeds, canned baked beans, stewed beef. But very exciting it was to lead off with the colonel or capture one of the St. Louis society boys from the St. Louis Battery, or a captain, and flaunt him in the face of a home beau who was only a sergeant.

The Sunday after we returned from St. Louis the boy who had pulled my hair ribbons took me out driving. I asked him what he meant by driving around and around the square. "I just want to show I'm still on the job."

Our idea of the purposes of the militia got a jolt. Came the Spanish-American War, and our regiment with its gallant, charming colonel, its handsome captains and lieutenants, its nice enlisted men, marched off to a camp in Georgia. Still we did not quite take it in. No one went who did not want to. And very likely the militia would never get to Cuba anyway. A little more serious than a summer encampment, annoying possibilities to worry wives and sweethearts, but no emotional stress. We did not shed tears when we presented our company a new flag. We cheered and thought how well the men looked. To raise money for comforts for them we gave ice cream socials where we laughed and danced. And then reports came back of sunstrokes from marching, of bad food, of bad sanitation, of typhoid fever. And typhoid fever was dangerous, as dangerous as bullets. Men were dying of it and dying by hundreds. One of our boys died—one of our best-loved boys.[7] They brought him home and made a hero of him. His body lay in state. The funeral was held in the largest church. Orations were made over his body. The mayor, the city officials, the city fire department, the old soldiers, the home guard, followed him to his grave.

During these years I renewed my acquaintance with Joplin. The two towns do not like each other. Joplin thinks Carthage is smug and superior. As strangers are told when they ask about it, "Oh, Carthage—it's where dead men walk about."

And Carthage thinks that Joplin is crude and self-sufficient. I never shared the feeling of either about the other. Of course they were different.

When I told a Joplin woman that I was writing this book, she said, "Joplin's awful sensitive. You better be careful." Sensitive about what? I wondered. Because it started as a mining camp? Why, it owes to the mines the fact that it is the metropolis for a territory three hundred miles in circumference. That it has the appearance and the equipment of a town of eighty or a hundred thousand? Or sensitive because it has been called wicked?

In Seattle a Joplin citizen saw a scene thrown on the movie screen with the caption beneath it, "Wickedest City in the United States," and there was the corner of Main Street and Fourth Street in Joplin. At a large breakfast given at Houston, Texas, for the women delegates of the Democratic National Convention of 1924, Will Rogers paid his respects to me as one of the guests of honor by saying, "You know, my folks went out to Indian Territory as pioneers, but they was allus good folks and they tried to bring us up, us children, to be good folks. They tried to keep us straight and make us good and what they said to us there in Claremore was, 'Now whatever you do, don't you ever go to that bad place, Joplin!' and when I see Mrs. Blair here from Joplin leading all these women and they following her I say, 'How some folks can rise above their beginnings.'"

A town, no more than a person, can have everything. A mining town is a mining town, and to be sensitive about it is as foolish as for a self-made man to be ashamed of the things he has gone through to become what he is.

I have always liked both towns. But in my childhood days in Carthage I had seldom seen Joplin. Father, I knew, had business there, and Mother occasionally accompanied him. And sometimes when I came home from

---

7. On May 5, 1898, the Carthage Light Guard left for St. Louis to be mustered into service as Company A, Second Missouri Infantry. They arrived at the Chickamauga, Georgia, training camp on May 20 (Schranz, "Story of the Carthage Light Guard"). Sgt. Charles Wood died from fever at Camp Chickamauga. He was buried in Carthage on July 14, 1898 (Livingston, *History of Jasper County . . . People*, 1:344).

school strange ladies would be there for midday dinner. And they would say, "So this is Ginx."

By then an electric line had been built connecting the towns in the mining district. We could go to Joplin any half hour. And intercourse between the towns picked up. There was a playground, Lakeside, made available to the people of Joplin and Carthage, where for the first time we were able to attend outdoor entertainments and go canoeing and swimming in the river.[8]

We went to the theatre in Joplin and to the House of Lords for supper afterward.[9] Incidentally, waiters in New York, California, and Florida have greeted me by name and when I have expressed surprise have explained that they had waited on me in the House of Lords. I now remade the acquaintance of the girls who had come to Carthage with their mothers to spend the day. I visited them for a week and they me. We went to dances, house warmings, and weddings in Joplin. They came to Carthage for ours.

Another mining boom was on. More young men came out of the East, Boston Tech men. They discovered Carthage girls. The Carthage boys discovered the Joplin girls. And Joplin had another interest for me. The boy who had pulled my hair ribbons and sat next to me at commencement had developed an ever increasing desire for my company. He was now official court reporter. When court was in session his headquarters were there.[10]

---

8. On August 21, 1896, the Southwest Missouri Electric Railway began to run regularly scheduled cars between Joplin and Carthage every half hour. Previously, it had been possible to travel between the towns by train, but it had required changing at Carterville from the White Line of the Jasper County Electric Railway to the Inter-Urban of the Southwest (Allison Chandler, *Trolley through the Countryside*, 73–75). In the summer of 1895, the Jasper County Electric Railway opened Lakeside Park, eight miles west of Carthage. It became a center for regional recreation, eventually featuring facilities for boating, swimming, baseball, dancing, musical concerts, and carnival attractions (ibid., 73, 75–76).

9. Well known for its excellent cuisine, the House of Lords was located at 319 Main Street in Joplin. With the restaurant and bar on the first floor, it reputedly had gambling tables on the second and "soiled doves" on the third floors (G. K. Renner, *Joplin, from Mining Town to Urban Center: An Illustrated History*, 40, 42–43).

10. In 1897, Harry Blair was appointed official court stenographer of the Twenty-fifth Judicial Circuit of Missouri, located in Joplin ("Career of Harry Blair," typescript, Folder 109, ENB Papers).

13 Blessed Be the Dabblers

It was five years after my father's death. My brother had become a precocious young businessman. More and more he became the leader, and my mother followed him. She felt that the younger girls needed her at home, so she went to the office fewer hours each day.

Anna was the brilliant one of the family. She had graduated from high school and gone to Hosmer Hall preparatory to realize her ambition to go to Bryn Mawr. It then developed that we could not afford it, so Anna went to the state university at Columbia, where she completed the four-year course in three years.[1] Anna the brilliant, the good—and also the beautiful dancer.

Mother believed I had a gift for writing, as what mother does not whose daughter's essays have been praised in journalism. But I got only as far as the second lesson. Social engagements were too diverting. The excuse I gave her—and I think I believed it—was that I had nothing to say and there were too many writers already who had nothing to say.

My mother's idea of education seems to have been to give each child a tryout at everything and then when she finally came to something for which she had an aptitude to spare no money or pains to develop it. She began on us all with music. For according to her traditions every girl should of course learn to play the piano. Her practical mind saw no sense in wasting money on music lessons if the student had no talent, so she adopted the policy of putting us each at a certain age under a teacher. If, at the end of a year, we showed no inclination to practice or no gift, we dropped our lessons. I had had my chance at music early, but unfortunately did not pass Mother's test. Then it was Anna's turn at the piano.

I say "unfortunately," for many times after I moved into a home of my own I wished fervently that I had gone on with my music. I discovered when we

---

1. Hosmer Hall, which opened in 1884 in St. Louis, was described as "A High-Grade Day and Boarding School for Girls," which had prepared students for admission to such eastern colleges as Vassar, Wellesley, and Smith (*The Student Register, 1899–1900: A College Directory of the State of Missouri, Being a Register of Students of All Academies and Colleges in the State, Giving a Sketch of Each School and School Town, Calendar, Faculty, etc., and a Sketch of All Fraternities and Societies in the Schools* [St. Louis and Columbia: Students Register, 1899], 1:156–60). Anna Newell was granted a B.A. from the University of Missouri in 1902 (Gary Smith, director of admissions and registrar, University of Missouri–Columbia, to editor, December 27, 1996).

had no music in my new home how much it had meant in the old, and would have given much to have been able to play for my children as she had done for us. Without it the house seemed always to lack something.

Mother had had very little musical instruction herself—it was one of her regrets that she had not had more—but with a natural gift for it, she had made that little go a long way. She could play a pipe organ when a girl of sixteen. She could read music easily and spent many hours at the piano, giving herself and us pleasure.

My sister Julia developed a real talent. By the time she was ready to study there had come to Jasper County a man who was not only a real musician but also an unusual and excellent teacher.[2] Unable to tolerate anything but the best, with big and uncompromising standards and fine taste, he set himself to bring musical consciousness to our middle-western community. Ruthlessly he drove out ill-equipped and superficial teachers. At a financial loss to himself he brought pianists and violinists to us. With satire he flayed all others. As someone has said, "He found a county playing the 'Maiden's Prayer' and left it appreciating Bach." That may not be strictly true, but his influence was great. Artists like Kreisler have given public evidence that they found in Joplin one of their most discriminating audiences.[3]

That it was so may in large measure be charged to the missionary work of Professor Calhoun. His pupils went to conservatories in Boston, Berlin, and Vienna and had little to unlearn. I asked him once whether he had just happened to strike a pocket rich with talent in Jasper County or whether there was as much talent everywhere but no Professor Calhoun to develop it. He thought there was talent everywhere in all the arts, but it lay sterile unless someone tilled the soil. I have listened to people talk of the cultural mediocrity of the Middle West. Who knows how different it might have been if there had been more Professor Calhouns?

There was no limit to what Mother would have done for Julia. She went to Peabody, to Berlin, and was at one time a leader in the musical circles of her state (Colorado).[4] I had an aptitude for nothing, although I had my fling at everything, including elocution, china painting, and embroidery.

Fairness to my mother demands that I, remembering the plethora of

---

2. W. L. Calhoun established his music school in 1888. In 1902, he had 240 students, to whom he taught not only how to play but also theory, history, and composition (Calhoun Piano School File).

3. Fritz Kreisler (1875–1962) was born in Vienna, a child prodigy who became a world-famous violinist and composer. He made his first tour of the United States in 1888 and thereafter made nearly annual tours. In 1939, he made the United States his permanent home, becoming a citizen in 1943 (*DAB*, s.v. "Kreisler, Fritz").

4. Julia Newell attended the Peabody Conservatory's Preparatory Department during the 1903–1904 academic year. She studied piano (Elizabeth Schaaf, archivist, Peabody Institute, to editor, October 1, 1998).

elocution teachers who recited "Little Nell" and "Curfew Shall Not Ring Tonight," shall report that the elocution teacher—a Boston graduate—taught me, by reading Shakespeare, the value of quality and beauty of rhythm. Remembering the atrocities inflicted on china, I must note that the china painting was studied under a woman who had painted in the great Doulton and English potteries and in Paris, an artist to her fingertips, whose lovely cups and saucers in underglaze rose and blue and green could not be reproduced by anyone else in this country. Even today I value every stroke she put on the few pieces I have, and her friendship was such that my world has been poorer ever since she voluntarily left it, because, though she could make the world more beautiful to others, she could not face its ugliness herself. As for the embroidery, it brought me into contact with the town's Aunt Cora whose wit punctured so many pretenses and who taught me the value and beauty of handicraft lovingly and well done.[5] Today when someone says something complimentary about some article I have written or something I have done, she says regretfully, "And she used to do such beautiful embroidery!"

There are artists in everything. "Blessed be dabblers," someone has said somewhere, sometime. Well, I should be doubly blessed. But, for none of these things I dabbled in did I have an aptitude.

There was nothing for me to do then except teach school. That I should go into her office never occurred to Mother, or, I confess, to me. Experimentally, I helped a friend in her kindergarten at home. This work seemed attractive, and I went to St. Louis to visit the kindergarten there that was state approved and offered a two-year course that would entitle me to a State Kindergarten Teacher's Certificate.[6] But I decided I would rather teach in the public-school grades and after two weeks returned to Carthage, and enrolled as a substitute in the public schools. But, though I substituted several months in a primary grade and several weeks in the high school, I did not, evidently, make good, for I was refused a regular appointment the next year. The reason given was that I did not have enough "experience." So, to get the required experience, I decided to teach at a country school. In my conceit, I thought a country school board would jump at a chance to have me. But though I journeyed day after day over country roads behind our tongueless horse to interview farmers, I met always the same answers. Objection number one was that I was a society girl; objection number two, that I did not need the job. At last, when I had almost given up, the school board of the nearby town of Sarcoxie

---

5. Cora Harrison (1857–1950) was called Aunt Cora by most Carthage residents (Funeral Card File).

6. Because of his interest in the ideas of Swiss educator Friedrich Froebel, St. Louis Schools superintendent William T. Harris began a kindergarten program in the city in 1873. Susan Blow established a school for kindergarten teachers the following year (James Neal Primm, *Lion of the Valley: St. Louis, Missouri,* 342–43).

engaged me to teach the second and third grades housed in room 2, with the proviso that I take a summer course at the state university in pedagogy. This I did, adding to this required subject courses in political economy, history, and English literature, which I enjoyed much more.[7]

When I arrived in Sarcoxie the Saturday before school opened, I found that the classes assigned to me were grammar, geography, and literature, in the seventh grade; civil government and history in the eighth; and algebra, general history, and physical geography in the high school. I saw that I would need to mix much midnight oil with my teaching. Such work commanded a higher salary. But I had agreed, they insisted, to teach for forty dollars—that they had changed the work on me made no difference. Whereupon I retaliated by refusing to sign a contract, for which bit of spunk I was later to congratulate myself.

My superintendent was a morose, stern man who believed in keeping teachers under strict surveillance.[8] So, I was to discover, did the school board. As Carthage was only eighteen miles away I went home frequently for weekends, and then one Monday I was summoned to the office of the president of the school board. The townspeople, he said, resented my trips home. A schoolteacher was expected to attend church and teach in Sunday school. I told him I was not engaged to teach in Sunday school or to go to church and if they had no fault to find with the service I gave in my schoolroom, they had no ground for complaint. I dare say I felt like adding, "especially at forty dollars a month." But I went home more seldom. I attended church and Sunday school. I even attended revivals and joined the Rebeccas.

Still, the school board was not satisfied. The president interrogated me as to my methods of discipline. I was not as active with the rod as I should be. It had been reported that the children had thrown paper wads toward the front of the room, and I had not noticed. My teaching was questioned. I did not stick closely enough to the book. I did not hold examinations often enough. It was suspected I did not know my physical geography very well. As a matter of fact, I didn't. It was a crime for me to try to teach it. But I salved my conscience then, rationalized by thinking that I probably knew it as well as anyone else they might get for forty dollars a month, and tried to

---

7. Sarcoxie is about eighteen miles south of Carthage. During the 1898–1899 school year, ENB taught physical geography, literature, and rhetoric in the Sarcoxie High School, earning $280. In the 1899–1900 term, she taught a fifth-sixth grade of sixty-two students, ages ten to seventeen (*Fiftieth Report of the Public Schools of the State of Missouri for the School Year Ending June 30, 1899*, table: "Facts Concerning High Schools," 162; "Term Report for Room 4 for the Term Commencing September 4, 1899–April 20, 1900," Sarcoxie Record Book, Elementary and High School, 1899–1912). ENB attended summer school at the University of Missouri in the summer of 1898 (*Catalogue of the University of the State of Missouri: Fifty-seventh Report of the Curators to the Governor of the State, 1898–1899*, 209).

8. W. E. McElree was superintendent of the Sarcoxie schools.

compensate by firing my pupils with my own love of books, my interest in geography, and curiosity about history.

To do this, I planned the reading lessons carefully, bringing down from home magazines with illustrated articles in them about authors, places, and historical events. I hunted out old chromes of generals and battle scenes, Niagara Falls, and Chapultapec. I searched for funny little human-interest stories.

I organized a lending library of books and magazines for collateral reading and taught geography by pretending we were taking a trip, and history by trying to imagine we were presidents and generals, kings and queens. I dare say I was superficial and my pedagogy weak. But my pupils seemed to enjoy it, and for that matter I did, too.

Once more the president sent for me. It had been reported that I excused the pupils from the room oftener than was necessary. This was too much for me. I told the president that either I run my room as I saw fit or I resigned. The dear man tried to smooth me down. He was a dear man, and I suspect had his own troubles in trying to defend me to his fellow members. But I would have none of it. I went to each member of the board, beginning with the bachelor banker and ending with the blacksmith, taking in the barber on the way.[9] To each I issued the same ultimatum. Either I knew my business or I did not. Hands off, or I would resign.

Hot with indignation, I waited to see what action the board would take. I did not hear from it again until I was asked if I would return the next year.

Teaching was the last thing I should have done. By nature a latitudinarian, I have no desire to make others conform, and as for discipline, I am as easy with others as with myself. Nor have I any desire to impart knowledge. Always I have been more interested in learning about people than in instructing them, more interested, I fear, in what I thought about them, than in what they should know. I am sorry this is so, but it is.

At the time I took the teaching very seriously. I had an idea that a teacher should introduce her pupils to the wider world, give them a keener enjoyment of what it offered.

I could not, try as I would, please Sarcoxie. Remembering the drab appearance of my own schoolteachers, I wore my prettiest summer gown to school. "They think you are putting on airs," said my landlady to me.

Then I had some school dresses made, plain and tailored. "They say you think anything will do down here," she said. She was a sketchy housekeeper, and had an irritating habit of serving up for supper what had been left over from the noon dinner. One afternoon, when she was out at the sewing society, I took the soggy pudding left on the dinner table and threw it out. But at supper, there it was again. "You liked it so well," she said, "that I made some

---

9. W. T. Sabert was secretary of the Sarcoxie Board of Education.

more for you tonight." I never knew whether she thought I had eaten it, or had discovered the pudding in the alley. Sarcoxie was my first experience with unfriendly criticism. Doubtless there were people in Carthage who gossiped about the Newells—we were certainly vulnerable enough—but we never knew it. Probably plenty of people resented our airs and unjustifiable assumption of superiority. But we were never conscious of it. We had grown up in our little ingrowing circle sufficient unto ourselves, never thinking nor caring what "outsiders" might think about us. The complacence of a group like ours in a small town is amazing. It has the aristocratic indifference to the opinion of the mob. It feels itself to be an aristocracy, albeit a self-constituted one. And now the first settlers of Sarcoxie took the same attitude toward me. They did not seem to approve of my condescension in coming to them or concede the superiority of the young lady from Carthage.

Instead they resented me as a Carthaginian. Sarcoxie had been the first settlement in the county and Carthage had gone ahead of it and numbered almost ten thousand souls, while the population of Sarcoxie was still below two thousand.[10] Carthage put on airs. It was much richer. Sarcoxie took its resentment out on me. Nor was I uncritical on my side. I disapproved a society where no social lines were drawn, servants eating with the family, washerwomen accepted as social equals. I disliked being eyed by the boys who hung about the drugstore and laughed as one passed by. I resented the interest in every move I made and the curiosity of the postmaster about my mail. I scorned the enthusiasm over the protracted camp meetings and was shocked at the number of hasty marriages that followed them, occasions for glee rather than condemnation. I thought it a crude sort of life and, I dare say, showed it.

I had in those years since I was a child lost my appreciation of people for their quality. I had come to measure them by a certain pattern, thinking stupidly it was the only one. Such was the effect of those years of conforming, of adjustment to environment. What they had done to me! I had become undemocratic, unadaptable. I held aloof and expected them to meet me on my own ground. It never occurred to me to place myself on theirs. I still had curiosity about other people, but not a sympathetic interest in them. I was to gain it back again. Long years after I had left Sarcoxie I found myself one day with a man in the small parlor of a country woman. We were trying to interest her in war work. She was diffident and afraid of me. But I talked with her about her children, and her chickens, and her garden. When we had left, the writer turned to me in surprised approbation: "It was wonderful the way

---

10. The first residents of Jasper County founded the town of Sarcoxie in 1831 and established a post office in 1833. It was first incorporated as a village in 1868 and then again in the 1880s (Livingston, *History of Jasper County . . . People*, 1:8, 76; North, *History of Jasper County . . . Townships*, 658–60).

you got her; you just set down and put yourself on her level, and acted as if you'd never known anything else. I bet she's telling some neighbor now that you're just as plain and simple as any of them."

"But you don't understand. I am on her level. I liked her. She is charming. If that had been put on, believe me, she'd have known it in a minute."

But I did not feel that way about people when I was in Sarcoxie. My appreciation of them was to come back to me as a result of my suffrage work, and of all it gave me I am most grateful for that. When you want people to agree with you and give you something, you try to get their viewpoint; to understand how things look to them, you forget the things in which you are different and focus on the things wherein you are alike. Even after I had come to that point, I still had a long battle with my diffidence before I could achieve a friendliness with strangers. I well remember the first time I dropped casually into conversation with my seatmate on a local train. He was in trouble, and he began to tell me all about it. I rejoiced, not that he was in trouble, but that he should feel no barrier around me that prevented his telling me and that I could comfort him so frankly. I felt that I had overcome a great handicap, that I had burst out of a social chrysalis and become really a social being.

I hardly knew what to think, a few months later, when an old countryman on a day coach in Michigan told me that he had just buried his third wife and was looking about for another. "I always give them a fine burial," he said. "I like your looks. Would you be interested?"

This experience in Sarcoxie was my first contact with persons outside my own circle since I had been a child. If it did nothing more for me, it punctured my complacency. Nor was I entirely friendless. Big-bodied, big-hearted Martha Moore, jolly, wholesome, was a delightful companion for evening visits. And I really liked my school board president-doctor. The hospitable McNallies and Rices actually invited me to their homes.[11] And there was always Miss Sargent, the town enigma and eccentric. A maiden lady past middle age, she had landed in Sarcoxie out of nowhere with a middle-aged man, whose relationship to her was never explained, to take up residence on a rocky farm, which, it seemed, the old man and her father had once acquired in some deal. She had once had a career "on the concert stage," whatever that may mean. At any rate, there was left from it a tiny piano, some diamonds in old-fashioned settings, and some old shawls and laces. She was raising Plymouth Rock chickens, doing all the work herself. Her contempt for her neighbors was unconcealed. She took an unholy glee, in fact, in telling them

---

11. Martha Moore (b. 1882) lived in Sarcoxie with her mother, Sue Moore. Ella McNallie lived in Sarcoxie with her two children, Clifton (b. 1877) and Rosa (b. 1884). Johnny and Viola Rice had seven children, including a son Earl (b. 1878) and a daughter Margarete (b. 1881), both very near ENB's age (1900 Population Schedule, Jasper County, 1652, 1604, 1659).

exactly what she thought of them. Those opinions she couched in a cultivated English spoken with a Massachusetts accent interlarded with oaths that she had learned, she told me, during the early days of Denver.

At first, naturally, she was resented by Sarcoxians. There was a time when she was a town scandal. But she had a personality that could not be ignored. She challenged their curiosity and stimulated their emotions so that in time, in spite of themselves, they became friends with her. Years later a younger group, discovering that she had sung professionally, persuaded her to appear in a concert. I like to picture the scene: her tall, gaunt figure in its shabby black dress about which she had draped an old raspberry silk embroidered shawl, her diamond cross hanging from her thin neck, standing on the rostrum with the self-possessed air of one trained to tread the boards, and singing in her thin, quavering voice to these youths hungry for music the songs that had moved their grandfathers and grandmothers. Her full story I never knew, but incidents that she would recall now and then as we sat in her bare, unpainted little cabin of a cottage, she wearing a man's boots and overalls, showed it to have been tragic and colorful. I took her to Carthage to my mother's home, and then there began between us a long friendship. She was forever having difficulties over business, and after I was married would appeal to my husband for advice, always arriving, as is the way of such guests, at the most inopportune moment.

Years and years later an astrologer told me that I would inherit some money. I laughed at him. "Now I know there is nothing in it, for there isn't a soul in the world who could or would leave me a cent."

And then within a year I received a notice that I and my husband had each been left one hundred dollars in Miss Sargent's will.

During the year 1917 I went back to Sarcoxie under instructions from the Council of Defense to take young Campfire and Boy Scouts from Joplin, Webb City, and Carthage as berry pickers to save the berry crop. I visited dozens of farmhouses, made arrangements for the housing of the bands, assigned the bands to the farms, checked up on them. The night the crop was all in, the farmers and townspeople gave an ice cream and strawberry social to all of us in the town square. And they gave me a crate of strawberries, followed by that much rarer and more valuable thing, a crate of red raspberries—that of which there is no more luscious fruit. Today the son of one of its "old families" is my son-in-law.[12] Some of my staunchest friends live there. I have a fondness for it. And had I been wiser and older then, I would have understood it better and consequently liked it more. For our quarrel was not one-sided. I daresay I was smug and superior and offered provocation enough for its dislike of me.

---

12. Newton Melville "Dutch" Forsythe married ENB's daughter, Harriet, on December 31, 1926, in Joplin (Raymond Parker, "Descendants of William Blair [Traditionally Known as Robert I]").

As Sarcoxie was it did me a good service. The boy who had pulled my hair ribbons was desiring my company more and more. With eighteen miles between us his appetite for it had become keener. So keen indeed that rather than lose my society Sunday evenings, he would hire a team of horses and drive down to Sarcoxie. And tarrying too late to drive home again that night— it took three hours by horsepower—he would put his rented team in the livery stable and take the midnight train home. I've always entertained the suspicion that the inroads on his bank account for team hire for two days plus board and lodging for two horses for twenty-four hours in Sarcoxie, plus service and railroad fare of the driver, plus railroad fare for himself, four times a month, suggested to him the fallacy that matrimony might be cheaper.

The schools in Sarcoxie closed in May, as there was only an eight-month term. And I hurried home to Carthage, for Jim was to marry Jessie Caffee on May 3.[13] We had all played "wedding" on the side steps of the old Baptist church, and Jessie was usually the bride and marched down the steps in regal splendor to be met by the bridegroom standing at the foot of the steps on the sidewalk. But now it was real, and the wedding was an eight o'clock affair in our own church with six bridesmaids and six ushers—the ushers in their first swallowtail coats. I was maid of honor, and Jim's best man was Harry Blair, who had pulled my hair braids at the old Benton School.

Jim had a stickpin of a ruby surrounded by small diamonds and set in gold. Just before the wedding he gave it to me and said, "After this I shall give everything to my wife, but I want you to have this now as a remembrance."

---

13. ENB's brother, James P. Newell, married Jessie Caffee on May 8, 1900 (Marriage Records, Roll 5, Book 5: 9/14/1899–6/26/1900, Jasper County Recorder of Deeds).

14 *On to Matrimony*

The greatest stroke of luck I ever had was my husband. When I say this people laugh. For if anything, they think, is a deliberate act of will, it is one's choice of a husband, and certainly I would not contradict George Bernard Shaw by suggesting that I had no part in that.[1] But to choose a husband is one thing, I have discovered. To have him turn out satisfactory is quite another, as the divorce courts bear witness. I suppose every girl thinks she is lucky when she gets the man she wants. The question is, does she think herself lucky thirty years from that day? Nor does her answer to that question have anything to do with his qualities of character and temperament, his tastes, and his bank account.

A man may be honest, valiant, loyal, kind, and rich, yet completely fail to give satisfaction as guaranteed. For this satisfaction depends not so much on his qualities as on whether she finds these qualities functioning in a way to make life agreeable for her. This is what is meant, I take it, by compatibility.

And how is any young woman who doesn't know herself what she is going to consider the agreeable life, what she wants to do with it or get out of it, what stimulations she will react to, what motives will dominate her, how is she to know that she will find compatibility in a young man who hasn't decided upon his idea of the good life, does not know what will guide him in decisions, what his possibilities and limitations are, what tastes or weaknesses he will develop?

If they are clever, these pathetic young persons may suspect that experience will make of both of them very different persons from what they want or expect or hope to be. But no vision under any circumstances will be vouchsafed them as to what kinds of persons they will be.

What most girls do, I imagine, is to say to themselves, "I may not be happy with him, but I know I can't be happy without him, so I'll take a chance."

Certainly the Emily Newell who married Harry Blair never in her wildest dreams expected to do the things or become the kind of a woman she was at fifty. And certainly Harry Blair never expected her to do so. If anyone ever drew a surprise package at the altar, he did. What is more the wrappings stayed

---

1. "The whole world is strewn with snares, traps, gins and pitfalls for the capture of men by women" (Shaw, *Man and Superman* [London: Constable, 1903], Epistle Dedicatory).

on the package for ten years, and all that time he thought the wrappings were the real woman. That he was able, when the woman inside it emerged, to adjust himself to her and help her become more and more unlike the woman he had married I count as good luck.

And the fact that not another young man this Emily Newell knew would have been able to do it, that not another one of them would ever have let the wrapping slip, makes her choice all the more extraordinary.

Not that she knew they were wrappings. She did not. If anyone had told her what was inside she would have thought him crazy. I know very well what kind of woman she appeared to Harry Blair, for she appeared the same to herself.

She expected to do the same things her mother had: bear a family, run a house, and spend her husband's money. She hoped to be an inspiration to him, keep him fit, encourage him, and fill creditably any position to which he would carry her. She did expect him to carry her far. That should have given her away. But it didn't, either to him or to herself. When she talked as she did about his ability and discussed a future in which he would do great things, he should have sighted right away that taint in her and fled her like the devil. But perhaps he did not know he would hate to have a wife using him as an outlet for such qualities. Certainly she did not. She should have known by the look of his square jaw and long nose that he was not the man to serve as that most pitiful of beings: a football to a wife's ambitions.

Someone should have said just then to that Emily Newell, "Aha, you are again waiting for your carriage." Not that it would have stayed her. For her imagination as it played with her future life was too entirely out of bounds. Too active to pay any heed to those wise relations of her husband-to-be who saw in his early marriage to a society butterfly like her an end to all his future prospects. So active that she felt it no risk at all to marry a young man with his legal education yet to finish, who expected, without reserve capital, to essay a legal career. And oh, how glad she has always been that she did have that imagination.

Our wedding was one of those simple home affairs where the house is done over from top to bottom and then friends decorate it out of all resemblance to itself: candles are made to take the place of electric lights, an altar replaces the furniture, bedrooms are turned into dining rooms, and the list of guests begins with the immediate family and increases until there are one hundred or more to sit down to a wedding supper.[2] It was on Christmas Eve, a date for which my sisters have never forgiven me. But Harry had only the Christmas vacation from court work, and it must be then or wait until spring. Even

---

2. Emily Newell and Harry Blair were married by Episcopal rector Charles J. Sniffen on December 24, 1900 (Marriage Records, Roll 6, Book 5: 6/27/1900–6/29/1901, Jasper County Recorder of Deeds).

if it was inconvenient, the Christmas season with its red holly, red candles, red ribbons, and Christmas greens did furnish a beautiful background for the chiffon wedding gown that reached from ears and fingertips to the end of a long train, and made me look far more matronly than I did at fifty. Sentimentally—and this I put in as typical of both me and the period—lovers' knots of lace were worked into the chiffon. Annie was my only attendant, regal as always with the American Beauties she carried in her arms as she would a baby.

So we started off. Harry's family, though they accepted it, were not too well pleased at our marriage. Harry expected to practice law, had already studied it in the evenings and was ready to enter the bar, and they knew there would be years of hard sledding before he was financially established. A frivolous girl such as they considered me to be would not be helpful to him.

I did not give them much encouragement, I am afraid, to believe otherwise. Mother had given me a very generous sum with which to buy my trousseau, and I had indulged in a clothes debauch. One of the new—and slightly shocking—short skirts, at least four inches from the floor, with which I wore high-laced shoes. But this, of course, was only for the street. The afternoon party dresses of broadcloth, swept the ground with pinked silk ruffles inside to catch the dust. For evening, there was a white broadcloth skirt with blouses of chiffon and silk, boned stiffly to a pointed front, which you hooked down onto your corset to give the "straight front" effect, and for dances a net over taffeta with the bust pushed out by means of starched ruffles sewed inside. Most amusing to me now is the number of negligees thought necessary— among them was actually a "wrapper" of red cashmere, the lining close-fitted but folds of the cashmere hanging from the high collar to the floor. Not a garment, it would seem, in which to relax. Perhaps its usefulness lay in the fact that it had no division at the waist, and so one could temporarily dispense with a corset. The desired figure with the stomach pushed into the vertebrae and the abdomen into the hips was not comfortably attained. But there was also something called a "kimono"—the first time I had heard the word—of pale-blue dotted challis with enough of the material gathered onto the yoke to house a family. Then I had handmade ruffled petticoats, silk stockings in weird drop-stitched designs that would have made your legs appear tattooed if they had ever been seen, underwear (we did not call it "lingerie"), coats, etc. This was supposed to be my last fling, and I should do as I pleased. But it was more than that. It was the beginning of an extravagance that was to ride me all my days.

There were the usual number of mishaps to be retold afterward whenever weddings were mentioned. Such as the arrival at the last minute of a large picture that was placed by some assistant in a conspicuous place among the wedding gifts and there, after the last guest had gone, discovered by the family as the old family chromo that had been sent down to be reframed for the hall.

There were the kisses that a dear old friend had made to be served with the wedding supper. "Didn't you like them?" her daughter asked me on my return from my honeymoon. "Mother spent all day making them." An interrogation of every member of the household followed, and my grandmother recollected that she had received a large package at the front door that she, to save bothering anyone, had put on top of the china closet cupboard and forgotten. A search discovered the three large pasteboard boxes filled with little mounds of powdered sugar. One day's hard labor gone to naught.

Harry and I went to St. Louis and returned for a postponed family Christmas celebration on New Year's Day. We hoped that the gifts we had spent our honeymoon buying would compensate my sisters for having to eat their Christmas dinner off the card tables set up in the midst of the wedding debris—a vain hope, I fear.

On the next day, Harry's parents celebrated their fortieth wedding anniversary.[3] "Think," I said to Harry as we drove over for it, "of being married *forty years*." It seemed an eternity—no less.

My husband was official reporter of the circuit court. It was his business to set down in shorthand every word of testimony in the cases on trial. On demand from either party to a case he must prepare a typewritten copy of this testimony called a transcript.

Only an expert stenographer could qualify. He had learned shorthand when a mere boy. Often in school I had seen him studying his Graham, concealed from the teacher's eye by textbook or desk. By the time he was fourteen he was able to substitute in the courtroom for his brother who was the official reporter. When he was sixteen he was deputy reporter and when nineteen became himself the official reporter.

Jasper County Circuit Court had two divisions that sat serially six weeks in Carthage and six weeks in Joplin, practically the year through. The January session was held in Joplin, so there we repaired, taking two rooms in a residence where we got our breakfasts on chafing dishes, eating dinners where we would. It was fun, but when spring came we decided we wanted to settle down in our own home, so we bought a house in Carthage whence Harry would have to go to and from the Joplin sessions by way of the electric cars.[4]

Saying sagely that I never wanted to go back and so should begin at the bottom, I was delighted at the little four-room house. I did not then know how many times we were to begin again.

With the itch for completeness I had not then learned to fear, we went to

---

3. John Blair and Mary Jane Pittinger had married on November 10, 1859 (Parker, "Descendants of William Blair").

4. In 1902 Emily and Harry lived at 308 West Fourth Street in Carthage. Harry had purchased a five-room cottage from N. A. Turner for fifteen hundred dollars (newspaper clipping, n.d., scrapbook in possession of Emily Forsythe Warren, Cleveland, Ohio).

work on it. A guest room of bird's-eye maple and pink organdy, very sickly sweet. A horrible golden-oak dining table and chairs, with a built-in corner cupboard. But a living room that, quite accidentally, was charming. Walls of green ingrain paper with a border of plain terra-cotta paper, pine bookshelves to hold Harry's rather considerable library, a mahogany table that by a stroke of fortune rather than taste is still good looking, some prints of Turner's misty harbors, and a Morris chair that came to us by way of a box of Mr. Larkin's soap.

You married in those days one man, the man you had seen all dressed up, devoted, charming, reserved, who treated you as if you were a queen or an angel. You found out slowly that you had married several men, the man tired and silent from work, the man annoyed at nonsense, the man who did not play at love all the time, the man who withdrew into himself when you felt sorry for yourself, the man who liked to be with other men sometimes, liked to hunt and fish. It was just luck when you liked the other men you had married or liked one of them enough to put up with the others.

The husband must have made his discoveries, too. We were, bride and groom, just romantic figures to each other, imaginatively endowed with characteristics neither had. Only with time did we come to know each other as human beings.

I began the serious business of homemaking that consisted for the first five months at least of showing off our wedding presents of cut glass, Haviland china, and silver by means of dinners and luncheons. Hours I pored over the menus and recipes in the women's magazines. It was the period of color schemes, with decorations, desserts, salads, and place cards all of the same pink, or yellow, or green. This did queer things sometimes to the flavor of the food, and the table often suggested a millinery shop more than a meal.

The experiences common to most young housekeepers were mine. Dumplings did not rise; we ran out of potatoes, and ice, and coffee at the very moment we wanted most to impress our guests. Never shall I forget one dinner. Our guests of honor were the parents of a Canadian, newly come among us, formal and "proper" to the last degree. I planned an elaborate meal beginning with canapés and running through innumerable courses to cheese and fruit. The day before this dinner I put on a large soup bone in a kettle full of water and went off to an afternoon party. When I returned at five a queer odor met my nose, with the unmistakable suggestion of creosote, and there seemed to be a haze in the atmosphere. Investigation revealed a heap of dry ashes in my kettle and a thin viscous scum on everything in the house. I had forgotten to turn off the gas.

"Thank fortune," thought I, "it is not tomorrow," and set valiantly to work. Everything in the house had, of course, to be washed. The curtains had to be laundered, the rugs sent posthaste to a cleaner's. It was all done. But every time we reentered the house that odor met our nostrils. We got a chemical deodorant and sprayed the air with it. Still the odor persistcd. There was no country club in those days to which we might take our guests, so we had to see it through, hoping that it would at least be mitigated by seven o'clock. But the lift of the nostrils of our guests told us our hopes were not confirmed. We tried, of course, to act as if nothing had happened, and so did they as they reached for their handkerchiefs, pressed them to their faces, coughed and sneezed.

As if this was not bad enough, the soup curdled, the chicken, although cooked for hours, was tough, the gelatin dessert did not congeal, and the coffee was as weak as water.

"Never again," I sobbed, as the last guest departed. "Never again." And not for many years did I essay a dinner like that.

Besides showing off my wedding presents, making my husband's bachelor friends regard our home as their own, and attempting the perfect hostess part, I had to utilize my trousseau. So to party after party I went, each one an occasion to spring a new "confection." There was in those days a wide gap between prenuptial and nuptial wardrobes. Never before had I had a dress for every occasion and everything to go with it.

I also intermittently ran a sewing shop. I would like to think—and did then—that it was a continuation of my maternal attitude toward my sisters that made me design and oversee the making of their clothes, but I know now it was my restless urge to achievement.

Dresses were not, in those days, merely cut-out forms run up at the seams, style and effect dependent on the line. They were intricate affairs with fitted and boned linings, high, wired collars, and tucks, insertions, embroidery, intricately worked in or onto them. My most difficult undertaking was a commencement dress for Julia of white organdy with a circular skirt tucked from hem to waist—the tucks graduated in size from bottom to top. The dollar-a-day seamstress who helped me said it could not be done, but it was.

I even made some dresses for myself, which must be charged to my clothes complex, for I did not need them at all. Since they amuse my daughter-in-law greatly today, it may be well to describe what I might call my chef d'oeuvre. It was a pale-blue silk striped grenadine over a white taffeta slip. Where the deep circular flounce joined the gored top of the skirt was an insertion that I considered the last word in ingenuity and workmanship. First a design of roses was carefully cut from a printed organdy and appliquéd with tiny stitches onto oval-shaped pieces of bolting cloth. These ovals were then basted on the skirt and outlined by scrolls that had been procured by taking apart some heavy ecru embroidery. This, too, had to be put on with stitches that did not show. When it was finally all placed, the dress underneath was cut out and you had what appeared to be hand-painted inserts edged with hand embroidery. This fetching creation was finished with a lace vest set into the bodice and outlined with more of the hand-appliquéd scrolls, a sash was made of ribbons the colors of the roses, blue and pink and white, whipped together, and, to top it all, a bouquet of handmade silk roses exactly like those on the panel was stuck jauntily on the shoulder.

Too bad that we had not been introduced to needlepoint or tapestry. For that expenditure of time I might have had seats for my dining room chairs. Of course, I did do embroidery. Hundreds of tiny daisies on corset covers, thousands of tiny stiletto-made holes buttonholed around, and miles of buttonholed scallops, and more miles of featherstitching so tiny that the lines seemed embossed. I even did some red carnations on a doily.

Then there was the weekly running of pink and blue baby ribbon in the beading of nightgowns and chemises. Someone ought to write a book someday on the tasks restless women have invented to occupy their time.

Harry and my brother owned some timber land in central Missouri. It had been infested by tie thieves, men cutting down the trees and selling them for railroad ties. We decided to look the land over. To do so we drove thirty miles off the railroad to a town bearing the inept name of Vienna.[5] No distance at all in these days, but then a long day's drive. My brother had written the innkeeper to expect us, and he had done his best to prepare for our coming. All the best furniture had been gathered into one large bedroom, even to the shell ornaments and the old clock on the mantel. In each corner stood a huge bed heaped with feather ticks and piled with patchwork quilts. My brother explained rather confusedly that he was sorry to put them to trouble, but really, while he and I were brother and sister, Mr. Blair and Mrs. Newell were no relation, and we would have to have separate rooms. This rather inadequate explanation did not satisfy them, but with insistence we were shown down the hall to two tiny cubicles in which were low beds with cornhusk mattresses, stands with tin water basins, and buckets for toilet purposes. Since it was the best we could do we went to sleep, only to be awakened by prickly sensations. When we scratched huge welts appeared. I lit the lamp. Little brown specks, too gorged to move, covered the sheet. We got up and stretched ourselves on the middle of the floor.

The food was just as bad. Eggs soggy with grease and biscuits huge as snowballs with a carbonic acid flavor and side pork. After one sampling we avoided the dining room and lived off the sweet crackers bought at the grocery store until some little black bugs came running out of the boxes. Then we depended entirely on the bologna to be had at the saloon, together with beer for the men and lemonade for us women. We drove from Vienna thirty miles more. Thirty miles sounds like nothing today. But over those Ozark hills along open spaces cut between the trees, the stumps left standing, through gullies, over rocks, it took us many hours to make them. We took lunch at Koeltztown, a German settlement, with a brick Catholic church, parish house, and school,

---

5. Vienna, Missouri, is in Maries County, about forty miles southeast of Jefferson City.

the hotel neat and clean, the houses spick-and-span, flowers in the yards.[6] It could not have been any larger than Vienna, or much richer, if any. The countryside was the same. I've often thought of the contrast between those two towns, one settled by so-called pure Americans, the other by Germans, when I've heard talk about 100 percent Americanism.

Back again we drove to Vienna, stayed the night, and next day drove back to the railroad. We were famished, and Dixon promised little better fare than Vienna. But up the line was a Harvey eating place.[7] We could catch the up-going train, eat there, and still have time to get our southbound train back. But we had no money. It had cost us as much, horses and all, to sojourn at Vienna as it would have at the Austrian city of the same name. Finally Harry persuaded a Masonic brother to endorse his check for five dollars. He told us that the last time he did so he was caught, but he would take a chance. So up to Mr. Harvey's we went.

I've had reason to bless Fred Harvey many times, but never more than that day.

---

6. Koeltztown is in Osage County, between Jefferson City and Vienna.

7. Dixon, in Pulaski County, is twenty miles southwest of Vienna and was on the Frisco Railroad line. The Fred Harvey restaurant was located in Rolla, Missouri.

15 Role of Wife

With an idea in my head that my interest in Harry's business would be more intelligent if I knew something about it, I set myself to make the acquaintance of Mr. Blackstone, and a tedious fellow I found him.[1] Some books in Harry's library on the Supreme Court and the Constitution I found more interesting, although I must confess that neither produced the effect I hoped for. I read some of Harry's transcripts and found them absorbing, boring him for many explanations of legal terms.

When the docket was long, night sessions of the court were held, and then I would accompany Harry, so fascinated by the mental agility of the lawyers with their cross-questionings that I was reminded that once long before my father had said to me, "Ginx, you ought to be a lawyer."

Murder trials, too, interested me, whether because of my curiosity about human nature or because of my appetite for drama, but rationalized then by my theory that a wife should know about the things that engaged her husband's attentions. If Harry had to follow these trials, so would I.

There were limits, I found, to putting this idea of mine into practice. Harry was asked by the sheriff to attend an execution to take down any statement the convicted murderer might make on the scaffold. I had to draw the line at that.

This amusing interest of mine in my husband's activities and work did not of course serve to help him. Indeed, it must at times have tried his patience. But it did, I know now, do a great deal for me. Not alone because of the knowledge I picked up thus scrappily of business methods, of justice and injustice, crime and criminals, and of people I would otherwise never have known about, but because it opened for me a window on the world outside the narrow walls of my home and social circle and thus kept me from being entirely absorbed by the trivial duties they demanded of me.

Nor would I wish to intimate that these high-flown theories of mine about the duty of a wife to take an intelligent interest in her husband's work prevented the usual adjustments that go with marriage. Neither I, nor my husband, were morons. I could be just as indignant when he was late for dinner, as hurt when he read his newspaper instead of talking to me, as

---

1. Sir William Blackstone (1723–1780) wrote *Commentaries on the Laws of England*, which became the foundation for legal education in England and the United States.

incensed when he ignored my new dress as any other bride. I can remember distinctly exactly how I felt when my ego was hurt, and I haven't the slightest doubt that I tried to hurt back either by speech or by silence. What I can't, somehow, recall are the occasions for it.

I remember how I felt one night when I opened the front door, stepped out into the dark, and the thought struck me, "What am I going to do when I get there? Tell them I have left Harry?" I sat down on the sidewalk, my feet in the gutter, and thought it out. Suppose he did not come for me—what then? Why, marriage was final. You could not play with it. Either you made a go of it or you did not. I got up and walked back to our own house.

We had not had a "honeymoon trip." Harry had been in court for months continuously and at nights typing his transcripts for the lawyers' "bills of exception," as I learned the phrase. He needed a rest. His sister lived in northern California and had written us glowing letters of the beauties of the redwoods, the fishing, the deer hunting.[2] And so we decided to visit her and call it our honeymoon. It proved to be a journey of mishaps, but was in retrospect all the more interesting.

We were gone six weeks and never once made a connection on time. From San Francisco we went by boat to Eureka, then without rail connections with the outside world. My sister-in-law's husband was a traveling salesman there for a wholesale grocery house. Once or twice a year he made the round of two counties—one of them as large as Illinois—by horse and buggy. Harry accompanied him to Coos Bay [Oregon], and Effie and I drove up the coast to meet them.

Next we took a six-hundred-mile driving trip with our relations. It took us up the shore, through the redwoods across the range, over the one county road that ran around the county. At night we stopped at the guest houses; places, that is, where they would put strangers up. You could not call them hotels, although they charged hotel rates. Once there was only a curtain between the various beds. Again, snuggled up in the hills was a charming little cottage, the walls hung with red cheesecloth on which were pasted illustrations from English papers. The host and hostess were English people exiled far from home. At another place, run by a retired fisherman and his wife, who had been cook to the Swedish royal family, the thin plank partitions ran only five feet up. I awoke in the middle of the night to hear a man breathing on each side of me. Carefully I put out my hands in the dark. The right one touched a rough plank. I breathed easily again, realizing the other man was beyond it.

Harry wanted a deer, so we stayed behind at a hog ranch on the top of a mountain. We got the deer and started home with our luggage, a camera and tripod, haunches of venison, the antlers, Harry's gun, and I do not know what else. We made the trip by stage—the stages had high four-seated chassis

---

2. Effie Blair Wall married Edward D. Wall in 1901. They lived in Eureka, California.

hung on leather springs that pitched them from side to side. Since they carried the mails, time was an item, and once the horses had swung into their pace, they slowed not for rock nor gully, man nor beast. Up one mountain and down another they dashed. At nine o'clock at night we had to change stages, and the second stage was already loaded with mailbags. We could not wait for another if we were to make our boat back to San Francisco. Harry had developed poison ivy and had so high a fever that he was delirious, so it fell to me to persuade the driver that we could get ourselves and our luggage into the space in the back seat behind the mailbags that were piled to the roof of the stage between us and the driver's seat. At last we plunged off, I holding camera and venison in my lap with one hand, and with the other clutching Harry who threatened to lurch out with every turn. Going down the mountain the horses stumbled. I could not see the driver for the mailbags piled between us. It was dark, but I could make out that on one side of us rose a dark wall and on the other was a drop of I knew not how many feet. I realized we were on one of those roads that hug a mountainside and knew there was a river below. I called to the driver, but he could not hear me for the clatter of the stage. I wondered if he were drunk. And then he stopped and got out to examine the horses. He did not begin to answer me, but I gathered from his curses that the stable boy had given the horses collars too tight for them. We were off again, and again the horses stumbled. He jerked them up, and we went on again. And so, again and again. But at last we stopped, mercifully still alive, and in a timber camp under the light of lanterns the men crouched over the mailbags, checking them off.

At one o'clock we reached a small lumber town and went into a dreary, drab hotel. So terrified was I by that time that I pulled the furniture against the keyless door and left my oil lamp lit. The next day we went into Eureka [California] on a bobtailed train that ran from that metropolis to the lumber camp, the engines and cars having been brought from Frisco, I was told, by boat.

But our troubles were not over. We had made our reservations on the boat before we left for our driving trip, but when we asked for tickets were told that we had not called for them in time so they had been resold. It was against the rules to sell a woman a ticket without a berth for her. Yet we had to be in San Francisco before the next boat left, if our return railroad tickets were to be validated in time. Somehow we must go on that boat. So Harry bought a floor ticket, and I became a stowaway. While my brother-in-law engaged the man at the gangplank in conversation I slipped on board. Whenever I saw a blue coat coming, I stepped into a stateroom. When it passed I slipped in another. The ship seemed, I thought, to have an enormous staff. Later I discovered a blue-coated band was on board returning from a street fair. After we got under way I hid behind some piled-up chairs. Then, when the bar was passed and there was no possibility of putting a boat back, Harry and I met.

"I feared this. We looked for you," said the purser.

"I'll sleep on the floor of the salon," I said, "beside my husband."

"But you can't," he said. "It's against the rules." It seemed also against the rules to place men and women in the same stateroom, and those for women were all filled. Nor would he put me in one with other men without my husband. He had therefore to find two berths. He would give one man his own berth, he said. The other man, I fear, found that there had been a mistake in his berth assignment and he would have to take floor space.

"Get into your berth early," the purser commanded, "and stay in it until the other man is up in the morning. Don't let him know a woman is in that stateroom."

My husband and I crept into the two upper berths early and waited for the third roommate to appear. When he did he began to climb into my berth. Before he thought, my husband had called out, "Don't get in there. My wife's in there."

With that the old German exploded. "Your wife—your wife—and I can't have mine—been on deck all this time with her. I'll report this—I'll—," but he went to bed.

San Francisco, Los Angeles, El Paso, we saw them all. But no part of the trip could equal those miles and miles of driving in that remote northern part of California. It was at that time the farthest frontier that those who wished to escape civilization could make. We ran into squaw men, men who wanted to forget, Indians, the digger—probably the lowest type. We ate in lumber camps. We drove beneath the arching redwoods on corduroy roads, and slid down mountain sides on grass as slick as ice. We rode up mountain passes. I daresay it is all settled and civilized today.

Even then, however, it had its native sons. In the remotest part a woman said to me: "And you've never been here before. Well, well, what do you think of that—she's never been here before." To get there I had gone a thousand miles by rail, almost two hundred miles by boat, and driven three hundred miles! There spoke the true provincial.

When we returned to our little house I took up again my round of entertaining, dressmaking, and law reading. But Harry, although he had been admitted to the bar that summer, wanted to test his knowledge by a law course in some university before he began to practice. To give up a five-thousand-dollar income and draw on our small resources seemed a hazardous thing to do, but after much discussion we did. So, after we had been married two years, Harry took a civil-service examination as a stenographer, and entered George Washington University—or Columbian, as it was then called—in Washington, D.C.[3]

---

3. Harry began his studies at Columbian College in the fall of 1902.

16 *Bleacher Seat*

We came to Washington in 1902 to see Aunt Fanny. The new Department of Labor and Commerce had just been established by Congress. George B. Cortelyou had been appointed secretary of the department.[1] He had been private secretary to President McKinley. Harry took a civil-service examination in an endeavor to get into the new department. He took the civil-service examination for a stenographer and having been a court reporter for several years passed the examination easily.

A very few days after the examination Harry received a note from Mr. Cortelyou asking him to call on him at the White House. The new department had not selected quarters, and the only personnel that seemed to be definitely determined upon was James R. Garfield, son of the former president, who was to head the Bureau of Corporations, and Frank H. Hitchcock, afterward postmaster general and chairman of the Republican National Committee, who was to be chief clerk of the new department.[2] When Harry called upon Mr. Cortelyou at the White House it developed that both of them wrote the same system of shorthand so that Mr. Cortelyou, who had Harry's civil-service examination papers, could read Harry's notes, and they both used

---

1. The Department of Labor and Commerce was created in February 1903. George B. Cortelyou (1862–1940), after studying at the New England Conservatory of Music, learned stenography and in 1895 was stenographer to Grover Cleveland. Earning his law degree at Columbian College in 1896, he then became secretary to William McKinley and continued under Theodore Roosevelt, who appointed him to head the Department of Labor and Commerce in 1903. Roosevelt then saw that Cortelyou was elected chairman of the Republican National Committee, and after managing Roosevelt's election, the new president appointed him postmaster general. His final government service was as secretary of the treasury, from 1907 to 1909 (*DAB*, s.v. "Cortelyou, George B.").

2. James R. Garfield (1865–1950), son of the former president, practiced law in Cleveland. He was elected to the Ohio State Senate in 1895 and 1897. After unsuccessful bids for the Republican congressional nomination in 1898 and 1900, Roosevelt appointed him to the Civil Service Commission in 1902. The next year, the president appointed him commissioner of the new Bureau of Corporations. His highest office came in 1907 when he became secretary of the Interior (*DAB*, s.v. "Garfield, James R."). Frank Hitchcock (1867–1935), received an LL.M. in 1895 from Columbian College. In 1903 he transferred from the Agricultural Department to the new Department of Labor and Commerce as chief clerk. In 1908 Hitchcock was chairman of the Republican National Committee and managed Taft's presidential campaign. As reward for victory, the new president appointed him postmaster general (*DAB*, s.v. "Hitchcock, Frank H.").

the same make of typewriter. Mr. Cortelyou was deluged with mail, and an arrangement was made for Harry to come to the White House daily for a few days and take dictation and write the replies to Mr. Cortelyou's mail.

The new department selected quarters in the then-new Willard Building, which is on Fourteenth Street, just across the street from the Willard Hotel. For the first few weeks Harry did stenographic work for all three: Mr. Cortelyou, Mr. Garfield, and Mr. Hitchcock. He arranged to attend Columbian University Law School, and as the personnel of the new department was expanded and built up he was able to stay with Mr. Garfield at the Bureau of Corporations, the forerunner of the present Federal Trade Commission, which was expected to be a legal bureau devoted to the investigation and study of corporation problems. Harry's salary was fourteen hundred dollars a year, and it was shortly raised to eighteen hundred dollars.[3]

Mr. Garfield was in the so-called Tennis Cabinet of the strenuous president, the members of which often met in his office. So I would hear about them: Gifford Pinchot, Jacob Riis, Nicholas Murray Butler, and others.[4] Righteousness in government, as everyone knows, was the first Roosevelt's specialty. One had only to report to him some irregularity and at once he set about getting the facts. His methods of doing so we learned one day, when Mr. Garfield instructed Harry to go with a Secret Service man to the office of the secretary of the Interstate Commerce Commission, turn away the employees, lock the doors, make an investigation, and report to him.[5]

---

3. In September 1914, Congress created the Federal Trade Commission, replacing the Bureau of Corporations.

4. Some of the men who played tennis regularly with Theodore Roosevelt often stayed to discuss governmental policies and thus came to be dubbed "the Tennis Cabinet." Among them were Gifford Pinchot, Jacob Riis, and Nicholas Murray Butler. Pinchot (1865–1946) earned his B.A. from Yale in 1889. After attending the French National Forestry School at Nancy for a year, he was appointed in 1896 to the National Forest Commission of the National Academy of Sciences to develop recommendations for the use of western public lands. In 1898, he was appointed chief of the Division of Forestry in the Department of Agriculture. He was elected governor of Pennsylvania in 1922 and 1930 (*DAB*, s.v. "Pinchot, Gifford"). Riis (1849–1914), born in Denmark, came to America in 1870. His career in journalism began in 1877 when he worked for the *New York Tribune* (1877–1888) and the *Evening Star* (1888–1899). A leading muckraker, he wrote about the poor, immigrants, and the slums. Although Roosevelt offered him various jobs, he did not take a government position (*DAB*, s.v. "Riis, Jacob"). Butler (1862–1947), president of Columbia University from 1902 to 1945, though not a government appointee, was known as "an 'insider of insiders'" and an important adviser to both Roosevelt and Taft (*DAB*, s.v. "Butler, Nicholas Murray").

5. Edward A. Moseley (1846–1911) was the secretary of the Interstate Commerce Commission (ICC). He was the first secretary appointed and served until 1911 (C. A. Miller, *The Lives of the Interstate Commerce Commissioners and the Commission's Secretaries*, 169–70). Martin A. Knapp (1843–1923) was chairman of the ICC from 1898 to 1911 (*DAB*, s.v. "Knapp, Martin A.").

It grew rather exciting when the enraged secretary put a detective on Harry's trail to see if he could not get something on him. I would watch him through the window as he followed Harry down the street.

One feature in connection with this experience impressed me. We were comparative strangers in Washington, our circle extremely limited. And yet, there was Florence Fabyan's husband who worked for the commission, who, of course, was interested in the investigation. Letters from Aunt Fanny's boss were in the files. And one of our fellow boarders was found to be a boon companion of the accused secretary. I learned then how tangled are the threads in Washington departmental life, and never since have I dared to use proper names when repeating anecdotes or gossip in a public place.

The story of this and subsequent investigations belongs in a story of Harry's life, not mine. Yet they have a place in my story, deepening as they did my interest in matters political.

We did the things that all newcomers to Washington do. One of them came about through an invitation secured by our congressman to attend a presidential reception. When we came opposite Mrs. Roosevelt, a sweet-faced woman, who seemed about to faint, I heard her whisper to her husband, "How many more?" The president caught my hand fiercely, thrust out his teeth at me, and we hurried on. A group of women in brilliant gowns stood back of a velvet rope and watched us go by. One of them raised her fan and whispered to another behind it, and they both laughed. It struck me suddenly that we were the show, not they, as we trudged by to shake the hands of people we did not know and who did not know us. I felt humiliated and never since have attended a public reception where I had no reason to be except that I could. Yet I am glad I had that close-up of Theodore Roosevelt. The only other time I saw him was when he drove down Main Street, in Joplin, standing in a car and singing, "There'll be a hot time in the old town tonight."[6]

Our congressman was M. E. Benton, nephew of the great Benton, more distinguished today as the father of Tom Benton, the iconoclast artist who paints Missouri mules on the walls of state capitols.[7]

---

6. Edith Kermit married Theodore Roosevelt on December 2, 1886. Theodore Roosevelt came to Joplin on September 23, 1912, and gave a speech at Miner's Park to a crowd estimated at ten thousand (*Joplin Globe*, September 24, 1912).

7. Maecenas Eason Benton (1848–1924) came to Neosho, Missouri, after service in the Confederate army and gaining a law degree from Cumberland University in Lebanon, Tennessee, in 1870. Prosecuting attorney of Newton County from 1878 to 1884, he was U.S. attorney from 1885 to 1889. He served in the United States House of Representatives from 1897 to 1905 (*Biographical Directory of the U.S. Congress, 1774–1989* [Washington, D.C.: U.S. Government Printing Office, 1989], 612). Well-known artist Thomas Hart Benton (1889–1975), born in Neosho, Missouri, was the son of Congressman Maecenas Benton (*DAB*, s.v. "Benton, Thomas Hart").

Mr. and Mrs. Benton were very kind to us.[8] An old-school statesman adorned with a square beard, long and thickish, he was an orator of the table-whacking, voice-volume variety, of which abilities he thought highly. Thinking to compliment him I told him what my cousin Alex had said of him: "He's an indefatigable committee worker with real influence. That's what counts, not speeches on the floor."

Quickly, Mr. Benton returned, "Has he never heard me speak?"

I have thought of this as I have seen administrators want to become orators, and research specialists administrators. It seems a human facility to think you are what you are not.

Mr. Benton's wife, much younger than he, beautiful, charming, and most efficient, made quite a place for herself socially, a success that was materially to help, unfortunately, toward his defeat when an opponent charged her with living beyond a congressman's means, and this though she made her own clothes, managed expertly with one servant, and otherwise made a dollar do the work of three.[9]

Their Missouri home was a large old southern house set on a hill in a town just south of Joplin, where they were the big people of the town, if not the district. This was the way people thought of congressmen in that day before the direct primary. They may not have been more able then, but they were far more important at home.

Missouri had an unusually strong representation in the Congress. Three of our congressmen had national reputations: Champ Clark, who afterward became the Speaker of the House; DeArmand of Nevada, who had so tragic an ending when with his grandchild he was burned to death on a sleeping porch; and Dick Bland. In the Senate were Vest and Cockrell, men who brought glory to the state by their reputation for wisdom and integrity and were, in turn, revered by the state.[10] We knew these congressmen only through a casual

---

8. Lizzie Wise married M. E. Benton in 1888 (*History of Newton, Lawrence, Barry, and McDonald Counties, Missouri* [Chicago: Goodspeed Publishing, 1888]).

9. Cassius M. Shartel of Neosho (1860–1943) defeated M. E. Benton in the 1904 election. A Republican, he did not stand for reelection, serving only from 1905 to 1907 (*Biographical Directory of the U.S. Congress*, 1797).

10. James Beauchamp "Champ" Clark (1850–1921) moved to Bowling Green, Missouri, in 1876. He was elected to his first state office in 1889, serving until 1891 in the Missouri House of Representatives. He was elected to the United States House in 1893. Defeated for reelection, he then served from 1897 to 1921. He was Speaker of the House from 1911 to 1919 (*Biographical Directory of the U.S. Congress*, 782). David A. DeArmand (1844–1909) moved to Missouri in 1869. He served in the state senate (1879–1883) and was circuit judge (1886–1890). A Democrat, he served in the United States House of Representatives from 1891 to 1909. He was from Butler, Missouri (ibid., 888). Richard Bland (1835–1899) came to Missouri permanently in 1865, residing first in Rolla and then in Lebanon in 1869. He was a Democratic member of the United States House of Representatives from 1873 to 1895. Author of the Bland-Allison silver purchase act of

introduction and the senators not at all. Representatives and senators were not the wet nurses for the constituents they have since become, nor their agents before federal bureaus. There were not so many of these bureaus. What they could do for you at most was to see the Pension Bureau or the Patent Office once the postmaster and local U.S. commissioner were appointed. Important patronage such as a position on the federal bench or a district attorneyship was no concern of the local people, like ward workers, precinct leaders, and plain voters, but of the state bosses. Our contact with the congressional representatives at Washington was not close. We thought of them, whether they were or not, as statesmen concerned with passing legislation, remote and somewhat superior to us and our personal needs. It had never occurred to us to ask any one of them about an appointment when we got to Washington.

Yet I gained some idea of what went on at the Capitol. Cousin Alex McDowell had become clerk of the House of Representatives, an important position of much patronage. He made us welcome in his little office at the Capitol off Statuary Hall where John Quincy Adams had died.[11] He loved an audience, and from this affable, catholic-minded, realistic Republican I learned much that was one day to be useful, not the least of which was an insight into how the political mind works.

My cousin also said to us: "It is a pity that you western people never learn the importance of keeping the same man here term after term. You change too frequently for anyone to gain influence. The East knows better. No wonder it puts things over on you." And we noted that the men who counted had been there many terms.

So Harry wrote a letter to our local paper reporting what he had heard about Mr. Benton, praising his work and mentioning the importance of keeping the same man there. And one morning he found a marked copy of this paper on his desk with a letter to Mr. Garfield from the Republican candidate for Congress from our district. "It is hard enough to fight Democrats here at home without fighting them in the administration," it said.

When he had received his appointment Harry had said to Mr. Garfield, "I'm a Democrat, you know."

1878, he was defeated in 1894 but reelected in 1897 (ibid., 632). George G. Vest (1830–1904) graduated from Transylvania University law department in 1853 and moved to Boonville, Missouri, in 1856. Elected to the state House of Representatives in 1860, he served in the Confederate Congress during the Civil War. Returning to Sedalia, Missouri, after the war, he moved to Kansas City in 1877. Vest was a Democratic U.S. senator from 1879 to 1903 (ibid., 1983). Francis M. Cockrell (1834–1915) also served in the Confederate army, gaining the rank of brigadier general. He returned to his home in Warrensburg, Missouri, after the war to practice law. He served as a Democrat in the United States Senate from 1875 to 1905 when Theodore Roosevelt appointed him to the ICC where he served from 1905 to 1910 (ibid., 802).

11. John Quincy Adams died on February 23, 1848.

"I'm not interested in your politics or religion," he answered.

Just the same he was nervous as he took the clipping and letter in to Mr. Garfield.

"Been getting into politics, I see," Mr. Garfield said. "Well, write an answer and I'll sign it."

I renewed my interest in genealogy, egged on by Aunt Fanny who had a passion for her ancestors. Queer what an interest they always seem to have for those without descendants! Hours I spent in the Congressional Library and even did a little original research work.

I journeyed to the county seat of Prince George's County, an hour then on the train. In colonial days a shipping point, it had become a dusty, forgotten little town almost a mile from the water. But the records in the old courthouse went back to the middle of the seventeenth century. A queer feeling it gave me to see the very signatures of great-great-great-great-grandparents who had been in their graves two centuries.

Among Aunt Fanny's treasures—for she had acquired much of the family's old furniture and other heirlooms, some by inheritance and some by purchases from the inheritors—was the wedding dress of Madame Sally McDowell, the young wife of Col. Alexander McDowell.[12] She had performed a surgical operation on the craw of her one and only hen to rescue the rare and precious cucumber seed that Biddy had picked off the windowsill. The dress was a lovely pale-green silk. Fancy, I thought, being married in that gown in a Philadelphia church and going off to the wilds of Pennsylvania on horseback to live in a stone house with paper windows.

I have that dress now. My daughter was married in it, and I wore it myself at the Bicentennial Ball in Alexandria in 1932 with a wig that duplicated Madame Sarah's hair arrangement in the portrait that came down to another cousin. Since the guests each were supposed to represent someone who had attended the last ball that George Washington had attended at this tavern, I used the name of Madame Sarah. Well, she might possibly have been there since bachelor brother-in-law John McDowell was president of St. John's College in nearby Annapolis. To give the idea verisimilitude, my husband took his name. The rooms of the old tavern had been restored as nearly as possible to what they were in Washington's time, and the ball reproduced the other as far as costumes, refreshments, servants, and furnishings could. It was a picturesque affair with the blackfaced men standing by the open fires, the long table laden with roasted whole pigs and hams, the huge punch bowls, the fiddlers, the gay and gorgeous dresses of the women and velvet and satin coats of the men. But we were not good actors, any of us, I fear. Instead of dignified poise, what we registered was curiosity.

---

12. Alexander McDowell married Sarah Parker of Philadelphia in 1795 (Folder 104, genealogical files, ENB Papers).

My old friends Colonel and Mrs. Caffee, who had taken me to the National Guard encampments, were spending the winter at Annapolis to be near their son, Arthur, who was to meet an early death at the Indian Head testing grounds when a gun blew out backward.[13] He was then midshipman at the Academy, and very popular. Mrs. Caffee, always a delightful hostess, drew round her, of course, his classmates and their girl visitors of the moment. It was fun to visit them weekends, after, that is, we recovered from the shock of our first visit when I found myself rated as a contemporary of Mrs. Caffee and Harry was addressed as "Sir." This was the first and only time in my life I have ever felt my age.

It was in Annapolis under Mrs. Caffee's tutelage that I discovered an interest in "antiques." I bought there my first: a hexagonal American empire table. It was not, I know now, either good looking or old (about 1820). But it did set me to studying furniture and haunting the auction sales.

Just as Mrs. Caffee with her southern drawl and her Madame De Sevigne conversation was my idea of the hostess of a salon, so Colonel Caffee with his brisk military gait, his dignity and courtesy was my ideal of the "parfit gentil knight."[14] Walking with him one spring morning around one of the Annapolis circles, I stumbled on the uneven sidewalk and sprawled on my hips.

There was almost nothing in those days more destructive of a young woman's self-respect than a tumble in the street, and little more ludicrous to the spectators. Colonel Caffee, however, acting as if I had merely performed a new figure in a cotillion, raised me to my feet, dusted off my dress, and gave me his arm.

"No harm done," he said to Mrs. Caffee later. "She is too plump to be hurt by it."

"She is something more than plump now," returned Mrs. Caffee, who made me lie down and smell her lavender salts.

Memory of my first summer in Washington is one of delicious solitude. We took a small furnished house on Rhode Island Avenue below the fashionable zone in which to await the birth of our first child.[15] I had, of course, the layette to make by hand. The rest of the time I spent reading. In the closet of the house were old files of *Harper's*, and *Century*. Through them I came to know Cole's *Woodcuts of the Old Masters*, my first real knowledge of pictures. I discovered in them, too, William Dean Howells, and Henry James, who opened to me a new school of literature.

I read their other books, went from them to Meredith and finally to Balzac. It was as if a fresh breeze had swept into my mind. As a result, with all the zeal

13. Arthur Gill Caffee entered the Naval Academy in September 1900 (Callahan, *List of Officers*, 674).

14. Madame De Sevigne (1626–1696) was one of the brilliant women in the Paris salons, setting the cultural standards of the day.

15. The Blairs lived at 946 Rhode Island Avenue in the District of Columbia.

of the convert, I turned my back on romance and went fanatically realistic. Amusing this seems today when by a later school they are dismissed as either trivial or sentimental, but it does make me understand the equally fanatical reactions of this younger school with its profanity and social resentments against them.

As this was Harry's first trip to Washington, he went in for historic landmarks. After doing the Revolutionary ones—Gunston Hall, Mt. Vernon, Alexandria, and Arlington—he came down to the Civil War period. There he lingered. As a boy, two old neighbors, one a Union soldier, the other a Confederate, had interested him with their stories of this war. Somewhere in his wanderings he discovered Robert E. Lee and conceived a great admiration for the Confederate general. From General Lee he went on to the Johnson-Reconstruction era. With the Congressional Library to draw on, we read book after book about it. Claude Bowers had not then popularized this period of our history.[16] This must seem strange in this day of debunking literature, but in our school days pupils were taught only the pleasant things about our nation's past. A queer way to improve a nation, it would seem, if one is to learn from experience what to avoid, and watch symptoms of it.

This was the first of many sorties into history I have undertaken. As an educational method, these self-directed courses of reading have their advantages. You undoubtedly read more carefully and remember longer when you undertake to satisfy an aroused curiosity than when you study a course set for you by others. But they do leave great gaps in your knowledge. Of certain periods you probably know far more than many a student who has majored in history, but of others you may be woefully ignorant.

As soon as our daughter arrived, as so often happens at such times, everything so carefully organized to go right went wrong. The cook left when the baby was two days old. The day after, the nurse went home. Mother, who was with me, seriously burned her hand. Faced with the difficulty of finding a dependable servant, we moved to the boardinghouse.[17]

After Mother had settled us, she left for Carthage. Never in all my life have I felt so inadequate as when she went down the boardinghouse stairs, leaving me standing at the top with my baby in my arms. Years later, I left that same

---

16. Claude Bowers (1878–1958) began his career in journalism in Indiana, moving to New York as an editorial writer for the *Evening World* (1923–1931). He wrote two best-sellers, *Jefferson and Hamilton* (1925) and *The Tragic Era* (1929) about Andrew Johnson and Reconstruction. In 1928, at the Jackson Day dinner in Washington, he "rallied desperate Democrats in a spectacular performance," which led to his choice as keynote speaker at the 1928 Democratic convention. From 1931 to 1933, he was a political columnist for the *New York Journal* until FDR appointed him ambassador to Spain. From 1933 to 1953, he was ambassador to Chile (*DAB*, s.v. "Bowers, Claude").

17. ENB's daughter, Harriet, was born on October 7, 1903. Their boardinghouse was on K Street in Washington.

baby grown into a woman with her first baby in her arms, and when I went back for something I had left, she was crying as I had long ago.

After that I hardly seemed to have a husband, for every evening after office he was at school until nine-thirty or ten at night. Yet I got a very special satisfaction out of waiting for him with chocolate and sandwiches ready. This was how I had dramatized marriage.

And there was the boardinghouse, presenting the Washington social picture by hearsay. For each boarder could call at least one prominent member of the administration by his first name, and quote him casually. Everyone had access to some station on the grapevine telegraph. So I, as do most of Washington's inhabitants, learned many things about people in public life and politics that were not so at all. I almost felt as if I knew Alice Roosevelt and the Countess Cassini, so many were the tales I heard.[18]

The theatre, too, was a source of great delight. Like all hinterlanders when they go to a city, I felt that I must see every play. It was a surprise to discover that some of the longtime residents looked upon the theatre as an extravagance, and went to it as to an occasion. Aunt Fanny was ever ready to go with me, and a cousin, Billy McDowell, who was in and out of Washington, served often as an escort. Besides, there were the matinees. In time I began to discriminate myself, and did not grow enthusiastic at everything behind a footlight. I have some of the programs now pasted in a memory book. Mrs. Fiske in *Mary of Magdala*; E. H. Sothern in *The Proud Prince*; Henry Irving in *The Merchant of Venice*; Denman Thompson in a revival of *The Old Homestead*; Grace George in *Pretty Peggy*. And there were, too, those fantastic new musical comedies, *The Wizard of Oz* and *The Prince of Pilsen*, Reginald de Koven's new opera, *Red Feather*, and my first Shaw play, *Man and Superman*, with Robert Lorraine.

Aunt Fanny was our fairy godmother and mentor in one, bringing me a new dress one day, and on another suggesting delicately that it was immodest to nurse my baby before my husband.

One afternoon when we were entertaining the Sewells from home in our room, we heard the cry of "Extra." We thought that Mark Hanna, who was then very ill, had died, but when we saw the paper, the headlines announced that Baltimore was burning.[19] Harry caught the next train and

---

18. Alice Roosevelt was the daughter of Theodore Roosevelt. Russian ambassador Count Arthur de Cassini had brought the sixteen-year-old Marguerite to Washington with him in 1898 and had called her his niece. Cassini had been secretly married to her mother, a Dutch singer. In 1901, he finally acknowledged that Marguerite was his daughter. She was a good friend of Alice Roosevelt and her father's official hostess at the embassy (Kathryn Allamong Jacob, *Capital Elites: High Society in Washington, D.C., after the Civil War*, 134–38).

19. William J. Sewell (b. 1866) married Mary Taggart in 1893. He purchased a one-third interest in the *Carthage Evening Press* in 1890 and became sole owner and editor in

from that confused and terror-stricken city brought back my sister Julia who was studying at the Peabody Conservatory of Music.

In February I went home with the baby. Harriet we had called her because Harry insisted he would never permit a boy to be named for him. A diminutive for Henry he seemed to think it, which is amusing today when so many men of prominence bear it, and his daughter-in-law chose it for her son. A healthy, happy baby, Harriet was the joy of everyone. Nor did the company and the changes in habitation seem to upset her. If she had been my only child, I would have thought, I fear, that any child cared for properly would be healthy like that.

Yet my trip home had its difficult moments. There was no through sleeper from Washington to St. Louis, so we had to go to Harrisburg in a parlor car and change there to the train from New York. Our train from Washington was late, and the conductor by mistake wired the Harrisburg stationmaster that he had no passengers beyond Indianapolis. So when we arrived in Harrisburg, the Limited from New York had gone and with it my reservation and my brother whom I was to join there. The stationmaster, all apology, insisted that he would give me the same reservation on the Express and wired the Altoona station agent to get my brother off the Limited to wait for me there. But when I got on the Express, there were no reservations at all. Harry, who had taken us up to Harrisburg and was returning to Washington, ran back to get the stationmaster, and before he returned the train started. So there I was: no berth and no surety of my brother's awaiting me, with a baby and a basket of bottles to be taken care of. I dropped down in the end section not yet made up. The Pullman conductor said I might sit there until we reached Altoona where its occupants would get on.

I pulled up the window curtain. It was a moonlit night. The ground was snow covered, with the little Pennsylvania towns seeming to cuddle up to the hills for protection. It must have been a beautiful scene, but to me, sitting there in the dark car, my baby in my arms, it seemed a very cold and remote world.

Of course, Jim did get on, and of course they found a lower berth, and Jim made the dining car take care of the bottles, although the milk soured and

---

1896. He retired in 1944 (*Carthage Evening Press*, March 25, 1922, June 2, 1956; McGregor, *Biographical Record of Jasper County*, 129–30). Mark Hanna (1837–1904), a Cleveland businessman, became the primary supporter of William McKinley in Ohio politics, managing his election to the governorship in 1891. Chairman of the Republican National Committee in 1896, Hanna was instrumental in gaining the Republican presidential nomination for McKinley. When the new president appointed John Sherman as secretary of state, Hanna was appointed to fill out Sherman's term in the Senate. In 1897 he was elected to the Senate and reelected in 1903 (*DAB*, s.v. "Hanna, Mark"). On February 7, 1904, fire raged through the business district of Baltimore, destroying 150 buildings and burning blocks of buildings. It was "the worst conflagration in its history" (*New York Times*, February 8, 1904).

Harriet cried with hunger before we reached St. Louis, where my sisters met us with a new basket of formula-filled bottles.

Harry thoroughly enjoyed and profited by his work with Mr. Garfield. He was anxious to minimize his shorthand work and devote himself to legal matters, and Mr. Garfield very graciously appointed him a special agent of the bureau and assigned him to the examination of the state records and reports of various corporations. After his graduation in June, Harry came out to Missouri to make a study of the records and annual reports of various Missouri corporations.[20] At Columbian University he had done two years' work in one. Being practically brought up in a courtroom evidently had its advantages.

Among the instructors, or perhaps they called them lecturers, at the school were two Supreme Court justices, Justices Harlan and Van Devanter.[21] Years later, in 1934, at a judiciary reception at the White House, Justice Vandevanter, who had once been an assistant attorney general assigned to the Interior Department and fulfilled many of the duties Harry then performed as assistant attorney general in charge of the Lands Division, was discussing with Harry the work in connection with the Interior Department: reclamation, irrigation, Indians, and national forests. Harry had recently argued some cases before the Supreme Court, and the justice had written the decision in one of them, expounding and explaining the applicable law. Harry reminded the justice that his opinion as a justice was enlightening and instructive and that Harry had gone to school to him before—at Columbian University.

"Now you're trying to tell me that I'm old," said the justice, over eighty.

"Not at all," said Harry. "I'm trying to say that I've gone to school to you twice—once at the law school and again this year before the Supreme Court."

This seemed to amuse the justice, but he must have been even more pleased,

---

20. Harry graduated from Columbian Law School in 1904.

21. John Marshall Harlan (1833–1911) studied law at Transylvania University in Lexington, Kentucky. Admitted to the bar in 1853, Harlan was elected judge of the Franklin County court in 1858. After serving in the Union army during the Civil War, he was elected attorney general of Kentucky, serving from 1863 to 1867. He ran unsuccessfully on the Republican ticket for governor in 1871 and 1875. After his support of Rutherford B. Hayes, he was appointed to the Supreme Court in 1877. From 1889 to 1910, he lectured at Columbian University Law School on constitutional law (*DAB*, s.v. "Harlan, John Marshall"). Willis Van Devanter (1859–1941) was Wyoming's chief justice from 1889 to 1890, then turned to partisan politics, serving as Republican state chairman from 1892 to 1896 and national committeeman from 1896 to 1903. His hard work for President McKinley was rewarded with an appointment in 1897 as assistant attorney general in charge of Indian and public lands in the Department of Interior. In 1903, Theodore Roosevelt appointed him to the federal circuit court of appeals, and in 1911 Taft placed him on the Supreme Court. His retirement in 1937, after strenuous opposition to New Deal programs, contributed to the defeat of FDR's court-packing plan (*DAB*, s.v. "Van Devanter, Willis").

if sensitive about his age, when a columnist who apparently overheard the conversation reported that Harry had reminded the justice of when they went to school *together*, a misversion that has found its way into one of those "inside Washington" books.

In these later days when the justices of the Supreme Court are treated as if they have retired from all contacts except those of the dinner table, I remember those justices who eked out their incomes by adding teaching to their Supreme Court decisioning.

Harry had just completed his study of corporation state reports at Jefferson City when he received a wire calling him back to Washington at once. I was at Carthage at my mother's with the baby, so I met him at St. Louis, and we returned to Washington.

Harry was recalled to go to New York to take part in the investigation of the *General Slocum* steamship disaster there.[22] The gruesome details of the *Slocum* disaster were revealed day by day. Harry, with his sensitiveness to suffering, could not forget them. An excursion boat filled with more than a thousand people off for a holiday had caught fire in midstream. Six hundred passengers had drowned. Examination revealed that the life preservers had been filled with cotton instead of cork, and that those supposed to be made of compressed cork contained a piece of iron inserted to give them the proper weight. Both fire hose and preservers had rotted, but there was no law fixing a penalty for not replacing them. We were not then so inured as the *Slocum* fire, the *Titanic* wreck, and finally the world war were to make us. The account of a capsized boat at the Washington regatta, where five men and a woman were drowned, upset us for days. We had not become accustomed to take a daily quota of automobile accidents as a matter of course.

We had moved for the summer into a furnished house out in Mount Pleasant near the zoo, with a large yard around it, and a convenient car line.[23] In twenty years that ground was to be so completely covered with apartment buildings that you could not even find the location of our house.

Across the street from us lived the retired president of the National Baseball League.[24] Making friends with me over Harriet's baby carriage, he asked me

---

22. *General Slocum*, a wooden paddle-wheel steamer, caught fire in the East River on June 15, 1904. In total, 1,021 lost their lives. The investigation revealed the captain's errors in judgment and lack of safety precautions.

23. They lived at 1626 Howard Avenue, Mount Pleasant (ENB Diary, October 1, 1904, Folder 50, ENB Papers).

24. Nicholas Emanuel Young (1840–1916) worked as an auditor in the U.S. Treasury Department after the Civil War. In 1871, he was instrumental in organizing the first professional baseball league, the National Association of Professional Base Ball Players. He became president of the National League in 1885, serving until he resigned in 1901 when he returned to government work (*Biographical Dictionary of American Sports*, s.v. "Young, Nicholas Emanuel").

if I liked baseball. I did not know much about it, although I had seen two league games in St. Louis, but I was willing to learn. So he initiated me, taking me not only to the big-league games and explaining the plays, but up our street where a Sunday-school league played several times a week under his enthusiastic auspices. It seemed, and still does, interesting that a man who had known all the big and best professional ballplayers of his time should so enjoy the efforts of those amateur boy players. When I said as much, he answered, "It's the game, not the expertness, if you really care for it, and it's interesting to see these boys do so well." The attitude of sportsmanship, I take it, before professionalism had wiped it out.

One incident of that period indicated to me how undeservedly and fatally reputations may be lost. My sister-in-law, the one whom we had visited in California, had lost her husband and was staying with us, the baby offering her some diversion.[25] We had a maid of all work, a colored woman, who in the winter served as cook in a large establishment. She was devoted to Harry and at first to me, but gradually she became disapproving in her manner, verging at times on impertinence. I had decided she would have to go when accidentally I discovered the cause. When Harry was away he asked some man who was unmarried or whose wife was away for the summer to come out and look after us, our grounds being large and remote from the neighbors. He usually came in about ten or eleven, after the maid had gone, but appeared at the breakfast table with me and my sister. I realized that the maid was rather rude to him, but put it down to annoyance at an unexpected guest. Then one Saturday night Harry came home unexpectedly and was present at the breakfast table, where he thanked the young man for inconveniencing himself just to relieve Harry's mind about our being safe. Later in the day Hattie came to me with an apology, saying she had not understood, and when I pressed for an explanation, explained that she'd seen enough in Washington houses not to be surprised at anything a wife did when her husband was away, but what she couldn't forgive was any wife fooling as nice a husband as I had. Suppose I had dismissed her, and suppose she had given her version of any "goings-on"!

While Harry was in New York on the *Slocum* disaster investigation, I went up to visit him. One of Harry's fellow stenographers had been drafted from the Immigration Service at Ellis Island and took me over one day to see its herded thousands. Young girls dressed in the latest American fashion met their mothers shawl wrapped, hatless, in the gay skirts of the peasant. They were of every nation, it seemed to me, some of them aggressive, others scared, distraught. Through a gate they passed single-file, a man lifting their eyelids as they passed through, looking for eye trouble. In one place were those who had been detained because they had not enough money or were considered

---

25. Edward Delemaine Wall, Effie's husband, died on November 5, 1903.

morally undesirable. Some of these people were defiant, others in tears. Seeing the difficulty they had in expressing themselves, their fear and confusion, I realized the pressure that must have sent them over here. Jacob Riis was just then agitating the immigration problem through his book.[26]

Either one likes Washington or one does not. I was one who did. I would have been satisfied to stay. But Harry was eager to get home to the practice of law. When it was intimated to him that he might later be attached to the White House staff in a shorthand capacity, he felt that he was likely to be sentenced for life to stenography and secretaryships. Besides, he was told that a Washington job ruined a young man: he lost initiative and never amounted to anything. Champ Clark had just made his speech stating that above the entrance to all government departments should be an inscription, "Leave Hope and Ambition Behind, All Ye Who Enter Here." I have often wondered what would have happened had he remained. For Mr. Garfield became secretary of the Interior; Frank Hitchcock, the chief clerk, became postmaster general; the assistant commissioner, Herbert Knox Smith, became commissioner of corporations.[27]

Still, Harry was a Democrat, the only employee who said he could not vote for Roosevelt's reelection. This might have made a difference.

Sometimes in recent years, after a lecture on life in Washington, I have been asked, "But how about people like us who would have no place in official society? What could we do to enjoy ourselves?"

Well, we found a great deal to enjoy, and this though there was less than there is today, and underlings were so much more restricted in their social activities. They were, in fact, almost looked down upon as inferiors. When President Roosevelt made Mr. Loeb his private secretary, social dowagers discussed seriously the question of whether or not his wife could be received, with her father only a government clerk.[28] Today some of the most popular hostesses are themselves in some office. A stenographer may be the daughter of a cabinet member, and clerks, accountants, typists rub elbows at the White House and exclusive functions with ambassadors, senators, and the "haute monde."

---

26. Jacob Riis's best-known works are *How the Other Half Lives* (1890), *The Making of an American* (1901), and *Children of the Tenements* (1903).

27. Herbert Knox Smith, part of Roosevelt's "Tennis Cabinet," succeeded Garfield as commissioner of the Bureau of Corporations in 1907 (Lewis L. Gould, *The Presidency of Theodore Roosevelt*, 198, 218).

28. At thirty-three in 1901, William Loeb Jr. was one of two assistant secretaries (along with B. F. Barnes) on Roosevelt's staff. Having been Roosevelt's secretary in Albany, Loeb became the president's private secretary in 1903 after Cortelyou moved into the cabinet (ibid., 15–16).

One like myself who had lived in a small town where she felt herself among the socially elite did not find this social exclusion entirely pleasing to her ego. Yet I have always been glad that I saw Washington as I did from a bleacher seat.

Harry resigned in late October, and we returned to Carthage. The election was held the next week after we returned, and Judge Perkins, under whom Harry had been court reporter, was defeated for reelection.[29] So the judge and Harry formed a partnership, Perkins and Blair, and Harry was at last launched on the active practice of law. When I left Washington I supposed it was forever. If I had thought of life at all as a design I would probably have considered it a series of stripes, here the one for girlhood, there one for Sarcoxie, and one for this Washington experience. But it was not a stripe. There were set certain stitches in a part of the design to which I would come back again and again, each time to add a few more of a deeper shade. Not that I realized that any stitches had been set in my life. For my part in Washington then was wholly that of a spectator who is a wife and the wife who sees the outside world through her husband's eyes. No young wife, I verily believe, any more completely submerged herself in her husband than I at this period. All my ambitions had been transferred at marriage to his future. I had no thoughts, no interests, of my own. I lived in and through him. For that experience I have always been grateful. It was a restful experience, that shirking of responsibility, that negation of the ego, that abnegation of individuality.

Afterward when I was tempted to grow impatient with women so immersed in their husbands' lives that they would placidly accept the wrongs of other women or of society's injustices, I had only to remember those years to understand and excuse it. I knew, in time, that had my husband wanted and enjoyed a carbon-copy kind of wife, I would have continued to be that kind. It was only as I learned how she bored him that I changed. Oh, this adaptability in women! Does it come from something deep in woman's nature, springing instinctively out of her physical helplessness? Or has it been bred in her by the centuries of her economic dependence on men? How many times I have smiled to myself, remembering those days and my enjoyment of them, when men masculinists have by word or act suggested that I was "different" from their wives.

For who knows better than I how many different women a woman has it in her to be. Already I have shown myself as the imaginative child, the queer young wallflower, the conventional young bride. Adaptability seems to have been my name. Am I, sometimes I have asked myself, a chameleon, or did I need to go through all these phases, appear in these different guises, on my way to what I am, as the embryo passes through all the biological stages of life? And if so, why? Other women, at least many of them, seem able to choose a part early and stick to it throughout their lives. Why did I have to

---

29. Joseph D. Perkins was Harry's law partner from 1905 to 1911.

essay so many? And yet I do not regret the varied roles. Quite otherwise. For whatever understanding I have gained has come from having myself played at one time or another all these parts, and so too, probably, whatever of interest my life may have for others. For though no one role was in itself outstanding, the variety may be illuminating.

Main Street, Joplin, 1900. From Art Work of the Lead and Zinc Region of Missouri and Kansas, *part 2*

Third Street on the square of Carthage, 1900. From Art Work of the Lead and Zinc Region of Missouri and Kansas, *part 3*

Emily Newell, about 1896. Courtesy of the Western Reserve Historical Society, Cleveland, Ohio

Harry Blair, 1900. Courtesy of the Western Reserve Historical Society, Cleveland, Ohio

Emily Newell, 1900. Courtesy of the Western Reserve Historical Society, Cleveland, Ohio

From left, *Harry Blair, daughter Harriet Blair Forsythe, granddaughter Emily Blair Forsythe, and Emily Newell Blair. Courtesy of the Western Reserve Historical Society, Cleveland, Ohio*

Emily and her children, Newell and Harriet. Courtesy of the Western Reserve Historical Society, Cleveland, Ohio

124

"The Golden Lane," the woman suffrage demonstration at the 1916 Democratic National Convention in St. Louis. Courtesy of Western Historical Manuscripts Collection, St. Louis

Suffrage leader Carrie Chapman Catt. Courtesy the Library of Congress

Dr. Anna Howard Shaw, president of the National American Woman Suffrage Association. Courtesy of the Western Reserve Historical Society, Cleveland, Ohio

Emily Newell Blair stands next to Clem Shaver, chairman of the Democratic National Committee, 1924. Courtesy of the Western Reserve Historical Society, Cleveland, Ohio

Emily Newell Blair's counterpart, vice chairman of the Republican National Committee, Harriet Taylor Upton. Courtesy the Library of Congress

Emily Newell Blair with Mrs. Woodrow Wilson and national committeewomen, January 11, 1928. Courtesy of the Western Reserve Historical Society, Cleveland, Ohio

The Woman's National Democratic Club, 1927. Courtesy of the Woman's National Democratic Club

Emily Newell Blair at work on her Good Housekeeping *column. Courtesy of the Western Reserve Historical Society, Cleveland, Ohio*

BOOK 2

Twentieth-Century Life

1 The Fertile Years

At last we were fairly started. My husband hung out his shingle, and I set to work homemaking. This brings me to the events in my life that are the most difficult to write about. The growth of a community is interesting in retrospect, the habits and customs of the past amusing to the eyes of today. But the affairs of home life are neither picturesque nor amusing.

Yet this was the most fertile period of my life. Before it had come the planting of many seeds. During it they took root. Out of them came first only tiny sprouts. During this period I made those readjustments that life forces on everyone. The rain of trouble fell; the sun came. It was the most intensely realized period of all my life, and I look back on it as, in many ways, the happiest.

But the experiences were only those common to every wife and mother who tries to make a home, who bears children, and strives to share her husband's burdens.

How dramatic my emotion, as sitting on a stone in my garden one summer morning, filled with a fear I dared not meet, I turned in on myself, and, stripping aside all words and formulas, sought earnestly to find a faith in God that would meet my needs? I came away from the spot a different woman. Much that I thought I believed was left behind, but what I took with me was my own, not the Church's, not St. Paul's, nor my mother's.

Or that painful and slow acquisition of the philosophy by which I live? It came out of many hours of meditation, hours of reading, hours of prayer. But they are not exciting incidents.

Or the momentous discovery of answer to prayer. Comes a moment of utter helplessness, a cry for help, a merging of the finite with the infinite. Peace descends, you know not whence. You get up and go about your business. And then, long afterward, comes the realization that the conditions changed, the trouble is past, the danger is removed. How to explain it? You do not know. A request granted? Or a demand honored? Nothing so simple as that. Utter self-negation; entire yielding of will; and then it happens.

It is of such experiences that these years are full. Yet on the surface of all that appears are houses furnished, children nursed, and bills paid.

Sitting over the register with a gasping child held between your husband and yourself. A doctor telling you that your husband has tuberculosis. A fee not paid. An election lost. Seeing your husband submerged in worry, thinking he does not love you, and finding out that he does. How silly it sounds—and yet such things rock your world and put it back again.

The birth of a son—well, it has happened to millions.[1] A sick baby that cries every hour he is awake unless he is joggled. Seven months of joggling. Every known baby food tried on him. At last a formula arrived at by weeks of experiment and the perusal of every book in the doctor's office. Nothing interesting in that!

A baby who weighs at five months less than when he was born. A floor worn out from walking him. Your husband and you taking relays at the walking. Finding yourself screaming in a chair from nerves and loss of sleep. Your arms moving up and down even when empty. Your mother's return from abroad and dividing the night with you. Sisters taking over the housekeeping. Sanity returned. The baby growing stronger. A crisis passed in three lives. Yet what dull reading it makes.

Years after, when the baby is a sturdy young man, someone says to you: "Well, there's one child that has never given a moment's worry."

"Oh, no," you answer, "he weighed just eleven pounds when twelve months old, fell out of a second-story window when he was two, was bitten by a mad dog when three, and run over by a Ford when he was five."

You may know his survival for the greatest achievement of your life. But what interest has that for others?

A trip East with an invalid sister-in-law. Making Christmas for the children. Helping organize a kindergarten for your children. Planning May fetes to make the money to support it. Church work. Gardening with its disappointments and joys. The ups and downs of business. Of one of the downs we have a relic to this day, our "thousand-dollar pepper boxes" we call them. Promised that amount by some clients, my husband bought them to commemorate his first large fee. But alas, the fee was never paid, and the bill for them must be.

An activity connected with church work stands out as indicating our naïveté in those days. I hated church suppers, food sales, and bazaars. I could never feel that moneymaking served the Lord or induced spirituality. Several of us had been to St. George's, an institutional church in New York, and become imbued with the idea that a church should do something more than give its members a place to worship. As a result, we organized in the church in Carthage what we called a "Parish Guild" to make a contribution to the needs of the town.[2]

---

1. James Newell Blair was born on April 5, 1907 (Parker, "Descendants of William Blair").

2. The Parish Guild of Grace Church was organized in March 1906. Its object, according to its constitution, was "to promote the welfare of the Parish of Grace Church through the building up of the social and industrial life of the Parish." ENB was its first president (Constitution and By-Laws of the Parish Guild, Minutes of the March 26, 1906, meeting, Parish Guild Book, Archives, Grace Episcopal Church).

Among our undertakings, such as furnishing a maternity bag for the indigent mothers, was the later astonishing one of burying the deceased paupers of the poor farm. Under the law they were simply put in an unmarked hole in the ground without a casket. This seemed, to our sentimental minds, cruel, and to them, especially the superstitious, a dire end. By an arrangement with the undertaker, we managed to get a simple casket, a marker, and a funeral. Such revolutionary ideas as to the function of a church were not, of course, accepted by all the church members. Much more important did they think it to make altar cloths and raise money for church improvements.

A year after our return from Washington, my brother gave me an old house that he was moving off the lot where he intended to build his new home. He gave me, too, a vacant lot in the same block, together with a sum of money to spend in making the house over.[3] I set myself to studying old numbers of *Country Life* and *House Beautiful*. Alas, my plans, at least so the contractor said, were impractical. Partitions could not be taken out across the dining room without weakening the roof. Casement windows would leak. Pine could not be waxed or stained brown. Side lights could not be placed where I wanted them. The stairs could not go beside the chimney. Yet these things were all done, even if the contractor did walk out on the job and leave me to finish it with two men working by the day. The brick mason who laid my chimney said to me: "You ain't like my wife. I says to her when I built our house, 'You can have the kitchen jest the way you want it,' and she says to me, 'Tom, I want you to have it jest the way you want it.' "

No, I was not like his wife. I wanted my house just as I wanted it and felt myself justified, in spite of having spent more money than we had and running into debt, when I stood in my blue and white living room, or sat in my dark-stained dining room with the French door I had so fought for leading to the pergola-topped porch, or slept in my organdy-hung bedroom. The outside was, I know, hideous, but the Jarvie brass lights, the built-in seats, the white red-bricked fireplace made the inside charming enough to make up for that.

It seems queer today, when casement windows are a commonplace and every hardware store shows colonial doorknobs, and colonial light fixtures may be had from any electrician, to remember how difficult it was to convince the local tradesmen that there were such things. Not that I was the only one building a house in Carthage. On the contrary, it had just passed through another building period. But conformity was still the fashion. White stone houses with wide circling verandas, supported by Grecian columns of marble, were the thing for the recently successful: erstwhile machinists who now owned factories, farmers who had become bankers, and blacksmiths who were now lawyers. For the recently married, there was the two-story eight-roomed square house, with varnished brown or green woodwork, green-walled living

---

3. In 1905 the Blairs lived at 109 North Maple Street.

room, and brown-walled dining room, with willow furniture in the first and a mission oak dining room set in the latter.

Carthage had spread out. Our house was a mile from the square, on the ground where I had once picked May apples and violets under oak trees. Now it was all built up. White stone sidewalks paralleled the macadamized streets with the hard-maple trees in the parkway. Fences were a thing of the past, and everyone was planting shrubbery with here and there a real garden.

On this block lived five young "married couples," and not far away several others who had gone to school together and moved in the same social set ever since. Our young children were nearly of an age, our social and cultural backgrounds were the same, our problems similar: the men's that of getting ahead in the world, the women's of making satisfactory homes. We had about the same status in the community. So we naturally formed an intimate social circle, an intimacy that has never lapsed through the years. Indeed, the Saturday-evening supper card club, then organized, still continues to meet, having never missed a winter in thirty-five years.[4] We "girls," as we called ourselves, had also a Domestic Science Club, which, since it was unique in that we each prepared a luncheon to cost not more than twenty-five cents a piece, I was later to describe in a magazine.

I worked hard those days at the cooking end of my housewife job, but did it characteristically. Day after day I drew up a menu and prepared and served the food. Seeing my efforts my husband said one day, "Why do you work so hard? I would be satisfied with steak and potatoes every night."

"But I wouldn't be satisfied to cook it," I said. "That would be drudgery. To try something hard and different each day and see what turns out makes a game out of it."

It seemed a great achievement when I could cook and serve by myself a four-course dinner for eight people.

There was a wider social life, too, in which we had our part. For there were a dozen or more groups like ours overlapping here and there, and on occasion coming together in huge parties, where two or three, or sometimes six, hostesses pooled their social debts and paid them all at once by entertaining eighty or a hundred guests. Hospitality was, as it were, being put on a commercial basis.

The social pattern had changed. Those who stood out in my youth as social leaders had become submerged in the mass. A few still felt themselves superior and strove to practice exclusiveness, but the superiority unrecognized avails nothing. Strangers no longer waited to be taken up by the old group. They formed their own. Where there had once been three women's clubs, there

---

4. Six couples formed the Garrison Avenue Club: the Blairs, Harry and Ann Putnam, Miller and Pauline Bryan, Henry and Anna Cowgill, Roger and Grace Webster, and John and Cara O'Keefe (Newell Blair, interview with author, June 2, 1998).

were now at least twenty. Instead of the Dinner Club, there were ten dinner clubs. And each one, in the minds of its members, was as important as the others.

If I seem to make much of the social life in Carthage, it is because social life in the small towns looms large. It is—or was—the only way one could get entertainment before the day of country clubs and movies. Beginning as a diversion, it ended as a business until the war put an end to it.

I had a very definite conception of what my life should be. I had, I thought, a brilliant husband, a brilliant sister-in-law who lived with us.[5] I was to make the home that served them. I was to encourage and help them. I had two children. I was to make them fit for life. Any part I would take in public undertakings was to be directed to the purpose of furthering their interests. I thought of myself—and I did think of it—as the woman behind the scenes, the inspiration, the helpmate of them all. I had no desire to do anything in my own name. I felt no need for self-expression. Looking back with a better knowledge of psychology I know now that what I really was doing was expressing myself through them. I know, too, what I never guessed then, that this effort of mine was not acceptable to my husband. He did not want anyone working through him. If I had been wiser, I might have guessed at times, but I was imbued with the old ideal of women's work. Yet a queer thing happened. In Washington I had learned to do without society. I found it just as hard now to interest myself again in it. I missed the pageant of city life, the shops, Congress. The first year back in Carthage was again a time of adjustment.

Life was having its way with me. Circumstances were weaving in their stitches. And the political threads fell again into the pattern.

One of the circuit judges resigned. The vacancy was in the division of the court that, by common consent, was always filled by a Carthage man, but the older lawyers did not want to try for a short term. The Democratic lawyers of the county, with the exception of two, drew up a petition urging Harry to run.

Although the idea of running for office was uncongenial to his temperament, it seemed folly not to take an unopposed nomination. So he announced his candidacy. And then, at the last moment, one of the two who had not signed the petition entered the race.[6]

This was the year the new primary election law went into effect in Missouri. It had been tried in only a few states. No one knew how it would work out, or how to conduct a primary campaign. All the elaborate system of letter writing, person-to-person canvassing, placards on the countryside, billboard and newspaper advertising was yet to be devised. I suspect the

---

5. Effie Blair Wall's husband, Edward Wall, died on November 5, 1903, and Effie lived with Harry and Emily for a time after his death.

6. Harry's opponent in the primary race for circuit judge was Robert A. Mooneyham.

proponents of the law thought innocently that candidates would simply announce themselves and leave the voters to find out for themselves the best man.

The first thing you had to do, under the law, was to get a certain number of signatures on petitions asking you to run, and file them by a certain day. Well, that was not hard. But as soon as that was done, common sense told you it would be wise to write to these men and thank them for their support. That made several hundred letters. In the meantime, the candidate was being urged by his friends to come here, there, everywhere and meet their friends. It was apparent that Harry would have to do a lot of visiting about the county.

But there was the mail to be answered. It was laden with letters offering support and asking for suggestions as to how to work, from newspapers asking for information about him and insisting on his taking some paid space, from men who did not want any money themselves to support him but knew where a little would do some good, from churches asking for subscriptions, from Negro clubs asking for a contribution for a new roof for their church or club room, from groups wanting money for rent for a place to meet. Someone had to answer them.

He could not attend to these letters and be out in the county all the time. So my dining room was turned into an office, two stenographers were engaged, and I undertook the management of the letter campaign. All day we got them out. In the evenings my sisters came and stamped and sealed them.

Naturally he came more and more to discuss with me the developments of the campaign. By the time he was nominated I had added a great deal to my knowledge of practical politics.

But we found that the campaign had not even begun. There was now the election, and it had to be done all over again, the same men to see, cards to be handed out again, and even more letters to be written. Day after day I got them out. Evening after evening we stamped and mailed them. At twelve or one o'clock he would wearily stumble in from some political meeting where the candidates had "lined up" and "said a word." I would give him some food and listen to his report of developments. It was all very exciting and interesting, but the money was giving out. For the same demands for contributions for every known sort of thing came in again. I've wondered sometimes if the innocent ladies asking candidates and officials for contributions to their pet charities know it for the blackmail it is. And disgusting things happened, too. Once a drunk man was found waiting for us on our porch one Sunday morning to ask for a quarter to get back to Joplin because he was campaigning for Harry and had been "celebrating" for him.

"You'd think you could at least keep your home clean of it," Harry said.

The Saturday night before election we were confident that he would win. Then, we said, we could economize and pay back the money we had borrowed, and all would be smooth and easy again. Harry was popular, he had grown up in a courtroom, and it was said that he had the judicial temperament and was cut out for a judge. I fear I let my fancy roam and saw him marching steadily toward a chief justiceship. Republicans by the hundreds had told him they would vote for him. But, unfortunately for us, "word came down the line" to the Republican headquarters that same Saturday night that there must be no scratching of ballots. And by Tuesday midnight we knew the worst. The Republican ticket had been carried from top to bottom. A Republican governor would sit in Jefferson City for the first time in many years. Taft was elected president.[7]

Harry ran six hundred ahead of his ticket, but that was small consolation to us as we met our disappointment, thought of the months wasted, and counted up our debts. For of course we had spent more money than we intended to, or had.

At the time we called ourselves all kinds of names. Harry said: "I've always said a man was a fool to run for office, and I see no reason to change my opinion."

But it contributed much to my political education. For one thing, I learned a lesson in sportsmanship. I was inclined to be bitter, but my husband said to me: "Someone would have to lose. If we had won, would you expect him to be bitter? Not at all. We had no business going into the fight unless willing to accept the fortunes of war."

This lesson stood me in good stead when later I went into politics myself, and time after time hard political effort went for naught. Without it I might have descended to personalities. They say that women do. But having seen in my husband the spirit that could oppose without antagonism, differ without resentment, I had learned how to fight impersonally. A very necessary lesson for a politician, for otherwise he degrades himself, weakens his cause, and wastes valuable emotional energy on nonessentials. Many times during the bitterly waged campaign of 1928 I had occasion to think of that.

Nothing was further from my thoughts in those days than politics and education. I had only done what I could to help my husband. And I continued to do the same. We had our fun. Now we must pay the piper. So the cook was dismissed. I resigned from my social clubs and set myself to do my housework and make over my old clothes.

But shortly another mining boom came on. The old Webb City field where my father had dropped eight thousand dollars during my childhood, and

---

7. William Howard Taft garnered 1.27 million more votes than Democratic candidate William Jennings Bryan; the electoral vote was 321 to 162. Herbert Spencer Hadley defeated Democratic congressman William S. Cowherd of Kansas City for the governorship. Hadley (1872–1927) was a progressive Republican who was the first Republican governor of Missouri since Reconstruction (*DAB*, s.v. "Hadley, Herbert Spencer"). Harry lost to Republican Henry L. Bright.

where Harry, before we were married, had once made a few thousand dollars, was opened up again. Miners were going to still lower levels for the ore. Fewer the "pick and shovelers" who could start with nothing and end with a fortune. My brother had gone into the mining business and engaged my husband as his attorney. Prosperity once more came to Carthage, carrying us up with it. Investors from the East came and went. At my brother's house in the same block was a constant succession of visitors. Business deals involving millions were discussed at our dinner tables. The atmosphere was charged with success. The present seemed pregnant with great fortune. During all my early life my father had a fortune just around the corner. Now we saw one in the same place. Ever and again I had an intuition that all was not on a sound basis. A sense of impending disaster, even in the midst of some gaiety, would seize me. And then I would forget it under the stress of all there was to engage my attention.

Servants were becoming a problem. Wages had risen from two dollars a week to three and three and a half, with no laundry. Someone suggested that we try a cooperative kitchen, meaning a cooperative eating place.[8] We did. Twenty families, I think. And there were other undertakings, in all of which I took part, but I was in no sense a leader, nor did I have any particular urge to become one.

Once I went East to New York with a sick sister-in-law. My sisters were in eastern colleges, and I visited them there.[9] I owe a great deal to these sisters. But never more than at this period. For their activities kept me in contact with a younger generation. Moreover they widened my world. I could not be entirely submerged in domesticity when they came and went, as they did, now to college, now to Europe, coming home with new ideas, stimulating me to keep up with them as far as possible. My interest in them still partook of the maternal. My husband had taken on the same attitude toward them.

Into all this life I felt tightly knit, and completely satisfying I found it. Yet toward the end of this decade I found that though the threads that held me to it were never to break entirely, they were often thereafter stretched. The first discovery was that I had a mind. I realize how silly this must sound, but if I am to be truthful, I must tell the truth about myself. And that was the way I felt about it.

Of course, if I had ever *thought* about it, I would have known that I was always cogitating on the whys and wherefores of things, and realized that I loved to argue. My sisters and I were given to ragging ideas to death, as a

8. The Cooperative Kitchen served its first meals on September 16, 1909, and closed its doors on January 1, 1912.

9. Margaretta Newell graduated from Vassar and earned an M.A. at Columbia University in New York City (Marion Banister to Charles E. Mills, letter of recommendation, December 6, 1941, Marion Glass Banister Papers). Julia attended Peabody Conservatory of Music in Baltimore. Anna graduated from the University of Missouri.

brother-in-law was later to complain. But I had early learned not to do so in mixed company. When I was a girl, visiting a friend, another guest had said: "Oh, for heaven's sake, Emily. I thought we'd lost that subject. You don't know when to let a thing drop."

I'd never forgotten her comment.

Especially was I imbued with the idea of deferring to the opinions of men. I don't know where I got it. Certainly my father had always listened to my mother and treated her as an intellectual equal. My husband treated me the same way. But it was not, in the society I knew, the attitude of men toward the opinions of women. There was one brand of conversation for the men, another for the women, and still another when men and women talked to each other. Women were to be entertaining, not argumentative. I tried to conform to this requirement.

If, occasionally, I did venture an opinion, it was to my discomfiture. One evening at the cooperative kitchen I had said to two politicians that it seemed to me as silly to elect your county recorders and treasurers and collectors as it would be to elect your butcher, baker, or banker; why didn't we elect one board, turn the county business over to it, and let it engage clerks to do the work? By manner, rather than words, they indicated that such an idea was too infantile, impracticable, and silly to merit serious consideration. Yet later I wrote an article about the primary law, discussing the shorter ballot, an article that is often referred to in college textbooks.

But there was one man in town who did not hold this opinion of mixed conversations: the music teacher, Professor Calhoun. One evening he came by with a book he wanted to read to us, G. Lowes Dickinson's *Modern Symposium*. It had made such an impression on him that he had bought thirty copies and then, being in Oxford, had dropped in on the author to tell him so. This book played a great part in my life, but in a way to have surprised Mr. Dickinson had he ever known of it. Our friend read beautifully, and we had such an enjoyable evening that we invited two other couples to join us in weekly meetings. Now one of these gentleman, Allen McReynolds, was a believer in democracy.[10] Mr. Calhoun was a believer in aristocracy. Arguments ensued. And almost before I knew it, I was taking part in them. And the men listened to me. Not only that, they answered me. More, Mr. Calhoun flattered me by saying that I had a man's mind. I had not then heard Dr. Shaw's famous retort: "Show me the man before I feel flattered."

I was flattered. For I had a high opinion of Mr. Calhoun's intellect. That he valued mine made it suddenly seem worthwhile.

---

10. G. Lowes Dickinson (1862–1932) published *A Modern Symposium* in 1935. Allen McReynolds (1877–1960) was Harry's partner in the law firm of McReynolds and Blair from 1919 to 1933. He served as Jasper County's state senator from 1934 to 1942. A political and civic leader in the state, McReynolds ran unsuccessfully for the Democratic nomination for governor in 1940 (*Joplin News Herald*, September 29, 1960).

My husband was responsible for my second discovery. It was that I could write.

I had been reading an article in the *Cosmopolitan* called "Confessions of a Rebellious Wife."[11] "I'm tired of reading about these unhappy wives," I said to my husband. "Why doesn't someone write about the contented ones?"

"Why don't you?"

"Nonsense, I can't write."

"But you could. Your letters show it."

I laughed. "Every husband thinks that about his wife."

"No," he insisted. "The last time I was in New York I read an extract from one of your letters to clinch some point in the conversation, and everyone commented on the way you put it. We can be discussing something, you and I, for hours. I go away and your first letter puts it more clearly than all our conversations made it. You could do it if you tried."

I could not get his words out of my mind. As I went about my household duties, I kept thinking about the happy wife. She could not tell about her contentment. That would not carry conviction. She must reveal it without any apparent intention of doing so. But how could she do this? In letters, of course, but letters to whom? To her sisters? One does not write about her married life to sisters, but only to her husband. Well, why not let her reveal her contentment in some letters to her husband? The letters might at least serve to amuse Harry. So one afternoon I sat down at the dining room table with the two-year-old baby playing on the floor beside me, and wrote a letter from a young wife to her husband, discussing their first separation and their hopes. That night I read it to my husband. He praised it. The next afternoon I did another in the same way. Presently I had ten, each one discussing some matter of adjustment between the husband and wife. They covered a period of twenty-five years. In young innocence I thought that by the time people had been married that long all problems would be solved, and nothing left for them but a happy Darby and Joan old age.

When Harry took them downtown for his stenographer to copy and sent them to *Cosmopolitan*, I looked upon it as a joke, and thought no more about it. The first and last manuscript I was ever to treat so lightly. Afterward I had my share of counting the days, and waiting for the postman, but that manuscript I actually forgot. So I was surprised one afternoon to find in the mailbox a small brown envelope with the *Cosmopolitan* address on the corner. I read the letter through in amazement and then raced to the telephone.

"*Cosmopolitan*'s taken them, the letters," I shouted.

"Of course they have," Harry said. "What did they pay for them?"

I glanced down hurriedly.

---

11. The anonymous article, "Confessions of a Rebellious Wife," appeared in *American Magazine* 62 (July 1909): 210–19.

"Fourteen dollars and forty-two cents. Oh no, Great Scott, Harry, it's one hundred and forty-two dollars and forty-two cents!"[12]

With that I dropped the receiver and rushed hatless up the street to show the letter to my brother. Then I telephoned Mother.

That day was certainly one of the greatest in my life. I went to a dinner party that night and was acclaimed the rising young authoress.

The editor had asked what else I had written and apologized because he had missed it. I wrote back that I had never written anything before, didn't have the equipment to write, knew nothing about composition, was a poor speller, and probably didn't write the English language correctly. He answered at once that I must write. They could get plenty of college clerks at a hundred dollars a month to revise my English. They couldn't find persons who could write about the emotions of everyday people so convincingly. And I did not know enough to appreciate how rare an editor Roland Phillips was, nor how lucky I, that he had read my first manuscript.

But I did think that I had found a gold mine. If it was as easy as that, I would write. Shortly afterward I awoke one night from a dream with a title fixed in my mind: "Evolution of a Lady." I wrote it down, and slowly an idea began to gather around it. The rough "pick and shoveler" who had "struck it rich" was a commonplace with us. Many tales had been told of how the different ones had spent their money, of the way they and their daughters and wives behaved. I tried to imagine myself in the place of one of those daughters, and how I would feel. And one evening I sat down to write such a girl's experiences. I thought they would sound more authentic—although I did not then know this meaning of that word—if I let her tell them herself, so I decided to put them in diary form. As I wrote, incidents kept coming to my mind, things I had heard and forgotten. And some I never remembered to have heard at all. When it was done Harry's stenographer copied it and sent it to Mr. Phillips. He told me that it would not do for *Cosmopolitan*, but perhaps *Harper's Bazaar* would like it. And they did.[13]

Another title occurred to me, "Heart of a Wallflower." And I wrote a story around that, in the form of letters from a daughter to her dead mother. Mr. Phillips took that.[14] Well, I thought myself made—no less. I began to compute how much I might make a year. I saw myself a coming novelist.

And then the blow fell. My brother's property went into the hands of a trustee, and the financial structure of our lives went with it. We had less than we had to start with, our confidence in ourselves was gone, and our pride laid low.

---

12. ENB's article, "Letters of a Contented Wife," was published in *Cosmopolitan* 50 (December 1910): 130–38.

13. "The Evolution of a Lady," *Harper's Bazaar* 45 (December 1911): 572–74.

14. "Heart of a Wallflower," *Cosmopolitan* 51 (September 1911): 536–48.

2 Small-Town Writer

Once more we began again and the new beginning involved renting our house and cutting down our outgo. My mother, a sister, and my small family combined households in a small cottage. When the old home was broken up, the clearing of the attic was, of course, a task. Files of *Harper's Weekly* with the Nash cartoons went on a bonfire; the old spindle Victorian bed on which I had surreptitiously read summer afternoons went to the second-hand store. Even my father's old captain's sword disappeared. Yet out of it we salvaged enough to manage two trousseaus that year.[1]

True to Mother's character, when the crash came she had enough cash in whatever was her substitute for a stocking to pay all her own household bills. With a small pension to live on, she set to work to build a world of thought for herself in which she thereafter lived. On that small pension she maintained her economic independence to the end.

She lived with me often for months at a time, but never did she stay long enough to make me feel that she had settled down with us. When she thought it was becoming too much accepted she suddenly announced that she was off on a visit to one of the other sisters. She did the same with them. She was of great assistance in the household, but when anything, from the family darning to responsibility about the children, seemed to be taken for granted, she let it lapse while she went to a picture show or made some calls. Yet what she did for my children cannot be estimated. Not in the usual way of a grandmother. Their physical care was no concern of hers, nor did she ever humor them. She was always more of a disciplinarian than I. But she read to them and what was more important answered their questions. When people called my young son precocious it was because he was that unusual child who had his questions answered. With a wide knowledge of facts—since whenever she did not know a thing she had always looked it up—she answered them. Facts had a preciousness for her for their own sake. For me they were only interesting for the conclusions they led to. Once they had served their purpose I was very likely to forget them.

---

1. Julia Porter Newell married Philip W. Chappel on May 5, 1910, and Ella Rebecca Newell married Ralph Putman on September 18, 1910 (Folder 103, genealogical files, ENB Papers).

To help meet our needs I set to work to garner some of the money that seemed so easily to be earned merely by writing down the happy thoughts that came to you. But I discovered literature to be a fickle goddess. When you needed to write, thoughts did not come to you—not the ones that editors wanted. Hoping to improve matters I took on a literary agent. Now, all the evidence given by more successful writers than I shows the literary agent to be the fairy godfather of struggling writers. On the basis of this evidence I recommend them often to the hopefuls who ask my advice about marketing their brain children. But my agent proved a.100 percent failure.

Her criticisms were helpful, and I needed criticism, for no trained critic had ever read a line of mine before it was submitted. But not a manuscript did she sell the entire year. Yet nearly every one of those stories I myself sold later.

Ideas for stories came to me easily, and were almost as easily written, and after my surprise that editors were not waiting impatiently for anything I wrote, I settled down to writing as a business. To prevent the deadly discouragement that comes from rejection slips, as soon as I sent out a story I made out a list of magazines, determined not to give up until the manuscript had journeyed, if need be, to the last on the list. Few had to be withdrawn from circulation, but perhaps this is not surprising in view of the number of magazines to which I sent them. One—and I think one of my best—was accepted on its thirty-first trip. This was the record.

On one of its earlier trips it came back with a door key in the envelope and a letter from the assistant editor of *Cosmopolitan* saying that as he did not expect to be out my way soon, he was returning it, though he was glad my latchstring hung out. I could guess what had happened. I had carried the envelope downtown unsealed, expecting to buy the stamps to include for its possible return, and forgotten to take out the door key I had slipped into it. The name signed to this letter was that of a man who would one day give me a great opportunity, and be for years my chief: my good friend William F. Bigelow, editor of *Good Housekeeping.*[2]

Having sold my first three stories to magazines of large circulation, I thought that if they did not take my work, the smaller-circulation magazines would jump at the chance to get it. But in this I was mistaken. The subjects and the handling that made stories available for the large-circulation magazines made them unavailable for those that wanted other subjects and snappier handling. And this was a misfortune. In selling to better magazines I had to compete with trained and practiced writers, and I was the veriest tyro, whereas

---

2. William F. Bigelow (1879–1966) was managing editor of *Cosmopolitan* from 1909 to 1913. In 1913, he was made editor of *Good Housekeeping*, where he remained until his retirement in 1940 (*Dictionary of Literary Biography*, vol. 91, *American Magazine Journalists, 1900–1960*, s.v. "Bigelow, William F.").

the writers for the others were mostly beginners like myself. I learned that I was not good enough for the best, and perhaps—at least I liked to think so—too good for the second best.

Then a great piece of luck came my way. A letter arrived from a complete stranger, signing himself William H. Hamby.[3] He was, he explained, by way of being a writer himself, having written some two million words in the past ten years, and as he was passing through my town would like to call on the author of the stories he had enjoyed. I had never seen a real writer. Harry invited him to dinner. He came at seven and left at two A.M., carrying with him several of my manuscripts to criticize. Thus began one of the most valuable and valued friendships of my life.

I have thought how queer it is that I, who owe so much to the friendly help of men, should have become so ardent a feminist, believed, I suspect, by the politicians I have fought in behalf of women's recognition in politics to have a violent antipathy to men. Nothing is further from the facts. Beginning with my father, men have helped me—far more in the aggregate than women. My feminism stems from a different root.

But to return to Mr. Hamby.

"I won't attempt to tell you what is right or wrong about these stories from a literary point of view," he said. "You may know better than I. But I can tell you whether or not they will sell, and where."

And so he did, not only those manuscripts, but many others that I sent him month after month. Nor did he do this only for me. Writers all over the country, some who have done work of distinction, owe their success to his encouragement and help. Generous to a fault, he never spared time or effort to develop any talent he found, and he had an uncanny gift for seeing it where others would pass it by.

Without his encouragement, I should have given up many times, but the fact that he had faith in me seemed always to warrant my going on. When later I went into the suffrage fight, he did his best to dissuade me. For writing was to him a jealous god. It was far better, in his opinion, to be a second-rate, struggling writer than to work for any cause. And perhaps he was right. Who knows? At least the editor of a metropolitan paper agreed with him. Long afterward, he wrote me, "I regard you as one of the sacrifices made to the suffrage fight. Notwithstanding your exceptional personal success in politics, it is a poor equivalent, so it seems to me, for the place you could have had in letters had you burned your candles solely at that shrine."

---

3. William H. Hamby (1875–1928) was educated at Drury College in Springfield and the University of Missouri. An editor and owner of several newspapers, he had worked for a time for the *Carthage Evening Press*. He published eleven books and many magazine articles (*Missouri Historical Review* 22 [April 1928]: 395; *Carthage Evening Press*, March 25, 1922; *Carthage Weekly Press*, June 17, 1897).

My debt to Mr. Hamby I was never able to pay to him. But when would-be authors come to me for advice, I remember it. Within two years of my meeting with Mr. Hamby my sales had greatly increased. The writing was going fairly well, and then I hit a snag that may have had some effect on any reputation I might have won as a short-story writer.

A story of mine, "The Bonds of Matrimony," appeared in the *Blue Book* magazine.[4] The theme occurred to me when three middle-aged married couples were divorced, all within a few months. "Haven't they," I thought, "in all these years forged some bonds of habit and dependence that make them necessary to each other?" The theme in hand, the story to carry it developed naturally with no thought of these people.

It was sold, published, and forgotten by me. But some good ladies of the town chanced to buy an old copy of this magazine on the train. They saw a resemblance to a particular husband and wife in Carthage who had been divorced. When they came home they told these people I had "written them up." They also told everyone else. The drugstore had to buy back copies of the magazines, and the tongues of Carthage wagged. Suddenly they saw me as a dangerous woman let loose in their midst. They went back over my other stories to discover who they were about. Even my harmless "Evolution of a Lady," born of a dream, was claimed by three persons as having violated their privacy.

The funny thing about the matrimonial story was that by the time the magazine reached Carthage, more than a year after it was written and sold, the man they thought they recognized had come back to his wife. They also, unknown to me, had a fire, and the wife had telephoned her husband just as my fictional characters had. Worse than that, it developed that the man had made a confidant of my husband. That my husband had never told me, just because he was a confidant, people of course did not believe. Only a fellow fictionist would understand that once you embark on a theme, your subconscious mind ties into it logically the incidents and details that will develop it. The result often strangely duplicates life.

When I told the editor of *Blue Book*, Ray Long, about this, he said, "Why, we bought it because there is a story like this in every town."[5]

But the man and his wife would not have believed that. They never spoke afterward either to my husband or to me. And it had been a friendship my husband valued.

I have wondered often about this experience of mine. Undoubtedly I did get my theme from these home people's lives. I wrote more of them into it

---

4. "The Bonds of Matrimony," *Blue Book* (April 1914): 1238–43.

5. Editor of the group of magazines *Red Book*, *Blue Book*, and *Green Book* from 1911 to 1918, Ray Long (1878–1935) was editor of *Cosmopolitan* from 1918 to 1931 (*Dictionary of Literary Biography*, vol. 137, *American Magazine Journalists, 1900–1960*, s.v. "Long, Ray").

than I knew or realized. Yet how is one to write otherwise? It is a question that baffles me to this day. To take a confidential matter and disclose it, one knows is unethical; to hold up the idiosyncrasies or failings of friends is unkind. But to use the material that is available to anyone who reads his papers, to give your own imaginative analysis of a situation that is public property— especially as only those who already know the situation can possibly recognize the individuals—is there anything culpable in that?

Whatever the answer, I did not mean to repeat this experience. So, when-ever I saw the slightest possibility that neighbors might recognize a situation or a character, I signed the story by a pen name. To be doubly safe, I used many different ones. Not that this stopped the gossip. My townsmen suspected me of every unsigned story they read, some I had not even seen. But my real stories got by, even one based on their propensity to suspect me. In two years I had published twenty-five stories. Whether or not it would have helped to establish me as a writer had they all had my own name on the byline is open to question, though Mr. Hamby did write me, "You are selling your heritage of a national reputation for a mess of Mrs. Grundy's greens." So much for the penalty exacted of the small-town writer.

If I had been aiming at a career, I might have felt the use of my own name more important than the goodwill of my neighbors. But a career had never occurred to me. That this writing showed any great gift I never thought. If I had, I might have scorned the gossips, felt superior to them, and talked about the freedom of art to enrich life! It must be wonderful to feel yourself the vehicle of a great talent. But nothing is more pathetic to me than the man or woman who has the feeling without the talent, and deludes himself to feed his ego. I had no desire to add myself to this list. Apparently there was a demand for the kind of writing for which I had a knack and no good reason I should not supply it. Also, an income was greatly desired just then.

Yet my writing was no mere diversion to be picked up and put down as you would fancywork. Every day found me four or five hours at my typewriter, hours sandwiched in between household tasks. Soon after my first story was accepted, the typewriter and an office desk had arrived one morning to surprise me. "You must have the tools of your trade," said my husband, whose gift they were. I owe it to him that I took a professional attitude toward my work. Had he not taken me seriously I doubt that I would. I have admiration for women who, against great opposition at home, have set out to do work of one kind or another. But to jeopardize harmony and peace at home where most of a woman's life is spent, one must have a strong urge to express one's self. And this urge I did not have. Home, husband, and children seemed to offer all the media I needed. Indeed, the gradual abandonment of these means of expression in favor of others came so gradually that I did not know what was happening until long afterward.

With my writing, the conversation around the dinner table shifted slowly to my interests—returned manuscripts, acceptances, themes and ideas for stories—and I came to see that discussion of them entertained my husband as accounts of housework, of women's parties, never had.

Once, years later, I said to him rather petulantly after a period of housework with no outside interests, "You know, you are always bored with me when I go domestic. You only find me entertaining when I do outside things?"

"Did it ever occur to you," he retorted, "that you are more entertaining when you are doing outside things?"

It was longer before I realized that my absorption in writing released him from my hitherto too intense interest in his affairs, an interest that now I know irked him greatly. The time was to come when we discussed those interests freely. But it was after I could discuss them as a companion who had interests of her own, not as a wife who had her entire personality in marriage and felt she had a vested right in her husband's every act.

It was a struggle to beat our way out of debt, never an easy thing for me. I can spend money recklessly, or I can do without everything. But I seem never able to attain the middle ground of getting the most out of my money. So now, as at other times when the need for retrenchment came, I punished myself relentlessly, changing my entire standard of living, resigning from all my social clubs, refusing invitations, and doing without everything but the barest necessities.

Perhaps I could have made a game of it, but I did not. I took it as an ascetic does a discipline, getting a sort of satisfaction out of the pain of it. Not the denial of things for themselves. This is not what poverty means, except when the denial involves actual privation, and ours did not. The agony of poverty comes from what it does to your self-respect, the way it separates you from those you have always considered your equals, the things you cannot do that you are expected to do, the kindnesses you must accept or seem ungracious that you cannot return, the things you see others able to give their families you cannot give yours, the economies you must keep secret lest they affect your standing, and, more than all, the conversations you cannot take part in because they deal with things that are outside your experience: new clothes, trips, cars, new house furnishings. Some natures can rise above such things, but mine is not one of them. There were times when I thought I would scream if I heard once more the words: "I'm going to get _____." I am afraid I grew a little bitter as I saw my girlhood friends having and doing things I could not. And I would have grown more so if it had not been for my writing. It was one way of "waiting for my carriage."

One thing I did learn from that personal depression period of ours: there is no truth in the phrase "fair-weather friends." Friends are friends whatever your fortunes, as ours all too generously proved. The only difference ever indicated was on my side, not on theirs. Sensitive people who have suffered financial misfortune do not make it easy for their richer friends to approach them, but ours were very patient with our pride and came not only three-fourths but often all the way.

Of course there were exceptions. An ugly side of human nature I had not suspected was shown to me. I saw cruelty look out of human eyes and saw fingers that enjoyed pressing into wound prints. I learned how mean self-righteousness can be. But I was sane enough, in spite of occasional brainstorms, to know that the kindness and the generosity far outbalanced the meanness.

Gradually things brightened for us. We were able to move back into our old house. And my writing brought me new contacts and widening opportunities.

One morning a letter arrived apprising me that a number of Missouri writers were to gather in Springfield to form a club. Except for Mr. Hamby I had never seen another writer, and it had never occurred to me that I was so listed. There was to be a luncheon, and they wanted me to make a speech. I had never made a speech before, but I chose the only subject I could think of—"The Husband of a Literary Lady"—wrote a rather facetious essay, and committed it to memory. With it in my head, and a new hat and suit in my bag, I went to Springfield, quaking inside but rather excited. All went well until luncheon when I discovered that the chamber of commerce, which was our host, was also entertaining Governor Hadley and the state officials, and had combined the two guest lists. I gazed up and down the table. Impossible to refuse and write myself down a quitter. I made that awful speech. The important thing to me was that I got through.

The day after the luncheon, the chamber of commerce took us down to view the dam then under construction among the Ozarks on the White River. Thus I gained my introduction to the Ozark Mountains that lie south of Joplin and Carthage along the Missouri-Arkansas line.

I say "among them" because it would be exaggerating to say "up." For, instead of climbing a mountain range, we seemed rather to find ourselves snuggled down into a nest of hills. We felt ourselves up in the world only when we clambered to the top of the dam, or stood on the bluff on which was located the clubhouse where we took residence for two days. A big log house, it had been the state of Maine's building at the St. Louis World's Fair, and removed log by log to the Ozarks by some St. Louis fishing enthusiasts.[6]

Later I was to know better this Ozark country with its hill people who refuse to accept the outsider, but on this trip I was content to see only the historic spots where the Bald Knobbers were caught, and the house where

---

6. The meeting was held at Hollister, Missouri, where, in addition to "informal talks and round table discussions on literary work," there was a "program of dinners, dances, outdoor hikes and excursions to various points of interest in the White River country" (*Carthage Evening Press*, November 13, 1913). At the Hollister meeting, ENB was elected president of the Missouri Women's Press Association (ibid., December 1, 1913).

Harold Bell Wright's "Old Matt" had lived.[7] No one, of course, like Mr. Wright's patriarch ever really lived there, but, as an editorial friend said, "If he gave so many people pleasure, what difference does it make whether he lived or not?" And after all, why should one cavil at romanticized versions of the hillbilly when he has developed such a spy-proof technique to prevent others from knowing what goes on behind his opaque face?

On this trip my companions were just as new to me and far more interesting than hillbillies. First of all there was Winifred Black, at that time the wife of editor Bonfils, of the *Kansas City Post*, known to millions of readers through her syndicated column.[8] Not only was she the first established writer I had ever met, but the first woman I had ever seen smoke a cigarette! A woman who used familiarly such names as Frank Norris, Gertrude Atherton, William Randolph Hearst, she stood to me for the great open spaces of the literary world.[9] She told stories, too, as I had never heard stories told, of her entrance into Galveston under a tarpaulin when the city was under martial law, of her visit to Father Damien at the leper colony on Molokai, of her investigation of the southern cotton mills in the guise of an old woman looking for a lost child—tales of little children at work that made my blood freeze. A capacious woman, carrying her loose, uncorseted pounds as jauntily as a girl, with wise, sibyl-like eyes that seemed at once to understand and forgive all the follies of

---

7. After a childhood of abject poverty, Harold Bell Wright (1872–1944) experienced a religious awakening and became a Disciple of Christ. Although he never finished his ministerial studies, he came to the Ozarks to preach, in Christian churches in Pierce City; Pittsburg, Kansas; Kansas City; and Lebanon. He retired from the ministry to write novels, which were best-sellers. His most famous was *Shepherd of the Hills* (1907) about the Ozarks and its peoples (*DAB*, s.v. "Wright, Harold Bell").

8. Winifred Black (1863–1936), known as journalist "Annie Laurie," had worked for William Randolph Hearst on the *San Francisco Examiner* and the *New York Journal* from 1890 to 1895. In 1901, she married Charles Alden Bonfils who became managing editor of the *Kansas City Post* in 1909. She continued as a Hearst feature writer and was one of the most sensational women journalists of the period. At the time of the Galveston tidal wave in 1900, she was the first outside journalist (and only woman) to get herself into the city (*Notable American Women, 1650–1950: A Biographical Dictionary*, s.v. "Black, Winifred"; hereafter cited as *NAW*).

9. Benjamin Franklin "Frank" Norris (1870–1902) became a correspondent for *Mc-Clure's* in 1898. He was best known for his muckraking novels, *The Octopus* (1901) and *The Pit* (1903) (*DAB*, s.v. "Norris, Benjamin Franklin"). Gertrude Franklin Horn Atherton (1857–1948) published the first of many novels in 1899. Among them were *The Conqueror* (1902), a fictionalized account of the life of Alexander Hamilton, and *Julia France* (1912), which dealt with the issues of feminism and women's rights (*NAW*, s.v. "Atherton, Gertrude Franklin Horn"). William Randolph Hearst (1863–1951) began his newspaper career when his father allowed him to take over as publisher of the *San Francisco Examiner* in 1887. He bought the *New York Journal* in 1895. He built his newspaper empire in the following years, buying papers in Chicago, Boston, Los Angeles, and Atlanta. He also created news services and purchased magazines such as *Cosmopolitan* (1905), *Good Housekeeping* (1911), and *Harper's Bazaar* (1912) (*DAB*, s.v. "Hearst, William Randolph").

human nature. Years afterward I was to see the same look in the little birdlike eyes stuck between the smiling wrinkles of Dorothy Dix's small face. Do the many Beatrice Fairfaxes, I wonder, have the same look in theirs?[10]

Then there was Alice Mary Kimball who was to write that long poem "The Devil Is a Woman," which ought to have created a sensation and did not. "A magnificent achievement," Achmed Abdullah once said to me.[11] "Why hasn't it been recognized?" Why, indeed? Will not someone, sometime, gather together some of those gems to which a blind generation has shut its eyes and give their makers posthumous acclaim?

A new type to me Alice Mary was then, and to others also of our middle-western mind. A gleam in her shining eyes, a dance in her foot, eager curiosity in her mind, and a soul daring and unafraid. What were our conventions to her, our pursuit of the safe middle road, our worship of the great god, Propriety? Out of Vermont she had come, on her own two feet, to see the world as it was, with only faith to pay her way. An itinerant newspaper reporter, now in the West Virginia coal fields, now in the Arkansas fruit lands, again in Springfield upholding the IWW's. Small wonder she shocked, surprised, and charmed me all in one. Typical she seemed, of that half-mad, vine-crowned rebel crew that inhabited Greenwich Village. And sure enough, she gravitated there and ran the Village gossip sheet. Ah, but what queer things life does to us all! The last time I saw her, she was sedately keeping house in an old colonial mansion retrieved down in King Street, New York, dripping domesticity and opposing conservative views to what she considered my radical ones.

---

10. Father Damien (1840–1889) was a Belgian Jesuit missionary who ministered to the lepers on Molokai from 1873 to his death from leprosy (Wheeler Preston, *American Biographies*, 218). Elizabeth Meriwether Gilmer, under the pen name of Dorothy Dix, was an extremely popular advice columnist. Starting out in New Orleans writing for the *Daily Picayune*, she moved to Hearst's *New York Journal* to become a crime reporter. Dix was an ardent suffragist and in 1917 returned to New Orleans and her advice column (*NAW*, s.v. "Gilmer, Elizabeth Meriwether"). Marie Manning (1873?–1945) wrote an advice column under the name Beatrice Fairfax for the *New York Journal*, beginning in July 1898. She continued the column until 1905, when she married, and then resumed it in 1929. She also wrote regular news for the paper, short stories, and romantic novels (*DAB*, s.v. "Manning, Marie").

11. Alice Mary Kimball, born in Vermont, began her newspaper career in 1910. She was a staff contributor to the *Kansas City Star* from 1914 to 1917 and a staff writer for *Country Gentleman* from 1918 to 1920. She also wrote short stories, articles, and poems for popular magazines. "The Devil Is a Woman" was published in 1929 (Durwood Howes, ed., *American Women, 1935–1940: A Composite Biographical Dictionary*, s.v. "Kimball, Alice Mary"). Achmed Abdullah (1881–1945) was a well-known novelist and playwright. Among his books are *The Red Stain* (1915), *Man on Horseback* (1919), and his autobiography, *The Cat Had Nine Lives* (1933) (W. J. Burke and Will D. Howe, comps., *American Authors and Books, 1640 to the Present Day*, 2). Many of his works were based on his experiences in the British Indian and Ottoman armies (*Current Biography: Who's News and Why* [New York: H. W. Wilson, 1945], 2).

And there were others, a poetess who wrote for the *Masses*, that highly sophisticated and mildly radical journal, a quiet, gentle little woman who ran a chicken farm; and women editors of country papers, with weird stories and vibrant personalities.

We enjoyed ourselves so much that we women organized ourselves into a Missouri Women's Press Association. And, somehow, in a year I found myself its president, for no reason at all except that I could not say "no" to Old Man Opportunity whenever I thought I might catch his forelock.[12]

A merry chase he has led me, too! The next spring he took me up to Columbia, where, during Journalism Week, all the press associations of the state met at the state university. Our Women's Press Association had to have a dinner, and I smile, now, at how rashly I went about it in my inexperience. Interesting occasions these Journalism Weeks were to a novitiate like myself. Publishers from New York, successful authors and journalists, editors from all over the state, and would-be writers one after the other telling the students how they started and what they thought. Dean Williams, threading the program with his bon mots, his generous introductions, his sprightly wit.[13] And the students interviewing you for the town paper that the School of Journalism published, treating you as someone who had arrived where they would like to be someday. Talks, too, *à deux* at lunch and dinner and on long walks with those who had really "arrived," men and women from St. Louis, from Boston, from New York. I never did know how Dean Williams persuaded these people to come, but he did.

As one of his protégées, he always put me on some program and said nice things about me. At one of these meetings I paid my respects to him as "the horticulturist who cultivates our sprigs of talent." He returned: "I don't know anything about horticulture, but I know a peach when I see one." This I have always thought was about the nicest compliment I ever had. These days at Journalism Week did a great deal to strengthen my self-confidence. They brought me into contact with people who had really accomplished something in the writing game. Among other things, they gave me an acquaintance among the editors of the state, who seemed to take a paternal interest in me.

---

12. At its meeting in Hollister, the Missouri Women's Press Association elected ENB its president in 1913 (*Carthage Evening Press*, November 13, December 1, 1913).

13. The annual Journalism Week at the University of Missouri began in 1910. In 1915, Dean Walter Williams of the Journalism School formed the Missouri Writers' Guild, and ENB was a charter member, serving as second vice president (Missouri Writers' Guild Organization and Charter Members, May 5, 1915, Folder 90, Missouri Writers' Guild Papers). Walter Williams (1864–1935) had been president of the Missouri Press Association and editor of the *Boonville Advertiser* and the *Columbia Herald* prior to his selection as dean of the University of Missouri School of Journalism in 1908. He was chosen president of the university in 1931 (*Who Was Who in America* [Chicago: A. N. Marquis, 1942], 1:1355).

When I came later into the suffrage campaigns, this acquaintance was to be very helpful.

Before another year, the Missouri Women's Press Association melted into the Missouri Writers' Guild, which continued to hold spring meetings at the university, and fall outings in the Ozarks. At these fall outings there were no formal programs. In the daytime we walked over the hills together, or boated; in the evenings we gathered around an open fire while some writer talked to us about our problems or told of his early experiences. Sometimes these experiences were amusing. Maude Radford Warren, for instance, confessing that her first poem, written when she was seven, had the title "How Sad It Is to Sit and Think about the Days That Are No More." An interesting crowd: Robertus Love, of the *St. Louis Republic,* authority on Jesse James; Lee Shippey, the lovable, half-blind verifier, later on the *Los Angeles Times,* and author of *The Great American Family;* Arthur Killick of the *Kansas City Star* whose humor as "Fatty Lewis" has rocked thousands; Breckinridge Ellis, who, from a wheelchair, turned out his best-sellers year after year.[14]

One fall was made forever memorable by a visit to Rose O'Neill, whose Kewpies were then at the height of their popularity.[15] She was spending the year at her old home, set away back in the hills. Miles we paddled down a

---

14. Maude Radford Warren (1875–1934) earned a master's degree from the University of Chicago. Among her publications were *King Arthur and His Knights* (1907), *The Land of the Living* (1908), and *Peter Pan* (1909). She was a war correspondent from 1916 to 1919, a special correspondent for the *Saturday Evening Post* in the Near East (1919–1920), and the first white woman to cross Great Bear Lake, Northwest Territory, Canada, in 1930 (ibid., 1:1303). Robertus Love (1867–1930) began his newspaper career in Louisiana, Missouri, in 1886, moving to Wichita, Kansas, the next year. In 1900, he became a staff writer for the *St. Louis Post-Dispatch* and spent most of his career with that paper, though he worked a few years as a special writer for the *St. Louis Republic.* In 1927, he became the literary editor for the *Post-Dispatch* and wrote verse based on current events, the Ozarks, and general themes. He also wrote a life of Jesse James (*St. Louis Globe-Democrat,* May 8, 1930). Lee Shippey (1884–1969), journalist and author, titled his autobiography *The Luckiest Man Alive* (1959). Beginning in 1927, his column in the *Los Angeles Times* was called "Lee Side o' Los Angeles" (Burke and Howe, *American Authors and Books,* 672). Arthur Killick (1880–1939) was a reporter for the *Kansas City Star.* He published "Fatty Lewis" stories in the *Star* for twenty years (*Missouri Historical Review* 33 [July 1939]: 591). John Breckinridge Ellis (b. 1870) wrote numerous novels and biographies. He lived in Plattsburg, Missouri (*Who Was Who among North American Authors, 1921–1939,* 2 vols. [Detroit: Gale Research, 1976], 1:481).

15. In early December 1913, ENB visited Rose O'Neill (O'Neill to ENB, December 18, 1913, Container 2, Folder 15, ENB Papers; *Carthage Evening Press,* December 1, 1913). Not only a commercial illustrator, Rose O'Neill (1874–1944) was also a serious painter, sculptor, poet, and novelist. She first published her Kewpie cartoons in *Ladies Home Journal* in 1909, and thereafter made a fortune from Kewpie dolls and related products. Having homes in Connecticut, on the Isle of Capri, and in Washington Square, New York, she returned frequently to Bonniebrook, her family home in the Ozarks, north of Branson, Missouri (Lina Mainiero, ed., *American Women Writers: A Critical Reference Guide from*

river, marched up hills and down dales, to make a call upon her—William Hamby, Alice Mary, and I. We knew she had come out from New York to work uninterruptedly on her second book. We meant to stay only an hour. We remained two days! And what a visit.

Surprise enough to find this house set down there on an Ozark hillside with a running brook under bay windows that extended over it. Balconies hung here and there where someone had a fancy to watch the sunrise or the birds. Wings were thrown out in this place and that to meet some need. A reading room with windows all around, seats under the windows and bookshelves under them, and a fireplace brought or copied from one in Capri. Rose's own studio was at the top of the house. Kewpie dolls everywhere, peeping out from behind doors, between the pillows on your bed. Drawings on the walls of weird gnomes and demons.

Rose and Callista, the one fair, the other dark, in their flowing auras of pink chiffon over blue, over lavender, over yellow; long peaked-toed, heelless satin slippers on their feet; and curls, such as one saw then only on bisque dolls.[16] Could it be possible such people were real? Wouldn't they vanish away like dream pictures? Could they really live thus day after day?

Seeing a photograph of Rose's painting *Paolo and Francesca*, which had been bought by the Luxembourg, a picture of weird power and superb drawing, I asked Rose how she felt about doing Kewpies after a canvas like that. "They make little children happy," she said, and could have added, "and feed a large family."

Her great ambition was to be of that select company who have both written and painted, of which Leonardo da Vinci stands at the head with William Blake a close second. One novel she had already written, two more, I think, have appeared since then.[17] Weird they are, like her drawings, fanciful and with a touch of genius, but caviar to the general taste.

"Now we must dance," said Callista after lunch, and down the front walk and onto the lawn they tripped, making graceful steps of their own devising.

We had supper—plebeian food of fried eggs and country bacon—and then a long evening with talk about Capri and Paris and London, about Joplin, the Ozarks, about books, the mot juste and difficulties of writing, the rewards of it. I had never known such talk existed outside of books. Later in the studio, Rose read to us some of her verse, "not to be sold for lucre," she explained,

---

Colonial Times to the Present, 3:307–8. See also Shelley Armitage, *Kewpies and Beyond: The World of Rose O'Neill*).

16. Callista, Rose O'Neill's sister, acted as Rose's business manager and caretaker. She died in 1946.

17. Rose O'Neill wrote *The Loves of Edwy* (1904), *The Lady in the White Veil* (1909), *Garda* (1929), *The Goblin Woman* (1930), and a book of poetry, *The Master Mistress: Poems* (1922).

"but to be given as a gift sometime." And at last music, music improvised by Rose. All mediums of expression seemed open to her, and beauty flowed out through them, some beauty that was in herself. A free soul, she seemed to me to be, untrammeled by the trappings, physical, mental, social, in which everyone I had known was bound. No wonder fairies spoke to her! No wonder she saw visions! Suddenly, I found myself talking to her as I had to no one else, and wishes, thoughts, hopes I did not know I had came speaking out of me. "Be yourself," she said to me. "Be yourself. You have it in you—the sacred fire. I can see it. I can feel it. Follow the gleam. It only is real. But to do it, you must be yourself."

Just what she poured into me or drew out of me I do not know. But I was never afterward quite the conformist I had been.

When I went home, my first act was to flood my house with color, bittersweet and orange. Always I had loved color and always I had subdued my taste to the quiet coloring demanded by the mode, although I had never been quite able to essay the popular monotone greens and browns. I did not know then that Rose was as rare, as exotic a figure in Washington Square, New York, in Paris, or in Capri, as she was in the Ozarks. I had an idea that the literary circles of New York and Paris were made up of people like her, and I longed to make my way to them and see more of her and them.

After the election of 1924, I was coming down from New York to Washington in the train, and a plump lady sat down beside me. She took off her hat, and chestnut curls fell down upon her neck.

"You aren't," I said, "you can't be Rose O'Neill?"

"But I am," she replied. "How did you know?"

I reminded her of that visit, and the years fell away. There still hung about her the same glamour, and I talked to her with the old frankness, the old longings pouring out of me. No, not in any circle have I seen anyone like her.

To these meetings of the guild came newspapermen from the St. Louis and Kansas City papers. When news was scarce they mentioned my stories. So much for luck! For many Missouri writers have done far more important work than I and never had one-tenth the notice given them, and it was the publicity, not the stories, that led me into the suffrage campaigns, and then politics, and so it is responsible for all that came afterward.

One of the first questions newspapermen always asked me was, "Are you a suffragist?" Now, I had gone into clubs as a matter of course. One was a nice society of socially congenial women that met at houses and either ended or began with a meal. The other was the town's one federated club, which met at the public library, to which anyone interested could belong. It concerned itself not only with studies of past civilizations, but also with approving social measures such as pure-food laws, sane Fourth of July celebrations, sanitary drinking cups, prison reform, fire protection for workmen and -women, free textbooks. I joined, I fear, in a spirit of condescension, feeling one should take part in civic affairs. I soon found myself, however, deeply interested. Soon I was made publicity chairman for our district, then sent as a delegate to a state convention.

Temperamentally I was a feminist. But of feminism as a cult, or a theory, or a belief, or whatever it is, I knew nothing at that time. Before I answered the newspapermen, it seemed I should look into it. So I got out of our town library all the books they had about it: William Hard's, Charlotte Perkins Gilman's, Olive Schriener's, Ellen Key's.[18] Their arguments seemed reasonable enough. But to be sure, I did what I always do before I decided upon my position. I read the opinions of those opposed to it. When I found that people like Mrs. Humphrey Ward and Elihu Root could make no arguments that I, with my inexperience and far less able mind, could not answer, I decided that I was in favor of it.[19] This was as far as I expected or intended to go.

---

18. William Hard, muckraking journalist who wrote for *Everybody's* and *Delineator*, contributed four substantial series of articles on women's issues from 1908 to 1914 (*DAB*, s.v. "Hard, William"). Charlotte Perkins Gilman (1860–1935), feminist, author, and lecturer, was best known for her advocacy of independence for women in *Women and Economics* (1898) and her short story, "The Yellow Wallpaper" (1899) (*NAW*, s.v. "Gilman, Charlotte Perkins"). Olive Schriener (1855–1920) was a South African novelist and essayist. Her best-known work was *The Story of an African Farm*, which was partially autobiographical. A feminist liberal, she wrote extensively on social problems (*Benét's Reader's Encyclopedia*, s.v. "Schriener, Olive"). Swedish feminist Ellen Karoline Sophia Key (1849–1926), who wrote *The Century of the Child* in 1900, attacking the traditional role assigned to women, published *The Woman Movement* in 1912 (Beverly E. Golemba, *Lesser-Known Women: A Biographical Dictionary*, s.v. "Key, Ellen Karoline Sophia").

19. Mary Augusta (Mrs. Humphrey) Ward (1851–1920) was a well-known English novelist and antisuffrage leader. She wrote for the *Times* of London, in addition to publishing twenty-five novels and three plays. Although she founded a social settlement, she was the first president of the Anti-Suffrage League in 1908 (Jennifer S. Uglow, comp., *The Continuum Dictionary of Women's Biography*, 568–69). Elihu Root (1845–1937) served as William McKinley's secretary of war (1899–1903), overseeing the administration of Cuba and the Philippines after the Spanish-American War and instituting fundamental reform of the army. In 1905 he returned to the cabinet as secretary of state, resigning in 1909 when he was elected to the United States Senate from New York. In 1920 he was chairman of the board of the Carnegie Endowment for International Peace (*DAB*, s.v. "Root, Elihu").

3 Woman's Suffrage—1914 Style

Woman suffrage is today such a finished issue that it seems like digging up a mummy to bring the subject into my story. But to omit it would make the rest inexplicable.

"Suffrage?" said a woman in my living room the other day. "Why, I've never even thought of it. I take women voting for granted as I do the flag and the Constitution."

To women like this it is well-nigh impossible to convey what the fight for it meant to women like me, pushed by it into a limelight as unpleasant as a klieg light, yet feeling ourselves missionaries of a new day for women. They cannot see us as we were, both timid and courageous: courageous with the bravado of the soldier who said his knees would shake more if they knew where his head was taking him.

This woman in my parlor could never understand my feelings when asked by a club of serious-faced, determined-looking women suffragists to tell them why I believed in it. I hated to come out and speak for it, but hated more to acknowledge myself a coward while feeling myself a martyr because I did it at all.

Nor is there at this late day any way to indicate to these younger women, accustomed to speaking their minds and commanding political attention, the drama of a scene in an office in the Missouri State Capitol when thirty little-known, unimportant, and inexperienced housewives in white dresses and yellow sashes handed to the secretary of state a petition that would challenge not only men's centuries-old prejudices but all the resources of astute politicians, and even such interests as the national brewing companies.[1] They cannot know it for the David and Goliath act it was. They cannot envisage these women at all: ladies bred to the drawing room, ladies whose only forum had been a church sewing society, timid schoolteachers, and self-abnegating farm women. Nor can they know what it meant to such women to go into stores and offices and factories to ask men to sign their petition, or vote for their amendment, and be told to go home and attend to their babies,

---

1. In 1914, the Missouri Equal Suffrage Association led the campaign that garnered fourteen thousand petition signatures, forcing a ballot on woman suffrage. Despite their slogan of "Suffrage for Missouri in 1914," the issue was defeated (Elizabeth Cady Stanton et al., eds., *History of Woman Suffrage*, 6:347).

or to put on the pants if they wanted to. They don't understand why these women sold their jewelry and melted down their wedding rings to get money for their campaigns.

How can such things seem revolutionary in a day when women are running campaigns of one kind or another all the time? With young women everywhere doing difficult jobs, deferred to and putting their elders on the defensive, how can I make anyone understand how scared a youngish matron like myself felt when she almost tiptoed into her first state suffrage meeting and found all eyes on her yellow lace dress and pink hat, or appreciate her dismay when she heard a stern old warhorse exclaim: "What! That young thing to run our publicity campaign!"[2]

One cannot convey to the reader of today the sense of great endeavor that these suffrage campaigns had for us women of that time—at least I cannot.

But before this several other things had happened that had a bearing on it. We had long had a poorhouse in our county that was a crying disgrace to our humanity. Grand juries had again and again declared it so, but it seemed impossible to vote a new one because the politicians of the county would not agree to call an election. Some of them refused to vote an almshouse to be located near Carthage unless the others would agree to vote a detention home and a courthouse to be located in other towns in the county. In the meantime the poor victims of poverty languished in conditions that were unspeakable. At last a philanthropic woman roused the women of the county to undertake a campaign to vote bonds for an almshouse.[3] True, the women did not have a vote, but they did have tongues. So they set out to talk the men into voting the bonds. Meetings of women were held in every hamlet and town in the county. The women organized and made a house-to-house visitation telling the women at their front doors about the poor farm and urging them to make their husbands vote for a new one. Just how it happened I do not remember, but somehow I found myself in the thick of this campaign. And among other things I had to do was to make speeches. True, I had never made any speeches—except the one before the governor at Springfield—but it was not hard to make an appeal for these poor unfortunates, though no one was as surprised as I when the Booster Club in a neighboring town jumped en masse to its feet when I had finished.[4]

---

2. March 1915 saw the beginning of the publication of *Missouri Woman* with ENB as its first editor. She resigned in March 1916 (ibid., 348).

3. In 1913, the club women of Jasper County organized a campaign to build a new almshouse. Through their publicity, they forced a county vote that passed by a five-to-one margin in favor of a direct tax to raise seventy-five thousand dollars to provide a new home for the poor. It was dedicated on January 25 and 26, 1916 (ENB, "Jasper County Almshouse," *Missouri Woman* [September 1916]).

4. The *Carthage Evening Press* reported that ENB's talk before the Joplin Noonday Lunch Club resulted in an endorsement of the issue (February 4, 1914).

Before the campaign was over I had gained some reputation as a speaker, though it was far from deserved. In fact, I have seldom made as good a speech since, and there were other women who were much more effective than I. But I had discovered that it was possible to get up and speak in public if there was something you simply had to say. Also, before we won the election by a four-fifths majority, I had made the acquaintance of a large number of women all over the county. I had never worked before in a large group like this, and I found it interesting to know women of all kinds. Never afterward was I to be content to limit my social intercourse to my own small social circle. I felt suddenly part of a larger whole. I know the joy of common work for a bigger purpose than a personal interest. That childhood interest of mine in people generally was suddenly revived, the sympathies I had then felt were reawakened, and I began to feel a responsibility for social conditions. Some of our experiences with the men politicians, and the attitude of other men to our work as women, roused my incipient feminism. But I was not yet an avowed suffragist.

About this time some of my friends in Carthage who were very interested in suffrage asked me to write down my reasons for supporting the movement. This I gladly did with no thought of a speech in mind. But one of these friends who liked the paper sent it to my dearest childhood friend, Winifred Whitsett, married to Maj. Henry Julian and living in Kansas City. The next thing I knew, I received a letter from Winifred insisting that I come up and give the paper as a speech in Kansas City. Helen Guthrie Miller heard me, and that is when I first met her.[5] Mrs. Miller promised me a secretary. What she wanted in exchange was my name for what it was worth to the editors of the state. Since magazines did pay for my work, these editors, thinking they were getting something for nothing, might, she thought, use what I sent them. I would like to think now it was my zeal for suffrage that made me accept this job, but truth compels me to state it was the secretary. Utterly unaware in my verdant ignorance of all that was involved, I thought that a secretary would really give me more time for my writing. She would not only do most of my suffrage work but also have time to type my manuscripts, thus releasing me to do more stories.

---

5. Henry S. Julian (b. 1862) was a lawyer in Kansas City, active in Democratic politics. He managed James Reed's mayoral campaigns in 1900 and 1902. He married Winifred Whitsett of Carthage (William Rufus Jackson, *Missouri Democracy: A History of the Party and Its Representative Members, Past and Present*, 3:365–67). Helen Guthrie Miller (b. 1861) married Dr. Walter McNabb Miller, a professor of bacteriology at the University of Missouri, in 1889. She served as first auditor and first vice president of the National American Woman Suffrage Association (NAWSA). She was president of the Missouri Equal Suffrage Association when the suffrage amendment passed (Mary K. Dains, ed., *Show Me Missouri Women: Selected Biographies*, 1:232–34; Stanton et al., eds., *History of Woman Suffrage*, 5:402, 425).

Why I got into the suffrage campaign I do not really know. Helen Guthrie Miller was, of course, partly responsible; for no one, so far as I know, ever refused to do anything this patrician, urgent, charming suffrage leader asked her to. You just could not refuse a woman who was so evidently giving her whole self to put over what she made you feel to be of vital importance to the world. Then there was pride that such a woman had picked you out. And an urge to escape domesticity and express my ego made me susceptible to the other appeals. I have never been able to analyze it, though I said to my husband that if one believed in a thing, one must be willing to throw what influence she had in favor of it.

At any rate, I made one of the most important decisions of my life, one that was to change its whole tenor, almost wreck my happiness, and bring me into national politics. Whether it would have been richer or poorer had I made a different decision, I cannot know; but it would have been different.

I didn't know what I was getting myself into. I did not know that an infantile-paralysis scare would send most of our best workers up north with their children, or that the war scare—it was in 1914—would so reduce our contributions that we would have only five thousand dollars in all for a statewide campaign, and my entire budget for publicity would be eighteen hundred dollars. Nor did I realize that I would spend eight, ten, or sixteen hours a day for five months in a little back office downtown, or foresee the reams of yellow handouts, the pages of "boilerplate" I would write, and the newspaper gift I would have to edit.

All this may seem nothing today to the many women who in each political campaign do as much. It turned my life upside down. Mother took my children out to my sister Julia in Colorado for the summer. I walked downtown at eight each morning with Harry, ate my lunch out of a box, and stayed often all evening, Harry helping me seal and stamp the releases. He said he got lots of fun out of it. I hope he did. He gave much to it. My friends lifted their eyebrows and thought my home was headed straight for disaster. Of them, in all these months, only one ever came to my office to see me. She gave me a contribution of ten dollars.

When it was all over and I made my report of the work done (only eleven of the seven hundred and some papers in the state were for suffrage at the beginning of the campaign, and at the end only thirteen openly opposed it) and the women stood up and cheered me, I thought I had done a great deal.

Two experiences may serve to give some idea of how I approached the campaign.

I had not expected to make any speeches, but someone got the idea that if we could just get a suffrage speech made on the platform at William Jennings Bryan's meeting at Joplin, the Associated Press, which had ignored our campaign, might mention it.[6] This was to be Mr. Bryan's first appearance in the state. The Democratic county committee, after much urging, finally agreed—if I would be the victim. Their choice may have been because of my Democratic husband and brother. Again it may have been because of my speeches in the almshouse campaign. Anyway, some women had gone all the way to Pittsburg, Kansas, to ask Mr. Bryan's permission, and I did not see how I could let them down, though I could see my husband was not enthusiastic about my doing it. He knew political audiences better than I did. Imagine then, walking all the way down the aisle of the enormous barnlike auditorium saying to myself, "I can—I can—I can—."

Imagine about three thousand miners out of work, who have been waiting forty-three minutes for Mr. Bryan. Hear the county chairman tell them there would be a ten-minute talk on suffrage by a Mrs. Blair. Try to see me standing up, small, hesitant, and hear a shout, "We want Bryan." Hear the others take it up until it becomes a chant to stomping feet: "We want Bryan—We want Bryan." See me try to speak—stop—begin again. Ashamed to give up. Unable to go on. And imagine, if you can, my feelings as Mr. Bryan comes to my side, lifts his big hand, and his voice booms out above their chant: "You will hear the lady first!" You may understand then that it took me only four minutes to say all I had to say, and that when I sat down I had to clench my hands and hold my feet to the floor to stop the trembling.

Years later I reminded Mr. Bryan of this experience as I sat between him and Governor Smith at the dinner given the delegates to a national Democratic convention in New York City. "If you had not stopped them," I said, "I would probably never have made another speech and so not be here tonight!"

"Then there is something the Democratic Party does owe me," he returned gallantly.

The second experience is of the same kind.

The suffragists wanted me to go to a state editorial convention in St. Louis, buttonhole the editors, and have a table of "literature" in the hall outside the convention. It seems a simple enough thing to do. But each morning I would walk around the block several times before I got up the courage to go inside the hotel and up the stairs.

"I never knew before," my sister Anne, with whom I was staying, said to me, "how diffident you really are—I can see you set your lips the minute you get out of bed and whip yourself up into going to your job."

A newspaper friend one evening warned me that the president of the editorial association—himself opposed to suffrage—intended to bring up my

---

6. On October 19, 1914, William Jennings Bryan made an appearance in Joplin before a crowd of between three and five thousand. The newspapers substantiate ENB's account (*Joplin News Herald*, October 20, 1914; *Joplin Globe*, October 20, 1914).

presence there at the next morning's session as violating the nonpartisanship rule of the association. Terrified, I called up some editorial friends.

"Go to sleep and forget it," they said. "Your friends will take care of you."

I went to bed, but not to sleep. Silly, that seems now. What possible harm could it have done me if I had been asked to leave? But diffidence is not rational.

But it was not all hard work. Sometime during it, Ruth Hanna McCormick, later Mrs. Simms, asked me to come to a conference in Chicago.[7] This was, to me, all pleasure. Pleasure, first, because their publicity man, C. T. Hallinan, who had been editor of the *Chicago Post*, said that I was a genius in publicity, and if I did not wholly believe him, it did make me feel important. Pleasure, too, because we sat one night until two o'clock beside the ice-skating rink at the College Inn, he and I, and talked about writing. I saw him later in London, and he referred to it as a red-letter evening in his life. I don't know why, unless a small-town idealistic woman who believed in sweetness and light was as much a curiosity to him as a cynical, realistic gentleman of the intelligentsia was to me.

Upon me, at once, Ruth laid her spell. How, indeed, could I resist it? An insignificant, unknown little woman from the country I felt myself, and here this glamorous person, moving in a world I had only dreamed about, powerful, rich, free from all the limitations that held me and the inhibitions that restrained me, invited me to her home, accepted me at once as a friend, talked to me confidentially, so that the glamour enveloped me, too. When she waved her wand, a pumpkin did turn into a coach. She could make Cinderellas into princesses. No handicaps for her. Through obstacles she could ride at will; realities vanished at her touch.

She had wanted a friend, who lived in a suburb, to go out with us.

"But I can't, Ruth. My husband is to meet me at the train."

"We'll telephone him."

---

7. Ruth Hanna McCormick (1880–1944), daughter of Mark Hanna, married Joseph Medill McCormick in 1903. Progressive Republicans, they both were politically active. He was elected to the United States House of Representatives in 1916 and to the United States Senate in 1918. A supporter of the Women's Trade Union League (WTUL) and the Illinois Consumers' League, she chaired the NAWSA Congressional Committee and in 1914 coauthored the Shafroth-Palmer amendment that emphasized state action in the suffrage amendment fight. In 1919, she was the first chairman of the new women's executive committee of the Republican National Committee (RNC) and served on the executive committee of the RNC from 1920 to 1924. In 1924 she was Republican national committeewoman from Illinois and organized women's Republican clubs. Elected to Congress in 1928, she then ran for the Senate in 1930, losing to Hamilton Lewis. Her husband died in 1925, and she was married again in 1932 to Albert Gallatin Simms, former congressman from New Mexico (*NAW*, s.v. "Simms, Ruth Hanna McCormick").

"You can't. He'll have left the house by this time."

"We'll send a telegram to the station agent."

"There isn't any station. It's just a stopping place."

"But there must be some way. We'll get the city depot and have the conductor get off the train and tell him."

Here was someone after my own heart. No such word as *fail* in her vocabulary. But here, too, I saw, was the daughter of Mark Hanna, with a long experience of getting what she wanted. I did not know then how this very trait was to prove her undoing when she ran for the United States Senate.

It was after this trip to Chicago, or it may have been a year later, that I went up to see my sister at Wisconsin University, and a young professor at the School of Journalism asked me if he could dramatize my story "The Bonds of Matrimony." I was delighted and saw it as a successful play on Broadway. I have the drama today that he wrote, I changed, he rewrote. But, although it was submitted to Ethel Barrymore herself through a friend, who is now a very successful play broker, it never saw the boards.

These early days of work and writing, as I look back on them, seem to have been sprinkled with such high hopes. Every new writer, I suppose, meets the same thing: writers who come to see and praise them, editorials in local and maybe city papers, attentions from editors, requests for a book, a suggestion of dramatizations, compliments, prophecies. And the few realize on them.

It was a step out, that trip for me. It was there, I think, that there came to me the thought, ambition, or temptation, whatever it was, that my life need not be bounded by the four walls of a home. Another way to put it would be that the cocoon of Victorianism was beginning to crack. Still another that I first saw that life even for me could be wider.

We did not win the 1914 suffrage amendment. We never expected to. But we had changed the attitude of thousands. Kansas City was the largest city ever to have gone for suffrage, and our congressman thereafter did vote for submission of the federal amendment in the House of Representatives. If we could do so well with practically no money, they probably thought a campaign well financed might have won.

As a reward for the campaign work, the state suffrage association sent me to the national suffrage convention that met that year in Nashville, Tennessee. I was accompanied by one of our most enthusiastic local workers. She had burst upon our smug community like a breeze, defying our prejudices, scoffing at our taboos. She lived a dramatic life, with trips to Tahiti and Paris, even going at last to Soviet Russia, where she served as dietitian for the Kuzbah Colony. Through her I learned to value the pleasures of the senses, as Willa Cather reports them—touch, taste, smell, sound. I, who had to intellectualize everything, found a new world of sensation to be enjoyed. What she did to my puritan soul cannot be measured. My life would be much poorer if I had never known Nathalie Ortt.[8]

Here I hesitate. For how can I make plain to readers to whom national conventions are a chore that I went into that group of women as a debutante to a royal court, or a senator to his first appearance on the floor? All eyes, all ears, for Mrs. Norman de R. Whitehouse and her strands of pearls, for Mary Ware Dennett and her booming voice, for oratorical little Antoinette Funk rolling up her sleeves as she defied her verbal opponents, for M. Carey Thomas, president of Bryn Mawr, leading a caucus, for Madge Breckinridge, long and lank, swaying an audience of five thousand as had her grandfather Henry Clay.[9]

If I could just convey what it meant to this self-conscious, unimportant little woman from her small Missouri town to sit beside Jane Addams at a

---

8. The NAWSA national convention met in Nashville on November 12–17, 1914 (Stanton et al., eds., *History of Woman Suffrage*, 5:398–438). Nathalie Ortt (Mrs. Spencer) was a lifelong friend of ENB from Carthage and Joplin. Her husband was in the mining business, but eventually sold out and became an ore buyer for Eagle Picher Company. In 1921–1922, she ran a restaurant in Joplin on the alley between Moffet and Byers and between Third and Fourth Streets. ENB probably enjoyed Nathalie as much as anyone she ever knew (Joplin City Directory, 1925; Newell Blair, interviews with editor, June 4, October 19, 1996).

9. Vira Boarman (b. 1875) married Norman de R. Whitehouse in 1898. In 1916, she was president of the New York State Woman Suffrage Association. In 1918, she was sent by the government to Europe to combat German propaganda. In 1920, she wrote of that experience in her book, *A Year as a Government Agent* (Stanton et al., eds., *History of Woman Suffrage*, 5:507; *Who Was Who in America*, 5:1969–73). Mary Ware Dennett (1872–1947) served two years as field secretary of the Massachusetts Woman Suffrage Association before her election as corresponding secretary of NASAW in 1912. Her opposition to World War I brought her the position of field secretary of the American Union Against Militarism, and in 1917 she resigned her position as executive secretary of the Women's Section of the Democratic National Committee to become a founder of the antiwar People's Council. Active in birth control, she opposed Margaret Sanger for her radical tactics (Barbara Sicherman and Carol H. Green, eds., *Notable American Women, the Modern Period: A Biographical Dictionary*, s.v. "Dennett, Mary Ware"; hereafter cited as *NAW-Modern*). In 1914, Dennett was corresponding and executive secretary of NAWSA (Stanton et al., eds., *History of Woman Suffrage*, 5:403). Antoinette Funk, of New Mexico, was admitted to the bar in 1904. Active in the suffrage movement, she had chaired the congressional lobby of NAWSA. After working for Theodore Roosevelt in the 1912 campaign, she had supported Woodrow Wilson in 1916. During the New Deal she was assistant land commissioner (1933–1939). She died on March 27, 1942, in San Diego (*New York Times*, March 29, 1942, 45:2; "Thumbnail Sketches of Women You Hear about in the New Deal," Box 8, Mary Dewson Papers). Martha Carey Thomas (1857–1935) earned her Ph.D. from the University of Zurich in 1882. When Bryn Mawr was established in 1885, she was appointed dean and professor of English. She served as president of the institution from 1894 to 1922. Active in NAWSA, she was the first president of the National College Women's Equal Suffrage Association. After suffrage, she supported the National Woman's Party (*NAW*, s.v. "Thomas, Martha Carey"). Madeline McDowell Breckinridge (1872–

dinner![10] Miss Addams's hour of trial that the war was to bring her had not yet come, and so I did not know then the full stature of her greatness. But I did feel, as I looked into those eyes, in which the sorrows of the world seemed to be mirrored, that here was a woman to reverence. Hers is a transcendent pity for the woes of men and women. And so she was, her pity so responsive that it made her endeavor to assuage every separate pain that she saw, and yet so broad that she labored to do away with the social causes of the pain. Not many are there who can in one life serve as she did the immediate and the further good at once.

There was also Pattie Jacobs, a slim young woman who was to be called the first citizen of Alabama for her prison-reform work; Esther Ogden, also young and slim, who for so many years served the Foreign Policy Association as its wise and loved secretary; Kate Waller Barrett who had founded the Florence Crittenton Homes for friendless girls, a Virginia aristocrat with a voice of silver.[11] Seeing all these and other women I realized how narrow had

---

1920), great-granddaughter of Henry Clay, was on the board of directors of General Federation of Women's Clubs and from 1912 to 1915 was president of the Kentucky Equal Rights Association. From 1913 to 1915, she was vice president of NAWSA (*NAW,* s.v. "Breckinridge, Madeline McDowell").

10. Jane Addams (1860–1935) founded the American settlement-school movement with the establishment of Hull House in Chicago in 1889. Beginning in 1907, she worked for suffrage, and after World War I, she devoted her energies to the peace movement (*NAW,* s.v. "Addams, Jane").

11. Pattie Ruffner Jacobs (1875–1935) was president of the Alabama Equal Suffrage Association 1912–1916 and 1918–1920. She served as second auditor of NAWSA and was on its congressional committee. In 1920, she was Alabamba's first Democratic national committeewoman. She held two paid jobs during the New Deal: head of the women's division of the Consumers' Advisory Board of the National Recovery Administration and as a speaker for Tennessee Valley Authority in Alabama (*NAW,* s.v. "Jacobs, Pattie Ruffner"). Esther Ogden (1867–1956) was elected third vice president of NAWSA at the 1915 convention. She also headed the National Woman Suffrage Publishing Company. She was active in the Foreign Policy Association, serving as its secretary from 1928 to 1937. A member of the Board of Trustees of the Woodrow Wilson Foundation and on the executive committee of the National Committee on the Cause and Cure of War, she was vice chairman of the women's bureau for the Democratic national convention in 1920 (Stanton et al., eds., *History of Woman Suffrage,* 5:456, 481–82; *New York Times,* January 15, 1956, 92:4). Kate Waller Barrett (1857–1925) earned her M.D. degree in 1892 and opened a home for unwed mothers in Atlanta the next year with money provided by millionaire Charles N. Crittenton, who financed other similar homes, naming them after his daughter. In 1896, Barrett began working for the National Florence Crittenton Mission, supervising the fifty homes throughout the country. When Charles Crittenton died in 1909, she became president of the organization. She was also a member of the Virginia Equal Suffrage League and a delegate to the Democratic National Convention in 1924 (*NAW,* s.v. "Barrett, Kate Waller"). At the 1914 convention, Barrett gave a speech on the attitude toward suffrage of the International Council of Women (Stanton et al., eds., *History of Woman Suffrage,* 5:410).

been my viewpoint, how little it mattered what Carthage thought and did, how selfish and vain had been my life.

It is almost as if two women did exist: one who was the creature of her environment, her training, and certain traits of character, such as the desire to conform, to be as like others around her as possible, and another inside of her who was struggling always to free herself, to develop, to come into her own.

I also added to my repertoire of "writers I have met." Ida Clyde Clarke, afterward the founder of *Pictorial Review*'s five-thousand-dollar annual award for the woman of achievement. Almost as new as I to such affairs, she had a mind fertile with ideas on publicity, though it was years before she found a market for them. And to talk to Cora Harris, the ironically witty author of *Letters of a Circuit Rider's Wife*, and watch her sibyl-like face; to listen to Zona Gale, as wistful looking as the love stories that brought her so many literary prizes; and Mary Johnston, who seemed too quiet and demure ever to have written such romantic adventures as *To Have and to Hold*.[12]

Perhaps a small-town woman going to her first national convention of the League of Women Voters, or a young political idealist attending his first national convention and seeing for the first time his idolized leaders, may understand.

Here were women who to me were brilliant, self-immolating. Here was a cause so big that women were willing to give their money until it hurt, their energies, their time, their very lives. You cannot pass on such an early enthusiasm to those of another generation. But I would like to express what it meant to ours, a devotion and merging of the self into a common cause

---

12. Ida Clyde Clarke attended the University of London and Columbia University. She was on the editorial staff of the *Nashville Tennessean* until 1909, was the managing editor of *Taylor-Trotwood Magazine* in 1910, on the staff of the *Nashville Banner* 1910–1913, and contributing editor of *Pictorial Review* 1916–1927. A Democrat, she was the first president of the Business Women's Equal Suffrage League. (Howes, *American Women, 1935–1940*, s.v. "Clarke, Ida Clyde"). In 1909, the *Saturday Evening Post* published a serial by Cora Harris (1869–1935), "A Circuit Rider's Wife," about the life of a rural Methodist minister. It then came out in book form. From 1910 to 1927, she published a novel a year. In the 1920s, she wrote popular romances and travel stories for the *Saturday Evening Post* (*NAW*, s.v. "Harris, Cora"). Zona Gale (1874–1938) was a novelist, playwright, and essayist. Earning a B.A. (1895) and M.A. (1899) from the University of Wisconsin, she moved to New York to work for the *New York Evening World*, 1901–1903. Thereafter, she worked as a freelancer, publishing stories in *Atlantic, Woman's Home Companion*, and other magazines. She was a member of the WTUL and in 1914 a vice president of the Wisconsin Woman Suffrage Association. In 1921, she won the Pulitzer Prize for drama for her play *Miss Lulu Bett* (*NAW*, s.v. "Gale, Zona"). Mary Johnston (1870–1936), author of twenty-three novels, published her most popular work in 1900, *To Have and to Hold*, about women at Jamestown. She also wrote short stories for *Harper's Monthly*. In 1909, she was a founder of the Equal Suffrage League of Virginia; during World War I she was a pacifist, joining the Women's International League for Peace and Freedom (*NAW*, s.v. "Johnston, Mary").

that made all other endeavors for long to come seem empty and flat. In view of my later political activities, I must record this: Strangely, I never thought of suffrage in terms of women in political organizations, or women holding office. To me it means the removal of a handicap upon women so that they might easier realize their own potentialities. "I am working," I used to say, "for my granddaughters, so that they may never have to soft-pedal their opinions or restrain their ambitions, so they will never know what it is to feel intellectual inferiority just because they are women." This, I thought and said, would benefit the race. I did think, too, that it would add to the electorate great numbers of voters who could and would take a personally disinterested attitude toward social measures.

Now that women have had the vote for nineteen years, I am sometimes referred to as a pioneer suffragist. This is amusing. I was no pioneer. When I came into the fight, only one among the thousands working at it, victory was almost in sight. True, there were always to the last men and women who jeered at us. And there was criticism of my activities that made me feel that I was pioneering among these critics. In a sense, too, with my background, I felt myself a pioneer. But all that does not make one a pioneer. The pioneers were those who had started the fight fifty years before I was born, and endured scorn and even outrage because they dared to say women should be equal politically with men. When I came into the struggle the rewards were far greater than the sacrifices. And I am profoundly grateful to have had my small part in it.

For through it was released in me a force I did not know was there. I do not try to explain it, but I have observed that when one works for something he believes to be for the general good, he seems to be lifted into something beyond himself. This is what suffrage work did for many women. The difficulty is that one must believe that what he is working for will accomplish good, and, with the modern confusion of thought about desired ends, it seems well-nigh impossible for people to convince themselves that anything will accomplish sufficient good to make it worthwhile for them to spend themselves for it. We were, in those days, either more simple or more credulous.

This is not the place to make an argument for feminism. I merely want to set down that I did believe that what I was working for was a fundamental thing worth working for. Activity for activity's sake has never appealed to me, nor have I ever been much interested in measures that merely relieved symptoms. This is the reason, I take it, that I have never been interested in charity work, except to relieve my own discomfort when individual cases appealed to my sympathies. I have always had to persuade myself that what I did would some way reach to causes. And the conclusion to which I had come was that the granting of the vote to women would remove a handicap that would in turn affect the position generally of women in society.

Lest I grow prosy by relating the many incidents that dot the suffrage work, I will confine myself to one that indicates the different social-political climate of that day.

It took place at one of Ruth McCormick's conferences. She wanted to prove to Chicago by way of the society columns that suffrage had at last become fashionable. So, by hook or crook, she had persuaded some of the city's most conservative and privileged social leaders to serve as hostesses at a large dinner on the roof of a downtown hotel. Some of these women were more for Ruth than for suffrage.

Everything was done that could be done to make it elegantly conventional, so that these leaders would not be scared off by any suggestion of radicalism. We got out our best evening dresses and keyed our conversation to the safe and bromidic. But Ruth had made one mistake. She had asked a Chicago University professor, then much in the public notice because of a book, *Sex and Society*, to speak, hoping probably to give the program a dash of the intellectual.[13] But she had reckoned without Professor Thomas. Either because he had a puckish humor, slightly Rabelaisian, or he could not miss such an opportunity to make the front page, he delivered a series of verbal "bombshells," such as these: Men got more than they bargained for when they extolled virginity. The superiority of monogamy has never been proved. Every woman—married or not—has the right to have a child.

The suffragists sat stunned. We could almost see the headlines in the morning papers: "Suffragists for Free Love!"

The other speakers rallied, said something politely contradictory, but it was not until the very end of the program that the situation was saved. A little anemic-looking lady, Miss Alice Stone Blackwell, dated by her iron-gray hair worn like my grandmother's, and the red cashmere shawl around her shoulders, turned to Dr. Thomas.[14] "I agree with you, sir," she said. "Every woman is entitled to a child, but I think she is entitled to a husband, too." At this from a New England miss of very certain years, the audience rose and cheered. By so much did Ruth and the suffragists find themselves saved from headlines that they knew would ruin them. But it took many telephone calls to editors and publishers before they felt really safe.

---

13. Professor William Isaac Thomas of the University of Chicago published *Sex and Society* in 1907.

14. Alice Stone Blackwell (1857–1950) edited the *Woman's Journal* for thirty-five years and, beginning in 1890, was the recording secretary of NAWSA for twenty years (*NAW*, s.v. "Blackwell, Alice Stone").

4 *The Middle of the Bridge*

During the year I was peddling my novel about, suffrage activities involved increasingly board meetings, speeches at state conventions, conferences of many kinds. Doubtless I found in them balm for my disappointment over the book. At any rate, I enjoyed them. Before this phase of my life came to an abrupt and not exactly pleasant end in the fall of 1916, I had learned to know my state from end to end, city, town, and hamlet.

I had moved out onto the national suffrage scene, had become to a small extent an actor, and very much a spectator. I had also widened my acquaintance, always worthwhile to me, who have an insatiable curiosity about people, their ways of life and thought. Both in my state and out of it I had come to know some of the women leaders of that day. The most picturesque was undoubtedly Dr. Shaw.[1] I had seen her first at Nashville, a small woman with a rotund figure and white hair. On the platform she usually wore a black velvet dress with a large Venetian-lace collar. It has always seemed to me one of nature's sardonic jokes that this woman, who was accused of wanting to act like a man, should look like a picture on a postcard for Mother's Day.

But with her looks this similarity to the conventional idea of motherliness vanished. She had pioneered in all the fields held sacred to men: medicine, theology, and law. Her barbed wit could prick the toughest prejudice; her gift for the trenchant phrase lands a thought in the most barricaded brain; and her voice was one of the most dramatic of all time. Had she not been a born evangelist, she might have gone on the stage, a combination of Marie Dressler and Duse.[2]

---

1. Dr. Anna Howard Shaw (1847–1919) graduated from the divinity school of Boston University in 1878 and was ordained by the Methodist Protestant Church. In 1886, she earned her M.D. from Boston University. After working for the Massachusetts Woman Suffrage Association and the WCTU, she became a national lecturer for NAWSA in 1891. From 1892 to 1904, she was vice president of NAWSA; she served as president of the organization from 1904 to 1915. During World War I, she was chairman of the Woman's Committee of the U.S. Council of National Defense (*NAW*, s.v. "Shaw, Anna Howard").

2. Marie Dressler (1869?–1934) debuted in New York in 1892. She was extremely popular as a musical comedienne whose humor was a little crude but good-natured. During World War I, she sold "millions of dollars worth of Liberty Bonds" (*NAW*, s.v. "Dressler, Marie"). Eleanora Duse (1858–1924) made her New York debut in 1893. A brilliant actress, comparable to Sarah Bernhardt, she became a star known for her realism and subtlety. She made a second American tour in 1896 (Young, *Famous Actors and Actresses*, 1:316–23).

"I have heard all the great speakers of our day," a Tennessee jurist once said to me. "I wanted to test her against them. She is the greatest."

Though she was wont to say drolly that God must love the men because he never entrusted one to her, the men who knew her adored her. She once went to visit a friend of mine in St. Louis. Unknown to her, my friend's husband, an important middle-aged banker, said that although he would, as befit a courteous host, greet her at dinner on her first night, he would thereafter dine at his club. At the end of the first evening, he asked if he might bring a friend to dinner the next evening to hear her stories. The second evening he added another; the third the two of them came again. When she left at the end of a week, the whole group accompanied her to the train, each bearing a bouquet of flowers.

She had one feminine trait: a love of precious stones. She did not have the means to indulge this taste, nor would she have considered it good for the cause to have appeared in jewels. Friends, however, knowing this love of hers, had given her at various times a diamond, a ruby, a sapphire, and an emerald. These stones, unset, she carried in a little pillbox, and after a lecture, when she reached her hotel bedroom, she would take them out and enjoy them all by herself.

And there was Carrie Chapman Catt, whose last name, bestowed on her by a husband, was the butt of so many witticisms.[3] Then in her heyday, she was a very handsome woman. Tall, with blue eyes and gray hair, she had an exquisite neck and a line from it to shoulder you never forgot. I met her first in St. Louis whence she had summoned some of us Missouri suffragists to plan a demonstration for the Democratic convention of 1916 to convince the delegates that women really wanted the vote. For the Republican convention she had already planned a parade, but southern Democrats, she felt, would not take kindly to women marching in the streets.

Suddenly I saw a picture in my mind. "Why not," I said, "line the way to the Coliseum with women holding out their hands in mute appeal?" So was born the idea of "the Golden Lane." The women must, of course, look feminine. Very well, they could be dressed in white and carry yellow parasols. Next to a fan, nothing is more feminine than a parasol. And their request? It could

---

3. Carrie Chapman Catt (1859–1947) earned her B.S. from Iowa State College in 1880. After the death of her first husband in 1886, she became active in the Iowa Woman Suffrage Association. In 1890, she married George W. Catt who agreed that she would spend two months in the fall and two months in the spring working for suffrage. In 1900, Susan B. Anthony chose her to become president of NAWSA, but she had to resign in 1904 when her husband became ill. After his death, she returned to suffrage work, becoming president of NAWSA again in 1915, and saw the passage of the Nineteenth Amendment. In 1925, she was a founder of the Conference on the Cause and Cure of War (*NAW*, s.v. "Catt, Carrie Chapman").

be printed on their yellow sashes: "Votes for Women." Nothing unladylike about a yellow sash.

We parted from Mrs. Catt at five o'clock in the afternoon. At dinner at seven she took out her notebook. In it was jotted down the whole plan, including the number of women required, with a quota fixed for each state, the number of parasols and sashes to be ordered.

That done, Mrs. Catt turned to me and asked, "How do you suppose they make this cornbread? It's better than ours." And so began a conversation about cornbread recipes.

In spite of my two-year association with suffragists, I was amazed. Others of us straight from our kitchens might be expected to talk about recipes, but that the leader of the stupendous New York initiative campaign, veteran of a hundred conventions, who was said to have the brains of a statesman and the voice of an orator, should talk about recipes! Often since then, when I have seen her standing majestically before an audience of thousands who hung on her words, I have thought of that dinner. Yet, in spite of her interest in cornbread, I realized that here was a woman who lived in and for an idea. "I have no hesitancy in asking women for money," she said that day, "because I first give all I can possibly afford myself." And so she did: ten thousand dollars a year of her own money, her time, eight hours in a downtown office, more hours at night for the international suffrage association of which she was president. And this though the doctor had warned her such work was dangerous for her.

It was this unselfishness that made her such an incomparable leader of women, incomparable because no other woman anywhere has been followed so unquestioningly, obeyed so implicitly, admired so prodigiously. Yet never has she assumed the prerogatives of a leader. When great honors came to her, as they did later, she always had the naive surprise of a child. I was with her when she was notified that she had been named as one of *Good Housekeeping's* "Ten Greatest Women." She was actually surprised. There is no exhibitionism in her. Neither would I say she has magnetism as we usually understand it. Rather is her attitude one of friendliness, the friendliness of equal to equal. She is not what you call a dominant personality, yet she has dominated.

All this I did not know that night, but I am a little proud—or should I say vain—that I had the sense to know I was in the presence of greatness even if it was devoted to cornbread recipes.

The Golden Lane came off as planned. Martha Taaffe, of Carthage, an enthusiastic suffragist and in time to become very active in Democratic politics, and I stayed with my deaconess sister Anna in her small apartment at the Cathedral House in St. Louis.[4] For six hours we stood along the sidewalk,

---

4. Martha Coffin Taaffe (1868–1957) was a founder of the Carthage, Missouri, Suffrage League in 1914. She served on the Missouri Suffrage League board and was a delegate to

blocks and blocks of us, women from the tenements and some from New York mansions, teachers and housewives, factory workers and factory owners. The delegates and visitors joked us as they took to the streets and marched between us to the convention; some uncomfortable, some annoyed, and some nodding approval according to their opinions on the subject.

This Golden Lane was only an introduction to our real purpose, which was to obtain a suffrage plank in the party platform. The chairman of the Resolutions Committee was my father's old friend William J. Stone, and I was detailed to keep in touch with him, so I sat on the front row at the open meetings of the Resolutions Committee, and listened to the antisuffragists make their talks against a suffrage plank. Queer business, I thought. Privileged women urging that other women should not have equality. And then I sat outside the closed doors behind which the men wrestled about the plank until early in the morning. Funny, it seems now, to think that a plank favoring woman suffrage was as much a matter of serious debate as later the Klan and repeal planks were to be. The politicians should have been grateful to us, for it was the only question in debate in the whole convention, and what would a Democratic convention be without a controversy? The fight was between the western delegates, who said they could not carry the western states, where women already voted, for Mr. Wilson unless a suffrage plank was adopted, and the southerners who would not have one.[5]

Two reports were brought to the convention, the majority report with a mild suffrage plank, and a minority one disapproving suffrage. When it came to the convention, Senator Stone was too worn out to present his committee's report, and turned it over to a slim Adonis from the West with melting brown eyes, Senator Pitman of Nevada. Like a young Lochinvar, he seemed to the suffragists as he spoke for the suffrage plank with dash, force, and brilliance. Then came the opposition report presented by Senator Nugent, the boss of New Jersey, supported by Governor Ferguson of Texas, ironically enough, the one, boss of a state that was to give the United States its first Democratic congresswoman, the other the man whose wife was to become one of the two woman governors we have had.[6]

---

the 1920 Democratic National Convention. Joining the Missouri Federation of Women's Clubs in 1908, she held every office on the state board except president. In 1926, she was unsuccessful in her bid for election to the Missouri House of Representatives (Dains, *Show Me Missouri Women*, 2:177–78). Anna Newell had graduated from St. Faith's Deaconness Training School in New York City and had been ordained at Christ Church Cathedral in St. Louis in 1911. She was on the cathedral staff for ten years, involved in social service work (typescript, Anna Gray Newell biographical sketch, Archives, Grace Episcopal Church).

5. In 1916, the Democratic platform supported woman suffrage but called for its adoption on a state-by-state basis.

6. Key Pitman (1872–1940) joined the Klondike gold rush and practiced law in Alaska 1897–1901. He then moved to Nevada and was elected as a Democrat to the United States

We sat on the platform, we suffragists, and listened amazed, at least I was, to the violence of the opposition to "our" plank. At last, worn out by his all-night committee session, hungry, sleepy, our young supporter from Nevada lost his temper, and said abruptly that if they wanted to reelect Woodrow Wilson they would have to take this plank—that was the long and short of it—or words to that effect.

Anger was in the air. The men tense. When the vote was taken man after man gave his delegation's vote for the majority plank with gritted teeth, some even saying, "If we have to do it for Woodrow Wilson."

On the way back to the hotel, a pleasant Boston Irishman, who had spoken on the floor, came over to me on the streetcar and said, "I saw you on the platform. Were you satisfied with the suffrage plank?"

I told him it was not as strong as we wanted, but it was all we expected.

"That's what I told the fellows," he said. "If we'd given you women suffrage in the first place, you'd just have voted and that'd be all there was to it. We've given you time to learn politics while you're getting it."

This may have been what politicians thought, but it was far from true. Women had not learned how to play politics, as I was to discover. At that

---

Senate to fill a vacancy. He was consistently reelected, serving from 1913 until his death in 1940 (*Biographical Directory of the U.S. Congress*, 1652). John F. Nugent (1868–1931) was admitted to the bar in 1898. He served as an Idaho Democrat in the United States Senate 1918–1921 and was not reelected. Woodrow Wilson appointed him to the Federal Trade Commission where he served 1921–1927 (ibid., 1578). Frank Hague (1876–1956) worked his way up through New Jersey politics. In 1913, he worked for civic reform in Jersey City, which led to the adoption of the commission form of government, and Hague was elected one of the commissioners. In 1917, he was elected mayor of Jersey City and controlled the Democratic Party of the state until the late 1940s. In 1924, he was chairman of the Democratic National Committee (*DAB*, s.v. "Hague, Frank"). James Edward Ferguson (1871–1944) was elected governor of Texas in 1914 and reelected in 1916. He fought against Prohibition and woman suffrage. Impeached in 1917 and removed from office, he ran his wife as his stand-in in 1924 (*DAB*, s.v. "Ferguson, James Edward"). Mary Teresa Hopkins Norton (1875–1959) entered politics with the help of Mayor Frank Hague, who convinced her in 1920 to represent Hudson County on the Democratic State Committee of New Jersey. She was the first woman on the state committee, and from 1921 to 1944, she was either chairman or vice chairman. When she was elected to the United States House of Representatives in 1924, she was the first woman Democrat elected without being preceded by her husband. In 1937, as chairman of the Labor Committee, she was instrumental in getting the Fair Labor Standards Act passed (*NAW-Modern*, s.v. "Norton, Mary Teresa Hopkins"). Miriam Amanda Wallace Ferguson (1875–1961) began her political career after her husband, James E. Ferguson, was impeached as governor of Texas in 1917. Running for governor as his stand-in in 1924, she was easily elected. Taking office only weeks after Wyoming's Nellie Tayloe Ross, "Ma" Ferguson was the second female governor of a state. Defeated in the primaries in 1926 and 1930, she was again elected governor in 1932 and was a strong supporter of Franklin Roosevelt (*NAW-Modern*, s.v. "Ferguson, Miriam Amanda Wallace").

time, however, I was not interested in politics, but only in women having their opinions counted.

This was my first experience with national conventions, and I did not find them alluring. But I was pleased when Mrs. Catt said to me when we parted, "Could you come to New York and help me with our publicity?"

"Goodness, no," I said. "I've a husband and two children at home."

"That's always the way, when I find a woman I can use," she said with her amused smile. But she made me promise that if ever I was free to come I would let her know. I promised that I would, little dreaming that in two years I would do that very thing.

I had grown a little less self-conscious. I was still frightened whenever I made a speech, but I could converse at times on equal terms with men. I felt it, I remember, quite an accomplishment when on the way to the convention, I dropped into conversation with our congressman from home and a local politician, and engaged them in a debate about suffrage. That I remember that talk so well with all its details indicates what it meant to me to be able to do it. I could even—and this I considered a great advance—talk casually to strangers on the train.

In the fall of 1916 Mrs. Catt called a special suffrage convention in Atlantic City.[7] I had no right to go to that convention. My husband had opened a new law office. Newell was up North with my mother, but Harriet had to be looked after. But my sister who insisted I needed a rest and perhaps suspected I needed a new perspective on my homework, which only absence could give, offered me the trip. A suffrage friend asked me to be her guest at the Marlborough-Blenheim. The temptation was too great. I went through the form of asking my husband's permission and, sending my daughter to a friend, I turned Harry out on the world and went.

I had twinges of conscience. But I enjoyed the convention. I had many friends among the delegates by this time. Meeting them again made the convention almost like a college class reunion. Besides, the work had gotten into my blood. I was, I suspect, more completely an extrahome woman, what is usually thought of as a career woman, than ever before or since, though I did not realize it. I threw myself into the discussions with eagerness, and was passionately concerned with the outcome of our deliberations.

One of the things that stands out in my memory was meeting Mrs. Raymond Robins and becoming interested in the Woman's Trade Union League she was mothering. It was my first acquaintance with the problems of the working women. Another was Elizabeth Bass taking me into a small caucus of Democratic women, at which they talked of the 1916 campaign and

---

7. Carrie Catt called the emergency convention to meet in Atlantic City on September 4–10, 1916. It was there that she announced her "Winning Plan."

the western woman vote.[8] Knowing that my husband was a Democrat, she took it for granted I would be.

The Atlantic City Suffrage Convention in 1916 was the occasion of President Wilson's appearance. The suffragists, with their flair for dramatization, made the most of it. For the cordon of honor they had chosen their best-looking women, beauteous Katrina Tiffany, impressive Mrs. J. Borden Harriman, statuesque Mrs. Guilford Dudley, and others formed an aisle. The president, with Mrs. Catt on one side and Mrs. Wilson on the other, walked through it to their seats.[9]

The women in their seats sat hushed in expectation. This was the first time a president of the United States had come to them. It was also the first time most of them had seen Edith Bolling Wilson. She wore a white gown with a corselette of mother-of-pearl sequins from which billowed ruffles of chiffon,

---

8. Margaret Dreier (1868–1945) joined the WTUL in 1904 and married Raymond Robins, a Chicago settlement worker, the next year. Both were independently wealthy and devoted their efforts to reform. She served as the president of the Chicago WTUL from 1907 to 1913 and was also president of the national WTUL until 1922, giving that organization her money, leadership, and organizational skills. Active in the women's division of the RNC in 1919–1920, she supported FDR in the 1932 election (*NAW*, s.v. "Robins, Margaret Dreier"). Elizabeth Bass (d. 1950) married George Bass in 1894. She had been president of the Chicago Woman's Club and a member of the original Juvenile Court Committee of Illinois. In 1916, she ran the Woman's Bureau of the Democratic national campaign. From 1916 to 1945, she was chairman of the National Woman's Bureau of the Democratic National Committee (*Who Was Who in America*, 3:54).

9. Katrina Tiffany (1875–1927) earned her A.B. from Bryn Mawr in 1897. Living in New York, she was president of the College Women's Equal Suffrage League and recording secretary of the Woman Suffrage Party of New York, traveling and speaking for the cause. She was active in the League of Women Voters and the Democratic Party. A founder of the Woodrow Wilson Foundation and a member of the executive board of the Foreign Policy Association (1918–1927), she was active in numerous philanthropic causes for social justice (*DAB*, s.v. "Tiffany, Katrina"). Florence Jaffray (1870–1967) married New York banker J. Borden Harriman in 1889. Rewarding her support in the 1912 election, Woodrow Wilson appointed her to the Federal Industrial Relations Commission, and she moved to Washington. After her husband's death in 1914, she became active in the suffrage movement. During World War I, she chaired a committee on women in industry for the Council of National Defense and after the war headed a committee of the National Consumers' League opposing the equal-rights amendment. In 1922, she was one of the founders of the Woman's National Democratic Club and was president of it for eight years. Beginning in 1924, she served thirty-two years as national committeewoman from the District of Columbia (*NAW-Modern*, s.v. "Harriman, Florence Jaffray"). Anne Dallas (Mrs. Guilford) Dudley (1876–1955) was the first president of the Nashville Equal Suffrage League (1911–1915). She served three years as president of the Tennessee Equal Suffrage Association. From 1917 to 1921, she was third vice president of NAWSA. Turning to partisan politics, she was the first woman associate on the Tennessee State Democratic Committee in 1920 and was a delegate-at-large to the Democratic National Convention in that year (*Who Was Who in America*, 3:240). Edith Bowling Wilson (1872–1961) married Woodrow Wilson in 1915 (*NAW-Modern*, s.v. "Wilson, Edith Bowling").

her dark, lustrous hair formed an aura for her radiant beauty. A lovely being to look at, and as remote, as detached from that scene as if she had come from another world. As she sat there, her small feet crossed, an invisible line seemed to separate her from all these women. They knew without her having said it that she did not sympathize with them.

Julia Lathrop, chief of the Children's Bureau, an appointee of the president, led off.[10] There was almost coquetry in her deft references to Wilson's interest in her work, his support of all that was helpful to women and children, her appreciation of his greatness. I came to know her well. No woman could better seize a moment and extract from it all its possibilities. Many times have I heard her speak since, moving from sardonic wit to gay glee and then to pathos that gripped one's throat. She had a voice with cadences to fit any emotion. But never was a speech better suited to its purpose than that. There was subtle flattery in her feminine deference to masculine superiority, still more flattery in her skillful suggestion of the importance and the intellect of the women who so deferred.

In contrast, Katherine B. Davis of the House of Corrections, a woman of generous proportions, standing squarely on her feet, who made no concessions to masculine vanity, seemed almost to arraign it without circumlocution as she talked about the double standard of morals and its unfairness to women. I can imagine how the president squirmed. I know I did, thinking it was maladroit to say the least. Yet its effect was good. For if Julia Lathrop conveyed woman's dependence on man's generosity for justice, Dr. Davis suggested their growing resentment at injustice, and resentment is an emotion to which candidates are sensitive. Other speakers employed the Lathrop motif, Owen Lovejoy, Robins.[11] By the time they were through, the president, if

---

10. Julia Lathrop (1858–1932), associated with Jane Addams in the formation of Hull House, was the first woman appointed by Gov. John Altgeld to the Illinois Board of Public Charities, serving from 1893 to 1909. In 1912, President Taft appointed her to head the new Children's Bureau, where she worked until 1921. A proponent of suffrage, Lathrop was active in the League of Women Voters, serving as Illinois president in 1922 and working for the organization at the national level (*DAB*, s.v. "Lathrop, Julia").

11. Katherine B. Davis (1860–1935), chief of the Parole Commission in New York City, presented "A Necessary Safeguard to Public Morals" (Stanton et al., eds., *History of Woman Suffrage*, 5:496). Receiving her A.B. from Vassar in 1892 and her Ph.D. in 1900 from the University of Chicago, Davis was appointed superintendent of the State Reformatory for Women at Bedford Hills, New York, beginning her career as a prison administrator and reformer. Commissioner of Corrections for New York City, she played a significant role in the passage of the parole law that established the New York City Parole Commission and was its first chairman (*DAB*, s.v. "Davis, Katherine B."). Lathrop's speech was called "Mothers in Politics." Dr. Owen Lovejoy, general secretary of the National Child Labor Committee, offered "Working Children." Robins's speech was titled "The Call of the Working Woman for the Protection of the Woman's Vote" (Stanton et al., eds., *History of Woman Suffrage*, 5:496).

he had his share of masculine vanity, should have felt as soothed as a well-stroked cat.

His own speech was as calmly delivered, as logically thought out, as perfectly phrased as his speeches always were. He reviewed briefly the history of his attitude toward suffrage, showed the processes of his mind as facts had developed that attitude, gave as clear and concise an argument for woman suffrage as had ever been made. When he wrote the speech he had doubtless had his mind upon the opponents, as well as the adherents of equal suffrage. But his climax was directed solely to these women. "We differ not on principle, but on method. You will not find me unfriendly to your cause." When he had finished, the women rose and applauded. It was not all they had hoped for, yet it was more than any president had ever given them.

Then Mrs. Catt had an inspiration. "I think on such an occasion as this we must have a final word from our own Dr. Shaw."

Mrs. Catt's personality seemed always to typify the reasonableness of the appeal for suffrage. Listening to her one could not but feel it ridiculous to deny such a woman a place in political life. Dr. Shaw's was the emotional appeal. She must have been inspired that night. For, turning to the president, she ended her appreciation of what his speech had meant to them in these words: "It is true that it is coming, Mr. President, but I, as one of your humblest followers and admirers, crave for you the glory of having this great act of justice done during your administration."

As with one movement, the women rose and fixed their eyes upon the president. For a moment there was silence, and then they broke into applause. If they had held out their hands to him, the appeal could not have been more dramatic. The president rose. "I think," he said, "that we will no longer quarrel about the method."

It has been said it was at this moment that Woodrow Wilson was converted to the Nineteenth Amendment. That this is so I do not know, but if so, it was a historic moment because the aid he thereafter gave the movement, even breaking all precedents to appear before the Senate to make a plea for it, did much to bring its success.

I am glad I was present that night. For not often do you participate in a moment of such high emotion. Those standing, taut, appealing women unconscious of what they did, little Dr. Shaw, dynamic, with that voice that could pierce any heart, and the president, the very picture of intellectual power and poise with beautiful Edith Wilson beside him, suggestive of another approach to life.

After the convention I went to a small, cheap hotel just off the boardwalk for a week. Atlantic City with its teeming crowd, its noisy beach, its raucous auctions would hardly seem the place for a rest cure. But each morning I went out upon the beach and lay down by myself where I could see no one. Each afternoon I went to the end of the longest pier and gazed at the water. Each evening I was wheeled as far up the walk away from the crowds as my guide would take me. I spoke to no one. I did not even open a book. I never entered a shop or pavilion. At the end of the week I was a new woman.

A brief visit to New York City to see editors, my first of many pilgrimages to them, followed, and then the prodigal mother and wife returned home.

But no fatted calf was killed for her. There was no feasting or rejoicing. She was welcomed, of course, but with an undertone of forbearance. The erring sinner was being received but her lapse not condoned. She was not to be allowed to forget that she had sinned. This was something new in my experience and decidedly unpleasant. I resented it, of course, but my conscience did not support my resentment. My husband had needed me. My daughter should not have stayed so long with my friend. My son had returned from his vacation. School had opened. He, too, had to stay with a friend. Try as I would to justify myself by my mental and physical weariness and need for a change, the importance of seeing these editors, and attending that convention if I was to do successful suffrage work, the fact was that my suffrage activities had come in conflict with my domestic duties, and I had put the suffrage activity first. Although never put into words, I knew my husband felt this. Something had gone out of our relationship. The realization was bitter medicine. And as I tasted it, I knew what was the most important thing in my life. What had gone meant more than any success in anything ever could. And I set out to retrieve it. Never one for half measures or moderation I resigned from all my clubs and organizations. The *Missouri Woman* found another editor. My typewriter ceased to click. I settled down again to being a wife and mother. A year I continued at my self-set program of renunciation, not always, I fear, graciously.

Never was there any question as to my decision, nor was there really a decision to be made. Nor would I refer to it here, with some embarrassment to myself, if it were not that many women in these later years have written me to ask help in a similar conflict between home and work.

Such conflicts are part of the problem of almost every married woman with children who essays extrahome activities. The demands of the two on her are not easy for her to resolve and adjust without either failing her home or handicapping her in her work. I did not attempt it. I simply capitulated. What the result would have been if the war had not come to work the change in our lives that it did in so many I do not know. Knowing better now than I did then my restless mind, my itch toward accomplishment, I cannot believe I would forever have been content with the role I then set myself of limiting all activity to my household. Had I done so, I hesitate to think what a dominant mother and nagging wife I might have become. But as it was, my capitulation served slowly to win back what I had so rashly forfeited, and circumstance solved my problem for me.

Circumstance and, I should add, my husband. I doubt that any woman can solve it alone. There must be concessions on both sides. The husband must be broad enough to appreciate his wife's point of view. He must be generous enough to yield what he prefers when yielding makes for her happiness. It is harder, I notice, for many husbands to give up these things than to confer material gifts. But a woman's happiness often depends far more on generosity as to her time and interests than generosity with money. The wife on her side has to make concessions, adjustments that only she can make. She has little to guide her. Now she sacrifices her work, now her family. It takes wisdom to know how far she can sacrifice her family without danger to something more valuable than her work, and how much she is really required, in justice to all, to sacrifice her work to her family. But then any happy marriage is the result of concession made on both sides. It is a work of collaboration in which each contributes the thing that he or she alone can. Nor is it an easy, simple task, although it seems so to the young bride and groom. The pity is that when its difficulties become apparent to them, they have no realization of how rewarding success will be and so do not feel it worthwhile to work hard enough to overcome or adjust them. Unfortunately, only those who enjoy the satisfaction of a happy marriage—and by a happy marriage I mean a completely satisfying relationship between a man and woman of fifty or past—know that it is the greatest thing life has to offer. But it is such a private thing that it is not exhibited to the bystander. It cannot be without doing violence to the thing that makes it what it is: the two-in-one-ness. To explain it spoils it, to proclaim it smirches it. Small wonder that young people looking on never suspect its meaning in the lives of those who have it, still less what has gone into its making. For it has to do with what a husband and wife mean to each other and that no one but themselves can guess. They themselves could never interpret it to anyone else, for no one else understands or looks at either one of them as each one of them does the other. They do not even examine it closely themselves lest it break into parts and is not the thing it was.

All this delicate adjustment is more difficult when there enters another factor, that of the wife's extrahome, extrahusband's interests. All a wife who has these activities can do, I think, is to meet each situation as it comes. If she knows which means more to her—the marriage or the work—her way is easier. If the wife's happiness is paramount with the husband, the solution is still easier. Fortunately for us I did know, and my happiness did come first with him.

5 World War I

I was not enthusiastic about the war, for I was temperamentally a pacifist. I do not know that I would ever have had the courage to do as did Jeanette Rankin, the woman congressman who voted against the declaration of war, but I admired her for doing it.[1] I felt Jane Addams had hold of some mystical truth that I almost but did not quite grasp.

Yet, in the end, I, too, was to be caught by the bait that this was a war to end war, and was willing to fight for victory. Looking back I find it difficult to remember just what my attitude was in September 1917 when I accepted the vice chairmanship of the newly appointed Missouri Woman's Committee of the Council of Defense.[2] I remember that my husband urged me to do it, feeling keenly that we should all do our part. I recall a conversation I had with my old friend Helen Miller in which I said that I suspected the government's attitude toward women in the promotion of the war was to keep them busy so they would not get hysterical—a suspicion I was later to find verified by facts. I resented the reorganization of the Red Cross that took it out of the control of women executives and put it under that of captains of industry or bankers, and even more the order that came down to our local organization that the local chairman should be a man, an order our chapter refused to obey, saying that the woman who had organized our chapter was as efficient and capable as any man. The insistence that bandages should be cut and folded exactly seemed to me ridiculous, as if the difference of a single thread or the way they were folded made them unfit to stop a wound. If they really needed bandages, numbers would certainly be more important than accuracy. I was to learn later how those bandages our women so slaved over, making a religion of their perfection, were used to wipe noses and guns. And the whole military

---

1. Jeanette Rankin (1880–1973) earned a B.S. in biology from the University of Montana in 1902. After working briefly as a social worker, she joined the suffrage campaign, becoming a field secretary for NAWSA in 1913. The first woman elected to the United States House of Representatives, she took office as a Republican in 1917. After her defeat, she was active in the Women's International League for Peace and Freedom, working as a field secretary. She also served as field secretary for the National Consumers' League (1920–1924). In 1940 she was again elected to Congress. Rankin voted against U.S. entry into both world wars (*NAW-Modern*, s.v. "Rankin, Jeanette").

2. ENB served on the state executive board of the Woman's Committee (Missouri Division) of the Council of National Defense. She was chairman for southwest Missouri.

paraphernalia of apron, cap, with the equally militaristic autocracy, offended my instinctive democracy. But I could understand that the soldiers and the allies must be fed, so into the conservation work I threw myself. Then, too, that something in us for which there is no name, perhaps just a yearning for a better, more perfect world, stirred in me, and I threw myself into the whole program for the improved social conditions that were to make this terrible sacrifice of life worthwhile.

I made speeches by the dozens all up and down my congressional district— on food conservation, Liberty Loans, child welfare—organized parades and strawberry pickers, entertained speakers, and got up meetings for them, and even educated people on the causes of the war and Germany's plan to come over and take the United States after she got through with Great Britain and France, all according to the "Red, White and Blue Books" issued by the government, to which later—God forgive me—I contributed myself.

We worked hard and intensively, so intensively that we sometimes seemed to forget our object in the technique. I was aghast one day to have a letter from a clear-minded county chairman that ran: "You cannot really mean it, Mrs. Blair, that it is as important to report the work as to do it." So I had unfortunately phrased my insistence on reports.

Those evening meetings in the German farm communities were especially hard. In the dimly lighted one-room schoolhouses they sat before us, men and women, stolid but bewildered as we tried to explain that it was not a war against the German people, knowing that they knew how those people were almost starving.

The war came home to me. My husband wanted to go. I knew this long before he told me, and I had decided what I was to say. Patriotism had nothing to do with it. I had no idea I was sacrificing him to my country. I only knew that I could not sacrifice him to me, and to keep him, feeling as he did, would do just that. So when Harry told me that he would like to offer himself to the YMCA, I told him I could manage.

Whether this was wise or foolish in me I do not know. How can one ever know? He came back a disillusioned man, far more pacifist than I. Life has never looked the same to him. Between him and the men who never saw the things he did, a chasm has always yawned. He does not give to things the values they do. If I had objected even by an expression he would not have gone, and this would have been spared him. And yet, not knowing what the experience would show him and mean to him, he would always have regretted that he did not go.

When he had been accepted I wired Mrs. Catt and a friend in Washington that I would be available for work. An answer came by wire asking if I could report in a week for work in the publicity department of the Woman's Council of Defense. I wired back that I could. Annie and Margaretta came in from Colorado to pack up the house. Harriet went to boarding school as she would have in any case that year. Annie brought Newell on later to join me in Washington. Of my work in Washington I shall tell in a later chapter.

Harry spent a week with me there before he went on to New York.

How thousands faced those partings in two world wars they themselves do not know. They remain as queer dreams. You cannot believe, looking back, that you did as you did. Harry left Washington on the midnight train. As I passed on the way upstairs, my landlady's husband and his friends were playing cards in the living room. I spoke to them and went up to my room. There at last my emotions swept up and out and over me like a thunderstorm. I had a firm conviction that I would never see my husband again. And yet, in a year, I was meeting him in New York, and my landlady's husband had died in that very house of typhoid fever.

Ten days after he left me in Washington, Harry sailed from Montreal. We had a signal, something he would send me, the day he left as they were not permitted to notify anyone of the vessel or the date. From that moment until the Armistice, it was as though I had no husband. For he had gone straight to the front, and if I thought of what that might mean, my imagination was too much for me. The only way to control it was not to think of him at all. And for those months I put him out of my mind entirely except when I read his letters and at night when I said my prayer. In our office was a map on which was daily traced the campaigns, as well as they could be deduced from the newspapers. Everyone went the first thing in the morning to look at it. I never did. My every effort was to forget what was going on in France. Those terrible weeks seem to have dropped out of my fifty years of marriage as if they had never been.

When the news of the false Armistice came to me, I was copying proof. I laid down my pencil and my first thought was, "Now I can think of him again." And not till then did I realize how completely during that time had I really lost him. It was as if he had been given back to me from the dead. The wild exuberance of that day I have never understood. My own reaction was so different. Mercifully, it never occurred to me that he might have been killed that morning and I not yet have known. He was, on that day, with the troops before Sedan.

Fortunately, I had a stiff job, one quite beyond me at first. The effort to fill it occupied my days, and in the evenings I visited furiously with friends. My memory of that period is confused as of no other part of my life, and I think of the Washington of that day as something like a nightmare with its awful crowds, the soldiers in uniform, the departmental conflicts, the flu, and the really terrible living conditions.

For, while Harry was fighting for democracy, Newell and I were fighting for housing. We first took a room in a two-room apartment belonging to a lady and her daughter, who moved us out overnight to make room for a guest. A secretary in our office, whose father's absence offered a temporary room, put us up for two weeks. We went from that to a Vermont Avenue lodging house. Finding the Fourteenth Street restaurants thereabouts impossible, we tried a small hotel, to be routed after one night's stay by the tiny inhabitants of the bed. We shared for a time another two-room apartment, kitchen, and sleeping porch with two girls until the army landlord returned, and finally ended by renting half a house—three rooms and a porch—below Fourteenth Street on V. It may have been poor management, but with rents what they were and the crowded conditions, it seemed all we could do on our income.

The house, a frame one, sat back in a yard at the other end of which a studio had been made into two apartments. The army officers who occupied them and the lady who had the other part of our house were the only white people on the block. Our landlord was an artist, and the house was furnished with museum pieces. Good to look at, but in our joy at getting the place we had not noticed that the beds were hung with rope mattresses, that you could not see yourself in the old mirrors or reach the drawers in the old highboys. When Mother, who had come to visit me, left, she said she hoped never to see an antique again.

One night I was awakened suddenly, my mother saying, "Something terrible is happening; get up quick." I jumped up and had just found my dressing gown in the dark when the door opened and a sailor in whites burst into the room. "Now be calm, ladies. It's all right. Calm right down. You're perfectly safe."

Just then the door flew wide open, and I saw a blaze and firemen carrying hose.

"My trunk!" cried out Mother. "My money and my bonds are in it. Here, help me throw it out of the window."

"But you can't," I said. "We're three stories up, and it would burst. It won't burn now with the firemen here, but the smoke might get us." And I told Newell to put on his coat. He thought the whole performance a great adventure and was not the least afraid.

As if we could not walk ourselves, the sailor took us each by the arm and led us down the stairs and out into the front yard. He even pulled down a shutter and made us stand on it.

We looked around. A fire engine was puffing in front of the house; an ambulance was drawn up. Policemen stood at the gate, and the fence was lined with black faces.

Newell surveyed it all carefully and then, with deep satisfaction, remarked, "Well, I guess Mr. Palmer has nothing on us."[3] It was the night after the attorney general's house had been bombed!

---

3. A. Mitchell Palmer (1872–1936) was a Democrat first elected to the United States House of Representatives in 1908 and reelected in 1910 and 1912. He was Pennsylvania's national committeeman in 1912. A supporter of Woodrow Wilson, he was appointed

When we finally returned to the house, we learned that our cotenant had been badly burned. While she had been in the bathroom a paper she had put around the gaslight had caught fire and dropped onto a fiber chair under it. When she attempted to throw the chair through the window it had fallen back on her. The landlord, alas, just that morning had put up the screens. Our sailor was passing by and had seen the blaze, turned in the fire alarm, and climbed up the porch to the rescue.

Mother had told the world that she had money and bonds in her trunk, and we thought it advisable to sit up the rest of the night to watch it, as our windows had all been broken.

The need to make my outgo balance with my small income was a severe discipline. I had to watch literally every single cent. I do not like to think even now of those economies.

Yet I did occasionally have an extravagant spree. When life seemed too utterly dull and I at a stopgap, I went out, as a man does for a drink, and bought something I did not need at all. When Christmas came with just Newell and me—Harriet spent it with an aunt in Chicago—in the small two-room apartment with no gifts from Harry (YMCA men were not permitted to send packages in the crowded boats), I bought myself a set of painted glass plates for ten dollars and sent them to myself with a card from Harry I had written. Our Christmas dinner, Newell's and mine, was eaten at a rotisserie.

I have always regarded those war months in Washington as a black, and a very black, mark against my motherhood. They were not fair to Newell. Overwhelmed mentally and repressed emotionally, I did not give him even the time and companionship I could. That his character survived them as it did is of no credit to me. He got, I think, some satisfaction from the thought that he was helping his father to win the war, but he might well have been a casualty himself of that war except for some deep unexpressed pride in him.

The lady who had the other part of our house had an adopted son almost Newell's age. He was an amazing little fellow, very independent, with ideas of his own. Newell did not care for him. Though the child would sit and visit with Mother and me, astonishing us with tall tales, Newell avoided him. To our questions he would say only, "Oh, he isn't my kind."

One night when I was out, Newell answered the door. A policeman stood there. "Does Newell Blair live here?" he asked.

Newell said he did.

"Is his mother here?"

Newell said no.

"Is any grown-up here?"

---

attorney general in 1919. At the 1920 Democratic convention, he was a contender for the presidential nomination (*DAB*, s.v. "Palmer, A. Mitchell"). On June 2, 1919, a bomb was thrown against the front door of Palmer's house, breaking all the windows (Stanley Coben, *A. Mitchell Palmer: Politician*, 205–7).

Newell said his grandmother was.

Mother was called.

"Is Newell Blair your grandchild?" asked the man. "Yes," she said.

"I am sorry to tell you that he is under arrest in Alexandria."

"But this is Newell, here beside me," she exclaimed. It developed that a boy with a suitcase bearing Newell Blair's name on it had broken into a shop and stolen some fishing tackle. Thus Newell was proved right about the other boy, who had run away and taken Newell's suitcase.

Immediately after the Armistice, Harry wrote that he would be home by Christmas. He was much worried for fear the Armistice would affect my job and I would not know what to do. Our house at home was leased, and to live on his YMCA allowance of sixty-five dollars a month would be impossible. A cable sent to me was undecipherable. My answers never reached him.

He did not land until the last day of the following April. When I went up to New York to meet my husband on his return from Europe, the first thing I said was, "Why, what have they done to your hands?" The tapering fingers that had made such infinitesimal stenographic hooks and crooks were thick and stubbed, the palms twice as large as normal.

"Why, this is nothing," he laughed. "You ought to have seen them at their worst. Your husband's been a porter. I can carry a piano from the basement to the attic. And I've learned to run a grocery store—in fact, five grocery stores, at one time."

I had put on my best, worn a veil and a flattering fur. As we came up from the boat on the subway, I noticed the men who had been with Harry in France eyeing us curiously. "Why didn't you tell us," one of them asked, "that you had a wife like that!" When I heard them call him "Grandad," I understood what they meant. I was fairly young for a grandmother. Yet he, with his hair gone white and his leather face, was exactly the same age as I.

We went down to Washington, where I had my work on the committee to do. In a week Harry had to return to New York's official welcome to his division. He had been with the 77th, made up of New Yorkers, and the officers of his regiment (the 308th) honored him by asking him to march with them. It was by a special request from the colonel to the war authorities that he had been permitted to return with his regiment. He was very popular with them. Reaching his assignment with the 308th shortly before the day that some of them were lost in the Argonne, he had been among the first to reach Major Whittelsey's "lost" battalion, which Harry always insisted was not "lost" but "beleaguered." Newell, then twelve years old, went back with Harry. He remembers that trip in every detail and how proud he was of his father.

6 *Point and Counterpoint*

While Harry was gone I threw myself wholeheartedly into my job. Those months may seem relatively unimportant in my marriage and my life, but this position oddly enough proved to be a most valuable stepping-stone in my work, without which I might have never taken such an active part in politics later on.

This job of mine, as I look back at it, was an interesting, if trying, one. The "Woman's Committee" had been a happy thought of the Council of Defense; it consisted of ten women with Dr. Shaw as chairman.

Mrs. Catt; Ida Tarbell; Mrs. Philip North Moore, president of the National Council of Women; Mrs. Josiah Cowles, president of the General Federation of Women's Clubs; Miss Maude Wetmore, chairman of National League for Women's Service; Mrs. Antoinette Funk, lawyer; Mrs. Stanley McCormick; Mrs. Joseph R. Lamar, president of National Society of Colonial Dames; Miss Agnes Nestor, vice president of the International Glove Workers Union; and Hannah Patterson.[1] They were all women of dominant personalities, brilliant,

---

1. Ida Tarbell (1857–1944) joined the staff of *McClure's* magazine in 1894. She became best known for her *History of the Standard Oil Company*, published in book form in 1904. She left *McClure's* in 1906 and joined the *American Magazine* where she worked until 1915; thereafter she freelanced. A supporter of Woodrow Wilson, she was not enthusiastic about suffrage. She served on the Woman's Committee of the U.S. Council of National Defense (Joseph P. McKerns, ed., *Biographical Dictionary of American Journalism*, s.v. "Tarbell, Ida"; *DAB*, s.v. "Tarbell, Ida"). Mary Eva Perry (Mrs. Philip North) Moore (1852–1931), a graduate of Vassar, was president of the National Council of Women from 1916 to 1925. She served as vice president of the International Council of Women 1920–1930. From 1917 to 1919, she was a member of the Woman's Committee of the Council of National Defense (*DAB*, s.v. "Moore, Philip North"). Ione Virginia Hill (Mrs. Josiah) Cowles (b. 1858) was president of the California State Federation of Women's Clubs in 1905–1906. She then moved to national offices: treasurer, 1906–1908; first vice president, 1908–1912; and finally president of the General Federation of Women's Clubs, 1916–1920. She was a member of the Woman's Committee of the Council of National Defense (*Who Was Who in America*, 4:208). Miss Maude Wetmore (1873–1951) was the daughter of a Rhode Island governor and senator. She was appointed to the Republican Women's National Committee in 1919. She also served as president of the Women's National Republican Club in 1928 and 1929 (*New York Times*, November 4, 1951, 85:1; *Who Was Who in America*, 3:906). Katharine Dexter (Mrs. Stanley) McCormick (1875–1967) attended MIT as a special student and earned a B.S. in 1904. In 1909, she became active in the suffrage movement and served as treasurer and vice president of NAWSA. During World War I, she was chair

full of ideas, the leaders of women in the country. And they took their job seriously. They supposed they had been appointed to organize the women to do real work. They did mobilize them. In every state women responded to their call, experienced women of ability.

The Woman's Committee and the States Relations Sections were amalgamated into the Field Division of the council. A man was made chairman, Grosvenor Clarkson, with Dr. Shaw vice chairman.[2] The acting director was Hannah Patterson, who had been director of the Woman's Committee. To be under a woman outraged the pride of these young men. Coming into the large room where we all worked one morning I was just in time to see one of them hold up an apple and say to the whole room. "See. I'm going to put it on her desk and say, 'Look, teacher, at the big red apple I've brought you.'"

Yet they were young men just out of college, and Hannah Patterson a mature woman, who had had a wide experience as manager of her father's extensive coal mines.

I thought of this when in the NRA twenty years later I was directing the activities of sixty men who took my chairmanship of the Consumers' Advisory Board as a matter of course, helping me in every way possible.

On the Woman's Committee, I had been in the Publicity Bureau, acting for Miss Tarbell who was then in Europe, after Mrs. Alline Wilkes (of the

---

of the NAWSA War Service Department and a member of the Woman's Committee of the Council of National Defense. With inherited money from her father and husband, she gave generously to suffrage, higher education for women, and the birth control movement (*NAW-Modern*, s.v. "McCormick, Katharine Dexter"). Clarinda Huntington Pendleton married Joseph Lamar in 1879. He was appointed to the United States Supreme Court in 1911. She held several offices in the National Society of the Colonial Dames of America: secretary, 1902–1910; vice president, 1910–1914; and president, 1914–1927. A member of the Woman's Committee of the Council of National Defense in 1917–1918, she wrote a history of the Colonial Dames (*Who Was Who in America*, 2:310). Miss Agnes Nestor (1880–1948) was a labor organizer, speaker, and administrator. She began her association with the International Glove Workers Union as vice president in 1903; in 1906 she was elected secretary-treasurer of the union, a paid position. In addition to her union association, she was also active in the National Women's Trade Union League, serving on its national executive board 1907 to 1948; she was president of the Chicago League from 1913 to 1948 (*DAB*, s.v. "Nestor, Agnes"). Hannah Patterson (1879–1937) was state chairman of the Woman's Suffrage Party of Pennsylvania, 1912–1915. In 1916, as corresponding secretary of NAWSA, she was a significant factor in getting both party platforms to endorse suffrage by state action. From 1917 to 1919, she was resident director of the Woman's Committee of the Council of National Defense. She was assistant to the secretary of war in 1919 and active in the Pennsylvania Federation of Republican Women (*NAW*, s.v. "Patterson, Hannah"; *Who Was Who in America*, 6:317).

2. Grosvenor Clarkson (1882–1937) was appointed assistant to the director of the U.S. Council of National Defense in February 1917. In the following month, he was made secretary of the council; in July 1918, he became acting director and finally served as director from December 1918 to March 1920 (*Who Was Who in America*, 1:227).

beautiful red hair) resigned.[3] With the consolidation, Miss Tarbell became titular head of the new Publicity Bureau, with a man acting for her, and I was under him. Since, however, he spent most of his day about town, the routine fell to me. Through this "Ivy Lee of the Western Coast," as he was called, I learned much about a new kind of publicity that, if I was never able to practice, I did learn to recognize. He was far more effective than I with all my bulletins and statements, some of which I realized had only the purpose of keeping me from interfering with him. But his method had at least the advantage of being painless to his coworker. When he left he confided to me that I had been a liberal education to him. What he meant I do not know. If he ever knew how much he taught me, he did not reveal it.

All of this was not without its effect on my feminism nor the discovery that, though I received only sixteen hundred dollars a year, a man subordinate to me was paid almost twice that much. Yet when it was desirable to get an article into print, I had to do it, even though it was his business.

I should not cavil at that, for these articles led an editor to ask me to do some for him. I was delighted.

But to get an order for an article was one thing. To get the article quite another, as I was to discover. The first article was about Mary Van Kleeck, the chief of the war emergency Women's Labor Bureau.[4] With my suffrage-made ideas as to the value of publicity, I expected her to be delighted at an opportunity to publicize her work. To my chagrin, I found her far more interested in preventing any misinterpretation of her work than in advertising it. Facts had to be pried out of her with a dentist's drill, and no words of hers could be quoted unless she herself OK'd the manuscript before the editor saw it. By the time she had transposed the sentences, it sounded more like a legal document than an article to woo readers!

I still wonder at the public official's fear of the printed word in those days. Journalists were to them species to be avoided if possible, and always to be censored and kept in their place. Human-interest stories were anathema.

In doing this article I had learned much about the problems of women in industry. A later one, "The Minimum Wage for Women"—there were eight in all covering many of the social subjects interesting to women—had a queer history. The editor of the *Ladies Home Journal* refused it with a letter saying that as they had ordered it, they would pay for it, but inasmuch as

---

3. Alline T. Wilkes was part of the administrative staff of the Woman's Committee of the Council of National Defense, serving as executive secretary to Ida Tarbell (ENB, *The Woman's Committee, United States Council of National Defense: An Interpretative Report*, 87).

4. Mary Van Kleeck (1883–1972) earned her A.B. at Smith College in 1904 and began her career as a social researcher. In 1910, she founded the Russell Sage Department of Industrial Studies, which she directed until her retirement in 1948. By the time of the New Deal, she had become an advocate of fundamental change in the economic system and admired Soviet collectivism (*NAW-Modern*, s.v. "Kleeck, Mary Van").

their conscience would not let them publish it, they were sending it back for me to use as I wished.[5] It would, they said, make the working women too discontented. Later I revamped it for the *Woman Citizen*.

When my first article came out, the magazine had printed below my name the words "of the Council of Defense." At once my chief sent for me. This would never do. Such a mention of my governmental connection was against all rules. As I had had nothing to do with using it, the incident was forgiven provided it did not happen again.

Amusing, this seems, in view of the way magazine pages today are strewn with the bylines of cabinet members and private secretaries. Dr. Shaw, who wrote each month a page for a monthly journal about "Women and War Work," felt that the money she received for it must be turned over to the committee. Even so, she was criticized for writing the articles, and especially for seeming to make the magazine a medium for reaching the women.

My work on the committee brought me into close contact with this remarkable woman, for it fell to me to compose the circular letters that went out under her signature. She would tell what she wanted to say, I would read several pages of her autobiography, *Story of a Pioneer*, to get her style, and make a draft for her approval.

"How can you make them sound like me?" she asked one day.

"If I were doing conversation in a story," I said, "I would make the characters talk as they would, not as I do."

Sometimes she penciled at the bottom of the sheet, "as I'd like to write and can't." Then I knew that I had failed. Again it would be, "Thanks for making me so elegant." I treasure these little notes as I do the letters from Woodrow Wilson that hang framed on my walls.

She was a great admirer of President Wilson even before the League of Nations. But that organization appealed to her for itself. She had long been an ardent member of the League to Enforce Peace. When she was asked to accompany William Howard Taft and President Lowell of Harvard on that historic tour to rouse the people's support of the League of Nations, she was just recovering from pneumonia.[6] We who loved her begged her not to go,

---

5. Edward Bok (1863–1930) became editor of *Ladies Home Journal* in 1889, retiring in 1920. Under his leadership, his magazine flourished, offering American women middle-class values and a sentimentalized vision of women. Although he gave thorough and laudatory coverage of women's contributions to the war effort, he opposed suffrage (*Dictionary of Literary Biography*, vol. 91, *American Magazine Journalists, 1900–1960*, s.v. "Bok, Edward").

6. Abbott Lawrence Lowell (1856–1943), who earned his law degree from Harvard in 1880, began teaching there in 1897. He was elected president of the university in 1909 and served in that capacity until 1933. An independent Republican, he supported Wilson and the League of Nations (*DAB*, s.v. "Lowell, Abbott Lawrence").

but she would not listen. "A good use for an old woman," she said. "Why should I spare myself when men have died for peace?"

The trip was her death sentence. She returned to be ill again, to get better, and then to drop off suddenly when we all rejoiced that she was getting well. The last thing she did before the final collapse was to listen to my friend, and hers, Caroline Reilley, read my "History of Woman's Committee."[7] I like to think how delighted she was with this account of the struggles of the committee. It had not been easy to do, that "interpretative report," as it was called. To get the information it was necessary for me to read all the minutes of the meetings of the council beginning with its organization in the August prior to the American declaration of war, and go over all the correspondence between the members of the Women's Committee and the council, as well as much of the correspondence of Dr. Shaw and Miss Patterson. It also required a thorough study of women's organizations, and finally a knowledge of what the women had really accomplished.

When I was through, I had covered the whole realm of women's war endeavors. From it came an interest I was never to lose in the effort of organized women to make life more safe and satisfactory for human beings.

It took me months to get my material and, when written, it, too, had to be so composed that there could not possibly be a misinterpretation. Finally it had to be approved by the secretary of war, Newton D. Baker, who wrote the foreword, and by each of the eleven members of the Woman's Committee.[8] The purpose of publishing it was to leave some record of the administrative problems involved for the benefit of those who might in the future be faced with similar problems.

Alas for this hope! When in 1933 the NRA was faced with a similar problem in connection with the organization of women, the little brochure was never once remembered, was not even known to exist by those who attempted the new work. By that time I had become accustomed to the hit-or-miss method of governmental endeavor. My idea of learning by mistakes and slowly evolving methods had been scrapped by experience.

Twice, only, I saw any of the people prominent in public life. When President Wilson spoke to the Senate for the suffrage amendment, Mrs. Bass took me to hear him. He sat, I remember, on the president's row of

---

7. Caroline Reilley was secretary to Dr. Shaw, the chairman of the Woman's Committee, Council of National Defense (*Boyd's 1918 Directory of the District of Columbia* [Washington, D.C.: R. K. Polk, 1918]; Council of National Defense, Woman's Committee Papers, introduction, M1074).

8. Newton D. Baker (1871–1937) practiced law in Cleveland, where he worked in the legal department in Mayor Tom Johnson's administration. In 1911, he was elected mayor of Cleveland and reelected in 1913. An early supporter of Woodrow Wilson, he was appointed secretary of war in 1916 (*DAB*, s.v. "Baker, Newton D.").

the senators' family gallery. The president I thought as superb a figure as I had ever seen. The day after the congressional elections of 1918 brought Republican victories. As I walked to work I noticed a wide-backed man ahead of me who was being stopped every few minutes by someone who shook his hand. I could see his wide back shake from side to side. When I came opposite I turned and looked over. He was ex-president Taft.

New methods of publicity and governmental methods were not all I learned this year. Under Miss Patterson's tutelage I learned the technique of administration. After many experiences with executives, I think I can safely say that she is one of the best I have ever known. Accurate, cautious, courageous, methodical, objective, she made work under and with her joy. Perhaps the most important thing of all I learned was that administration is a means, never an end. The end she ever kept in view both for herself and for her subordinates, so that you saw how your own work dovetailed into something bigger. To this patient, wise, and capable woman I have always been very grateful.

The actual work of the committee members who nominally headed the divisions was done by assistants, young college women experts, as the committeewomen were not often in residence. I think I got my dislike then of the system whereby one person heads an undertaking, or an organization, and takes the credit for its accomplishments while an underling does the job. I made up my mind that never would I let my name be used for anything I could not personally supervise, a promise to myself I have sometimes had to break, though never without discomfort.

I also noted with dismay the chances some of these members took with their reputation by allowing assistants to sign their names to letters and documents they had never seen. I always signed "Ida Tarbell" myself with fear and trembling and watched my man associate do it with suspicion.

During this year in Washington, two things happened that were to have an important bearing on my future work. At the time they seemed unrelated, but they were to join at a common point much later.

The first was a bit of personal publicity that was to dog me for many years, and give me an importance I would not otherwise have gained yet to be of much regret to me.

It happened this way:

When the resolution to submit a suffrage amendment to the Constitution was before Congress, Mrs. Catt sent for me and asked if I had any influence with Senator Reed of my state.[9] I told her I did not, but that as my husband and brother had very ardently supported him, he would, at least, listen to

---

9. James A. Reed (1861–1944) moved to Kansas City in 1887 to practice law. He served as prosecuting attorney of Jackson County 1898–1900, mayor of Kansas City 1900–1904, and Democratic U.S. senator 1911–1929 (*Biographical Directory of the U.S. Congress*, 1701).

what I said. She wanted me to ask him if he would refrain from speaking against the resolution, since she feared if he did speak, he would be vitriolic, and she hoped to key the argument to a different tone. As a result of this talk I wrote him a note saying, in effect, that I and many of his friends would be very happy if he felt he need not speak to the motion. Whether he ever got my note or not I do not know, though it was sent special delivery. At any rate, he did make the speech. I did not hear it myself, but I read in the papers that night under headlines all about it. The impression that the papers gave me—and I am a reader of average intelligence—was that he had attacked the suffragists personally, referring to the petticoats in the gallery who had come even to the halls of Congress.

As I read it, I felt that Missourians also had a right to resent it, as it did not express what I believed to be their sentiments.

Nor was I long in hearing from my suffragist friends. They were incensed by the tone, the manner, and the words of the attack. I got the *Congressional Record* and read it carefully. I felt the words used unpardonable in a serious discussion of a political measure. They revealed a contempt for women, an insult that should not, I believed, go unchallenged.

I wrote my friend Helen Miller to this effect, calling attention to the implication of his remarks that one did not know whether to receive a women with "kisses or kicks," and that only a little group of Missouri women were for it (though our state Democratic committee had endorsed it). I thought she would phrase any statement she might make herself, after reading the *Congressional Record.* Great was my surprise, therefore, to find a few days later that parts of my letter had been taken verbatim and broadcast throughout the state. Mrs. Miller had been absent from the office, and an overzealous subordinate had read my letter and sent it out.

Before I learned this, however, an old friend of Writers' Guild days, then sergeant at arms in the Senate, came to see me.[10] "Have you seen this?" he asked, showing me a Missouri paper.

I said I had not.

He then told me that I must have been misinformed. The senator had not attacked women, but only Sen. J. Hamilton Lewis, the senator from Illinois, when he used the words: "When a man comes upon you with doubled up fists and with the glare of battle in his eyes, you know what to do, but when you catch a flutter of lace, and your nostrils are intoxicated with a delicate perfume, you do not know whether you ought to resort to blows or embraces."[11]

---

10. Charles P. Higgins, from Missouri, was elected sergeant at arms of the United States Senate March 13, 1913. He served in that position until May 1919 (ibid., 295).

11. James Hamilton Lewis (1863–1939) served in the territorial legislature of Washington in 1887–1888 and as a Democratic member of the United States House of Representatives from Washington from 1897 to 1899. Moving to Illinois, he was an unsuccessful

He had come to me as a friend. He knew I would want to retract what I had said. Oh, no, the senator had not sent him. He had come on his own volition. He showed me a copy of the *Congressional Record.*

But the senator, even if he had not sent this emissary, was greatly annoyed. He meant to bring this up on the floor of the Senate, but was willing to give me time to make an apology. My friend was giving me the opportunity. He advised me to talk it over with people, find out how mistaken I was, and then give him a statement. He could persuade the senator to wait a few days.

I felt myself in a hole. I did not want to let the Missouri suffragists down, but neither did I want to be responsible for untruths. And I certainly did not want to be attacked on the floor of the Senate. I took his advice and discussed it with other people. What had the senator actually meant? I went to my usual source for honest, nonpartisan statement of fact: the newspapermen who sat in the press gallery. Opinions disagreed, but one of those expressed by a *New York Times* man seemed to me probably the correct one. "Those of us in the press gallery," he said, "who knew how the senators sometimes twitted the senator from Illinois because of his fastidious apparel might realize that Senator Reed referred to Senator Lewis, but those in the galleries who know nothing of this might well think he referred to the ladies."

This, I saw, was an old oratorical tactic: to imply one thing while technically saying another, to be able to claim one did not attack a person or a measure and yet leave all the stigma of attacks upon them.

"Certainly he meant to insult women. That is his usual method," said another newspaperman who admired the method.

I read the *Congressional Record* again. The application of his phrase depended upon the emphasis given the word *man.* As it read it could easily mean that the speaker did not know whether to meet women with a kiss or a kick. This to women, at least, did constitute an insult. To make a statement without indicating this would be cowardly and unfair to the suffragists. But to make this plain would partake of a further attack. This I did not want to make, gratuitously.

So when my sergeant-at-arms friend returned, I told him I was willing to make a statement, but that Senator Reed should make a request for a statement before I gave one.

"You realize," he said, "that what you wrote was libelous. You can be sued on it."

This was rather terrifying with my husband in France, but I stuck to my statement that there must first be a request from Senator Reed.

---

candidate for governor in 1908 and 1920. He served in the United States Senate from 1913 to 1919, was defeated, then reelected to serve from 1930 to 1939. From 1933 to 1939 he was the Democratic whip (ibid., 1369).

"Very well," he said, his friendliness disappearing. "You will have the request."

And so I did, but not until four years later, when I was on the Democratic National Committee.

But with the fear of a libel suit in mind, I appealed to lawyer friends in Missouri. They went over my letters and told me to refer the senator to them. And Senator Lewis gallantly took a copy of my letter and offered to defend me on the floor if it came up.

I have always regretted that I did not make that explanation, unsolicited. It would have been an attack, for I can be fairly vitriolic myself on occasion. But it would have left the issue clear. As it was, the senator could protest his innocence as to the literal application of those words, and thus seek to escape indictment on the insult to women that they really contained. My own position would have been clearer if this had been pointed out. Moreover, had it not been for this encounter my future opposition to him on the League of Nations question would have been on an impersonal basis.

Yet—so queer are politics—that incident was to prove an asset to me. I might have opposed the senator on questions of policy, and no more attention would have been paid to me than of thousands of others who disagreed with him. But this incident dramatized me as an opponent. Those who opposed him on other grounds put me forward as their spokesman; and those who agreed with him opposed me. Thus I gained a following and notoriety I would probably never otherwise have had. When I went to Washington three years later as vice chairman of the Democratic National Committee, it was the opposition of Senator Reed to me that made my appointment of interest, to politicians and newspapermen, and so gained me a hearing. That incident that I had never planned, indeed regretted, did more to make me considered a political leader than years of hard work could have done![12]

---

12. In a partial and incomplete draft of this section, ENB wrote more forthrightly: "Senator Reed never forgave me. He would have forgiven me still less if I had written the second letter. My subsequent opposition to him, so he has always charged, was motivated solely by that incident. As a matter of fact it was not. While I could never admire his type of oratory, nor his particular method of attack, I have followed other public men whose manners and temperament I do not commend because they stood for the same principles and measures I do. For many men who opposed suffrage on rational arguments I have spoken and worked. After it was won and they could not hurt it, I could support them for what they would support next.

"But when Senator Reed opposed the League of Nations I was bound to oppose him. I could never have supported anyone who led a fight against what I believed would make for peace unless he had stood for something else to my mind of equal importance. And he never has. All the things I believe in, he had opposed.

"And yet I must be honest. There is a deep antagonism between my temperament and the senator's. He is a masculinist through and through. I am a feminist. We stand at the opposite poles of thought as to what are the desirable things."

The second incident also dealt with politics. With the imminence of the passage of the suffrage resolution, the political parties were becoming aware of the potential woman vote. To win it, the Democratic organization had installed Mrs. George Bass as chairman of the Woman's Division and placed her on its Executive Committee as vice chairman. The Republicans had named my old friend Ruth McCormick to head a Woman's Republican Executive Committee.

Mrs. Bass, knowing of my Democratic family, had taken it for granted that I would be a Democrat. Mrs. McCormick, however, thought that I might choose my party on the basis of belief rather than tradition. Perhaps this flattered me. Perhaps her friendship did. At any rate, I rebelled at joining a party just because my family belonged to it. So I let them both talk to me. Strangely, their reasons for their party alignment seemed very much alike. But Ruth did have one argument that appealed to me. She was outlining a program of social reform to attract women to her party that she optimistically thought she could persuade Mr. Hays, the chairman of the Republican Committee, to accept.[13] Dear Mrs. Raymond Robins, with her heart open to all the world, but particularly to labor, was another member of this committee. Her idea that the government should set a minimum standard for citizenship appealed to me. I saw or thought I saw that the Republican belief in a centralized government made it possible for it to stand for such things as abolition of child labor, national minimum-wage laws, and a national workmen's compensation, which the Democratic Party, with its states' rights doctrine, could not.

I have one of those outmoded minds that likes to start with a philosophy or theory, and work from that to a program. The Republican theory gave me that opportunity. All the more receptive was I when Ruth asked me to help her draw up the program. With the assistance of Arthur MacMahon, a professor from Columbia then working in the Council of Defense, I did so.[14] Often I have wondered what some of my Republican opponents would think if they knew that I once tried to outline Republican policies. Ruth made a plausible case for what we could do together. She wanted me to help with the publicity. It seemed an opportunity to do something worthwhile. And the idea of such a program on either party was very inviting. I fear I had a wild idea that the

13. William H. Hays (1879–1954) had been active in Indiana local and state Republican Party politics before serving as chairman of the state central committee from 1914 to 1918. In 1917, he was chairman of the state Council of Defense. From 1918 to 1921 he was chairman of the Republican National Committee. He was Harding's postmaster general in 1921–1922 (*Biographical Directory of the U.S. Executive Branch, 1774–1971* [Westport, Conn.: Greenwood Press, 1971], 156–67).

14. Arthur MacMahon (1890–1980) earned his Ph.D. from Columbia University in 1913. A professor of public administration at Columbia, he was assistant secretary, chief of field division, of the Council of Defense from 1917 to 1919. He served on the U.S. Civil Service Commission from 1947 to 1950 (*Who Was Who in America*, 7:366).

Democrats might try to meet it, and we would have both parties falling over themselves in an effort to win the woman vote. Alas, for these impracticable dreams! We reckoned without the politicians. Whatever happened to our program I do not know. For, by the time Mr. Hays got around to tell Ruth, I had written her a letter that put an end to my possible Republicanism.

President Wilson had presented his plan for the League of Nations, and I realized that there were other things besides the welfare measures to be considered in making a party alignment. Ruth and I sat up until three o'clock one morning discussing it. She says with that taunting smile of hers that if she had kept me until four she would have had me. We were to finish the talk the next day at lunch, but the morning of that engagement I had a heartbroken note from her. Theodore Roosevelt had died suddenly the night before, and she was on her way to Sagamore Hill.[15] Before she had returned, the attack on Mr. Wilson had been launched, and I could not support that.

There were other things, too. I had grown up in a belief that a high tariff was wrong. I had argued the Bryan side as to trusts and railroads and the money question. I could not really become a Republican. So I wrote to Ruth that she could lay it to early prejudice if she wished, but I could not be with her. What I really had, I supposed, was one of those awful mugwump minds she abhorred.

But I was not through, as it happened, with the problem of political alignment. Almost immediately after this letter to Ruth, the Democratic National Committeeman from Missouri, Edward Goltra, arrived in Washington, sought me out, and asked me to be the Democratic associate national committeewoman from Missouri.[16] He did not know me himself, but mine was the name that had been suggested to him by the Missouri suffragists he had consulted. I told him frankly that I did not desire to go into politics. He asked me to think it over.

As a means of thinking it over, I went to the woman at the national Democratic headquarters, and Ellis Meredith, then acting for Mrs. Bass, took me in hand.[17] For hours she talked to me. "If women like you do not take these appointments," she said, "what complaint can you make about dirty politics?" I told her I was not even sure I was a Democrat. "But you are not a Republican," she said. "You know that. You may not like everything in the Democratic Party, but if you go in, you throw your influence there for the

---

15. Theodore Roosevelt died at Sagamore Hill on January 6, 1919.

16. Edward Goltra (1862–1939) earned his A.B. from Princeton in 1887. The owner of various iron and steel businesses in St. Louis, he became the national committeeman from Missouri in 1911 (*Who Was Who in America*, 1:466).

17. Ellis Meredith (1865–1955) married Henry H. Clement in 1913. A Colorado journalist and author, she wrote several novels and contributed to newspapers and magazines. She was a member of the Woman's National Democratic Club in Washington, D.C.

things you do want." She herself was a Progressive, and she believed firmly the Democratic Party more progressive than the Republican.

"You are a Progressive," she said. "Go in and make the Democratic Party more progressive." So she convinced me that I should accept the appointment. Then commenced for me a miserable week. No matter what the party did I would have to accept it. I felt I had yielded my liberty of conscience. I realized that Ellis had done just as Ruth had, concentrated on the things she liked in her party, and skipped lightly over the other things. I did not want to be like that. I wanted to stand outside both parties, and go for the candidate who gave me more nearly what I wanted.

By this time my husband had returned from abroad. I told him how I felt. "Then don't [do] it," he said. "Wire Mr. Goltra you have changed your mind." I wired Mr. Goltra and felt again a free woman. So, free forever, I hoped, of political entanglements, I went back to Missouri to join my husband.

7 Edging into Politics

I was not overjoyed to go back to Carthage. At what to me was a large salary, an assistant editorship of a magazine had been dangled in front of me.[1]

But home was where the husband was, and my husband's business was in southwest Missouri. During the war the mines in northern Oklahoma had opened up. In one year we had seen this land a prairie with grass waist high. In another, mining camps had sprung up, three towns had sprouted there of five thousand inhabitants each, mining towns with rows of shacks along the dusty streets, each house with a water barrel beside its door. And everywhere were the derricks and tracks and tramways of the mines.[2]

In ten years more some of them would be deserted, the schoolhouses closed, the houses crumbling. Such is a mining district. Almost overnight houses were put on wheels and carted off to some new camp, shopkeepers literally picked up their stocks, the machinery in the mills was dismantled to go groaning down the road. All that was left was an uncovered boiler too rusty to salvage, standing like a lonely symbol of the past. In our own county were many of these abandoned relics of mining camps.

Since Harry's chief clients were mining companies, Joplin was more convenient as his business center. It was eighteen miles from Carthage. So we moved there. Joplin was having another boom. The center of it was the Connor Hotel, with men surging back and forth, engineers, promoters, ore buyers.

"Why," asked the eastern promoters and investors, who sat at my dining table, "will they live in those awful shanties? They make four or five dollars a day." No use to explain that they do not work every day, not always a whole day at a time. A job today, none tomorrow! All day today, knocked off tomorrow! And the insecurity! Swinging down in the bucket into a deep shaft. Perhaps never coming up. A fallen slab. A pillar taken out by a greedy owner. A roof falling. The stope sliding down. A broken windlass. And miners' consumption, the dreaded "tiz," as they called it. How many weeks till it gets them? Why worry about a house? Live for the day—that's the ticket! But a

---

1. Possibly *Green Book* offered her an assistant editorship. She was on their staff in 1920–1921. *Delineator* may also have offered her a position (Newell Blair, oral history, Archives, Woman's National Democratic Club).

2. The last major ore discovery of the region was made at Picher, Oklahoma, in 1914. Production began in 1916 (Everett Ritchie, *Guidebook to the Tri-State Mineral Museum*, 2).

happy crowd, a carefree crowd, an uproarious crowd on Saturday night, all American born. Not a foreigner or a union man among them.

Such was the mining town in boom time. Then the decline of the boom. Mines shut down. Men out of work. Houses abandoned. A trek to another camp. Or a tent. Or a sullen staying without paying rent. The agitator. Meetings. The soup line. The welfare chest. The Connor lobby empty. Plenty of room on Main Street Saturday night. Engineers, managers going away; people you've known and liked, silently like the Arab. Stores empty.

Never mind. It would come back. It always had. It always would. Some of the miners would go to work picking berries, working in yards, or on the road. Some grub in the tailing piles. Prospectors hunting for "pockets" of ore. Practical mining men leasing the big abandoned properties. They would work them in their small, their primitive way, just enough work to prevent forfeiture and so be ready for another boom, when they might sell them to the eastern broker who would issue bonds for suckers to buy and put in again new and expensive machinery and mine in the approved, the mining-school, way, until again the boom declined. It had always been that way. It always would. At least, so they used to say.

Joplin was still in her boom when we went there. A busy place and colorful, with people from many places, interested in music, in languages, in new houses, in books, and in social welfare. The mining companies, guided by a young man from the Public Health Service, the Dr. Parran who was to become the surgeon general of the United States, were putting on a fight begun in 1917 by Dr. Royd Sayers against tuberculosis.[3] Rules and regulations had been adopted, baths installed, an educational campaign waged, a county sanitarium was being urged. Into this I threw myself with interest.

We took an apartment at the Olivia, and I settled down to write again.[4] Two articles for the *Ladies Home Journal*, then a trip to Washington to read proof on my government book, a two-months' publicity job for an antituberculosis state campaign that took me to St. Louis, and it was 1920, the campaign year, with suffrage nearly won. But still I had no thought of politics as I struggled on with my not very successful writing.

In February came a suffrage convention in Chicago, a jubilation convention with the women so relaxed that they even had a fashion show at the Congress

---

3. Thomas Parran (1892–1968) earned his M.D. from Georgetown University in 1915. He was surgeon general from 1936 to 1948. He was dean of the graduate school of public health, University of Pittsburg, 1948–1958 (*Who Was Who in America*, 4:734). Royd Sayers (1885–1965) was professor of electrochemistry at the University of Buffalo, 1911–1913. He then served as medical director of the U.S. Public Health Service and chief of the Division of Industrial Hygiene, National Institute of Health, from 1933 to 1940 (ibid., 7:503).

4. The Olivia Apartments were located at 320 Moffet Street.

Hotel, girls appearing in old dresses of the styles worn since the first suffrage convention in Seneca Falls in 1840.[5] It was then Mrs. Catt made the statement that gave such pleasure to Mrs. Bass and Mrs. McCormick as heads of the Democratic and Republican Women's Committees. "The time has come," she said, "when I must urge you to go where I cannot follow—onto the political parties." So jubilant was Mrs. Bass that, as we left the hall, she caught my arm and led me into her headquarters. Still, I had no intention of becoming part of the Democratic organization.

After the convention I stayed on to attend Mrs. Catt's "Citizenship School," where university professors and practical politicians instructed us in the game of politics. The *Green Book* had asked me to do a series of articles orientating women in politics, nonpartisan articles.[6] I meant to keep nonpartisan as I thought a journalist should. I went back to Joplin still on the political sidelines. When I finally got into politics, it was not because of any conviction that I should, but for the reason that I was being kept out of them.

The state convention of the League of Women Voters, an organization formed as a residuary legatee of the suffragists' hopes and ideas, was meeting in Joplin. I took an active part in it. Immediately, the local politicians decided that it was a new women's party and proceeded to fight it and the women connected with it. Came the state Democratic convention to Joplin.[7] A state convention promised to be an interesting show. As a journalist I wanted to see it. With some friends I presented myself at the door. The doorkeeper, a Joplin politician, refused to let me in. While I still protested, a Carthage friend came by.

"What!" said Gene Roach, editor of the Carthage paper.[8] "Emily Newell kept out of a Democratic convention! Come with me."

The doorkeeper still barred the door.

---

5. The national suffrage convention, held in Chicago, February 12–18, 1920, was a joint convention with the League of Women Voters.

6. Beginning in May, each month ENB published an article in *Green Book* on politics: "What Shall We Do with It?" (May 1920): 20–23; "I Nominate—" (June 1920): 79–82, 107; "Platforms for Women" (July 1920): 22–24, 96, 98; "Where the Money Comes From" (August 1920): 42–45, 103, 104; "Women Planks in the Platforms" (September 1920): 30–32, 111; "Your Candidate and Mine" (October 1920): 52–55, 116; "The Woman Vote" (November 1920): 20–23; and "Paying Election Debts" (December 1920): 46–49.

7. The state League of Women Voters met in Joplin on May 18, 1920. The state Democratic convention opened in Joplin on April 22, 1920.

8. Eugene B. Roach (1869–1939) came to Carthage in 1910 where his brother Cornelius owned the *Carthage Democrat*. Gene became the editor and publisher of the *Carthage Democrat* and the *Jasper County Democrat*. He was president of the Ozark Press Association in 1924 and of the Missouri Press Association in 1925. He also served as state publicity manager for the Democratic Party in 1925 (*Missouri Historical Review* 34 [October 1939]: 131; "Cornelius Roach and Descendants, as of September 1968," ed. Constance M. Roach, Box 9, Edna Gellhorn Papers).

"You can't keep her out," said Mr. Roach. "She has a Carthage proxy." He pushed me on in front of him.

"But I haven't any proxy," I told him.

"Of course you have," he said, leading me up to the gallery where the Jasper County delegation sat. A sergeant at arms came up to question my right to be there. "She's a Carthage delegate," said Mr. Roach. "She has a proxy." He thrust a paper in my hand. So I found myself a labeled Democrat.

Why these men wanted to exclude me was not exactly clear. The reason given was that I was a member of the League of Women Voters, and so could not be a Democrat. But there was more to it than that. Instinctively, some of them feared the suffragists with their reforming ideas.

Harry was as usual a delegate to the convention. He was also the manager of a friend's candidacy for the Democratic nomination as state supreme court judge. In later years Harry was to laugh that his politics were like some men's religion—in his wife's name. But he was always a delegate to conventions, always interested in someone's candidacy, always a worker at elections, always in the know, and his contributions expected. Without his knowledge and his advice I could never have gotten into politics myself. For politics was a man's game. A woman on her own had as much chance in them as a Du Pont to sit in President Roosevelt's cabinet.

The convention was a revelation to me as to political method. Away down on the platform a man rose to speak. He was met by hisses and groans. Feet stomped. Not a word could be heard. The din continued, an hour, two hours. We adjourned for supper, reconvened. The noise began again. The Kansas City delegation was refusing to let the convention go on unless it would ratify its choice of Senator Reed as one of its district delegates to the national convention. Ordinarily, of course, a United States senator was one of the state's four delegates at large, but because of the senator's opposition to President Wilson and the League of Nations, the convention had refused to name him. His district was determined to have him as a district delegate. The convention would not even have that.[9]

At last a stout, motherly woman was put on the platform. Whether in curiosity or surprise, the noise ceased. "There are more women voters in Missouri than all the Democratic votes in Kansas City," Mrs. Martin began.[10]

---

9. James Reed's opposition to the League of Nations, combined with his refusal to support woman suffrage, united his opponents with the result that the state Democratic convention refused to name him as a delegate to the national convention.

10. Katherine (Mavity) Martin (b. 1872) taught at the State Normal University in Normal, Illinois. She was married to Professor W. W. Martin, who had been dean of education at Cape Girardeau, Missouri, State Teachers School. President of the Missouri Federation of Women's Clubs, she was a member of the first Women's Democratic State Committee. Active in the suffrage movement, the WCTU, and a member of the Missouri Writers' Guild, she published several short stories and articles. In 1920, she was

Why, she was talking politics. Not a word of sentiment—just common sense. When she finished, the whole audience stood and cheered. "It was," said one of the delegates, "just like Ma talking to Pa."

After that there were more speeches. The Kansas City delegation must either have become worn out, or the leaders have come to some agreement. We on the floor did not know. But at six in the morning, a vote was taken. Not, however, as at any women's convention I had ever attended. Up in our gallery a local leader appeared; the others huddled around him. He told us how we should vote. Another man postulated. The first outvoiced him. A woman protested. He told her to keep still. He spoke so loud and fast that no one could get in a word. He put the question. Came a chorus of no's and aye's. I had no idea how we stood, nor did any one else but, when the secretary of the convention called for our Jasper County vote, it was given.

At eight o'clock in the morning my husband and I went across the street to the station lunchroom for breakfast, and I caught a train to Cassville, a town about forty miles away, where I made two speeches on women in politics. Returning home on the midnight train I went at once to work on an article that had to be in the mail the next night. When it was off, I went to bed and slept for twenty-four hours.

In June I went to the two national political conventions. The National League of Women Voters had planned a pilgrimage to them to urge certain planks in their party platforms that they believed would be of interest to women. They had asked me to go with them to act as a courier. They were also desirous that I give some publicity to their planks. I had already promised an article on the conventions to *Green Book*. I hoped to do another that ultimately I sold to *Current History* magazine.[11]

The Republican convention was held in Chicago when the city was having one of its hot spells. I had only one thin gown, a brown organdy. At the end of the convention it was a rag. Something different, this convention, I discovered, from the St. Louis convention of 1916 just four years before. The suffrage resolution had not been ratified by the thirty-sixth state, but it seemed only a matter of weeks until it would be, and the politicians, knowing that the women would undoubtedly vote in November, were wooing them industriously. Herbert Hoover, who was one of the candidates for the Republican nomination, had a whole floor of the Auditorium Hotel set aside

---

a delegate to the Democratic State Convention in Joplin and the Democratic National Convention in San Francisco. She also served in the Missouri Constitutional Convention of 1922 (*Missouri State Journal,* January 21, 1922, clipping in Folder 21, Box 23, Edward Goltra Papers; *Missouri Manual, 1923–1924;* "Biographical and Genealogical Sketches of Members Attending the Missouri Constitutional Convention, 1922–1923," typescript, State Historical Society of Missouri Library, Columbia, Missouri).

11. "Women at the Conventions," *Current History* 13 (October 1920): 26–28.

for women's organizations. Mrs. Lowdon and her daughter received the women daily in a hotel suite; Mrs. Harding did the same in a ballroom at another hotel.[12] These candidates had paid the women a high compliment, that of selecting for their women managers women of attainment. One, a woman professor from the University of Chicago; another, the woman editor of a national magazine.[13] The men delegates were gracious to the women, welcomed them, sought them out. Even the representatives of the League of Women Voters were treated as honored guests and their proposed planks given a courteous hearing. It was the same when later we came to the Democratic convention in San Francisco. Women were everywhere. Their leader, Mrs. George Bass, even presided at a convention session. Every candidate's nomination was seconded by a woman, and their short, clever speeches were given tremendous applause. At the great debate of the convention on the Prohibition plank of the platform, Anna Dickey Olesen of Minnesota divided honors with the party's most eloquent speakers, William Jennings Bryan and Bourke Cockran. When Senator Glass presented the report of the Resolutions Committee, he said, "Ladies, if we have forgotten anything you want, just ask us again."[14]

---

12. The Republican convention opened on June 8, 1920, in Chicago. Herbert Hoover (1874–1964), a successful international mining engineer, had headed the Commission for Relief in Belgium in 1914. When the United States entered World War I, Wilson appointed him food administrator. In 1920, there was mild support for him to be the Republican presidential nominee. In 1899 he had married Lou Henry (*DAB*, s.v. "Hoover, Herbert"). Florence Pullman, daughter of railroad car manufacturer George Pullman, married Frank Lowden in 1896. Mr. Lowden (1861–1943) served in Congress 1906–1919 and eight years on the Republican National Committee, ending in 1912. In 1916 he was elected reform governor of Illinois. In 1920 he was a leading candidate for the Republican presidential nomination (*DAB*, s.v. "Lowden, Frank"). Florence Kling (1860–1921) married Warren G. Harding in 1891. Ambitious for her husband, she actively promoted his political career. The Congress Hotel housed the Harding Women's Headquarters (*NAW*, s.v. "Harding, Florence Kling").

13. ENB was possibly referring to Marie M. Meloney (1878–1943), who was editor of the *Delineator* from 1921 to 1926. She was a close friend and supporter of Herbert Hoover (*NAW*, s.v. "Meloney, Marie M.").

14. The Democratic national convention met in San Francisco, June 28–July 5, 1920. Anna Dickie Olesen (1885–1971) had served as vice president of the Minnesota State Federated Women's Clubs, 1916–1918. A member of the advisory board of directors of the Minnesota League of Women Voters in 1920, she served on the Democratic National Committee from 1917 to 1924. She was the Democratic nominee for Minnesota's U.S. senator in 1922 and a candidate for the House in 1932. She was postmaster of Northfield, Minnesota, 1933–1934; state director of the NRA, 1934–1935; and a member of the National Emergency Council, 1934–1938 (*Who Was Who in America*, 7:435). William Bourke Cockran (1854–1923) emigrated from Ireland to the United States at age seventeen. After practicing law in New York, he was elected as a Democrat to the United States House of Representatives and served 1887–1889. Not a candidate for reelection, he was then elected to fill a vacancy in the House in 1890. Reelected, he served from

In 1920 the men did respect and fear the woman vote. So did they believe that women voters would respond to recognition of women. They really believed that women had brought a new factor into politics. They had yet to learn that there are as many kinds of women as there are of men and that they are subject to the same motivations as their husbands, fathers, and sons.

Prominent at the Republican convention were Ruth McCormick and Alice Longworth. Ruth was staying at the Harold McCormick house on Michigan Avenue. Having breakfast with her there one morning in her room, she twitted me with my Democracy, talked with her old frankness.

Alice Longworth drove with us to the convention. "I don't think I can stand those nominating speeches," she said.

"Be careful," Ruth said to her. "Emily's a Democrat."

Alice peered at me with those Mona Lisa eyes of hers. "But she can't be that!" she exclaimed.

She had for me a peculiar fascination, has today. It springs from the suggestion of daring she conveys, the air of mystery. But it is not subject to analysis. One either feels it or one does not. To me she explained those historic women of the boudoir and the salon who have exerted their informal influence on events. When I reached home, I found that Mr. Harding's nomination had given me a reputation as a political prognosticator.[15] Why, away back in the early spring I had predicted that he would be the nominee! I dug into my memory and recalled that sure enough, on the theory there would be a convention fight and that he would be very acceptable to certain leaders, I had thought of him as a logical compromise. As the preconvention fight for delegates went on, I had forgotten all about it, and was as surprised as anyone else when he was nominated.

On our way to San Francisco the league delegation made a tour by way of Omaha, Denver, Cheyenne, Great Falls, Spokane, Seattle, and Portland, holding meetings at each place. So I saw for the first time the Northwest, and fell completely in love with it. The queer feeling of being high up in the world

---

1891 to 1895. After bolting the party in opposition to free silver and support of McKinley, he returned in 1900 to the party and served again in the House 1904–1909 and again from 1921 to his death. He was a delegate to the Democratic National Conventions in 1884, 1892, 1904, and 1920 (*DAB*, s.v. "Cockran, William Bourke"). Carter Glass (1858–1946), a newspaper publisher in Virginia, was first elected to the United States House of Representatives in 1902 where he served as a Democrat for sixteen years. A member of the Banking and Currency Committee, he became known as the "Father of the Federal Reserve System." In 1919, he was appointed secretary of the treasury and in 1920 to fill a Senate vacancy. He remained in the United States Senate until his death (*DAB*, s.v. "Glass, Carter").

15. Although Warren G. Harding had won the Michigan presidential preference primary, he was not considered a major contender. When the major candidates—Leonard Wood, Frank Lowden, and Hiram Johnson—deadlocked, the convention turned to dark-horse Harding.

experienced on the Wyoming plateau. The mountains of Montana rising out of the lush green. Seattle with its ocean front yard and lake backyard, with mountains thrown in for a backdrop. I remember a most charming women's club where we stayed while there. Portland with its enormous pink roses growing in the parkways, its Stanford White hotel, its fresh salmon and strawberries. The daughter of an old pioneer took us up the Columbia River to a Midway House for lunch, and I was distraught because I wanted not to miss a moment of the scenery on either side of the car, and at the same time not a word of hers as she described her mother's pioneer trip to Oregon in a covered wagon.

None of it looks so lovely to me today, and I wonder if it is because it is more familiar or not quite so new and fresh itself.

One incident at Portland amused us greatly. We were sitting at the wide hotel window watching the parade of the Shriners, who were holding a national convention.

"Shriners?" said a Boston lady, shocked at the bizarre costumes. "Never heard of them. We don't have them in Boston."

At just that moment the flag of Boston came in sight, the men the most spectacularly garbed we had seen.

She led the laugh on herself.

Then, at San Francisco, the Fairmont, a hotel of another day when there was time for space and looking out of wide windows and walking up and down wide staircases laid with red carpet.

The women in the group were interesting. Maude Wood Park, president of the league, looking like a madonna in her blond, braided coronet, whose keen mind had led the congressional lobby for the suffrage resolution; Dr. Valeria Parker, with a penchant for speaking out on hygiene that gave our Victorian prudery moments of great embarrassment; Pattie Jacobs, globe-trotter and state politician; Dr. Rude, late of the Children's Bureau, returning to California where, she said, women could really be well groomed, because their feet did not swell with the heat and their gloves stick; and Mabeth Paige, who was to be so many years in the Minnesota legislature. In San Francisco we were joined by Mary E. McDowell, director of the University of Chicago Settlement with her droll wit; Mrs. Pennybacker, the fiery orator of the General Federation of Women's Clubs and later president of the famous Chautauqua Woman's Club; Mrs. Edwards, the inventive publicity genius who helped to run the Harding campaign; and last but far from least to anyone who knew her, Mrs. Gifford Pinchot, colorful and frank.[16]

---

16. Maude Wood Park (1871–1955) graduated from Radcliffe in 1898 and became president of the Massachusetts Woman Suffrage Association in 1900 and was active in organizing college women. In 1901, she accepted a paid position as executive secretary

Edna Gellhorn, the Brunhild of the suffragists and later the darling of the league, had left us at Omaha.[17] It was there that Mrs. Pinchot convulsed her audience by saying, "After hearing all these others tell what they have done, I have come to the conclusion that the only thing of importance I have ever done is to marry my husband." Since then, she has done many things, even running for Congress.

The San Francisco convention stands out as the most enjoyable I ever attended. Not only was it delightfully cool, the hotels uncrowded, the food marvelous, but there was the beautiful auditorium with its great organ. It was, moreover, the most harmonious Democratic National Convention I was ever to attend, although that impression may have sprung from my lack of personal responsibility, inasmuch as all I had to do was to speak to the

---

for the Boston Equal Suffrage Association. In 1917, she went to Washington to work for NAWSA's congressional committee, and in 1920, she was elected the first president of the League of Women Voters. A Republican, she became head of the Women's Joint Congressional Committee, lobbying Congress for social reform and feminist causes (*NAW-Modern*, s.v. "Park, Maude Wood"). Dr. Valerie Parker (1879–1959) received her M.D. from the Chicago Homeopathic Medical College in 1902. After serving as field secretary for the Connecticut Social Hygiene Association, 1914–1919, she joined the staff of the American Social Hygiene Association from 1919 to 1936. She was executive secretary of the U.S. Interdepartmental Hygiene Board in 1921–1922 and director of the Institute on Marriage and the Home, 1936–1937. She was president of the National Council of Women of the U.S., 1925–1929, and served as third vice president of the Democratic Woman's Club (*Who Was Who in America*, 3:957). Dr. Anna E. Rude, a physician with the Children's Bureau, headed the Division of Maternal and Infant Hygiene when it was formed in 1922. Mabeth (Mrs. James) Paige received her legal training at the University of Minnesota College of Law in 1900. She was a Republican member of the Minnesota House of Representatives, 1923–1945 (*Who's Who of American Women, 1958–1959* [Chicago: A. N. Marquis, 1959], 1:976). Mary Eliza McDowell (1854–1936), born in Cincinnati, moved with her family to Chicago, then Evanston, Illinois. There she met Frances Willard and became active in the WCTU. In 1890, she moved to Hull House. In 1894 she became head resident of the University of Chicago Settlement, remaining in that position until she was seventy-four. In 1923, reform mayor William Dever appointed her commissioner of public welfare where she remained until 1927. The first president of the Illinois WTUL, she was connected with the national WTUL from 1903 until her death (*DAB*, s.v. "McDowell, Mary Eliza"). Anna J. Hardwicke (Mrs. Percy V.) Pennybacker, from Texas, was national president of the General Federation of Women's Clubs, 1912–1916 (*Who's Who in the Nation's Capital, 1926–1927* [Washington, D.C.: W. W. Publishing, 1927], 452). Cornelia (Bryce) Pinchot (1881–1960) married Gifford Pinchot in 1914. In 1918–1919 she was secretary of the Pennsylvania Woman Suffrage Association. A Republican, she served on the state committee. Beginning in 1928, she made three unsuccessful attempts at election to Congress. In 1934, she ran for governor (*NAW-Modern*, s.v. "Pinchot, Cornelia").

17. Edna Fischel (1878–1970) graduated from Bryn Mawr in 1900 and married George Gellhorn, professor of obstetrics and gynecology at Washington University in St. Louis. An officer in the St. Louis and Missouri Equal Suffrage Associations, she was always a volunteer. Active in the organization of the League of Women Voters, she became vice

Resolutions Committee for the Women in Industry plank offered by the League of Women Voters.

The only real conflict was over the seating of Senator Reed, whom the Kansas City delegation presented, in spite of the action of the state convention, as its delegate. First, before the national committee, and again before the Credentials Committee, it argued its case for him, the Mrs. Martin who had won the state convention at Joplin appearing to oppose it. The real fight on seating Senator Reed was not, of course, based on his opposition to women, but on his opposition to President Wilson and the League of Nations. And of this Mrs. Martin made good use. But it gave suffragists satisfaction to know that it was a woman's wit and oratory that had furnished the chief weapon against him. Again Mrs. Martin spoke, and again she was effective. When she sat down, Senator Glass said, "I apologize for ever opposing suffrage." And the leader of the Kansas City delegation named her the ablest "man" on the other side.

Had I known Ed Moore, the national committeeman from Ohio then as I did later, I would have taken the nomination of his candidate, Governor Cox, as a foregone conclusion. For never was there a floor manager to compare with him as he padded about on his tennis shoe–clad feet. And there was Bernice Pyke, working with the women, Ohio's beautiful, white-haired, and brown-eyed committeewoman, who is perhaps the most astute woman politician produced by suffrage.[18] The chant from the gallery that rose at every opportunity, "O-hi-o, O-hi-o," is as associated with that convention as the words, "Alabama Casts Twenty-six Votes for Oscar Underwood" were to be with the deadlock convention of Madison Square Garden.

Mitchell Palmer was also a candidate, with Justina Wilson buttonholing the women delegates and urging his "progressivism" on them, and Mrs. Owen, the wife of the Oklahoma senator, campaigned for her husband by means of afternoon receptions, while little Antoinette Funk took delegations aside

---

president of the national organization and the first president of the state branch (*NAW-Modern*, s.v. "Fischel, Edna").

18. Edmond H. Moore (1862–1925) was mayor of Youngstown, Ohio, from 1896 to 1900. He served on the Democratic National Committee, 1912–1920 (*Who Was Who in America*, 1:859). The leading Democratic presidential candidates were Attorney General A. Mitchell Palmer, Wilson's son-in-law William G. McAdoo, and Ohio governor James Cox. Requiring forty-four ballots, the nomination finally went to Cox. Bernice (Mrs. Arthur B.) Pyke (1879?–1964) moved from the suffrage campaign to partisan politics in the Democratic Party. From 1932 to 1933, she was Cleveland's director of public welfare; from 1934 to 1953, she was collector of customs for the Port of Cleveland. She had been a vice president of NAWSA, a delegate to the Democratic National Convention in 1920, and a member of the Democratic National Committee in the 1930s (Marian J. Morton, *Women in Cleveland: An Illustrated History*, 197; Ruth Neely, ed., *Women of Ohio: A Record of Their Achievements in the History of the State*, 3:1085).

to whisper that when the moment came William Gibbs McAdoo was really the man.[19]

I had there my first sight of Franklin D. Roosevelt, an Adonis in modern dress.[20]

With the opening speech of the convention by Homer Cummings, the chairman of the Democratic National Committee, setting forth cogently in English of the classical tradition the progressivism of Woodrow Wilson, I wondered that I could ever have hesitated to be a Democrat.[21] I list this as one of the three greatest political speeches I have ever heard. The others, the League of Nations speech of Newton Baker at Madison Square Garden, and the Jackson Day–dinner speech of Claude Bowers in 1928.

One of the pleasant experiences was a dinner with my old friend Winifred Black in her bungalow on the bluff facing the Bay. She had had much sorrow since I had seen her, and her rich personality had mellowed, deepened. There I met Helen Grenfell, for so long Colorado's superintendent of schools.[22] I remember how pleased I was when the chairman of the Colorado delegation told me that on anything in regard to women or their interest in legislation he took Mrs. Grenfell's advice. In my ignorance or innocence I thought it would be only a short time until all political leaders would thus defer to their women associates.

And there was a dinner given by a local forum to the visiting newspaper "trained seals" as they called the feature correspondents: William Allen White, Edna Ferber, Dorothy Dix, Mark Sullivan. I was not familiar then with this pleasant custom of making such guests pay for their supper by a speech, and certainly never expected to be one of them. Edna Ferber, with her imitation of a nominating speech, was amusing, but only one of these "talks"

---

19. Justina Leavitt (Mrs. Halsey) Wilson (1870–1955) received her A.B. from the University of Minnesota in 1913. She served as national secretary of NAWSA in 1917. She was director of education for the Democratic National Committee (1922–1924) and conducted suffrage schools and schools of democracy (Howes, *American Women, 1935–1940*, s.v. "Wilson, Justina Leavitt"). Daisy Deane Hester married Robert Owen in 1889. In 1907, the new state legislature of Oklahoma elected him to the United States Senate. He was reelected in 1912 and 1918 (*DAB*, s.v. "Owen, Robert").

20. Franklin D. Roosevelt had given a speech in favor of Al Smith, but when Ohio governor James M. Cox was finally nominated, he chose FDR to be his vice presidential running mate.

21. Homer Cummings (1870–1956) was national committeeman from Connecticut from 1900 to 1925. He was vice chairman from 1913 to 1919 and chairman from 1919 to 1920. In 1920, he gave the keynote address in support of Wilson. Floor manager for FDR in the 1932 convention, he was named attorney general in 1933 and served for six years (*DAB*, s.v. "Cummings, Homer").

22. Helen L. Grenfell (d. 1935) was Colorado superintendent of public instruction from 1899 to 1905. A suffrage leader and Democratic political leader, she also served on the Colorado prison board for two terms (*Denver Post*, July 26, 1935).

has remained in my memory, that of Simeon Strunsky, who seems himself to have been forgotten, though he wrote that really fine book *Akhnaton*.[23]

At the convention a resolution was passed requiring each state to present the name of a national committeewoman. Up to that time the women on the committee, having been only associate committeewomen, had been appointed by the committeemen. Missouri had had two of these associate committeewomen since I had turned down Mr. Goltra's appointment: beautiful Barbara O'Neil of St. Louis and Mrs. Burris Jenkins of Kansas City, the wife of an eloquent minister.[24] To conform to the new rule, the delegation had now to elect a committeewoman. I was approached and asked to become a candidate. But though I knew now that I was a Democrat, my part, I felt sure, was to be merely that of a sympathetic private in the ranks.

In this mind I went home to Joplin.

I have sometimes pondered what it was the war did to my situation. It is hard to put into words, but it was something like a Rubicon I had passed, or maybe more like a flood that had wiped away certain prejudices and sentiments. For thereafter it was taken for granted by myself and everyone else that I should pursue extrahome activities to any extent I wished, even if they took me away from home for weeks.

----

23. William Allen White (1868–1944) bought the *Emporia Gazette* in 1895. After the turn of the century, he supported progressive measures. In 1924, he ran for governor of Kansas when neither major party candidate would oppose the Klan (*DAB*, s.v. "White, William Allen"). Edna Ferber (1885–1968) worked for the *Milwaukee Journal* until 1905 when ill health forced her to quit. She then began writing novels, plays, and short stories. In 1912 and 1920, she reported on the political conventions (*DAB*, s.v. "Ferber, Edna"). Mark Sullivan (1874–1952), muckraking journalist and progressive Republican, was the Washington correspondent for the *New York Evening Post* from 1919 to 1923. He then moved to the *New York Tribune* where he had a syndicated column (*DAB*, s.v. "Sullivan, Mark"). Simeon Strunsky (1879–1948) published in 1928 *King Akhnaton: A Chronicle of Ancient Egypt*. A collection from his *New York Times* column, "Topics of the Times," from 1933 to 1947 was compiled and published in 1956.

24. Barbara Blackman married David N. O'Neil in 1903. Active in the suffrage movement, she was president of the St. Louis League from 1912 to 1916, first vice president of State Association, and acting president in 1918–1919. She was also a member of the executive committee of NAWSA. In 1919 she was the first woman appointed to the Democratic National Committee for Missouri. In the 1916 suffrage demonstration at the Democratic convention in St. Louis, she portrayed the Statue of Liberty in the tableau on the steps of the Art Museum (Mary Semple Scott, ed., "History of Woman Suffrage Movement in Missouri," 283; Avis Carlson, *The League of Women Voters in St. Louis: The First Forty Years, 1919–1959*, 6; John Leonard, ed., *The Book of St. Louisans: A Biographical Dictionary of Leading Men of the City of St. Louis*, s.v. "O'Neil, David"). Mattie Hocker married Burris Jenkins in 1894. A writer and minister, he was an editor of the *Kansas City Post* and the minister of the Linwood Boulevard Christian Church. When Barbara O'Neil resigned, Mattie Jenkins replaced her on the national committee (*Missouri Historical Review* 39 [July 1945]: 571–72; Walter Williams and Floyd Shoemaker, *Missouri: Mother of the West*, 5:424–45).

Another thing the war did. It organized and gave a direction to my
theretofore rather sketchy and unrelated social efforts. Up to the time of the
Woman's Committee work, I had done my stint of personal charity helping
others, largely, I suspect, because it made me uncomfortable to see people
suffer on my doorstep; and I had also given my vocal support to such remedial
measures as were brought to my attention by the federated clubs. But after
the Woman's Committee work I thought in terms of longtime programs on
such things as child welfare, women in industry, high cost of living, prison
reform. I began to consider the social system, its injustices and casualties, and
what might be done to improve it. Yet I felt sure my own work was, except
for local activities, to be confined to writing.

On my return from the conventions the demands of homework crowded in
upon me. The children being home on vacation, there was plenty to occupy
my time.

Then I received a visit from my suffragist friend Laura Brown.[25] She was
alarmed, not to say annoyed. The positions on the county and Democratic
committees that had been newly created for women were to be handed by the
men leaders to their wives and some women they had picked out, women who
though very nice themselves were not at all interested in women becoming
effective in politics.

At once my feminism was up in arms. It was not in order to give these
men two votes instead of one in party matters that we women had worked for
the vote. Something, I saw, had to be done about it. Consulting my husband
I soon learned what it was. We women interested in women's activities and
opinions would have to select our own candidates for these positions and
get them elected. It was not so difficult. Through our almshouse campaign
and our war work, we had made the acquaintance of the women who had
an interest in public affairs, not only in the precincts of our own county,
but throughout our congressional district. All we had to do was to find out
which ones were Democrats, and tell them what was at stake. So, getting into
Laura's motorcar, she and I spent the afternoons visiting our friends. There
were jaunts into the country to those living in the farming precincts, others
to Carthage, Webb City, and Sarcoxie. After that, to the county seats of the
other counties in our district. When we explained matters to these women,
they were quite willing to run themselves or to find someone who would.

When the newly elected Jasper County committee met, we had such a
majority of women in favor of our candidate for the woman county vice

---

25. Laura (Mrs. Thornton) Brown had been a civic leader in Joplin and became a
national organizer of women when ENB became vice chairman of the DNC. She was later
a member of the Board of Appeals, Veterans Administration, in the New Deal (ENB to
Marion Banister, n.d., Box 1, Marion Glass Banister Papers; Susan Ware, *Beyond Suffrage:
Women in the New Deal*, 139).

chairman that the men withdrew their candidates. But the women who had been ousted never forgave me, although I explained to them as pleasantly as I knew how that there was nothing personal in my fight, that I esteemed them personally, but believed these offices should go to women interested in women in politics. They did not, I could see, believe me.

What we had done in our county, our friends in the other counties had done in theirs, so that the night before the county chairmen and women vice chairmen would meet to elect the district's members of the state committee, a local male leader called me up and said, "They're trying to put me off the committee, Mrs. Blair. You've got the votes to save me. Will you help me out?" Such a question, as any politician knows, meant victory.

It had been a hot month's work. The opposition to us, and particularly to me, was that I was not really a Democrat. Not that these local leaders knew anything about my effort in Washington to choose my party on the ground of belief instead of tradition. But they had decided that you could not be a Democrat and a worker for the League of Women Voters. Besides, they had a temperamental fear of suffragists.

I was not myself elected to any office. I did not even go to the state committee meeting, though a woman who was working with the men did approach me and suggest that we unite our forces and control it. With that one effort I retired, so I thought, from active politics.

I was surprised, therefore, in the fall when the state committee asked me to help in the campaign. They were trying a new plan, that of sending into every county a man and a woman to stimulate the local work. I was asked to go to Richmond in Ray County and put myself at the disposition of the county chairman. Ardent for the League of Nations, I was glad to do anything I could. I found the chairman a delightful person, but he seemed to have no more idea what to do with me than I did myself. The hotel was a funny one with a bare room at the end of a wide and desolate corridor. I spent much of my time in it. No local women came to see me. I made a few speeches and that was that! Later I was sent with Champ Clark, who was running for reelection to the House, to tour some counties along the Missouri River. Thus I was with him on that last campaign of his that ended in his defeat. It was a sad experience. The ex-Speaker of the House, a man as greatly beloved in Missouri as any citizen it had ever boasted, was neither young nor well. Some of our audiences were strongly German. They had been loyal citizens during the war, but now they visited on him their resentment of the peace. Here was a man whose district had adored him for years and who had brought great credit to it, certainly its greatest citizen, and yet, for something he was not in the least to blame, they punished him by sitting glum and silent without a single clap of applause. It was a great lesson to me on the fickleness of voters as we went back unattended to our country hotels, where I pulled a chair for Mr. Clark before the stove, took his red muffler, and brought him a cup of coffee.

On my way home I stopped the day before election at the St. Louis headquarters, and learned from the faces of the few left there that defeat awaited us.

I was greatly disappointed. For I had become an ardent Democrat. Much as I might desire the intellectual detachment of nonpartisanship, my Democracy was, I suppose, bred in me. Those years when I had worn a Cleveland and Hendricks cap as a child, debated the tariff in the civil-government classes at school, listened to my father discuss the money question with Mother, sent out letters for Harry on imperialism, helped my husband in his campaign for judge had won out.

The case of Governor Cox has always interested me. Immediately after his nomination he went to see President Wilson and then and there decided to wage the fight for the League of Nations, losing the Hearst support when he did it. And he made a good fight for it. His speeches were all that could have been asked, and he himself grew in stature as he made them. Of his sincerity and his willingness to go to defeat for it there was no doubt. This is the stuff of which leaders are made, the leaders to whom men rally even in defeat as the proponent of their cause. Yet the thousands of men and women who believed passionately in the league long after the campaign was ended never again looked to Governor Cox as their leader.

I do not know Governor Cox, having met him only casually when speaking on the same platform, but he seems a vigorous personality, and he is certainly able. I ask myself, why did he fail to become a leader of the party, or of the nation? Was it because he failed in some way to identify his personality with the cause he fought for? Does he lack that something that enables an individual to use the cause to dramatize his leadership? This ability is something that Democratic nominees, it seems, must have or become mere political incidents. So many times this has happened that one wonders why Democratic conventions so frequently forget it and add to the number of Democratic candidates whose leadership dies with a campaign.

After the campaign, I settled down in the apartment house to write again, but early in 1921 the University of Florida asked me to give a course of lectures on "Women and Their New Citizenship" for their Extension Department. This engagement, like many of my endeavors, was the result of an accident. A woman had disappointed them at the last moment; they had appealed to the League of Women Voters to suggest a substitute; they named me.

My study for the *Green Book* articles, which had involved the reading of every book on politics I could get from the St. Louis libraries, including the memoirs and journals of statesmen such as Hoar, Blaine, and Benton, and even the autobiography of Tom Platt, had given me a fair preparation for such lectures, although it was something of a task to inform myself in a few days on the Florida laws as affecting women and elections that, based on the old English common law, were quite different from our Missouri ones.[26]

Florida was delightful then as now, but in a different way. I hardly suppose, for example, that it would now take anyone four—or was it five—hours to go from Bradenton to Arcadia, or that the only route through those turpentine forests was by way of a little one-car train that burned wood picked up every few miles by the engineer and conductor. The first time I made the trip I arrived at the Arcadia Hotel just as a Chicago Goodwill Tour was leaving. I noticed that everyone stared at me. When I looked in my mirror I understood why. One side of my face was smoked like the inside of a lamp chimney. I had sat next to the open window of the car.

For six weeks I had to make a bus circuit of the same eight towns, giving a lecture a week in each: Tampa, Tarpon Springs, Dunedin, Largo, Clearwater, Petersburg, Bradenton, and Arcadia. I enjoyed it, except for the lectures. Though I had learned to assume assurance, that queer complex of mine still made me approach each audience as if it were composed of enemies I had to appease. No evidences of kindly appreciation—and there were many— seemed to rid me of it. Each new audience or lecture I approached with the same feeling of being thrown to the lions.

One of the most interesting things to me was the flatness of the rivers. In my Ozark country, rivers ran downhill. The land lying parallel to the sky seemed to me peculiarly restful.

After I finished this tour I went inland and across the state to give other lectures, stopping at sleepy old towns buried in live oaks, down to Apalachicola, then a deserted seaport forgotten by the present, to Pensacola with its English and Spanish forts.

One weekend I went over to New Orleans. Thence, I went into Mississippi up from Gulfport through the middle of the state to the Delta country, which I discovered to be not the Mississippi delta, as I had supposed, but the Yazoo delta in the northwestern corner of the state.

Swampland there, I discovered, had been turned into gold a few years before by an Aladdin's lamp in the way of a drainage system. So much money had flowed in that people could not spend it fast enough. Italian villas had sprung up beside roads deep in mud. Reproductions of Irene Castle met me at the stations with Rolls-Royces. Rooms were furnished in Chinese lacquer from San Francisco and draperies from Marshall Field's.[27] Children wore ermine bonnets. And on every finger shone diamonds, their "four carats" or

---

26. George Hoar, *Autobiography of Seventy Years* (1903); James G. Blaine, *Twenty Years of Congress: From Lincoln to Garfield* (1884); Thomas Hart Benton, *Thirty Years' View* (1854– 1856); and Thomas Platt, *The Autobiography of Thomas Collier Platt* (1910).

27. Irene Castle (1893–1969) and her husband, Vernon, were famous dancers on Broadway and in film. Their story was portrayed in the 1939 film starring Fred Astaire and Ginger Rogers, *The Story of Vernon and Irene Castle* (*NAW-Modern*, s.v. "Castle, Irene").

"five carats," they called them, as the case might be. Even the Negroes had their "flivvers," encouraged to own them by the planters in order that they might be held to their landlords by debt. But evidently the Aladdin's lamp had been mislaid, for cotton had gone down, land values, which had increased so enormously that everyone had sold land and bought more with their profits, had decreased, and banks were calling in their notes and withholding credit. So, by five years the Delta anticipated the Florida boom.

Sleepy old towns and beautiful old houses, and fresh commercial towns, also, I took in my stride, coming at last to Vicksburg. This river town had a sentimental interest for me because my father had been invalided home from there during the Civil War siege. In fact, the Mississippi River had always been invested with romantic appeal to me. How could it be otherwise when I had been brought up on Mark Twain's *Huckleberry Finn,* and *Tom Sawyer?*

As a child the South was to me a glamorous country, whether because of the stories my mother told of her childhood on a Kentucky plantation, or the books of Mary J. Holmes.[28] Many wordy battles I had fought for it when I studied history, my teacher a staunch New Englander. My northern father had laughed at my partisanship. He did not know that when with southerners I suddenly went northern. It must be comfortable to be so securely embodied in a tradition that you can see but one side of a controversy.

More than all else, however, I enjoyed the women I met. They stand out today, when I have met women all over this country and from some others, for a certain quality of gallantry. One, my own age, taking on herself the responsibility of ending the lynch method of controlling the Negro; another getting up at four each morning and writing for four hours before the family awoke to do the book she felt needed to be written; still another who, to support her growing family had, when widowed, opened a boardinghouse and, too frail to do anything else, had not gone downtown in twenty years. Women, all of them, with a long heritage of public service behind them, descendants of United States senators, or Supreme Court judges, who had given their lives in one way or another to the South.

While on this trip I received one day a telegram that placed me with both feet in politics. My old friend and coworker Laura Brown wired me: "National Committee-woman resigned. Women agreed want you. Will you accept?"

I wired her I would.

When I returned home my husband expressed surprise. "You do not usually change your mind," he said, "and you were so relieved when you turned it down before!"

Marshall Field (1834–1906) established his wholesale and retail dry goods firm in Chicago in 1881 (*DAB*, s.v. "Field, Marshall").

28. Mary J. Holmes (1825–1907) was a sentimental novelist who wrote about domestic life. She was a prolific novelist and had huge sales (*NAW*, s.v. "Holmes, Mary J.").

"It has been pursuing me so," I answered, "that I decided I could not escape it." And then added, "You know Mother always says that the reason Moses never saw the Promised Land was because he held back when the Lord called him."

There was more to my decision than that. As I thought it over down there in Florida, I realized that I must practice what I had been preaching to other women. I had no right to try to effect results without assuming responsibility. This, at least I would have said, was what motivated me. With the better knowledge of myself the years have given me, I realize that I did really want to do it. But so much was I held by my Victorian training that women did not do things just because they wanted to, that, feminist though I had become, the thought of doing anything for self-realization had to be well padded by rationalization.

When Laura wired me, I thought she was offering me a position. Too late for me to back out came the knowledge that I had only accepted a candidacy. And between a candidacy and an election a wide gap is to be breached.

8 Standing the Gaff

The new national committeewoman for Missouri had to be elected by the state committee, vested with the authority of filling such vacancies. The committee did not meet until November. During this time my friend Laura Brown kept up her campaign urging the committee of which she was a member to meet and elect me to the position. My own contribution was limited to letters to two men, one an old friend of Father's, and the other an editor of Missouri Writers' Guild days. As Laura lived only a block away from me, she would rush down every day with an answer to show me or some new lead to discuss, often growing impatient with my lack of cooperation.[1] I do not understand it now myself. For I did wish to be elected. Early in the summer had come a letter from a Washington friend saying that she and other women there felt that I should be put in charge of the national organization of the Democratic women, and though I could not see how I could leave home to do it, so great still was my faith in fairy godmothers that I hoped some way it would work out.

After my return from Florida I had come to the conclusion that if I was ever to make a success of writing, I had to learn my craft. I must do the studying that I had thought, because my first story was accepted, could be evaded. So I laid out two courses of study, one in short-story writing and the other in literary criticism. Nothing was to be allowed to interfere with these studies. Social life of every kind was eliminated. We had moved from the apartment hotel to a house, but even my housework came second. For the first and only time in my life I neglected it, but the neglect was deliberate.

It seemed to me that I had to find out once and for all whether or not I could learn to write well enough to derive an income that would enable me to organize my household so I could write. Otherwise I would forever be doing a little of both and neither very well. Better for the household to suffer for a time than always.

For nine months I kept at these studies. Before they ceased I had written almost a million words of copy and read a great many books. I had my discouragements. A professional authors' critic to whom I sent a story answered

---

1. Laura Brown lived at 603 North Pearl Street, and ENB lived at 501 North Pearl in Joplin.

that it was done all wrong but that he would give me twenty-five dollars for the plot—a story that incidentally I sold to *Liberty* thirteen years afterward.[2] An instructor of Columbia University's short-story course advised me that I had better take some courses in English composition before I began on hers. Little I thought that I was not to write again for four years. Yet it was the work I did then that prepared me for the book reviewing I was to do for *Good Housekeeping* magazine. Without it I would never have dared attempt it, nor could I have answered the thousands of letters of inquiry my work in that department brought me.

Surely it is not strange that I have a faith in a power, not ourselves, directing our circuitous ways, or that I advise the women who ask me how they shall set about preparing themselves for some career to do the thing they feel "led" to do.

When the state committee meeting was at last held the matter of the new national committeewoman was settled, as such matters are usually settled in politics, by the men. Another woman had been put forward. My husband's new law partner, Allen McReynolds, who had gone up to St. Louis for the meeting, and a friend who had been on the supreme court of the state, went into conference with her supporters. I have been told that my friends convinced them that as the majority of the women wanted me it was not wise to antagonize them. Whatever happened, the other woman's name was not presented at the committee meeting, and so I was elected, as the saying goes, "without opposition," although I have an idea that not all of those present voted.[3]

My reception, when I came into the committee, was not exactly cordial, but I thanked the committee quickly and made way for Sen. Pat Harrison to make one of his amusing speeches that, I hoped, made the committee forget this irritating injection of women into politics.[4]

---

2. "The Mob," *Liberty* (September 14, 1935): 28–35.

3. Early in 1921, Mrs. Burris Jenkins resigned as Missouri's national committeewoman; ENB was not elected to replace her until immediately before the national committee meeting on November 1. Although there was overwhelming support for ENB by the women of the state, her earlier disagreements with Senator Reed were the primary stumbling blocks to her election (telegram, Edward Goltra to George White, February 17, 1921, Folder 2, Box 16, Goltra Papers; Mary Semple Scott to Goltra, October 14, 1921, Folder 20, Box 20, Goltra Papers).

4. Byron Patton "Pat" Harrison (1881–1941) was admitted to the bar in Mississippi in 1902. He served as a Democrat in the United States House of Representatives from 1911 to 1919 and was elected to the Senate in 1918, where he served until his death. A supporter of the League of Nations, he was temporary chairman of the 1924 Democratic convention and keynote speaker. He was an early supporter of FDR, and in 1933 as chair of the Finance Committee played a critical role in getting New Deal legislation passed. In 1941 he was elected president pro tempore of the Senate (*DAB*, s.v. "Harrison, Byron Patton").

Often I have wondered how I, who have the weakness to like to be liked, have managed so frequently in politics to find myself the center of a conflict. When I have seen women acclaimed by their state organizations, I have been inclined to envy them, for such was never my good fortune. Though I was to have ardent support from women friends and men have come to my rescue again and again, never while I was national committeewoman was I cordially welcomed at any Missouri caucus or convention. Yet I stayed on the committee for seven years, and this though Ruth McCormick said to me when she heard of my election, "I give you six months only, Emily. You're too thin-skinned to last in politics." And Annie, with whom I was staying in St. Louis, said: "It will be all right until you have to stand the gaff, Emily. I'm afraid you cannot take the punishment."

Some years later I went, at the invitation of the Missouri women, to a regional conference of the Democratic National Committee, then meeting in St. Louis. The mayor of St. Louis was there; the governor of the state and his wife; and the wife of our senior senator, Bennett Clark. As they welcomed me back into the state with flattering phrases I realized that this was the first time in my seventeen years of connection with politics that I had not been on the defensive with some group or other of Missouri Democrats; now a Reed following, again a local organization. I began to feel something like a relic, or an antique.

For the benefit of the unpolitical, I should explain that the national political committees are the between-conventions functioning organizations of the national parties. Composed of a man and a woman from each state they fix the date and place of the national nominating conventions and decide the representation there. They also, through executive committees, direct the campaigns of their party's nominees for president and vice president. When and if desired, they maintain a national headquarters between campaigns to further the interests of their party. These members are further expected to raise funds for the national campaign and act as a liaison between the national and state organizations. Their importance is often rated higher than it really is, but if their party has no United States senators from their states, committee members may have something to say about patronage. But of this more later.

After the election of Mr. Harding in 1920, which gave the Democrats almost as great a defeat as the Republicans sustained in 1932, the Democratic national organization, left with a large debt, had closed its national head-quarters and practically ceased to operate. By the fall of 1921, however, there was a revival of hope, and a meeting of this committee was called. It was this meeting, to be held in St. Louis, which had finally brought the Missouri state committee to the point of electing a national committeewoman. Nor had it done so any too soon. I was elected one afternoon. The national committee met the next day. Thus, almost at once I had a taste of committee tactics. Both amazing and confusing I found them.

After the state committee meetings I went over to the Jefferson Hotel to meet the visiting committeewomen. Instead, I met a committeeman, Wilbur Marsh of Iowa. And this was fortunate for me. For he sat down with me on a davenport, and of all the things we might be expected to talk about, we hit upon cattle and Rudyard Kipling. He had, it seemed, introduced Guernsey cattle to America. My brother had had a prize herd of shorthorns. We compared their points. Kipling was his favorite author. I, too, was enthusiastic over him. So, we forgot politics, and I learned you could really enjoy politicians. An old acquaintance came over and asked me to dine with Governor Folk's party.[5] An invitation came from Senator Glass who, his hat stuck defiantly on his head, walked back and forth across the lobby. I saw that it would not be altogether unpleasant.

A fight was on, it appeared, for control of the committee. It centered around the chairmanship. The chairman, George White, afterward governor of Ohio, an endearing person, was personally liked by nearly every man on the committee.[6] But personal fondness cut little ice, apparently, in politics. A goodly number of the committee wanted to depose him. He was one of the most amiable men I have ever met. But neither does amiability count in politics. For he had no intention of surrendering to his opponents. So two caucuses were held that night. One was presided over by Senator Glass who set forth with characteristic energy the reasons for having a new chairman; and the other by Senator Harrison. What he presented I do not know. I was not as catholic in interests as the committeewoman who attended both caucuses.

Who the new chairman should be Senator Glass could not tell us. Daniel Roper, whom they had hoped to elect, was not eligible, as it had been

---

5. Wilbur W. Marsh (1862–1929) was a prominent Waterloo, Iowa, businessman and dairy rancher. He was a delegate to the Democratic National Conventions in 1912, 1920, 1924, and 1928. A member of the DNC from 1915 to 1924, he was treasurer from 1916 to 1924 (*Annals of Iowa* 17 [July 1930]: 393–94). Joseph W. Folk (1869–1923) graduated from Vanderbilt Law School in 1890 and entered practice in St. Louis. Attorney for the Amalgamated Association of Street Railway Employees in the 1900 strike, he was then elected circuit attorney for St. Louis and worked on city investigations of corruption in the state legislature. A Democrat, he was elected governor of Missouri in 1904, leaving office in 1909. He lost his bid against William Stone for the primary nomination for the United States Senate. After supporting Woodrow Wilson in 1912, he was appointed solicitor general of the State Department, serving from 1912 to 1914, when he became counsel for the Interstate Commerce Commission (*Biographical Directory of the Governors of the U.S., 1789–1978* [Westport, Conn.: Meckler Books, 1978], 2:858–59).

6. George White (1872–1953) began his political career by serving in the Ohio House of Representatives as a Democrat, 1905–1908. He was elected to the United States House in 1910 and 1912, losing in 1914, winning in 1916, and losing in 1918. He was chairman of the Democratic National Committee in 1920, managing the Cox campaign. He was elected governor of Ohio in 1930 and reelected in 1932 (ibid., 3:1230–31).

discovered that the rules of the 1920 convention provided that the chairman must be a member of the committee and the committeeman from his state was in Europe and could not be reached to be persuaded to make a place for Mr. Roper.[7] Accustomed to women's organizations, it struck me as queer that the men who wanted Mr. Roper had not discovered this before. But I was not yet familiar with the pleasant little custom of slipping jokers into convention resolutions, nor the way politicians, far from laying the deep plans with which they are credited, let the cards fall as they will and then use their ingenuity to play them. It was evident to me that I had been lined up for the faction led by Senator Glass, for I received no invitation to the other caucus about which I heard from the committeewoman who went to both.

The next morning Mr. Goltra, the same Mr. Goltra who had once asked me to be associate committeewoman, gave a breakfast to the ladies. He had not, however, given me any support in my recent election, as he frankly told me after the breakfast. He would, he assured me, always be ready to talk things over with me, but each would, of course, be free to vote as each pleased. Just why he thought this necessary I never knew. He did keep his promise. For three years we were on the committee together, but never did he ask anything of me or tell me anything of his own plans, though we collaborated in the most friendly way over the arrangements of the Missouri delegation at the Madison Square Garden convention.

Most of us went to bed after these caucuses. But as is the way in politics, there followed another smaller caucus between Senator Glass and Senator Harrison. What they discussed I can only gather from what happened when the committee met next day.

In a roundabout way I was apprised that Mr. Goltra had been approached to resign from the committee to make way for Breckinridge Long to become the chairman; but it would take more than that, I felt, to pry Mr. Goltra from the committee membership that he apparently prized greatly.[8] Personally, I

---

7. Daniel C. Roper (1867–1943) was elected to the South Carolina House of Representatives in 1892. The following year he was appointed clerk to the United States Senate Interstate Commerce Committee. In 1911, he was clerk of the House Ways and Means Committee and worked for Woodrow Wilson's election. His reward was appointment as first assistant postmaster general. In 1917, he became commissioner of internal revenue and in 1924 supported William McAdoo for president. In 1932, he swung the McAdoo votes to FDR at the Democratic convention and was rewarded with appointment as secretary of commerce (*DAB*, s.v. "Roper, Daniel C.").

8. Breckinridge Long (1881–1958), born in St. Louis, married Christine Graham, a granddaughter of Frank Blair, and thereby gained social position and wealth. While practicing law in St. Louis he became a major contributor to the Democratic Party, which resulted in his appointment as an assistant secretary of state in 1917. The intraparty fight in 1920 with Senator Reed had left the Missouri Democratic Party in disarray, and Long lost his bid for the United States Senate. In 1922, he ran against Reed who, with the backing of Pendergast, won the contest and ended Long's elective political career in Missouri. An early

had always a feeling of gratitude toward him. Not only had he paid for the special train that brought the vote to Jefferson City, necessary to enable the Missouri legislature to ratify the suffrage, but he was always wholeheartedly behind the organization and recognition of Missouri Democratic women.

When the committee convened, I was all set to watch a row. But to my surprise, when it was called to order Mr. White rose and said that press of business made it impossible for him to give more time to the chairmanship and so he must present his resignation, much as he regretted doing so. My mouth fell open, and remained so. Then followed a motion accepting with great regret Mr. White's resignation and thanking him for his fine work. Came speeches in high praise of Mr. White, his character, what the party owed him, made by the very men who had been opposing him last night. I pinched myself. I just couldn't understand it. The name of Cordell Hull of Tennessee was put in nomination.[9] Speeches were made about him, his character and ability; speeches by the very men who had been supporting Mr. White the night before. I was hopelessly confused. In an hour the committee adjourned.

So, I had a practical demonstration of Mrs. Catt's dictum that when you marched into the hall of politics you would think things were being done on the platform, so you would go up there; but when you got there you would think they were being done in the room behind it and would march in there, only to discover that they were really being done in the washroom upstairs.

In the afternoon Mr. Hull had a conference with various women who were eager to have a woman at the national headquarters organizing the women. Among them was Miss Mary Archer of Pennsylvania, an enthusiastic Wilsonite, and myself.[10] Mr. Hull listened to all we had to say and looked down his long nose, his lips pressed. I thought to myself, "Why, he looks like a judge," not knowing that he really was addressed as "Judge Hull."

In 1920 Mrs. Bass had left, and there was no leader of the Democratic women. Then in 1921, three vice chairmen were elected, two men and one

---

supporter of FDR, Long was a floor manager at the 1932 convention, and the new president rewarded him with the ambassadorship to Italy (*DAB*, s.v. "Long, Breckinridge").

9. Cordell Hull (1871–1955) was elected in 1906 as a Tennessee Democrat to the United States House of Representatives. He held that seat (except for 1921–1923) until he was elected to the Senate in 1930. A supporter of Wilson and the League of Nations, he served on the Democratic National Committee from 1914 to 1928, serving as chairman from 1921 to 1924. After supporting FDR in the 1932 convention, he resigned from the Senate in 1933 to become secretary of state, serving until 1944 (*DAB*, s.v. "Hull, Cordell").

10. Mary Archer (1881–1963) died March 28 in Reading, Pennsylvania. She was Pennsylvania's first woman member of the DNC (*New York Times*, March 30, 1963, 7:7). When Archer was defeated for reelection to the national committee in 1924, a newspaper report described her as a "widely known wealthy farmerette and horse woman" (*Kansas City Journal*, June 28, 1924).

woman. These were honorary positions, with no active duties assigned, but providing for succession in event the chairman should die or resign. Miss Charl Williams was the woman selected.[11] She was from Memphis. Tennessee was the last necessary state to ratify the amendment, and she had been active in suffrage. She also had been head of the National Educational Association, and was a very prominent and capable person.

After the meeting I went back to Joplin and my studies. In February, after some correspondence, Judge Hull asked me to come to Washington. Years later I asked him how he happened to choose me, and he said, "of all the women mentioned, most people wanted you." And then my faith in fairy godmothers seemed to be justified. My husband told me that in all probability his business would take him much to Washington that winter. The land in Oklahoma, perhaps I had best explain, on which the mines are located, belongs to the Indians, and the leases of the mining companies must be made with the Indian Bureau. That at least is what he said. Later, he put it differently, saying that as I had agreed to his going to France, he thought it only fair that he agree to my going to Washington, if I wished to go.

It seems rather amusing to remember how I rationalized this move of mine as if it were a reflection on Harry, when young and glamorous Dorothy McAllister who filled that same position lived around the corner from me later, with her two young children and her husband, a Michigan Supreme Court judge, ran back and forth to Washington.[12] My difficulty was that I had the feelings and the urges of the new women then emerging, along with the inhibitions and the sentiment of the old.

---

11. Charl Ormond Williams (b. 1885) was the first Democratic National Committee-woman from Tennessee and the first woman vice chairman of the DNC. She served as president of the NEA in 1921–1922 and as president of the National Federation of Business and Professional Women's Clubs from 1935 to 1937 (*Who Was Who in America*, 7:615).

12. Dorothy Wonderly (Smith) McAllister (b. 1899) earned her A.B. from Bryn Mawr in 1920 and her A.M. from the University of Michigan in 1950. She was director of the Women's Division of the DNC from 1937 to 1941. In 1921, she had married Thomas McAllister. Appointed to the Michigan State Liquor Control Commission in 1933, she was a member of the Michigan State Social Security Commission in 1937 (*Who's Who of American Women, 1958–1959*, 836). Thomas Francis McAllister (1896–1976) earned his J.D. degree from the University of Michigan in 1921, the same year he married Dorothy Wonderly Smith. He was elected to the Michigan Supreme Court in 1937. In 1941 he became judge of the U.S. Circuit Court of Appeals, 6th Circuit, and was chief judge of the U.S. Court of Appeals from 1959 to 1963 (*Who's Who in America, 1976–1977* [Chicago: Marquis Who's Who, 1977], 2:2069).

9 The "Outs" Were the "Ins"

The headquarters of the Democratic National Committee in 1922 reflected the state of the Democratic Party. Four crowded, small rooms. Once, I was told, the committee had had luxurious quarters, but they had gone the way of the Democratic majorities. With them had gone, too, any records that might have been left of the previous women's organization.

There had been such records, for Mrs. Bass, my predecessor together with her assistants Esther Ogden and Ellis Meredith, had done brilliant work in the campaign of 1920. To Mrs. Bass must be credited the form that women's participation in politics has taken. For it was she who persuaded the Democratic National Committee to put women on it and thus designed what is known as the "fifty-fifty" representation of women on party committees. But her records had been destroyed. The Woman's Bureau had been closed. As far as headquarters were concerned it was as if there had been no woman's organization. Nor did the staff take kindly to my advent.

The day after I arrived I went into the publicity department to ask if they wanted any information about me to use in announcing my appointment.

"It is not our custom," said the director, "to use the committee for personal publicity."[1]

For a second I was nonplused, hardly realizing what he implied. Then I rallied and said: "But don't you think if it is important enough to appoint a woman to organize the Democratic women, that it is important to tell women that you have?"

Grudgingly he consented to issue a short announcement of my appointment. It consisted of three lines. To me, accustomed to the suffragists' use of publicity to gain their end, the incident seemed incredible. I had thought I was to be used to win women to the Democratic Party, to give them a woman leader, to advise the men how to appeal to women. It was borne in on me that my first job was going to be to make these men at headquarters accept me as a coworker, and then make my position one of leadership of women. It was difficult because the one defeated the other. It was woman leadership the men instinctively feared.

---

1. Richard Linthicum (1859–1934) wrote articles and short stories for various magazines. A journalist, he became news editor of the *Chicago Chronicle* in 1904. He served as director of publicity for the DNC in 1922 (*Who Was Who in America*, 1:733).

I was given a room, a desk, and a chair. After a few conferences with Mr. Hull, I had a secretary and another desk. When I asked for a rug to cover the old floor, consternation was registered on all faces. Then a stroke of luck came my way. Mr. Hull disclosed that he had in mind an assistant for me. Some friends came to see me about her. Finally she came herself. And there happened one of those rare miracles that give light to life. The moment I looked at Marion Banister, I knew that I had found my complement, and then and there began one of the deepest and most satisfying friendships of my life.[2]

In a few weeks we had what looked at least like a going concern. Newspaper girls and even men dropped in to see us. Democratic women came, too. Sometimes their words were a bit disconcerting, as when a woman I had known in suffrage days, a wise woman, too, advised me never to have anything, anything at all, to do with any Democratic woman in the District of Columbia. When, a few days later, one of them commanded me to make no move nor hold any conference with any District women without her presence I began to realize what she meant.

In a month we had outlined a plan for the organization of Democratic women's clubs and printed a pamphlet of instructions. A few weeks later, Mrs. Banister had a biweekly news sheet for them.

The reason for this organization was simple. One of my first acts after getting stationery and a secretary had been to make a survey of the organization of women in the states to find out how many women had a place on the state or local Democratic committees. In most states there were none. I had also circularized the county chairmen asking them to send in the names of the women on their committees. Of the more than three thousand, only eleven answered, and of those, one said, "None, thank God," and another, "We don't have any or expect to have any."

In reply, Judge Hull, as chairman, had written to the state chairmen urging them to make provision for women in their committees, even, when it was necessary, to instigate legislation to that end. But we could not wait to organize women until this was done.

We had other reasons for the clubs. Not only could we thus attract women who might not otherwise be drawn into party work, but it was a technique of organization that women understood. In addition, the clubs offered us

---

2. Marion Banister (1875–1951), sister of Sen. Carter Glass, worked on the editorial staff of the Public Information Service, Department of Labor, during World War I. She served as assistant to ENB from 1921–1924 and was a founder of the Woman's National Democratic Club. From 1924 to 1928, she was publicity director for the Mayflower Hotel in the District of Columbia. She was publisher and editor of the *Washingtonian* magazine, 1929–1933. FDR appointed her assistant treasurer of the United States in 1933, and she served until her death (Banister Papers; *Who Was Who in America*, 3:47; James S. Olson, *Historical Dictionary of the New Deal: From Inauguration to Preparation for War*, 33).

an opportunity to publicize the party policies by informing the women about them.

I thought of the clubs myself as a proving ground for the development of woman leadership. To me leadership meant leadership that women themselves would follow. In this I was undoubtedly motivated by my feminism, the same thing that had made me in Joplin defeat the plan of men to put their own wives on the committees. But I also thought it good for the Democratic Party. To win, we needed the votes of women, and women would, I believed, follow more readily leaders whom they themselves had chosen. As I often put it to the men: "There is no point in my working for the votes you would get anyway, by marriage. My only value to you is to bring in those you might not otherwise win."

Since I knew my own state best and had many friends there who wanted my work to be successful, I naturally began my club organization there, the first club being organized in Springfield, a neighbor to Joplin. Immediately, and it was to my surprise, a cry of protest went up from the friends of Senator Reed who was going into a senatorial primary that summer for reelection that these clubs were designed to defeat him. Now I was not unaware that women's clubs in Missouri might not work to the senator's advantage. I may even have hoped that they would not. But the club plan was not designed only for Missouri. Before we were through we had nearly three thousand of them scattered over the country, only two hundred of which were in Missouri. Our organizer, Mrs. Laura Brown, had traveled from Montana to Maine on the job. The instructions to the clubs stated specifically that they should take no part in primary elections. Nor did they ever do so, as far as I know.

I really leaned backward in order to be neutral in Senator Reed's campaign, for by going to Washington I had, I felt, forfeited all opportunity to take part in this primary contest. But this, I realized, as their protests came in to the chairman, the Reed supporters did not believe.

The opposition, however, did me good service. I was involved in a fight. Thus I became news. Newspaper correspondents found their way to my office. My old fight with Senator Reed was remembered and retold. Politicians, too, looked me up. This was the kind of politics they understood. I had become one of them.

While all this was going on I had been busy in other ways, for there is no chronology in political organization. It goes on like a four-ring circus.

The League of Women Voters was having a convention in Baltimore.[3] It was to be a Pan-American conference with representatives from all the South American countries, Canada, and Mexico. The State Department and Pan-American Union had cooperated. There would be gathered many American politically inclined women, among them many Democrats, old friends with

---

3. The League of Women Voters convention in Baltimore was held April 20–28, 1922.

whom I had worked and whom I might interest. I would have headquarters there, entertain these Democratic women at tea, interest as many as I could, and get publicity on it. By so doing I would indicate to the world at large that the Democratic committee was making a bid for the woman vote, was friendly to the things the league stood for, and would incidentally through the publicity make my intentions known to the women of the country.

I unfolded my plans to Mary Archer, my staunch supporter on the committee. The trouble was that the committee had no funds available for such a purpose. So, to finance it, she gave me a check for one thousand dollars. As the law provided that all money spent must be reported to the clerk of the House of Representatives, this contribution had, of course, to go through the committee's books. So it was given to me; I gave it to the treasurer's office; it "advanced" me back the amount; in due time I returned an itemized account of the way it was spent to be copied into the books. By this laborious process was handled all the money I personally raised for my work. Eighty thousand dollars it amounted to in two years. This was a tedious performance and involved keeping a complete set of books of my own. But it was necessary. The committee—as is the way of political committees—had great difficulty raising money. Often it was in the red and knew not how to meet its weekly payroll. If my money was deposited in the committee's account, there was a possibility it would not be there when I needed it. Since it was given me for a specific purpose I had to assure myself and the donors that it would be used for that purpose.

With my thousand dollars I went to Baltimore. Miss Archer and other committeewomen went with me. We created quite an excitement. The publicity was plentiful, but what was my surprise to find much of it suggesting that I had come to influence the League of Women Voters in declaring for the League of Nations. If not that—said one reporter—then what? This was my first experience with the attitude that back of every political performance there must be an ulterior motive.

During the convention the League of Women Voters put on an enormous dinner. It was held on the Century Theatre roof. Even the gallery was filled with tables. The speakers' table was on the platform. On one side of me sat the secretary of commerce, Herbert Hoover. That I found him difficult to talk to is not perhaps surprising, for next to him was Lady Astor, the guest of the league, who was really responsible for the crowd. On her other side was Governor Ritchie.[4] She managed to keep them both laughing, that is, when

---

4. Lady Astor, Nancy (Witcher Langhorne) Astor (1879–1964), married in 1906 Waldorf Astor who was the son of an American who had been made a British peer. In 1910, Waldorf had been elected to Parliament and when he succeeded to the title of viscount in 1919, she was elected to his place in the House of Commons. The first woman M.P., she served from 1919 to 1945 (Uglow, *Continuum Dictionary*, 33; *Dictionary of National*

they were not looking down her marvelous back. Just before the dinner was finished, however, she got up and made an impromptu speech, telling them all how sorry she was to leave.

"No wonder," I heard the women who escorted her away say to her, "you don't need a press agent."

Still I had no opportunity to talk with Mr. Hoover, for the other speeches began at once. There were a great many of them, but I did not listen well, except to Governor Ritchie who was so handsome one had to look at him and, looking, listen. Later I was to confer with him at his office at Annapolis and learn that he is one man, at least, who can combine the manner and attitude of talking to a charming woman with the words and thoughts of a man talking as man to man.

During the other speeches my mind was on my own. An ordeal, I knew, was before me. It was customary then for this league on such occasions to have a Republican woman and a Democratic woman each represent her party. At this dinner the Republican representative was Mrs. Harriet Taylor Upton, who as vice chairman of the executive committee of the Republican National Committee was authorized leader of the Republican women, and I, who as resident committeewoman (as I was then called) of the Democratic National Committee was authorized leader of the Democratic women, was to speak for the Democratic women.[5] Mrs. Upton and I had played vis-à-vis before. The night after I had reached Washington I had spoken after her on a public platform. Now Mrs. Upton is large and rotund, wears her straight hair in a bun on the top, dresses in the long skirts and indeterminate lines the portly woman of sixty-five or after is likely to affect, and never in her life, according to her own reports, laid any claim to looks. But nature had compensated her with a wit that can convulse her hearers, and she, wise woman, uses it to capitalize both figure and face. Had she essayed a career as a comedian instead of following her congressman father into the law and politics she could have far outshone Marie Dressler on stage or screen.

When she arose that night in Washington—it was a meeting of women employees of the government to urge that the principle equal wage for equal

---

Biography, 1961–1970, s.v. "Astor, Nancy Witcher"). Albert Cabell Ritchie (1876–1936) began his four terms as Democratic governor of Maryland in 1919. During the 1920s, he was an opponent of Prohibition and a part of the conservative wing of the Democratic Party. He was a professor of law at the University of Maryland until his election as governor (DAB, s.v. "Ritchie, Albert Cabell").

5. Harriet Taylor Upton (1853–1945), a lifelong Republican, had served as her father's hostess for thirteen years when he was in Congress. In 1890 she joined NAWSA and served as treasurer from 1894 to 1910. From 1899 to 1908 and again from 1911 to 1920, she was president of the Ohio Woman Suffrage Association. In 1920 she was appointed vice chairman of the Republican National Committee, serving for four years (NAW, s.v. "Upton, Harriet Taylor").

work be incorporated in the proposed Re-Classification Bill—she began her remarks something like this: "Here we are, Mrs. Blair and I. You know every time the Democratic Party selects a woman to speak opposite me she turns out to be a little woman and a young and a pretty woman. There was Mrs. Pyke and Mrs. Bass, and now they've chosen Mrs. Blair to lead the Democratic women. You can see her for yourself and now look at me. But I remember the emblem of my party." She was interrupted by laughter and applause. Followed some stories and more laughter and applause. Then came her sentiments about the equal wage also presented wittily. When she sat down the applause was deafening. "What a grand old girl," the hands and faces of her audience said. It looked pitying at me. "Now, poor little woman, how can you equal that?" Such was its thought, I knew well. It was also my own. I was bound to be an anticlimax! But there was naught to do but to go through with it. And so I said the words that came:

"I don't deny the smallness, and I'm grateful for the young and pretty, but I do hope Mrs. Upton does not mean to insinuate that I suggest the emblem of my party." Laughter, applause. Hurrah, luck is with me, so I go on. "Anyway I belong to the party that does not believe that God is on the side of the heaviest battalions." More laughter and applause. A few of my sentiments. And then as deafening applause as Mrs. Upton's. "The dear little thing," the faces in my audience said, "she managed wonderfully." Yes, I had got through, but would I again? This was the thought in my mind at that Baltimore dinner. What might not Mrs. Upton spring this time?

And then at last, far into the night, before the tired, bored audience she rose. And Eureka, she was saying the same thing, adding the remark that we were the political Gold Dust Twins under the political big tent. Hurrah again! I had only to make the same retort. But the audience did not know, of course, it had all happened before, and my Democratic women were so relieved that my applause was again quite equal to hers, someone calling, "Bravo, little girl!" And I realized that to come after her on a program had an advantage all its own. The audience felt so sorry for the position I was in that pity predisposed it to be kind to me!

As many of the women members of the Democratic National Committee were attending this convention of the League of Women Voters, I had called a meeting of the national committeewomen in Washington immediately after it. The money for it, too, coming out of Miss Archer's donation. I wanted to meet them and put my plans before them. I smile now to think how rashly I rushed into things a seasoned politician would have feared to undertake. Now I would consider carefully all the possibilities for trouble such a conference held. Then I thought only of its usefulness to my purpose, expecting it to go off like a Missouri Suffrage Association meeting. But the trouble came.

The national committeewoman for the District of Columbia was the widow of that Croesus Thomas Walsh. She had been named in 1920, but after the election of Mr. Harding and the defeat of Mr. Cox had ceased to function. Neither would she resign. She even refused to answer letters. My invitation to the meeting was not, therefore, acknowledged. There was another woman in Washington who had served the Democratic committee of the District of Columbia as vice chairman.[6] For some reason she got the idea that if Mrs. Walsh refused to act, she, ipso facto, assumed her position. In vain I explained to her that under political rules and custom this was not possible. I was authorized to recognize only Mrs. Walsh or someone having her proxy. Vice chairmen of state committees had not been invited, and I could not recognize the vice chairman of the District. There was even a question if she really held that position. She had, however, her own ideas about political organization. She considered not only that she should be recognized as leader at any and every political meeting held in the District, but that I could call no meeting or caucus inside the District, even in my own office, until she had censored the list of conferees. I was not even to receive there any ladies with whom she was not on good terms, and there were, it appeared, a number of them. When she heard about this meeting, she served notice she would come in Mrs. Walsh's place and if not recognized make a disturbance. From what I had heard about her I believed she would. And a fine beginning that would be to my work. After the meeting there was to be a tea at which Mrs. Woodrow Wilson was to be the guest of honor. This woman demanded also a place in the reception line. Other women in the District advised me they would not appear if she did. I was in a quandary. D_____ if I did and D_____ if I didn't, it seemed. And so hours that should have gone into planning my program were devoted to solving this problem.

The night before the meeting came, and the problem was still not solved. And then I had an inspiration. I called up a friend who was also one of Mrs. Walsh's and begged her to get a proxy from Mrs. Walsh early the next morning. She said she would and did. But Mrs. Walsh kept her waiting so long that when she finally arrived with it at the meeting, the lady vice chairman was already at the door and forcibly removed my friend's hat before she was able to get in. All very funny it seems now, but it is situations like that, keeping attention off the main issues, that make political meetings so often ineffective. As I presided at the meeting, my mind was far more occupied in watching for

---

6. Carrie B. Reed (d. 1932) married wealthy Colorado mine owner Thomas F. Walsh in 1879. In 1900, they moved to Washington, D.C., where she became a well-known philanthropist. She was also national committeewoman for the District of Columbia. They lived at 2020 Massachusetts Avenue NW (*National Cyclopedia of American Biography*, s.v. "Walsh, Carrie B."; *Social Register: Washington, 1929*). Mrs. Mary Wright Johnson was the state campaign director of the District of Columbia Democratic Committee, 1916–1922. She was the D.C. Democratic National Committeewoman to the New York national convention in 1924 (*Who's Who in the Nation's Capital, 1926–1927*, 315).

fear she would make a scene and being on the alert to prevent it than on the program I had planned.

Not content with the meeting and the tea, I had planned a Democratic dinner for the evening. And so innocent—not to employ a less complimentary word—was I that I did not know how rash I was. I simply rented the room in the Washington Club, ordered the dinner, engaged the speakers, invited the guests, and without publicity or committees and all the ballyhoo I now know to be necessary for working up attendance at such an affair expected a crowd. By a sort of miracle it appeared. Not the two or three thousand of a Jackson Day dinner, of course, but a fairly creditable showing so soon after the whacking defeat of 1920, for Democrats were in a pitiful minority then in Washington, and even those left over from the Wilson administration were not proclaiming publicly their Democracy.

Our party was making a tariff fight then in Congress, and I had conceived the idea of featuring the tariff question on our program. I had asked Judge Hull to suggest the best men to make the speeches, and he had named the best informed on the tariff without regard to their wit or terminal facilities. So we listened I won't say how many hours to the intricate and involved discussion of schedules that we could as well have read in the *Congressional Record*. However, two persons, at least, enjoyed the dinner, Elizabeth Marbury and Senator Heflin.[7] For during it they had time to exchange all their stories, each proclaiming the other the best storyteller he or she had ever met. The only trouble was that the other diners, witnessing a glee that they could not share, resented even more the speeches. Nevertheless, next day this dinner found a place on the front pages of all the newspapers.

The reason for this affords an amusing example of my ignorance of what constitutes political news in Washington. I had of course invited ex-President and Mrs. Wilson. He had, of course, declined. As his gracious letter contained a message to the Democratic women, I read it to them at the dinner.

In a few moments a crowd of men in street garb appeared at the door. In a few minutes more they were behind me. Did I have press copies of the letter? They hadn't received one. No, I hadn't sent out any. Might they see the letter? I let them copy it, holding onto the paper all the while. They were, I gathered, newspapermen.

---

7. Elizabeth Marbury (1856–1933), theatrical producer and author agent, became active in New York City politics in 1918–1919. A delegate to the Democratic National Convention in 1920, she became national committeewoman. Her final convention was 1932 (*DAB*, s.v. "Marbury, Elizabeth"). James Thomas Heflin (1869–1951) was elected to the United States House of Representatives as a Democrat in 1904; he served for sixteen years. Opposed to woman suffrage, he was elected to fill a Senate vacancy in 1920. Reelected in 1924, he lost his party's nomination in 1930 after he had opposed Al Smith's candidacy (*DAB*, s.v. "Heflin, James Thomas").

And the next morning every metropolitan paper quoted the letter verbatim. The wires, I learned, had been held open for it. This, it seemed, was the first public message the ex-president had sent since he had left the White House. It was news in capital letters, and I had not known enough to show it to our publicity man. Perhaps, even if I had, I would have thought it better taste not to capitalize on it. But at least I would have known I had a sensation up my sleeve.

10 Wooing the Minority

I set to work to build up two things: a place for myself and an organization of women. The first because I knew what the men evidently did not: that women were not waiting to fall over themselves to work for the Democratic Party just because an unknown woman suggested it to them. Little I might know about national politics, but I knew a lot about women, and one thing I knew was that women might follow men directly, but they were not going to be delivered as so many bobheads by an agent of the men. But if I could make them see me as one who could lead them according to the tactics they were familiar with, they might treat me as their leader. At least the kind of women I had worked with were like that, and these were the kind, so I thought, that could build up the party: the women who had qualities of leadership themselves, and ability and experience with women to bring to the service of the party. It is the inability of men in politics to understand this that is back of the weakness of the political party organization of women. The men want quiescent agents, and able women will not follow that kind. If political male leaders had been wise, they would either have refused to recognize the woman voter as being any different at all from the man voter and left those who wanted to go into politics to fight their way against men to committeeships, or have picked out women of initiative and given them authority to lead the women. As it was, most of the male political leaders tried to have their cake and eat it. They depended on women to mobilize the woman vote, yet they chose the acquiescent kind whom women would not follow.

I saw that I had an opportunity—it was nothing more than that—to show eligibility for leadership. But the women must know me, they must have evidence of my ability to accomplish things. To show them such evidence, I discovered, was like raising myself by my own bootstraps. I would have no help from the men, for they never suspected my needs, nor could I have made them understand these needs. They had risen to their positions of leadership by the survival-of-the-fittest method, they had a wide acquaintanceship, the positions they had held or might hold gave their words and thoughts weight. I was only a stranger from the past, "a little wren perched on the windowsill," as one newspaper correspondent called me, although a later one did repeat that he had heard in Missouri that I was like the drink called Southern Comfort that goes down so smooth and easily but has an awful kick afterward. I had no political record, no fortune to put at the party's disposal, no social position to be capitalized. What chance had a woman like that to build up a position of leadership? If I was not to remain a supersecretary, I saw I had to create for myself some other position.

As a matter of fact by no rule or precedent did I have any right to demand recognition for myself or my office. I was simply engaged to do a job. And yet to do the job, so I thought, it was necessary for me to insist on being included in the councils of the committee. As Mr. Hull's appointee it was just as important that I do all I could to make his work successful as that I represent the women. I could not sacrifice one for the other. Yet necessarily they were often in conflict as, for instance, when it was necessary that he win some man who was opposed to women. His program was the simple, but not easy, one, of keeping the committee neutral as to individual candidates for nomination, and during the 1922 congressional elections, I think I made him realize that I understood this. In time he came to talk over his problems with me. In the beginning I felt I owed him a loyalty because he put me there, and as time went on I came to give to him a great personal loyalty as I realized and came to understand what the world found out afterward, that he was a great man. Consummate politician as he is, he also is a man of democratic convictions. The party was a matter of faith with him, Democratic success a concern for the welfare of the country. And these things came always before his own political fortunes. Had Mr. Hull had the gift for dramatizing himself, he might have been president. He is one of those all too few men in politics who thinks as a statesman and regards politics as a calling. Madison and Jefferson, I think, would have found him a kindred soul. Hamilton and John Adams would have respected him.

Once a woman from the Republican organization came to me. "Before we were partisans," she said, "you and I were suffragists together. Tell me how it is that you can get so much more from the men than we can?"

"It's simple," I said. "You haven't the talking points with your men I have with mine. Since your party has already won an election without giving the women any special recognition, your men think they don't need to do so. We, the minority party, have to woo the women. Also," I added, "you don't have a Judge Hull." For it was to his fairness as much as anything else that Democratic women owed his acceptance of us. Whatever he may have thought of the federal amendment, he was a Democrat. If women were voters, equal participation in party matters seemed to him only just. Being a practical politician he knew that the only way the committee could bring about such participation was by making special provision for it.

I have always had a sympathy for those men who were active in political organization when suffrage came. Here we were, we women, suddenly to be dealt with, insisting on being heard and seen, asking to take part in a game we did not know, mussing up their rules. Naturally they were baffled as to what to do with us.

Once there was a conference of some leaders to discuss affairs, at which I had been left out. I protested my exclusion to Mr. Hull. Discomfited, he said to me: "To tell you the truth, Mrs. Blair, I forgot you."

"But what am I to do?" I asked. "I don't want to come where I am not wanted, but if the women feel that I do not represent them, they will insist on a woman who does."

"I'll tell you," he said, looking down that nose of his. "Come in every day or so and say: 'I'm here, Mr. Hull.' "

The situation was not any easier for him than for me. Some of the men did resent having me around, and he of course knew it. In a contest of factions for control of the committee, I was just an extra wheel quite in the way. And there was no basis technically for my insistence on being consulted and counted in. I was, after all, only an appointee of his. But I would, I felt, do neither him nor the party any good by serving merely as a supersecretary. To win the women I must really represent their ideas and viewpoint there. At least, so I argued to him and to myself. We had many discussions on the subject with the result that, in a few months, he took a letter vote of the committee on a resolution to elect me as a vice chairman of the committee.[1] He believed as firmly as I that the greatest appeal the party could make to women was an indication that it recognized women. It was a fallacy held by many men and women in those days.

When Mr. Hull took the chairmanship, he had expected to be well financed, but so deep was the cleavage between the two factions in the party—those for Mr. McAdoo and those against him—so much did they mistrust each other—that neither side would contribute lest it accrue to the advantage of the other. To both Mr. Hull was meticulously fair, but he would give no advantage to either. The committee, he believed, was the party's, not a faction's. Perhaps this was not what either side wanted. Perhaps not knowing him as they did later, they did not believe it. At any rate, day after day he walked the floor of his little office, his head down.

"I will tie a rock around my neck and jump into the Potomac, Mrs. Blair," he said to me one day, "before I will sell out this committee to either side."

When some Democrat from the country would come in, Mr. Hull would be sitting at his desk looking as if he hadn't a care in the world. He would ask about the man's family, outline at length the party's policies and prospects, and listen to his opinions. Of course, they usually wanted something, and

---

1. Cordell Hull wrote to all Democratic National Committee members asking authorization to change ENB's status from resident committeewoman to a regular vice chairman of the DNC (Hull to Carter Glass, August 2, 1922, Box 169, Carter Glass Papers). See also Hull to Edward Goltra, August 2, 1922, Folder 12, Box 16, Goltra Papers.

he had nothing to give them, but when they left they took with them a knowledge that Chairman Hull was absolutely fair and impartial and that the committee would not be swayed or controlled by any individual candidate for nomination.

When, two years afterward, he left the chairmanship, he said to me: "I always gave you everything you asked for, Mrs. Blair, except money, and I never had that."

This was true, and never would I have succeeded in what I did accomplish—less though it was than I wanted to do—except for his help. No, the troubles that I had were not due to my chief. They inhered in the situation. And indeed many of the difficulties of women in politics are more due to that than to the opposition of men.

One of my duties was to endeavor to secure Democratic support in Congress for the things in which women were interested. The Children's Bureau was of interest to all women, and so I sought to impress upon Democrats in Congress the importance of support for it. In line with this endeavor I went to see Sam Rayburn, of Texas.[2] A southerner, a bachelor, I approached the subject with him with some trepidation. He was courteous, polite, and patient at first, but as we talked he became interested. He is a true Jeffersonian Democrat. As we talked and I explained the importance to women of the Children's Bureau and of our party supporting the movement to establish it, he became greatly interested and was most helpful. Afterward I went to him often for advice and assistance. Always he was understanding and helpful. I regard him as one of the finest men I have known. Shortly after the Roosevelt administration came in, I was in a restaurant in Washington, and he came across the room to me and asked what I wanted in the way of an appointment. When I laughed and told him nothing, that already I had had all I wanted from politics—lots of fun, lots of work, and lots of fine friends—he said: "Well, if you change your mind and I can help, let me know, for if anyone is entitled to the fruits of victory you are that one." He was the only person who ever suggested to me that I was entitled to a political appointment because of my political activities. Afterward he became Speaker of the House, and no one rejoiced more than I. I shall treasure always my friendship with Sam Rayburn, which has continued through the years.

---

2. Samuel T. Rayburn (1882–1961) was elected to the Texas House of Representatives in 1906 as a Democrat. In 1911 he became Speaker of the Texas House, and the following year he was elected to the United States House of Representatives. A southern progressive, he was elected House majority leader in 1936 and served as Speaker of the House from 1940 until his death (*DAB*, s.v. "Rayburn, Samuel T.").

11 My Fairy Godmother

In June I took a house out on Albermarle Street between Cleveland Park and Chevy Chase. It was on a high terrace, surrounded by trees, and quite cool. My sister Margaretta came to look after it, my children home from school, and my mother to stay with me. We had a happy summer there, although my husband's plans had suffered a change, and instead of being in Washington, he was detained in Joplin by unexpected business there. Still we managed to see each other every month or so. Sometimes he would join me on my way West, and we would visit on the train. Again he would rush on to Ohio to spend a day with me. And several times I would make a stop for a few days in Joplin. The time was soon to come when it would seem a natural arrangement for a wife's business to take her one place and a husband's another, but I felt very apologetic, not only to him, but to the world at large.

In Washington I had been existing more or less in a social vacuum—an environment I never enjoy for long. For I am by nature a social person. Although never satisfied with the social life as an end or aim of activity or interest, my interest in people, my pleasure in conversation, make me crave social intercourse. It exhilarates me and stimulates my mental activity. Perhaps the fact that I grew up in a large family where there was constant entertainment had something to do with it. Even in those days in Carthage when I was writing and doing suffrage work I had made many sacrifices to keep in touch with my own social group.

But there was a special reason I wanted social contacts in Washington. I knew how much easier it was to exchange views over a dinner table than a desk, that breaking bread with anyone put him or her on a different footing with you. Great corporations did not keep expensive contact men to entertain visitors for nothing. Theirs was a technique I knew well from my experiences back in Carthage when we entertained eastern bankers and brokers in our home, and from those days in suffrage work. And Washington, I knew, was a place in which these social contacts played a great part. Meeting me as a guest, or hostess, those men with the shut-out look I met in offices might change their attitude toward me. Besides, I longed to know the inside stories of what was going on in Washington. I felt the need of more information than I was acquiring at my desk.

Of course I was invited to the large official dinners and luncheons of which there are so many in Washington when you sing for your supper with a speech.

But they did not serve the purpose. True, at the first private dinner to which I was asked I had been buttonholed by a senator's wife to hear about her ill health, and not a man had approached me. But I did not disdain wives or even conversations about surgical operations. The best way of all to a man was often through his wife. As a politician who had long evaded me once explained his final capitulation to me: "You got my wife, and I had to like you."

But the Democratic wives were coy. None of them had been suffragists. They had no interest in politics and ignored women politicians. How I was to manage to make the necessary social contacts I did not know, but someway I must.

And then my fairy godmother took a hand. Into my office one day walked Mrs. J. Borden Harriman, later to be known to me as "Daisy." Rather overpowering she was, with her splendid figure, her aquiline nose, but that was before I knew her soft, melting smile and what Arthur McKeogh calls her delightful naïveté.[1]

"I heard you speak the other night," she said, "and I've come to offer any help I can give you. What can I do?"

I told her I had two things in mind. To explain to her the first, I confided to her my difficulties, telling her how and why I needed to meet these senators offstage and explaining, further, how much it would profit the Democratic Party if there was some Democratic drawing room where our senators—they were few in number—congregated socially, discussed things informally. I recalled to her Mark Hanna's breakfasts and Ruth McCormick's Saturday evenings. At such social affairs as these were, I pointed out, Republicans were so in the majority that Democratic talk was never possible. She appreciated that, for she had found herself time and again the only Democrat at a social function, although it is safe to say she never failed to give evidence of her Democratic faith. She would not have hesitated to take on a roomful of the enemy at once. And then and there we planned those Sunday-evening suppers of hers that have become an institution in Washington society, the nearest thing to a political salon that the capital offers.

The Senate was sitting that summer. It was very hot. Many of the senators were living in hotels, their families having left for their homes. There were few parties and little entertaining. To sit under the canopy in Mrs. Harriman's garden on F Street behind the brick walls and eat her delicious food was a treat to them.[2] Naturally they expanded. Mrs. Harriman's social instinct had

---

1. Arthur McKeogh (1890–1937) began his journalism career as a reporter for the *New York Evening Sun*, 1912–1914. On the editorial staff of the *New York Sunday World*, he was the associate editor and art editor for the *Saturday Evening Post*, 1919–1923. Editor of *Cosmopolitan* in 1925, he was editor of *McClure's* from 1925 to 1927. From 1927 to 1929, he was New York editor of *Red Book* magazine. After 1929, he was managing editor of *Good Housekeeping* (*Who Was Who in America*, 1:816).

2. Mrs. Harriman lived at 2017 F Street.

kept her from limiting invitations to senators or even to Democrats. Her hospitality must not savor of the caucus, but be, in fact, merely informal social diversion. Correspondents of the metropolitan newspapers, good conversationalists all, were invited and many others, men or women whom Mrs. Harriman found interesting. The invitation lists varied with the week, though always chosen with a nice balance and congeniality of companionship in view. The inclusion of the newspapermen was a stroke of genius. It served the party in a way I, at least, had never thought of. What it was I realized one night when a well-known Republican columnist said to me after the men returned to the drawing room: "You know I never heard these men talk as they did up there in the library. Why, Cordell Hull actually believes in democracy. The primary and income tax law mean something to him. He's in deadly earnest."

I saw, then, that these contacts served to reveal some of our men to reputation makers in a way that would be helpful in presenting them to the country. And I do not doubt that they had something to do with the changed evaluation thereafter given some of our leaders in the public press. Neither was the plain speaking and wit of the correspondents without its effect on the Democratic politicians. Many an idea they picked up there.

But nothing was further from Mrs. Harriman's mind than exploiting any of her guests for the benefit of others. Her only purpose was to be a good hostess, and for that she is superlatively fitted. Utterly spontaneous, with a gift for drawing people out, saying just what she thinks, and thinking just at the right time the thing that will provoke a laugh, she gives a festive air even to the most serious discussion. Winston Churchill and many other foreign visitors have said they found one of her suppers their most delightful entertainment in Washington.

She herself thinks their success is due to her lack of plan. Never does she prepare beforehand what direction the discussion shall take or even think of the subject. She simply waits until the conversation at dinner suggests something to her. Then when the dessert is served and everything but the finger bowls removed from the table, she pushes back her chair, raps for quiet, asks her guests to make themselves comfortable, insisting that they rearrange their chairs so no one's back is to another's, and fires some question to a guest.

It may be: "Dr. Lubin," speaking to an economist from the Brookings Institute, "the secretary (referring to a cabinet member) would like to know what you think the Reconstruction Finance Corporation will do to the depression?"[3] Or she may turn to me with: "Emily, the governor (referring to

3. Isador Lubin (1896–1978) earned his Ph.D. in economics from the Robert Brookings School of Economics and Government in 1926. He had worked for the government as an economist in World War I, with the War Industries Board, and had taught at Brookings and the University of Missouri. In 1928, he was an adviser to the Senate committee on

Governor Ritchie) isn't in favor of our Unemployment Bill." Thus we are off. As soon as one talker—speeches are taboo—is through, interrupted by sallies of wit or questions or objections, someone answers him and someone else him. If no one does, "Daisy" is ready to pull someone else into voice. And so the evening passes. Nothing is ever settled. "Daisy" finishes with a quip perhaps, or someone must go. But in that charming dining room with its old pine paneling and candlelights and bare tables, men and women who might never otherwise have met have exchanged views on national questions, or listened to those they would never otherwise have heard. It is, perhaps, the only clearinghouse of opinion like this in the whole country. Cabinet members, ambassadors, judges of the Supreme Court, foreign ministers, governors, senators meet and argue with newspapermen, college professors, welfare workers, socialists, economists, publicists, novelists, capitalists, artists, poets, and plain Washington residents. Alice Longworth is often there, though always silent.

"Daisy's" acquaintanceship is wide. All she asks of anyone is that he shall be interesting. Economically, it offers a cross-section of American life. A man or woman living on three thousand dollars a year may sit beside Owen D. Young or a Du Pont.[4] Socially, it offers a cross-section of Washington. A mere government clerk, expert in some subject like oil geology, may engage in controversy with the scion of the most exclusive Knickerbocker family. All this, it seems to me, has a real political and social value. A sociology professor of Chicago University once said to me that one of the worst things about America, politically speaking, was that Americans lived in watertight social compartments between which there was no interchange of opinion. Capitalists did not know professors; writers did not know politicians; laborers did not know farmers; welfare workers did not know politicians; and thousands of little groups all over the country were composed of people who thought exactly alike politically and sociologically. He blamed our intolerance as well as our political and economic ineptitude on it. If he is correct, then Mrs. Harriman must be doing something of real value in bringing all these people together and especially in bringing the rulers of the country, lawmakers as well as national bankers and industrialists, into touch with each other and with the economists, professors, and writers.

Education and Labor. FDR appointed him commission of Labor Statistics in 1933, and he modernized the Bureau of Labor Statistics (*DAB*, s.v. "Lubin, Isador").

4. Owen D. Young (1874–1962), a Boston lawyer, became general counsel and vice president of General Electric in 1913. Chairman of the board of Radio Corporation of America in 1919, he also became chairman of GE's board in 1922. In the 1920s, he was a significant figure in international diplomacy, helping to formulate the Dawes Plan and the Young Plan to reduce reparations. In 1932, he was mentioned as a possible Democratic presidential nominee, but he became a close adviser to FDR. From 1923 to 1940, he was a member of the Federal Reserve Bank of New York (*DAB*, s.v. "Young, Owen D.").

That these suppers have served me is beside the point—except to me. At them I could evaluate the abilities of the men as I never could from a *Congressional Record*. I saw the whole man, not only his political front. I saw how his mind worked, learned his temperament and prejudices. I had a chance to establish points of contact. I was also able to disarm some of them of their prejudices against me as I became to them a human being, not an example of the type they feared. I learned what was really going on, sometimes what was going to be done before it was, could put a word in occasionally, got a better grasp of political policies, heard much about men in public life I did not know, learned to admire some greatly and distrust others, met the wives of many, made friends with them. Some of the men grew to have a protective feeling about me, to understand my problems. I began to understand things before perplexing. And I got over my fear of these men, my timidity. I made friends, too, with the newspapermen who can tell you more and advise you better than anyone in Washington. I enlarged my viewpoint, could take politics less seriously in some ways, more seriously in others. If one has a mighty purpose, is single-eyed and single-minded like Senator Norris, he may succeed, although never leaving his own goldfish bowl. But if one is dealing with people, works in and with propaganda, I do not see how he can. The unprinted, the conversational gossip, is often more important to his purpose.

And, I acknowledge frankly, there is in me a desire for camaraderie, for approval, for friendship. A man in public life may find this among his fellow workers. A woman working with women, or in positions or professions where men give it to their women coworkers, may find this in their work hours. But a woman thrown among men politicians is not likely to get it there, not unless they have met her on some other ground and come to accept her there as a friend. A political office run and staffed with men is not the place for it. There is too much instinctive resentment at her invasion.

The first suppers back in the summer of 1922 were small—only one table— the talk general, and no need to start discussion with a question, as when they were enlarged to take care of twenty or thirty guests seated at small tables. The dinner talk simply continued as we lingered around the table. Among those I remember meeting there—whether at the first or successive suppers—is Sen. Joseph Robinson, discovered to be a charming raconteur of stories, old and new, about the Senate.[5]

He had a charming social manner. "Sweet," the ladies called him because he had such a natural and endearing way. Later he and his equally natural

---

5. Joseph T. Robinson (1872–1937) was a Democratic member of Congress from 1903 to 1913. Elected governor of Arkansas in 1912, he was then elected to the United States Senate in 1913 to fill a vacancy. In 1923, he was elected Democratic leader of the Senate. In 1928, he was nominated for vice president (*DAB*, s.v. "Robinson, Joseph T.").

wife became social favorites, but up to this time they had not mingled much in society, living, as many congressmen in Washington do, a quiet, retired life in a hotel.[6] "We could not afford society on our salary," Mrs. Robinson confided to me. "Mr. Robinson enjoyed his work, and I was satisfied just to be near him and make him comfortable." She had never "made her calls," as the official calling of a newcomer on her husband's superior in rank is known. But now some early investments were paying. They had a car, could take an apartment and go out more.

The next year I campaigned with the senator through country towns, when we had to change trains at any hour of the night, put up at funny hotels, travel in day coaches. It is a trying situation for a man and woman and a test of both manner and manners. But Senator Robinson passed it with a high mark. He talked just enough to relieve the tedium but never long enough to bore me or make me feel I was boring him with the need to be entertained. Naturally courteous to ladies, his thoughtfulness never seemed a strain. Every situation was met in such a natural, simple, easy way that embarrassment was impossible. It takes an innate gentleman to do this, and that he seemed so unaware he was doing it was all the more indicative of his innate fineness.

Senator Harrison, it appeared, was also a storyteller and a good one, but his quips on current politics were still more amusing, his irrepressible humor seeing always the comic side, and so making politics a source of never-ending amusement to him. No man in public life whom I have met has ever seemed to enjoy them more. There was a captivating boyishness about him in spite of the tinge of old-fashioned gallantry in his manner to women and patriarchal benevolence to men.

Senator Walsh, then paying devoted court to Mrs. Harriman, emphasized the serious side of politics, listening to persiflage with the patient tolerance of a schoolmaster watching the antics of the young, but always when he spoke, with careful diction and in a modulated voice, he commanded instant attention.[7] As thousands have seen him preside at national Democratic conventions, so he performs at a dinner table, courtly, gracious, precise, weighing each thought and word.

Senator Jones, on the contrary, moved from a ponderous exposition of tariff intricacies that might follow the simplest question about it to a delightful exchange of personal experiences.[8] It was as if he had certain stops. You turned

---

6. Ewilda Gertrude Miller married Joseph Robinson in 1896.

7. Thomas J. Walsh (1859–1933) was elected as a Montana Democrat to the United States Senate in 1912. Reelected three times, he served until 1933. A delegate to every Democratic National Convention from 1908 to 1932, he was permanent chairman in 1924 and in 1932. He died en route to Washington to accept an appointment as attorney general in FDR's cabinet (*DAB*, s.v. "Walsh, Thomas J.").

8. Andrieus A. Jones (1862–1927) had been mayor of Las Vegas, New Mexico, in 1893–1894. A member of the Democratic National Committee from 1908 to 1922, he was

on one and he became a public official; you turned on another and he was a boy out of school ready for a conversational lark.

Senator Walsh of Massachusetts, of the grandmotherly face, in spite of his Irish blood, seemed almost aching in humor, but in society left the forum behind him and could seldom be inveigled into a political discussion.[9] Just a nice old lady, he appeared dignified, reciprocative—fond, however, of society, especially that of the socially elect and highly placed. He is a bachelor, as to her discomfiture my daughter discovered when, giving a telephone invitation for Mrs. Harriman, she asked "Senator and Mrs. Walsh." Her terrible blunder was made apparent in his secretary's shocked voice.

Senator Pomerene and his wife, the most graciously mannered woman I have ever met, conveying always the cordial interest of one naturally reserved, which is the subtlest flattery, were frequent guests.[10] Like a courtly gentleman from the eighteenth century was the senator, with his high collar and wide black satin bow tie.

It was a moment for me when I met Mark Sullivan who had interested me ever since he had been editor of *Collier's*. For some reason I had expected to find a sprightly man, bubbling over with friendliness and interest. The dignity of the gray-haired man surprised me, his cynical attitude toward politics was a shock to me, and his indifference to a woman politician unflattering. Later I was to learn that he had his own enthusiasms. He could unbend, too, as when he dropped me a note saying that if my table was not full he would like to take back his regrets for my dinner for Senator and Mrs. Glass; his admiration for Senator Glass was so great he hated to miss an opportunity to see him, but would I please not tell his wife he had committed such a social error.

The discovery that cynicism toward politicians was the usual attitude of

elected to the United States Senate in 1916 and reelected in 1922 (*Biographical Directory of the U.S. Congress*, 1276).

9. David Walsh (1872–1947), lieutenant governor of Massachusetts in 1913, he served as governor in 1914–1915. He was elected as a Democrat to the United States Senate and served from 1919 to 1925. Defeated for reelection, he filled the vacancy at the death of Henry Cabot Lodge in 1926. Reelected in 1928, 1934, and 1940, he was defeated in 1946. Walsh was a lifelong bachelor (ibid., 2001; *DAB*, s.v. "Walsh, David").

10. Atlee Pomerene (1863–1937) graduated from the Cincinnati Law School in 1886. Associated with the reform group in Cleveland, he was convinced by Mayor Tom Johnson to run for governor in 1908. Although he lost, he was elected lieutenant governor of Ohio in 1910, after which the state legislature elected him to the United States Senate. He was reelected in 1916 but defeated in 1922 because of his opposition to the Eighteenth and Nineteenth Amendments. He became a national figure when he served as one of the special prosecutors of the Teapot Dome scandals in the Harding administration. In 1928 his name was placed in nomination for the presidency at the Democratic convention. Chair of Hoover's Reconstruction Finance Corporation, he then became a critic of the New Deal. In 1892 he married Mary Helen Bockius, daughter of a Canton, Ohio, manufacturer (*DAB*, s.v. "Pomerene, Atlee").

newspapermen was at first disconcerting. As also was the assumption on their part that I was just another one of the same stamp, made plain to me by their answers to my questions, and expressed in so many words by Willmot Lewis (now Sir Willmot Lewis) of the London *Times* in words something like these: "I came tonight just to meet you. I have been stationed in every capital of the world and met the politicians of every country, and without exception I have found them despicable, and I wanted to see what a woman politician would be like."[11]

Not as rude as it reads, however, did it sound, delivered in Sir Willmot's charming, whimsical way. For Sir Willmot, be it noted, shares with the late Mr. Richard Victor Oulahan of the *New York Times*, known affectionately as "Dick," the distinction of being the most polished "gentlemen" of the organized press.[12]

Yet these correspondents became in time my best friends in Washington, and I owe much to them, both men and women. You could, I discovered, discuss frankly with them any problem, putting all your cards on the table, and never would they betray a confidence. Advice, if asked, they would freely give. Their private opinions and estimates of other politicians were yours, not in turn to be betrayed. When I wanted to know the inside dope or get a real opinion on the outcome of some business, it was to them I went. Nonpartisan—if not without prejudice since they were human—their viewpoint made these opinions and estimates of real value. And always they were entertaining and delightful, with a gift of friendship.

The fear so often expressed of newspaper reporters I have never understood or shared. Their success depends upon winning the confidence of those who are the sources of information. If once they betrayed such a confidence, a source would be closed to them. So all I had to do was to tell them what was not for publication "in confidence," and give them the right to use the other more freely. How they managed after a long and involved conversation to keep the two separate in their minds was to me a wonder, and also how exactly they could report you. Only once was I seriously misquoted, and since the young woman did no more than to make me ridiculous, and at that was having a honeymoon, I felt no resentment.

Among the correspondents met at those first suppers at Mrs. Harriman's was Charley Michelson of the *New York World*, afterward the most brilliant

---

11. Willmot Harsant Lewis (1877–1950) became Washington correspondent for the *Times* of London in 1920. A leader of the Washington press corps, he was knighted in 1931 (*Dictionary of National Biography, 1941–1950*, s.v. "Lewis, Willmot Harsant").

12. Richard Victor Oulahan (1867–1931) became head of the Washington Bureau of the *New York Times* in 1912. The "dean of the capital corps of correspondents," he had covered every national convention of both parties since 1892 (*New York Times*, December 31, 1931, 1:3).

political publicity man, perhaps, in history when he served the Democratic National Committee prior to and during the campaign of 1932. His "Out of the Frying Pan" column that ran for years in the *World* deserves to rank with the column of Frank Kent of the *Baltimore Sun*, the "Great Game of Politics."[13]

Frederick William Wile, the popular radio speaker, was a frequent and always entertaining guest, constantly on the alert for a story for his radio talks and syndicated column, quick with a bon mot. And also Fred Essary, the genial representative of the *Baltimore Sun*, gregarious, generous, a thorough student, and probably the best informed of all on certain economic questions such as railroads.[14]

It was there, too, that my friendship with the Hards, Bill and Anne, began, although I had met William Hard in St. Louis on my way to Washington, discovering thereby how these correspondents run down their stories.[15] With a few members of the local League of Women Voters who were all brilliant women I was invited to meet him for tea at Barbara O'Neil's. As if incidentally, he threw out a few questions about Senator Reed. Answers from the women invariably led away from the subject to the League of Nations. I noticed that he adroitly brought them back, usually with some clever repartee, but thought nothing of that. Mindful of my newly acquired position with the Democratic

---

13. Charles Michelson (1868–1948) covered the Spanish-American War for the *San Francisco Examiner* and became that paper's managing editor in 1906. In 1917, he was the chief Washington correspondent for the *New York World* and wrote a column, "The Political Undertow." In 1929, Michelson went to work as publicity director for Democratic headquarters. After holding several jobs in the New Deal, such as publicity director of the NRA, he returned to party publicist in 1934 (*DAB*, s.v. "Michelson, Charles"). Frank Kent (1877–1958) started with the *Baltimore Sun* as a cub reporter in 1900. He became one of the top political reporters and was one of the first daily columnists with his "Great Game of Politics" (*Dictionary of Literary Biography*, vol. 29, *American Newspaper Journalists, 1926–1950*, s.v. "Kent, Frank").

14. Frederick William Wile (1873–1941) was a correspondent in Europe from 1900 to 1919. After his return to the United States, he became a news analyst and one of the first radio commentators. In 1920, he was chief of the Washington bureau for the *Philadelphia Public Ledger*. In 1923, he became an editorial writer for the *Washington Star* and began a column, "Washington Observations." In the same year he started his radio commentary, a fifteen-minute weekly show called *The Political Situation in Washington Tonight* (McKerns, *Biographical Dictionary of American Journalism*, s.v. "Wile, Frederick William"). J. Frederick Essary (1881–1942) was Washington correspondent for the *Baltimore Sun*, starting in 1912. He was president of the National Press Club in 1928 (*Who Was Who in America*, 2:177).

15. Anne Hard (1877–1961) graduated from the University of Wisconsin–Madison in 1898. Starting as a reporter for the *Madison Cardinal*, she worked for the *Chicago Evening Post* in 1903–1905 and also freelanced until the mid-1930s. She contributed articles, fiction, and interviews with political personalities to many popular magazines, did radio commentaries and newscasts, and wrote a column for *Town and Country* under the pseudonym Hyde Clement on activities in the capital. A Republican, she campaigned for Hoover in 1928 (*National Cyclopedia of American Biography*, s.v. "Hard, Anne").

National Committee I, myself, kept still. The guests had to leave, and the party broke up.

An invitation was immediately given for an impromptu dinner at the club downtown. I found myself seated next to Mr. Hard. Again the conversation got around to Senator Reed. Again I kept still. The hour grew late. But some of the crowd were going out to the Grossmans' and I must come along. The conversation somehow got on Wilsonianism and party loyalty and the league. Again I kept still. When a breakup seemed imminent Mr. Hard would plunge at once into another story as if to hold us longer. At last departure could not be postponed—trains did not tarry. To my good-bye in the hall, "so nice, etc.," he said abruptly, "Don't you have any opinions about Senator Reed? Or do you never talk?"

I had plenty, I explained, but I did not think this the time to express them publicly. But if he wanted to know for his private information I would tell him; although not, of course, for publication. And I did. He listened graciously, though with, I thought, a shade of discomfiture. When I met him in Washington he referred to this meeting. "You gave me a merry chase that day," he said, "and then at the last moment you told me what I'd been after all day and like a veteran promptly sewed me up. I knew then you were an A-1 politician." I let him think so. But until that moment I hadn't an idea of the purpose of those impromptu parties, nor what I had done to Bill Hard's story. My fairy godmother must have been on her job.

I had never met anyone like William Hard, then the author of a syndicated column, now the brilliant radio analyzer of politics. Nor have I since. Small, coming only to my shoulder, with a head so large that it seems on that body the largest you have ever seen, an emaciated face in which big eyes stare out at you and the mouth seems very large, he had enough intellectual energy and personality to have made a seven-foot body seem like a dynamo. The moment he raises his loud voice in emphatic, clear-cut words, everyone else keeps still. He has a laugh that reaches through the house and a sense of humor that constantly exercises it. Not that he monopolizes conversation. He is the most seductive listener I know. But when an opinion is expressed with which he disagrees, he is instantly ready with a retort. As a dialectician he has few equals. With many of his opinions I disagree, but I have never dared to get into an argument with him. Yet in spite of the force with which he discusses them and the vigor of his convictions he is one of the most popular men in Washington. Absolutely honest and frank, there is no pretense about him, and he, as well as his wife, the brilliant correspondent of the *New York Tribune*, has that gift for instant appreciation and understanding of others that makes for immediate friendship.

Frankness and open speaking such as theirs seldom make for popularity, yet they are as sought after for dinner guests as anyone in Washington. Living out at Georgetown in an unpretentious house on what cannot be a large income, entertaining simply, driving about in a Ford, they gather about them as brilliant a company as is to be found in the capital. Theirs is one of the most popular houses. There one may meet sooner or later everyone who counts politically or socially. Nor is all this surprising to anyone who has heard the conversation around their table, at which guests often linger all evening, and found himself suddenly uttering brilliant persiflage or expressing opinions that command attention, seen tired cabinet members become gay and senators sparkling, and realized that here is what social entertaining was meant to be and all too seldom is.

I have sometimes thought that if I were ever to be born again into this world I would like to be a finished, decorative, great lady like Mrs. Bourke Cockran; again a languorous siren like Mrs. Blaine Beale; or someone dripping charm like Eleanor Patterson, for women like these, I am convinced, exercise far more influence upon this man-made world than any others; again someone like Alice Roosevelt Longworth with a compelling personality and a gift for enjoyment of the passing panorama with no itch to take part, for this I know to be the most rewarding part a woman can play; or a real beauty like Mrs. Ogden Mills, giving pleasure by her mere presence; but more often I would choose to be Anne Hard, for all of these women owe something to their setting, their opportunities, and background, and Anne would be Anne wherever she found herself, witty, enthusiastic, compelling, owing nothing to anything but her own intellect and personality, yet dominating any scene in which she found herself, dashing here and there, finding interest in all things and people, able to write when she wishes, play, converse, entertain, think, and adjust herself to any environment, generous, fearless, unself-conscious.[16]

At our first meeting there had passed between us that queer electric spark that betokens affinity of spirit, and though we think alike about few things, our friendship has developed, fed by that generosity of hers that, seeing my need, has done so much to enlarge my Washington circle and done

---

16. Annie Ide married Bourke Cockran in 1906 (*New York Times*, March 2, 1923). Harriet S. Blaine, the youngest daughter of James G. Blaine, was divorced from Truxton Beale in 1896 (Marie Beale, *Decature House and Its Inhabitants*, 123). Eleanor Medill Patterson (1881–1948), called Cissy, was the granddaughter of Joseph Medill of the *Chicago Tribune*. In 1904, she married Count Joseph Gizycki, a Polish nobleman; they were finally divorced in 1917. She was a well-known society hostess at her home on Dupont Circle. In 1930, William Randolph Hearst hired her as editor and publisher of the *Washington Herald*. In 1939 she bought the *Washington Times* and the *Herald* and combined them (*NAW*, s.v. "Patterson, Eleanor Medill"). Dorothy Randolph Fell married Ogden Livingston Mills in 1924. He had served in Congress as a Republican from New York, 1921–1927. Undersecretary of the treasury from 1927 to 1932, he was secretary of the treasury in 1932–1933 (*Biographical Directory of the Executive Branch*, 243; *Who Was Who in America*, 1:846).

me so many kindnesses, not the least taking in my son one spring vacation from Yale.

And all this—with much more yet to be told—came from that call of Mrs. Harriman's. Without those suppers my life in Washington would never have been so interesting nor my work as effective. But it was not all that came out of her visit to me. I had said there were two things she could do. And the suppers planned, we went on to the other.

Washington was, as I have noted, at that time completely dominated by Republicans. Not only had we very few Democrats in Congress, but everywhere you went, all you heard was Republican doctrine. The Democratic stranger coming there must go away not only with the impression that the Democrats simply did not count but also impregnated with Republican doctrine. Even Democrats did not talk Democracy. When the DAR, the National Federation of Women's Clubs, and other organizations held their annual meetings, it was Republican hostesses who entertained them, Republican speakers who addressed them, Republican men and women they met. The drawing rooms of Republican women, I knew, were at the disposal of their party as Democratic women's seldom have been. There women from away might meet Ruth McCormick or Alice Longworth or cabinet leaders and go home charmed and, yes, influenced by them. Hadn't I long before seen Ruth employ this tactic when she kept open house at her Republican headquarters and Alice Longworth had said when I first met her, "Oh, surely not a Democrat!"

There was available no Democratic hostesses with big houses and a desire to use them so. But there were Democratic women in the District, wives of senators and representatives and permanent residents who had no opportunity in the voteless District to serve the party. Why, I had thought, couldn't they be organized to promote a Democratic Woman's Clubhouse to serve us in this way? And so the second thing I told Mrs. Harriman I wanted and she could get for me was such a clubhouse.

She saw the possibilities in it at once. And like me, having faith in fairy godmothers, was willing to undertake it. Only women with more faith than practicability would ever have done so. For surely no project could seem wilder, in those days of '22 when publicists were prophesying that the Democratic Party was dead, when hardly anyone in Washington seemed willing to acknowledge themselves Democrats, when we had no financial angels to draw on. But Mrs. Harriman discussed it with ex-President Wilson. He took an interest in it. Cordell Hull encouraged us and thus enthusiastically joined us. We found a few women to go in with us. And so we began. Mrs. Harriman says the idea was mine. But the enthusiasm, much of the work, and the prestige were hers. And those are the essentials that made it go. Afternoon after afternoon we met in her drawing room, Mrs. Charles Hamlin, wife of the then-governor of the Federal Reserve board, Democrat to her backbone; Mrs. Andrieus A. Jones; and Mrs. John B. Kendrick; senatorial wives who felt, they said, glad to do something for a party that had done so much for them. Marion Banister; Antoinette Funk; Mrs. Stephen Bonsal, to whom Democracy was almost a religion; Catherine Filene Dodd, Mrs. Alvin, a bride and newcomer to Washington from Boston; Mrs. Frank Hiram Snell, a Washingtonian leader of women. Many were the difficulties and snags, but finally we issued invitations for memberships. It was to be financed—well, there is no reason for giving away our methods or our troubles to Republicans—but in time we were established in a house on Eighteenth Street, almost across Jackson Square from the White House.[17] Mrs. Wilson was one of our first members. Mrs. Harriman was president. We opened with an evening reception, the first time Democrats as Democrats had gotten together for a long time. We planned a series of Monday luncheons at which Democrats would speak, thus furnishing an opportunity for Democratic women to get together and for the dissemination of Democratic doctrine.

Many were the vicissitudes we had—those who operate on faith must expect them—but slowly we grew. In time Minnie Fisher Cunningham came to manage and help us, the national committee assisted us financially, and at last, due to the generosity of Mrs. Edward B. Meigs, we were able to buy a beautiful house near Dupont Circle. Mrs. Hamlin brought out of storage priceless old furniture for it. And now, with Mrs. Herrick its president, it

---

17. Huybertie Lansing Pruyn married Charles Hamlin in 1898. President Cleveland had appointed him assistant secretary of the treasury in charge of customs in 1893; Wilson also appointed him to that job in 1913 and the next year appointed him to the first Federal Reserve Board. He was reappointed for ten-year terms in 1916 and 1926 (*DAB*, s.v. "Hamlin, Charles"). In 1902, Natalie Stoneroad married Andrieus Jones, senator from New Mexico (*Who Was Who in America*, 1:645). Eula Wulfjen, daughter of a Texas and Wyoming rancher, married John B. Kendrick in 1891. He served as governor of Wyoming in 1914 and was elected to the United States Senate in 1916, the first Democratic senator from Wyoming. He served until his death in 1933 (*DAB*, s.v. "Kendrick, John B."). Henrietta Fairfax Morris married journalist Stephen Bonsal in 1900 (*DAB*, s.v. "Bonsal, Stephen"). Catherine Filene of Boston (b. 1896) married Alvin Dodd in 1921 and then Jouett Shouse in 1932. With an A.B. and a M.Ed. from Vassar, she was the author of *Careers for Women* (1920). A founder of the Woman's National Democratic Club, she was editor of the *Democratic Bulletin* and the *Democratic Digest*, 1929–1933. She was a member of the DNC from Massachusetts in 1920 (*Who Was Who in America*, 3:230; *Who Was Who among North American Authors, 1921–1939*, 1:515–16). Mrs. Frank Hiram Snell was on the organizing committee of the Woman's National Democratic Club. She served on the Board of Governors in the 1920s and was the first life member (Adalyn Davis, *The Woman's National Democratic Club: The Place Where Democrats Meet* [Washington: WNDC, 1992]; Minnie Fisher Cunningham to ENB, May 12, 1927, ENB Papers). Although the Board of Governors voted on February 8, 1923, to authorize the "lease and purchase" of a house at 1724 I Street, the club evidently never moved there. On December 14, 1923, the board voted to lease 820 Connecticut Avenue, holding their opening reception on January 15, 1924 (Scrapbook, Club Letters and Minutes 1922–1926, Archives, Woman's National Democratic Club).

is one of the centers of social life in Washington with a constantly growing membership.[18]

To the dinners of the Democratic governors and Mrs. Harriman's round-table dinners came the elite of Washington, Republicans as well as Democrats prizing an invitation to them. How much it has done to popularize Democracy socially, one cannot, of course, know; but the fact remains that, though we have not yet at the time I write in the summer of '32 had a Democratic administration, it is not any longer de trop to talk Democracy or to be a Democrat in Washington, and Republicans frequently express their envy of our house, our entertainment, and the interest we create. Nor was this its only service to the party. Democratic senators and representatives bring there as a matter of course their constituents from home for the weekly luncheons and the monthly dinners. These visitors return home with an idea that the Democratic Party, even though in the minority, is active and alive in the capital. There they see, meet, and talk to the Democratic leaders, and hear discussed Democratic policies that they will in time discuss when they go home. Thus is deepened and tightened their ties to their party and their sense of its national scope.

During that summer of 1922 we, of course, only laid our plans. It was the fall of '23 before we opened our clubhouse. But much time went into these meetings and plans.

---

18. Minnie Fisher Cunningham (1882–1964) earned a degree in pharmacy in 1901. When the Texas state suffrage organization began in 1903, she worked as a speaker and became the state president in 1915 and succeeded in getting the woman vote in primaries in 1918. In 1919, Catt brought her to Washington to be secretary of NAWSA's Congressional Committee. After passage of the Nineteenth Amendment, she became executive vice president of the national League of Women Voters. In 1923, she became executive secretary of the Woman's National Democratic Club and editor of its *Democratic Bulletin*. In 1927, she made an unsuccessful run for the United States Senate, the first woman to do so in Texas. In 1944, she lost in the governor's primary to Coke Stevenson (*NAW-Modern*, s.v. "Cunningham, Minnie Fisher"). Margaret Wister Meigs was the wife of physiologist Dr. Edward Meigs. They lived at 1445 Rhode Island (*Who's Who in the Nation's Capital, 1926–1927*, 397; *Social Register: Washington, 1919*). Fannie Field (1883–1962) married lawyer Samuel Herrick in 1907. Her grandfather had been attorney general of Virginia and the vice presidential candidate on the Populist ticket in 1892. A graduate of Wellesley in 1904, she served as president of the Woman's National Democratic Club in 1931–1933 (*Washington Post*, June 7, 1962; *Prominent Personages of the Nation's Capital: A Work for Newspaper and Library Reference* [Washington, D.C.: *Washington Times*, n.d.], 277, 338).

12 *Campaigning for Congress*

Throughout this summer I made flying campaign trips. The first was to Maine, the state where as the election is in September campaigning becomes also summer resorting. Perhaps that is one reason for the perennial activity of Democrats in that hopelessly Republican state. For no matter how hopeless it may seem, Democratic orators are delighted to have a try at converting these stony-headed Republicans. At that time there was, however, another reason. The perennial gubernatorial candidate was a William R. Pattangall who, had he lived in another state, might ere this have become a Democratic nominee for president. Brilliant in intellect, with a biting wit and oratorical fervor, passionately a Democrat, his campaigns became great public events. Even Republican newspapers detailed reporters to accompany him that his game of wit might be recorded. The countryside turned out to hear him. Never expecting to win he went into these campaigns partly, I think, for diversion and partly to educate the people. They should at least hear Democracy. When he and his energetic, capable wife asked a national committee for speakers and campaigners, they could not be said nay. So up to Maine I went to have a very good time campaigning with Judge Pattangall. That I did not make a good speech did not bother me, for who needed to say anything when Judge Pattangall had said it all; and the drives in their car, the old houses with barns attached, the smiling hills and blue surf beating against the rocky shore afforded all the joys of vacationing. In spite, too, of the Republican majorities, the Pattangalls could always stir up enthusiasm and had a slew of workers. Strange as it may seem, I have never in any state found as active and devoted a political organization of Democrats. No wonder the Republicans decided to eliminate Mr. Pattangall as a candidate by placing him in the supreme court of Maine. It was a great loss to the Democratic Party if only that no longer were national conventions treated to one of his speeches like that he made in Madison Square Garden against the Ku Klux Klan—his wife, by the way, voting against the plank he was favoring.[1] Oh, yes, they had

---

1. William R. Pattangall (1865–1942) had served in the Maine House of Representatives from 1897 to 1911. Chairman of the Democratic State Committee in 1916 and 1919, he was Maine's attorney general 1911–1913. He ran unsuccessfully for governor in 1922 and 1924 and was appointed associate justice of Maine's Supreme Court in 1926. From 1930 to 1935 he was chief justice. He served on the DNC in 1936 (*Who Was Who in*

their convictions, sometimes on opposite sides of a question and again on the same side.

Sometimes at parties we play a game in which each member tells the most embarrassing moment of his life. My contribution came from an earlier trip to Maine. Judge Hull and I went up together to a meeting of the state committee. We got off the train at eight in the morning to be met by a reception committee, large in number and properly pompous in manner, facing us on the platform. He alighted first and turned to help me. And just as I took the first step my supporter broke from my corset. I made an ineffectual grab for it. The weight of it carried down my stocking. Stopping the procession I had to gather it up again and clutch it through my skirt. Yes, skirts were fairly long then, perhaps seven inches from the floor, but bare ankles were not common even on beaches and dangling stockings never will be. Still clutching my stocking I got into a car. It was full of men. Now I would, of course, frankly take off the offending supporter and roll my stocking, but rolled-below-the-knees hose were then a very private matter. The hotel, a summer resort, sat far back from the street. The walk was bordered with spectators. But up the long walk I went beside Judge Hull, slightly bent at my hips, my hand clutching my garter. The entrance hall was large, the desk a long way off. But, finally there I excused myself and hurried to the first door. Whether Judge Hull or any man wondered why I stooped all that long way, I do not know. At least they gave no sign.

After my trip to Maine I dashed out to New Mexico. Mrs. Jones, who took a great interest in her husband's reelection to the Senate, had persuaded Judge Hull to send me to the state convention that met at Albuquerque. I missed my connection in Kansas City, and the only train that would get me there on time was the Mail Express, which carried only the mail car and one day coach. My husband who had come up to St. Louis to ride from there to Kansas City with me ran to get me a thermos bottle of coffee and some sandwiches. I arrived at Albuquerque just in time to run hurriedly to a dinner of women kept waiting for me. My speech next morning was the first on the program, and so I had had no opportunity to acquaint myself with New Mexican ways.

The large barnlike auditorium was filled with a dusky mass of men, many in blue shirts and khaki trousers with shining brown faces—Mexicans, of course. Only a few women. I was introduced and began my speech. Imagine my amazement after my first sentence to hear a fine voice interrupt me and speak a sentence in a foreign tongue. I looked around, and there stood a handsome cream-colored young man. He stopped. I said another sentence. Again he interrupted, and I realized that I was being interpreted line by line. I had never heard that in New Mexico public political meetings and the law courts

---

America, 2:415). Gertrude McKenzie married William Pattangall in 1892. The Democratic National Convention opened in Madison Square Garden on June 24, 1924.

are conducted in two tongues. Not much chance for fire, emotional appeal, halted thus; and continuity was hard to maintain. But I got along until the last. For my peroration I had borrowed a metaphor of William Jennings Bryan, calculated to bring a rousing applause. This time the applause anticipated my last sentence. The young Spanish interpreter, acquainted with Bryan's oratory, had finished my quotation for his Spanish hearers without waiting for me to say it first in English.

I was, however, a little mollified when the blue-shirted Mexicans crowded up to express volubly, if not comprehensibly, to me at least, their appreciation and gratitude. "They are delighted," Mrs. Jones explained enthusiastically. "Many of them, you know, never heard a woman speak in public before. The man in front of me turned to his neighbor and grabbed his hand. 'My God,' he said. 'She's got brains in there,' putting his hands on his own head."

Mrs. Jones was enthusiastic over the success of her experiment. She had evidently been nervous about the new women voters. She was, it developed, the personal conductor of the senator's campaign as well as the senator. That he was popular with his constituents was evident when he rose to speak. The interpreter was no impediment to his fire and continuity, for he never stopped. He simply pitched his voice in one key while the interpreter trailed him in another, and so the speech went on like a duet, the Americans listening to one and the Mexicans and Spaniards to the other.

The speech was a great success and the applause deafening. But the most important part of campaigning to the senator was speech making. He was absentminded, had a bad memory for people's names, and was too weary to grow enthusiastic over strangers. Never mind, Mrs. Jones was there, ever at his elbow, whispering names into his ear, reminding him of this, insisting that he accept this invitation, apologizing profusely that he must refuse the other.

When I was afterward asked, as I often was, what part a wife should take in a husband's campaign, or by wives of candidates how they could help their husbands, I have always remembered Mrs. Jones, to me the perfect pattern of a candidate's wife. Quiet, unobtrusive, she accompanied the senator on all his trips, always herself in the background, but seeing that no trick in the game was missed, sparing him when she could, yet firm about essentials. He was not strong. The food at out-of-the-way hotels did not agree with him. Without offense to anyone she censored his diet, saw that he rested when he should, as buffer, valet, physician, the first and greatest ally of his manager. Yet apparently, and this was her greatest achievement, no one except myself ever seemed to realize all this, not even the senator himself.

Seeing her in Washington, apparently engaged wholly in the social life, quiet, diffident, and sensitive, one would never suspect how much she had to do with getting the senator there. Yet, as president of the National Woman's Club, she later played a part herself on the political stage.

From Albuquerque I went up to Colorado Springs where for an afternoon

I saw my husband again on his way to Denver on business. We caught each other as we could in passing, so difficult was it to fit our engagements and itineraries. And then on to Minnesota where Anna Dickey Olesen was waging a fight for the senatorship with the able assistance of redheaded, vigorous, effective Mabel Wiesner, always on the firing line to elect a Democrat.

The first woman to run for senator, Anna Olesen was waging her campaign with a voice. Without any organization to speak of—the Democrats were greatly in the minority and quite hopeless with hardly any funds—she had taken on single-handed Senator Kellogg, the Republican nominee, and Henrik Shipstead, the Farmer-Labor candidate.[2] Into a town she would go in her little Ford—the gift of some women friends—make her fiery oratorical speech on the tariff, on farm relief, on foreign policy, take up a little collection, and on to the next. I don't know whether her opponents were ever afraid of her or not, but she drew large crowds and evoked great enthusiasm. Deadly earnest, she was an emotional orator, impressively sincere, and a masterly campaigner. I should like to have seen her in the Senate, for she would have come into it like a wind from the prairies and, undaunted by precedent or political expediency, brought into it that feminine note that suffragists hoped so vainly to put into government.

I opened her campaign with her in an enormous auditorium in Creekston on the northern border of the state. And thereby acquired what my family calls my political affinity.

After I returned to Washington I found my secretary chuckling one morning over a letter in my mail.

"Dear Lady," it began. "Perhaps you do not remember me. I was in the back of the gallery (remember the size of that auditorium), but I liked your looks fine. Will you give me political advice about this here campaign?" It was signed by a name unknown to me.

I dictated an answer advising him to vote for Mrs. Olesen.

In due course came another letter on similar paper, dated from another place.

"Dear lady," it ran. "I saw Mrs. Olesen too, but you was the one that went to my heart."

The correspondence ceased, or so I thought. But four years later when I was dated to speak at a Democratic dinner in Minneapolis arrived another

---

2. Frank Billings Kellogg of Minnesota (1856–1937), a progressive Republican, served in the Senate 1917–1923. Coolidge apppointed him ambassador to Great Britain in 1924–1925 and then secretary of state in 1925. He won the Nobel Peace Prize in 1930 for his role in the Kellogg-Briand Pact (1928), renouncing war as an instrument of national policy (*DAB*, s.v. "Kellogg, Frank Billings"). Henrik Shipstead (1881–1960) was elected to the United States Senate on the Farm-Labor ticket in Minnesota in 1922. He defeated incumbent Kellogg. He was reelected three times before his defeat in 1946 (*DAB*, s.v. "Shipstead, Henrik").

letter on the same kind of stationery. Enclosing a clipping of my picture, my old correspondent recalled himself to me, expressed joy at my being in Minneapolis so soon, and asked me to name the place and hour he could see me. I answered, saying the public was invited to the dinner at a certain hotel, and thought no more about it.

Before the dinner, however, a man called over the telephone announcing he was downstairs and ready to see me. I did not catch the name, but at once I remembered my unknown admirer. And rather curtly said I could not see anyone before the dinner. Nor did I go down to it until the last moment. And when I did, a prominent politician told me with equal curtness that he was sorry I had not been able to give him the conference he desired. The admirer, of course, never appeared.

Followed other campaign tours. One into Ohio gave me my first experience of that hit-or-miss way state campaign managers have of shuttling a speaker across a state wherever someone asks for one, without knowing whether one is needed or not. Such appeals had been made to me to come into Ohio that I had canceled other engagements to go, supposing there was some special need for my services. When I arrived at Columbus I was told to report the next day at a little town in the northeastern part of the state. To get there I had to go into Indiana, get off my train at six A.M., take an electric road back to Lima, and then, after another wait, a local to the town. When at last I arrived I found myself unexpected, no meeting had been planned, nor was one especially desired. But finally a few people were gathered in a small lodge room, made up mostly of women who told me they would never vote for Senator Pomerene on any account because he was anti-Prohibition. I checked that meeting off as an accident such as might happen to any campaign manager. My itinerary took me back to Columbus to report to state headquarters. Thence I was sent back to the eastern part of the state to speak at a mill town on the Ohio River, across from Wheeling where, as there was no hotel in the town, I was advised to stay the night. The meeting was in a Bessemer Steel–plant suburb. The hall was filled with workmen, hardly a woman was present. I was not prepared to speak to such an audience, nor was it prepared to listen to a woman like me. What they wanted was a man, preferably a labor man, who spoke their own language. I tried to revamp my speech as I went along, but I do not flatter myself that I turned any votes. The next night I spoke in the northeastern part of the state. With me was billed a congressman from Texas who made so long a speech that there was time for me to say only a few words. Back again then to Columbus and a small unadvertised meeting of women. Then, since there was a day when they had nothing whatever to do with me, out to a small town with a gentleman who was to tell the women how to organize. As a matter of fact, that was just the kind of a meeting I could have been helpful at. But the man did not know that, and introduced me, after he had spoken, merely as an afterthought.

One of the women asked him what they were to do about Florence Allen who, though a Democrat, was running as an Independent for supreme judge.[3]

He explained to them, as if speaking to children, that as she was not running as a Democrat, they would, of course, have to vote against her and for the man the Democrats were supporting. It was just too bad, but she could have gone in for the Democratic nomination and she hadn't. Maybe next time she would, and they could vote for her. As Democrats they must work against her.

On our way back to Columbus he asked me how I thought he had handled that Florence Allen business. It was giving them lots of trouble, as she was popular with the Democratic women.

"I don't know your election laws here or anything about your judiciary," I said, "but it occurs to me, after what you said and the way they talked, that perhaps your method of electing judges was designed to have a nonpartisan bench and Miss Allen is running deliberately as an Independent because that is the intention of the law, although by agreement the political parties are getting around it."

He said yes, that was the case.

"Well, don't you think these women who live in Ohio will see that as clearly as I, a stranger, did?" I asked. He allowed that perhaps they would. Her election proved they did.

Once more I was sent across the state into the northwest corner and thence to Zanesville, arriving just as the meeting at the fairgrounds broke up. But at that I had a pleasant visit with gay-hearted Eleanor Bailey, a young matron who had been campaigning with Senator Pomerene, a charming, unexperienced speaker who made a great hit with her audiences and was cut out for politics but not, I could have told the senator, one to win over these middle-aged dry women.

Thence I went back to Washington, a hard week without a single vote affected. Such was, and is, the way men utilize women to win the women's vote. There were in Ohio a number of Democratic women's clubs, active and efficient, who would have welcomed me and whom I might have stimulated and helped. But the campaign managers—men all—had not thought of them. A place ought to have a speaker. Here was one. Send her out.

Other more successful trips followed. A speech in Boston after which Professor Dallas Lore Sharp came up to me and said, "Why, you speak good English. If only we'd known you would be like this, we would have had you

---

3. Florence Allen (1884–1966) graduated from New York University Law School in 1913, worked for suffrage, practiced law in Cleveland, and became an assistant county prosecutor in 1919. After passage of the Nineteenth Amendment, she ran for the Court of Common Pleas judgeship and won, the first woman on any general jurisdictional court. In 1922, she was elected to the Ohio Supreme Court by a large majority. In 1934, FDR appointed her to the Sixth Circuit Court of Appeals (*NAW-Modern*, s.v. "Allen, Florence").

a real audience who could appreciate you."[4] One in Philadelphia to a club of ladies when an aristocratic member of an old family said, "Even if she is a Democrat she's a lady." Once in Rhode Island I spoke to an Irish group where I tried to overcome the damage done by a previous speaker who had extolled Cromwell. Others in Detroit, Chicago, New Jersey, Delaware, Tennessee, and New York.

Yet all the time constant work was going on at the office, what with the correspondence, the organization of women's clubs, the furnishing of women speakers where they really were wanted, the preparation of a weekly news sheet sent to women's clubs and newspapers, and literature. Nine o'clock frequently found us at our desks. We rarely left until seven, and often it was much later. I still marvel at the work we did with our small force. Fortunately for me there was no law against slave driving.

Several organizers were kept on the road, making reports, organizing clubs. Connecticut, Maine, and other states had followed Missouri in forming state federations of Democratic women's clubs. Women speakers were sent out. Requests came in so constantly for education on organization and Democratic policies that Mrs. Halsey Wilson of New York was kept busy holding three- to six-day schools modeled on the citizenship schools of the League of Women Voters.[5] Schools of Democracy they were called in which instruction in speech making, organization, and Democratic policies was given. Very popular they proved, too, Mrs. Wilson having a faculty for rousing enthusiasm and zeal and giving an idealistic interpretation of policies that appealed to women. Her students were devoted to her.

If response was any indication, my theory that women preferred to work in clubs was justified. But ever and again there was difficulty with the men state-controlled organization. Sometimes, too, with women in the state organization who feared the clubs might weaken their control, especially women who owed their position to the men. In vain I would point out to them that there had always been men's clubs and that in every campaign such clubs were advocated, promoted. I called attention to the Young Democrats' Club of Oklahoma, the National Democratic Club in New York, and many others. Some state vice chairmen advanced the idea that the vice chairmen of the local party committee should become ipso facto the president of the women's club.

---

4. Dallas Lore Sharp (1870–1929) graduated from the theological school of Boston University in 1899. He was a professor of English there until 1922. He published numerous books of essays, including *A Watcher in the Woods* (1903) and *The Better Country* (1928) (Preston, *American Biographies*, 922).

5. Halsey Wilson (b. 1868) began the *United States Catalog* of books in print in 1899 and also established *Readers' Guide to Periodical Literature*. In 1902, he organized the H. W. Wilson Company and in 1904 began the *Book Review Digest* and other bibliographic sources. He married Justina Leavitt in 1895 (*National Cyclopedia of American Biography*, s.v. "Wilson, Halsey").

Nor could I make them see that if a club was denied the opportunity to elect its own officers, it then lost its character. The naive proposition was once put to me by a national committeewoman that no clubs should be formed until she had censored all the officers.

Fear, I saw then, was the great enemy of effective organization, fear that someway, somehow, power would be generated that would not be controlled by those already having power. My objective—to organize the women for victory—was not that of these politicians. Theirs was to keep themselves in power.

And then there were the complications due to the topsy-like way that political organizations had developed. The state organizations were supreme in their states. The national organization could not, against their will, organize Democratic women's clubs in their states. Yet the national organization was supposed, urged, expected to promote organization. How could it do nothing then in states that would not undertake or perfect organizations of women themselves or opposed—as some did—any organization of the women. Women were voters. And the very states with active organizations were often the very ones that opposed our doing any work in them. It was all quite confusing to a woman who had been trained in organizations that concentrated on victory for their cause rather than control by a clique. Still, in spite of difficulties, the number of clubs was increasing.

At last the congressional campaign ended. Election night came. We gathered in headquarters to hear returns; the chairman and his force, senators, congressmen, District Democrats. No private wires, of course. We could not afford that, but a telephone connection with some source of information and telegrams continually being delivered with someone to add up figures. And soon we knew we were winning. We gained both congressmen and senators. Not the majority of Congress, but a great gain.[6]

To one who knows the difficulties under which Chairman Hull worked, the lack of money, the disrupted conditions in which the campaign of 1920 left the party, the hopeless attitude of many Democrats, the little assistance given the committee, it was a remarkable victory. There was no depression to be capitalized. The Harding administration was still in full swing. The tariff was the sole issue, and the Fordney-McCumber Tariff Act had not been in operation long enough to be a very good object lesson.[7]

Yet there had been steady pounding by a publicity department that supplied

---

6. The 1922 congressional elections left the Senate with 51 Republicans to 43 Democrats and 2 Farmer-Laborites; the House division was 225 Republicans, 205 Democrats, and 1 Socialist (John D. Hicks, *Republican Ascendancy, 1921–1933*, 88).

7. The Fordney-McCumber tariff of 1922 restored protection to a level comparable to preprogressive tariff reductions. The tariff made it difficult for foreign countries to sell goods to the United States, thus harder to repay war debts.

seventy-two hundred country papers frequent and heavy broadsides from Cordell Hull, an energetic stiffening of county and state committees, literature, speaking tours, and constant correspondence. When newspapers generally referred to the work of the national committee under Chairman Raskob and Executive Chairman Shouse in 1929 as the first between-campaign work to be undertaken by the national committee, I remembered those months of work in 1922.[8] When the Democratic victories in the congressional election of 1930 were hailed as evidence of what splendid between-campaigns work they had done, I recalled those victories in the 1922 congressional campaign. How short is political memory, public and private!

---

8. John Jakob Raskob (1879–1950) was a financier associated with the Dupont Company and General Motors. In 1928 he became chairman of the DNC to run the Smith presidential campaign. He opposed FDR's nomination in 1932 (*DAB*, s.v. "Raskob, John Jakob"). Jouette Shouse (1879–1968) was elected to the United States House of Representatives from Kansas as a Democrat in 1914 and placed on the Banking and Currency Committee where he became a friend of Carter Glass. Reelected in 1916, then defeated in 1918, he was appointed assistant secretary of the treasury at the suggestion of Glass. After working with Raskob on the Smith campaign, he became chairman of the DNC after the 1928 election. Although he supported FDR in 1932, he opposed the New Deal; in 1934 became president of the American Liberty League, an isolationist organization and thereafter supported Republicans (*DAB*, s.v. "Shouse, Jouette").

13 *Jug of War*

In December I went home for Christmas, my children returning from school for the holidays. At once I went domestic. Politics and politicians were forgotten. I might, so far as thoughts and interests went, never have left my Joplin home. There were the Christmas celebration to plan and bring off, wardrobes to be seen to, parties to give, attend, and chaperon, meals to superintend. I started as a domesticated woman, and when I went into writing and public work, I continued to be one. I seemed, indeed, to be a double-barreled person. For periods one barrel might not be used while I concentrated on the other, but each one was ready to be shot when it was needed. At other periods I have employed them both simultaneously.

Nor is this as hard as it may seem. It requires only a faculty for concentrating on the one you are using while you are using it and having a real interest in both kinds of work. I have always liked housekeeping. There is no task it involves I do not enjoy, whether it is cooking, cleaning, sewing, furnishing, or entertaining, although I grow weary of one if my interests are held to it exclusively for too long a stretch, not because of the tasks themselves but because routine work always becomes boring and it leads to no definite end—no job ever finished. Perhaps, too, the other parts of my nature, the desire to accomplish a definite job, reach an objective, and other parts of my brain after lying long dormant insist on exercise.

There is a very real fillip to the ego in knowing you are making people dependent on you for making them happy and comfortable. No other accomplishment brings as much satisfaction as is mine when I look about a room or house that is as I would have it be.

I came back to domesticity as a businessman goes on a fishing trip or putters about his farm or garden for diversion. When a woman is double-barreled this way, or divides her interest, perhaps she is not as successful in either job as if she had concentrated on one. It may handicap her to try. On the other hand I am not sure it is not a help; one may serve as diversion from the other and so enable her to bring a freshness into each when she attacks it. Few men have ever tried this way of working. I doubt if they could even if they wanted to. But women—at least domesticated women—have served a long apprenticeship in flitting from job to job, keeping three things going at the same time. The traditional work of the sex has demanded it. Perhaps by some survival-of-the-fittest method it has become a feminine faculty.

At any rate I always came back to domesticity with pleasure, and never was I willing to forfeit a home and the expansiveness it gives me for any amount of success in some other work.

To Washington I returned by way of Oklahoma to see Jack Walton's governor's inaugural barbecue at which were one hundred thousand people.[1] He promised well, Jack Walton; I was impressed both by his speech and by an interview I had with him. A man with his jaw should have succeeded, and Oklahoma likes its governors rugged and picturesque. But there were evidences, even then, of trouble. Even the inauguration ceremonies suggested an armed truce. The Democrats seemed divided into two camps: those who had voted for him and those who had not—the first determined the others should have no recognition, and the others determined he should not succeed. State elections are not verdicts in Oklahoma. They merely name the parties to a tournament—the governor and the legislature a tournament that frequently ends in unseating the governor. Even the women I met were divided into groups that scarcely spoke to each other. In an effort not to play favorites I sashayed between the two, but it really was time wasted, for they scarcely knew I was there. Perhaps it was natural, seeing they were all more or less newcomers themselves, that they felt no obligations of hospitality. Many states have their own particular cultural idiosyncrasies growing out of their history, but none are more unique than Oklahoma's. Starting as Indian Territory, which to this day I call it when I do not stop to think, with its Indian citizenry and much of its land still owned by the federal government's wards, colonized all at once by the spectacular "runs," closer than any other to its own frontier days, becoming a state at a period when political fads and fancies were the fashion, and suddenly through the discovery of oil turning out millionaires overnight; it is different from not only any other part of the United States but also the world.

Not that it is "all of a piece." In one place it reminds me of the Delta country of Mississippi, in another of Reno, in still others of western Kansas, the Far West of Deadwood Dick, a section of New York City. An English university professor said to a friend of mine that she was so glad to have read *Cimarron*. She had always wanted to know what the Middle West was like, and now she did! I thought of our prim and smug little town of Carthage, of the placid farms of Iowa, of central Missouri's southern culture, of the gaunt lands of Nebraska, of Illinois' rich mud farms and prosperous industrial towns and mouldering

---

1. John C. Walton (1881–1949) was elected governor of Oklahoma in 1922. To stop the Klan, he put the entire state under martial law, which led to his impeachment and removal from office in 1923. In 1924, he was the Democrats' unsuccessful nominee for the United States Senate. He lost his race for mayor of Oklahoma City in 1931 and his bid for the Democratic nomination for governor in 1934 and 1938 (*Biographical Directory of Governors*, 3:1244–45).

Springfield, of the thrifty towns in Kansas, like Emporia and Lawrence with their academic backgrounds; and I smiled. The Middle West? Oklahoma is a composite of southern prejudice, the far-western independence and outlaw spirit, the go-getter attitude of New York City, and Indian traditions. Yet it is in the Middle West, a part of it, and not the poorest or least important. Living within twenty miles of it all my life, I had seen it in the making, and this proximity brings it into my own picture and impression of the Middle West.

I stopped at Tulsa. Different from Oklahoma City, which is a small town that has expanded gradually into a large one, keeping the town appearance and ideography, which incidentally became the state capital, Tulsa is a mushroom city, sprung into being overnight, with a ten- or fifteen-story building or hotel patterned after Broadway or Fifth Avenue next to a vacant lot filled with rubbish, shops that equal or surpass in merchandise any to be found in Palm Beach or Atlantic City, a city air, a city complex. And as I looked at it, I recalled that even after we were married, my husband had hunted deer upon its site. If he had taken seriously the old codger who brought him a bottle filled with a dark, thick fluid that he had gotten out of a hole when he drilled for water, this might have been a very different story of mine!

Back in Washington I settled into the business of organizing the Democratic women for the 1924 campaign. One of my theories—I am given, it must be apparent, to them—was that it was a mistake to wait until after a presidential nomination to organize for victory, that there should be a permanent, continuous, working party organization, like a standing army, ready to start the moment a national convention was over. I thought of the fight between the two parties as a war in which each campaign was only one battle. To me, a political party was not a horde of hungry office seekers hunting every four years for some new bait to catch voters so they could get the offices, but an organization devoted to a political philosophy and program, seeking to make converts to both, with each campaign an opportunity to win more converts until it had enough to enable it to put both into practice in governmental policies. The current idea that political parties must take a position pro or con on any matter of public interest or discussion at the moment in order to give people a chance to express themselves on it has never appealed to me, nor its corollary that if they do not, well, they are afraid to face an issue. Here, for example, is the Ku Klux Klan. Some people favor it; some oppose it. So the political parties in their platforms must declare themselves one way or another. Here again is the Eighteenth Amendment! Some want it retained; others want it repealed. So the political parties must take a stand for retention or repeal. And if they do not, why, there is no difference between the parties and party leaders are cowards.

If a political party really has a philosophy of government, it will naturally present certain economic and social programs embodying that philosophy. It will care so much to put these programs over that it will not be diverted to any other questions. This idea of a political party may be idealistic or naive. But imagine Jefferson being diverted by a wet-and-dry issue, or Hamilton, or Pitt. Fancy Mussolini, or Lenin, or Cromwell, waging a campaign on such an issue.

They want to win, of course, but not for victory's sake, but to put their program over, and would rather be defeated than abandon it. But if a party has no philosophy or program, these issues naturally take possession of its machinery just as the ten devils in the parable entered into the empty man.

Not that social questions like religious intolerance and Prohibition are unimportant. They are not. But there are ways to solve them without diverting a political party from its real business. The Eighteenth Amendment could be repealed by the same process it was passed. No major political party ever had a plank for Prohibition. No national campaign was fought on it.

I do not write this because I am opposed to the repeal of the Eighteenth Amendment. I am not; of that, however, in its appointed place. But if a political party has no program based on a philosophy of government, perhaps it is just as well to use it as a referendum on some matter engaging the public interest.

I know that my theory of a political party did not accord with the facts. Instead of being an organization made up of people believing in a philosophy, in America at least, political parties were only a means to power. Someone wanted something, an office, or a policy. He could get it, under our system, only through belonging to or working in a party, so he joined the one that was in the majority in his locality or that would more likely adopt the policy he favored. He selected it, regardless of his own philosophy (everyone has one even if he has never formulated it). And so inside both parties there were men who had conflicting philosophies of government, and periodically they indulged in a tug of war called national conventions in which those with one philosophy pulled hard against those who had the other. When one side won, the party would be "radical" or "progressive"; when the other it would be "conservative" or "standpat." But even so, I held to my theory of what a party should be. I thought that if I presented my idea of a party to women, I might persuade enough of them to come into the Democratic Party to make it stand more definitely for a philosophy and so develop economic and social programs.

I would present to them what I considered the Jeffersonian philosophy and the Wilsonian application of it, and ask the women who believed in it to join us. Well, this is not the place to make my speech, but I may say that I was fair to the Hamiltonian philosophy and advised those who favored it to go Republican.

I failed to take into consideration, I see now, the combative spirit that is strong in women—as well as men—the instinct that prefers dramatization of a personality to an idea or a principle, and how few people like to think in terms of philosophy. Political organizations cannot be effected that way; certainly conventions are not controlled by any such ideas and appeal. Prejudice and tradition are far more effective. But if I had not been able so to idealize my work it would not have interested me.

Nor was it without results. Before the Madison Square Garden convention I had organized twenty-five hundred women's Democratic clubs and persuaded many women in many states to go into active politics, taking places on committees. I had reason, I think, to be proud of my woman's organization. It was drilled, earnest, even ardent, ready for the next campaign. Then came the 1924 convention in Madison Square Garden, New York, the long weeks of struggle in which women no less than men had a part and my two years of work went for nothing.

The day the minority report of the resolutions committee on the Klan was brought in I ran into Judge Hull upon the platform by accident. He looked pale and worn. "Our work has been useless," he said. "It's all wiped out, and the nomination won't be worth a tinker's dam." And people wonder why political organization is so ineffective!

He had worked much harder than I. He had an even better organization among the men. There were hundreds of Victory Clubs in countless towns, a national organization of young Democrats had been started, thousands of names had been card indexed, county committees had been stimulated. He had also waged a fight in the public press on the Republican tariff bills. Thousands of Democratic papers had been supplied with literature about the investigation at Washington.

It will be remembered that Democratic prospects looked bright in the spring of 1924. Newspapermen were encouraging in their prognostications. The Republican nomination for vice chairman went begging.

Mr. Hull, with his political foresight, saw that in those clubs, in these counties, would be repeated what was to take place in Madison Square Garden in the next few days, members turning against each other, a bitter religious fight started that would cripple and almost disrupt the party.

But of course I could not know all this before the convention when I went about the country, making speeches, sending out organizers, and holding conferences of women, getting out our pamphlets on the tariff.

To stimulate the organization of women, stir up their enthusiasm, and exchange ideas, I called the national committeewomen, women executives of the state organizations, heads of the Federation of Clubs, and congressional committeewomen into regional conferences. Again I was rash, not realizing the factional fights I would get into or the contest of personalities.

The men, poor dears, in a perfectly honest desire to do the right thing by the women, were the innocent causes of many of these. When they had first put women on the national committee only a few of the state committees had any women on them. And so the men had asked these national committeewomen to organize the women in their states, which they did.

Later, in some of these states a woman vice chairman was appointed to do this work. Some of these national committeewomen felt they had been shorn of some of their authority and resented it. Some kept up their own organization work. And there were conflicts between the national committeewoman and the state vice chairman, each perfectly sincere in her contention that hers was the right to do this work. Sometimes new national committeewomen, in all innocence, undertook to do the work their predecessors had done only to find a vice chairman telling her she was encroaching on her territory. Nor was this the only cause for misunderstanding. In addition to the national committee there was a national congressional committee made up of members of Congress from each state, and in their desire to give the women full equality this committee hit upon the generous idea of adding a woman from each state. For some of these women members, told that they were to organize the women in the congressional districts, went to work to build up another organization of women in their states. So we sometimes had three women from the same state, each one in all honesty claiming that she was responsible for and in charge of all the organization of women in it. When all three came to the regional conferences with their followers there was battle, especially if one was on the program and another not. I was the center around which the conflict raged. There were states where there were self-appointed women leaders who had started organizations of their own and refused to recognize the women leaders whom the men who headed the state committee had designated. Sometimes there were two of these from the same state. They came to the conferences and insisted on being heard.

At one place it was so bad that I feared for the success of the dinner that was to open the conference. Fortunately I had just heard the story about Mrs. O'Mally and Mrs. Flannery: "What branch of the Flannerys do you spring from?" asked Mrs. O'Mally. "I'll have you know the Flannerys never sprung from nobody. They sprang at 'em!" said Mrs. Flannery. Due to the racial sense of humor of the contesting factions this story saved the day and conference.

These self-appointed leaders usually sprang up in states where no provision had been made for the election of women leaders or where chairmen had arbitrarily named some women to organize the women. Often these men would bitterly complain to me that women could not keep the peace, that they were just naturally quarrelsome. But when I suggested to them that if they would revise their system so that the women have some voice in choosing these women who were to organize them, they at least would have the rule of the majority on their side of the argument. They preferred, it seemed, to keep their difficulties and their power. I told them, which was true, that there was not this trouble where they had passed the fifty-fifty rule.

This fifty-fifty rule (or law where state committees were created by law) provided that there be both men and women on all political committees in equal numbers.

It had first passed in Colorado, and with the able assistance of state senator McCawley of Carthage I had worked hard and successfully to have the fifty-fifty principle enacted into law in Missouri, and it worked effectively.[2] I was, with Mr. Hull's cooperation, urging our state chairmen everywhere to adopt it in practice where possible.

I would not give the impression that all states had such troubles or that there was no effective organization of women. For it would not be true. There were brilliant women on the committees, and much splendid work reported, but no picture of the entrance of women into politics is complete that ignores these complications; and when the success or failure of women in politics is discussed they must be taken into consideration. Many of them inhered in the situation, but others were the result of the determination of some men—often instinctive rather than planned—to have the women in politics on the men's terms and to keep the women in their place.

In spite of all these troubles, these regional conferences were helpful. We usually ironed out the complications. I got to know the women, became acquainted with their difficulties, and learned a great deal myself as I saw women locally meeting their problems.

In Cleveland, for instance, I saw how Bernice Pyke, probably the most successful Democratic woman politician in the country since she not only has continued as national committeewoman for twelve years, been a delegate at large to every national Democratic convention, but also sits in at all the caucuses of her local organization and has been appointed to two of the highest-paid offices in its gift, put her women to the front, and kept herself in the background, how she achieved cooperation with the men, had their confidence and deserved and earned it. At this conference Newton D. Baker made the address. I have heard him many times and always with admiration and pleasure, but never did he more move his audience than that night.

During the conference at Salt Lake I discovered a new interpretation of hospitality. I had left Washington with a bad attack of sinus trouble, my doctor advising me to have a treatment at every stopping place. Incidentally I may remark here that I could write an article on the varieties of sinus treatments, for the specialists at Chicago, Kansas City, Salt Lake, Pueblo, Joplin, and Springfield, Missouri, each gave me a different kind. But the Salt Lake physician distinguished himself above all others. I was there four days, and each day in a most up-to-date office, with an extensive equipment he treated me for—well, it seemed an hour each time. And when I asked for my

---

2. A. L. McCawley (1876–1966) was elected to the state senate from Jasper County in 1922 and reelected in 1926. In 1928, he vied for the Democratic nomination for governor but lost to Francis Wilson. Beginning in 1932, he served one term as a state representative from the eastern district of Jasper County (*Carthage Evening Press*, January 5, 1966).

bill he said, "Well, if you could come all the way out here in this condition I think we ought to take care of you for nothing."

It was on this visit that I made the acquaintance of Mr. George Henry Dern and his wife, another political team like the Pattangalls of Maine, the Jacksons of New Hampshire, and the Franklin Roosevelts.[3] Mr. Dern was regarded as the leader, if unofficially so, of the men. Later he became governor of Utah and was urged by his state for the vice presidential nomination at the Democratic convention of 1932. He was secretary of war in President Roosevelt's cabinet.

---

3. George Henry Dern (1872–1936), a Utah mine operator, was elected governor in 1924. Reelected in 1928, FDR appointed him secretary of war in 1933. He married Lottie Brown in 1899 (*DAB*, s.v. "Dern, George Henry"). Robert Jackson was chairman of the New Hampshire State Democratic Committee in 1919–1920 and a member of the DNC from 1928 to 1936. He married Dorothy Witter Branch in 1909 (*Who Was Who in America,* 6:209).

14 *The Dog's Tail*

I essayed another rash undertaking, nothing less than a National School of Democracy to be held in New York City. Now, I knew little about cities, city people, and city political organizations, and nothing at all about New York City. Not that I had found this ignorance a disadvantage. Political organizations in a city and the country are quite different. To be effective with one kind helps you not at all in the other. But large, successful city organizations feel superior to their country cousins and regard any suggestions from them as impertinent, much as if the tail were trying to wag the dog. It is the state and county organizations that want help and like advice from the national committee. So it is more important in a position like mine to know your country and small town than to know the city, and to be familiar with county and town organization methods rather than the city's.

Since being vice chairman I had been to New York, of course. Soon after I was appointed, a Democratic club of women had given a luncheon for me. I had established contacts with Miss Elizabeth Marbury, New York's national committeewoman, who had delightfully entertained me in her doll-like twenty-foot house in Sutton Street that has so often been described in magazines with its drawing-room windows made into two conservatories filled with blooming plants—Easter lilies and pink ramblers when I saw it first—and its English paneled dining room opening onto a terraced garden.

Mrs. Roosevelt, as vice chairman of the New York State Committee, had been most cooperative, putting her city home at my disposal. She was doing an interesting piece of work. Voting at her upstate home at Hyde Park, Dutchess County, she had come on the Democratic State Committee representing a rural community and so was not expected to play with the city organization. This city organization (I use this word instead of Tammany, for there are five counties in New York City and Tammany is the organization of one only) felt about the state organization as those in other cities: that the state organization was unimportant—merely the tail it wagged, except in big cities like Buffalo. And since the city delivered most of the Democratic votes in the state, and upstate was largely Republican, the state committee had never bothered to do much organization in the state. In some counties Democratic tickets for county offices were seldom put into the field. The county chairman himself was inactive, more or less a figurehead. Mrs. Roosevelt conceived the brilliant idea that by building up an effective women's organization in these counties, it would be possible to invigorate the sleepy state organization and make it function. With the assistance of Mrs. Daniel O'Day, widow of a vice president of the Standard Oil Company, an ardent southern Democrat and idealist, she toured the state, not once but several times, persuading women to serve as vice chairmen of county committees and in this capacity to put an organization in the counties.[1] These county chairmen were then organized into a women's Democratic State Committee that demanded recognition by the state committee. With their active county organizations back of them they could not be refused. It was slow, arduous work, these county-by-county organizations, but the resuscitation of the New York State Democratic Committee may in large measure be traced to the stimulation given to men's county committees by the activities of the women's county organizations, and the large vote Governor Roosevelt polled when he ran for governor may, to some extent, be charged to it. Mrs. Roosevelt had been astute enough to see something that too many women's organizations never have. If the men hold the purse strings and pay the bills, they have the upper hand. Women cannot ask that their work be financed by men leaders and then refuse to do what those men ask. Realizing this, Mrs. Roosevelt raised her own funds, paid her own bills, until the organization could finance itself.

It must be noted that Mrs. Roosevelt had the knack of being independent of men without offending them. It is the prime requisite for a woman who would organize women in a political party.

I had attended, spoken to meetings of the New York women. But I had not met the women of the city organization except here and there as individuals or in clubs. And I had no idea of the power and control of this organization.

I broached my project of a national school to Miss Marbury and Mrs. Roosevelt. I interested individuals. We got together a committee. But before we could go forward we must, I discovered, have the consent of Mr. Murphy, head of Tammany. It was not hard to get. Mr. Murphy was not only a clever politician, but also a wise one. It was he who had seen that if Tammany was

---

1. Eleanor Roosevelt had organized the women in nearly every New York county by 1924. She served the Democratic State Committee as finance chairman of the women's division from 1922 to 1928 (*NAW-Modern*, s.v. "Roosevelt, Eleanor"; Joseph P. Lash, *Eleanor and Franklin*, 278–320). Caroline O'Day (1869?–1943) became interested in social work after her husband's death in 1916. She was associated with the New York Consumers' League, the WTUL, and the Henry Street Settlement. Gov. Al Smith appointed her to the State Board of Charities in 1923, where she served until 1935. In 1923, she was chairman of the women's division of the New York State Committee; in 1924, she was chairman of the state delegation to the national convention. In 1926, she was first vice chairman of the New York Democratic Committee and in 1934 she was elected to Congress, where she served until 1942. She was a close friend and associate of Eleanor Roosevelt (*NAW*, s.v. "O'Day, Caroline").

to continue in power it must make a compromise with the public interest. For one thing, it must develop and put forward men of real ability. That he recognized and pushed forward men of that type, the rare gifts for administration of Al Smith and the senatorial record of Senator Wagner prove.[2] It must also give the people efficient service. I make no defense of him or any political organization whose prime objective is private profit, whether it be by way of jobs for its members or gifts for the leaders. But when I think of the Tammany of Mr. Murphy's day, I recall what an editor of *Harper's* once said to me: "We have a choice in New York between a city administration which is corrupt but efficient and one that is honest but inefficient. We pay high for Tammany but it does give us good police protection, garbage collection, clean streets, and good water."

I recall, too, what Mayor Cermak of Chicago once said to my friend Amelia Sears, of the Cook County Board of Commissioners, when some reformer had approached them on his hobby: "If we did all the things these reformers wanted us to, we wouldn't be here to do them. It's our business to do all we can and yet stay."[3]

Mr. Murphy of New York also used rare judgment in his dealings with women. Immediately after suffrage was given women, he put a woman on his slate for one of the best-paying county offices, Annie Mathews.[4] What is more,

---

2. Charles Francis Murphy (1858–1924) came to power in the Tammany organization in 1902. He controlled both the city and the state for twenty-two years until his death (*DAB*, s.v. "Murphy, Charles Francis"). Alfred E. Smith (1873–1944) was first elected to the New York State Assembly in 1903 and became Speaker in 1913. He served four terms as governor of New York (1918, 1922, 1924, and 1926). In 1928, he was the Democratic nominee for president, losing the election to Herbert Hoover (*DAB*, s.v. "Smith, Alfred E."). Robert F. Wagner (1877–1953) got his political start through Tammany Hall. In 1911, he was a member of the New York Factory Investigating Commission formed after the Triangle Fire. He was elected to the United States Senate in 1926. He made significant contributions to designing New Deal legislation, particularly the Wagner Act, which created the National Labor Relations Board (*DAB*, s.v. "Wagner, Robert F.").

3. Anton J. Cermak (1873–1933) came up through the ranks of Chicago Democratic politics and in 1922 was elected president of the Cook County Board of Commissioners. From that position he created the Democratic machine in Chicago. In 1931 he was elected mayor of the city and in 1932 used his political influence to give FDR victory in Illinois. He died as a result of wounds sustained in the assassination attempt on FDR in February 1933 (Melvin G. Holli and Peter d'A. Jones, eds., *Biographical Dictionary of American Mayors, 1820–1980*, s.v. "Cermak, Anton J."). Amelia Sears (1874–1946) became director of the Woman's City Club of Chicago in 1913. She organized the Bureau of Public Welfare of Cook County, served as superintendent of the Juvenile Protective Association, and from 1918 to 1930 was assistant general superintendent of United Charities of Chicago. From 1930 to 1934 she was a member of the Cook County Board of Commissioners (*New York Times*, March 28, 1946, 25).

4. Annie Mathews (1866–1959) began as a suffragist and moved into the Democratic Party as a supporter of Woodrow Wilson. She was the first woman to be elected registrar of

he elected her. He also put women on his precinct committees and rewarded them for work well done. True, he picked his women and exacted obedience from them, but so he did the men. And he called women into conference with him and got their ideas, although, of course, he used his own judgment in adopting them. Frank Hague, the boss of the New Jersey organization, did the same thing, as witness the political rise of Mary J. Norton, who was an outstanding congresswoman for so many years. These men dealt with facts. The women had the vote. They were in politics for results and had no intention of jeopardizing them because of any private prejudice they might have against women in politics. Instead, they used the safe methods to win and control the women that they had found successful with men. Generally speaking, the boss-controlled machines have been more hospitable to women than those led by more idealistic politicians.

Mr. Murphy saw no harm in our National School of Democracy. But Tammany, it developed, was a democratic organization. We must win the consent—or at least the approval—of the women in his organization, and so a meeting of them was called at which I presented our plans. Miss Marbury presided. It was she who won them. For they were, it was apparent, a little suspicious of me, and the national committee and its woman vice chairman meant nothing at all to them. This was my first contact with the localism— some call it provincialism—of New York City. Like other colonials, I had seen New York only as an outsider and thought of it as the economic capital of the country and in that sense belonging to all of us, our New York. I had never realized that it had a life of its own in which we people who came to it periodically and paid our tribute to it had no part. I could have said that, like Palm Beach and Atlantic City, it was a visitors' city. But as I saw how these New York women viewed this school wholly in its relation to them and their organization, and considered first of all what they would get out of it and how it would appeal to New Yorkers, with little thought of the women who were coming from all over the country, I made acquaintance with the New York spirit. It was the dog, the rest of the country the tail. Neither in Atlanta, Philadelphia, St. Louis, Cleveland, Worcester, nor Salt Lake, where our regional conferences and school had been held, had there been this spirit. The local interest in every place had been made subservient to that of the visitors whom they were entertaining. I was to meet this spirit again in New York when the national convention was held there in 1924. Far more important was it that the New York Democrats receive seats and approve its platform and nominee than that the majority Democrats of the country should. Even at the entertainments given the delegates—and they

---

New York County in 1921 and reelected in 1925. She belonged to the Woman's National Democratic Club, the League of Women Voters, and the Woodrow Wilson Foundation (*New York Times*, October 25, 1959, 85).

were many and superb—the featured persons, the guests of honor, were the local leaders, not the national ones.

To the school came women from all over the country, two hundred of them, though I doubt if any New Yorker knew they were there. Mrs. Halsey Wilson conducted it. There was a brilliant dinner for which New York furnished the program, and since New York women had done the work for it that was of course right and proper. I was also, it appeared, necessary, Miss Marbury explaining to me that New York being accustomed only to the best and having the talent of the world to draw from would not be receptive to speakers or entertainment from the provinces. One state delegation did put on a little play, but she was right. The New Yorkers were very critical.

One of the most important features of this school was an open meeting held at the town hall. Governor Smith was the featured speaker. It was my first meeting with him, and naturally I was curious. His subject was "A Progressive State Program." I thought it a happy selection. It was a subject in which all citizens should be interested, and no one in the country was better fitted to speak on it than the governor who had so conspicuously put such a program into operation in the most important state. I was greatly impressed with his speech. Free from bunk, dealing directly with the subject, it showed a remarkable grasp of administrative problems, an unusual ability to solve them, and a rare appreciation of the duty of the state to humanize our modern industrial system. His earnestness, his fearlessness, his realism were apparent. No one concerned primarily with policies and results, instead of personalities and prejudices, could fail to see that here was that rare phenomenon, a man in politics who was really meeting the opportunities public office gave him to serve the public weal. And yet, as I watched the women who had come to the school from other parts of the country and heard them afterward I saw that a personality and a manner foreign to their experience so alienated their sympathies and roused their prejudices that what I saw was obscured from them. They interpreted his choice of subject and his frank account of what he had done as egotism, an exploitation of himself. They had eyes only for mannerisms so strange to them that they could account for them only by suspecting intoxication, just as in earlier days bystanders who saw Theodore Roosevelt standing up in an auto and waving his hat invented the same explanation. I was to see the same unfair reaction to Governor Smith later at the Democratic National Convention of 1924 and in the campaign of 1928.

When discussing the out-country prejudice against Governor Smith in the years before 1928, New Yorkers would always say: "But they've never seen him. Just let him go out and speak to them and they'll fall for his personality. They can't help it." What they did not understand, and could not, was that this personality, so different from what they were accustomed to, invariably alienated them. Its very vigor antagonized them, for he dramatized to them what they disliked and feared: the foreigner, the East sider, and Tammany. Thus, what he said and what he had done never got a fair hearing, and his very real abilities were ignored. That this was so is no compliment to the intelligence and the tolerance of the out-countries. Nevertheless, it is a fact, and therein lies the tragedy of the Democratic Party, and of Governor Smith, too. For, of course, he did not realize it. He understood the out-countryite and his looks and his manners no better than they his. And because of this, issues were joined, prejudices roused, antagonisms embittered that for a time destroyed the Democratic Party's usefulness, set section against section, and eliminated from public service a man superbly designed to serve it.

If Governor Smith had gone into the United States Senate and there given a demonstration of his abilities before the whole nation so that these people could have had evidence of his statesmanship before they saw or met him physically, his political career might have ended differently. He and his friends thought, quite naturally, that the demonstration he had given as governor of a great state, with its complex problems and enormous population, would do this. But they thought as New Yorkers who do not know the hinterland.

New York, knowing its own importance, living to and in itself, assumes that what happens there is nationally known, considered of national importance. It does not realize that, except for something like the Walker investigation, the country knows as little and cares as little about New York's internal affairs as New York cares about what happens out in the country.[5]

In touch with New York and New Yorkers as I became, I could understand and appreciate their viewpoint; growing up and living in the Middle West I knew and appreciated theirs. The result was that when I tried as I did to tell New Yorkers the situation they would say, "You're prejudiced against New York." And when I tried to make the middle westerner appreciate that of the New Yorkers, they thought I had become contaminated by my association with them.

Something else happened to impress me at this meeting in the town hall besides Governor Smith's grasp of public affairs and clearness in discussing them. Mrs. Roosevelt had left us at dinner, saying she must go down early to see that everything was right for the meeting. And when we arrived there she was in the foyer, greeting everyone in her affable way to make them feel welcome. "That's Eleanor," said the woman beside me. "She's got to make everyone feel comfortable and at home," and how well she did it! The

---

5. In March 1931, charges of malfeasance and negligence of official duties were leveled against New York City mayor James J. Walker. The Hofstadter Committee, created by the New York state legislature, began its investigations of Tammany Hall and Walker in June. Walker resigned in September (Bernard Bellush, *Franklin D. Roosevelt as Governor of New York*, 269–81).

Roosevelt gift for cordiality, for lack of self-consciousness, for saying the right word in the right place—in short for popularity.

The success of the school was due in large measure to her. Miss Marbury had helped greatly, as had the Democratic Woman's Club, with Mrs. Quin as president. Many New York women had contributed time and money to it. And Mrs. Halsey Wilson did a remarkable job as director. The two hundred women who had paid their own expenses to come felt rewarded. In fact they enjoyed it all so much that they wanted to make it an annual affair and effect a permanent organization. I explained that to build it into a permanent organization would take money and there was none available, and that the national committee could not sponsor it. However, as a group of individuals they had a perfect right to organize themselves into anything they wanted. In their enthusiasm they did organize and elected Mrs. Jobe of Detroit president.[6] But nothing came of it, as they could get no funds either.

It was sometimes difficult to make women realize the nature of political organization, especially the relation of the national committee to the party. Accustomed to permanent dues-paying organizations, many of them looked upon the party as an association they had joined, and the committee as its board of directors, the final authority, entrusted with the duty of perfecting party organization. They found it hard to understand, therefore, that there were no funds available for it except such as we might persuade people to give. It had no authority to impose plans or programs on the states or localities. Nor did women understand the lack of continuity in political work. They could not grasp the idea that what one chairman of a national committee proposed or started, a new chairman and committee might drop entirely. No one, indeed, can understand the machinery of political party organization who has not studied the history of its development, and learned how it came into being. Women, organized women, have learned organization after the federated method, by which method members are organized in local units, which are federated into a state organization, and the state organizations in turn into a national organization. Either that, or local units are directly connected with the national board. Political organization does not follow that method. The national political committee is a creation of each national convention. Any national convention could abolish it altogether by simply failing to pass a

6. Aylitt Buckner Conner (b. 1884) married Percy Edwards Quin in 1913. He was a U.S. representative from Mississippi, 1913–1932. She was a founding member of the WNDC but is not listed as a president. She served as president of the Colonial Dames of Washington, D.C., and was a member of the DAR and the CAR (Howes, *American Women, 1935–1940*, s.v. "Conner, Aylitt Buckner"). Grace (Mrs. Walter) Jobe of Detroit was a state organizer for and president of the Detroit Council of Parent-Teacher Associations. She had been state president of the Missouri branch of the National Congress of Mothers and Parent-Teacher Associations ("Parent-Teacher Association in Detroit," *Club Woman* 14:227).

resolution providing for a new committee. Having been created, it hangs in midair, having no connection with any other piece of party machinery. The state committees have no connection at all with it.

If I go into such detail about my political experiences and difficulties, it is because they may indicate why women are charged today with not being a success in politics.

15 *Women's Way of Winning*

In the summer [1923] I had a house in Georgetown.[1] It came to me in a curious way. Dining one night with Anne Hard, I spoke of the difficulty of getting a house that would have some grounds for my family. The other guest, a stranger, said that I could have hers.

"But you don't know me," I protested. "And maybe I can't afford it."

"Oh, I never charge for my house," said Dr. Erving.[2] "If I did, I would have to fix it all up. I just pick out someone and lend it to them. You're a friend of Anne's, so that's all right if you want it."

Of course I wanted it, for it was a large, old home set in an acre of ground just across from the beautiful Peters House, which was built by George Washington's adopted grandchild. It was filled with Dr. Erving's old furniture, the very pieces appearing in Wallace Nutting's books on "antiques."[3]

The first Sunday after we were there, my friend Robert Woolley appeared.[4]

"I've always wanted to get into this house," he said. "Now take me all over it." So we went through the four stories examining each piece of furniture, its brasses, its cornices, its patina. After he had gone, I took down one of the furniture books and read the descriptions of these pieces, until I could discuss each one like a connoisseur. I could then give a personally conducted tour ending at a sixteenth-century chest in the music room with the impressive claim, "The end, of course, is obvious."

Mrs. Banister and her daughter Margaret came to share the house with us, as did two of Laura Brown's daughters.[5] Newell came down from Exeter

---

1. They lived that summer at 1645 Thirty-first Street in Georgetown.

2. Dr. Emma Lootz Erving, with her husband, also a physician, had offices at 1621 Connecticut Avenue NW (*Boyd's 1921 Directory of the District of Columbia* [Washington, D.C.: R. K. Polk, 1921]).

3. Wallace Nutting wrote several books on antiques; the best known was his three-volume *Furniture Treasury* (*DAB*, s.v. "Nutting, Wallace").

4. Robert Wickliffe Woolley (1871–1958) was a lawyer and newspaperman. He was chief of the Bureau of Publicity of the DNC in 1912; director of publicity and a member of the Democratic National Campaign Committee, 1916; chairman of the National Democratic Council of D.C., 1935–1936. Wilson appointed him director of the Mint in 1915–1916, and he was a member of the Interstate Commerce Commission from 1917 to 1921 (*Who Was Who in America*, 3:940).

5. Margaret Banister (1894?–1977) was the daughter of Marion Banister and worked in public relations for Sweet Briar College and at the Pentagon. She retired in 1956 to

where he was in school, and Harriet from Goucher. With the gay friends of these young people, and a long visit from Harry, we had a happy summer, thanks to the generosity of Dr. Erving.

It was there I was awakened one night by the cry of "Extra—Death of President Harding."[6] We sat in the living room in our dressing gowns very much ashamed. For we had had a discussion that evening at dinner about the administration that was far from kind.

"I'll never again talk like that," said one of the girls.

"Wait," I said. "If it was true then, it is true now, isn't it? It is very sad about him, but it does not change facts, does it?"

She thought I was very hard, but politics was teaching me realism. However, his death did change manners.

"Heavens," said Mrs. Banister. "That bulletin we sent to press today!"

The next morning she went to the printers and destroyed the whole issue.

During this summer Harry Putnam and his wife and two children came to visit us from Carthage.[7] They were strong Republicans and had been dear friends for many years. When Harry saw all the activity and realized I was really doing something, he was amazed. "Why, Emily," he said, "Carthage must have a dinner for you when you come home." Later in the summer when I did go to Carthage, Harry and Martha Taaffe, a staunch Democrat, organized a lovely dinner in my honor. I was gratified to find as many Republicans present as Democrats.

Of the life I lead at my work my social friends in Carthage had always been, for the most part, ignorant. It was as if I lived on two tracks at once. On one I ran my house, did my parties, talked to my friends, determined that none of these activities should be affected by my office homework. The tribute I have in my day paid the god of respectability—what was expected of me! At it I must have been fairly successful. For, when I went to Washington to undertake the organization of women for the Democratic National Committee, one of those friends said to me, "Emily, if it is such an important position, how did they ever come out here and get you for it?"

Though I saw her at least weekly while I lived in Carthage and often after I moved to Joplin, she had not the least knowledge of my activities as a writer and leader in suffrage work, or my war work, or the experience they had given me and the contacts they had made for me.

Friends I did have who helped me at that time. Helen Fabyan McGee possessed an unselfishness that made her always interested in others, and she

---

write novels (*Contemporary Authors* [Detroit: Gale Research, 1981], 73–76:42; see also *Washington Post*, November 23, 1977). Laura Brown had two daughters, Dorothy, born in 1896, and Helen, born in 1900 (1910 Jasper County Census).

6. President Harding died on August 2, 1923.

7. Harry Putnam was an owner of Calhoun Putnam Lumber. He and his wife, Ann, lived at 1833 South Garrison Street and were lifelong friends of the Blairs.

read my first book in manuscript, the only one outside my family who did.[8] I have those friends now, and I would go to them in trouble. But they had no part in my outside-home life, regarding it, I thought, very critically, as did many others in Carthage. In fact, I am told that some of those others have said, "Well, you have to admit that her husband still loves her, and her children have turned out very well." It shows why I tried to keep my work sub rosa in those days.

In the fall we went to the Wardman Park Hotel, Mrs. Banister and I, and in February to the clubhouse, which needed badly to rent its bedrooms to meet its expenses.

Together we essayed some entertaining that had its funny incidents, as what entertaining does not. One of our difficulties was corralling enough unattached men for our unattached ladies. In desperation, one afternoon I thought of a congressman whose wife I had noted had died the past summer. We invited him, and he came. For our next supper we invited another congressman and his wife. When the hour arrived, the wife appeared, but with her, instead of her husband, was another woman. Putting names together we discovered that she was the supposedly deceased wife of the congressman we had invited to the first party. Whispered inquiries to other guests revealed that it was his brother's wife who had died. The two families who were friends lived in the same hotel. I have always enjoyed reconstructing their little scheme: "What are those women like who purloin other women's husbands?"

"Why not come and see? We're invited next week. My husband does not want to go. You come in his place."

Either one of these ladies was eccentric enough alone for one party to absorb. Two were a problem. Moreover, as the tables were arranged for four each, that meant that one table would have three women to one man. I chose roguish Paul Anderson, the brilliant correspondent for the *St. Louis Post-Dispatch*, for my victim.[9] Paul was equal to anything, and gave the two Victorian ladies the shock of their lives.

In January came the meeting of the national committee to plan for the convention. Trained by women's clubs, I prepared a detailed report of my activities and expenditures. I was proud of it and justly so, I think. But just before the meeting, word was passed to me that there was no time for

---

8. Helen Fabyan, sister of Florence Fabyan, was married to John McGee.

9. Paul Anderson (1893–1938) moved to St. Louis in 1914, working for the *Post-Dispatch* and assigned to East St. Louis. He gained national attention when he gave testimony before Congress on the East St. Louis race riots in 1917. In 1923, he joined the *Post-Dispatch*'s Washington bureau and was awarded a Pulitzer Prize for his reporting of the Teapot Dome scandal in 1928. Leaving the *Post-Dispatch* in early 1938, he joined the Washington staff of the *St. Louis Star-Times* and committed suicide in December of that year (*St. Louis Post-Dispatch*, December 6, 7, 1938; *St. Louis Star-Times*, January 25, February 28, 1938).

lengthy reports. We were just to say a few words on general lines. With disappointment I obeyed. The time thus salvaged was given to invitations from cities to hold the convention. Speaker after speaker indulged in glowing accounts of the city of his choice. At the end of this ballyhoo, a resolution was introduced to postpone action until tomorrow. I did not know until next day the reason. It seemed we were waiting for San Francisco to boost its offer in order to "up" New York.

Before we adjourned, I introduced a resolution that had been agreed upon at headquarters, designed to increase the representation of women at the convention by asking states to send eight, instead of four, delegates at large, and making four of them women. To my surprise it was turned over to a committee. I knew what the chairman did not: that the woman on that committee was opposed to my resolution, and the two men did not care for women in politics, period.

When I went to this committee to talk for my resolution, I was put on the defensive at once. The woman plied me with ridiculous questions. One of the men who had been imbibing became truculent. The other kept a discreet silence. I saw my resolution's defeat. I went to see Judge Hull. Mrs. Hull met me at the door of their apartment, and she must have seen that I was in "a state," for she made me sit down and tell her what was wrong.[10] She patted me on the shoulder and told me not to worry, it would work out all right; and I couldn't help believing she was right.

I had a dinner that night for the national committeewomen at my hotel, with Mrs. Woodrow Wilson as guest of honor. It was an expensive (for me) occasion, and a gala one, each woman beautifully gowned, and Mrs. Wilson most gracious and charming. I went through it as best I could, convinced it was my last, for it seemed just then hopeless to expect any cooperation from the men. A militant type of woman, I told myself, was needed in my place.

The next morning my telephone rang while I was dressing. It was Myrtle McDougal of Oklahoma.[11] "We're going to bring that resolution of yours through from the floor. I'm off to tell the women."

As I walked across the Lafayette Hotel lobby, Mrs. Robert Jackson of New Hampshire stopped me. "Do you really want that resolution?" she asked.

I said I did.

"All right," she said. "We've two votes for it."

When the resolution came up, Mrs. Benton McMillan was at once on her feet and made a glowing speech. Beautiful Mrs. Springs of South Carolina followed. Mrs. Farley of Kansas spoke for it, in spite of protestations from

---

10. Rose Frances Whitney married Cordell Hull in 1917.

11. Myrtle Archer (Mrs. Daniel A.) McDougal from Sapulpa, Oklahoma, joined the Democratic National Committee in 1922. She had been president of the Oklahoma Federation of Women's Clubs (*Who Was Who in America*, 5:478; DNC membership list, Folder 12, Box 16, Goltra Papers).

her national committeeman, as did Mrs. Pattangall and Mrs. Pyke.[12] I was asked to explain it.

This was not much, I knew. But it was the only way we were likely to get any large number of women delegates to the conventions, and even if these women would have only half a vote each, the men from their states must halve theirs with them. Once the men grew accustomed to seeing the women about, and having to count them in, it would be easier to get more. The first obstruction was a psychological one.

The resolution carried, though some of the men shook their heads.

After that came the question of where to hold the convention. Mr. Dockweiler had an offer from San Francisco to meet that of New York. New York boosted theirs to eighty thousand dollars. This eighty thousand dollars was necessary to meet the committee's deficit, and so was a great argument for New York to those who felt responsible for raising the debt. Yet there was something else involved in this decision, although discussion of it did not reach the floor. The committee members were already committed to their candidates for the presidential nomination. About half were for William Gibbs McAdoo, the rest were divided between other candidates: John W. Davis, Oscar Underwood, Alfred Smith, Senator Ralston.[13] The second half

---

12. Lucille Foster (Mrs. Benton) McMillin (1870–1949) was the first National Democratic Committeewoman from Tennessee. She served two terms. She had been president of the Tennessee State Federation of Women's Clubs. In 1924, Cordell Hull appointed her regional director of Democratic women of the southern states. During the New Deal, she was a member of the Civil Service Commission (*Who Was Who in America*, 2:364). Lena Jones (Mrs. Leroy) Springs of South Carolina (d. May 18, 1942) had been active in the South Carolina Equal Suffrage League, serving as vice president in 1917. She was president of the South Carolina Federation of Women's Clubs, 1918–1919, and district director of the South Carolina League of Women Voters, 1920–1925. She served on the DNC from 1922 to 1928 and was nominated for vice president at the 1924 Democratic National Convention (*Who Was Who in America*, 2:503). Florence Farley (1890–1962) was national committeewoman from Kansas from 1921 until the early 1930s. She was elected vice chairman of the DNC in 1928 and was in charge of the western headquarters in St. Louis for the Smith campaign. She later served as special assistant to Harry Hopkins, retiring from politics in 1941 (*New York Times*, March 25, 1962, 89).

13. Isidore B. Dockweiler (1867–1947), a Los Angeles lawyer, was the Democratic candidate for lieutenant governor of California in 1902. He was a member of the DNC from 1916 to 1932 (*Who Was Who in America*, 2:158). John W. Davis (1873–1955) served two terms in the United States House of Representatives, 1911–1915. A progressive Wilsonian, he was U.S. ambassador in London in 1918. He returned to his law practice until he became the Democratic presidential nominee on the 103rd ballot in 1924 (*DAB*, s.v. "Davis, John W."). Oscar W. Underwood (1862–1929) of Alabama served as a Democratic member of the House from 1897 to 1915 and the Senate from 1915 to 1927. In 1924, he failed to get an anti-Klan plank in the party platform (*DAB*, s.v. "Underwood, Oscar W."). Samuel M. Ralston (1857–1927) was Democratic governor of Indiana from 1913 to 1917. In 1922, he won a United States Senate seat where he served until his death (*DAB*, s.v. "Ralston, Samuel M.").

desired to stop McAdoo at any cost. The McAdoo men knew this. If the decision went to New York, it meant taking the convention into the city of McAdoo's opponents. But when a woman asked one of these McAdoo men how she should vote, he said it made no difference—New York was all right.

Thus, I had another instance of how the men whom we suffragists once credited with such deep-laid plans did not bother to forestall events, preferring to meet them as they came, and trusting to luck, or maybe brains. Almost anyone, it seemed to me, could have foreseen then what was to happen. I am sure the New York politicians did, as they gleefully accepted congratulations.

At some time during the committee meeting the members were received by ex-President Wilson at his home on S Street. I stood at one side of him to introduce the women, and Judge Hull on the other to name the men. To each of them in turn Mr. Wilson made some personal remark. To Sen. J. Ham Lewis of Illinois, I remember, "Not as pink as they were, Senator," referring to his greying whiskers; and to Frank Hague of New Jersey, who called him "Governor," he said, "It's like old days, seeing you, Frank."

The president, as we still called him, seemed frail, but alert and in good spirits. This was almost his last contact with anyone outside his family. The next month came his fatal illness.

Mother was staying with me at the time. She had always been an ardent admirer of him; not only did she approve enthusiastically his policies, but she also had a personal interest from the fact that his grandmother had been her mother's intimate girlhood friend, and had given her wedding. Yet I was surprised when she joined the group of women who remained a day praying on the sidewalk across from his door. It was so foreign to her nature to do anything like that. She went with me and Marion Banister to sit outside the church at his funeral. Among all his many mourners, none was more sincere than she.

I did not really know the ex-president, but he took a great interest in my work, sending me a special letter after the election of '22 that I still treasure. Once he had given me an opportunity to come and tell him about it. So historical did I regard anything about him, so impressed was I with him as a great tragic figure, that when I returned, I wrote down the conversation as well as I could remember it, as Frank Cobb wrote down that memorable conversation of his with President Wilson the night before the declaration of war, the most completely revealing picture of Woodrow Wilson's war attitude that we have.[14]

Often I would wait on the sidewalks after a Saturday-evening performance

---

14. Frank Cobb (1869–1923), chief editorial writer for the *Detroit Free Press* from 1900 to 1904, moved to the *New York World,* working there from 1904 to his death. He wrote the book *Woodrow Wilson: An Interpretation* in 1921 (*Dictionary of Literary Biography,* vol. 25, *American Newspaper Journalists, 1901–1925,* s.v. "Cobb, Frank").

at Keith's to see Mr. and Mrs. Wilson drive away from the side door.[15] When he waved his hand, I sometimes felt that he recognized me.

What he was to me and did for me in fixing my ideals of politics and public performance he did, of course, to thousands of others. Sometimes I have thought that this legacy of a public man like him far outweighs all factual accomplishment in the way of legislation and administration. The results of it in the lives of countless others, and future policies evolved by them, are not to be measured. It is today being felt, I am sure, and will be passed on and on.

In April came the state democratic convention in Missouri, which would elect the delegates to the national convention, and the man and woman who would sit on the national committee for the four years succeeding the convention. It was held in Springfield.[16] I was fairly sure of reelection as national committeewoman, as many county conventions had instructed their delegations for me, and I was almost the unanimous choice of the out-state Democratic women. But one never knows in politics until the votes are counted, so I went up to the convention with my husband and friends, sure but nervous, as candidates for office usually are.

My out-state friends were glad to see me, but I was very conscious of the unfriendly looks of the Kansas City and St. Louis delegations. They, with the exception of one St. Louis ward, wanted to defeat me, but could not find anyone to run against me.

The national committee members were elected the last thing in the evening.

When I came onto the platform after a dinner given me by the women, Harry came over to tell me that standing by the door he had overheard a delegate say they had found an opponent for Mrs. Blair. We sent a friend of ours, well versed in political scouting, to find out what was afoot. In a few minutes he was back with information that the city delegates were buttonholing the delegation chairmen, asking each one to give them, just as a friendly gesture, a few votes for some young lady in St. Louis. She was a stenographer in the office of a railroad lawyer. By adding these votes to the solid city votes, they thought they might win. But the argument to the county leaders was: "M____ can't win, of course, but we want to make a showing, that's all, and we'll remember this favor of yours." County leaders, who might need city votes sometime, were not proof against this appeal. Our opponents might thus pick up enough votes to win. This information was passed on to some women friends. The convention was already called to order. There seemed no time to do anything. But some of these women hurried down the side aisles and told a woman in each delegation what was planned.

---

15. Keith's Theater, an upscale vaudeville theater in Washington, was located at 619–21 Fifteenth Street NW (*Boyd's 1923 Directory of the District of Columbia* [Washington, D.C.: R. K. Polk, 1923]).

16. The state Democratic convention in Springfield was held on April 15, 1924.

When the roll was called, the first county was Buchanan. The man leader stood up to give its vote, but before he could speak, a young woman in the delegation jumped up and announced briskly: "Buchanan, *as instructed*, gives its votes for Mrs. Blair."

Thus shown how to do it, as each county was called, some woman in the delegation followed her example. The surprising thing was that this young Buchanan County lady had never been to a convention before and was very timid. To her quick thinking I really owed my election.[17]

Kansas City, to my astonishment, gave me sixteen votes. I asked the newly elected committeeman, who was succeeding Mr. Goltra of St. Louis, how it happened.

In the Kansas City caucus, William Kemper said, one of the woman delegates, a working woman named Sarah Green, had announced that the women would give sixteen votes for Mrs. Blair, and when the leader had objected she had repeated that it would be sixteen votes for Mrs. Blair or they would not vote for Mr. Kemper for committeeman.[18] As these women were delegates by the grace of this leader they had been very daring.

I went to Sarah Green and asked her why she had done it.

"You came all the way out from Washington," she said, "to speak to the Kansas City club women for our minimum-wage legislation. We don't forget our friends." How glad I was I had gone, even though I had had to pay my own way!

The loyalty of these women touched me. Many of them scarcely knew me. There is something humbling in knowing that you stand for something entirely outside yourself. Others gave me devoted, selfless friendship. I think especially of Florence Reid, a little pugnacious slip of a woman with an enormous heart. She did so many things for me, taking all her reward out of her pleasure in my success. Ella Jean Flanders of Excelsior Springs was another such friend.[19] I wish I could name them all.

---

17. The local newspaper reported that ENB was reelected "with but little support from Kansas City and St. Louis." She won over Mrs. Ann Carney of St. Louis, 704 to 311 (*Joplin Globe*, April 17, 1924).

18. William T. Kemper (1866–1938), a Kansas City banker, organized Commerce Trust Company in 1906. A member of the Democratic State Central Committee, he became Missouri's national committeeman in 1924, serving until 1936 (*Who Was Who in America*, 1:665).

19. Florence F. (Mrs. Fred A.) Reid was president of the Democratic League of St. Louis and a bitter opponent of Sen. James Reed. Ella Jean Flanders of Excelsior Springs was delegate-at-large from Missouri at the 1924 Democratic convention and a district delegate to the Chicago convention in 1940. An excellent public speaker, she served on various state committees and was chairman of the woman's division of the Stark for Senator campaign (Floyd Shoemaker, ed., *Missouri and Missourians: Land of Contrasts and People of Achievements*, 3:260–61; W. H. Woodson, *History of Clay County, Missouri*, 700–701).

16 *Tickets, Please!*

Shortly after the national committee meeting came the appointment of the "Arrangements Committee," which had the job of planning for the national convention in New York. By resolution of the national committee, this subcommittee was to be small in order to save as much as possible of the eighty thousand dollars for debt. After conferences between the managers of all the candidates for the nomination (at which I was not present) it was agreed that a committee of eleven be appointed. I was asked to name for it one other woman beside myself. When I protested that this was not a fair representation of women, it was explained to me that the committee had been carefully arranged to maintain balance between the various candidates. Five of them, since it was Mr. McAdoo against the field, were to be McAdoo men, the other five to go each to a single candidate. None of these candidates would be willing to entrust his fortunes to a woman; but the McAdoo forces, since they had five places, were willing to give two to women. This other woman must, however, come from a state that did not already have a man on this Arrangements Committee and be a McAdoo woman (one man had already been appointed). Fortunately Myrtle McDougal of Oklahoma filled the requirements.

This situation was, I felt, most unfair. The national committeewoman from the hostess state, New York, should, with the national committeeman, be on the committee. Miss Marbury of New York had a right to expect it. Could they not, I begged, increase the committee so that I could at least include her? No, they explained, that would make two members for Governor Smith. If they did that then each of the other candidates would demand two representatives, and the McAdoo people five more. This would make the committee too large.

The plea was for harmony, not to disturb things and start a row. Mr. Hull, to whom I felt my loyalty pledged, desired above all things to keep the peace between the factions, and give all a fair chance at the convention.

There was nothing to do but accept it with what grace I could, but if I had realized what difficulties it would raise for me I might even have dared the row.

The next thing to plan was about the convention expenses. Remembering the 1920 convention, I had ambitious ideas as to headquarters for the women. Also, the convention seemed to offer a splendid opportunity to make contacts with women delegates, supply literature, sell them our club plan, discuss organization. I wanted a group of women with me to do these things. Little I dreamed what this convention would be like with no time, in all the three weeks, for plans to win a campaign, so engaged would it be winning a nomination. But economy was the watchword, and Homer Cummings was told to explain it to me. I have to smile even today as I remember how he came into my room and adroitly went to work on me. I could imagine almost the very words with which the men in the other room had sent him in. "You've had experience with these political women. Go in and smooth her down."

There was no money, not even to pay the railroad expenses of the staff helpers, much less their hotel expenses. Not even Mrs. Banister could be provided for. Of course, like all committee members I would pay my own expenses, although the committee might provide a parlor for the women to gather in. Finally after much discussion, some parlors in a hotel across the street from Madison Square Garden were promised for women's headquarters and a lump sum allowed me for clerical help.

These headquarters came in very well for a meeting of a woman's committee I had planned, but they were not occupied during the convention.

This decided, we moved next to consideration of the housing of the committeewomen. It seemed a complicated business, so I sent Mrs. Cantrill, the committeewoman of Kentucky, up to New York to look after it, and also to act as liaison between our headquarters and a committee of nine women who were planning hospitality.[1]

This was, I know now, a mistake, for this Committee of Nine resented my seeking any connection with them. I made many mistakes at the convention. Some due to my ignorance of political conventions, and some to my ignorance of New York.

But all this I discovered was not what the Arrangements Committee was really for. Its real job had to do with tickets and patronage; how many sergeants at arms the committee members were to get for their states at ten dollars per diem, how many door keepers, how many tickets for the delegations and visitors, not to mention what they gave to friends.

There was also the fight over who was to be the temporary chairman of the convention, who the permanent chairman, who was to head the committees, for this committee recommended the officers to the convention. I saw then why the committee should be balanced.

This last did not, however, engage much of my time. The committee met in New York at the Waldorf, talked endlessly about tickets and boxes, and

---

1. Carrie Payne married James C. Cantrill in 1893. She died in 1913. He served as a Kentucky Democrat in the House of Representatives from 1909 to 1921. His second wife was committeewoman from Kentucky in 1922 and 1923 (*Biographical Directory of the U.S. Congress*, 740; *Who Was Who in America*, 1:190).

adjourned. Afterward, upstairs in Judge Hull's room was held the discussion, the argument, or whatever it was, as to who these chairmen should be, and I was not there. When asked why not, Mr. Hull's answer was always the same: "We will wait until they come to some agreement." By "they," he meant, I knew, the McAdoo men and those against him.

It hurt my self-respect, of course, to be left out of this discussion. I felt like a fraud having my picture taken with the committee while everything was decided without me.

"Why don't you," asked a woman on the judge's staff, "go on up to the room and join them? You're on the committee. They can't throw you out."

"No," I said, "but they can go on into his bedroom for the real conferences, and if I follow in there they will probably go into the bathroom, and what could I do then?"

I had not changed my belief that you could not demand confidence. You might win it or, if you had power back of you, force participation. I had neither the confidence nor the power.

But I did have faith in Judge Hull. I wanted him to achieve a compromise and prevent a fight on the convention floor, and would not really do anything to handicap him. To have me there might do that, if it prevented the men from talking freely.

I could see their side of it, too. It was a nuisance to have two women who had nothing really to contribute, when they would have liked another fighter on their sides. Mrs. McDougal would just vote with the McAdoo men, and I would go along with Judge Hull.

But I did explode occasionally, knowing what women like Bernice Pyke or Elizabeth Bass would say to being kept out. Waiting hours one night to hear what they had decided, I said to Homer Cummings, "I've always one ace I can play. It would make the front page and do the party no good if I resigned because the committee ignored me."

He laughed, but told me what I wanted to know. Senator Harrison was to be temporary chairman, and Senator Walsh permanent chairman. The decision was acceptable to both sides.

This decided, the ticket business began in earnest. How many for the McAdoo managers, how many to Norman Mack for Governor Smith's followers?[2] How many to the local New York committee?

"And how many for the women?" I would ask meekly.

There is something funny about convention tickets, something I have never understood. It ought to be possible to get them to those who want them.

---

2. Norman Mack (1858–1932) was the editor and publisher of the *Buffalo Daily Times* until his retirement in 1929. A delegate to six national conventions, he became the New York national committeeman in 1900. He was chairman of the DNC in 1908 (*Who Was Who in America*, 1:762).

There are always empty seats I've noticed. But a fear is built up deliberately, I think—that there will not be enough. They are announced as scarce. People grow hysterical and fight for them. Is it the sense of power it gives those who have them to make men plead for them?

I wanted, in addition to tickets for my Missouri delegates, tickets for the women who had contributed to my fund. I would take about three hundred. Why I should not have had them in time to mail them in an orderly way so that it would seem a compliment, I do not know. They were granted by the committee at the last moment. And an embarrassment they were to be to me, too, as were the twenty-three badges for assistant secretaryships given me at the meeting of the Arrangements Committee just before the convention met. These had been discovered when the badges were delivered to the secretary by the maker. We had not planned for assistant secretaryships, but in duplicating the order of 1920 they had been furnished.

"What shall we do with them?" asked the secretary.

"Give them to Mrs. Blair," said someone. "She can use them for some of these women she is always talking about who will not be taken care of by their local men."

"Yes," I said, "but might it not make trouble if I named women as secretaries of the convention without first asking the committee members from their states?"

"Nonsense," said Norman Mack. "We wouldn't care."

"You'll take the responsibility, then," I asked, "for those I give to New York women?"

I was nervous about it, so I tried to get in touch with committeewomen. One that I did not reach was Miss Marbury of New York. I was naming three women from that state: Nancy Cook, Esther Ogden, and Mrs. Halsey Wilson.[3] When their names were announced the next morning at the full committee meeting, I knew I had made a mistake even before her annoyance was voiced to the press.

Followed another unpleasant experience with tickets. On Sunday evening, I had set out with my folder of tickets to the caucus of the Missouri delegation. My national committeeman and I had talked it over, and I expected to meet him there where we would together turn them over.

Having been to a tea given by some socialite, I came in a bit late. This was unfortunate because Mr. Goltra had not come at all, and the delegates were indignant. I walked up to the front of the room and explained to them that I could not give out the tickets without Mr. Goltra. There followed

---

3. Nancy Cook helped organize the new New York Women's Division of the Democratic Committee in 1920 and became its assistant director. After 1925, she ran the Val-Kil furniture factory at Hyde Park, working closely with Eleanor Roosevelt and Marion Dickerman (Blanche Wiesen Cook, *Eleanor Roosevelt, 1884–1933*, 319–24).

an amazing performance. Someone had told them that I had been given three hundred tickets. They demanded them. I explained that these were not for Missouri, but were given me as vice chairman for the women who had financially supported my work. They rose en masse and moved toward me. I clutched my folder and pounded the table. They quieted enough for me to speak. The chairman of the meeting, who had been imbibing, attacked me again. Other delegates followed. I explained that if they would give me time I would get them all in. They ordered me to give those tickets to them then and there. It was at that time, I think, that Mr. Pendergast of Kansas City, rose and said: "I think you forget that Mrs. Blair is a lady."[4] Mr. Pendergast was opposed to me politically. I had never been a friend to him. It seemed to me an amazing thing that he of all the men there, some of them men I had long known, friends of my husband, should come to my defense. I have never forgotten it.

Another surprising item was that when the photographs that the Missouri newspapermen snapped of the rush upon me appeared, on one side of me stood Harriet, and on the other Newell. They had come over with my secretary to see "Mother" perform, and were standing in the very back of the room when I entered. How they managed to get through the crowd and join me neither I nor they knew.

The result of it all was that the delegates agreed to wait until next morning for another caucus at which I promised to deliver Mr. Goltra and the tickets. Then I walked over from the McAlpin to the Waldorf, a block away, a Springfield man who weighed about three hundred pounds by my side, electing himself my protector.

It was ten o'clock before Mr. Goltra showed up, saying he had been detained at a telegraphers' meeting. I delivered an ultimatum about the tickets. The delegation must decide itself by vote how they would be divided.

Then I went to the sergeant at arms of the convention, who had always been very friendly to me, and told him my predicament. There were seventy-two delegates, seventy-two alternates, and two hundred had come with them on the special train. I must have more than the seventy-two allotted me. He felt very sorry for me, he said, but he could not go back of the Tickets Committee's orders.

The next morning at seven-thirty I was at the caucus. Mr. Goltra was

4. Thomas J. Pendergast (1872–1945) followed his brother James in controlling Democratic ward organization in Kansas City. Coming to Kansas City in 1890, he worked his way up through the organization, from city superintendent of streets to the city council where he served from 1910 to 1914. After James's retirement in 1910, Tom took over leadership and built a machine; by the mid-1920s he was the boss of Kansas City. In 1932, he supported FDR in the general election (*DAB*, s.v. "Pendergast, Thomas J.").

there. I took charge, and stated that we had but seventy-two tickets. They could decide what to do. Someone moved that they be divided among the delegates. I called their attention to the fact that this meant that any delegate could give his to a New York friend, and none would be left for alternates. They voted unanimously to give them to the delegates.

I opened my bag and dropped the badges and tickets on the table preparatory to distributing them. The delegates rushed to the table. My secretary and Mr. Goltra and I had to cover them with our hands. One of the badges was stolen. I retrieved some tickets from another hand. At last they were distributed. Then some of the alternates and visitors who had been most vociferous in their complaints and attacks came at me for their tickets. Delegates demanded pages, and sergeants at arms for their sons and friends.

"Can you really," I said to one of these delegates, a woman, "ask me to give you a page's pass for your son after the way you have acted?"

When it was all over, I turned and there was my husband standing beside me. He had promised me when I went to Washington that if I ever needed him he could come. I had wired him: "I need you," and he had taken the next train, come in that morning, and found me at the caucus.

Without a word we walked over to the Waldorf. When we reached our room he started to kiss me. I turned away and walked up and down the room without speaking. After a few minutes I stopped and said, "Now you can kiss me."

I knew that anything as personal as a kiss then would have brought me to hysterics, and I was determined I would not break down.

The ticket business was not yet over. While he and I talked in the bedroom, a crowd of Missouri women walked into the sitting room next to it, and demanded to see me. My secretary, Olive B. Swan, barred the door to the bedroom. One of the women caught her arm, tearing the sleeve, and scratched until the blood came.

And who, of all people, quieted them? Harriet, my eighteen-year-old daughter. She stood up on a chair and made them a speech, and soon had them laughing, and, I hope, ashamed. She took their names and promised each one should have a ticket.

And she got tickets. She found out where new tickets were being printed for the Victory Club members, and made up to the people who handled them. She even went to Judge Hull himself and secured a platform ticket for a newly elected committeewoman whose own committee members of a different faction had not taken care of her.

Harry went to work. He got a Missourian put on as a door keeper, and at the beginning of every session stood beside him to point out the Missourians. He got more books of tickets from the Ticket Committee. Each morning he would take the tickets for that day over to the chairman of the delegation, ex-Governor Gardner, and hand them over, taking a receipt for the number delivered.[5]

There was still the matter of the lost delegate badge. The owner threatened to bring the theft up on the floor of the convention. He seemed to think I had it. I went to the secretary of the committee. He had one badge left, he said, but it was locked in the safe and he did not have the combination. At last we were able to open the safe, and the badge was delivered.

About the middle of the convention one of the Kansas City leaders stopped me in the garden and said: "Mrs. Blair, I want to tell you the tickets have never been so well handled before."

I could laugh about it then. "They ought to be," I said. "I've an expensive lawyer devoting all his time to them."

A newspaperman twitted me with the fact that I had to call on my husband to help me out. I recalled that, almost every time I had looked at Judge Hull, Mrs. Hull was somewhere near urging a glass of milk or crackers on him. The difference between us was only in the kind of help given a wife by a husband, and a husband by a wife. How either one of us survived that convention is a mystery, and I am sure neither of us could have without our spouses.

My phone rang every minute until three or four in the morning. It began again at five in the morning. The only thing that saved me was that Mrs. Constance Livingstone Hare had offered me her town house, which was in charge of a caretaker.[6] No matter how late the hour, four or even five in the morning, Harry would take me out there, help me to bed, give me my breakfast at eight, and take me to town again. Lunch and dinner I caught as I could; when I could not get to it, he urged a glass of milk on me. I have always thought that may account for my present allergy to milk.

We were not entirely done with tickets. One night Harriet, who had stayed over in my bedroom instead of going back to her own hotel, was awakened by hearing someone in the sitting room. She looked out and saw two men going through my desk. My sister, who was with her, called the desk downstairs, and after that they kept a detective on my door. We supposed from something they said that they were after tickets.

To add to my discomfiture, my friend Mary Archer, to whom I owed so much in my work, financially and morally, had a difficulty over her tickets that resulted in her refusing to go to the convention. In order to be sure the committeewomen would have their share of tickets, the committee had passed a rule that no state batch was to be delivered without a receipt signed by both

---

5. Frederick D. Gardner (1869–1933), a St. Louis businessman, was the Democratic governor of Missouri from 1917 to 1921 (*Biographical Directory of Governors*, 2:861).

6. Constance Parsons married Montgomery Hare in 1908. He was a well-established lawyer in New York City and active in Democratic politics (*National Cyclopedia of American Biography*, s.v. "Hare, Montgomery").

the state committeeman and the committeewoman. Her committeeman had, however, managed to get those for his state without her signature. When he doled out what he decided she should have, she refused any. I felt I should be able to do something to help her, but could not.

Before the convention was over the Missouri women made the *amende honorable* by giving me a breakfast with the hostess, Mrs. Gardner, the wife of our ex-governor, and the most popular mistress our Missouri mansion had.[7] They invited my whole family, sent me flowers, and made me nice speeches. The ticket difficulty was forgotten, wiped out. This, too, is politics. One does not get very far by hanging on to the past.

---

7. Jeanette Vosburgh married Frederick Gardner in 1894 (*Who Was Who in America*, 1:439).

17 *Emotional Spectacle*

My troubles at the Madison Square Garden convention did not end with the solution of the ticket problem. When the convention had been deadlocked for some time, Mr. McAdoo failing of enough votes to win a majority but enough to prevent anyone else from winning, a resolution was brought in designed to end the deadlock. This resolution, providing for a committee to consider some way to end the situation, had been drawn up in the little room off the platform and brought in suddenly. The men behind it had never even thought of the women. But the moment I heard it, I knew there would be trouble for me. As it was drawn, it would be impossible to get a woman on this committee, and the women in the convention would be furious if there was not a woman on that committee.

I went to Mr. Hull and to Senator Walsh, the chairman of the convention, to protest that this would never do. Politely but firmly they said that it might be too bad, but inasmuch as the convention had spoken nothing could be done about it.

The women did not feel that way about it. At once they visited me, singly and in groups. A plan for a protest meeting of women was set on foot. It was not easy to serve a party and the cause of women at the same time. The good of the party that threatened to be disrupted by this bitter nomination fight demanded that this resolution should not be thrown back on the floor of the convention for amendment by the women. Moreover, it would be almost impossible to amend it satisfactorily. No candidate would be willing to entrust his interests on that committee to a woman, and to have a woman for each candidate would make it unwieldy. Besides, some of these candidates would not have women. Such at least were the men's arguments. Yet to have a matter as important as this settled as if there were no women in that convention was intolerable to some of these women. It seemed to put a period to their effectuality, which they probably doubted anyway.

There was also the point that in overlooking me, as vice chairman of the committee representing the women, they had ignored the importance of women in their setup.

Facing this I realized that if I failed them here my effectiveness as their leader was gone. Already there had been talk of the fact that though Mrs. Bass had presided at a session of the 1920 convention, no recognition had been given me at this one.

Since I was not a delegate, and only delegates could preside, except by invitation of the convention, this was really all right. I should, of course, have realized this and asked for a place on our delegation, but I had not thought of it at the time of the Springfield state convention.

Then a solution came to me. Under parliamentary rules almost anything can be done by unanimous consent. I went to Mr. Hull and Senator Walsh and told them that if no one objected, there was no reason I should not attend the committee meeting. This meant that I had to get the managers of all the candidates to consent to my inclusion. So I went from manager to manager with my case. It was difficult for me, for I was still foolishly diffident. The last one to be seen was Tom Taggart, the Indiana boss.[1] It was the ambition of his life to name a Democratic president. His candidate at that convention was the greatly respected and beloved Senator Ralston.

"It is just stage setting," I said to him, "but politics is largely a matter of stage setting, isn't it?"

"I understand you," he said. "You speak my language. Of course you should attend the committee meeting."

I was waiting in the outer room surrounded by newspapermen who had made quite a bit of copy out of the situation when the sergeant at arms appeared and asked me in. I think I have never felt so foolish in my whole life as when the men stood up as I entered.

When I looked around, I saw that instead of one man for each nominee there were practically all of the McAdoo managers, and two or three for some of the others. I never did know how they got there, but I realized that convention resolutions when people had the nerve or strength to break them were not the ironclad things I had been told they were.

The question was over abolishing the two-thirds rule. A man from Alabama made a speech against breaking it, as rhetorical and impassioned as if he had been speaking to the convention itself. Realistically, I wondered how anyone could indulge in generalities and sentiment with men whose minds were already made up, and, to my surprise, these men stood up and gave him an ovation. I wondered then if oratory was to them anodyne or release. The next performance was a burst of profanity from one of the men. The others looked meaningly at the speaker, and he turned and apologized to me. The third was a small man jumping at a six-footer with doubled up fists saying: "Do I understand you call me a liar, Sir?" It was like a little game rooster attacking a lion. Men separated them. The meeting adjourned. I had

---

1. Thomas Taggart (1856–1926) began his political career in Indiana in 1886. He served as chairman of the Democratic State Committee, 1892–1894, and as mayor of Indianapolis for three terms, 1895–1901. He was national committeeman from Indiana from 1900 to 1916 and chairman of the DNC from 1904 to 1908. In 1916, he was appointed to fill a Senate vacancy (*Who Was Who in America*, 1:1214).

known what it was to be in a room where a word could produce instantaneous combustion.

All this time there had been another annoyance that went on day by day. It began when a newspaper said that Mrs. Blair would not be reelected, it was understood, as head of the women and Janet Fairbank was slated to take her place.[2] The same afternoon Mrs. Fairbank sent for me and told me that she was not a candidate and was supporting me for reelection. The next morning appeared an item that Mrs. Benton McMillan of Tennessee was to take my place. She stopped me and told me she had no intention of running against me. Another day it was Mrs. Leroy Springs, a very beautiful woman from South Carolina, who was later put in nomination for vice president. It was a simple matter, since the newspaperwomen were friends of mine, to run down the source of these interviews and reports. Miss Marbury had not taken placidly the appointment of these New York women as assistant secretaries.

At the time I was not even sure I wanted to succeed myself another term, but I was quite sure I did not want to be put out as a failure.

In view of all this the convention to me was largely a matter of confusion of tickets, marching, crowds, heat, conflict of egos, and continual balloting. But a few things stand out in my mind. The night Newton D. Baker made his speech for the League of Nations, and, not even noting the tremendous applause the audience gave him at the close, turned from the rostrum saying, "I haven't changed a single vote." The personal acclaim meant nothing to him on fire with his purpose. Senator Glass coming to stand beside him, though he knew this might lose his own nomination. I realized I had seen something rare in politics, where not often do men forget themselves for an idea.

The night the fight on the Klan plank was on I sat between lame congressman William Upshur of Georgia, and Joe Tumulty.[3] Each time the pro-Klanners made a point, Mr. Upshur would reach over and hit Mr. Tumulty with his crutch. When the anti-Klan speaker made a good point, Mr. Tumulty would reach across me and punch the congressman in the ribs.

---

2. Janet Ayer (Mrs. Kellogg) Fairbank (1879–1951) contributed articles to newspapers and magazines, among them the *Chicago Post*, the *New York Herald Tribune*, and the *New Republic*. She also wrote novels, plays, and short stories. Active in the suffrage campaign, she supported Theodore Roosevelt in 1912, acting as finance chairman of the western women's division of the Progressive Party. She served on the DNC from 1920 to 1928 (*National Cyclopedia of American Biography*, s.v. "Fairbank, Janet Ayer").

3. William D. Upshaw (1866–1952) was elected to the House of Representatives as a Democrat from Georgia in 1918. Reelected in 1920, 1922, and 1924, he was a strong Prohibitionist and publicly sympathetic to the Ku Klux Klan. Defeated in 1926, he did not support Smith in 1928 but switched to Hoover. In 1932, he was the presidential candidate of the Prohibition Party (*DAB*, s.v. "Upshaw, William D."). Joseph P. Tumulty (1879–1954) promoted progressive causes in the New Jersey General Assembly from 1907 to 1910 when he became an adviser to Woodrow Wilson. When Wilson was elected president, Tumulty became his secretary (*DAB*, s.v. "Tumulty, Joseph P.").

Mr. Bryan that same night made his last appeal to the Democratic Party on this same Klan issue. Returning from the lunch counter, I came into the hall just as he began, and stopped among the delegates to listen. He swung into rhetoric, it caught them, they applauded. Then immediately he dropped into the didactic as if he were addressing a Chautauqua crowd. He was met again by jeers and hisses. As if challenged, he swept again into oratory, and again won applause only to drop again into the didactic. It went on so for several minutes, the two Bryans spelling each other: the oratorical Bryan who had won a nomination with a speech, and the lecturer who had toured the Chautauquas.

In the bitter contest for the nomination I had no part, though I was, of course, deeply interested, and knew fairly well what was going on. My position, as I look back on it, seems incredibly naive. I felt that Mr. McAdoo would make the most invincible nominee, and was the choice of the majority of the Democrats. I had a deep personal interest in Carter Glass's candidacy both because he was Mrs. Banister's brother and because I admired him. I saw no conflict in these two feelings inasmuch as Senator Glass was available as a candidate only if Mr. McAdoo could not make it, and was himself friendly to Mr. McAdoo. But I had taken literally Judge Hull's dictum that the national committee staff was to be neutral. Nor did I see any inconsistency in this. Though I knew Mr. McAdoo's friends had supported my work—even urged my appointment in the first place—I thought they were looking forward toward the election. If Mr. McAdoo won the election as they confidently expected him to, they wanted the women organized; and not only the McAdoo women, but all the women, which meant that the leader should not be tied to him. Nor did any of the McAdoo men ever suggest anything different to me. Never was I taken into their councils. Only once in all that two years was I asked to do anything for the special benefit of Mr. McAdoo, and what they wanted me to do was to use my influence with someone to do what he had already ineffectually attempted.

As to the final vote of the convention that chose John W. Davis, I have heard three conflicting accounts, two of them by men involved and absolutely honest in their reports of the facts they print. This much I do know, however: that the current newspaper comment that the nomination of Mr. Davis was decided upon by a little group of bosses months before has no basis in fact. It is true that certain New Yorkers did not want Mr. McAdoo nominated, that certain political bosses were also opposed, and that they encouraged the susceptible ambitions of other men in order to block Mr. McAdoo's nomination. But it is also true that Mr. Taggart was deeply disappointed when his candidate, Senator Ralston, too honest to seek an election after the doctor had pronounced his death sentence, withdrew his name; that the Alabama delegation had every reason to hope that Senator Underwood would be the beneficiary of the blockade; and that Senator Glass missed the nomination by only a few moments. The desires of capitalists and bosses do not always agree—nor even, thank goodness, the desires of all bankers and all capitalists. The control of a nomination is not as simple as some commentators would have us think, men being individualistic and selfish. Often, too, an accident does what the best-laid plans of men cannot. It is easy for commentators to jump from desires to results and tie the two together, but their conclusions are seldom true.

The one really important thing I had tried to do at that convention was a flop. Early in the spring I had known that the League of Women Voters and other women's organizations would have certain planks they wanted the Democratic convention to include in the platform. It seemed to me that the planks of special interest to women ought to come from the Democratic women, that they should be the ones to propose them rather than those who had stayed outside the party. Was it not, indeed, that they might bring their party to accept such planks that women had come into the party? I talked it over with Judge Hull, and we appointed a committee of women to hold hearings on the planks the women's organizations wanted included, and then to propose such planks as they wished to the Resolutions Committee. Mrs. Franklin Roosevelt was asked to be chairman with Mrs. Minnie Fisher Cunningham and Mrs. Pattie Ruffner Jacobs the other members.

Several days were spent on these hearings in the rooms across from Madison Square Garden, and the committee worked very hard on their recommendations.

I expected that the Resolutions Committee would see this as an opportunity to strengthen our women and show women generally the value of being in a party. But it was more of my wishful thinking. Though Mrs. Roosevelt did present their planks, in the hectic fight over the Klan and League of Nations planks, these planks were given very cursory attention, and the women's committee appointed by the national committee was kept, like those of other organizations, cooling its heels outside closed doors.

This, I can see now, is inherent in the composition and purpose of a political party. Instead of being a group of people seeking the best program or the best candidate, it is made up of people who want to exploit it to express their own particular ideas, prejudices, and interests. Not a resolution of interests that will best serve the common weal, and not even victory for itself, is their prime concern, but to make it stand for their own preferences and purposes. As there are those with contrary interests and purposes, a bitter fight in the convention results, a fight in which the welfare of the state, or even the party, is forgotten in the desire to bend it to the desired uses. I do not say this because of the matter of these planks with which there might be honest disagreement, but because in the fight over the Klan and Prohibition planks there was no time or inclination to consider them as a contribution of Democratic women, either to the party's success or to the welfare of the country.

One little satisfaction I got out of the convention. When Senator Glass read the resolution providing for the composition of the national committee for the next four years, he had made a few small changes that went unnoticed as the weary delegates voted unanimously for it. The first vice chairman had to be a woman!

Just before the last session as I was passing along the hotel corridor, Mr. Goltra caught up with me, rushed me into the flower shop, filled my arms with all the red roses they had, and drove me out to Frank Polk's house, where the John W. Davises were staying.[4] The house was full of people. We went back to the room where the Davises were sitting. Their attitude, I would say, was one of bewilderment. They had given up all idea of Mr. Davis's winning. He had reached his peak some days before and had stopped there. He even told someone he had his tryout; now it would be the others' time.

I, myself, could only feel thankfulness that it was over. There remained only the nomination of the vice president. We went into a room where Mr. Davis and some men were talking about it. Just like that, I think, they decided. We went onto the platform. It was accomplished.

But the convention was not quite over for me. I got to my room and learned that my sister Margaretta and secretary, sitting together on the platform, had overheard a man behind them say to another, "Now we must get busy and get our friend in Mrs. Blair's place." They had named her. It was the first I knew she even wanted it, and the new committee was to meet the next morning.

We talked it over, Harry and I. Tired, worn out, disillusioned, with a party so split that there seemed little hope of victory, I was willing to call it a day and go home. But as we discussed the fight that had been waged on me—and it did rankle—it seemed like giving up under fire. The truth was I did not like to be licked, and by a surprise attack. I had to be at a women's breakfast at nine o'clock, at which I had asked Mrs. Davis to meet the women. There would be no time to do anything. Then I did a rather outrageous thing. I called up Mrs. Roosevelt and asked her if I might come out. She was in a dressing gown, calm as usual, when I told her what was afoot and asked her if she could catch Norman Mack before he got off to the committee meeting, and see if he could not restrain Miss Marbury from the attack she seemed about to launch. It must have been two o'clock in the morning.

When the committee meeting convened after the breakfast I had no idea what to expect. I had asked for no votes, not expecting a contest. I had

---

4. Frank L. Polk (1871–1943), a New York lawyer, was an independent Democrat opposed to Tammany. A supporter of Woodrow Wilson in 1912, he was appointed in 1915 as counselor in the State Department and was deeply involved in the transition from neutrality to war. In 1918–1919, he was acting secretary of state while Lansing was in Paris. In 1919, Congress gave him the title of undersecretary of state. In 1924, he was floor manager for John Davis at the Democratic convention (*DAB*, s.v. "Polk, Frank L.").

not had time to see anyone except Mrs. Roosevelt, not even my national committeeman from Missouri.

The committee organized by electing Clem Shaver as the new chairman.[5]

I waited for the next move and heard someone suggest that further organization be postponed until Mr. Shaver had consulted the nominee, and that the election of other committee officers be held at the notification meeting that was fixed for Clarksburg sometime later.

At least I had time. Harry left that day for Joplin. Newell and Harriet had gone sometime before. They had come to the convention straight from school. When it had lasted ten days and threatened to last weeks more, I did not feel we could afford the expense of indefinite hotel bills.

Both were deeply disappointed and left feeling aggrieved. Newell, who had been acting as a volunteer sergeant at arms on the platform, did not see why he should not stay and take the ten dollars a day for hotel bills offered by the sergeant at arms, who said he was one of the best assistants he had. My feeling that it would hardly do for my son to take remuneration from the committee Newell did not share, saying he did not think he should be penalized because of his mother. Harriet had a very grand time. Friends of ours had college sons about her age, and they ran about together. "It may be awful for you, Mother," she said, "but I'm having the time of my life."

When I came to the hall the day the convention opened, there sat Harriet, who really was a lovely-looking girl, in a chiffon dress and a big hat, in front of Mrs. Hull at the very edge of the platform. I sent her a note to the effect that she should not be in such a conspicuous place.

The chief sergeant at arms of the platform—an exuberant Irishman—had placed her there and she couldn't help herself, she wrote back.

I was glad someone was enjoying herself.

The social engagements I do not remember at all. Most of the functions I never saw. There was a very grand party, I believe, given by the Hearsts, but if I went I don't remember it. The Committee of Nine, I know, had a very large reception somewhere. Mrs. Smith and Mrs. Roosevelt were, I think, their guests of honor.[6] I did, I think, walk down the line. When the New York committee gave its large dinner to all the delegates, Judge Hull was ill, and I was asked to respond for the committee. That was the night I sat between Governor Smith and Mr. Bryan. It was the only time, so Governor Smith told me later, that the two ever met. They did not engage in any conversation that night, but both were pleasant to me. Governor Smith's many admirers

---

5. Clement Shaver (1867–1954) started the movement for John Davis at the 1924 convention after Smith and McAdoo had deadlocked. Active in West Virginia Democratic politics, he had served as chairman of the state committee and managed gubernatorial and senatorial campaigns. Chairman of the DNC after the 1924 convention, he served for four years (*Who Was Who in America*, 3:776; *New York Times*, September 3, 1954).

6. Catherine Dunn married Alfred Smith in 1900.

wanted his autograph in their menu card. Soon a steady line of them were coming to our table. Gallantly, though his friends did not care for it at all, he insisted that I must put my name down below his. Mr. Bryan's friends wanted his autograph. A steady line came up to him. Not to be behind Governor Smith in courtesy, he insisted on my autographing his friends' menus, so I was kept very busy. Very few of the delegates, I noted, wanted those of both Governor Smith and Mr. Bryan. I never, I think, changed my conversational gears as often as I did that night.

Just before the convention convened, the New York committee had given a dinner to the Arrangements Committee that, for the look on Miss Marbury's face, I have always remembered. It was a very elaborate dinner with wine and cocktails "and everything," as the children say. When dessert and liqueurs were over, Mr. Wanamaker, the chairman, arose and made a speech.[7] The committee wanted to make some expression to Judge Hull and Mr. Mack of their gratification at having the convention in New York, and particularly for the way the arrangements had been handled. They therefore wished to present to Mrs. Hull "this diamond watch, and to Mrs. Mack this diamond bracelet." Miss Marbury's face was a picture. She had worked as hard as Mrs. Mack, devoting herself for months to hospitality arrangements for the delegates and thrown her really exquisite house and garden open to them. I think both of us felt it more profitable that evening to be political wives than women politicians.

Elizabeth Marbury was a remarkable personality. With tiny bones wrapped in pounds of flesh, she could walk only with the help of two canes. Without apparent vanity—at least of the flesh—she wore her hair tossed carelessly on the top, and appeared in nondescript black dresses. But so pertinent and pungent was her wit that people crowded to be with her. Her experience was large. She knew everybody on two continents who was worth knowing. She was a successful businesswoman, a playwright broker, and had a house that was perfect in every detail, an exquisite bandbox of a place on Sutton Place. It was my misfortune that I failed to win her friendship.

Before I leave the convention I should say something of two men who I think, although one was not there and the other only the last night, dominated it. The first was William Gibbs McAdoo. I never knew him well, but when I met him I echoed what my sister said when I introduced her to him: "Why didn't you tell me he is absolutely fascinating?" Fascination was what, I think, he had, the same kind of fascination that Alice Longworth has: that of a personality that is never grasped and so always tantalizes. No man ever had a more devoted following. It partook almost of mysticism. He had a reputation

---

7. John Wanamaker (1838–1922) founded his department store in 1876, and it became one of the largest in the United States. A Republican, he was rewarded for his support of Benjamin Harrison in 1888 by appointment as postmaster general (*DAB*, s.v. "Wanamaker, John").

as a great administrator. His followers believed him to be a great progressive. As much selfless energy and generosity was poured out for his nomination as ever for anyone's. The other was Governor Smith, of whom I have written something before in this book. I saw him when he came up on the platform to make his speech the last night congratulating Mr. Davis. He, too, drew from followers intense personal devotion. More, he dramatized in his person two ideas deeply implanted in Americans: the rise of the poor boy to high place by his native ability, and the right of the individual to religious liberty. When the *New York World* and other New York leaders exploited this dramatization in order to "stop McAdoo," they started something that was perhaps as unfortunate for Governor Smith as it was for the Democratic Party, and perhaps for the country at large.

During the marching demonstration on the floor for Governor Smith, an editor of the *World* said to me: "You see, we have McAdoo stopped."

"Yes," I answered, "and there is not a state in your parade that has ever gone for a Democratic nominee except New York, and it not often."

He shrugged his shoulders. "We thought we did the right thing. Perhaps we were wrong."

"I should think you would have been sure," I answered.

Governor Smith's speech was largely the same one he had made to the women's conference about a progressive state government. It seemed to me proper for him to speak to the convention of what he knew and what was undoubtedly a real accomplishment. Those in the audience from other parts of the country, however, felt that it was the injection of something local on a national platform, and resented the emphasis on the "I." It was an evidence, I think, of Governor Smith's failure to understand the psychology of the out-country as opposed to that of New York, which had something at least to do with his subsequent defeats.

Both men have always seemed to me to be alike. Either one, had he been elected president, might have justified the promise he then gave and would have become a great national figure with achievements of great merit to his credit. But it was true of each that with defeat of his ambitions, something seemed to crumple in him so that power went out of him. Men may become great with success who cannot withstand defeat. I have myself known the deadening effect of failure that stops whatever in you is fertile. Neither of these men apparently had the something more than ability or strength that made men like Clay, or Bryan, able to defy defeat and continue as leaders of men.

Men and women in emotional undress do not present to me a pleasing spectacle. The uncontrolled emotions at this convention flayed my nerves far more than the deadly monotony of repeated ballots, and made Madison Square Garden something I hardly like to remember.

18 Magnificent—but Not Winning

Back in Washington again I awaited developments as to the election of the vice chairman. Mr. Shaver came to see me, and out of the blue sprang up supporters. Women wrote to Mr. Davis. Mrs. Roosevelt went to see him. A friend in headquarters wrote for proxies. When the committee met in Clarksburg, I knew that Mr. Shaver wanted me to continue.[1] I also knew that I had opposition for reelection.

At a luncheon given in Clarksburg to the committee, I sat next to Mr. Norman Mack. He asked me what all the trouble about me was. I reminded him of the assistant secretaryships, and told him about the Arrangements Committee. He had about six proxies he was supposed to vote against me, as Miss Marbury had not come to the meeting herself. A friend of my opponent had come to me with a proposition. "Why not elect you both?" he said. "You to have charge of the organization." I reminded him of the convention resolution that provided for only three vice chairmen, and said the men would not stand for two women to one man. I explained that this would take from the office of woman vice chairman the importance it seemed to me it must have if she was to appear to be the leader of the women. This, I pointed out, was of more importance than what woman held the position. If his candidate had the most votes, she should hold this position.

How I did cling in those days to the idea that the office conferred power. I had yet to realize that what counts in politics is not the official handle to your name, but your backing and actual power as an individual.

When the matter was settled at the committee meeting, it had been true to form, decided by a subcommittee sitting outside, and the meeting reported me as vice chairman and added two more committeemen in spite of the convention resolution.

Often I have wondered why I insisted on staying in my position on the committee. I had no longer any illusions that it was easy or even pleasant work. The hopes of success at the election were slight. It would be expensive. Mr. Shaver, looking forward to difficulty in raising money, offered me only my actual expenses of board and lodging while in Washington and my traveling expenses. These would be only a small part of what it would cost me to stay

---

1. The Democratic National Committee met in Clarksburg, West Virginia, on August 11, 1924.

away from home. The nominee, although not unfriendly, had no particular interest in my work or purposes. I would have to be separated from my children during their vacation, and they would be looked after by Ella and a friend.

There were probably two reasons I kept the position. One was that it seemed a justification of my work; the second that I still had hopes of finishing what I had started, the inclusion of women in politics.

Mrs. Banister and I stayed at the clubhouse on our return to Washington. The club was closed for the summer, but our room rents were needed to pay the house rent. So we huddled behind its drawn curtains with a cook we paid ourselves.

I was away much of the time making speeches, leaving Mrs. Banister in charge of the office, so the hot house was worse for her.

On the way home from the committee meeting, I had a jolt. Mr. Shaver told me he had promised Mrs. Robert Jackson (wife of the committeeman) that she could be in the New York office in charge of the women in the eastern states. This was directly contrary to my contention that the women responsible for the organization of the women should make their own appointments. Yet I could hardly make an issue of it, even if I did not know what it meant or what was back of it, since if I had been asked to name someone from those states I would undoubtedly have chosen her.

I went up to see her, told her all I knew. In a way it was a relief to me to have no responsibility for this area, for by now I knew I was not the one to work with the New York politicians. I did not understand them any better than they did me. The day I went into headquarters at the Belmont Hotel, I found the place completely staffed with the henchmen of the city organization. They were even posted at the door of Mrs. Jackson's office. It looked almost as if these headquarters had been put under their surveillance. Office desks were undoubtedly examined and mail looked over. I went back quite satisfied with things as they were, even though I knew that my leadership had been discredited.

There was at first some confusion from having the two sets of headquarters. The New York people thought theirs should run the whole campaign. While acceding to their demand that they have a headquarters, Mr. Shaver was insistent on keeping the control in Washington. I understand better now than I did then his reasons for it. The difficulty was at last resolved by leaving the campaign in New England, New York, Pennsylvania, and New Jersey to the New York office, while the Washington office oversaw the rest.

Poor Mr. Shaver! What he had to do was to drive in double harness two horses who balked at the union. His preconvention organization for Mr. Davis had been negligible. He could not depend upon that. He could only enlarge it by bringing in the McAdoo and anti-McAdoo men, and they did not trust each other. Yet he had to make them work together somehow.

After the La Follette convention our prospects were not bright.[2] The managers, in order to keep going, had to convince themselves that Senator La Follette's candidacy would draw more votes from the Republicans than from us. A difficult job of persuasion, but politicians are adept at convincing themselves by hope.

I, for example, was able to persuade myself that Mr. Davis was a liberal. Had he not voted for all Mr. Wilson's progressive legislation when he was in Congress in 1914? When Mabel Costigan, who was running the women's end of the La Follette campaign, sent me a list of progressive legislation fostered by Senator La Follette, I sent it back with a notation of the Democratic majorities by which each item had been passed.[3]

What happened is history. How the Republicans played upon the fear of throwing the election into Congress and making Charles Bryan president, until it almost seemed a contest between Mr. Coolidge and Mr. Bryan![4]

The difficulties in hitching the two groups together were duplicated in states and counties, and even in the women's clubs. The organizations so carefully built up by Mr. Hull and myself went to pieces, disrupted by the factional fights in the convention. The city organizations, realistic all of them, knew from the start they had no chance of victory and concerned themselves only with saving their local tickets.

Nor did our candidate help us. A dignified, reserved gentleman, he stated his position on all issues in short speeches that were masterpieces of English, but, as one correspondent put it, "They were so perfect that they did not touch the imperfect human beings to whom they were addressed." Admirable for a Supreme Court justice, they left private citizens cold. To them he was a statue. Except for Mr. Shaver, whose great ambition it was to give his country as president a man he considered of great intellectual stature, and

---

2. The national convention of the Conference for Progressive Political Action met in Cleveland, July 4–6, 1924. Robert La Follette was nominated for president and Sen. Burton K. Wheeler of Montana for vice president.

3. Mabel G. Cory married Edward P. Costigan in 1903. She had been prominent in suffrage, the National Consumers' League, and the Progressive Party. He had been a Republican but switched to the Progressives in 1912, and in 1916 supported Wilson. In 1930 he won a United States Senate seat as a Democrat from Colorado. She died on September 21, 1951, in Denver (*DAB*, s.v. "Costigan, Edward Prentiss").

4. Charles Bryan (1867–1945), a political adviser to his brother William Jennings Bryan, was elected governor of Nebraska in 1922. At the 1924 convention, he vied for the presidential nomination. When the deadlock between McAdoo and Smith resulted in the choice of Davis, Charles was given the vice presidential nomination to conciliate the Bryanites of the party (*DAB*, s.v. "Bryan, Charles"). Calvin Coolidge (1872–1933), a career politician, rose to prominence in Massachusetts politics and was elected governor in 1918. As Harding's vice president, he became president upon Harding's death. In 1924, he was the Republican nominee, beating Democrat John Davis and Progressive Robert La Follette (*DAB*, s.v. "Coolidge, Calvin").

those of us who were self-hypnotized, I doubt that a hundred Democrats cared enthusiastically for him. Through the campaign he walked, doing all he should and doing it perfectly, himself the least discomposed by his defeat. It was magnificent, but it is not campaign winning.

Yet I still believe that it was a national misfortune that John W. Davis was not elected. In 1925 it was not too late to have gone back to Woodrow Wilson's policy of regulation and control of big business and finance in the public interest. Mr. Davis, with his 1912 style of progressivism, believed in it. With his grasp of constitutional law and corporate organization, with his orderly mind and convincing logic, he might have deflected us from the excessive exploitation and financial brigandage that resulted from the do-nothingness of Mr. Coolidge's conservatism. In spite of his Wall Street connections, he would, I believe, with the United States as his client, have put its interests first, just as Chief Justice Hughes was to do when the United States became his client.[5]

Up to this time I had not understood the evanescent character of political work. Now I saw that one could not build for the future. Each campaign might be only a fight in a war that never ceased, but each fight was unconnected with others so that there could be no long-term planning. The men in control in one campaign might not be in the next. The fight for power inside the organization prevented that. This knowledge caused me far more disappointment than our defeat at the polls, for my whole idea of women's political organization crumbled.

In this, I think, lies a profound difference between women's and men's approach to organization. Men work by the job method. They have something to do and do it. When through, they rest until there is a new job to be done. Women work by the program method. They line it out, do a little each day, each month, each year, keeping everlastingly at it, satisfied if they approach only a little nearer their goal. So in campaigns. Men saw them simply as single jousts; women saw them as pieces in a long continued process of getting what you wanted. To men organization was merely a drive, useful for the fight on hand, and then to be scrapped; women, as something that moved slowly but surely to an appointed end, taking defeats by the way.

It may, of course, have been that I became too soon discouraged. In these later years a women's organization in the Democratic Party has been built up. It has a permanent program of what it calls "education," and its opponents

---

5. Charles Evans Hughes (1862–1948) began his political career in 1905 as counsel to a committee of the New York state legislature investigating New York City utilities. A progressive, he was elected governor in 1906 and reelected in 1908. President Taft appointed him to the Supreme Court in 1910, but he left the court to run for president against Wilson. In 1921, he became Harding's secretary of state, returning to his law practice in 1925. Hoover appointed him chief justice of the Court in 1930, where he served until his retirement in 1941 (*DAB*, s.v. "Hughes, Charles Evans").

"propaganda." It is designed toward a permanent objective. It may be that the Republican women have something in their party of the same kind. This may be something that women have contributed to political organization. Yet it may be that with the defeat of the New Deal, their organization, too, could be disrupted. For it, too, is dependent on the personnel in charge, and it changes. It will be interesting to see what comes of it.

There is another point about women and political work. Men have organized politics according to their fight technique. Decision by combat, and acceptance of the verdict. This is their way. When a campaign is over, it is over, and the issue settled. The defeated turn to another issue. Women are different. Having once decided they want something, they keep going until they get it. To them defeats are only temporary things to be taken in their stride. The verdict at the polls does not alter their opinions. It merely starts them on a new effort. So far they have not brought this habit of theirs into politics, but once they are really politically organized in the parties they may. It is perhaps the fear of this that makes men dread their real participation.

The weakness of my women's organization was that it had to operate through state and local organizations headed by men. My clubs, for example, though stimulated from our headquarters, were told to put themselves at the disposal of their regularly constituted official leaders. Much of my time and effort was directed toward persuading these local organization leaders to accept the help of these clubs. Sometimes their refusal sprang from a deliberate intention not to handicap their local ticket by any tie-up with the national ticket, which they considered a liability. Sometimes it was because the women in the clubs had not belonged to their particular faction. It was a fallacy, I discovered, to think that men in politics always want an effective organization; they much prefer defeat to the victory of someone they oppose in their own party. Men did not want women organized if they were not organized by them.

When the presidential nominee started out on his special tour, word was sent out from our headquarters to the state leaders that the state national committeewomen were to be included in the local group that rode across a state with the nominee. The men in charge of the tour were instructed to ask these women, and insist on their inclusion. Not a single one of these women, so far as I know, was included.

Some of my time was spent in the western headquarters at Chicago. In charge of the women's work was a woman politician who had had much experience in other campaigns assisting men leaders.[6] She was amazed and baffled to find herself as the head of the women's organization, set off in a

---

6. Mrs. Madge O'Neil, national committeewoman from Iowa, took charge of organization of women from the western headquarters in Chicago (Draft of Report of First Vice Chairman, DNC, August 11–November 1, 1924, Folder 98, ENB Papers).

cul-de-sac with no cooperation at all from the men, or news of what was going on.

I was baffled myself. Dinners and compliments on my hats and friendly persiflage from the men, while pleasant, did not compensate for lack of participation in their councils. They thought of me, as I well knew, in these Chicago headquarters, as a nice person to be humored if it did not involve any money, and the women as a nuisance to be put up with and kept quiet.

This did not apply to the headquarters in Washington. Mr. Shaver was genuinely and completely an equal suffragist. He did not even in his thoughts make any distinction between women and men in politics. Both were just people to him, so it was natural for him to talk over problems with me as his assistant and ask me to his conferences. The only problem of women in politics to him was the problem of new voters. He deferred to me as likely to know better than he what would appeal to women. I was, in fact, more inside politics during this campaign than ever before or since. The only trouble was that there was very little to be "inside" of.

He was a delightful man to work with, almost completely selfless, with interests as varied as fishing and iris culture, Boy Scouts and politics. He had a profound knowledge of American history and a passion for liberal democracy. Unfortunately for him, he had also that rare thing, an instinct for anonymity. He wanted others to have the recognition. Such a man had none of the self-dramatization that is such a help to newspapermen. They, in appreciation, naturally feature the dramatizer. It took a Will Rogers, who said that Mr. Shaver was the finest man in politics he knew, to appreciate the rare qualities of Mr. Shaver.

To Mr. Shaver it seemed a matter of course that I should preside at the notification of Mr. Bryan of his nomination for the vice presidency as he had presided at the notification of Mr. Davis of his nomination for the presidency.

These notification meetings were nonsensical holdovers from a day when men did not, openly at least, wage campaigns for nominations. Stage setting for the nominee's speeches opened the campaign. It was stage setting for me to preside at the meeting in Lincoln, Nebraska, in the university stadium. I remember it as the Meeting of Tall Men. I never saw so many together elsewhere. Arthur Mullen, the national committeeman with eyes and face—and, I have an idea, the political shrewdness—of Abraham Lincoln, a seven-foot director of the Omaha Chamber of Commerce, and Sen. Pat Harrison.[7] I have my picture standing among them, a little white wisp. When I took it

---

7. Arthur F. Mullen (1873–1938), a Nebraska lawyer, was Democratic National Committeeman from 1916 to 1935, with the exception of 1920–1924. In 1932 he was vice chairman of the campaign committee (*National Cyclopedia of American Biography*, s.v. "Mullen, Arthur F.").

home, some of my Joplin friends who had wondered why any woman wanted to go into politics decided there was really something to it.

This was my first and last meeting with Charles Bryan. A casualty of the calendar, he always seems to me, acclaimed a dangerous radical for espousing legislation that was in another generation to be accepted as commonplace. Unlucky, too, in his hard common sense, being overshadowed by a brother with a genius for phrasing and an evangelistic cast of mind. In another day he might have stood out as a rugged pioneer in a new frontier of thought.

As to my contributions to the campaign, they were of time and energy and worry, rather than of value. I took as my field those questions of social betterment that were supposed to be women's special interest, at least of the organized women of America. I studied them, made memoranda on them for our speakers and candidate, urged that support be given to the Child Labor Amendment and child-maternity legislation. Mrs. Banister prepared much literature that, though good, was not, I fear, much used by state committees that had neither the funds nor the organization, and sometimes not the desire, to distribute them. We kept women speakers on the road, held meetings of local women leaders in an effort to stimulate them. Trying to bring the national committeewomen into the work, we appointed them in charge of certain regions, but as we could give them little money, they could not do much.

Election night Mrs. Banister and I went up to New York to hear the returns. I had had a long letter from Harry that day in which he endeavored to prepare me for defeat, knowing as he did that with the self-intoxication of those who wage campaigns, I had persuaded myself to expect victory. But I was not prepared for the desolation at headquarters, nor the way the few who ventured there faded away by ten o'clock. At eleven Marion and I sat practically alone in the hotel at our late supper.

Our headquarters were at once dismantled. Only our faithful Eva Coulter was left of our large staff.[8] Mrs. Banister went to the Mayflower Hotel as publicity director. I went home.

I had not realized that in the necessity to cut expenses for rent and storage, our files would be destroyed until it was too late to make arrangements to store them. With their destruction our two years' work was wiped out as if it had not been.

---

8. Eva Coulter, a stenographer employed by the National Democratic Woman's Club, lived at 2003 I Street NW in 1923.

19 *Printer's Ink*

Only two years and ten months I had been in Washington, and ten chapters have been devoted to them. This is proper, for they were the busiest, most interesting, in some ways the most trying.

It was not easy to go back to Joplin. I did not see myself sinking into a life of domesticity, and it offered nothing else. But neither did I see myself breaking the bonds that made it my home. I knew my husband was aware of my feelings. Not one to accept a sacrificial wife, he was not happy over it. My sister Ella had moved us, before I came, into another house.[1] She had even curtained it for me. I was not as grateful as I might have been.

Joplin did not any more know what to do with me than I how to fit in. I was a maverick, half admired, a little suspected, and somewhat feared. But I belonged to a club that has always stuck by me, I had friends, and I set to work to make a life for myself there. A friend of mine asked me to take charge of a drive to raise funds for a lecture and concert course. This helped to orient me among them again.

A few weeks after my return, at a mass meeting of club women, a visiting woman made a speech against ratification of the Child Labor Amendment. Once the legislative agent for the League of Women Voters, she had become a "lecturer" for a state manufacturers' association. One of the audience moved that the women meet again the next week and hear from Mrs. Blair on it. Thus I was drawn back into what we called "social" or "civic" work.

I took to my writing again. I wanted to write on politics and especially women in politics.

But no woman's magazine thought women sufficiently interested in the subject. When I had done an article for the *Saturday Evening Post*, and two for *Harper's*, the market for that subject seemed exhausted.[2]

---

1. In 1925, the Blairs lived in the Cleveland Apartments, no. 4, at 801–807 First Street (Joplin City Directory, 1925).

2. In an article titled "Are Women Counting in Politics?" ENB was the anonymous author of the "Counted Out" portion of the article (*Saturday Evening Post* [July 18, 1925]: 7, 78–82). She published two articles in *Harper's* on politics: "Are Women a Failure in Politics?" 115 (October 1925): 513–22, and "Men in Politics as a Woman Sees Them" 152 (May 1926): 703–9. She also had an article in the *Independent*, "Are Women Really in Politics?" 119 (December 3, 1927): 542–44.

With summer the children came home for vacation, and the house was full of guests. Discomfited over some bills I had incurred doing over the sunporch, I wrote an article I called "The Pangs of Extravagance," and sent it off to *Cosmopolitan*.[3] They accepted it and sent me a check for four hundred dollars. After it was spent I had a letter from Ray Long, the editor, saying that they were in a dilemma. Not until they had scheduled the article for publication had they noted that it had been submitted anonymously, and it was absolutely against their rules to publish a first-person story unsigned. If they could not use my name, they would have to send it back. This meant I would have to return the four hundred, so I consented to the use of my name. When it appeared, the magazine had changed the title to "How I Cured Myself of Extravagance." This was a laugh since my family and friends knew I was not cured. A day or so after it came out, my husband was called on the telephone by the assistant cashier of the bank, who looked after my overdrafts.

"Tell Mrs. Blair," she said, "there's an article in this month's *Cosmopolitan* she should read."

"Overdrawn again?" he asked. "I'll be right over."

The answer to my desire to write I owe to my mother.

"Why don't you write about books?" she asked me one day. "You talk well about them, have original ideas."

Write about them for whom? Book reviewing was poor pay, and newspapers already had their reviewers. Then some of my friends asked me to recommend some books for their summer reading, and the thought struck me: "Why not try to get a department in some woman's magazine, recommending books for all the various tastes? No such magazine had one, but why not?"

I knew that Mr. Bigelow of *Good Housekeeping* was always open to new ideas, so I wrote him suggesting such articles. In answer he asked me to do a sample for him.

The day his request came, three of my family arrived on a visit. Not seeing how I could do this and manage the house, I made an agreement with Harriet. If she would take over the menus and ordering, I would give her a percentage of the first check, if and when I got one. So, in between visits, I did the article and sent it off. In answer came a telegram saying Mr. Bigelow would be out to see me the next week.

When he came, he told me he had been wanting this kind of department for ten years, but had never found just the woman to do it. This was not a compliment on my style or knowledge of books. When a literary critic asked him why he did not get a professor of literature, he said he wanted someone who approached books as his readers did, for interest and entertainment.

---

3. "I Am Curing Myself of Extravagance," *Cosmopolitan* (March 1926): 52–53. She also published "Why We Live beyond Our Means," *Forum* 77 (June 1927): 892–99.

He did not know how long he would run the articles; that would depend on the interest they stimulated—perhaps a year, perhaps six months. He ran them seven years.[4]

It was a difficult assignment, I realize now, though I did not then. I was not to evaluate, review, or criticize books. I was to pick out each month some ten, twelve, or fifteen volumes and tell about them in such a way that each reader would know which was the book for her. It had to be a varied list, one for every taste. This meant reading a great many more books—sometimes thirty, or even fifty during one month. As I wanted the best of its kind, I had to wait until the end of the month to choose, so I put aside and then eliminated and again eliminated.

I had to think up ways to introduce them to the readers and hang each book on the introduction; as the magazine went to press two months before it came out, my article had to be done at the last possible moment in order to get the latest books.

At first we bought them, but this made the articles follow so long after the issue of the books that I asked the publishers to send me advance copies. As our magazine had the largest circulation of any discussing books, publishers were soon sending me everything they published on the chance of my choosing one of their stock.

Packages of them came to the front door each morning. It took my houseman hours to unwrap them and then wrap up again the ones I did not want. We soon developed a system for handling them and a list of places to send them when through with the ones I used: missionaries in China, tuberculosis homes, penitentiaries. We never, of course, gave them to anyone who could or should buy them.

Frequently people have asked me if I actually read all the books I mentioned. I certainly did—and not only once, but often several times. I read them first for enjoyment, just as though I had no article to do. I knew that if I ever read them as a chore and not as a casual reader, I could not write about them as if their reading was a pleasure. Some that I started, I never finished, knowing they would not serve my purpose. Most of them, however, got at least a cursory reading because I am so constituted that I want to know how even the worst story ends. When the time for the article came, I went over the possible again. Finally, when the article was written I went over the books once more to check all the data and characters.

I had three secretaries during that time, each of whom had a gift for accuracy. They checked the spelling of characters and dates with the books. The day the article was finally posted was a hectic one. The last possible train—no airmail—went out at nine o'clock at night. Usually Harry or a secretary just managed to get the manuscript on the train.

---

4. Her first column in *Good Housekeeping* was titled "Tasting and Testing Books" 82 (February 1926): 43.

In addition to the reading and waiting, we had letters of inquiry to answer that ran into the hundreds a month. Often the answers required much research. At first I worked in a study in my own house, but in a year I had a little four-room cottage down the street.[5] I had no telephone, and people seldom came to call. There we worked. An income tax agent turned up one day to investigate my reported "office," suspecting the item of twelve-dollars-a-month rent.

The time schedule I then followed was to cause me trouble in later days because of the sleep habits formed by it. The reading I did at night. Beginning my book about ten-thirty when the rest of the family had retired, I finished it before I went to bed, at four or five o'clock in the morning. I stayed in bed until ten or half-past the next day. I did this for two reasons. One, I could cover more ground and get a much clearer idea in the night's quiet. Two, I thus got an uninterrupted space of four or six hours, but if I rose at seven or eight I found my morning hours frittered away by telephone calls and questions about household matters. As long as I was "asleep" I would not be disturbed by servants or friends; but if "up and around" nothing could protect me from interruption. At eleven o'clock I went to my office, and my houseman brought down my lunch at two. When I came home at five o'clock I went over the house, checking up on everything, rested for an hour, and was ready to give my husband the evening.

I tell all this in such detail because so many women have written me asking how you got a "job" of book reviewing like mine, and others have asked me how I managed to do so much reading.

Other writing, too, I did during those years; for it is true of writing, I have discovered, that no magazine wants your work, or they all do. You cannot sell anything, or you can sell more than you can write. So I did many other articles and even published two books.[6] What I had so longed for had come to pass: I had an income that justified my organizing my domestic life to make it.

At about the same time I did an article on "Why I Sent My Children Away to School."[7] It, too, had an amusing aftermath. When it was finally sold to *Harper's*, I had so many inquiries from parents as to the schools I chose that the cost of answering their letters ate up all my profits.

This may be as good a place as any to write about fan mail. Many writers, I understand, are superior to it. Now it is true that the answering of these letters is often a burden upon the time or the purse of a popular writer. Sometimes it is even impossible for him or her to manage it, for the financial rewards of even good and fairly successful writers are often far from large. But for myself

---

5. The first record of an office separate from her home was in 1928; it was a small house at 112 North Jackson Street in Joplin.

6. *The Creation of a Home: A Mother Advises a Daughter* came out in 1930 and a novel, *A Woman of Courage*, in 1931. Both were published by Farrar and Rinehart.

7. "Why I Sent My Children Away to School," *Harper's* 152 (March 1926): 428–36.

those letters seem well worth the cost. When you sit before a typewriter in your own room and aim your words at the horizon, it is certainly pleasant to learn that they reached someone. I would rather have criticism than no response. And I have had much criticism, even anonymous letters that were rather scathing. I have also had letters that were very helpful and have made epistolary friends I value greatly.

A word on the financial rewards of writing may not come amiss here, for so many correspondents through the years have seemed to think the business of professional writing yields a fortune.

The idea springs from the reports of best-sellers, or from the prices paid for serials to someone like Kathleen Norris, Mary Roberts Rinehart, Faith Baldwin, or Temple Bailey.[8] But these are the few. For one of them are hundreds of professional writers who are lucky if they average twenty-five hundred dollars, nor are they ever certain of this. Many are satisfied to pick up a thousand. It is easy to figure out. It takes six stories at four hundred dollars to make an income of twenty-five hundred dollars. How many of the few magazines that pay five hundred dollars a story want five in one year from the same writer? If the price is three hundred or less it takes more stories, and how many years can one turn out five stories, each worth five hundred dollars, to a magazine?

At the fifty to one hundred dollars paid by many magazines it will take ten to twenty stories to make a thousand dollars. When against this is set the fact that each story is a gamble—no one may want it—and that it costs paper and postage to market stories, the returns are small, the odds against reaching the high-income group very great. I would recommend professional writing to no one who does not have a salaried job or a contract with a magazine. Its disappointments and its hazards are too great. This, of course, does not apply to the genius who can afford to wait or is willing to live on bread and water, or to the amateur who regards an occasional check as pin money.

---

8. Kathleen Norris (1880–1966), married to the younger brother of Frank Norris, wrote eighty-one novels, in addition to short stories, poetry, magazine articles, and plays. She was "one of the most popular and commercially successful authors of her time" (*NAW-Modern*, s.v. "Norris, Kathleen"). Mary Roberts Rinehart (1876–1958) wrote more than sixty books, mainly humorous detective stories. She published many magazine pieces about the New Woman (*NAW-Modern*, s.v. "Rinehart, Mary Roberts"). Faith Baldwin (1893–1978) wrote about three dozen novels, many of which were serialized in *Good Housekeeping, Woman's Home Companion,* and *Cosmopolitan.* She also wrote short stories, poems, and features (*DAB*, s.v. "Baldwin, Faith"; *Who Was Who in America,* 7:27; Durwood Howes, ed., *American Women: The Standard Biographical Dictionary of Notable Women,* s.v. "Baldwin, Faith"). Irene Temple Bailey (d. 1953) wrote juvenile books and was a consistent contributor to *Cosmopolitan, Harper's, Scribner's,* the *Saturday Evening Post, Good Housekeeping, Ladies Home Journal,* and other popular magazines (*Who Was Who in America,* 1:77).

There were still responsibilities devolving from my vice chairmanship that kept me active in politics. At the time I was working on the book reviews, I was also giving speeches and attending political meetings and conferences.

In October of 1925 the Woman's Democratic Club got into financial difficulties. To close it in such a condition seemed "bad business" for the party. When I learned about it, I was in New Orleans attending a triennial convocation of the Episcopal Church with my sister Annie, the deaconess. It was while there I learned to know Genevieve Thomson, the daughter of Champ Clark.[1] A remarkable woman she is: frank, direct, realistic as few women are, and with a charm, a sweetness, and a depth that few have. It is a great pity that she was not elected to Congress when she ran for it. She could have not only gone far, but also carried women with her.

When the convention closed, I went to Houston to see Jesse Jones, the treasurer of the Democratic committee, and proposed to him that the committee give me enough money to put Minnie Fisher Cunningham at the clubhouse as an executive secretary to save the club and use it as a clearinghouse for the activities of the Democratic women.[2]

This was hardly what I would have chosen since I wanted women to function equally with men in the regular party organization, but with the organization not functioning at all, and no other place for the women to operate, it seemed better than nothing at all. Mr. Jones, I suspect, was glad to get rid of me so easily, and he agreed. Mrs. Cunningham, who had been executive secretary in the National League of Women Voters, and delegate at large to the San Francisco Democratic convention, undertook the job, and in two years had the club buying a new clubhouse.[3] In three years she

---

1. Genevieve Clark (b. 1894), the daughter of Champ Clark, was married to James M. Thomson, publisher of the *New Orleans Item* (Carla Waal and Barbara Oliver Korner, eds., *Hardship and Hope: Missouri Women Writing about Their Lives, 1820–1920*, 162; Bennett Clark Papers).

2. Jesse Jones (1874–1956), a Texas businessman and banker, was a major contributor to Wilson's 1912 campaign and became a behind-the-scenes adviser. During the 1920s, he was a major factor in keeping the Democratic Party financially afloat. FDR appointed him chairman of the Reconstruction Finance Corporation in 1933. From 1933 to 1939, he was a member of the National Emergency Council (*DAB*, s.v. "Jones, Jesse").

3. The new home of the National Democratic Woman's Club was at 1526 New Hampshire Avenue NW, in Washington, D.C.

was holding there a national conference of Democratic clubs, and in 1928 the committee, in gratitude, gave the club a sum of money to apply on the mortgage.

One of those years I allowed myself to serve as president for the club.[4] Not a happy idea, because I was not in Washington enough to make a good one, but at the time it seemed wise. Every winter I stayed there for a few weeks or months as the nominal head of the Democratic women.

I am not proud of those second four years as vice chairman of the committee. All that I can say in defense of them is that had I resigned there could not have been any women vice chairmen at all. It seemed better to stay and do what I could.

About a year after I had returned to Joplin, I announced to Harry one morning that I was going out that day to buy our house. We had been playing with the idea of building one on a hillside in the country, and had our plans for a two-level house with a spring bubbling out of the porch. But I knew it would take at least a year to get into it; and, realizing that the children might not be with us many more vacations, I did not want to wait that long for a house that, after all, was for them.

Harry said it was all right with him, but I would not find a house to suit me. We had several times combed the town for one—Joplin was then having a housing shortage—but I meant to take one this time, however short of our desires it fell.

I came upon one, contractor built, bungalow front and two-story back, so unattractive it had been waiting for a purchaser for six months.

"I don't like the color," I said to the builder.

"I'll restucco it."

"I would want different windows."

"I'll change them!"

"I don't want this large playroom upstairs; I need two more bedrooms."

"I'll make it into two."

"I'd use this room for a library, so it would have to be lined with book-shelves."

"I'll put in the shelves."

"Then this door should be wider."

"I will widen it."

"And this room, which is good only for a sunporch, should have more windows."

"I'll put them in."

"But I want it in ten days when the children come home from school."

"It will be ready in ten days."

---

4. ENB was president of the National Woman's Democratic Club in 1928–1929.

And so it was. We moved in the eleventh day.[5] The children came the twelfth. It was like buying a ready-made dress and having it fitted.

We had not told the children a word. When we met them at the station, we told them that Harry had to go by and see a man on business on the way home.

He went into the new house and called to them to come in for a minute. When they saw Uncle Dave, sitting in the front room beside the familiar table and lamp, they realized what had happened.

I have always rejoiced that I did it just that way. Though there was not a thing about it I would have had in the planned house, with the help of decorators and new paint, changes in the kitchen arrangements, and a new terrace off the dining room, it soon had the charm that fixed-over houses so often do. The arrangements designed to cover or make up for inadequacies might never otherwise have occurred to one. And because its lines were not good, I let myself go on curtains and rugs and chintzes.

Just a month after we moved in, my mother died, and I was glad to have room for all the visiting family, and a place to bring her.[6]

Eight years earlier Mother had had her first heart attack. She was in Lowell, Massachusetts, with Getta, who was teaching in a private school there. Mother had walked through the Royal Gorge that summer with the girls, so it was a great shock. Julia had gone back and brought her to my brother Jim's home in Chicago. Characteristically, when the doctor pronounced his verdict, Mother set herself to follow his rules and regulations meticulously as to exercise, worry, and food. Yet, never did she by a word or act suggest that she was an invalid or incapacitated. She was, I know now, often bitterly unhappy—occasionally, very occasionally, she would show it. One of the great regrets of my life is that I was not more tender and understanding of her. But strong, dutiful, and proud people do not win tenderness automatically. Mother, as I see it now, had virtues that in my day seem almost to have disappeared, virtues I cannot claim for myself. Yet they were not, unfortunately, the lovable ones.

Every year since she has gone, I have known better what I owe to her. I only wish she could have known of that realization. I was objective where I should have been subjective, realistic when I could have been sentimental. To each of us she gave something: me my writing and interest in politics, Annie her leaning toward a religious life, Julia her gift for music. But she had them all.

These pioneer women had something in them that gave them an integrated strength, and created a personality. I sometimes wonder if the women of our softer generation will ever achieve an old age that makes men lift their hats,

---

5. They lived at 717 Glenview Street in Joplin.
6. Anna Gray Newell died on January 21, 1926.

not just to a woman, but to someone they venerate. So everyone who knew her venerated my mother.

My sister Annie who was up from Mexico and barely restrained from returning was discovered to have a tuberculosis germ and spent a long time in my new guest room.

In this book I have said very little about illness, which indicates that whatever we had of it made little impression on me. And I think we did have less than our share, although I can remember our doctor bills were usually hefty. Perhaps we called him on too slight provocation. When Ella was taken—back in 1911 or 1912—with a desperate attack of appendicitis and rushed by two doctors to the hospital where they struggled for seven weeks with peritonitis, I remember saying to Dr. Gentry: "I see now how you can put up with the boredom of all our colds and stomachaches for the sake of a great battle like this."[7]

Harry, however, was always having pleurisy, tonsillitis, grippe, chills, or violent indigestion; once he was thought to have tuberculosis. And when he is sick, he is very sick, delirious with a high fever, or too weak to talk. I thought of him as being very delicate until he took the examination for the YMCA for France with a perfect mark and came back from the war strong and rugged after having had flu, sleeping in the mud under a "limber." Three different times I thought myself very miserable, and took long courses of treatments for an agonizing back that could be relieved only by lying on hot-water bags. Now I seem to remember that these attacks coincided with periods when I did not find the demands of life interesting. We did not know—at least I did not—of neuroticism and psychosomatic medicine!

For most of my life I have been able to punish my body relentlessly, sleep few hours, eat irregularly or not at all, work steadily without exercise or fresh air, and never feel a worse result than to have people tell me each time they saw me how much better I looked than the last time. I began to wonder how bad I did look that first time.

The children were spared any more serious illnesses than the usual mumps, measles, and adenoids, except for Newell's first year.

This, I realize, has made me unsympathetic and callous about the pains and illnesses of others. I have no bedside manners, cannot make others comfortable. So I did not understand what Annie was going through as she lay on her bed day after day, alone, as I did years later when I had my own experience with illness.

It is surprising the number of people you find you have failed when so much of your life, you think, is spent in ministering to others.

---

7. Dr. William Gentry (b. 1873) earned his M.D. from the Missouri Medical College in St. Louis in 1896. He moved to Jasper County in 1898, settling in Carthage (Livingston, *History of Jasper County . . . People*, 2:854).

During those years I learned to know the Ozarks better. My brother-in-law Burt Blair had a camp down on Bear Creek in the Ozarks.[8] I found it very interesting down there. Not only because it was a lovely spot—the purling creek below the house, the hills behind it, and the quiet of the country free from vibrations all about it—but also because of the hill people whom I came to know slightly. The young people used my brother-in-law's croquet ground below the bluff at the back of the house for a dance hall. They used to gather in their ginghams and store suits, raise their voices in that queer twang, and go through their strange figures to this music. One of the boys took a great fancy to Harriet. A natural flirt, she made the most of it until Burt's wife told her that his "girl" had the week before met another hill-Jane who had flirted with him on a country lane, pulled her off her horse, and given her a licking. The information that the boy was only recently returned from the penitentiary for stabbing another boy at a dance did not add to his attractions. Harriet's ardor perceptibly cooled.

I learned verses of the songs and with practice could even do the strange tonal lilt at the end of each line. If I had not, alas, forgotten it, the accomplishment might have made me popular in Washington when later this came into social vogue.

I also studied their phrases and words with interest. One of these phrases, often spoken to the children, was "Clabern'll get yeh ef yeh doant watch out." No one, on inquiry, knew what it meant. The mothers had it from their mothers, and they from theirs. We decided that it must have come down to them from the days when Claibourne had ravaged the Scottish border after Culloden, and had been held up to the children as a bogey. For these people had come to America from Scotland. They had gone first to the hills of North Carolina, then into Tennessee, and early in the eighteenth century had trekked on to the Ozarks where they had stayed ever since, closemouthed, inexpressive, living in the same old board cabins, on what they could raise in that thin soil, having no intercourse with the outside world until the railroad came in 1895. Even then they had as little as possible, resenting the "outsider." Their method of getting rid of outlanders was to trade them into poverty if possible, or annoy them by silence. Money they had never used—had hardly seen until some canning factories had set them to cultivating tomatoes on their small patches. These tomatoes they planted in the stumpy, rocky ground a year or two, and when the soil worked out, then moved on to another patch to do the same thing.

Great prosperity came to some of them when the state had passed a blind-pension bill. Blindness, prevalent among them, became a great asset. A blind mother-in-law or father-in-law brought in more cash than they had ever seen

---

8. Karl Burton Blair (1869–1940) was Harry Blair's brother.

before. One of Burt's neighbors had even traded his tomato patch to a brother in exchange for the old lady.

Burt had a book, printed by the government in 1852, that contained an account of a trip to this country made by a government agent in 1804. It had changed very little.[9]

Uncle Dave lived with us those years. We felt it a great privilege to have him. Extraordinarily well informed, he was a delightful companion. I read many books to him, tried out all my articles on him, and we discussed many things. With the years he had lost his rebellion at his blindness, and no longer refused to talk of it. He had a mellowed broad understanding of human beings, including himself. "I could not have said it once," he said to me, "but I can truthfully say that my life has been worth living."

This from a man nearing eighty who had been sixty years blind, who had buried, one by one, father, mother, two brothers, and a sister, all but one of them daily companions, who was frail in body and had lost his money.

I remember going into the pantry one day to hear a charwoman say to the cook: "Well, you have to hand it to her—she's good to the old man."

What had gone before I could not guess, but what an idea about Uncle Dave! Everyone who knew him was good to him. Only an utterly insensitive person could have been anything else.

Julia had married Philip Chappell and now lived in Canyon City, Colorado. Ella had married Ralph Putman and lived in Joplin.[10] Margaretta taught for a long time at Baldwin School in Bryn Mawr. She had graduated from Vassar and took her master's degree at Columbia University. Later she studied for her Ph.D. at University of California. As none of my sisters had any children, they were very generous and helped a great deal in caring for Harriet and Newell. Frequently Julia and Phil had Newell in Colorado; and I recall one time Ella took care of him when he was sick. The children adored their aunts, and Harriet once remarked, "How lucky I am—not many girls have four mothers." Certainly I could never have done all I have without them. No matter how far apart we lived, we managed to see each other quite often. An old friend once said, "Considering the fact that you girls haven't much money, you move around a mighty lot."

A matriarch by nature, I delighted in having my home the family clearing-house and stomping ground.

During the Christmas holidays of 1925 Harriet had met Newton Melville Forsythe. The first time he called for her, I knew, watching them together, that Harriet was falling in love—the young man was in love already but didn't know it. As they left I said to Harry, "This is it." Harry was quiet a

---

9. Moses Austin, *A Summary Description of the Lead Mines in Upper Louisiana* (Washington, D.C., 1804).

10. Ralph Putman married Ella Newell on September 18, 1910.

moment and then said, "Well, he's quite the nicest young man who has ever been in this house." The romance progressed through that winter and the following summer. At first they planned to be married in June and then in April of 1927. But in October Harriet decided that was too far off and she thought the Christmas season an ideal time. From past experience I knew it was about the worst, but we planned a 4:30 wedding in the Episcopal church of Carthage on New Year's Eve 1926. Between the two families we discovered we were related to half of southwest Missouri, so the reception presented a problem. We finally decided to have it at home, for we had six rooms downstairs. They had all the trimmings, bridesmaids, ushers, and the usual round of parties. Harriet wore her great-great-great-grandmother's gown. Sarah Parker McDowell first wore it in Philadelphia in 1795.

No mother is glad to see her daughter leave—we are never quite ready. But I wanted her to be loved, have a home and family of her own as I had. Just before Harriet left, she came to Harry and me and said the loveliest thing a daughter can say to her parents. "Mother and Daddy, I want you to know that I have had a perfect childhood and from now on it is up to me."

21 *Republican Game and Democratic Religious Revival*

It seemed a foregone conclusion that the nominee would be Governor Smith. His followers were enthusiastic. Others regarded this as a campaign that must be endured. They did not think he could win in the country, but until he had tried, the party would be torn in two. Some of them took it as bitter medicine. "The trouble," said a midwestern leader, a Catholic of high standing, "is that his nomination will lose us all our state and local tickets, but we've got to show that the Democratic Party is the party of religious liberty even if it costs us defeat."

The committee, in gratitude for Mr. Jones's success with its deficit, gave the convention to him to hold in Houston.[1] When they decided to go in the middle of the summer to south Texas, and to a town that did not even have a convention hall to house such a convention, I decided that anything Mr. Jones wanted, he was very likely to get.

As I had to have some Texas woman in Houston to look after hotels and arrangements, I sent down Mrs. Gretchen Dau Cunningham who had been recommended highly to me by members of the League of Women Voters in Cleveland, and was acceptable to the Houston committee.[2] Nor did I regret it, for in most difficult situations she proved invaluable, saving me many embarrassing moments.

As for the convention, it produced the same headaches over tickets as Madison Square Garden, with the addition of difficulties over housing the delegations and lack of hotel elevators to carry the crowds.

Houston had done itself proud, but it could not make a hastily built timber auditorium cool. Our offices, however, high up in a downtown building, were

---

1. The Democrats met in Houston, June 26–29, 1928.

2. Gretchen Dau Cunningham worked for R. G. Dun and Company from 1914 to 1918. After serving as a foreign correspondent in the Rhine Province in 1928, she was an associate editor of *Transportation* in 1931–1932. Active in Democratic politics, in 1933 she became chairman of the Southern California Women's Division of the NRA. From 1934 to 1935, she was economic adviser to the NRA textile section in Washington and then was appointed assistant state procurement officer, Procurement Division, United States Treasury Department, Los Angeles (Howes, *American Women, 1935–1940*, s.v. "Cunningham, Gretchen Dau").

always swept by the Gulf breezes, and the Houston committee gave me a house complete with servants. It even had ceiling fans. Unfortunately, I had a bad attack of hives. The minute I got into my room I threw myself on the bed and my sisters applied lotions. I would be under the fans until it was time to go back to the hot hall.

Somehow I do not remember this Houston convention as unpleasantly as the New York one. Perhaps I had become less sensitive, or took things more philosophically. Perhaps it was the gracious hospitality of the Texas ladies. Certainly nothing that could be done for our physical comfort or pleasure was left undone.

But it was a convention and I was in politics, which seemed to mean I was in hot water.

The Missouri Democrats that year had decided upon a truce or an armistice. It was generally accepted that Senator Reed was to have the delegation to the national convention, and Charles Hay, a Wilsonian, was to be the candidate for United States senator.[3] I do not mean to say a deal was made. I do not know anything about that. But the Wilsonians did not attempt to elect anti-Reed delegates—did not, in fact, have many of them even go to the state convention. Their assumption certainly was that if they let Senator Reed have the delegation, Mr. Hay would be unopposed for the senatorship, though I remember telling Mr. Hay that I thought he was being rather Pollyannaish if he thought a compromising attitude with the senator would work, a bit of futuristic thinking that was proved correct when Senator Reed later returned from a visit to the Democratic presidential nominee, and announced that Mr. Hay, being a dry, could not consistently run on a ticket headed by Governor Smith.

The Reed delegation to the convention was naturally suspicious of me, although I went to their headquarters and told Senator Reed's manager that, though I was not for Senator Reed as the nominee, as their national committeewoman I was ready to serve the delegation in any way I could.

Whether this Reed antagonism was the cause, or whether it was hurt vanities because they had not been invited to some functions for me, I do not to this day know, but the women of his delegation were "out" with me about something, so much so that they expressed themselves in the newspapers, and I was advised to withdraw some invitations to a breakfast I was giving the new national committeewoman. It seemed awfully funny to me that after all the really difficult things, I should come a cropper over social slights. But people at conventions do not behave as anywhere else.

---

3. Charles Hay (1879–1945), a St. Louis lawyer, was a delegate to the Democratic National Convention in 1924, chairman of the Democratic State Convention in 1924 and 1928, and the Democratic nominee for a United States Senate seat in 1928 (*Who Was Who in America*, 2:242).

The really trying part of the convention was over the Prohibition plank in the platform.

I felt very sorry for the "dry" women who, ardently Democrats, felt their party was being taken away from them to propagandize something that had no connection with what made them Democrats. It wiped out, of course, my whole argument for choosing a party and made it something different each campaign.

Nor was my position in regard to the nominee a comfortable one. Knowing what it would mean to us, I could not be enthusiastic about him as a nominee, even though I believed and said that as a president he had great possibilities. The trouble with a heated emotional attack like that made on Governor Smith is that few on either side look at the matter objectively. If you are not 100 percent for him, you are 100 percent against him; if you are not 100 percent against, you are 100 percent for. So, while my western and southern friends resented my support of Governor Smith, Governor Smith's adherents regarded me as an enemy. A position of sweet reasonableness is hard to maintain in politics.

When the governor, however, sent his repeal measure to the convention after his nomination, I thought he had gone too far. I did not believe he had a right when it had spoken to override it. It was too much as if he had swallowed the party, and I did not like to be swallowed. I went home resentful and disappointed.

Before I went to the Democratic convention, and I don't know how I happened to write about it first, I had attended the Republican convention in Kansas City as a press correspondent, for I was doing not only an article for *Good Housekeeping* on the two conventions, but also a daily story at both for the King Feature Syndicate.[4] It was fun, of course, at Kansas City, where I was merely a spectator. I had time to dress properly, to think things out, to go where I pleased. Besides, Republican conventions were usually more orderly and sedate than Democratic ones. Their fights—and they had one— were most incidental. They did not tighten the atmosphere, and the leaders were less irate.

Ruth McCormick was at Kansas City, for instance, leading a fight against Herbert Hoover, but she led it like a gay buccaneer. At her table every night (Republican conventions have time for dinner) were men and women of all factions, and even Democrats, who laughed together and told stories and passed biting repartee. I can't imagine any Democratic leader at New York or Houston, or later in Chicago, doing that.

---

4. The Republicans met in Kansas City, June 12–15, 1928. ENB's convention article was "May the Best Man Win," *Good Housekeeping* 87 (September 1928): 26–27. She also contributed an article on the Prohibition issue, "Neither Wet nor Dry: How the Non-Combatants Feel about It," *Century* 116 (October 1928): 760–66.

His opponents pushed violent diatribes against Mr. Hoover under the hotel doors of the delegates' rooms, but I did not see a single sheet of them in public view. It did not, I fancy, ruffle any forehead except, maybe, Mr. Hoover's. It is a game, presidential nominations, and Republicans play it as a game. The Democrats go at it like a religious revival.

The night Mr. Hoover was nominated, Anne Hard and I took a taxi and drove for hours through the park. It was the happiest night, she said, since she had her first baby. She felt it a great moral victory, the dawning of a new day. But she was solemn about it—serious. She did not want excitement and noise.

I can't imagine this end to a Democratic convention. The last note is usually utter weariness or noisy jubilation. My last night in Houston was a bit of both. Mr. Shaver gave a dinner for those of us who had been with him through the convention, or maybe someone else gave it. Fred Essary was there, Ted Huntley, a newspaperman, Gretchen Cunningham, Florence Farley, and Claude Bowers.[5]

We laughed outrageously, told amusing stories, were like children out of school.

I had put on a dress I had not worn before as being too feminine and fussy for a convention—a white chiffon with pink cabbage roses on it—and a big white hat.

"Why weren't you like this at the convention?" one of them said to me. "You're ten years younger, and gay and lots of fun."

It was because I was through. The responsibility, the worries, the difficulties were of the past. I was a free agent again, myself. For with the convention I ceased to be vice chairman, was no longer a committeewoman. When the state convention had met in the spring, I had not even been a candidate.

From Houston I went to Joplin, spent two days writing my *Good House-keeping* article, and went on to Pittsburgh to become a grandmother. This brought home to me as nothing else had done the difference between a man and a woman. What man, after a grilling convention like that, with articles to be written, would rush immediately to be present at the birth of his daughter's child? Nothing in the world would have kept me away.

There was a three weeks' wait. Harriet lived in a tiny apartment. I slept on an improvised couch in a little sunporch. It required adroitness to keep out of my son-in-law's way at bathroom hours. And it was hot, very hot. Some articles I had to do were written on my lap and sent home for copying. The joke was on me, I thought, remembering the office cottage in Joplin, the commodious house, the room and bath of my own. Though at last I had

---

5. Ted Huntley was the Washington correspondent for the *Pittsburgh Post* and the *Pittsburgh Sun.*

them, here I was. My sister said if I could laugh at that, I certainly had a sense of humor.

The baby was named for me.[6] When I saw the tiny bulging forehead like my own, the narrowness above the ears, and the widow's peak, it was a shock. No one can explain the sensation you feel when your first grandchild is put in your arms, nor the sentiment you feel for the child. It is like no other in the world. Sometimes I have thought that it springs from an inner yearning for immortality. At a time when you have abandoned hope of a pot of gold at the end of a rainbow, when the future is no longer a promised land, and ambitions cease to stimulate hope, you feel that in this small parcel you are moving into the future, life is not a dead end. Whatever the cause, there certainly is some mystical bond between grandparents and grandchildren.

I was not invited to Governor Smith's notification meeting. I had no communication from any of his friends. It was a strange situation. The new chairman and vice chairman had not yet been elected. That awaited the decision of the candidates. How the arrangements for the meeting itself were made I do not know, perhaps by self-appointed leaders, perhaps by the governor's preconvention organization. Mr. Shaver, for all I knew, may still have been acting.

My information of the election of Mr. Raskob as chairman of the Democratic committee, and the election of Governor Ross and Florence Farley as vice chairmen, came to me through the newspapers.[7]

It is a peculiar sensation to find yourself completely out of something you have been much inside of. You like to think that, as a person, you still have something to contribute. It is one thing to want to get out, quite another to find you are ignored.

At the same time I was receiving a number of letters urging me to come out for the Republican nominee, Herbert Hoover.

Now I would not in any case have done that. Whatever influence or effect my attitude might have would be the result of the position the Democratic Party had given me. That of the individual I was before my committee connection would have amounted to nothing outside of Missouri. I do not understand people who use an influence conferred by a confidential relationship to hurt the person or organization that conferred on them the influence. It would have been ridiculous as well as ungrateful for me to have publicly used the influence given me by the Democratic Party to oppose its candidate.

---

6. Emily Blair Forsythe was born on July 24, 1928.

7. Nellie Tayloe Ross (1876–1977) was born near St. Joseph, Missouri. When her husband died in office as governor of Wyoming in 1924, she won a special election to complete his term and then won the office herself in 1925. Defeated for reelection in 1926, she became vice chairman of the DNC in 1928 and served four years. FDR appointed her director of the Mint in 1933 in which position she remained until 1952 (*DAB*, s.v. "Ross, Nellie Tayloe").

Neither did I desire to do it. The repeal of the Eighteenth Amendment was not in my opinion the most important issue before the country. Nor did I think that the election of Governor Smith would accomplish it, inasmuch as the Congress would not go with him on it. What to me was most important was the direction our economic system was taking.

Of the theories and past performance of both Governor Smith and Mr. Hoover, I much preferred Governor Smith's. I knew, therefore, I would support Governor Smith, even though his position on the liquor question did not please me or some of the people backing him.

I dreaded the campaign, knowing that my position would alienate many friends to whom I was indebted. Missouri people would think, I felt, that I had sold out. When Mrs. Roosevelt asked me to be on her executive committee of five women, I declined. The reason I gave was that I did not think it advisable. What I argued to myself was that it would not help Governor Smith for me to go on that committee then. What help I could give would be much more valuable if it came from outside his own committee. From this distance of time, I realize I was rationalizing. I just did not want to align myself intimately then with the Smith forces.

Many things entered into this, among them undoubtedly the fear that if I did I would no longer be acceptable to my women readers. I can acknowledge this now, for when I went on the stump for Governor Smith, I did it knowing quite well that it might cost me my *Good Housekeeping* job. *Good Housekeeping* was for Prohibition, and so were the majority of its readers. If they disapproved, my usefulness to the editor was, of course, at an end.

The appointment of Mr. Raskob as chairman fell upon the dry Middle West like a blow. As a Catholic friend of mine put it to another in my presence, "If a man turned Catholic, you would not want to see him made pope the next day." The control of the campaign by New York men with New York ideas further irritated the West. I do not think those in control ever realized it, but the attitude among these middle-western and far-western Democrats was that a New York that they did not like or trust, regarded very much as a foreign city, was trying to dominate the rest of the country. The campaign managers did little to disabuse them. Everything was planned and decided there, and little account taken of the prejudices and fears of the outlanders.

The opposition to the Democratic nominee, in spite of the importance given to the liquor and religious questions, was fundamentally based on sectional antagonism and misunderstanding. The religious and liquor questions offered an alibi for an antagonism more fundamental.

The New Yorkers never understood this. One of their organizers suggested to us in Missouri a plan for organizing independent Smith clubs in empty store buildings. When asked my opinion of the plan, I said, "We are not bothered about the independent vote. If we can get the Democratic vote, we'll be lucky."

"But of course they'll be for Smith," she said. "You've only got to tell them what a good governor of New York he has made."

"Do you know what they will say?" I answered. "Well, maybe he is; it's half foreign anyway."

Asked for a plan for the women, I suggested that New York women of the highest type, old-line Americans, be sent to the towns of ten thousand or more, women who would gain an audience because of their prominence in national social welfare movements, to show the local women what type of women were supporting him; then when his candidacy had been made respectable they could organize Smith clubs.

Such women speakers came into the state, but too late. The opposition to Governor Smith had gained such headway as the result of Hoover meetings in every country church that no one came to hear them but the "yellow-dog" Democrats and the repealers, which only further antagonized the others.

The worst mistake the campaign managers made was in sending Governor Smith on his western tour. At Houston, when Mr. Van Namee had asked me if I had any suggestions for the campaign, I had told him that it would be wise, I thought, to keep the nominee at Albany, and sell him to the westerners by sending picked delegations to him to come back and tell them about him.[8] Westerners, I explained, were not familiar with his type. He would seem a foreigner to them, and they "would not heed what he had done and really was."

But his New York friends and advisers thought differently. They believed voters had only to see the governor to fall for his personality. Used to hundreds seen daily with his features and manners, they saw only his power, his ability to make abstruse problems understandable to the simple, his dramatization of the poor boy who makes good.

I went up to hear Governor Smith when he came to Sedalia, Missouri.[9] The crowd, of course, was enormous, and Governor Smith made as remarkable a speech as I ever heard, reducing the intricacies of a budget to terms comprehensible even to me, to whom figures are worse than Sanskrit. It was hardly short of genius. One could believe that he was one of those rare people who are born with a gift so great in one line that they do not need the intellectual background and study demanded of others.

---

8. In the push for the Smith nomination, George R. Van Namee was part of Smith's "War Board." He had been secretary of the New York Democratic State Committee in 1914, creating its publicity bureau, and served as Smith's secretary during his first gubernatorial term. On the state committee during the 1920s, he served on the executive committee of the DNC during the 1928 election (Elizabeth Israels Perry, *Belle Moskowitz: Feminine Politics and the Exercise of Power in the Age of Alfred E. Smith*, 161, 189, 194).

9. It was reported that thirty thousand people were at the state fairgrounds in Sedalia to hear Al Smith on October 16 (*New York Times*, October 17, 1928, 1:2).

But when he bent his knees and leaned toward that audience, banging one hand on another, and said in harsh guttural accents, "Let's look at the record!" these Missouri farmers and small-town businessmen and their wives simply gaped, as at a spectacle. The only explanation they could think of was that he must have been drinking. He hadn't, but what are facts against foregone conclusions?

I had a brief talk with the governor, in which he told me, among other things, that the people wanted repeal. I thought that he could not be sensitive to middle westerners and southerners if, after his trips to Oklahoma and Kansas, he could still think so. But he talked also about the utility problem, child labor, and other things I was interested in, in a way that pleased me very much.

Shortly afterward, Senator Hawes, who was running the western head-quarters in St. Louis, sent for me and told me that for Governor Smith to win it was essential that he carry Missouri, and I could help as much as any one person with the Democrats who were refusing him support.[10] I was asked to go into Kentucky and North Carolina, but Senator Hawes refused to let me leave Missouri.

To give newspaper publicity to my support, it was decided that I should speak with the vice presidential nominee, Senator Robinson, on his three speeches in Missouri. Some of the Missouri leaders had not apparently been consulted. Politicians, it must be noted, are frequently more concerned with their own fortunes than with victory for their tickets. This is what makes campaign organization so difficult. These unconsulted politicians did not welcome me to the meetings. It was not pleasant in Springfield to find some opposition to my appearance on the platform.

I left it up to Senator Robinson, telling him I wanted to do whatever he thought best for success. He insisted on my speaking. At Kansas City I was introduced by a chairman who presented first "a beautiful lady who, I am happy to tell you, does not want to make a speech," and then announced me as one who would speak, introducing me as "a lady who had done war work" with no mention of my political connections. At Columbia, where the meeting was at four in the afternoon, I was told I was to wait until after Senator Robinson had left. As the open-air audience was made up of farmers who would have to leave early, I did not see them waiting for a fifteen-minute aftermath by me. My family, who had driven me up, urged me not to speak at all, but I knew the interpretations that would be put on that. Those three

---

10. Harry Hawes (1869–1947), a St. Louis lawyer, was president of the Board of Police Commissioners for four years. He was a Democratic member of the United States House of Representatives from 1921 to 1927 and a U.S. senator from 1927 to 1933. He was the unsuccessful candidate for governor in 1934 (*Who Was Who in America*, 2:242).

speeches, incidentally, were about the best received I ever made, so does opposition stimulate you.

In spite of all that Mr. Hawes could do about it, for he wanted them to use me, insisted on it, the state committee kept sending me to little crossroads meetings and tiny towns that could not greatly affect the vote. When questioned about it, the Speakers Bureau said the larger places did not want me. Knowing these small places were opposed to Governor Smith, I could understand that. Then I received letters of indignation from the women of these towns because I had been refused them. I met, incidentally, a local politician of Cape Girardeau who begged me to give them a day. I had been told Cape Girardeau would not have me. I never did know what was behind all this. Sometimes politics seems a game of blindman's bluff, but I was, after some pressure from Senator Hawes, sent to the larger places.

I ended my tour the Saturday night before election in Maryville with a congressman from Oklahoma as cospeaker. I had spoken there several times and had many friends. When I rose they greeted me with enthusiasm. When I sat down there was hardly a hand clap. They did the same to the congressman. The applause at the beginning was courtesy to us as individuals. The lack of it at the end disapproval of our candidate.

When we sat afterward in the drugstore to drink a malted milk and talk it over, I asked the congressman how he could be away from his district this close to election day.

"The further away I can get," he said, "the better it will be for me."

My county, which has gone as high as a four-thousand majority for a Democrat, gave Mr. Hoover a majority of ten thousand. Never had Missouri Democrats had as much money, or as many excellent speakers as were sent from the national organization. The state went Republican. We lost the governorship, the senator, and the congressmen.

It was what they suffered and endured in this campaign that made it hard for Democrats to excuse Governor Smith's lukewarmness in 1932. I doubt that he ever realized it.

22 *All Things to All Men*

With the defeat of 1928 I was out of politics, at least so I thought. Nor was I sorry. The next four years passed quickly, and for the most part pleasantly. Interesting work, a house I loved, friends, and enough interests and trips to offer variety. One summer I spent in New York City with my secretary, Frances Ullmann, getting out a book, *The Creation of a Home*, made up from letters I had written to my daughter about her household problems and endeavors.[1] It was then I began this autobiography. I meant to call it "Transcript of a Lucky Life."

In New York I made new friends, very different from my political ones. It seems to be, indeed, that my friends have always been in watertight compartments so far as intercourse between them is concerned. My Joplin group, my political group, my writing group. John and Margaret Farrar, who had a house in Connecticut; Fulton and Grace Oursler, he the editor of *Liberty* and she, Grace Perkins, the writer and actress; Jean Wick and Achmed Abdullah, she an author's agent and he the dramatist and story writer; Margaret Widdemer; and many others. They were people very different from any I had known, clever, looking at life freshly, free of so many of our Victorian taboos. Through John Farrar, my publisher, I met many others: Hervey Allen and Beverly Nichols, and the Rineharts.[2] I enjoyed it all so much that I wanted to return and make my life there.

---

1. Frances Ullmann (1904–1984) was born in Springfield, Missouri. She earned a B.A. from Wellesley in 1925. After working as ENB's secretary, she edited the *National Parent Teacher Magazine* (1931–1941), the *Encyclopedia of Child Care and Guidance* (1951–1954), and the *Junior Literary Guild* (1954–1969). She wrote books for children and young girls (Collection summary, Frances Ullmann DeArmand Papers, Schlesinger Library, Cambridge, Mass.; *New York Times*, April 28, 1984).

2. John Farrar (1896–1974), a Yale graduate, began his career as a reporter on the *New York World* in 1919. In 1921 he became editor of a new literary magazine, the *Bookman*. Book publisher George Doran hired Farrar in 1925 as his editor. In 1929, he and fellow editor Stanley Rinehart established their own publishing house, Farrar and Rinehart. During World War I, he headed overseas publications for the Office of War Information. In 1926, Farrar married Margaret Petherbridge, the longtime editor of crossword puzzles for the *New York Times*. She was also a leader in the publication of crossword-puzzle books for Simon and Schuster (*DAB*, s.v. "Farrar, John"). Fulton Oursler (1893–1952) became well known for his involvement with the popular journalism of "crime, sex, fads, and public relations." In 1931, he became more conservative as editor of *Liberty* and, along with

I know now I don't belong in that lightsome crew, but always I hated the idea that I was a club-woman type. I wanted to camouflage it as I had my literary efforts to my domestic friends. Everything I wanted to be—all things to all men.

Newell finished his course at Sewanee in 1929. Winifred Julian's daughter, Laura Betty, came with me to his commencement exercises. The night of the graduation dance the boys and their girls had no food after dinner as the school was closed. Determined to feed them something, I sent William, our chauffeur, out to lay in a supply of eggs, bacon, toast, and coffee. Little did I know I would end up at 4:00 A.M. fixing breakfast for seventy-five starving youngsters. One of the boys came out to the kitchen of the fraternity house and offered to help me. "Well," he said, "never did I think I would see a politician turned chief cook and bottle washer!"

On the way home we stopped in Arkansas for lunch. The restaurant refused to let William enter, and Newell haughtily accompanied him around to the kitchen. Inside we noticed people staring and talking, getting more and more excited. We ate as quickly as possible. Afterward, Newell, Laura Betty, and I went with William into the garage to get some gas. The attendant said, "You'd better move outa here—we kill niggers around this town." We said we couldn't leave fast enough. It was a terrible thing to see a strong, fine man like William afraid of people like that. Newell stood right by him and stared the men down. We finally got the gas and gladly left. We couldn't understand why the people had been so furious and unreasonable and later learned that colored people had never been allowed to live in Boone County.

---

publisher Bernard McFadden, tried to make it a competitor of *Collier's* and the *Saturday Evening Post*. After divorcing his first wife, he married author Grace Perkins (1900–1951) in 1925 (*DAB*, s.v. "Oursler, Fulton"; Howes, *American Women, 1935–1940*, s.v. "Oursler, Fulton"). Jean Wick (d. 1939) was a well-known literary agent in New York City. She was also the wife of the author Achmed Abdullah (*New York Times*, February 4, 1939). Margaret Widdemer (1880–1978) wrote essays, short stories, and poems and novels. She shared the Pulitzer Prize with Carl Sandburg in 1919 for *Old Road to Paradise*. She was a Republican (Howes, *American Women, 1935–1940*, s.v. "Widdemer, Margaret"; *Who Was Who in America*, 8:612). Hervey Allen (1889–1949) taught at Columbia University and Vassar. In 1926 he published a biography of Edgar Allen Poe. Author of many historical novels, he was particularly well known for his 1933 *Anthony Adverse* (*DAB*, s.v. "Allen, Hervey"). Journalist (John) Beverly Nichols (1900–1983) was the author of numerous novels, children's books, plays, and nonfiction. In addition to writing articles for women's magazines, he wrote thirty best-sellers (*Contemporary Authors*, vols. 93–96, 110; *Who Was Who in America*, 8:300). Stanley Marshall Rinehart Jr. (1897–1969) married Mary Noble Doran in 1919. He, his brother Frederick, and John Farrar formed the publishing company of Farrar and Rinehart in 1929. In 1931, they bought the Cosmopolitan Book Corporation and gained numerous popular authors, including Hervey Allen (*DAB*, s.v. "Rinehart, Stanley Marshall, Jr.").

That summer Newell went to Europe. Harry and I had tickets three times, but something always interfered, so we finally decided to wait till the following year. Then came the depression.

Another summer I went to California, to speak at the NEA convention in Los Angeles, and then up to visit my sister Anna, who was then dean of St. Margaret's School in Berkeley.[3] She had gone back to her mission school in Mexico, and come home again to remain another year with a depleted thyroid. She had then undertaken the Training School for Deaconesses in California, which, with the help of the bishop and California churchwomen, had become a kind of church Hull House. She was an extraordinary woman, and not at all what one associates with the word *religious*. A gay nature with a great sense of fun, a profound understanding that could really forgive all, and a mind that could dig through anything, a "lovely mind" someone once called it. She made me understand the Gospel use of the words *grace* and *charity*, and that impersonal, unsentimental, encompassing *love*. We were very close all our lives, and though she was four years younger than I, she was the rock on which I leaned. Of all the women I have ever known, I think she made the most out of life—the experience of living. It was a beautiful visit.

We had sorrows, too, those years. My brother Jim's wife was drowned off the coast of Florida.[4] A girlhood friend of mine, she had come into our family when she and Jim were twenty. I went back to Florida with my brother to stay with him until he could readjust himself.

A brother-in-law's wife died suddenly, and he came to live with us—and in two years Harry's other brother lost his wife.[5] This left me the only woman of their generation in the family. Women, I have observed, can remake their lives when they lose their husbands, but men seem to be left adrift when wives of many years go. I suppose it is because so much that makes life, all the social part and the home part, is made by the woman.

---

3. ENB spoke at the National Education Association meeting in Los Angeles; her talk was titled, "Women in the Modern World" (National Education Association, *Proceedings of the Sixty-ninth Annual Meeting Held at Los Angeles, California, June 27–July 3, 1931*). Anna Newell came to Berkeley in 1927 and became dean of St. Margaret House, the training school for deaconnesses of the Western Province of the Episcopal Church. Its location across the street from the University of California was convenient for its attempt to expand its mission to include "working at the problem of making a religious contribution to educational life" (ENB to Eleanor Roosevelt, September 29, 1934, Box 1286, 1934, Series 100 Personal Letters, Eleanor Roosevelt Papers).

4. Jessie Caffee Newell drowned while swimming in the ocean near her home in Fort Pierce, Florida, on February 22, 1930 (*Carthage Evening Press*, February 24, 1930).

5. Christine Luscombs, wife of Karl Burton Blair, died on December 17, 1929; Lillian Cowgill, wife of Charles Allen Blair, died on January 19, 1931 (Parker, "Descendants of William Blair").

Twins came to Harriet.[6] She had moved to Cleveland. Newell had gone for his law degree to Washington University in St. Louis.

I had great pleasure in an unexpected honor that was paid to me during this period. I am not greatly impressed by honors. Often what is so considered is only an opportunity for hard work. But this one touched me deeply. The League of Women Voters, as a money-raising project, was placing the names of suffragists on a bronze tablet somewhere in Washington. To place the names there, the sponsors had to raise a thousand dollars. I do not know that it was a very happy idea. Some names that should have been there were not, and others less important probably were. What surprised and pleased me was that a group of young Joplin women placed my name there. Women I hardly knew. That they wanted to do it meant a great deal to me.[7]

In 1930, some men urged me to run for Congress. There was a factional fight in the Republican Party, and they thought that though mine was a Republican district, it might be possible for me to win. But I had no desire to be in Congress—certainly not for one session—and the Republicans would probably be united for the next election. To politics, in fact, I gave very little time. Each winter saw me in Washington for a few weeks at the club. I followed with interest the work that Governor Ross, as vice chairman, and her assistant were doing under Mr. Jouett Shouse, the director of the committee, especially the very fine speeches Mrs. Ross was making. Once in a while, I made a political speech, and for three months in the spring and another three months in the fall I went on a lecture tour. The Democratic women where I was speaking would often give me a luncheon. So I kept my contacts warm, but it was rather in memoriam than for any future use.

One political speech was made in Chicago. A friend of mine, Amelia Sears, who had for twenty years been director of Chicago's United Charities, was placed in nomination with three other women by the Cook County Democratic organization for the Cook County Board of Commissioners. There was a large meeting of independent women, sponsored by a Republican, and I was asked to speak. I was greatly complimented that these independent and Republican women wanted me—a "professional Democrat" as my sisters called me—to speak. It seemed to indicate that in spite of my partisanship, opponents believed in my integrity. Mayor Cermak, the head of the Democratic organization, had chosen women of a very high type. The office could offer them great opportunity. I felt it a step forward for women, and said so.

---

6. Harriet and Newton Melville Forsythe had twins, Anne Goodner and Margreta Newell, born on February 27, 1931.

7. The League of Women Voters unveiled a bronze plaque honoring suffrage pioneers during their annual council meeting in Washington, April 14–17, 1931. ENB's name was one of twenty-six Missouri women ("Notes and Comments," *Missouri Historical Review* [October 1930–July 1931]: 649).

They were elected and often, during Amelia's term of office, I stayed with her and my friend Clara Paige, who lived with her, and so learned much of her experience.[8] Clara Paige was a girlhood friend from Joplin who had become president of the Cook County Welfare Board.

I am always tremendously impressed with women who seem deliberately to have changed themselves or developed themselves, cast off prejudices of class or place and become larger, and broader. Clara is one of them: made not by environment or by inner urges, as I think myself to be, but by her will and mind. And what she has become makes her a most unusual friend, every hour with whom is a treat.

During the campaign of 1930, I made only a few speeches, and those for friends who were running for Congress. In fact, I took the whole campaign casually. When I heard the returns reported on the radio election night, I called to my husband: "Why, Harry, listen: we're actually winning!" I was so habituated to defeat I could hardly believe it.

I realized it was the first time since I had been in politics that I had been on the victorious side.

With all of this so satisfactory life, I was continually beset with a desire to live in the East. There were many reasons for thinking it more desirable. The many trips back and forth to see editors and keep in touch with affairs and people ate heavily into my profits. More and more editors were adopting the order-and-collaboration method of dealing with writers. The editor had the idea. He wanted someone to write it. He gave an order. You wrote the article. He corrected and changed it. Sometimes the writer had to do it over several times. The *Century* magazine was the last, I think, that gave the writer the opportunity to say what he thought even if the editor disagreed with him. Editors told me it was almost impossible for a writer to live away from New York, that only two or three writers in the country managed to do it. I felt it increasingly difficult to get enough material away from the centers. I believed I needed the stimulus of being with people who were doing the same thing I was, who talked my trade. It took a great deal of energy and time to live two lives simultaneously.

---

8. Clara Paul (b. 1878) married Nathaniel Page in Joplin in 1906 (*Joplin Globe*, August 31, 1906).

23 *Democratic Stock*

In the meantime I was growing interested in the preconvention campaign for the Democratic presidential nominee in 1932. In December of 1931 at a tea given by the Woodrow Wilson Foundation, of which I was a trustee, in New York, I had been approached in regard to Newton Baker's availability. I admired Mr. Baker greatly, and his known devotion to the League of Nations made an appeal to me. At the same time he had, it seemed to me, become very conservative as to domestic matters. I could not support his attitude on the utilities, for instance, and domestic problems appeared then crying for new and progressive answers.

This would be the first campaign since I had been in politics when I was free to advocate a candidate for nomination.

I had known the Roosevelts since 1922. Not very well, but when I was on the national committee, and Mrs. Roosevelt was an officer of the New York State Committee, we had worked together. I remember her giving me a luncheon to talk to some of the women about our club. She had asked me to stay at her New York house—under a caretaker for the summer—to save hotel bills. I had many talks after 1924 with Mr. Roosevelt about the future of the party. I believed that he had it in him to be the progressive Democratic president some of us had been working and hoping for. I wrote to Mrs. Roosevelt and asked if I might have an opportunity to talk to him. In answer she asked me to come up to Albany. Anne O'Hare McCormick of the *New York Times* went up on the same train with me. After dinner—it was their anniversary and the Morgenthaus were there—the governor signed some bills and then asked me to come to his little study off the dining room.[1]

---

1. Anne O'Hare McCormick (1880–1954) began sending articles to the *New York Times* in 1921 when she was traveling abroad with her husband, Francis. In 1922, she became a regular correspondent and eventually had her own column, "Abroad." In 1937, she won a Pultizer Prize for her reporting. In 1936, she became the first woman member of the *Times* Editorial Board, where she served until her death (*NAW-Modern*, s.v. "McCormick, Anne O'Hare"). Henry Morgenthau Jr. (1891–1967) married Elinor Fatman in 1916. Active in Dutchess County politics, he was a neighbor of FDR. In 1928, Governor Roosevelt appointed him chairman of the state Agricultural Advisory Commission and in 1930 to the state conservation commission. After serving as governor of the Farm Credit Administration, he was appointed acting secretary of the treasury in November 1933, becoming secretary of the treasury in 1934 (*DAB*, s.v. "Morgenthau, Henry, Jr.").

During our talk he took his pencil and wrote down six problems that were needing solution and outlined how, in general, they could be met. It was a sales talk, and the solutions were not blueprinted, but I felt that the direction was right, the intention to do something there. Later when he startled the country with his AAA, NRA, PWA, I realized that this had been indicated on the little slip. In my own mind, I had decided that Franklin Roosevelt was the progressive Democratic nominee we had been hoping for so long.

I say "in my own mind," because nothing had been asked of me, and I did not know what, if anything, I could do. Miss Dewson, who was in the New York headquarters in charge of the women's end, had talked to me stressing his availability, but to her I felt I was just another name.[2] We did not talk organization.

Sometime during those early months, the national committee met in Washington. I had a proxy and attended it. Mr. Raskob made a speech, I remember, which made a very fine impression. The Democratic stock was coming up, due undoubtedly to the intensive work of the national committee under Jouett Shouse, to Mr. Raskob's money, and to Charley Michelson's broadsides against President Hoover. When the Jackson Day dinner came off at the Mayflower Hotel, Mrs. Kahn, a waggish Republican representative from San Francisco, said to a friend, "Why, there are twenty-five hundred Democrats all dressed up and acting just like Republicans."[3] Men and women sensing victory were coming out of the woods.

The Roosevelt leaders were there. Miss Marbury received the women and talked to them; Louis Howe the men. I did not see either, though I wanted to talk to Mr. Howe about the Missouri situation. When my name was mentioned to him he said, "That little woman can stir up more hell in a minute than a dozen men can settle in a year." I mention it to show that any part I took in the campaign was gratuitous. There appeared to

---

2. Mary Williams Dewson, called Molly (1874–1962), graduated from Wellesley in 1897. After beginning her career in social work in Massachusetts, she became a leader in the woman suffrage movement and served with the Red Cross in France during World War I. After the war she was hired by Florence Kelley as her chief assistant at the National Consumers' League, and from 1925 to 1931, she was president of the New York Consumers' League. In 1928, she organized women in Al Smith's presidential campaign; she did the same for FDR's gubernatorial race in 1930 and his presidential bid in 1932. She became head of the Women's Division of the Democratic National Committee in 1933 and was in charge of securing jobs for women in the New Deal. She served for a year on the Social Security Board, 1937–1938 (*NAW-Modern*, s.v. "Dewson, Mary Williams").

3. The Democratic National Committee met in Washington on January 9, 1932. Florence Prag Kahn (1866–1948) was the wife of San Francisco congressman Julius Kahn who had been first elected to Congress in 1898 and served for twenty-five years, with the exception of the 1903–1905 term. After his death in 1924, she was elected to fill his place in a special election. She won reelection in 1926 but was defeated in 1936 (*NAW*, s.v. "Kahn, Florence Prag").

be some arrangement made when Mr. Farley came to attend a luncheon in Kansas City, whereby the Rooseveltians would not come into Missouri but would leave the convention delegation to Senator Reed.[4] This, naturally, irked the Missourians who were for Mr. Roosevelt. The senator, they felt, might hold his delegation until it would be too late to help Roosevelt. Personal ambitions, too, undoubtedly made them dislike to have the Reedites, whom they considered in the minority, accepted as the state's leaders. More than all else, however, they were motivated by a distrust of Senator Reed. They did not think he would play fair with Roosevelt in the end.

Sometime later, I told all this to Senator Hull and Homer Cummings when they undertook to line up for Governor Roosevelt the southerners and the old McAdoo crowd. Someone asked me the other day what one man was responsible for Franklin Roosevelt's nomination at Chicago. I said primarily it was Roosevelt himself who caught the Democratic imagination and made them think he was a winner. After that, there was no one person, but you could point to several men and say that if they had not done this or that, he would probably not have won the nomination. Among them are Cordell Hull, Homer Cummings, and Dan Roper.

The solution to the Missouri situation seemed to us Rooseveltians to be to get a delegation from Missouri that, though it was instructed for Senator Reed, would be made up of Roosevelt men, so that when the senator appeared to have no chance, they would go to Roosevelt. To do this it was necessary to get a pro-Roosevelt state convention. Unless we did, it might be that, as in 1928, anti-Reed men would stay away from it and let the senator have his delegation by default. There was not much time to work up a pro-Roosevelt convention, and it was still further shortened when the date of the convention was set two weeks earlier than was customary.

The man responsible for getting the pro-Roosevelt state convention was Ewing Mitchell of Springfield, a most indefatigable worker and persistent to the point that you had to do what he asked in order to have peace.[5] Within

---

4. Louis Howe (1871–1936) worked as a newspaper correspondent until he met Franklin Roosevelt in 1911. Beginning by writing publicity, Howe acted as FDR's closest adviser, working behind the scenes. When Roosevelt became president, Howe became a public figure (*DAB*, s.v. "Howe, Louis"). James A. Farley (1888–1976) was president of General Builders Supply Corporation (1929–1933 and 1949–1958), which he had helped form. An early supporter of Al Smith for governor, he had been elected to one term in the New York state assembly in 1922. A delegate to the Democratic National Convention in 1924, he became secretary of the Democratic State Committee in 1928 and chairman in 1930 and 1932. An important player in FDR's gubernatorial election, he was floor leader for FDR at the 1932 convention. He was elected national chairman of the DNC in 1932. FDR appointed him postmaster general, and he managed FDR's 1936 reelection campaign (*DAB*, s.v. "Farley, James A.").

5. Ewing Mitchell (1873–1954), a Springfield, Missouri, lawyer, was a longtime Democratic activist. A bitter enemy of Sen. James Reed, he managed Breckinridge Long's

two weeks he had covered the state. I helped as I could with letters, as I was in Washington, and Harry went to work in our and adjoining districts. We were both delegates.

The convention that met in St Louis came to a stalemate. The Kansas City delegation headed by Mr. Pendergast wanted an instruction that held the national-convention delegates to Senator Reed until he released them. The Roosevelt men wanted its instructions to read, "as long as Senator Reed has a reasonable chance." We sat for a day, two days, while they fought it out in the Resolutions Committee, one of our men, Gene Frost of Cassville, on the committee always ready to bring a minority report to the floor.[6]

It was very trying to Mr. Mitchell and me to sit about able to do nothing when we knew that the convention could easily be swung to a Roosevelt instruction. If I had been a spellbinder, I might have been tempted to try it.

Mr. Pendergast, although very strong, was not then the power in the state he later became. Though the fact that he could vote a Democratic majority of ninety thousand in Kansas City gave the out-state people a wholesome respect for him—especially office seekers—he did not control the convention. The St. Louis organization, for instance, refused to take his leadership, and many of the out-state Democrats were also quite independent.[7]

The Rooseveltians won. The delegation was instructed for Senator Reed as long as he had a reasonable chance. On it were men and women who had theretofore been opposed to Senator Reed.

In all this, so far as I knew, neither Mr. Farley nor Mr. Howe nor any of his official managers had any part. It was a volunteer movement on the part of Missourians who wanted Mr. Roosevelt nominated, and not, perhaps, entirely pleasing to the Roosevelt inner circle. But it was to have its value.

I went to the two conventions as a writer of a daily feature for a syndicate. Both were held in Chicago. The Republican convention was a sorry one, the delegates having no choice but to renominate Mr. Hoover, though they

---

senatorial primary fight against Reed in 1922. In 1932, he was an early supporter of FDR, chairing the Missouri division of the Roosevelt Business and Professional League. In 1933, he was appointed assistant secretary of commerce but was dismissed in 1935 in a dispute over departmental irregularities. In 1936, he switched parties, backing Alf Landon, and in 1940 ran unsuccessfully for the Republican senatorial nomination (Ewing Mitchell Papers).

6. The state Democratic convention was held in St. Louis on March 28, 1932. William Eugene "Gene" Frost (1890–1955) served as circuit clerk of Barry County, 1922–1926, and probate judge, 1926–1934. He was elected state senator in 1935 and was later prosecuting attorney of Jasper County. Active in Democratic Party politics, he was a delegate to the 1932 national convention (*Missouri Historical Review* 50 [October 1955]: 107; *Official Manual of the State of Missouri, 1937–1938* [Jefferson City: Secretary of State, 1938], 59).

7. For Pendergast's influence at the 1932 convention, see Robert Ferrell, *Harry S. Truman: A Life*, 125; and Alonzo L. Hamby, *Man of the People: A Life of Harry S. Truman*, 182–83.

knew his chances for election were slim. There was even very little to make good copy. But I had an amusing time sitting in the press gallery between William Allen White and Bill Hard, with Will Rogers just behind me. I wish I had written down their running comments. Anne O'Hare McCormick was there, and Alice Longworth and Frank Kent, and we had much fun dining together. The newspaperwomen—Genevieve Herrick of the *Chicago Tribune*, Maxine Davis of Scripps-Howard, Emma Bugbee of the *New York Tribune*, Doris Fleeson of the *New York Daily News*, Winifred Mallon of the *Times*, Bess Furman of the Associated Press, and others—were good company.[8]

Between the conventions I remained at the Blackstone and did my *Good Housekeeping* article. An amazing incident of that interim I shall never forget. When I gave the chambermaid a fair-size tip, she refused to take it, saying, "Oh, I couldn't. I know how hard you worked for it. I have heard your typewriter going night after night."

With the Democratic convention things started. It is not my intention to describe that convention even if I could. My memory is a hazy confusion of crowds, conferences, daily articles, and family. My daughter and son-in-law had come up from Cleveland with some friends. Harry and Newell and a brother-in-law were there. My secretary, Ruth Mardick, was with me. One day, after an all-night session, they were all in my small room. The deadline for my daily article had been reached, and it was not done.

"Get out of here," I said. "Get out, everyone, and don't come back until I send for you."

----

8. Both conventions were held in Chicago; the Republicans met June 14–18 and the Democrats June 27–July 2. Maxine Davis (d. 1979) was a newspaper reporter for the *New York World*, United Press Association, and the *Detroit Free Press* from 1924 to 1928. She had a syndicated column, "Capital News," from 1926 to 1930, and after 1932 was a freelancer. She wrote numerous books and contributed regularly to national magazines (*Who Was Who in America*, 8:145; *Who's Who of American Women*, 1:315). Emma Bugbee (1888–1981) was a reporter for the *New York Herald Tribune* for fifty-five years, retiring in 1966 as one of only two women staff members, Ishbel Ross being the other. Best known for her coverage of Eleanor Roosevelt, she also wrote children's books (*Encyclopedia of American Journalism*, s.v. "Bugbee, Emma"; *New York Times*, October 10, 1981). Doris Fleeson (1901–1970) worked for the *Pittsburgh Sun* in 1923, moving to the *New York Daily News* in 1927. In 1933 she and her husband, John O'Donnell, went to the Washington bureau of the *Daily News*, and their column "Capital Stuff" carried a double byline. In 1943–1944, she was a war correspondent for *Woman's Home Companion* (*Encyclopedia of Twentieth-Century Journalists*, s.v. "Fleeson, Doris"; *NAW-Modern*, s.v. "Fleeson, Doris"). Winifred Mallon (1879–1954) worked for the *Chicago Tribune* before becoming a correspondent for the *New York Times* in 1929. She was president of the Women's National Press Club in 1935–1936 (Howes, *American Women, 1935–1940*, s.v. "Mallon, Winifred"). Bess Furman (1894–1969) began her newspaper career with the *Omaha Daily News*. From 1929 to 1936, she was employed by the Associated Press in its Washington bureau and covered the House of Representatives. After FDR's election, Furman's principal assignment was Eleanor Roosevelt (*NAW-Modern*, s.v. "Furman, Bess").

My husband, walking down the hall with my secretary, said to her sadly (so she told me): "You might live with her ten years and never see her like that again."

The Missouri delegation was as usual a center of conflict. Senator Reed had headquarters. An old-time friend of mine, Jewel Swofford, a very lovely and gallant person, was in charge of the women's end of it.[9] I was not persona grata there, but through Harry I kept in touch with the delegates. A St. Louis delegate wanted to leave the senator almost at once. He was, I understood, knocked down by some Kansas Citian and went about afterward with a bodyguard. These Missouri delegates, especially the women, must have had a hard time of it, for every possible pressure was brought on them to stick to Senator Reed. Even tears, I was told, were employed.

The ardent Rooseveltians came to me for instructions. I am sure they thought I was much more inside and important than I was. But they did give votes as needed, as, for instance, for the Rooseveltians' candidate for permanent chairman, Senator Walsh, as opposed to Jouett Shouse, and an increasing number for Mr. Roosevelt as the ballots went on.

Mr. Farley was counting on Mr. Pendergast to come across in time, as, in time, he did. What we feared—and by "we" I mean Harry, Ewing Mitchell, and the strong Roosevelt delegates—was that the New York delegation, in an effort to hold Missouri off from Roosevelt, might give a few votes to Senator Reed. Once he received any votes from some other states, and so had a possibility of winning, the Missouri delegation could not in honor leave him. This fear, however, was entirely our own. One always exaggerates one's own contribution to a campaign, especially if there is a victory. What we did may not have been necessary. We thought so, and so did the delegates who dared to give their votes without waiting orders. It took courage, and they suffered for it, too. When Mr. Pendergast came into statewide power, they were punished. Those who were rewarded were those who stuck by Mr. Pendergast, leaving him to come across when he wished and take the credit.

Of that convention, the most poignant moment to me was not the one when Mr. McAdoo took the platform and announced that California went to Roosevelt—perhaps because I had already heard of his intention in the press gallery. It was when Cordell Hull faced the hisses of the "wet" galleries to speak against the repeal plank. I had called him on the telephone about six o'clock to ask his help in getting approval of maternity and infancy aid

---

9. Jewel Swofford, a Reed supporter, had been an active civic leader in Kansas City. She worked in the Democratic campaigns in 1928, 1930, and 1932. She was secretary of the state committee in 1930 and 1932. She was appointed to the U.S. Employment Compensation Commission in 1933 and served three six-year terms (Elsie L. George, "The Women Appointees of the Roosevelt and Truman Administrations: A Study of Their Impact and Effectiveness" [Ph.D. diss., American University, 1972], 79).

into the platform, and he had said that he had just discovered he would have to go on the platform that night to speak against the repeal plank. I realized he was much distressed. He had tried, he explained, to get the oratorical drys to make the speech. He had no knack for swaying an audience, but if no one else would, he must do what he could. Knowing him as I did, I realized what he suffered when he stood up before that wet-mad crowd booing him until Mayor Cermak threatened to clear the galleries. I felt for Mrs. Hull, too, who so adored him, sitting there behind him. When Governor Smith followed, his insults to Mr. Hull seemed unforgivable. One should, it seemed to me, deal gently with a gallant foe. I realized then that Governor Smith was not a sportsman.

The business about the wet-and-dry question was interesting to me. At the Republican convention I had heard it all argued—better argued, too, than it was at the Democratic convention, Sen. Hiram Bingham of Connecticut making one of the best talks I ever heard. The convention galleries had listened politely to both sides. The wets had gotten what they asked for. I had been to the wet mass meeting that gave Mrs. Sabin an ovation such as few women ever had.[10] It was a surprise to me to find the repealers at the Democratic convention asking for so much more, and Democrats willing to give it to them at the cost of ramming defeat down the throats of honest, convinced dry Democrats, and making them choose between their Democracy and Prohibition. To make the degree of loyalty for repeal the issue at that campaign seemed to me reckless and unjustifiable. That it was not is owing to the nominee and not to the wet plank in the platform. Had Governor Smith been the candidate, it would, no doubt, have been the major theme.

The night that Mr. McAdoo threw the nomination to Mr. Roosevelt, a man came up to the people in the press seats next to me. He wanted their railroad tickets.

"The party's off," he said. "We're going on the midnight train. I'm getting the special car now and must have your Pullman tickets."

---

10. Hiram Bingham (1875–1955) earned his Ph.D. in 1905 in South American history. He taught at Princeton, leading numerous exploring expeditions in South America and publishing accounts of his exploits. In 1922, he was elected Republican lieutenant governor of Connecticut. In 1924, after serving only one day as governor, he resigned to accept his election to fill an unexpired term in the United States Senate. He then won in the regular election of 1926, serving eight years in the Senate. He was an Old Guard, conservative Republican (*DAB*, s.v. "Bingham, Hiram"). Pauline Morton Sabin (1887–1955) was elected as the first woman full member of the Republican National Committee in 1923. She was a delegate to both the 1924 and the 1928 national conventions and headed the women's activities in the Coolidge and Harding campaigns. In 1929, she resigned from the RNC and helped form the Organization for National Prohibition Reform, serving as its national chairman. It became one of the first anti-Prohibition groups to endorse the 1932 Democratic ticket (*NAW-Modern*, s.v. "Sabin, Pauline Morton").

It seemed news to them. "How is Governor Smith?" they asked.

"Taking it pretty hard. Emily and Mrs. Smith are with him.[11] The door's locked."

I asked someone who the stranger was, and was told it was Major Warner, Governor Smith's son-in-law.[12] The conversation seemed to indicate how unprepared Governor Smith's friends were for the California switch.

I am not sure if it was this night or another that I was flooded with telegrams urging Newton Baker as the nominee, some of them from people I had not seen for ten years. The Western Union boys fell upon the convention aisles like locusts. It was a great telegram campaign.

A number of the people I saw much of at the convention were for Mr. Baker. Some of them were very violent in their antipathy to Mr. Roosevelt. One friend to whom I was devoted bore down on me in the Blackstone dining room one evening.

"I hear you're back of this Missouri business," she said. "You're working for him tooth and nail. How can you?"

I don't know why she was surprised. I had often been put on the defensive for supporting him in Washington. I remember one night taking on a whole roomful when it was demanded that I say how I could choose him. It was there, I think, in answer to an attack by Oswald Garrison Villard and some others, who called themselves progressives or liberals, that I articulated what I believed to be the difference between Mr. Baker's and Franklin Roosevelt's liberalism.[13]

Which night we sat in the Coliseum until daylight I cannot remember, though I recall how funny I felt at 3:00 A.M. sitting in our evening clothes on a stool in a little hole of a restaurant while Newell went behind the counter and brought cups of horrible coffee to Mrs. Hull and Mrs. Barkley and me.[14]

It is funny, the queer things that stick in your mind. Emma Guffey Miller saying to me—I can see the place—"Well, we're together for once on a candidate." Senator Barkley coming over to Mrs. Barkley to press her hand just before he made his keynote speech. A man beside an Ohio leader who said, "I don't care, anyone except Roosevelt." Walking up Michigan Avenue

---

11. Emily Smith was the second of Al Smith's five children and her father's favorite (Matthew Josephson and Hannah Josephson, *Al Smith, Hero of the Cities: A Political Portrait Drawing on the Papers of Frances Perkins*).

12. In June 1926, Emily Smith married John A. Warner, superintendent of the New York State Police.

13. Oswald Garrison Villard (1872–1949) was editor of the *New York Evening Post* from 1897 to its sale in 1918. A consistent opponent of war, he championed many reform causes, including woman suffrage, antilynching laws, prison reform, and government regulation of insurance and the stock market. He was editor of the *Nation*, the leading liberal publication, from 1918 to 1932 (*DAB*, s.v. "Villard, Oswald Garrison").

14. Dorothy Brower married Alben Barkley in 1903.

at one o'clock with Anne McCormick and a stranger beside me saying, "Where have I missed you all this time, dearie?" Alice Longworth saying that progressives like her could accept a man like Ritchie. Emptying a malted milk on a new dress in the drugstore. Mrs. Daniels, gracious and motherly, saying, "How can I remember you when you change your hats so often?" Meeting Belle Moskowitz on the steps of the Blackstone, speaking to the Norman Macks, and Mrs. Mack with a hat that had a chain of beads hung under her chin. These are what ramble into my mind rather than the serious moments of conference with Governor Ritchie, and Lavinia Engle, with Harry Byrd, with Carter Glass furious over the threat of abolition of the two-thirds rule, of speaking to the Resolutions Committee for a child-welfare plank, of the fight over seating Huey Long.[15]

One incident does stand out clearly. We were in the hall of the Congress Hotel between the elevator and the Roosevelt headquarters, Harry and I. The place was filled with milling people laughing, screaming to make themselves heard. Cordell Hull got off the elevator, saw us. He led us to a corner and there, as if we were on a desert island together, he told us why he believed

---

15. Emma Guffey Miller (1874–1970), sister of Pennsylvania senator Joseph Guffey, became active in the suffrage movement after 1910. In 1924 and 1928, she seconded the nomination of Al Smith for president. She was an early supporter of Franklin Roosevelt and seconded his nomination in 1932 and 1936. From 1932 until her death, she was Democratic National Committeewoman from Pennsylvania (*NAW-Modern*, s.v. "Miller, Emma Guffey"). Alben Barkley (1877–1956) served in the United States House of Representatives as a Democrat from Kentucky from 1912 to 1923. In 1926, he was elected to the Senate. In 1924, he was acting chairman of the Democratic National Convention and in 1928 was unsuccessful in securing the vice presidential nomination. A leading preconvention supporter of FDR, he was the keynoter at the 1932 convention. In 1937, he became Senate majority leader and was Truman's vice presidential running mate in 1948 (*DAB*, s.v. "Barkley, Alben"). Addie Worth (b. 1868) married Josephus Daniels in 1888. In 1920, President Wilson appointed her as U.S. delegate to the Woman Suffrage Conference of the World in Geneva. She wrote *A Cabinet Officer's Wife in Washington* (Howes, *American Women, 1935–1940*, s.v. "Daniels, Addie Worth"). Belle Moskowitz (1877–1933) began working for Al Smith in 1918 when he ran for governor of New York. She managed his campaign for the presidential nomination in 1924. After his failure to win the 1932 nomination, her political career ended (*NAW*, s.v. "Moskowitz, Belle"). Harriet Taggart married Norman Mack in 1891. Lavinia Engle was field secretary for the NAWSA (1913–1920), director of the Maryland League of Women Voters (1920–1936), and on the staff of the Social Security Administration (1936–1962), serving as its chief of field operations from 1940 to 1962 (*Who's Who of American Women, 1974–1975* [Chicago: A. N. Marquis, 1975], 273). Harry Byrd (1887–1966), Virginia's youngest governor in 1925, turned down FDR's offer of an appointment as secretary of agriculture. He began his senatorial career by filling a vacancy in 1933 and was then elected to six terms. After supporting FDR in 1932 and 1936, he never supported another Democratic national ticket (*DAB*, s.v. "Byrd, Harry"). Huey P. Long (1893–1935) was first elected governor of Louisiana in 1928. He was elected to the United States Senate in 1930. Although he had campaigned for FDR in 1932, he turned against him in the summer of 1933 (*DAB*, s.v. "Long, Huey P.").

Franklin Roosevelt should be nominated. He began with a review of the encroachments of the executive on the legislative branch of the government, explained why the legislative branch could not accomplish liberal measures, indicated where the country was going, what must be done to change it, and why Franklin Roosevelt could do it. When we left, my husband said, "He's the only one thinking like a statesman in this whole bedlam." He may not have been the only one thinking in terms of state craft, but he was the only one detached enough to talk about it.

After it was ended with Governor Roosevelt's speech of acceptance came the national committee meeting, me again with a proxy all fixed, I recall, for some contest about what I can't remember, except that it never came off, Mrs. Roosevelt reaching out from the aisle and catching my hand. I do remember that it was then I first met Malvina Thompson, Mrs. Roosevelt's astonishingly capable "man Friday."[16]

After the convention we drove up to Detroit to meet the parents of Greta Flintermann to whom Newell was engaged, down to Cleveland to see the grandchildren and home.[17] Home, but not to rest, for I had a job awaiting me.

---

16. Malvina Thompson (1893–1953) was a secretary for the New York Democratic Committee in 1922. She was personal secretary to Eleanor Roosevelt for twenty-five years (*DAB*, s.v. "Thompson, Malvina").

17. Greta Flintermann married Newell Blair on October 12, 1935.

Earlier, in June, I had written to a candidate for the Missouri gubernatorial nomination, offering my services to him at my own expense. I had done it for two reasons, either one of which might have sufficed. Russell Dearmont had been the leader of the state senate and fostered the best educational legislation Missouri had. I thought that as governor he would give us what Missouri badly needed: a modern legislative program along social lines. Opposing him was a very old and half-sick man whose campaign was being backed by Mr. Pendergast of Kansas City.[1] I had no objection to Mr. Pendergast, so long as he confined his politics to Kansas City, this being its citizens' business, but when he reached out to control the state, he should, I felt, be resisted. He had a slate for every office—if one included his support of Senator Reed's ambitions— from the president on down, including U.S. senators and Supreme Court judges.

I did not know Mr. Dearmont, but I argued to myself that this was a clear issue that the Democratic women should meet, and as one who had worked for suffrage, I owed it to them to pose it to them. I suspect that I looked upon it as something that would justify to myself my whole political performance, a sort of soul washing as well as a sop to my ego, a dramatization of myself, perhaps as a disinterested politician. For I had no personal antagonism to Mr. Pendergast, and wanted nothing from Mr. Dearmont.

At any rate, I did it. My first action was to write to the women on my mailing list asking them to join our committee of women. Out of one thousand, seven hundred responded. Not a bad record for a list eight years

---

1. Russell Dearmont (1891–1967) was a Cape Girardeau lawyer who was legal counsel for the Missouri Pacific Railroad Company. He served in the Missouri senate from 1929 to 1932. Opposed to the Pendergast machine, he ran unsuccessfully for the Democratic gubernatorial nomination in 1932 (*Who Was Who in America*, 4:238; Franklin D. Mitchell, *Embattled Democracy: Missouri Democratic Politics, 1919–1932*, 151). Francis Wilson (1887–1932) was a lawyer from Platte City, Missouri. His terms in the Missouri State Senate began in 1899, 1909, 1911, and 1913. The Democratic nominee for Congress in 1904, he was appointed U.S. attorney for the Western District of Missouri by Woodrow Wilson in 1913. He was reappointed in 1917, and his term ended in 1920. With the support of Pendergast, he won the Democratic nomination for governor of Missouri in 1932 but died before the general election (*Who Was Who in America*, 1:1360; March, *The History of Missouri*, 2:1365–66).

unused. On my return from the national convention in July, I made a speaking tour. Newell drove me. The Dearmont headquarters made the engagements. Sometimes I spoke on the courthouse steps, a thousand and sometimes more people in front of me. Always two and sometimes three meetings a day, far apart. Sometimes a local man introduced me. Oftener I was on my own. It was terrifically hot. At every place Newell had to go out and buy me new handkerchiefs, as I used three at a meeting to wipe off the perspiration, and then forgot to take them with me. He was a great cavalier. One afternoon I came into a town almost exhausted. "I think you'll feel better," he said, "when you've rested and had a bath." He drew the water for me, unpacked my bag, and got out my dress. Then he tiptoed out, and in an hour was back with a tray of food.

In Kansas City where I stayed two days with the Edgar Shooks and made four speeches, hardly one of the many women I had worked with before came out to see me.[2] Even the newspapers that had always been friendly to me either ignored me or gave me backhanded interviews.

I had never known the Shooks, but he had backed Mr. Dearmont's campaign there. A young lawyer, full of ideals, he continuously opposed Mr. Pendergast's organization. One night Mrs. Shook invited a number of young men and their wives to meet me: bankers, lawyers, businessmen. Each man told me that he would like to support my candidate but did not dare, for fear of retaliation on his business, a run on his bank, real estate values boosted for taxation purposes. It was easy enough for an outsider like me to come in; Edgar Shook was the really courageous one.

I realize now what was wrong with my campaign. I told the facts as I knew them. The people out in the state could not believe them to be so. If I had diluted them, they might have had more verisimilitude for my hearers. All the politicians told me I was a fool. Perhaps so, but I enjoyed that campaign more than any I was ever in. The issue seemed to me clear-cut. It was wholly individual. It was like suffrage days.

I ended my campaign in my garden before a group of Joplin women. Mr. Pendergast won overwhelmingly. He might have won anyway, but the situation in regard to congressmen gave him a great advantage.

After the census of 1930, Missouri lost two of its congressmen, having only thirteen instead of fifteen. The legislature having failed to pass a redistricting bill, these thirteen had to be elected by the whole state. There were fifty-four candidates for these thirteen nominations, all with their friends and neighbors. Whichever one of these got the Kansas City majority vote was pretty sure of success. Mr. Pendergast played them cannily. He waited until

---

2. Edgar Shook (1894–1970) earned his LL.B. from the University of Missouri in 1922 and practiced law in Kansas City from 1929 to 1970. He married Elizabeth Stone Harwood in 1928 (*Who Was Who in America*, 5:659).

a few weeks before the primaries, and announced that any one of twenty-six would do. The supporters of these men, their families, and friends were sold to Mr. Pendergast. On the day of election, the Kansas City organization, of course, got word of the exact thirteen to vote for.

The successful nominee for governor was a much liked and respected man, a politician of the old school. He probably did not understand my opposition, and believed his victory would not give Mr. Pendergast control of the state. Whether it would or not cannot be known, for he died before election day, and the place, filled by the state committee, went to a little-known circuit judge, the choice, of course, of Mr. Pendergast.[3]

His victory was complete, except for the election of Andrew Romjue, a congressman from north Missouri, who managed in some way to win without him, and the nomination of Bennett Clark for U.S. senator, a great surprise to everyone except, perhaps, himself and his sister.[4] He had come into the fight after two other men had been announced. One of them, Charles Hay, had run in 1928, and been defeated because of the anti-Smith feeling in the state. I had helped him open his campaign. I had said to Mr. Clark at the Chicago convention, "I'm with Mr. Hay, you know. But this is just a tryout for you. You'll run again next time, and then I'll be for you."

"I'll take that as a promise," he replied.

But he had won this time. The state's devotion to his father was, of course, a great asset. But his intensive whirlwind campaign in which his sister, Genevieve, helped, and his own forthright speeches caught the voters, fed up with platitudes. In my own county there was a complete right about-face.

With this primary campaign, I was, I thought, completely eliminated from politics. Even had I wanted to be in, I could not. It was a surprise, therefore, in September when I received a letter from Mrs. Roosevelt asking me to come

---

3. After Francis Wilson's death on October 12, Jackson County Democratic chairman suggested to Pendergast that circuit judge Guy B. Park of Platte County fill the vacancy. Pendergast traveled to Jefferson City when the state committee met and saw that Park was named to fill the vacancy (March, *The History of Missouri*, 2:1365; Lawrence H. Larsen and Nancy J. Hulston, *Pendergast!* 90).

4. Milton Andrew Romjue (1874–1968) practiced law in Macon, Missouri. A delegate to Democratic State Conventions from 1920 to 1940, he was a delegate to the 1928 national convention. He served in the United States House of Representatives from 1917 to 1921 and from 1923 to 1943 (*Biographical Directory of the U.S. Congress*, 1739). Bennett Clark (1890–1954), son of Speaker of the House Champ Clark, earned his law degree at George Washington University in 1914. After service in World War I, he returned to Missouri and joined the St. Louis law firm of Fordyce, Holliday, and White in corporate and trial practice. In 1932, he was elected to the United States Senate after defeating a Prohibitionist and Tom Pendergast's favorite in the primary. During his career, he alternated between opposition to and cooperation with the Pendergast faction. In 1945, Truman appointed him to the Circuit Court of Appeals for the District of Columbia (*DAB*, s.v. "Clark, Bennett").

on to New York to consult about the campaign. Miss Dewson, in charge of the organization of women, had in mind that this was the time to get in touch with the women's clubs I had once organized, and see what they could or would do. But eight years is a long time. The clubs, many of them, had disbanded—discouraged and disrupted by the party's factional fights. The response was not encouraging. Lena Madesin Phillips made an effort to revive them. After a few weeks at headquarters, I set out on a campaign tour. The committee was economical with its speakers. Governor Ross, Ruth Bryan Owen, Anna Dickey Olesen, and I among us were to cover the country, while Emma Guffey Miller concentrated on Pennsylvania where her brother Joe Guffey was a candidate for Congress.[5] We were the grandstanders, good for publicity purposes and attracting crowds. The real campaigning, in Mary Dewson's plan, was to be done by what she called the "grass trompers," women who went into a district and stayed long enough to get up meetings, start an organization, speak at every ready-made occasion. She had dozens of them, and they were far more effective than we.

Mary Dewson, "Molly" we all called her, might well have been God's gift to Franklin D. Roosevelt and the Democratic Party. She was utterly without personal ambition, and completely objective in her approach. Furthermore, she had had wide experience in nonpolitical organization, knew it up and down. Forthright, frank, direct, with a passionate belief in her cause, she could make the most obstinate and indifferent do what she wanted. Free, too, as she was from connections with the lower-rung political organization, she did not have to waste time with their intrigue and personalities. She had but one job to do—elect Franklin Roosevelt—and she kept at it. Never, I am sure, had there been a more intensive and effective organization of women for any undertaking than the one she built up in 1932, unless it was her even better one in 1936. She had a way, too, with men. They liked her directness, her humor. She said once, humorously, that men like two kinds of women. For her to have essayed the charmer role would have been ridiculous, but they all had a fondness for the motherly.

---

5. Lena Madesin Phillips (1881–1955) was the first woman to graduate from the University of Kentucky Law School. The founder of both the National and the International Federations of Business and Professional Women's Clubs, she became a leading lawyer in New York City (*NAW-Modern*, s.v. "Phillips, Lena Madesin"). Ruth Bryan Owen (1885–1954) was elected to Congress from Florida in 1928, the first southern woman in Congress. After her defeat in 1932, Roosevelt made her the first woman to hold a major diplomatic position when he appointed her minister to Denmark. In 1936, she married Borge Rohde (*NAW-Modern*, s.v. "Owen, Ruth Bryan"). Joseph Guffey (1870–1959), a businessman, became chairman of the Democratic State Committee of Pennsylvania after Wilson was elected president. He was known as the "boss" of Pennsylvania Democrats. An early supporter of FDR, he became a staunch New Dealer. Elected to the United States Senate in 1934, he lost his bid for a third term in 1946 (*DAB*, s.v. "Guffey, Joseph").

To work with her was fun, but it was work. I had my "run-ins" with her. My political feud with the Kansas City organization she never understood. But she was loyal to her workers and not to be diverted by attacks on them. When, during the campaign, she was told that Senator Reed considered it an unfriendly act to have me at headquarters, she answered that she had not interfered with the men having whomever they wanted, and she wanted me.

She had also a deep loyalty to women. That their services be recognized, that they be counted in, she demanded, and it is largely because of her insistence and promotion ability that women today have what place they have in government.

I learned a great deal from her that, had I known it before, might have made my previous work more effective and me much less uncomfortable.

That campaign trip of mine is something never to be forgotten. How I survived, I wonder today. First into Connecticut, New York, Ohio, Wisconsin, Indiana, and Iowa. Big and small meetings; old friends and new ones; meetings stuck in at the last moment; automobile drives fifty, a hundred miles to some place I just must go.

I had asked for three days off in Missouri to write a *Good Housekeeping* article, for I kept up my reading, doing a book in my berth or hotel at night, or in a railroad station between trains. But I had two engagements in Missouri, for, to my amazement, a request had come from the new state chairman saying I must speak there—it was essential. The amusing thing was that his wire came to headquarters the very day the chairman of the Speakers Bureau had told the chairman of the women's Speakers Bureau that Missouri leaders objected to my being sent out, saying that I had no following in Missouri.[6] For answer she had shown him the telegram from the Missouri chairman demanding me.

I knew that what he wanted was to put me on record as supporting the state ticket. Apparently, opposition did not necessarily eliminate you; it sometimes made you more important.

So before I began my article in Joplin, I went to Columbia. The speech was a failure. I knew it. What, I asked my husband as we drove the two hundred miles home that night, was wrong. "I'm not a speech maker," he said. "You are, but I could make a speech this campaign." He told me what he would say. Instead of writing the *Good Housekeeping* article, I spent the two days at my typewriter composing the new speech.

The next day I started on the second lap of my trip, and what had gone before was, in comparison, a leisurely saunter.

By plane to El Dorado, Kansas. A speech in the afternoon; a fifty-mile drive and an evening speech in Winfield; another drive and a luncheon in Anthony; another drive and a speech in Hutchinson. The train there and a

---

6. The Democratic Speakers Bureau chairman was Robert Jackson of New Hampshire; the chairman of the women's Speakers Bureau was Lavinia Engle.

luncheon speech in Denver; a radio speech and the train again for Salt Lake. It was Sunday, and I spent it in my rooms doing the *Good Housekeeping* article and got it off at two o'clock Monday morning. At six I took a plane for Pasco, Washington.

When we came down in the smiling valley at Boise City, I asked the pilot who sat in an open cockpit behind the cabin I occupied alone, "How long before you would know it if I died?"

"When we landed," he answered.

"Do you call this a smooth or a rocky trip?"

"Rather rocky," he replied.

When they had brought out the little plane at Salt Lake, I had protested that I thought it was to be trimotored, only to be told that this was really much safer as there was no place to land a big plane in the mountains. Comforting thought. I had remembered this as we flew between peaks so close I felt I could touch them with my hand.

At Pasco a tea and speech, the train to Spokane and another speech; a night train to Yakima and a speech: a night train to Seattle and two speeches. I had expected here to find an audience of club women. When I walked onto the platform I saw that the hall was filled with men quite evidently off the streets. They had evidently come to hear their idol, Lioncheck, who had been given five minutes on the program. I threw away my written speech and set to work to talk to my audience, expecting momentarily a walkout, but there wasn't any. The night train to Portland, Oregon, and five speeches; a night train to Marshfield and another speech; a three-hundred-mile drive to Medford and a speech; a plane to San Francisco; a drive to Sacramento and a speech. Sunday at Berkeley and a tea; a luncheon Monday at San Francisco with a speech; the train to Bakersfield that night and three speeches; the night train to Los Angeles, a luncheon and a speech there; a tea, a radio speech the next day. Speeches at Long Beach and at Pasadena. A plane at three o'clock in the morning for Kansas City; my husband there to meet me. A cold, a doctor, and an osteopath; a drive to Warrensburg, Missouri; a speech and home in time to vote. Fifteen days, twenty-five hundred miles, and twenty-eight speeches, not to mention the conferences, the organization talks, the dinners, teas, and luncheons.

My written speech had worked out very satisfactorily. To the same introduction I had tied a speech on the tariff, one on the utilities, one on welfare, one on the depression and need for relief, one on the agricultural problem, another on taxation. I had only to pick out at each place the subject of most interest to that community—utilities, for instance, in Seattle, tariff in Denver—and hitch it on to my opening and closing sections.

This was my first presidential campaign, I realized, that I had spoken to enthusiastic, sympathetic audiences. There was something pathetic about their intense concern, the avidity with which they ate up statistics as if hanging their hopes on facts. In every way it was the most satisfactory political speaking I have ever done. Yet it was then I realized that the day of the campaign speaker was over.

Those who can listen to the principals in the contest on the radio, who can turn on their dials and feel present at a Madison Square Garden speech or a great rally, can hear senators and publicists any night, would not long, I knew, go out on a bad evening and sit on an uncomfortable chair to listen to some unknown person talk about the personality of someone else and what he would or would not do.

This campaign tour was in a sense my political swan song, though I did not realize it then. I did go out again in 1936 when President Roosevelt ran for reelection, scampering like twenty other women over Kansas, Iowa, Wisconsin, Nebraska, Ohio, and Michigan, the doubtful states we must carry. There were exciting times, as when the Republicans sprang their attack on the Social Security Act on almost my last day, and in Iowa Mrs. Ryan and I sat up all night to do a question-and-answer radio dialogue for the middle of the state.[7] I enjoyed it, too, for I was especially at home in these middle-western states, and felt a kinship for the women of these small towns, but the work was more or less a routine. There was not the excitement of combat, or winning converts, and I was not, perhaps, the evangelist I had been. One does not keep it up forever. Besides, I had changed greatly during these four years. Political success creates new problems. This, with the Democratic victory and our removal to Washington, I was to learn.

---

7. Evelyn Althea Murphy (1869–1951) married Charles Gaston Ryan in 1896. A public-school teacher from 1889 to 1896, she was a delegate to the Democratic National Convention in 1928 and a Democratic National Committeewoman from Nebraska (*Who Was Who in America*, 3:750).

25 So Far

At last we were living in Washington on a permanent basis. Harry was appointed assistant attorney general in the Department of Justice. I found my social life for the most part built around his interests, and the center was the attorney general, Homer Cummings, and his pretty wife.[1] It was another of my many strokes of good luck that brought me to know Cecelia Cummings. The moment I met her, the February before the election of 1932, I knew that there was one of those bonds between us that presage friendship. There is something very special about a friendship established suddenly with a stranger of whose background and previous life you know nothing, for it is based wholly on what you give and take from each other's personality, and it is therefore deeply satisfying. It exists outside of time and place.

Homer Cummings I had known on the national committee, but I was to discover that knowing a man "in politics" was very different from knowing him as a friend. Mr. Cummings is one of the most social persons I have ever known. By "social" I mean adapted to and able to make contacts with other human beings. While he looks dignified and aloof—*urbane* may be the word—he "gives up" admiration, appreciation, understanding, affection. He is the one man I have ever known who could employ toward other men the word *love* without seeming sentimental. He is also completely integrated.

I have written elsewhere of the Washington social scene at this time; suffice it to say that there were countless balls, luncheons, teas, and dinners to keep one as busy as one chose.

The second summer, Homer, Cecelia, Stanley and Mrs. Reed, Harry, and I went to Hawaii together. The men went on official business, but Harry was allowed only six hundred dollars' traveling expenses. Fulton Oursler offered me one thousand dollars for an article I wrote for *Liberty*, and this paid my way.[2] Although it proved rather expensive, as Harry had to spend five hundred dollars of his own money, we had a grand time.

---

1. Harry was appointed assistant attorney general of the United States in January 1934 (Homer Cummings to FDR, January 3, 1934, Roll 48, Alphabetical File, 1933–1946, Franklin D. Roosevelt Papers). Mary Cecelia Waterbury married Homer Cummings in 1929; she died ten years later.

2. Stanley F. Reed (1884–1980) married Winifred Elgin in 1908. He was general counsel to the Federal Farm Board, 1929–1932, and to the Reconstruction Finance Corporation, 1932–1935. In 1935, FDR appointed him solicitor general; in 1938, he

Women had finally stepped off into the promised land, but they had found it preempted by those who had never been on the other side, indeed did not even know there had been another side. These women had wisely spent their time learning something to do in that promised land and instead of building one bridge had already taken possession. As this was what we bridge builders had worked for, we had no reason for complaint, but it did leave us feeling somewhat marooned. Our kind of organization was not necessary with the Roosevelts in the White House, and it was a little late for some of us to learn another craft. We were adrift, lost.

I thought I knew what I needed: some new undertaking that would make the same demands on me in the way of study and struggle that the political work, writing, and suffrage work in their time had done. After some months, I thought I had found it.

Through the help of Mr. Roper, then secretary of commerce, I was added to the Consumers' Board of the National Recovery Act, which was a group of men and women.[3] Here was a new field. I would have to work and study to understand the consumers' problems, and, what was equally necessary, I believed one of the most important problems facing our economic system was that of getting the goods made by our industrial system to the people who needed them. I thought I had found my next sphere of endeavor. Malcolm Rose in his *Death of a Yale Man* has written more entertainingly than I can what I would wish to say of the effort of the Consumers' Board to serve this purpose through the amazing and conflicting decisions of the NRA. By nature and experience an evangelist, I threw myself into the protection of the consumer under the NRA and the promotion of his interests in our system with as much enthusiasm as I had once had for the inclusion of women in politics. I committed myself to a new purpose. It was difficult to grow fervid about something that rested on economic facts and theories as did the interests of consumers. The economists on whose figures and facts we had to base our endeavors held us down a bit from conclusions. The research they did took so long that by the time the huge pile of facts and figures was accumulated the situation we wished to remedy had changed. They involved us in such details as to procedures and methods and techniques that we had to read reams of notes before we realized that they had after all arrived at these conclusions that

---

was appointed to the Supreme Court where he served until his retirement in 1957 (*DAB*, s.v. "Reed, Stanley F."). Their trip to Hawaii was July 22–September 5, 1934 (Homer Cummings Diary, Box 234, Homer Cummings Papers). "Is the Home on the Way Out?" *Liberty* (February 22, 1936): 41–43.

3. The Consumers' Advisory Board of the NRA was established on June 16, 1933. ENB's appointment came in the first week of August. She headed the consumers' protective bureau, handling price complaints (ENB to Dewson, August 8, 1933, Box 16, Dewson Papers; ENB to FDR, August 18, 1933, Alphabetical File, 1933–1946, microfilm roll 48, Franklin D. Roosevelt Papers).

had already been perfectly apparent to an uninformed person like myself. The facts and figures were so conflicting that they seldom came to a conclusion or could be utilized to produce conclusions, and they ignored the most important factor—which was the human variable concerned. But it was all interesting and seemed to me greatly worthwhile. I felt, too, that I had a contribution to make. If I did not know economics except those that I had learned long ago at the University of Missouri, at least I knew as much as the politicians and businessmen who were determining the codes at the NRA, and I did know how to work with men and politicians. As the other members of the Consumers' Board either lived elsewhere and came to Washington only for board meetings or were primarily devoted to some other job, I found myself more and more called on to help Mrs. Rumsey, the able and earnest chairman of the board, who had all the attributes of knowledge of business affairs, executive ability, and charm of personality the Harriman family possesses in such abundance. Since I had been her coworker on administrative problems, it was considered advisable for me to go on in her place, when she so tragically died from a fall from her horse, at least until the Supreme Court's decision decided the future of the NRA.[4] Because of Harry's position it did not seem to me wise to take a salaried position (how different things are today!). But as the work entailed added expenses at home, I agreed to a ninety-day appointment by which time we hoped to hear from the Court. The waiting period dragged on thirty days longer. When at last the NRA was put out of business, I was named by the president as one of the NRA board of six to liquidate it. This board functioned about thirty days more. I was then adrift again.

Other things led to my discomfort. Few experiences are more trying to the ego than that of becoming a "has-been." To have been in the center of events, have had even a small part in determining them or trying to determine them, and find them going on without you is decidedly annoying. No actor enjoys becoming a spectator, as was the fate of so many of us who found ourselves watching the "youngsters" in the New Deal. When an actor, you long, so you think, for the ease of a seat in the audience. What you do not realize is that it will not be you, the actor, sitting in a box seat, but you as a spectator on the back row of the peanut gallery!

When you work for a campaign, it is "we." "We" will be elected, "we" will do this and that. When the candidate is elected it is "he." His is the

4. Malcolm Ross (1895–1965), *Death of a Yale Man* (New York: Farrar and Rinehart, 1939). Mary Harriman Rumsey (1881–1934), daughter of Edward Henry Harriman, railroad financier, began work in social welfare when she helped found the Junior League. After her husband died in 1910, she became active in politics. She, along with her brother Averell, supported Al Smith in 1928 and was a personal friend of both FDR and Frances Perkins. In June 1933, FDR appointed her to be chairman of the Consumers' Advisory Board of the NRA (*NAW,* s.v. "Rumsey, Mary Harriman"). On November 17, 1934, Mrs. Rumsey fell off a horse during a fox hunt. She died on December 18.

responsibility, his the reputation that is at stake, and his the decisions. This is as it should be. But the severance was a jolt to me.

A letter I wrote to Molly Dewson just after the campaign comes back to me as indicating how little I knew about all this. It was as naive as it was presumptuous, suggesting that "we women get together and decide upon the right woman for the right job" and see that she was appointed to the end that the administration give a great example of what women could and should do in government. Little did I know the pressure upon a new administration—of the politicians with their women candidates, the senators with theirs, or the tramping that Molly herself would have to do from one official to another, combing their appointments and urging them to give certain ones to women. She made a grand job of it, one that I know I could never have done. Miraculously, considering the grab-bag manner of getting and making appointments, she frequently got the right women for the job. Even the appointees of the politicians—call it Roosevelt luck if you will—have turned out as well and sometimes better than our handpicked ones might have done.

Strangely, at every decennial you pass you have a certain readjustment to make, a sense of something gone and of something strange and not altogether pleasant to come. You do if you are an adult—only the infantile or adolescent hold on to the past. Ten years before I had written an article, "I Prepare to Face Fifty." I tried to do one now on approaching sixty.[5]

It was then that I came upon some articles for a magazine about a group of people who employed a certain technique and method to find what I was seeking. The criticism in the articles did not, I could see, invalidate the efficacy of the technique. I had never met a member of this group. But as these things happen, once I had read about them I began to run across them. A woman at a garden party. A woman who roomed next to me at my club in New York. And my sister Annie who came on to visit me.

I decided to try it. It was very personal and private all this. But miraculously the technique seemed to work. I was asked to speak at a luncheon in New York given by some of their members. Thus I found myself aligned with the Oxford Group under the direction of Dr. Frank Buchman.[6]

There has been little in my book about my political convictions or the social problems crying for solution. Yet I had not been unmindful of those objectives. Quite definitely, I knew what I, and I thought women, wanted.

---

5. "I Prepare to Face Fifty," *Harper's* 153 (September 1926): 434–42.

6. Frank Buchman (1878–1961), an ordained Lutheran minister, had established an organization in the 1920s that came to be known as the Oxford Group. "A movement outside the established churches that sought to bring individuals to dynamic spiritual earnestness within the framework of their own religious traditions," it emphasized meditation as a means of self-improvement. In 1938, Buchman changed the name to Moral Re-Armament, with the goal of preventing war through individual spiritual renewal (*DAB*, s.v. "Buchman, Frank").

Briefly, it was to humanize our system. Mr. Roosevelt's interpretation of the way to do it, namely, by raising the standard of living of the submerged one-third, had not occurred to me. But when he brought forth his plan, I knew that this was one way to do it. Probably the only way it could be done. That all his methods were 100 percent effective or desirable, or that they went to the root of our social problems, of course I did not think; but his objective I knew was right, and I knew also that no one else on the public scene was trying to reach them. I was deeply sympathetic therefore with the New Deal.

Here I think is the difference between the man, or woman, who works through a party—becomes a so-called partisan—and the independent man or woman working for social ends outside a party. The party member, or partisan, goes along with an organization with the intention and desire of trying by means of it to get officials who will work toward the end he thinks desirable. He is content, knowing the political methods and the difficulties, if he can get 70, 60, sometimes even 40 percent of what he wants. The party member has his mind on the direction; he accepts the failures and mistakes as necessary to the process. The independent, on the other hand, is with the party only so long as it does what he wants. To him the party, like the officials, is something to be exploited to obtain certain specific things. As long as the party or officials work for those specific things, the independent is with them. In other words, the independent exploits the party and officials so long as it serves his end; the partisan tries to influence the party and lead it in the right direction.

This is something the New Deal administration has taught me. At long last, I have come to see what party organization and party work mean. What I was fumbling for way back in 1920, I have found through empirical methods.

It is not my intention, however, to write of the New Deal administration. It is too close in time to get a perspective, and I could not give a picture of Washington of the day if I tried. The unimportant has not yet been sifted from the important by memory. It would be a confusing, inconsistent, and fantastic picture.

You can write about your past because in a sense it has become detached from you. You see it as you do the life of another, or that of a character in a book. If you have lived a quick, busy life, its rancors and disappointments—even its sorrows—do not stay with you. I can say only that I would not have passed this period, even though it did not offer me a wholly pleasant experience.

So I confine myself to what it did for me and what connection it has with the woman who crossed the bridge. Even that is difficult, for, as I have said, the end of this bridge that women had been so slowly and laboriously building debouched upon a strange new world. The astonishing fact that women were there went unnoticed in the newness of the world itself. But the women there were new, so new that they seemed strangers, many of them, to the bridge builders.

Once early in this book I wrote that it was difficult to make the experiences of any everyday wife and mother interesting. To make the woman I now faced understandable is far more difficult. For to do so one must deal with reality, and that is not easily reduced to words. Dramatization, emotions, experiences, and facts write themselves, create words. But what takes place inside you, things as they are in their essence, words conceal as often as they disclose. But I must try, as without it this book tells only of a life and a society that is gone, and I am still a living person in the world of today where men are engaged in a life-and-death struggle with realities.

Long ago I knew that a new day was coming although just when I could not say. It was about the time of the First World War that I saw its approach. Up to that time we had thought this not a perfect world, but one operated by a mechanism called progress. It worked somewhat slowly but surely. All we had to do was to move along with it, the more courageous and intelligent responding to its demands. In this progressive world men did not retrace their steps. When a thing was done, it was finished. Men went on to something still better in the steady slow race toward perfection. War was cast aside forever. Intolerance was obliterated. Oppression was done with. Cruelty belonged to another age. The world moved on to wider applications of justice, understanding, generosity, kindness. Freedom was something you had as surely as you breathed. One had only to apply it in larger areas. Liberty was a possession. One simply decided how and when to use it. This was our prewar idea, and so fixed were we in it that we took the idea for the fact. World War I opened our eyes, but seeing was not enough. It did not change our habits of thought, though we realized that something was wrong with our idea. Still we did not face realities, at least I did not. I knew that things were not as I had believed them to be, but I went along living in my old surface mold, holding the same values of the good life. Once in a while some book or some injustice bared would make me realize that I was wrapped in protective prejudices, manners, and desires that prevent me from reaching down into the actualities that I apprehended must be there. I knew that there were people who came to grips with life as I did not, that there was a world of feeling and experience I had not touched. But I had no time to find out what it was. I was too busy with getting the income to live in a certain approved manner to see the struggle involved in getting enough money to keep me alive. Too busy having a house what I wanted it to be to face the possibility of not having a roof over my head. Too busy making women effective in politics to face the eventuality of making politics serve man's needs.

I am not apologizing for myself in a spirit of self-incrimination. I am just trying to explain how living in the world of manners removes one from actuality. Once I would have said that this was true only of the specially privileged. I did not realize that I, too, was of the privileged, that below me were millions. I saw only how far I was from the top.

One does not, it seems, learn much except through experience. Sympathy with others, even understanding—good though they are—do not take the place of personal knowledge. Of course I felt sorry for others less fortunate. When they came under my eyes I tried to help them. And I was ready to back all the movements to improve their conditions with time and money. But I did not really know what they were up against or how culpable I was for leaving them against it.

Fortunately for me, I had had some actualities to meet myself. Not those of privation and desperation, but enough to show me in what a dreamworld I had lived and how unfit I was to meet the real thing.

I began to see more clearly what the fundamental problems of life are, and I realized that I had nothing in myself with which to meet them. I saw what counted was not what you got or accomplished, but what you were. I felt myself, for all my background and possessions, very poor indeed.

Looking back on my life, I remembered that day I had sat in my garden. I had found something then not myself. In memory I retraced the years. When I started out, I was working for something outside, greater than myself. I had known exaltation. I had regarded my public work, my political work, as for the good of others rather than myself. But somewhere along the line, perhaps influenced by the ability to earn money and popularity, I saw I had changed tracks. Though I had camouflaged this to myself and to others, I had really come to work for a person known as Emily Newell Blair.

The realization now as the newcomers took over that perhaps I was not looked upon by them as the person I had been building up through the years was a bitter but a salutary experience. It seemed rather sardonic, however, for this self-realization to come when what I had honestly envisioned so many years ago was being realized. Women were at last being recognized in politics. The progressive administration had come. I was living at last in Washington.

We lived in three places during these years. A little house in Georgetown, a place out in Spring Valley, and the Wardman Park Annex. It was while we were there that my sister Anna died of pneumonia while on a vacation in Arizona with Margaretta.[7] Anna was too vivid a personality to die. One could no more think of her dissolving into nothingness than one's mind can conceive a vacuum. The world grew suddenly more empty.

My brother, Jim, lived then in Florida and had married Betty, whom we all admired. Jim was with the governor and fulfilled the duties that in other states devolve upon a lieutenant governor.

Women wanted Miss Perkins in the cabinet, and we thought the president

---

7. Anna Newell died on January 4, 1937.

did also.[8] She had never been in politics, but she was a most capable and experienced woman. She had difficulties with some union people and with some politicians, but I have always felt that what she accomplished was outstanding and will be more and more so recognized as time passes.

Another appointment over which women rejoiced was that of Florence Allen as a judge of the Circuit Court of Appeals. She has demonstrated her ability and reflected great credit on her sex.

In 1935 Newell had married Greta Flintermann of Detroit. I have always thought Greta was Newell's greatest stroke of luck, as Harry was mine.

In the fall of 1936 Harry resigned to go into private law practice again. It did not seem convenient just before the election to have a vacancy to fill, and so at the request of the attorney general he held it back until after election. The president then asked that he hold it until after inauguration. At the end of January it was accepted.[9] Harry's reason for leaving was the very practical one that with the upturn of business conditions he could no longer afford to confine his earning powers to the government salary. He had enlisted, as he put it to the attorney general, for the duration of the term, and the first administration was coming to a close.

We finally took a house in Alexandria, Virginia, George Washington's old town across the Potomac. I brought on my things from Joplin, including the boxes and boxes of books. Harry commuted between Joplin and Washington; a grandson came, Harry Wallace Blair II.[10] I wrote now and then; I had completed the circle and was back again to the purely domestic life of my early married days.

I come to the end—so far—of my life. It is one that can never happen again. For no young woman like me with the same repressed ego and urge for self-expression and attainment will be hampered by the Victorian concepts that

---

8. Frances Perkins (1880–1965), with an A.B. from Mount Holyoke (1902) and an M.A. from Columbia University (1910), was secretary of the New York Consumers' League, working with Florence Kelley from 1910 to 1912. After the Triangle Fire, she became secretary of the Committee on Safety of the City of New York working for factory-inspection legislation. Working closely with Al Smith in New York reform, she was appointed by him to the New York State Industrial Commission in 1918. During Roosevelt's governorship, she was part of his inner circle, working to improve conditions of depression in New York. In 1933, Roosevelt appointed her secretary of labor, the first woman cabinet officer. In that position, she was instrumental in drafting much New Deal legislation, including the Federal Emergency Relief Act, the National Industrial Recovery Act, the Civilian Conservation Corps, the National Labor Relations Act, the Social Security Administration Act, and the Fair Labor Standards Act (*NAW-Modern*, s.v. "Perkins, Frances").

9. Harry resigned as an assistant attorney general, effective January 31, 1937 (Harry Blair to Homer Cummings, January 13, 1937, Box 80, Cummings Papers).

10. They moved to 323 South Fairfax Street in Alexandria. Harry Wallace Blair II was born on March 29, 1935.

hampered me. The young woman of today starts free to be and do what she wishes. She does not have the same concessions to make to respectability, the same compromises between domesticity and marriage. For both she and her husband feel that she has a right to pursue the outward course if she wishes. She does not have to discover herself through experience or learn by doing. Where women like myself without special training struggled along and managed a sort of success, since there was no competition from trained women, today's woman sets herself to prepare for her chosen work. Never again, I believe, will the volunteer woman worker have such innings as she has had in my time.

Perhaps her problems will be greater, and the difficulties, too, but they will not be the same.

I think I know what some of them will be. Such knowledge is the compensation of experience and age. Many women, most women, perhaps, will simply go on in the economic, the political, and the social worlds, exploiting their opportunities. But the pioneer souls, the evangelistic, creative ones, of the same type and in the tradition of the feminists of my day, will see the next step for women. They will know that it is to write into our thinking and our system the values that are peculiarly those of women, the values that enable the individual soul: those of honesty, purity, and unselfishness and love in human relations. They will know that the holding and the promotion of these values have always been women's contribution to civilization. I base this prophecy on what has happened in and to myself. For, after this long journey, and all these essays after personal realization, after all my efforts to improve social conditions by law and movements, I have come at last to the knowledge that it is only as I express these values in my own life that I experience fulfillment and realize the potentialities of womanhood—of humanity itself. It is a lesson I was long in learning. But this life of mine following the movement of women in our time, and, in a small way, epitomizing it, has taught me that this is the message of the women's movement. Our generation freed women that they might go on to this, their next step. To tell them this has really been the purpose of my book.

Bibliography

Selected Publications of ENB

"Our Cooperative Kitchen." *Woman's Home Companion* (October 1910).

"Letters of a Contented Housewife." *Cosmopolitan* (December 1910).

"Nelly Howard's Daughter: A Story of the Confederate Reunion." *Sterling* (February 1911).

"Every Man His Own Campaign Manager." *Outlook* (February 25, 1911).

"Safety Valve." *Lippincott* (May 1911).

"A Successful May Fete." *Woman's Home Companion* (May 1911).

"Heart of a Wallflower." *Cosmopolitan* (September 1911).

"Evolution of a Lady." *Harper's Bazaar* (December 1911).

"The Year of the Trial." *Ladies' World* (June 1912).

"A Belated Rosebud." *Lippincott* (August 1912).

"Progressive Rainbow Dinner." *Woman's Home Companion* (April 1913).

"A Country Woman's Rest Room." *Independent* (June 19, 1913).

"Little While." *Lippincott* (July 1913).

"An Incurable Dissipation." *Outdoor World and Recreation* (September 1913).

"My Son's Wife." *Housewife* (March 1914).

"The Bonds of Matrimony." *Blue Book* (April 1914).

"Summer Economies." *Missouri Magazine* (May 1914).

"The Grandmother (Story for the Aged) as Told by Herself." *Holland's Magazine* (June [1914?]).

"We Love and Learn." *Blue Book* (September 1914). [Under pen name John Stewart Rodgers.]

"The Man with Love Enough for Two." *Blue Book* (October 1914).

"The Backslider's Wife." *Red Book* (1915?).

"The Triumph." *Woman's Home Companion* (March 1915). [Under pen name Sydney Carter.]

"Front and Back Doors." *House Beautiful* (April 1915).

"The Obtuse-Angled Triangle." *Green Book* (April 1915).

"When a Man Marries." [journal unknown] (April 1915).

"What One Woman Chose." *Blue Book* (May 1915).

"Developing a Prospect." *Green Book* (June 1915).

"Her Sense of Honor." *Green Book* (July 1915).

"A Dangerous Woman." *Green Book* (August 1915). [Under pen name Marcia Corwin Follansbee.]

"The Measure of a Man." *Holland's Magazine* (December 1915).

"Houses and Character." *Countryside Magazine* (January 1916).

"The Journey of His Heart." *Blue Book* (January 1916).

"Love's Indian Summer." *Green Book* (February 1916).

"The Knight and the Dragon." *Smith's Magazine* (April 1916).

"Domesticating a Genius." *Romance* (June 1916).

"The Cost of Peace." *Smith's Magazine* (July 1916).

"Southwest Missouri Women Organize for War Work." *Missouri Woman* (February 1918).

"Women in War Industries." *Current History* (January 1919).

"Where Are We Going?" *Ladies Home Journal* (March 1919).

"Should a Woman Get a Man's Pay?" *Ladies Home Journal* (April 1919).

"The United States Council of National Defense." *Current History* (May 1919).

"What Are We Women Going to Do?" *Ladies Home Journal* (May 1919).

"What Shall I Do with It?" *Ladies Home Journal* (September 1919).

"What the War Did to Wives." *Ladies Home Journal* (December 1919).

The Woman's Committee, United States Council of National Defense: An Interpretative Report. Washington, D.C.: U.S. Government Printing Office, 1920.

"What Shall We Do with It?" *Green Book* (May 1920).

"I Nominate—." *Green Book* (June 1920).

"Platforms for Women." *Green Book* (July 1920).

"Where the Money Comes From." *Green Book* (August 1920).

"Woman Planks in the Platforms." *Green Book* (September 1920).

"Your Candidate and Mine." *Green Book* (October 1920).

"The Woman Vote." *Green Book* (November 1920).

"Paying Election Debts." *Green Book* (December 1920).

Democratic Women's Clubs: Organization Plan. Washington, D.C.: n.p., 1922.

"What Women May Do with the Ballot: An Address by Mrs. Emily Newell Blair before the Democratic Women's Luncheon Club of Philadelphia." Philadelphia: privately printed by Maria Lansdale, 1922.

"What Women Have at Stake." *Woman Citizen* (October 18, 1924).

"What Is Non-Partisanship?" *Woman Citizen* (March 7, 1925).

"Are Women Counting in Politics?" *Saturday Evening Post* (July 18, 1925).

"Are Women a Failure in Politics?" *Harper's* (October 1925).

"I Am Curing Myself of Extravagance." *Cosmopolitan* (March 1926).

"Why I Sent My Children Away to School." *Harper's* (March 1926).

"This Business of Wifehood." *Harper's* (April 1926).

"Men in Politics as a Woman Sees Them." *Harper's* (May 1926).

"The Congress and the Country." *Woman Citizen* (September 1926).

"I Prepare to Face Fifty." *Harper's Magazine* (September 1926).

"The Novel with a Purpose." *Creative Reading* (1927).

"A-Careering." *Woman Citizen* (January 1927).

"Why Clubs for Women?" *Forum* (March 1927).

"Why We Live beyond Our Means." *Forum* (June 1927).

"'Boring from Within': An Answer to 'The Lady and the Tiger.'" *Woman Citizen* (July 1927).

"The College Woman on the Farm." *Country Gentleman* (July 1927).

"How Magazines Are Raising the Standard of Living." *Magazine Advertiser* (July 1927).

"Living beyond Our Means." *Garard Review* (July 1927).

"The Professional Point of View." *Ladies Home Journal* (August 1927).

"Protest from the Big Congregation." *Independent* (August 6, 1927).

"The Job of a National Committee Woman." *Woman's Democratic News* (October 1927).

"Wives in Politics." *Forum* (October 1927).

"No Answer—Dusty or Otherwise." *Forum* (December 1927).

"Are Women Really in Politics?" *Independent* (December 3, 1927).

"Americans We Like: Florence E. Allen." *Nation* (December 7, 1927).

"Driving Through: Fit and Misfit Rural Homes that the Passer-by Sees." *Country Gentleman* (January 1928).

"The Magnificent Adventure: Marriage." *Red Book* (January 1928).

"Why I Prefer to Live in a Small Town." *Bookman* (January 1928).

"Margotry." *Forum* (February 1928).

"Another Job for the Supersalesman." *Independent* (March 10, 1928).

"Meat without Manners." *Forum* (March 1928).

"Political Platforms." *Outlook* (March 1928).

"Case for the Opposition." *Woman's Journal* (April 1928).

"May Day." *Century* (May 1928).

"A New Role for the Donkey: In which He Might Win Leadership and Gain Power." *Century* (May 1928).

"Realistic Detail in the Novel." *Creative Reading* (May 1928).

"At the End of the Rainbow." *Household Magazine* (June 1928).

"Looking Forward." *Bulletin of the Women's National Democratic Club* (June 1928).

"May the Best Man Win." *Good Housekeeping* (September 1928).

"Many Roads Lead Women into Politics." *New York Times Magazine* (October 1928).

"Neither Wet nor Dry: How the Non-Combatants Feel about It." *Century* (October 1928).

"The Job of Being a Feminist Small-Town Style." *Outlook and Independent* (April 1929).

"Must Our Children Start Where We Did?" *Harper's* (May 1929).

"Women in the Political Parties." *Annals of the American Academy of Political and Social Science* (May 1929).

"Case of Mrs. Willebrandt." *Woman's Journal* (June 1929).

"New Styles in Feminine Beauty." *Outlook and Independent* (June 26, 1929).

"Dilemma of the Democratic Party." *Outlook and Independent* (July 24, 1929).

"Married Feminist's Predicament." *Outlook and Independent* (September 4, 1929).

The Creation of a Home: A Mother Advises a Daughter. New York: Farrar and Rinehart, 1930.

"Future of the Hinterland." *Outlook and Independent* (January 29, 1930).

"In Defense of the Spendthrift." *Outlook and Independent* (April 16, 1930).

"Jobs after Motherhood." *Outlook and Independent* (June 4, 1930).

"Trial Balance for Homemakers." *Better Homes and Gardens* (October 1930).

"Profits for Wives." *Outlook and Independent* (October 1, 1930).

"New Approach." *Outlook and Independent* (October 8, 1930).

"Is Marriage Worthwhile?" *Pictorial Review* (November 1930).

"Opportunity Rouses the Democrats." *Review of Reviews* (December 1930).

"Now Feminism Leads Back to the Home." *New York Times Magazine* (December 7, 1930).

A Woman of Courage. New York: Farrar and Rinehart, 1931.

"Why I Am Discouraged about Women in Politics." *Woman's Journal* (January 1931).

"Putting Women into Politics." *Woman's Journal* (March 1931).

"Discouraged Feminists." *Outlook and Independent* (July 8, 1931).

"How to Salvage Time." *Better Homes and Garden* (September 1932).

"Women and Political Jobs." *New York Herald Tribune Magazine* (April 23, 1933): 4.

"Women's Club Program." *Good Housekeeping* (September 1933).

"If You Were Gadding about Washington." *Good Housekeeping* (March 1934).

"Why New Deal Washington Fascinates Women." *Liberty* (December 1934).

"Because in War You Never Know What You Are Fighting For." In *Why Wars Must Cease*, ed. Rose Young. New York: Macmillan, 1935.

"The Mob." *Liberty* (September 14, 1935).

"A Who's Who of Women in Washington." *Good Housekeeping* (January 1936): 38–39.

"Is the Home on the Way Out?" *Liberty* (February 22, 1936).

"A Plan of Action." *Lecture Recorder* (April 1936).

"The Oxford Group Challenges America." *Good Housekeeping* (October 1936).

"How to Get into Politics." *Democratic Digest* (November 1937).

"Tomorrow Is Another Day." *Good Housekeeping* (January 1938).

"How Honest Is the Oxford Group?" *Liberty* (August 6, 1938).

"First Aides to Uncle Sam." *Independent Woman* (September 1938).

"Faith that Conquers Where Reason Fails." *Forum and Century* (November 1938).

"Democratic Women March On." Washington, D.C.: Women's Division, Democratic National Committee, 1945.

"Assisting Providence." *Pearson's Magazine* (May [n.y.]).
"Colorado Farmers' Club Runs Experiment Plot." *Grit* (n.d.).
"Growing Pains." *Holland's Magazine* (February [n.y.]).
"Knowing the Ozarks." *KCS Ozarks Outings* (n.d.).
"A Pioneer Woman's Garden." *Farmer's Wife* (n.d.).

Manuscript Collections

Archives. Grace Episcopal Church, Carthage, Mo.
Archives. Woman's National Democratic Club, Washington, D.C.
Banister, Marion Glass. Papers. Library of Congress, Washington, D.C.
Beimdiek Family Folder. Powers Museum, Carthage, Mo.
Blair, Emily Newell. File. Powers Museum, Carthage, Mo.
————. Papers. Western Reserve Historical Society Library, Cleveland, Ohio.
Calhoun Piano School. File. Powers Museum, Carthage, Mo.
Clark, Bennett. Papers. Western Historical Manuscripts Collection, Columbia.
Council of National Defense, Woman's Committee. Papers. Record Group 62. National Archives, Washington, D.C.
Cummings, Homer. Papers. University of Virginia.
Dewson, Mary. Papers. Franklin and Eleanor Roosevelt Library, Hyde Park, N.Y.
Funeral Card File. Powers Museum, Carthage, Mo.
Gellhorn, Edna. Papers. Washington University, St. Louis.
Glass, Carter. Papers. University of Virginia.
Goltra, Edward. Papers. Missouri Historical Society, St. Louis.
Grace Episcopal Church File. Powers Museum, Carthage, Mo.
Harriman, Florence Jaffray. Papers. Library of Congress, Washington, D.C.
Hull, Cordell. Papers. Library of Congress, Washington, D.C.
Missouri Writers' Guild. Papers. 1916–1980. Western Historical Manuscripts Collection, Columbia.
Mitchell, Ewing. Papers. Western Historical Manuscripts Collection, Columbia.
Reed, James A. Papers. Western Historical Manuscripts Collection, Kansas City.
Roosevelt, Eleanor. Papers. Franklin and Eleanor Roosevelt Library, Hyde Park, N.Y.
Roosevelt, Franklin D. Papers. Franklin and Eleanor Roosevelt Library, Hyde Park, N.Y.
Women's Studies Manuscript Collections. Series 2: Women in National Politics. Schlesinger Library, Radcliffe College.

Newspapers

Carthage Evening Press, 1895, 1896, 1903, 1908, 1909, 1910, 1911, 1912, 1913, 1914, 1922, 1937, 1956, 1966.
Carthage Weekly Press, 1897, 1935.
Denver Post, 1935.
Denver Times, 1900, 1902.
Joplin Globe, 1912, 1914, 1924.
Joplin News Herald, 1914, 1960.
Kansas City Journal, 1924.
Missouri State Journal, 1922.
New York Times, 1904, 1919, 1920, 1923, 1924, 1931, 1932, 1942, 1946, 1951, 1953, 1954, 1956, 1959, 1962, 1963.
St. Louis Globe-Democrat, 1924, 1930.
St. Louis Post-Dispatch, 1938.
St. Louis Star-Times, 1938.
Washington Post, 1962, 1977.

Other Sources

Alberti, Johanna. *Beyond Suffrage: Feminists in War and Peace, 1914–1928*. New York: St. Martin's Press, 1989.
Allen, Florence. *To Do Justly*. Cleveland: Western Reserve University Press, 1965.
Allen, Lee. "The McAdoo Campaign for the Presidential Nomination of 1924." *Journal of Southern History* 29 (May 1963): 211–38.
Anderson, Kathryn. "Practicing Feminist Politics: Emily Newell Blair and U.S. Women's Political Choices in the Early Twentieth Century." *Journal of Women's History* 9 (autumn 1997): 50–72.
Anderson, Kristi. *After Suffrage: Women in Partisan and Elective Politics before the New Deal*. Chicago: University of Chicago Press, 1996.
Anderson, Mary. *Women at Work: The Autobiography of Mary Anderson as Told to Mary N. Winslow*. Minneapolis: University of Minnesota Press, 1951.
Armitage, Shelley. *Kewpies and Beyond: The World of Rose O'Neill*. Jackson: University Press of Mississippi, 1994.
Baker, Paula. "The Domestication of Politics: Women and American Political Society, 1780–1920." *American Historical Review* 89 (June 1984): 620–47.
Barnard, Eunice. "Women in the Campaign." *Woman's Journal* 13 (December 1928): 7–9, 44–55.
Beale, Marie. *Decature House and Its Inhabitants*. Washington, D.C.: National Trust for Historic Preservation, 1954.
Bellush, Bernard. *Franklin D. Roosevelt as Governor of New York*. New York: Columbia University Press, 1955; reprint, New York: AMS Press, 1968.

Benstock, Shari, ed. *The Private Self: Theory and Practice of Women's Autobiographical Writings*. Chapel Hill: University of North Carolina Press, 1988.

Blair, Karen. *The Club Woman as Feminist: True Womanhood Redefined, 1868–1914*. New York: Holmes and Meier, 1980.

Breckinridge, Sophonisba. *Women in the Twentieth Century: A Study of Their Political, Social, and Economic Activities*. New York: Arno Press, 1972.

Brown, Dorothy M. *Mabel Walker Willebrandt: A Study in Power, Loyalty, and Law*. Knoxville: University of Tennessee Press, 1984.

———. *Setting a Course: American Women in the 1920s*. Boston: Twayne, 1987.

Burg, David F. *Chicago's White City of 1893*. Lexington: University Press of Kentucky, 1976.

Burke, W. J., and Will D. Howe, comps. *American Authors and Books, 1640 to the Present Day*. 1943. Reprint, New York: Crown Publishers, 1962.

Burkhalter, Nancy. "Women's Magazines and the Suffrage Movement: Did They Help or Hinder the Cause?" *Journal of American Culture* 19 (summer 1996): 13–24.

Callahan, Edward, ed. *List of Officers of the Navy of the United States and of the Marine Corps from 1775 to 1900*. New York: L. R. Hamersly, 1901; New York: Haskell House, 1969.

Carlson, Avis. *The League of Women Voters in St. Louis: The First Forty Years, 1919–1959*. St. Louis: League of Women Voters, 1959.

Catalogue of the University of the State of Missouri: Fifty-seventh Report of the Curators to the Governor of the State, 1898–1899. Columbia, Mo.: n.p., n.d.

Chafe, William H. *The Paradox of Change: American Women in the Twentieth Century*. New York: Oxford University Press, 1991.

Chambers, Clarke. *Seedtime of Reform*. Minneapolis: University of Minnesota Press, 1963.

Chandler, Allison. *Trolley through the Countryside*. Denver: Sage Books, 1963.

Coben, Stanley. *A. Mitchell Palmer: Politician*. New York: Columbia University Press, 1963.

———. *Rebellion against Victorianism: The Impetus for Cultural Change in 1920s America*. New York: Oxford University Press, 1991.

Conway, Jill. "Women Reformers and American Culture, 1870–1930." *Journal of Social History* 5 (winter 1971–1972): 164–78.

Cook, Blanche Wiesen. *Eleanor Roosevelt, 1884–1933*. Vol. 1. New York: Viking Press, 1992.

Cott, Nancy F. *The Grounding of Modern Feminism*. New Haven: Yale University Press, 1987.

Craig, Douglas. *After Wilson: The Struggle for the Democratic Party, 1920–1934*. Chapel Hill: University of North Carolina Press, 1992.

Dains, Mary K., ed. *Show Me Missouri Women: Selected Biographies*. 2 vols. Kirksville, Mo.: Thomas Jefferson University Press, 1989.

Deland, Margaret. "The Change in the Feminine Ideal." *Atlantic Monthly* 105 (March 1910): 291, 293.

Eaton, S. J. M. "City of Franklin." In *History of Venango County*. Chicago: Brown Runk, 1890.

Evans, Timothy K. "This Certainly Is Relief: Matthew S. Murray and Missouri Politics during the Depression." *Missouri Historical Society Bulletin* 28 (July 1972): 219–33.

Ferrell, Robert H. *Harry S. Truman: A Life*. Columbia: University of Missouri Press, 1994.

Fiftieth Report of the Public Schools of the State of Missouri for the School Year Ending June 30, 1899. Jefferson City: Tribune Printing Company, State Printers and Binders, 1900.

Fisher, Marguerite J., and Betty Whitehead. "Women and National Party Organization." *American Political Science Review* 38 (October 1944): 898–99.

Flexner, Eleanor. *Century of Struggle: The Woman's Rights Movement in the U.S.* Cambridge: Harvard University Press, Belknap Press, 1975.

Fowlkes, Diane L. *White Political Women: Paths from Privilege to Empowerment*. Knoxville: University of Tennessee Press, 1992.

Freedman, Estelle B. "The New Woman: Changing Views of Women in the 1920s." *Journal of American History* 61 (September 1974): 372–93.

———. "Separatism as Strategy: Female Institution Building and American Feminism, 1870–1930." *Feminist Studies* 5 (fall 1979): 512–29.

Furman, Bess. *Washington By-Line: The Personal History of a Newspaperwoman*. New York: Alfred A. Knopf, 1949.

Golemba, Beverly E. *Lesser-Known Women: A Biographical Dictionary*. Boulder, Colo.: Lynne Rienner Publishing, 1992.

Gould, Lewis L. *The Presidency of Theodore Roosevelt*. Lawrence: University Press of Kansas, 1991.

Gruberg, Martin. *Women in American Politics: An Assessment and Sourcebook*. Oshkosh, Wis.: Acadmia, 1968.

Hamby, Alonzo L. *Man of the People: A Life of Harry S. Truman*. New York: Oxford University Press, 1995.

Hareven, Tamara. *Eleanor Roosevelt: An American Conscience*. Chicago: Quadrangle Books, 1968.

Harriman, Florence Jaffray. *Mission to the North*. Philadelphia: J. P. Lippincott, 1941.

Hartmann, Susan M. *The Home Front and Beyond: American Women in the 1940s*. Boston: Twayne, 1982.

Hicks, John D. *Republican Ascendancy, 1921–1933*. New York: Harper and Row, 1960.

"The History of the Women's National Democratic Club." *Democratic Bulletin* (June 1928): 4–12.

Hoff-Wilson, Joan, and Marjorie Lightman, eds. *Without Precedent: The Life and Career of Eleanor Roosevelt.* Bloomington: University of Indiana Press, 1984.

Holli, Melvin G., and Peter d'A. Jones, eds. *Biographical Dictionary of American Mayors, 1820–1980.* Westport, Conn.: Greenwood Press, 1981.

Howes, Durwood, ed. *American Women: The Standard Biographical Dictionary of Notable Women.* Vol. 3. Teaneck, N.J.: Zephyrus Press, 1974.

———. *American Women, 1935–1940: A Composite Biographical Dictionary.* 2 vols. Detroit: Gale Research, 1981.

Jackson, William Rufus. *Missouri Democracy: A History of the Party and Its Representative Members, Past and Present.* 3 vols. Chicago: S. J. Clarke, 1935.

Jacob, Kathryn Allamong. *Capital Elites: High Society in Washington, D.C., after the Civil War.* Washington, D.C.: Smithsonian Institution Press, 1995.

James, Edward T., ed. *Notable American Women, 1650–1950: A Biographical Dictionary.* 3 vols. Cambridge: Harvard University Press, Belknap Press, 1971.

Josephson, Matthew, and Hannah Josephson. *Al Smith, Hero of the Cities: A Political Portrait Drawing on the Papers of Frances Perkins.* Boston: Houghton Mifflin, 1969.

Kent, Frank R. "Senator 'Jim' Reed." *Forum* 78 (July 1927): 62–70.

Laas, Virginia, Everett Ritchie, and Daniel Stewart. *An Introduction to the Tri-State Mineral Museum.* Joplin, Mo.: World of Printing, 1985.

Larsen, Lawrence H., and Nancy J. Hulston. *Pendergast!* Columbia: University of Missouri Press, 1997.

Lash, Joseph. *Eleanor and Franklin.* New York: Norton, 1971.

Lemons, Stanley. "The Sheppard-Towner Act: Progressivism in the 1920s." *Journal of American History* 3 (July 1969): 776–86.

———. *The Woman Citizen.* Urbana: University of Illinois Press, 1973.

Lens, Sidney. *The Labor Wars: From the Molly Maguires to the Sitdowns.* Garden City, N.Y.: Doubleday, 1973.

Leonard, John, ed. *The Book of St. Louisans: A Biographical Dictionary of Leading Men of the City of St. Louis.* St. Louis: St. Louis Republic, 1906.

Leuchtenburg, William E. *Franklin Roosevelt and the New Deal, 1932–1940.* New York: Harper and Row, 1963.

Livingston, Joel T. *A History of Jasper County, Missouri, and Its People.* 2 vols. Chicago: Lewis Publishing, 1912.

Mainiero, Lina, ed. *American Women Writers: A Critical Reference Guide from Colonial Times to the Present.* New York: Frederick Ungar, 1979.

March, David D. *The History of Missouri.* 2 vols. New York: Lewis Historical Publishing, 1967.

Marzolf, Marion. *Up from the Footnote: A History of Women Journalists.* New York: Hastings House, 1977.

Matthews, Glenna. *The Rise of Public Woman: Woman's Power and Woman's Place in the United States, 1630–1970*. New York: Oxford University Press, 1992.

McGerr, Michael. "Political Style and Women's Power." *Journal of American History* 77 (December 1990): 864–85.

McGregor, Malcolm G. *The Biographical Record of Jasper County, Missouri*. Chicago: Lewis Publishing, 1901.

McKerns, Joseph, ed. *Biographical Dictionary of American Journalism*. Westport, Conn.: Greenwood Press, 1989.

Miller, C. A. *The Lives of the Interstate Commerce Commissioners and the Commission's Secretaries*. Washington, D.C.: Association of Interstate Commerce Commission Practitioners, 1946.

Mitchell, Franklin D. *Embattled Democracy: Missouri Democratic Politics, 1919–1932*. Columbia: University of Missouri Press, 1968.

Morgan, David. *Suffragists and Democrats: The Politics of Woman Suffrage in America*. East Lansing, Mich.: Michigan State University Press, 1972.

Morton, Marian J. *Women in Cleveland: An Illustrated History*. Bloomington: University of Indiana Press, 1955.

Mott, Frank Luther. *American Journalism: A History, 1690–1960*. New York: Macmillan, 1962.

Mowry, George E. *The Era of Theodore Roosevelt, 1900–1912*. New York: Harper and Brothers, 1958.

Muncy, Robyn. *Creating a Female Dominion in American Reform, 1890–1935*. New York: Oxford University Press, 1991.

Murray, Robert K. *The 103rd Ballot: Democrats and Disaster at Madison Square Garden*. New York: Harper and Row, 1976.

National Education Association. *Proceedings of the Sixty-ninth Annual Meeting Held at Los Angeles, California, June 27–July 3, 1931*. Vol. 69. Washington, D.C.: NEA, 1931.

Neely, Ruth, ed. *Women of Ohio: A Record of Their Achievements in the History of the State*. 3 vols. [Chicago]: S. J. Clarke, n.d.

Nestor, Agnes. *Woman's Labor Leader: An Autobiography*. Rockford, Ill.: Bellevue Books, 1954.

North, F. A. *The History of Jasper County, Missouri, Including a Condensed History of the State, a Complete History of Carthage and Joplin, Other Towns and Townships*. Des Moines: Mills, 1883.

Offen, Karen. "Defining Feminism: A Comparative Historical Approach." *Signs* 14 (autumn 1988): 119–57.

Olney, James, ed. *Autobiography: Essays Theoretical and Critical*. Princeton: Princeton University Press, 1980.

Olson, James S. *Historical Dictionary of the New Deal: From Inauguration to Preparation for War*. Westport, Conn.: Greenwood Press, 1985.

O'Neill, William. *Everyone Was Brave: The Rise and Fall of Feminism in America.* Chicago: Quadrangle Books, 1969.

———. *Feminism in America: A History.* 2d ed. New Brunswick: Rutgers University Press, 1994.

Parker, Raymond. "Descendants of William Blair (Traditionally Known as Robert I)." Grosse Point, Mich.: Anne Blair Dalby, 1987.

Parrish, William. *A History of Missouri: Volume III, 1860–1875.* Columbia: University of Missouri Press, 1973.

———. *Turbulent Partnership: Missouri and the Union, 1861–1865.* Columbia: University of Missouri Press, 1963.

Perry, Elizabeth. *Belle Moskowitz: Feminine Politics and the Exercise of Power in the Age of Alfred E. Smith.* New York: Oxford University Press, 1977.

———. "Training for Public Life: ER and Women's Political Networks in the 1920s." In *Without Precedent: The Life and Career of Eleanor Roosevelt,* ed. Joan Hoff-Wilson and Marjorie Lightman, 28–45. Bloomington: University of Indiana Press, 1984.

Pole, William. *The Evolution of Whist: A Study of the Progressive Changes which the Game Passed through from Its Origin to the Present.* New York: Longman, Green, 1894.

Porter, David L., ed. *Biographical Dictionary of American Sports.* Westport, Conn.: Greenwood Press, 1987.

Pratt, Ruth Baker. "The Lady or the Tiger." *Ladies Home Journal* 45 (May 1928): 8, 119.

Preston, Wheeler. *American Biographies.* Detroit: Gale Research, 1974.

Primm, James Neal. *Lion of the Valley: St. Louis, Missouri.* Boulder, Colo.: Pruett Publishing, 1981.

Renner, G. K. *Joplin, from Mining Town to Urban Center: An Illustrated History.* Northridge, Calif.: Windsor Publications in cooperation with the Joplin Historical Society, 1985.

Ritchie, Everett. *Guidebook to the Tri-State Mineral Museum.* Nixa, Mo.: A. J. Printing, 1986.

Robinson, Alice M., Vera Moury Roberts, and Milly S. Barranger, eds. *Notable Women in the American Theatre.* New York: Greenwood Press, 1989.

Roosevelt, Eleanor, and Lorena Hickok. *Ladies of Courage.* New York: G. P. Putnam's Sons, 1954.

Ross, Charles G. "Reed of Missouri." *Scribner's* 83 (February 1928): 151–62.

Ross, Ishbel. *Ladies of the Press: The Story of Women in Journalism by an Insider.* New York: Harper and Brothers, 1936.

Rothman, Sheila. *Woman's Proper Place: A History of Changing Ideas and Practices, 1870 to the Present.* New York: Basic Books, 1978.

Rucher, Frank W. *Walter Williams.* Columbia: University of Missouri Press, 1964.

Ryan, Mary P. *Womanhood in America: From Colonial Times to the Present.* New York: Franklin Watt, 1975.

Schnell, Christopher. "Missouri Progressives and the Nomination of FDR." *Missouri Historical Review* 68 (1974): 269–79.

Schranz, Ward. "The Story of the Carthage Light Guard: Some Historical Facts about a Famous Organization of This City." Carthage, Mo.: Carthage Public Library, October 10, 1931. Microfiche.

Scott, Anne Firor. "After Suffrage: Southern Women in the Twenties." *Journal of Southern History* 30 (August 1964): 298–318.

————. *Natural Allies: Women's Associations in American History.* Urbana: University of Illinois Press, 1992.

————. *The Southern Lady: From Pedestal to Politics, 1830–1930.* Chicago: University of Chicago Press, 1970.

Scott, Anne Firor, and Andrew McKay Scott. *One Half the People: The Fight for Woman Suffrage.* Urbana: University of Illinois Press, 1975.

Scott, Mary Semple, ed. "History of Woman Suffrage Movement in Missouri." *Missouri Historical Review* 14 (April/July 1920): 282–384.

Shaner, Dolph. *The Story of Joplin.* New York: Stratford House, 1948.

Shapiro, Michael Steven. *Child's Garden: The Kindergarten Movement from Froebel to Dewey.* University Park: Pennsylvania State University Press, 1983.

Sharf, Lois. *To Work and to Wed: Female Employment, Feminism, and the Great Depression.* Westport, Conn.: Greenwood Press, 1980.

Sharf, Lois, and Joan Jeson, eds. *Decades of Discontent: The Woman's Movement, 1920–1940.* Westport, Conn.: Greenwood Press, 1983.

Shoemaker, Floyd Calvin. *Missouri and Missourians: Land of Contrasts and People of Achievements.* 5 vols. Chicago: Lewis Publishing, 1943.

Showalter, Elaine, ed. *These Modern Women: Autobiographical Essays from the Twenties.* Old Westbury, N.Y.: Feminist Press, 1978.

Sicherman, Barbara, and Carol H. Green, eds. *Notable American Women, the Modern Period: A Biographical Dictionary.* Cambridge: Harvard University Press, Belknap Press, 1980.

Solomon, Barbara Miller. *In the Company of Educated Women: A History of Women and Higher Education in America.* New Haven: Yale University Press, 1985.

Stanton, Elizabeth Cady, Susan B. Anthony, Matilda Joslyn Gage, and Ida Husted Harper, eds. *History of Woman Suffrage.* 6 vols. 1881–1922. Reprint, New York: Arno Press, 1969.

Stoner, Kathryn H. *Twenty-Five Years of a Great Idea: A History of the National League of Women Voters.* Washington, D.C.: League of Women Voters, 1946.

Strom, Sharon Hartman. "Leadership and Tactics in the American Woman Suffrage Movement: A New Perspective from Massachusetts." *Journal of American History* 62 (September 1975): 296–315.

————. "Practical Idealists: Women's Politics and Culture in the New Deal Years." *Reviews in American History* 16:4 (1988): 604–11.

Tilly, Louise, and Patricia Gurin, eds. *Women, Politics, and Change.* New York: Russell Sage Foundation, 1990.

Trattner, Walter. *Crusade for the Children: A History of the National Labor Committee and Child Labor Reform in America.* Chicago: Quadrangle Books, 1970.

Uglow, Jennifer S., comp. *The Continuum Dictionary of Women's Biography.* New York: Continuum Publishing, 1989.

Waal, Carla, and Barbara Oliver Korner, eds. *Hardship and Hope: Missouri Women Writing about Their Lives, 1820–1920.* Columbia: University of Missouri Press, 1997.

Wagner-Martin, Linda. *Telling Women's Lives: The New Biography.* New Brunswick: Rutgers University Press, 1994.

Ware, Susan. *Beyond Suffrage: Women in the New Deal.* Cambridge: Harvard University Press, 1981.

————. "ER and Democratic Politics: Women in the Postsuffrage Era." In *Without Precedent: The Life and Career of Eleanor Roosevelt,* ed. Joan Hoff-Wilson and Marjorie Lightman, 46–60. Bloomington: University of Indiana Press, 1984.

————. *Holding Their Own: American Women in the 1930s.* Boston: Twayne, 1982.

Wheeler, Marjorie Spruill, ed. *Votes for Women! The Woman Suffrage Movement in Tennessee, the South, and the Nation.* Knoxville: University of Tennessee Press, 1995.

Williams, Walter, and Floyd Shoemaker. *Missouri: Mother of the West.* 5 vols. Chicago: American Historical Society, 1930.

Woodson, W. H. *History of Clay County, Missouri.* Topeka: Historical Publishing, 1920.

Young, William C. *Famous Actors and Actresses on the American Stage: Documents of American Theater History.* 2 vols. New York and London: R. R. Bowker, 1975.

Index

Abdullah, Achmed, 150, 150*n11*, 327, 327*n2*
Adams, John, 232
Adams, John Quincy, 106*n11*
Addams, Jane, 163–64, 164*n10*, 175*n10*, 179
Allen, B. B., 37*n2*
Allen, Florence, 254, 254*n3*, 356
Allen, Hervey, 327, 327*n2*
Almshouse campaign, 157, 157*n3*
Altgeld, John, 175*n10*
Anderson, Paul, 276, 276*n9*
Ankeney, J. S., xii, 44, 44*n2*
Archer, Mary, 220, 220*n10*, 225, 227, 288
Arnold, Philip, 6, 6*n6*
Astor, Lady Nancy, 225, 225*n4*
Atherton, Gertrude, 149, 149*n9*
Autobiography, xix, xx, xxi
Ayers, Amy, 12
Ayers, Emily, 11

Bailey, Eleanor, 254
Bailey, Temple, 310, 310*n8*
Baker, Newton, 189, 189*n8*, 264; and League of Nations, 207, 292; as presidential contender, 332, 339
Baldwin, Faith, 310, 310*n8*
Baltimore, burning of, 110, 111*n19*
Banister, Margaret, 274, 274*n5*
Banister, Marion, 279, 283, 293; and ENB, 223, 223*n2*, 274; in 1924 campaign, 305; and Woman's National Democratic Club, 223, 247, 276, 300
Barkley, Alben, 339, 340*n15*
Barkley, Dorothy Brower, 339, 339*n14*
Barrett, Kate Walker, 164, 164*n11*
Barrymore, Ethel, 162
Bass, Elizabeth, 173, 174*n8*, 189, 195, 199, 227, 284; at 1920 Democratic convention, 202, 290; as organizer of women, 194, 220, 222
Beale, Harriet Blaine, 245, 245*n16*

Beebe, Joe, 22
Belmont, Perry, 74, 74*n2*
Benton School, 23*n8*
Benton, Lizzie Wise, 105, 105*n8*
Benton, Maecenus E., 104, 104*n7*, 106
Benton, Thomas Hart (senator) 104, 211, 212*n26*
Benton, Thomas Hart (artist), 104, 104*n7*
Betts, Nannie, 37, 37*n2*
Bingham, Hiram, 338, 338*n10*
Bingham, Richmond F., 52, 104
Bigelow, William F., 143, 143*n2*, 307–8
Black, Winifred, 149, 149*n8*, 207
Blackstone, William, 98, 98*n1*
Blackwell, Alice Stone, 167, 167*n14*
Blaine, James G., 25, 25*n2*, 211, 212*n26*
Blair, Burt (brother-in-law), 315, 315*n8*
Blair, Christine, 329, 329*n5*
Blair, Emily Newell: ancestry of, 9–13, 107; birth of, xi, 6; and brother, 18, 21–23, 45, 89; and campaigns, 210–11, 345, 346–48; childhood and adolescence of, 3, 9, 57, 60, 64, 65, 73–74, 76, 77, 78; and Consumers' Advisory Board, xvi, 350, 351; death of, xvii; early political efforts of, 28, 136, 157, 158; education of, xiii, 18, 19, 61, 64, 69, 84; and father, 27, 29, 45, 66–67; feminism of, xv, xxii, 209; health of, xx, 314; and homemaking, 57–58, 69, 133, 134–35, 258, 275–76; and James Reed, xiv, 191, 193*n12*, 224, 319; marriage of, xiii, 90, 91, 91*n2*, 92–93, 94–96; in Missouri Democratic politics, 199, 200–201, 216–17, 342; and mother, 43, 68–69, 142, 313; on news reporters, 242; organizes Democratic women's clubs, xiv, 223–24, 231–32, 255–56, 262–63; personality of, xii, xiii, 21–22, 43, 52–53, 59, 64, 86–87, 91–92, 231; photos of, 119, 121, 122, 123, 125, 127, 128; on political organizing, 209, 260, 261, 272–73; and prohibition, 261;

reading of, 39–40, 49, 75–76, 108; and religion, 46–47; and Republican Party, 194, 201; and sisters, xiii, 22, 138; and Southern Comfort, 231; suffrage work of, xiv, 156–57, 157n2, 159, 162–66, 169–70, 173, 225–27, 330; teaches school, xiii, 83, 84; urged to run for congress, 330; and Woman's National Democratic Club, xv, 246, 312; and working with men, 74–75, 139, 144; and World War I, xiv, 179–80, 181, 187, 189, 190, 354; and World War II, xvi, xvii; writing career of, xiv, xv, xix, xxi, xxii, 140, 141, 143–47, 150–51, 198, 199, 199n6, 215–16, 307, 308–10, 327, 335–36
—And Democratic National Committee: elected to, xiv, 195, 196, 213, 216; meetings of, 217, 333, 341; reelected to, xv, 280–81, 295, 299; as resident committeewoman of, 221, 222–23, 227, 233; resigns from, xv, 327; as vice chair of, xv, 233n1, 304. See also Democratic National Committee; Democratic Party conventions; Woman's National Democratic Club
Blair, Harriet (daughter), 122, 123, 173, 315; and aunts, 316; birth of, xiii, 108, 109, 109n17, 111; education of, 61, 180, 275; manages Blair household, 307; marriage of, 316–17; as mother, 321, 330; at national conventions, 286, 287, 296
Blair, Harry (husband), 89, 96, 99–101, 109, 312, 316–17; career of, xiii, xvi, 80n10, 93, 98, 102–3, 112, 113, 114, 116, 138, 349, 356; education of, xiii, 101, 110, 112, 112n20; and ENB, 60, 89, 90–91; and ENB's career, xix, 140, 147, 221; health of, 314; marries, xiii, 92–93; photo of, 120, 122; and politics, 135, 200, 287, 295, 296, 335, 336, 340; and World War I, xiv, 180, 181, 184
Blair, Harry Wallace II (grandson), 356
Blair, John (father-in-law), 93n3
Blair, Mary Jane Pittinger (mother-in-law), 93n3
Blair, Newell (son), 173, 329, 339; at 1924 convention, 286, 296; and aunts, 316; and autobiography, xx; childhood of, xiii, 132, 132n1, 314; in Dearmont campaign, 343; education of, 274, 328, 330; marries, 356; photo of, 123; and

segregation, 328; and World War I, 181, 183
Bland, Richard, 105, 105n10
Blow, Susan, 83n6
Bok, Edward, 187, 188n5
Bonfils, Charles A., 149, 149n8
Bonsal, Henrietta Fairfax Morris, 247, 247n17
Boon, Sallie, 15, 15n4, 30, 52, 59
Bowers, Claude, 109, 109n16, 207, 321
Breckinridge, Madge, 163, 163n9
Briles, B. S., 54, 54n4
Brinkerhoff, Anna, 15, 15n4
Brookings, Robert, 33, 33n3
Brooks, Sarah, 18n1
Brown, Anne Goodner Forsythe, xx, 330, 330n6
Brown, Dorothy, 275n5
Brown, Helen, 275n5
Brown, John, 74–75, 74n3
Brown, Laura, 209, 209n25, 213, 215, 224, 274
Brown, Lou, 44, 44n2
Bryan, Charles, 301, 305
Bryan, Miller, 134n4
Bryan, Pauline, 134n4
Bryan, William Jennings, 30, 30n9, 195, 202, 251, 298; Cross of Gold speech, 75, 75n4; in Joplin, 159–60, 160n6; on Klan, 293; and Al Smith, 296–97
Buchman, Frank, 352, 352n6
Bugbee, Emma, 336, 336n8
Butler, Nicholas Murray, 103, 103n4
Byrd, Harry, 340, 340n15

Caffee, A. H., 41n8
Caffee, Anna Belle, 33, 33n2, 73, 73n1, 78
Caffee, Arthur, 107
Caffee, Jessie, 15, 15n4, 22, 30, 96; death of, 329, 329n4; and ENB, 52; marries, 89, 89n13
Caffee, Lacie, 30
Caffee, William, 33n2
Caffee family, 108
Calhoun, W. L., xii, 82, 82n2, 139
Cantrill, Carrie Payne, 283, 283n1
Carney, Ann, 281n17
Carthage, xi, xiii, 197; businesses in, 26, 26nn3,4; Cooperative Kitchen, 138, 138n8; description of, 14–15, 25–26, 29, 41; and ENB, 276; history of, 7–8, 7n11; and Joplin, 79; photos of, 118; schools

in, 19–21, 22–24; society in, xi–xii, 32–34, 37, 38, 54–55, 133–34, 134–35
Carthage High School, xiii
Carthage Light Guard, 32, 32*n1*, 53
Cassini, Marguerite, 110, 110*n18*
Castle, Irene, 212, 212*n27*
Catt, Carrie Chapman, 170, 176, 185, 185*n1*, 190; description of, 169–70, 169*n3*; and ENB, xiv, 173, 180; photo of, 124; and politics, 169–70, 174, 199, 220
Cermak, Anton J., 268, 268*n3*, 330, 338
Chappell, Julia. *See* Newell, Julia
Chappell, Philip, 316
Chicago World's Fair, 58–59
Children's Bureau, 175*n10*, 234
Church, Henry Seymore, 34*n5*
Church, Katherine Gray, 34*n5*
Church, Margaretta, 34
Churchill, Winston, 237
Civil War, in Missouri, 29, 29*n8*
Clark, Bennett, 217, 344, 344*n4*
Clark, James Beauchamp, 105, 105*n10*, 115, 210–11, 311
Clarke, Ida Clyde, 165, 165*n12*
Clarkson, Edna, 34, 34*n4*
Clarkson, Grosvenor, 186, 186*n2*
Clarkson, James D., 34*n4*
Clarkson, Mary, 34, 34*n4*
Clarkson, Pearl, 34, 34*n4*
Clay, Henry, 163, 298
Clement, Ellis Meredith. *See* Meredith, Ellis
Cleveland, Grover, 25, 25*n2*, 211
Cobb, Frank, 279, 279*n14*
Cockran, Annie Ide, 245, 245*n16*
Cockran, Bourke, 202, 202*n14*
Cockrell, Francis, 105, 106*n10*
Collins, Margaretta Forsythe, xx, 330, 330*n6*
Consumers' Advisory Board of NRA, xvi, 164*n11*, 350–51, 350*n3*
Consumers' League, 161*n7*, 179*n1*
Cook, Nancy, 285, 285*n3*
Coolidge, Calvin, 301, 302
Cooperative Kitchen of Carthage, 138, 138*n8*
Corbett, Jim, 44
Cortelyou, George, 102, 102*n1*, 103
Costigan, Mabel, 301, 301*n3*
Coulter, Eva, 305, 305*n8*
Council of National Defense: men on, 194*n14*; women on, 168*n1*, 179*n2*, 185*n1*, 186*n1*, 187*n3*, 189*n7*. *See also*

Woman's Committee, Council of National Defense
Cowgill, Anna, 134*n4*
Cowgill, Henry, 22, 22*n5*, 75*n4*, 134*n4*
Cowles, Ione Virginia Hill, 185, 185*n1*
Cox, James, 206, 206*n18*, 207*n20*, 211, 228
Creation of a Home, xv
Cromwell, Oliver, 261
Culahan, Richard, xxi
Cummings, Cecelia, 349
Cummings, Homer, 207, 207*n21*, 283, 284, 334, 349
Cunningham, Byrd, 15, 15*n4*
Cunningham, Gretchen Dau, 318, 318*n2*, 321
Cunningham, Minnie Fisher, 247, 248*n18*, 294, 311

Damien, Father, 149, 150*n10*
Daniels, Addie Worth, 340, 340*n15*
Daugherty, James F., 48, 48*n7*
Davis, Ellen Graham Bassell, 295
Davis, John W., 278*n13*; and ENB, 299, 301–2; and organizing women, 300; as presidential candidate, 278, 293, 295, 298
Davis, Katherine, 175, 175*n11*
Davis, Maxine, 336, 336*n8*
DeArmond, David, 105, 105*n10*
Dearmont, Russell, 342, 342*n1*
Democratic National Committee: and Dewson, 333*n2*; and ENB, xi, xiv, xv, xvi, 193, 217; meetings of, 218–20, 277, 299, 333–34, 333*n3*; men on 195*n16*, 206*n18*, 207*n21*, 218*n6*, 240*n8*, 284*n2*, 291*n1*, 296*n5*; organization of, 222, 282; purpose of, 217; and state committees, 263; women on, 163*n9*, 207*n19*, 221*n11*, 227, 229*n7*, 263, 277*n11*, 278, 292*n2*, 322, 322*n7*, 340*n15*
Democratic Party: 50–50 rule, 263–64; in Missouri, 199, 200–201, 200n10, 216–17, 280, 280*n16*; in New York, 266–67; and organizing women, 223–24, 260, 262–63
—Conventions: in 1916, 171–72, 171*n5*; in 1920, 202, 202*n14*, 204–8; in 1924, 216*n4*, 262, 269, 282–83, 292, 294; in 1928, 318, 319, 320; in 1932, 334–35, 339, 341
Dennett, Mary Ware, 163, 163*n9*
Dern, George Henry, 265, 265*n3*
Dern, Lottie Brown, 265, 265*n3*

Deutsch, Albert, 55, 56*n6*
Dewson, Mary, 333, 333*n2*, 345, 352
Dix, Dorothy, 150, 150*n10*, 207
Dockweiler, Isidore, 278, 278*n13*
Dodd, S. C. T., 49, 49*n8*
Dressler, Marie, 168, 168*n2*, 226
Drew, John, 62, 62*n2*
Dudley, Anne Dallas, 174, 174*n9*
Duse, Eleanora, 168, 168*n2*

Edwards, Elizabeth, 204
Ellis, Breckinridge, 152, 152*n14*
Ellis Island, 114
Embree, Frances, 37, 37*n3*
Engle, Lavinia, 340, 340*n15*
Erving, Emma Lootz, 274, 274*n2*, 275
Essary, Fred, 243, 243n14, 321

Fabyan, Florence, 52, 52*n1*, 59, 104
Fabyan, Helen, 275–76, 276*n8*
Fairbank, Janet, 292, 292*n2*
Fairfaix, Beatrice, 150, 150*n10*
Farley, Florence, 277, 278*n12*, 321, 322
Farley, James A., 334, 334*n4*, 335, 337
Farrar, John, 327, 327*n2*
Farrar, Margaret, 327, 327*n2*
Farrar and Rinehart, xx
Federal Trade Commission, 103, 103*n3*
Feminism, xv, xxii, 155, 158, 187
Ferber, Edna, 207, 208*n23*
Ferguson, James E., 171, 172*n6*
Ferguson, Miriam Amanda Wallace, 172*n6*
Flanders, Ella Jean, 281
Fleeson, Doris, 336, 336*n8*
Fleming, Emily Gray, 6, 6*n7*
Fleming, Joseph Allen, 6, 6*n7*
Flintermann, Greta, 341, 341*n17*
Folk, Joseph, 218, 218*n5*
Fordney-McCumber Tariff, 256, 256*n7*
Forsythe, Harriet Blair. *See* Blair, Harriet
Forsythe, Newton Melville, 88, 88*n12*, 316, 336
Franklin, Pa., xi, 3, 4, 49, 50
Fred Harvey Restaurant, 97, 97*n7*
Frick, Henry, 50, 50*n9*
Frick, Lulu, 64, 64*n6*
Froebel, Friedrich, 83*n6*
Funk, Antoinette, 163, 163*n9*, 185, 185*n1*, 206–7, 247
Furman, Bess, 336, 336*n8*
Frost, Gene, 335, 335*n6*

Galbraith, William, 12

Gale, Zona, 165, 165*n12*
Gardner, Frederick, 288, 288*n5*
Gardner, Jeanette Vosburgh, 289, 239*n7*
Garfield, James R., 102, 102*n2*, 103, 106, 107, 112, 115
Gellhorn, Edna, 205, 205*n17*
General Federation of Women's Clubs, 164*n9*, 205*n16*
General Slocum, 113, 113*n22*
Gentry, William, 314, 314*n7*
George Washington University Law School, xiii
Gilman, Charlotte Perkins, 155, 155*n18*
Glass, Carter, 257*n8*; and Democratic Party, 202, 203*n14*; 218, 219, 293, 340; ENB gives dinner for, 241; and League of Nations, 292; and political women, 206, 295
Golden Lane: ENB suggests, xiv; photo of, 124
Goltra, Edward: and ENB, 195, 195*n16*, 208; and national committee, 219, 281; at 1924 convention, 285, 286, 295; and suffrage, 220
Good Housekeeping, xi, xv, 346
Goucher College, xii, xiii, 64
Grace Episcopal Church, Carthage, 15, 15*n3*, 45, 45*n3*, 132, 132*n1*
Gray, Carl R., 53, 53*n3*
Gray, Elisha Burritt (grandfather), 10*n3*, 12
Gray, Emily Jane (cousin), 61, 61*n1*
Gray, Josephine Cecelia McDowell (great-aunt), 61*n1*
Gray, Margaretta Rachel McDowell (grandmother), 10*n3*, 11
Gray, Margaretta (aunt), 11*n4*
Gray, Philander E. (great-uncle), 61*n1*
Greeley, Horace, 3
Greene, Sarah, 281
Grenfell, Helen, 207, 207*n22*
Guffey, Joseph, 345, 345*n5*

Hadley, Herbert, 137, 137*n7*, 148
Hague, Frank, 171, 172*n6*, 269, 279
Halliburton, J. W., 27, 27*n5*
Hallinan, C. T., 161
Hamby, William H., 144, 144*n3*, 145, 146, 148, 153
Hamilton, Alexander, 232, 261
Hamlin, Huybertie, 246, 247, 247*n17*
Hanna, Marcus, 110, 111*n19*, 162, 236

Hard, Anne, 243, 243*n15*, 245–46, 274, 321

Hard, William, 155, 155*n18*, 243, 244–45, 336

Harding, Florence, 202, 202*n12*

Harding, H. H., 15, 15*n3*, 36, 37*n2*

Harding, Warren, 203, 203*n15*, 217, 275, 275*n7*

Hare, Constance Livingstone, 288, 288*n6*

Harlan, John, 112, 112*n21*

Harriman, Florence (Daisy), 174, 174*n9*; gives Democratic dinners, 236–40; and woman's National Democratic Club, xv, 246–47

Harris, Cora, 165, 165*n12*

Harris, William T., 83*n6*

Harrison, Byron Patton, 216, 216*n4*, 219, 240, 284, 304

Harrison, Cora, 83*n5*

Harrison, D. A., 37, 37*n2*

Hawes, Harry, 325, 324*n10*, 326

Hay, Charles, 319, 319*n3*, 344

Hays, William, 194, 194*n13*

Hearst, William Randolph, 149, 149*n9*, 211

Hendricks, Thomas, 25, 25*n2*, 211

Heflin, James Thomas, 229, 229*n7*

Herrick, Fannie Field, 247, 489*n18*

Herrick, Genevieve, 336

Higgins, Charles, 191, 191*n10*, 192

Hitchcock, Frank H., 102, 102*n2*, 103, 115

Hoar, George, 211, 212*n26*

Hobby, Oveta Culp, xvii

Hodges, Leigh, 43, 43*n1*, 44, 45

Hodges, Sybil, 43, 43*n1*, 44, 45, 59

Holmes, Mary J., 213, 213*n28*

Homestead strike, 49

Hoover, Herbert, xvi, 226; and ENB, 225; as presidential candidate in 1920, 201–2, 202*n12*; in 1928, 321, 322, 324, 326; in 1932, 333, 335

Hoover, Lou Henry, 202*n12*

Hosmer Hall, 81*n1*

Houston, Mrs. Fred B., 33, 33*n3*

Howe, Louis, 333, 334*n4*, 335

Hughes, Charles Evans, 302, 302*n5*

Hull, Cordell, 229, 250, 277, 287, 288, 293, 301; as chairman of DNC, 220, 220*n9*, 256, 257; and ENB, xiv, xv, 221, 223, 232, 233, 233*n1*, 234; ENB on, 232, 338; insulted by Al Smith, 338; at 1924 national convention, 262, 282, 284, 287, 290, 291, 294, 296, 297; at 1932 national convention, 334, 337, 340–41; political views of, 237; supports women in party, 220, 223, 246, 264

Hull, Rose Frances Whitney, 277, 277*n10*, 288, 296, 297, 339

Hull House, 164*n10*, 175*n10*, 205*n16*

Hunt, Bessie, 15, 15*n4*

Huntley, Ted, 321, 321*n5*

Jackson, Dorothy Witter Branch, 265, 265*n3*, 277, 300

Jackson, Fannie, 15, 15*n4*

Jackson, Robert, 265, 265*n3*, 346*n6*

Jacobs, Pattie, 164, 164*n11*, 204, 294

James, Jesse, 7, 7*n10*

Jefferson, Thomas, 232, 261

Jenkins, Mattie (Mrs. Burris), xiv, 208, 208*n24*, 216*n2*

Jobe, Grace, 272, 272*n6*

Johnson, Mary Wright, 228*n6*

Johnston, Mary, 165, 165*n12*

Jones, Andrieus, 240, 240*n8*

Jones, Jessie, 311, 311*n2*, 318

Jones, Natalie, 246, 247*n17*, 250, 251

Joplin, Missouri, xi, 4, 198; and Carthage, 79; House of Lords in, 80, 80*n9*; and mining, 4, 4*n1*, 5, 7, 197–98; photos of, 118; W. J. Bryan visits, 159–60; T. Roosevelt visits, 104*n6*

Julian, Henry, 158, 158*n5*

Julian, Laura Betty, 328

Julian, Winifred Whitsett, 158

Kahn, Florence Prag, 333, 333*n3*

Kansas City, Mo., 3, 162

Keith's Theater, 280, 280*n15*

Kellogg, Frank Billings, 252, 252*n2*

Kemball, Alice Mary, 153

Kemper, William, 281, 281*n18*

Kendall, Madge, 62, 62*n2*

Kendrick, Eula Wulfjen, 246, 247*n17*

Kent, Frank, 243, 243*n13*, 336

Key, Ellen, 155, 155*n18*

Killick, Arthur, 152, 152*n14*

Kimball, Alice Mary, 150, 150*n11*

Kipling, Rudyard, 218

Knapp, Martin A., 103*n5*

Kreisler, Fritz, 82, 82*n3*

Ku Klux Klan, 260, 292, 293, 294

Labor and Commerce, Department of, 102, 102*n1*

La Follette, Robert, 301, 301*n2*

Lamar, Clarinda Huntington Pendleton, 185, 186*n1*

Langtry, Lily, 62, 62*n*

Lathrop, Julia, 175, 175*n10*

League of Nations, 195, 207, 294; Reed opposes, 200*n9*, 206; support for, 210, 216, 292, 332

League of Women Voters, 175*n10*, 202*n14*, 205*n17*, 208*n24*, 311, 318; citizenship schools of, 255; conventions of, 199, 199*nn5,7*, 224, 224*n3*, 225–27; and ENB, xiv, 211, 330, 330*n7*; and political parties, 201, 202, 206, 210, 294

Lee, Robert E., 109

Lenin, Vladimir, 261

Lewis, J. Hamilton, 191, 191*n11*, 192, 193, 279

Lewis, Wilmot Harsant, 242, 242*n11*

Linthicum, Richard, 222, 222*n1*

Loeb, William, 115, 155*n28*

Logan, John A., 25, 25*n2*

Long, Breckinridge, 219, 219*n8*

Long, Huey, 340, 340*n15*

Long, Ray, 145, 145*n5*, 307

Longworth, Alice Roosevelt, 110, 100*n18*, 203, 238, 245, 246, 297, 336, 340

Love, Robertus, 152, 152*n14*

Lovejoy, Owen, 175, 175*n11*

Lowden, Florence, 202, 202*n12*

Lowell, Abbott Lawrence, 188, 188*n6*

Lubin, Isador, 237, 237*n3*

Mack, Harriet Taggart, 297, 340, 340*n15*

Mack, Norman, 284, 284*n2*, 285, 295, 297, 299, 340

MacMahon, Arthur, 194, 194*n14*

Madison, James, 232

Mallon, Winifred, 336, 336*n8*

Marbury, Elizabeth, 267; and DNC, 266, 282, 333; and ENB, 297, 299; on New York, 270; at 1924 convention, 285, 292, 295, 297; personality of, 229, 229*n7*; and School of Democracy, 269, 272

Mardick, Ruth, 336

Marsh, Wilbur, 218, 218*n5*

Marshall Field's, 212, 212*n27*

Martin, Katherine, 200–201, 200*n10*, 206

Mathews, Annie, 268, 268*n4*

Matthews, Daniel, 20*n2*

McAddo, William G., 38, 38*n4*, 233; ENB on, 297–98; at 1920 Democratic convention, 206*n18*, 207; and 1924 Democratic convention, 278, 279,

282, 284, 290, 291, 293, 300; at 1932 Democratic convention, 219*n8*, 337, 338

McAllister, Dorothy, 221, 221*n12*

McAllister, Thomas Francis, 221*n12*

McCawley, A. L., 264, 264*n2*

McCormick, Anne O'Hare, 332, 332*n1*, 336, 340

McCormick, Katharine Dexter, 185, 185*n1*

McCormick, Ruth, 236, 246; and ENB, 194–95, 217; ENB on, 161–62, 161*n7*; at Republican conventions, 203, 320; and Republican Party, 194, 199; and suffrage, 167

McDougal, Myrtle Archer, 277, 277*n11*, 282, 284

McDowell, Alexander (great-great-grandfather), xi, 11, 11*n5*, 107, 107*n12*

McDowell, Alexander (cousin), 65, 65*n8*, 105, 106

McDowell, Frances Galbraith (great-aunt), 50, 50*n10*, 62–63, 62*n3*, 102, 110

McDowell, John, 64, 64*n7*, 107

McDowell, Mary E., 204, 205*n16*

McDowell, Sarah Parker, 107, 107*n12*, 317

McDowell, Thomas Skelley, 11

McDowell, William, 110

McDowell, Willis, 64*n6*

McElree, W. E., 84*n8*

McKeogh, Arthur, 236, 236*n1*

McKinley, William, 30, 30*n9*, 102, 111*n19*

McMillan, Lucille Foster, 277, 278*n12*, 292

McNallie family, 87, 87*n11*

McReynolds, Allen, 139, 139*n10*, 216

McReynolds, Samuel, 27, 27*n5*

Meigs, Margaret Wister, 247, 248*n18*

Meloney, Marie, 202*n13*

Meredith, Ellis, 195, 195*n17*, 222

Michelson, Charles, 242–43, 243*n13*, 333

Miller, Emma Guffey, 339, 340*n15*, 345

Miller, Helen Guthrie, 158, 158*n5*, 159, 179, 191

Mills, Dorothy Randolph Fell, 245, 245*n16*

Mining, in Tri-State District, 5*n5*, 137–38, 197–98

Missouri Democratic politics: and ENB, 346; in 1928, 319, 326; in 1932, 335, 337, 342–44; and Pendergast, 342, 343–44

Missouri Equal Suffrage Association, 156*n1*, 158*n5*

Missouri Woman, xiv, 159, 177

Missouri Women's Press Association, 148*n6*, 151, 151*n12*

Missouri Writers' Guild, 151*n13*, 152, 200*n10*

Mitchell, Ewing, 334–35, 334*n5*, 337

Modjeska, Helena, 58, 58*n7*

Moffet, E. R., 4*n1*

Montgomery, Mrs. R. A., 33, 33*n3*

Mooneyham, Robert A., 135

Moore, Edmond, 206, 206*n18*

Moore, Martha, 87, 87*n11*

Moore, Mary Eva Perry, 185, 185*n1*

Morgantheau, Elinor, 332, 332*n1*

Morgantheau, Henry, 332, 332*n1*

Morris, Clara, 47, 47*n5*

Moseley, Edward S., 103*n5*

Moskowitz, Belle, 340, 340*n15*

Mullen, Arthur F., 304, 304*n7*

Murphy, Charles Francis, 267, 268–69, 268*n2*

Murphy, Patrick, 4, 4*n2*

Mussolini, Benito, 261

National American Woman Suffrage Association: Citizenship School of, 199; conventions of, 162, 163, 173, 174–76, 198–99; and Golden Lane demonstration, 170–71, 208*n24*; officers of, 158*n5*, 161*n7*, 163*n9*, 164*nn9,11*, 167*n14*, 168*n1*, 169*n3*, 179*n1*, 185*n1*, 205*n16*, 206*n18*, 207*n19*, 208*n24*; subsidiaries of, 163*n9*, 164*n9,11*, 165*n12*, 168*n1*, 169*n3*, 170*n4*, 174*n9*, 205*nn16,17*, 227

National Committee on the Cause and Cure of War, 164*n11*

National Consumers' Advisory Board. *See* Consumers' Advisory Board of NRA

National Education Association, 329, 329*n3*

National Recovery Administration. *See* Consumers' Advisory Board of NRA

National School of Democracy, 266, 272–73

Nestor, Agnes, 185, 186*n1*

New Deal, 353

Newell, Anna (sister), 9, 170, 180, 352; birth of, xi, 3, 9*n1*; career of, 171*n4*, 311, 311*n1*, 329, 329*n3*; childhood of, 35, 57, 70; death of, 314, 355; death of father, 69; education of, 81, 81*n1*, 138*n9*; on ENB, 160

Newell, Anna Gray (mother), xi, 142; death of, 313; death of husband, 66, 71–72; and employment, xiii, 5, 6*n6*, 40, 68–69; marriage of, 3, 4, 4*n3*; personality of, xiii, 5, 29–30, 35, 40, 43, 56–57, 59, 68–69, 81, 82, 142, 313; and religion, 45, 71–72; and society, 34, 54; suggests ENB review books, 307; and Woodrow Wilson, 279; and World's Fair, 58

Newell, C. Edward (uncle), 50, 50*n11*

Newell, David (uncle), 9, 9*n2*, 313, 316

Newell, Ella (sister), 300, 306, 314; birth of, xi, 35, 35*n6*; childhood of, xiii, 35, 71; death of father, 66, 69; marries, 142*n1*, 316

Newell, Huey (grandfather), 9–10, 9*n2*

Newell, James Patton (father), xi, 4, 213; and Civil War, xi, 6, 6*n9*; death of, xiii, 66; description of, 3, 6, 29; employment of, xi, xiii, 6*n8*, 8, 8*n12*, 41; and ENB, 29; marries, 4; and religion, 45; and World's Fair, 58

Newell, James Patton (brother), 9, 30, 57, 111, 313; birth of, xi, 6*n7*; and business, xiii, 68, 81, 138; death of father, 66; and ENB, xii, 16, 21–23, 44, 45, 60; marriages of, 89, 89*n13*, 329, 355; and mother, 45

Newell, Jennie (aunt), 10

Newell, Jessie Caffee. *See* Caffee, Jessie

Newell, Julia (sister), 138*n9*, 313; birth of, xi, 16, 16*n5*; childhood of, xiii, 71, 95; death of father, 69; education of, 82, 82*n4*, 111; marries, 142*n1*, 316; on Missouri, xiii

Newell, Louisa Hoosey (grandmother), 9, 9*n2*

Newell, Margaretta (sister), 180, 235, 295, 313; birth of, xi, 35, 35*n6*; childhood of, xiii, 35, 69, 71; education of, 138*n9*, 316

Newell family, xii, 38–42

New Orleans, 212–13

New York, 177, 266, 269

Nichols, (John) Beverly, 327, 327*n2*

Norris, Frank, 149, 149*n9*

Norris, George, 239

Norris, Kathleen, 310, 310*n8*

Norton, Mary J., 172*n6*, 269

Nugent, John F., 171, 172*n6*

Nutting, Wallace, 274, 274*n3*

O'Day, Caroline, 267, 267*n1*

Ogden, Esther, 164, 164*n11*, 222, 285

O'Keefe, Cara, 134*n4*
O'Keefe, John, 134*n4*
Oklahoma, 5, 5*n4*, 259–60
Olesen, Annie Dickey, 202, 202*n14*, 252, 345
O'Neil, Barbara, 208, 208*n24*, 243
O'Neil, Madge, 303*n6*
O'Neill, Callista, 153, 153*n16*
O'Neill, Rose, 152–54, 152*n15*
Ortt, Nathalie, 163, 163*n8*
Oulahan, Richard Victor, 242, 242*n12*
Oursler, Fulton, 327, 327*n2*, 349
Oursler, Grace, 327, 327*n2*
Owen, Daisy Deane Hester, 206, 207*n19*
Owen, Robert, 207*n19*
Owen, Ruth Bryan, 345, 345*n5*
Oxford Group, 352
Ozarks, 315

Paige, Clara Paul, 331, 331*n8*
Paige, Mabeth, 204, 205*n16*
Palmer, A. Mitchell, 182, 182*n3*, 206, 206*n18*
Park, Guy B., 344, 344*n3*
Park, Maude Wood, 204, 204*n16*
Parker, Valeria, 204, 205*n16*
Parran, Thomas, 198, 198*n3*
Pattangall, Gertrude McKenzie, 249, 249n1, 265, 278
Pattangall, William, 249, 249*n1*, 265
Patterson, Eleanor, 245, 245*n16*
Patterson, Hannah, 185, 186, 186*n1*, 189, 190
Paul, W. S., 6*n8*
Pendergast, Thomas, 286, 286*n4*, 335, 342, 343–44
Pendergast machine, xiv
Pennybacker, Anna Hardwicke, 204, 205*n16*
Pere Marquette Railway, 4
Perkins, Frances, 355–56, 356*n8*
Perkins, Joseph D., 116
Phelps, William, 28, 28*n6*, 37
Phillips, Lena Madesin, 345, 345*n5*
Phillips, Roland, 141
Pinchot, Cornelia Bryce, 204, 205, 205*n16*
Pinchot, Gifford, 103, 103*n4*
Pitman, Key, 171, 171*n6*
Pitt, William, 261
Platt, Thomas, 211, 212*n26*
Plumer, Arnold, 12, 12*n6*
Political parties: nature of, 353; organizing

methods of, 302, 303–4; purpose of, 261, 294
Polk, Frank, 295, 295*n4*
Pomerene, Atlee, 241, 241*n10*, 253, 254
Pomerene, Mary Helen Bockius, 241, 241*n10*
Presidential campaign of 1924, 300, 303, 305, 345
Prohibition, 202, 253, 260, 261, 294, 320, 323, 338
Putnam, Ann, 134*n4*, 275
Putman, Ella. *See* Newell, Ella
Putnam, Harry, 134*n4*, 275, 275*n7*
Putman, Ralph, 316, 316*n10*
Pyke, Bernice, 206, 206*n18*, 227, 264, 278, 284

Quantrill, William, 7, 7*n10*
Quay, Matthew, 65, 65*n8*
Quin, Aylitt Buckner, 272, 272*n6*

Ralston, Samuel M., 278, 278*n13*, 291, 293
Rankin, Jeanette, 179, 179*n1*
Raskob, John Jakob, 257, 257*n8*, 322, 323, 333
Rayburn, Samuel, 234, 234*n2*
Reed, James A., 217; and ENB, xiv, 192, 193, 216*n3*, 224, 243, 244, 319, 346; and national conventions, 200, 200*n9*, 206, 319, 334–35, 337; opposes woman suffrage, xiv, 190, 190*n9*, 191; and Pendergast, xiv, 342
Reed, Mary Cecelia Waterbury, 349
Reed, Stanley, 349, 349*n2*
Reed, Winifred, 349, 349*n19*
Rehan, Ada, 58*n7*, 62, 62*n2*
Reid, Florence, 281, 281*n19*
Reilley, Caroline, 189, 189*n7*
Republican Party: national committee, 161*n7*, 185*n1*, 194*n13*, 202*n12*; national conventions, 201–2, 202*n12*, 203, 320, 335–36
Rice family, 87, 87*n11*
Riis, Jacob, 103, 103*n4*, 115, 115*n26*
Rinehart, Mary Roberts, 310, 310*n8*, 327, 327*n2*
Rinehart, Stanley M., Jr., 327, 327*n2*
Ritchie, Albert, 225, 225*n4*, 226, 238, 340
Roach, Gene, 199, 199*n8*, 200
Robins, Margaret Dreier, 173, 174*n8*, 175, 175*n11*, 194
Robinson, Ewilda G. Miller, 240, 240*n6*
Robinson, Joseph T., 239, 239*n5*, 240, 325

Rockefeller, John D., 49
Roessler, Reuben, 37, 37*n2*
Rogers, Will, 79, 304, 336
Romjue, Andrew, 344, 344*n4*
Roosevelt, Alice. *See* Longworth, Alice
  Roosevelt
Roosevelt, Edith, 104, 104*n6*
Roosevelt, Eleanor, 265; at 1924
  convention, 294, 296; description of,
  271–72; and ENB, 295, 299, 323, 332,
  341, 344–45; in New York politics, 266,
  267, 267*n1*
Roosevelt, Franklin D., 265; campaigns
  of, xvi, xi, 267, 348; and Dewson, 345;
  and ENB, 207, 207*n20*, 333; and 1932
  convention, 207*n21*, 334–35, 339, 341
Roosevelt, Theodore, 115, 270; death of,
  195, 195*n15*; Tennis Cabinet of, 103,
  103*n4*, visits Joplin, 104, 104*n6*
Root, Elihu, 155, 155*n19*
Roper, Daniel, 218, 219*n7*, 334, 350
Rose, Malcolm, 350, 351*n4*
Rose's Store, 8, 35, 35*n7*, 43
Ross, Nellie Tayloe, 171, 172*n6*, 322,
  322*n7*, 330, 345
Ross, Sadie, 15, 15*n4*
Rude, Anna, 204, 205*n16*
Rumsey, Mary Harriman, 351, 351*n4*
Ryan, Evelyn Althea, 348, 348*n7*

Sabert, W. T., 85
Sabin, Pauline Morton, 338, 338*n10*
Salt Lake City, 264
San Francisco, 99, 100
Sanger, Margaret, 163*n9*
Sarcoxie, xiii, 84–86, 87–88
Sargeant, Miss, 87
Sayers, Royd, 198
Schriener, Olive, 155, 155*n18*
Sears, Amelia, 268, 268*n3*, 330
Sedalia, Mo., 324, 324*n9*
Sergeant, John B., 4*n1*
Sewanee, Tenn.: University of the South,
  xix
Sewell, Mary, 110, 100*n19*
Sewell, William J., 100*n19*, 110
Shafroth-Palmer amendment, 161*n7*
Sharp, Dallas Lore, 254, 255*n4*
Shartel, Cassius, 105*n9*
Shaver, Clement, 301, 322; as chairman of
  DNC, 296, 296*n5*, 299, 300, 321; and
  ENB, 299, 304; ENB on, 304; photo of,
  125; Will Rogers on, 304

Shaw, Anna Howard: and Council of
  National Defense, xiv, 185, 188, 188–89;
  death of, 189; description of, 168–69,
  168*n1*, 176; on flattery, 139; photo of,
  125
Shaw, George Bernard, 90, 90*n1*
Sheffield, Jeannie, 35, 35*n7*
Sherman, John, 63, 63*n5*, 111*n19*
Shippey, Lee, 152, 152*n14*
Shipstead, Henrik, 252, 252*n2*
Shook, Edgar, 343, 343*n2*
Shouse, Catherine Filene Dodd, 247,
  247*n17*
Shouse, Jouette, 257, 257*n8*, 330, 333, 337
Smith, Alfred E.: and Bryan, 296–97;
  ENB on, 268, 268*n2*, 270–71, 298, 338;
  insults Hull, 338; in 1924 presidential
  race, 160, 270–71, 278, 282, 284; in
  1928 presidential race, 257*n8*, 318, 322;
  and prohibition, 320, 323, 338; public
  reaction to, 270–71, 323–25; religion of,
  323; in Sedalia, Mo., 324
Smith, Catherine, 296, 296*n6*, 339
Smith, Emily, 339, 339*n11*
Smith, Herbert Knox, 115, 115*n27*
Snell, Mrs. Frank Hiram, 247, 247*n17*
Snowdon, George, 49, 50*n9*
Sothern, Edward A., 47, 47*n5*
Springs, Lena Jones, 277, 278*n12*, 292
Stone, William, 28, 28*n7*, 171, 218*n5*
Strunsky, Simeon, 208, 208*n23*
Suffrage: and ENB, 156–57, 159, 162,
  165–66, 173, 195; and Missouri 1914
  campaign, 162; amendment passed, xiv;
  Shafroth-Palmer amendment, 161*n7*.
  See also National American Woman
  Suffrage Association
Sullivan, Mark, 207, 207*n23*, 241
Swan, Olive B., 287
Swofford, Jewel, 337, 337*n9*

Taafe, Martha, 170, 170*n4*, 275
Taft, William Howard, 137, 137*n7*,
  175*n10*, 188, 190
Taggert, Thomas, 291, 291*n1*, 293
Tammany Hall, 268
Tarbell, Ida, xiv, 185, 185*n1*, 186, 187, 190
Taylor, Fletch, 7*n10*
Thomas, M. Carey, 163, 163*n9*
Thomas, William Isaac, 167, 167*n13*
Thompson, Malvina, 341, 341*n16*
Thomson, Genevieve, 311, 311*n1*, 344
Tiffany, Katrina, 174, 174*n9*

Tulsa, Oklahoma, 260
Tumulty, Joseph, 292, 292*n3*

Ullmann, Frances, 327, 327*n1*
Underwood, Oscar, 206, 278, 278*n13*, 293
University of Missouri, xiii, 84, 151, 151*n13*
Upshur, William, 292, 292*n3*
Upton, Harriet Taylor: and ENB, 226, 226*n5*, 227; photo of, 126

Van Devanter, Willis, 112, 112*n21*
Van Kleeck, Mary, 187, 187*n4*
Van Namee, George R., 324, 324*n8*
Vest, George, 105, 106*n10*
Vicksburg, 6, 213
Villard, Oswald Garrison, 339, 339*n13*

Wagner, Robert, 268, 268*n2*
Walker, James, 271, 271*n5*
Wall, Edward, 99, 99*n2*, 114*n25*, 135*n5*
Wall, Effie Blair, 114, 135
Walsh, Carrie Reed, 228, 228*n6*
Walsh, David, 241, 241*n9*
Walsh, Thomas F., 227, 228*n6*
Walsh, Thomas J., 240, 240*n7*, 284, 290, 291, 337
Walton, Jack, 259, 259*n1*
Wanamaker, John, 297, 297*n7*
Ward, Mary Augusta, 155, 155*n19*
Warner, John A., 339, 339*n12*
Warren, Emily Forsythe (granddaughter), xxii; and autobiography, xx; birth of, 322, 333*n6*; photo of, 122
Warren, Maude Radford, 152, 152*n14*
Washington, George, 107
Washington Club, 229
Webster, Grace, 134*n4*
Webster, Roger, 134*n4*
Wetmore, Maude, 185, 185*n1*
Wheeler, Burton K., 301*n2*
White, George, 218, 218*n6*, 220
White, Peter, 4

White, Stanford, 33
White, William Allen, 207, 208*n23*, 336
Whitehouse, Vira, 163, 163*n9*
Whitsett, Winifred, 52, 52*n2*
Wick, Jean, 327, 327*n2*
Widdemer, Margaret, 327, 327*n2*
Wiesner, Mabel, 252
Wile, Frederick William, 243, 243*n14*
Wilkes, Alline, 186
Williams, Charl, 221, 221*n11*
Williams, Walter, 151, 151*n13*
Wilson, Edith Bowling, 174, 174*n9*, 176, 228, 229, 247, 277; photo of, 127
Wilson, Francis, 342, 342*n1*
Wilson, Halsey, 255*n5*
Wilson, Justina Leavitt, 206, 207*n19*, 255, 255*n5*, 270, 272, 285
Wilson, Woodrow, 190, 207, 207*n21*, 279, 301; at 1916 Democratic convention, 171, 172; at 1916 suffrage convention, 174, 176; and ENB, 188, 229, 280; and League of Nations, 195, 200, 206, 211
Woman's Committee, Council of National Defense, xiv, 179, 185, 186–87, 189, 209
Woman's National Democratic Club, xv, 127, 195*n17*, 223*n2*, 246, 247, 247*n17*, 248, 251, 272, 311–12, 311*n3*
Women's Christian Temperance Union, 168*n1*, 200*n10*
Women's International League for Peace and Freedom, 165*n12*, 179*n1*
Women's Trade Union League, 161*n7*, 165*n12*, 174*n8*, 186*n1*, 205*n16*
Wood, Charles, 79*n7*
Woodrow Wilson Foundation, 164*n11*, 332
Woolley, Robert, 274, 274*n4*
Wright, Harold Bell, 149, 149*n7*

Young, Nicholas E., 113, 113*n24*
Young, Owen D., 238, 238*n4*
Young Men's Christian Association, xiv, 180, 183, 184, 314